A Fast Track to Structured Finance Modeling, Monitoring, and Valuation

A Fast Track to Structured Finance Modeling, Monitoring, and Valuation

Jump Start VBA

WILLIAM PREINITZ

WILEY

John Wiley & Sons, Inc.

For general information on our other products and services, or technical support, please contact our Customer Care Department within the United States at 800-762-2974, outside the United States at 317-572-3993 or fax 317-572-4002.

Wiley also publishes its books in a variety of electronic formats. Some content that appears in print may not be available in electronic books.
For more information about Wiley products, visit our Web site at http://www.wiley.com.

Library of Congress Cataloging-in-Publication Data:

Preinitz, William, 1950–
    A fast track to structured finance modeling, monitoring, and valuation : jump start VBA / William Preinitz.
        p. cm.
    Modeling with Visual Basic Application language.
    Includes index.
    ISBN 978-0-470-39812-8 (cloth/online)
    1. Finance–Computer simulation.   2. Risk assessment–Computer simulation.
3. Finance–Mathematical models.   4. Microsoft Visual BASIC.   I. Title.   II. Title: Structured finance modeling jump start VBA.
    HG106.P74 2009
    332.01′5195–dc22
                                                                    2008040318

10 9 8 7 6 5 4 3 2 1

Contents

Preface

Welcome!
I am glad that you have picked this book off the shelf or clicked on a link or done whatever it was that brought you here! I assume that you are reading this because you want to have some idea about what this book is about.

Broadly speaking, this book is about modeling. Specifically, it is about structured finance modeling. As of this writing, the practitioners of "structured finance" are living in a very challenging environment. The capital markets have been shaken by a sharp rise in the delinquency and default rates of residential mortgages. Structured finance deals, dependent on the cash flows generated by the monthly mortgage payments, have seen varied results based on the creditworthiness of the mortgagees. Certain types of structured finance deals such as Collateralized Debt Obligations (CDOs) will never enjoy their one-time popularity again. Be that as it may, a wide Range of structured products remains and will continue to be, a significant part of the financial landscape. I have spent the last 30 years of my life in this industry. Most of that time was directly spent in the activity of financial modeling. I have personally modeled over 70 different types of cash flow-producing assets and have managed people who have added another 50 to 60 types to that list. Having said that, we should now say this:

This book is a modeling book. It is not a primer on structured finance. It uses structured finance as the vehicle to present the modeling ideas, but it is not a textbook on how to structure investment banking deals per se. In fact, the example shown in the text is deliberately designed to be as generic as possible. It is intended to be a book to teach you the fundamentals of financial modeling. In the book you will build two models, the first will be used to structure and originate a deal. The second model, using many components of the first, will perform a risk assessment and valuation activity on the deal after it has been created. You will learn:

- How to design and implement a model to access information from the environment, either in the form of data or in the form of user choices and inputs.
- How to design a financial calculation engine to perform the steps necessary to generate loan-by-loan cash flows for a collateral portfolio.
- How to design and manage a complex reporting capability to convey the results of the model to the user.
- Lastly, how to take the components of one model, a structuring model, and quickly reconfigure them to produce a model for risk assessment and valuation. This second model will measure the performance of our deal against its at issuance expectations. It will also provide an ongoing valuation process that will allow us to compare the value of the deal against others of its kind in the market place.

The modeling techniques taught in this book can be applied to almost any real-world situation and activity. You will find them equally applicable and useful if you want to model systems as different as the movement of thousands of rail cars over an intercontinental network.

If modeling a financial structure or a rail car network is not sufficiently interesting, then how about these two alternatives? The first might be a model that is a historical simulation of the 1939–1945 Battle of the Atlantic between the Allied merchant convoys and their escorts and the German submarine fleet. The second might be a model to test various hypotheses about the mass extinction of over 50 species of Ice Age mega-fauna from North and South America that occurred 40,000 years BCE.

My point is, once you learn a set of robust modeling techniques, you are only limited by the information available and your own creativity.

What I will do in this book is to lead you through an analysis and implementation process. You will start with a real world set of objects and relationships. From this collection you will identify key processes and elements that drive a system. When I say "system" I will use the term in a high degree of abstraction. A "system" is a group of objects that interact with each other and themselves through a series of definable relationships of cause and effect. You will use your judgment to select a subset of these components and relationships and incorporate them into a simplified system that becomes the basis of the model. If these elements are selected carefully, the model will retain the critical core characteristics and behaviors of the larger, progenitor, system. The selected elements of the model will then be translated into a set of inputs and the relationships expressed in the language of the model. The model will then be tested, validated, and run, and the initial results produced. These results will be examined and further development of the model will occur until you are satisfied that it meets the needs of the project.

As mentioned early on, the example in the book is of a structured finance deal. If you are interested in other types of modeling DO NOT LET THAT DISCOURAGE YOU! Focus on the processes and learn the techniques and you can apply them anywhere.

This book is not written to address any particular problem, such as where to place the next 50 locations of an expanding hamburger franchise. It is not written about modeling what could have happened at the Alamo if Colonel Travis had had 200 more riflemen to man the south wall. It is instead written about structured finance.

As such, this book will start with a particular perspective. It will assume that you are a new analyst or associate and have entered a department of an investment or commercial bank after completing your corporate training cycle. In your training you will have been exposed to the various business activities of the organization and acquired a fundamental knowledge of financial theory and calculations.

You are replacing a person who is leaving in two weeks. You need to sit with them and come up to speed on the current set of projects you will assume. One of these projects is the modeling support for an asset-backed securitization (ABS) deal that the department feels highly confident of winning. The modeling for the deal must be complete in about two months.

The person you are replacing has gotten the project off to a good start. They have built an Excel spreadsheet that correctly models the debt structure of the deal.

One part of the model that is *NOT* complete is the calculation of the amortization, payments, defaults, and recoveries of the several thousand loans comprising the loan portfolio. The requirement to model these cash flows has the current analyst completely stumped. With only knowledge of Excel, this person has tried a number of different spreadsheet solutions. None of these solutions have proved feasible. The analyst has been unable to develop a spreadsheet application that can amortize thousands of loans across a wide variety of assumptions.

"Well, you seem pretty bright!" he says as he is leaving. "Good luck. It is your problem now!"

Indeed it is.

You have the Excel spreadsheet, but the columns that will receive the cash flows from the loan portfolio are blank. You have the client's data file, which contains the initial loan portfolio information. You are very lucky concerning this data file. It contains extensive demographic information about the loan portfolio in addition to all the information you need to calculate the monthly payment streams. From prior deal write-ups done by your new department, you know what types of reports are needed for the decision makers both internal and external.

Best of all you have this book!

This book will walk you through, on a step-by-step basis, the construction of a robust, flexible, and easy-to-run model. It will teach you how to wrap the Excel model in a series of menus to bring in information. It will teach you how to read data from other Excel files and how to write reports from the results produced by the model. It will help you build a valid, working model that will accomplish more in a single afternoon than your predecessor would have been able to accomplish in a month using Excel alone. The model you will build will allow you to answer a wide Range of questions and to adroitly manage the risk assessment and structuring requirements of the deal. The model will be capable of producing a very rich and extensive set of results. There will therefore also be a set of ancillary programs developed along with the model to help you manage and summarize the results to improve your efficiency.

Once the deal has been created there will be a need to track its performance. The bulk of the book, the first 21 chapters, will have taught you how to build a model to structure a deal. The last three chapters teach you how to create a monitoring program from the structuring program we have already developed. We can then use this program to track the ongoing performance of the deal over its life. This program will also serve to generate many of the criteria we will need to consider in determining the current value and prospects of the deal.

Having accomplished all this you will look like a star to the other members of the deal team and the management of your department. You will create an analytics engine that will describe the financial risk of the deal, serve the client, and answer the questions of your own risk personnel and the rating agencies. You are a lucky guy, but only if you work hard. When you have completed this process you will have acquired a significant additional skill to add to your probably already considerable repertoire.

By the way, when your predecessor left, did he say it was "Your problem now!" or "Your opportunity now!"? I forget.

I am particularly sympathetic to this set of circumstances because, as I will later relate in Chapter 1, I *have* been in *exactly* this situation. I hope that this book will save you from some of the more painful parts of the modeling learning curve that nearly all of us have had to endure.

What I intend to do is teach you how to build a basic structure that is applicable to every type of analytical exercise. It will provide you with an application that will be flexible and robust. You will learn how to construct VBA code in a professional, organized, and highly effective manner. You will learn how to open files, read data from them, build menus, error check the menus you have built, compare collateral against a set of acceptance standards, report the eligible and ineligible collateral, build a cash flow generator, run the cash flows through a waterfall spreadsheet, calculate the spreadsheet for each scenario, read the scenario results and store them, and finally, report the results. By learning these specific things you will also learn a lot about the VBA language and how to use it for a wide variety of purposes.

Just remember, model building is not a be-all and end-all in itself. It is just one skill of many.

It is, however, a skill that can greatly leverage many other skills you already have. It will force you to think about problems more precisely and concisely. It will enhance your ability to break complex, seemingly insoluble problems down into a set of manageable tasks. These tasks can then be attacked and completed one-by-one.

I will warn you now. You get from this material proportionately what you put into it. You should expect to work. The more VBA code you write on your own, instead of just reading it from the chapters, the faster you will learn. The more you emulate the style, format, and organization of the VBA you see in the book, the cleaner, clearer, and more supportable your models will be. As you see examples in the model we will construct, try to independently apply them to your own work. Start slow and build up by trying out small things first. Walk your way through the code instead of just reading it. Have fun exploring the examples.

This book will also show you how to build a second model from the framework of the first. The emphasis of the first model is the assist in the creation of new securities, the second one to track their ongoing performance and determine their health and value. I hope this will clearly demonstrate the value of this modeling approach: The ability to transform one model into another, related but different model, of equal utility and value and in a much shorter time than to begin from scratch.

Although it can be very difficult at times (especially your first several experiences in debugging), model building offers opportunities for creative and rewarding work. It will also raise your productivity, allowing you to do much, much more in less time. This is always a consideration in today's world, where there is just never enough time.

I hope you buy this book. Leaving aside for the moment the fact that I will get paid if you do so, I want you to for another reason.

Modeling can be real fun. It can instill in you a sense of accomplishment and self-worth. There is nothing so satisfying as a job well done, especially if none of your peers can accomplish as much! I have had a lot of fun modeling over the years and I would like you to share in the experience.

WILLIAM H. PREINITZ
December 2008

About the Web Site

With this book you get access to a Web site (www.wiley.com/go/vba).
The Web site for this book contains supplemental material that tracks the contents of the chapters. Not all chapters have Web site material but many of them do and some contain quite a bit of material that you will find interesting.

After we have discussed the more general topics of the Introduction and Chapters 1 and 2 we begin to build the model. As each chapter comes to a close, an incremental amount of Excel or VBA has been added to the model. These increments are fully backward integrated. This is to say that at the close of each chapter you have added a piece to the working program that existed at the end of the previous chapter.

You will be able to take each of these partially completed models and run it. It will perform all of the functionality it possessed at the end of the previous chapter and the functionality that was built into it in the current chapter. There is a section at the end of each chapter entitled "On the Web Site." This section delineates the names and numbers of files or other materials on the Web site relevant to that chapter.

A brief overview of this material is as follows:

Chapters 1 and 2	No material.
Chapter 3	The data file containing loan-by-loan information about the collateral of the deal.
Chapter 4	The Excel spreadsheet containing the basic deal structure and waterfall.
Chapter 5	No material.
Chapter 6	The first VBA code in the model. Creating and naming the VBA modules to hold the code.
Chapter 7	There are a collection of recorded macros. There is also a Web chapter to walk you through the process of constructing a small model from these macros. This model replicates all the basic functionality that you will later see in the main development effort.
Chapter 8	Menus are now added to the existing model.
Chapter 9	No material.
Chapter 10	Menu error checking code is added to the model.
Chapter 11	Template files for the model's reports are created.
Chapter 12	The Main program is begun and the code to read the menu inputs is added.
Chapter 13	The code that selects the eligible collateral and generates our first report package is added.
Chapter 14	The loan-by-loan cash flows of the collateral are generated.
Chapter 15	The capability to use the cash flows to run the structuring waterfall is added to the model.

Chapter 16	No material.
Chapter 17	We add a report to trace and validate cash flows at the loan-by-loan level.
Chapter 18	The completed model! All the material we need to structure, size, and issue a deal are produced. We also build an ability to run multiple scenarios in a batch mode. Lastly, we build a standalone program to parse output files extracting targeted data from each.
Chapter 19	Additional capabilities are added to the model. There will also be a set of new template files for the new modified report package.
Chapter 20	No material.
Chapter 21	We write a standalone program to help compare output files generated when we compare a new version of the model to an old version of the model.
Chapter 22	We build a new model using the code we developed from the first model. This model is a Monitoring & Valuation model.
Chapter 23	The quarterly historical portfolio performance files for the first 24 months of the deal. You will also find the monitoring reports and valuation output for the deal based on these inputs.
Chapter 24	We provide the monthly collateral files used to run the model, the results of each of these quarterly analysis, some suggested exhibits for use in dealing with the rating agency inquiry, and the solution to risk management's question and how to arrive at it.

As you can see, there is quite a bit of material to guide you along the way of learning how to model in VBA! If you study this material you will significantly increase both the pace of your learning and the content of what you will learn.

The password for the Web site is: preinitz

# PART One

Introduction

## CHAPTER 1

Why? What? Who? Where? and How?

THE IMMORTAL QUESTION(S)

If you use the Search feature for Amazon.com and search for the combination of subjects "Excel," "VBA," and "Modeling," it currently returns a total of almost 500 results. Some of these are essentially duplicate entries. A book with three editions will show up once for each of the editions.

What makes this book different?

Why should you spend the time reading it, and even much more time learning the concepts and practices laid out within?

What do you need to know even before you start?

If you are already proficient or even expert with Excel, what possible advantage can you gain by learning the Visual Basic Application (VBA) language?

What can you do with this knowledge and how will that help you?

Is learning a programming language as difficult as everyone says it is?

These questions are all reasonable and valid. Except for the specific reference to Excel, they are the broad questions that any author should be prepared to answer whatever the subject of their work.

I am prepared to do just that.

Why Is This Book Different?

This book is different because it is the only book that equally balances the mindset of modeling with a code intensive approach, and at the same time is aimed at the complete novice.

What do I mean by that?

Although this book has as its subject a structured finance model application, its intellectual focus is to get you to start thinking about dynamic problem solving. We will take a moderately complex set of rules and relationships and help you to break them down into some very small components. The process of the book will work with you to implement these discrete elements without losing sight of the bigger picture.

To accomplish this you will be exposed to VBA code, more VBA code, and even more VBA code! You will see a few, then tens, then hundreds, and finally thousands of lines of VBA code. At the end of each chapter you will see the model in a progressive and additive state of development. First there will be just the Excel workbook of a single worksheet containing the deal waterfall and nothing else. Then over the course of the following chapters we will add one piece of code and then another and another until at last we have a finished model. I will tell you now that you cannot learn VBA by just reading it. At the end of each chapter you need to take the code out and play with it. Step through its operations using the VBA debugger tool. Look at the structure and the types of VBA statements used to achieve the results of the incremental addition of the chapter. Then take the code copy it, muck around with it and see if you can replicate its functionality on your own. Start simply and start small. Don't attempt to build an elaborate menu error-checking subroutine the first time out. Make a scaled down version of what you are seeing and then try to build up once you have it working. If you do this you will make much more progress and at a faster rate than you would if you don't. Don't worry, I will provide you with lots of code to look at! You will see practically every single line of VBA code used to create the model. It is up to you to dive in and start swimming. In fact it is the only way to learn.

There will be little or no theoretical discussions about anything. There will be no discussions about the Zen of design, or the Tao of programming. That can wait! It can wait until you have mastered a critical minimum subset of the VBA language. It can wait until you can fashion problem-solving code in a manner that will not be a danger to yourself or others. It can wait until you know enough to have your own informed opinions. That time is *not* now.

I have strong opinions about what works and what does not work, all based on 25 years of experience. You will hear them expressed from time to time in the material to come. The focus of this book is on concrete, immediate, measurable progress toward problem solving through the use of VBA.

The two effects that this will have are:

1. You will become much more facile in jumping between the specific and the general scope of decomposing and reconstructing complex problems. In a phrase, you will increase your mental agility.
2. Upon recognizing specific problem elements, you will be able to reflexively choose the correct and concise VBA code to express its logical or computational solution.

By the end of this book I would hope that you have substantially improved your mental acumen in problem decomposition and synthesis, and that you have begun to think in VBA. Here I will make one final point. When learning a foreign language, one starts with basic vocabulary and the rudimentary syntactical rules and works from there. As one builds upon this early knowledge, the vocabulary is expanded, and certain short expressions are integrated into one's repertoire. There, then, is a stage where entire sets of sentences spring to mind as complete entities. Final mastery of the language is accomplished when one dreams in the language.

I do not expect you to dream in VBA by the end of this book, but I do expect you to at least catnap in it.

In a word, this is not a book about a computer language.

It is not a book about structured finance per se although the applications are particularly relevant to the conditions in the financial markets today.

It is a book aimed specifically at improving your complex problem solving abilities.

It is a book about giving you the ability to translate your thoughts into a medium that is relatively easy to learn and that can be powerfully applied across a wide Range of practical problem solving processes.

It is a book whose goal is to add to the inventory of your personal tool kits an increasingly valuable, and monetarily rewarded, dimension. By the way, in case you missed it, the crucial word in the preceding sentence was the word **monetarily**.

I want everyone who reads this book, who does the work, and who perseveres in the pursuit of this knowledge and these skills to understand that this book will make you more valuable. It will do so by giving you an added dimension that many of your peers do not have. These skills will improve your personal market value and your career potential.

Who Is This Book Aimed At?

In order of immediacy, this book is aimed at the following people:

- Men and women working in the financial industry, especially at the levels of vice president and below, who want or need to develop their modeling skills in a self-paced environment. This especially relates to the current environment. The volumes of structured finance deals being currently created and issued is significantly less than it was last year or two years ago. Much of the analytical effort is now directed to helping risk managers understand what they have and the prospects for their positons in the current market environment. For people involved in these activities the book packs a double punch! You will see the development of a structuring model that will teach you the fundamental elements common to all structured finance deals. You will then see the transformation of the structuring model we will create into a monitoring and valuation model. This is an especially valuable twofold experience for people working in today's marketplace.
- Intermediate level managers who supervise these people but have little or no knowledge of, or experience with modeling. They want to know what is possible, and how it is to be accomplished. More importantly, they need to be able to form realistic ideas of what is possible in a given time frame. There is a saying about tradeoff: "I can be fast, accurate, and cheap. The problem is that you can have only two of the three." As mentioned above, in today's environment the aspect of risk management and portfolio monitoring is critical. Intermediate level managers will need to be up-to-date as to the current health of their businesses. Modeling in VBA/Excel providers them with an excellent platform to improve their information flows and knowledge of the sensitivity of their holdings.
- Students in graduate or undergraduate programs wishing to develop modeling skills.
- Anyone that wants to have the ability to intensively explore problems that require a quick, fluid medium of analysis. This includes anyone in the financial world dealing in risk and especially those that seek to measure it and evaluate risk arbitrage through modeling.

- Anyone in any commercial, nonprofit, government, or military function that needs a tool for dynamic problem solving.
- Anyone that is a regular Excel user and wants to significantly expand the scope of their ability to address issues that the use of Excel alone cannot.
- Anyone that wants to ask the question "What If?" and needs a powerful, easy-to-learn tool to translate their thoughts into concrete quantitative reality.
- Lastly, anyone that thinks they know and are good at VBA. I am certain that you will find many useful techniques here that you may have overlooked.

What Assumptions Do I Make About You?

- Basic computer literacy.
- A working, although not expert, knowledge of Excel.
- A working knowledge of algebra is required to understand some of the bond math and mortgage amortization processes.
- A positive attitude and a willingness to mentally engage in the process. It is assumed that the reader is willing to put in the work and to think about the work that they are doing. Learning a programming language, especially VBA, is not easy. It is however, not that difficult either. This of course posits two assumptions:
  1. You really want to learn.
  2. You will continue to want to learn and will persevere beyond the first, second, or third setback.
- That you are a professional in the broadest sense of the word.
  - That you want to produce a quality product and that you will take the time and make the effort to do so.
  - That you will feel a sense of responsibility to yourself and others not to produce a model that is hard to work with, easy to make mistakes with, or inaccurate in its function.
  - That you will take responsibility for your work by completely testing and validating the model results.
  - Lastly, that you will take the time to protect yourself and others by providing a minimum of documentation necessary to prevent the model from being inappropriately applied.

WHAT ARE THE ADVANTAGES OF LEARNING VBA?

When I was ten years old I announced to my grandfather, who was a plumber, that I felt that I had mastered enough mathematics to last me the rest of my life. The scene of this revelation was a modest summer cottage by a lake. I was feeling rather reflective. It was a hot day in July, and the reality of returning to school was a distant idea. My conclusions seemed quite reasonable.

He smiled at this and made little in the way of return comment.

The next day he asked me to dig a hole off to the side of the front yard. He gave me a small plastic coffee scoop and an old table knife. He led me over to a stake he had placed in the ground about three feet from a hedge. He told me the hole must be exactly one foot on each side with sharp clean corners. I was to do nothing else until I had finished the task. Nothing else specifically included playing with friends, swimming, and fishing with him.

At first everything went smoothly. I cut through the sod and the first six inches of topsoil. I then hit the roots of the hedge, a rock the size of dinner plate, and lastly a mixture of clay and pebbles. Two-and-a-half hot days later, complaining, bored, frustrated, and angry I finished.

The next day he had me repeat the process using any tool I wanted from the shed. I was finished in 15 minutes. That, he said, was the difference between life with and without the knowledge of mathematics.

I did not think about this incident for years until I was called to travel to the London office of the investment bank with which I worked to debrief a leasing specialist who was leaving the firm. He had created an Excel model to run the cash flows of a structured finance asset-backed securitization (ABS) deal. This model was viewed by everyone in that department with a mixture of awe and reverence. The fastest PC in the office was dedicated solely to the running of this model.

We spent the first two days reviewing it. It consisted of over 65 spreadsheets that amortized 1,900 individual leases. He indicated to me that he had made some changes to it recently. These changes had decreased the runtime from its original eight to nine hours to the present six and a half hours. At the moment, however, we needed to produce 15 scenarios for one rating agency and nine for another. Eight more were required for internal credit approval and four by the credit wrap provider of the deal. In total, that was 216 hours of runtime, not factoring the setup times for each scenario, and assuming that everything went well thereafter. The vast majority of the computational time was taken up in determining the monthly cash flows from the existing lease agreements and then calculating additional cash flows from a re-leasing agreement that served to extend the terms of the original contract. The uses of the cash from the collateral were straightforward and represented a small portion of the computational burden of the program.

I began by replacing the thousands of columns of Excel that calculated the individual leases. Using amortization subroutines that I had previously written in VBA (very similar to those in this book), we were able to eliminate all but seven of the spreadsheets. Five of these spreadsheets were menus; one displayed the monthly collateral cash flow summary and one the performance of the debt supported by those cash flows. This moved the vast majority of the computational burden of the model from the Excel spreadsheets and into the VBA code.

The runtime of the new program, (even before we tried to optimize the VBA calculation sequences), was now reduced to eleven minutes per scenario. This was a 97% reduction in the time it took to produce a single scenario. We next implemented a simple looping structure that allowed the model to run groups of related scenarios without human intervention. Finally we separated the output reports from the model itself into standalone Excel files that used a common report format. This allowed us to produce up to 50 variants of a base scenario without human intervention. Now we could put in the scenario specifications, turn the model on, and go to a series of well-deserved extended lunches. Upon our return we would find various sets of files, each containing a unique scenario. The model had finished, printed the files including graphics, sorted the scenario files based on their characteristics into particular directories, and produced a summary report resident in the model.

Some holes can be dug far more efficiently with knowledge of VBA than without such knowledge. There are also entire classes of problems that cannot be solved by Excel alone!

The combination of Excel and VBA is far more powerful than either product alone. Excel is a wonderful medium for quickly changing report configurations. It also offers a wide Range of options for the graphic display of information.

VBA can be used to control the Excel environment in a surprisingly wide Range of activities. It can also replicate complex sequences of tasks that an Excel user would have to perform manually. This frees the analyst for other, more valuable work (interpreting all that newly available data), and increases individual and team productivity.

VBA allows the user to explore a wider Range of situations and to pursue the analysis to a deeper level than would be possible by using Excel alone.

There is one further lesson to be emphasized from the above. The key to the rapid rewrite of the model was the fact that I had previously written a collection of VBA subroutines that performed cash flow amortization for leases. The VBA code was written for leases on railroad cars, not aircraft, but was easily changed to meet the somewhat different aspects and conditions of the second deal. I also had a set of preconfigured report files and VBA code to transfer the information from the model to these files. All of this work we were able to employ immediately in the aircraft model. It was intact, tested, and available to the new model. The ability to transfer previously developed work to new projects is an enormous productivity boost. We will engage in just this kind of activity late in the book. We will use a structuring model as the basis for the development of a risk assessment and valuation model for the securities we created with the first model.

As you learn and practice VBA you will find that two things will happen. First, you will be able to develop new VBA modules faster. (Practice may not make you perfect, but it will make you formidable.) Second, if properly written, you will be able to repeatedly reuse VBA code you have previously developed in new projects. These two factors will synergistically interact, allowing you to dramatically reduce your model development times.

WHAT ARE THE DISADVANTAGES OF LEARNING VBA?

As enticing as I hope you have found the preceding section to be, we must balance it by presenting the disadvantages and barriers to learning VBA.

The first and most obvious is the natural fear of change. This seems paradoxical if one believes that the change will ultimately be beneficial. There is still a hesitation to abandon the tried and true, the familiar ways of doing something. There is always comfort in the ways of the devil that you know, as opposed to the one that you do not. Different ways of doing things can change relationships, workflow, and the perception of relative value between peers and managers. New ways can leave some people who are not a party to them feel excluded and disenfranchised. They can also create new classes of problems for others who are not directly involved in the change but who are affected nonetheless.

My answer to the above dilemma is simply that LIFE = CHANGE. Change occurs whether we want it to or not. The one thing that is known is that those who have more capacity to deal with change deal with it better. VBA can improve your productivity, which will, in the long run, give you more time, not less. It also gives you another response option to business problems. I am not representing that learning VBA is a panacea that can be applied against all possible future career situations. Learning VBA will *not* solve all your troubles. It is self-evident, however, that having more resources rather than fewer are better when dealing with change.

The second is the issue of time. I can barely keep up with my work now. I need to balance time spent on my career and time spent on my family. I feel that I am overburdened at present and now you want this and me to do everything I'm doing now, too? Taken as a whole, VBA has tens of thousands of features, methods, objects, commands, and rules. You do not need to know all of them to be quickly productive in a meaningful sense. You need to know fewer than four dozen statement types, variable types, objects, and methods to produce the model we will develop in this book. I have selected the most critical and the most widely useful elements of the language as the focus for creating the model code. This is a fast track to real, working VBA code.

The third issue is the entire concept of learning to program at all. You will become a programmer. Does this mean you will immediately begin wearing plastic pocket protectors and sport inch-thick glasses? No. You will be the same person you now are, except you will have an additional and valuable skill at the end of the learning process.

Is it easy to learn how to program? Yes and no.

Yes, if the material is properly selected. Yes, if there is a manageable subset of basic concepts that is progressively developed. The pace must be manageable so that the material can be understood and internalized by the student. Most important is your commitment to learn. The first program I ever wrote had 16 statements. As it turned out it also had 25 errors! Learning how to program in VBA is not simple, *but it is not impossible*, or even terribly difficult for that matter! It is a precise process. You need to be careful. It can be frustrating to have the model produce results that are clearly wrong when you are sure you have programmed it correctly. As you practice you will become better, faster, and much more confident. We will build that confidence through the examples at the end of each chapter. If you have the patience and the commitment you will find the process rewarding.

No, if you are bombarded by too much too soon. VBA has thousands of features that you will never need to learn, or if you do, you would be better off not knowing. Why? There is a tendency in some beginner programmers to try to find a use for every feature they read about. This practice is not only counterproductive, it is also danger-ous. It leads to overly elaborate programs that are nearly impossible to understand by anyone other than the original author. In a fast-paced and demanding business environment, it means that it will be difficult and time-consuming to understand and to modify. That type of code is mostly characterized by the use of the object-oriented features of the VBA language, which are inappropriate for beginning modelers to tackle their first time out. It also makes the VBA models they write less accessible to other modeling generalists, who lack a formal computer science education and who may inherit the code after them.

Lastly, there is the issue of too much of a good thing. If the model can produce five scenarios, why not run 10, 20, 50, 100, 500, 1,000, 10,000? Why not run all possible value combinations of each of the 30 dependent variables and the 10 independent variables that are the model drivers? There is a tendency for some managers to ask for too much information simply because they can get it. It is possible to miss the relevant trees through the forest of too many scenarios. The situation can also arise where the analyst wishing to demonstrate their technical skills produces so much information that the decision maker is swamped by sheer volume of the model results. This, at best, leads to confusion and delay, at worst to errors, missed opportunities, and losses. This is not as uncommon as you may think it is.

The answer to whether VBA is easy to learn is common sense. Some work will be required, some will be optional, but common sense and communication should serve to ameliorate the worst of these situations.

So having weighted the alternate advantages/disadvantages, we now must decide. To learn VBA or not to learn! I vote for learn! I believe it is always the best course to try to improve and grow. We need to stretch ourselves and push out our boundaries. Learning VBA is a way to do that. Your problems may change, but you will have one more tool to deal with them. It has worked for me and thousands of other people.

If you have continued to read to this point you have de facto accepted that the advantages of VBA just might outweigh the disadvantages. With that premise in hand let us address the next question.

WHAT IS A MODEL?

The Basic Concept

A model is an abstraction of a real world situation. That is what everyone can agree upon. Unfortunately past that point of agreement you can find yourself in the position of the person who asked the nine blind men what an elephant was and received nine very different answers, each based on personal perspective.

My view is that a model is a computer program that is configured for investigative purposes. This is the classic "WHAT IF (conditions 1, 2, 3) = RESULTS." Its goal is to allow the model user to move from the known into the unknown. It is different in this way from a program that balances your checkbook or keeps track of the medical histories. The function of these programs is rather simple and one-dimensional. They tend to exist merely for the manipulation and reconfiguration of static information.

Models are dynamic. They tend more towards the consideration of complex problems rather than simple ones. They produce a Range of results as opposed to a single answer. They focus on the effect of multivariate degrees of change. They also seek to illuminate the interdependencies of the components of the phenomena they are built to describe. They seek to produce an informationally "dense" or "rich" result, on several different layers of complexity or of several dimensions (especially time).

More often than not they will raise just as many questions as they answer.

Difference between a Spreadsheet and a Model

A common question is "When does an application stop being a spreadsheet and start being a model?"

Spreadsheets develop a set of answers from a set of equations. This set of answers represents a single descriptive entity, or scenario. That is, however, as far as it goes.

If you have purchased a portfolio of assets and know their empirical performance as to payments and losses, a spreadsheet can produce the expected case. You can change one assumption, run the spreadsheet, and get another case.

A model, however, will be designed to produce sets of scenarios. These scenarios will have value in and of themselves if viewed in isolation. Their value will significantly increase if viewed as elements of a unified set. They may be taken as a series of risk points along a continuum from what is desirable, through acceptable, to catastrophic. The value of the individual scenario results is greater because they form the descriptive elements of a much greater whole. It is this type of collective result that is most characteristic of models versus spreadsheets. The other defining characteristic of the model is that it provides for a collective interpretation of this result set—the ability to look at one result, several results, or all results, and conceive a framework for thought or a unified perspective. That perspective might be as simple as a grid exhibiting a single result parameter for each of the component analyses, or as complex as a three-dimensional graphic.

Complexity, Synergy, Dynamism, Sensitivity

Models are particularly important for capturing and describing complex systems. Complex systems tend to exhibit behavior that is not always incrementally uniform or predictable.

They are also excellent at capturing synergistic relationships between various independent and dependent variables. Depending on the Range of scenarios produced and the degree to which the model's report package is designed, all kinds of interesting interrelationships can be described and studied. This is especially true of VBA models used in Monte Carlo simulation analysis, where the result set can contain thousands, tens of thousands, or even hundreds of thousands of scenarios, which combined together, comprise the whole of a single model run.

Dynamism is very difficult to capture with the use of a spreadsheet alone. When a model produces a collection of scenario results, it is possible to measure the degree and type of change triggered by variations of the value of a single variable. The time it takes an analyst to run a properly designed model and capture the results of as few as 25 scenarios is tiny compared to the effort required to replicate those same results from a spreadsheet model. Why is this so? Models, because they are designed to produce a set of scenarios, will have the results at hand. A spreadsheet produces one scenario at a time. The results must then be correlated and displayed in a manual process. This tends to bog the analyst down in the mechanics of data collection and presentation, instead of freeing him to focus on what the results are saying.

Sensitivity analysis is the last element that separates models from spreadsheets. Not only can we see broad trends from a collection of scenarios, we can look at incremental change between any pair-wise comparisons of available results. We can see if a given set of linear changes in an independent variable produces a similar set of changes in the value of any of the dependant variables. This is particularly important when a high degree of analytical granularity is required. How thinly can a change process be sliced before it becomes significant to the decision? It is these observations that are sometimes the most important output of the modeling effort.

WHY IS MODELING A VALUABLE SKILL?

Modeling is valuable because it is the most powerful tool we have to describe systems that are too complex for manual computational solutions.

In the business world, modeling is preponderantly focused on the issue of financial risk. Describing a continuum of risk is virtually impossible without the use of computer models. There are entire fields of finance that were created only after computers became fast enough and financial analytics became robust enough to describe the risk inherent in the products. This risk not only had to be measured, it also had to be described, and then packaged in a way that was comprehensible to the non-specialist. This often involved extensive "What If?" analysis from a wide Range of constituencies both internal and external to the business unit originating the financial product.

Learning to model will improve your analytical and product skills. You have to know what you are to model before you can model it! Modeling forces you to decompose complex systems and then rebuild them from the ground up in the world of VBA. The combination of the development of these general intellectual skills coupled with the specific skill of modeling is a useful package to have.

Having said all of the above, let us finally get to it. **How does one model?**

WHAT ARE THE STAGES OF MODEL DESIGN AND CONSTRUCTION?

Stage 1: Defining the Deliverables

The emphasis of this book is on concrete deliverables. What am I going to learn, how do I put it to use, what will be the end product?

Begin the modeling process by describing the successful end product. How will you know when you are done? This sounds sophomoric, but many modeling efforts bog down and then self-destruct because people do not set clear concise goals. As the project evolves, goals are changed, and changed, and changed again. You find yourself chasing a moving target. You can never succeed because you can never finish.

You need a set of goals to be able to point to as the deliverables! You can then claim success when they are achieved.

What Do the Decision Makers Need to Know?   What are the concise, finite, and, above all, specific results you need the model to produce in order to enable the decision-makers to decide? Get a list; check it twice (even if you are not Santa Claus). Be very careful to specifically layout the calculations and form of the results the decision-makers want you to produce. Make sure that you have specific agreement as to form, Range, and granularity of the desired results.

Then get explicit signoff, by e-mail or some other document if possible.

What Is the Scope of the Modeling Effort?   Is the model to address a specific case or a set of more general cases? How much effort is willing to be spent in terms of personnel, money, and time? Is this going to be a prototype for a series of models or is it for a unique situation that is unlikely to occur again? Will you need to cooperate with other personnel? What external constituencies will be involved? Do any of them have special requirements that will have to be addressed by the model in addition to your own requirements?

Who Is the Target Audience?   Who, other than yourself, will see the output? Will other parties require special outputs or, more importantly, special methodologies that are not in the original internal plan for the model? What is the level of knowledge, sophistication, and need for detail of all the parties who will see the output? Will the results have to be packaged differently for other parties in your firm, including members of the management team up the line? This last point is particularly important in that senior managers often require that an entire briefing fit on one side of a single sheet of paper.

What Will Be the Frequency, Intensity, and Longevity of Use?   Who will run the model? Will there be error checking, reasonableness checking, checking for conflicting computational options, checking for infrastructure issues (for instance, is the data file where you said it was?)? How frequently is the model to be run? Will the model produce several scenarios, tens of thousands of scenarios, hundreds of thousands of scenarios? This will be particularly important when it comes time to determine how much optimization effort you will put into designing and writing the VBA code.

Is the model a one-trick-pony, or is it anticipated that it will be continually developed over many years as part of the ongoing effort for a product line? Will the model be needed to perform ancillary functions such as monitoring the deals after they are created for either risk or regulatory purposes? Remember that if the business is subject to rapid change, the model will have to continually reinvent itself to keep pace with the evolution of product development in the business environment. It will be linked to the successive challenges the business faces and must be robust enough to meet them in a timely and accurate manner.

Is the expected profit (or avoidance of losses) from the use of the model substantial enough to warrant extraordinary measures in its development? This has significant impact on the degree, extent, and complexity of the validation effort. It may also necessitate the involvement of third parties to replicate and verify the model results.

Stage 2: Research and Abstraction of the Real-World Problem

What to Put In, What to Leave Out   One of the most critical early-stage decisions in model development is what aspects of the real-world problem to include in the scope of the models and which ones to ignore. Some items are obligatory, some discretionary, and others a matter of judgment. Obviously this question is intimately related to some of the issues we laid out above. What are the resources and time frame of the development effort? Will it accommodate extensive study of all the real-world elements we seek to model? Can we learn more about the impacts of the various inputs? Can outside parties give us guidance or education on these items?

A specific case in point is regulatory issues. Any insurance product in the United States or the United Kingdom is a highly regulated item. To correctly understand the behavior of various reserve accounts requirements, we hired a consulting firm.

In the end, we had a team of three insurance specialists spend over 80 hours each educating the deal group and especially myself in how to calculate certain of these requirements.

One is also faced with the absence of data or the absence of data in a directly useable form to the modeler. It then becomes necessary to make a judgment as to at what level of abstraction or approximation is sufficient or acceptable to include in the model. In another instance, we had to analyze a portfolio of home equity lines of credit. When we received the data, a key item was missing. Inquiring of the client, we found that they did not capture this information anywhere in their systems. They would be happy to do so going forward, but not retroactively, on the 10,000-loan portfolio. Unfortunately this information was critical to both an internal risk analysis and one of the rating agencies. We therefore assembled an audit team, and with the deal team, flew to the client site. We had called them beforehand and had them assemble sets of 25 randomly selected loans. We read the missing information from each loan file and then constructed a statistical estimate of the values for the portfolio as a whole. These were then used in the analysis. VBA was critical in this instance in helping to develop a statistical distribution of this data. This population was sampled repeatedly, and its new values inserted into the collateral files, allowing an estimate of the risk that a specific parameter introduced into the deal.

Description of Key Interactions   There needs to be a list and description of all-important activities that make up the real-world event. The sequence of these should be determined and the computational or data manipulation requirements described in as much detail as possible.

Mathematical Formulae   Any phenomena that can be reduced to mathematical formulae should be described in as precise a manner as possible. If there are existent standards for the calculation or measurement of the process, these should be strictly employed and earmarked for special validation efforts. If there are industry-accepted methods for the implementation of particular algorithms, these should be determined and adopted. If the client or any of the internal or external constituencies require an idiosyncratic calculation or approach, it must be researched and validated. It cannot be stressed enough that you *must know these things* before you start writing the VBA code. You can have 80%, 90%, or even 95% of the model building process complete and yet hit a snag that may force you to undo or discard hours and hours of work.

Human Element   If there are judgmental issues in the modeled process, one must make allowances for them. This is to say that decision branching caused by human decisions must be anticipated and allowed for. If collective or cascading human behavior (the madness of the crowds) is a significant factor in the modeled issue, you must make allowances to include it. If it cannot be explicitly included, it may be possible to implicitly include it by allowing manipulation of the behavior of other variables.

Chance   Some tasks and behaviors are deterministic and some are probabilistic. You may need to determine how you will model items that are subject to chance. Mortgage defaults are a perfect example.

Most mortgage default behavior is probabilistic. Unless there is a specific economic factor causing systemic default stresses, borrowers default in a random manner. A portfolio may consist of 20,000 mortgages that share common demographics, similar balances, and payment terms. Individual defaults that occur are generally modeled in this portfolio by deeming a certain fractional percentage of each loan to have defaulted. This is in fact standard industry practice and an accepted risk measurement approach. What happens if, instead, 20% of the portfolio is contained in 10 of the loans? If even one of these loans defaults we will see a huge increase in default rate for the period. If measuring such volatility is important (and it is), we will have to consider other methods. In the preceding case we may wish to separate these 800-pound gorillas from the rest of the zoo and treat them as a separate portfolio unto themselves. We may wish to model the defaults of these large balance loans by using a Monte Carlo technique that would randomly default their entire balance, rather than subjecting them to the proportionate attrition techniques generally applied.

Environmental or Regulatory Risk   If the modeled process is subject to changes in law or regulatory modification, elements reflecting those potential changes may need to be provided for.

Organizational Constraints   The last items that may need to be considered are constraints affecting the modeled phenomena by self-imposed organizational practices. One such issue is sector risk. How many companies in a particular industry are we willing (or allowed) to do business with? How much business with any one of them and how much with all of them in aggregate? What will be the maximum duration of our involvement?

Another factor to consider is the organizational policies that govern the development of models in general. Are there specific testing and development milestones that will require you to seek signoffs from other parties within the organization? Are there independent model validation groups that will need to certify the accuracy and scope of the model prior to its deployment and use?

The above are not meant to be an exhaustive list of considerations, but ones to start you thinking broadly about this part of the process.

Stage 3: Develop the Fundamental Framework

Sequence Functional Procedures of the Model   Now the process begins to move from the abstract to the concrete. Having completed the initial fact-finding, you next will sequence all the activities the model will have to perform from the beginning of its run to the end.

Broadly, these will fall into three macro phases common to all computer programs of whatever type: input activity, computational activities, and output of the results.

In regards to input, you will need to determine the sources, volume, character, and method of input that the model will require. Will the inputs be in the form of menu-specified data and choices from the user, files, Internet feeds, or randomly generated information? Will the data be sparse or voluminous? Will it be simple in form, or will it require extensive preprocessing inside the model to become useful?

Will it be numerical, alphabetical, or mixed? Will it all be available at the beginning of the model run or will some of it be developed along the way?

For the computational aspects, you will have to determine the sequence and timing of all calculation activities. You will need to identify, specify, and pair each calculation with each portion of the computational activity associated with it. You will need to think through sequential dependencies. One aspect related to this will become vitally important as you become more familiar with the use of looping structures. These structures allow the repetitive execution of specified VBA statements contained within the boundaries of the loop. Model performance can be severely degraded by placing computational activities within a loop when they can be done more efficiently outside of it.

Output of results also needs to be carefully considered. In the initial stages, develop a conservative plan for the minimum amount of output that will satisfy the decision criteria. Do not be too aggressive. Carefully survey the exact scope and detail needed in the output. Confirm with the intended audiences that these results are both sufficient and robust enough to satisfy the requirements of the project. This is an excellent time to begin design of the actual form and content of the reports that will present this information.

Define the Major Activity Blocks   The next step in the planning process is to move from the three phases described above to a specific breakdown of activity units. For example, at the first level, the input phase now becomes the following:

1. Read the menu worksheets of the model.
2. Verify and conduct error checking of the contents of the menus, returning the user to the input phase if errors or inconsistencies are found.
3. Read the names of any data files and determine if they are in the locations specified.
4. Open and read the data.
5. Read the names of any links to external systems; verify the pathways or site names.
6. Establish connection and download the required information.
7. Move this information to the variables of the model so that they are available for the computational phase to follow.

This degree of specification will then allow us to decompose the problem further. In the case of item 1 we can now design VBA routines to read each of the individual menus. This process of detailing will then give us a list of specific tasks that need to be accomplished at the micro level.

Writing Pseudo-Code (at least once)   The final activity will be to write pseudo-code or lines that describe the activity that you will later replace with actual VBA language. Pseudo-code is an excellent way to organize and structure your model. It is, however, time consuming. Do not worry! Writing pseudo-code is a skill that you may well find valuable when faced with planning and writing horrifically complicated models.

I recommend it to beginners as a way to clarify your activities at a very macro level. For the first time modeler it will probably save more time than it will cost. It can also be a useful practice for the experienced modeler when you have to venture into new practices or a different application area. This is especially true if you are seeking complicated issues for the first time. It can be particularly useful when used to walk others through what the model will do and how it will do it. This allows them to be part of the organization of the model with no need for programming or technical involvement, and also assures you that the correct steps are being taken in the correct order to solve the problem.

Stage 4: Implementation into Software

Translating Functionality into Code Now you will have to translate the overall macro design into a first cut at a model. Determination of what to construct in Excel and what to construct in VBA is the big decision here.

What to Implement in Excel Implement in Excel those portions of the model that have high visibility. There is a significant efficiency in being able to look right at a portion of the model and see what is going on. In the VBA sections you will need to use a facility of VBA itself to do this. It is called the debugger. In Excel you can literally see all the ancillary functionality already built into the product to assist you. Such features as the "Trace Dependents" option in the Tools menu can be invaluable as a fast, accessible, and easy-to-use diagnostic tool.

Extend the visual concept to all menus and user specifications. Use Excel to express those elements of the model most subject to change. If you are going to provide the user with any type of intermediate results, provide Excel spreadsheets to display this information.

Lastly, all of the output should be created and displayed in Excel. This will allow you to make rapid changes in formatting. It will also allow you to fully exploit the tremendous Range of visual effects Excel has to offer.

What to Implement in VBA VBA should be reserved first and foremost for the most computationally intense portions of the model calculations. This is especially true of complex calculations that have a high frequency of repetition. If, for instance, you have to sort through 30,000 items and make multiple determinations on each item, do it in VBA. Likewise, if you have to perform a complex, repetitive task, such as the lease amortizations I alluded to earlier, use VBA.

As you gain experience you will develop an instinctive nature of which parts of the model to place in what medium. What I intend to do is to provide you with enough examples so that you are well on your way to this goal by the end of the book.

Compilation and Debugging After you have finished writing the Excel and VBA portions of the model, you will need to compile the program and debug it. Debugging is the skill (and some would say art) of identifying errors in your program. I have devoted an entire chapter, Chapter 16, "Debugging the Model," to this subject. VBA has an excellent, powerful, and informative debugger capability. You may or may not have heard horror stories about debugging models. They are all true. (Just kidding.) With patience and common sense, most VBA programs can be debugged in relatively short order. With practice you will learn to avoid common mistakes in writing VBA code. This will substantially decrease the number of errors the debugger will find. You will be able to concentrate on those types of errors that are more difficult to identify and fix. Once again I would emphasis that **patience and practice** are 90% of the key to mastering debugging techniques.

Stage 5: Model Validation

The task of model validation is as unique as each model you will create.

Some elements of validation are actually accomplished in the debugging phase immediately above. That is the phase in which most simple errors are caught and fixed. These as a class are generally basic arithmetic mistakes. Often tables of results from independent sources are available to directly compare your results to. This is the case with handbooks and Web sites that deal with bond math. Many of these sites offer numerous specific examples that can be easily checked in considerable detail against what your model is doing.

For more complex issues you can sometimes use other previously validated VBA models, or you can replicate portions of the analysis in Excel. You can also enlist others for second perspectives, especially if they have more product knowledge or experience. You will find that these people (and you will soon be one of them) have an instinctual feel for what is a reasonable set of results and what is not.

If others will use this model, you should involve them from the design process onwards. It is imperative that you reconfirm that the design, scope, and computational content of the model meet their requirements before proceeding. Walk the potential users through the model and explain how it is to be run. Get their feedback. Make suggested changes now to marshal support for the model. Like the model debugging process, the model validation process has a separate chapter devoted to it, Chapter 17, "Validating the Model."

Finally, when you are satisfied with the results, you can release the model.

Stage 6: Initial Deployment of the Model

First Use   Start simple. Do not overreach or over-promise in the early stages. Establish credibility for yourself and the model. If other people are going to use the model, make sure you take the time to lay out the series of steps needed to run the model correctly and then sit with them as they run the model. This will tend to defuse any negative feelings should problems arise because you are there to help and guide them. It demonstrates that you are equally invested in the process of using the model, not just in the process of developing it.

Interpreting the Results   Get buy-in as soon as possible from the decision makers that the model addresses the core requirements in a sufficiently detailed and accurate manner. Listen to what they say and do not let pride of ownership interfere with your ability to hear their comments. Take criticism constructively; remember if they do not succeed, you do not succeed! Use the initial results as a framework that leads to thinking about the next steps in the model development.

Documentation   This is the time to complete whatever documentation efforts you have decided are appropriate. The term "complete" is used because if you follow the practices of this book, you already will have performed a substantial amount of documentation in writing the model. This documentation will be completely contained inside the model itself. Most of it will take the form of comments. Comments are notations that are made in the VBA code, but which are not VBA statements that the computer can act upon. Comments are for the benefit of the person who has responsibility for maintaining and expanding the code. In all likelihood that person will be you. You will be the "expert" on the model for some time to come. By leaving yourself these explanatory notes and identifying remarks you protect both your firm and serve your own interests. We will discuss commenting in much more detail later.

If there is to be additional documentation produced that is resident outside of the model, now is the time to do it. Do not procrastinate! This is especially true of training and user documentation, the dos and don'ts of running the model. The documentation you create will hopefully put bounds around what is acceptable user behavior. Despite this, you may find all manner of aberrant behavior being practiced on your helpless model! Curb these practices with guidance, training, and documentation.

There is a tendency to feel that the initial deployment of the model is a time to take a break after the development stage. Documentation can be a pain and is generally underappreciated. Despite this, get it done now, while the ideas are fresh in your mind and not dimmed by the passage of time. Documentation has much in common with a serious dental problem. It doesn't get any better by ignoring it or deferring it. It only gets harder and more painful to correct the more time goes by.

In addition you must realize that it is an ongoing process! As you make each change to the model you must update a Change Log to tell everyone (and yourself later) when and where additional changes to the base model were made.

Stage 7: Mature Deployment of the Model

Segregation and Protection   Once the model has weathered its first set of deployment issues and has become temporarily stable, it is time to lock it up like a prisoner in a maximum-security jail! (You can console yourself that this is for its own good . . .)

Create a copy of the model, along with any validation runs and supporting material. Place it in a secure directory inaccessible to the user community. Even you should not have the ability to change this first copy. Many companies refer to this copy as the "gold copy." It can be copied but not modified. This is for several obvious reasons:

- It protects the original work from corruption by you or others (more emphasis on the others!).
- It provides a measurable base line to compare any legitimate changes you may make in the future. If you develop other expanded versions of the model, it can be used to immediately validate the parts of the model that did not change. This is important because you do not want the incremental work to affect the existing work unless it was meant to do so. In either case, you have an immediate benchmark to measure the change, or lack thereof. This process is called "back testing."
- It provides a history of the model building activity and links the model to a specific time period and analytical approach.

Training of a General User Group   If you are going to roll the model out to a wider user group, this is the time to conduct more formalized training.

Stage 8: Continued Evolution of Model Scope and Complexity

Adding Methodologies   Well-constructed models often create the need for change. They excite thought and facilitate creativity. This is especially true if they are economically valuable, generating revenue or preserving or expanding competitive advantage.

At some point, and probably sooner than you think, you will be called on to expand the model. You will add new methodologies and the process of model development will begin anew. If you follow the general precepts we have talked about, this will not be traumatic. Challenging work, perhaps, but not traumatic. A set of improvements to the basic model that we will build are presented in one of the final chapters of the book. These are broadly representative of the typical kinds of model capability extension that you may be called on to implement. Chapter 19, "Building Additional Capabilities," can be a guide to what you might face.

Improving the User Interface   One of the most common immediate demands is to change the way the user deals with the model through interfaces such as menus. Repeated use will suggest other and better ways to do things that were unforeseen in the original design conception. This is a positive development and far superior to one in which people use the model for a short while, become dismayed or disgusted, and abandon it.

The most common immediate improvements to the interface involve providing the user with the ability to specify more independent variables. You may also want to allow the user to combine the independent variables into combinations that were not possible in the previous version of the model.

Another issue is increased granularity of the model's inputs. For instance, inputs that were expressed as annual rates may next need to be specified on a weekly or daily basis as well.

Expanding the Model to Other Analytical Tasks

Over time the model may be applied to other tasks that are related to, but different from, the model's original role. A model that originally began life designed to structure securities may be transformed into a model that accepts historical data to monitor the ongoing, and project the future, performance of the original deals over time. The same may be said of an issuance model that is transformed into a pricing model to support trading activities in the secondary markets of the security.

OTHER ASPECTS OF MODELING

Productivity Enhancement for Follow-on Modeling Efforts

There is a very interesting, synergistic, aspect to modeling. If you build reliable, efficient VBA code for the first model, you will find that you will be able to reuse significant portions of it for the next model. Not only that, but as you build up a library of models, you may eventually get to the point where a significant portion, (30 to 50%) of the model is comprised of reusable code. This is equally true whether you are writing models for a business that has a series of similar deals or one with only a single specialty deal. How can this be?

Let us take the case of an individual input menu. The role of this menu is to perform the standard menu tasks of receiving user inputs and choices. It then transfers them into VBA variables that make the information available to the model. Many of the fields of this menu will be common across all applications because every application needs to execute a certain irreducible set of tasks to function. Filenames and pathways must be read from the menu. Runtime options must be specified: do this, do that, do not do this. Data arranged in time periods must be ordered and made available to the VBA for calculation purposes, and so on and so forth. The VBA code that performs these functions will be virtually identical across models. All you will have to do is change the names of the variables to be better able to identify their contents in respect to the specific application. If the original names of the variables are generic enough you might not even have to rename that many of them!

It is therefore possible to design generic menus, report generators, sorting routines, and selection routines.

Similarly, it is possible to pre-configure files containing templates for frequency distributions or cumulative loss curves. Day-count methodology menus also fall into this category of reusable technology.

Report files can incorporate previously configured graphics that can be used across many different types of models. Your VBA code will simply supply the idiosyncratic results of the specific model and the titles, spacing, scaling, and color of the various components that you wish to be automatically displayed. This is especially true of graphics that display the timing and magnitude of the cash flows of the model. All amortizing assets such as loans and leases have scheduled principal repayments, coupon income, defaulted principal, prepaid principal, and recoveries of defaulted principal. Standardized graphics can be prepared and set aside to be integrated into any model that requires these performance criteria be visually displayed.

The last subject of the book is the process of using an application, the initial model, that you have already produced, to quickly build another, related, but different application. Here we will take the model that we spent the entire book building and in one chapter transform it from a structuring model for deal issuance into a risk assessment and valuation model. This second model will monitor the health of the deal. It will provide a means of placing an ongoing, (and changing), value to the securities as they respond changes in the performance of the collateral pool and market conditions.

These are only a few of the many examples of the use of replicable VBA code. If you design the code well, you will eventually construct a box of generic spare parts and components, from which you can quickly develop new and different VBA engines.

Risk Control

"Key Person" Risk   One of the nightmares of everyone working on a team with tight deadlines and high financial risk reward issues is the loss of a key team member. While there is nothing that VBA can do to defeat the loss of human capital, VBA's very design can mitigate the departure of a valued team member.

A well-planned, well-commented model, with supporting documentation, will at least preserve the essence of the analytical approach to the problem. From a managerial perspective this tends to provide a solid starting point for recovery. VBA is a straightforward language. It lacks some of the sophistication of its rivals such as C++ and Java, but is easier to maintain and learn than either of them.

PERSPECTIVE OF THIS BOOK

The preface of this book outlines the perspective the author intends to follow.

This book will assume that you are a new analyst or associate who has completed the corporate training cycle in an investment or commercial bank. In your training you will have been exposed to the various business activities of the organization and acquired a fundamental knowledge of financial theory and calculations.

You are replacing a person who is leaving in two weeks. You need to sit with them and come up to speed on the current set of projects you will be assuming. One of these projects is the modeling support for an asset-backed securitization deal that the bank feels highly confident of winning. The modeling for the deal must be complete in about two months.

The person you are replacing has gotten the project off to a good start. He has built an Excel spreadsheet that correctly models the debt structure of the deal. One part of the model that is NOT complete is the calculation of the amortization, payments, defaults, and recoveries of the several thousand loans that constitute the client's loan portfolio. Expert in Excel, the outgoing analyst has tried a number of different spreadsheet solutions. None proved feasible—the analyst is stumped as to how to develop a spreadsheet application that can amortize thousands of loans across a wide variety of assumptions.

"Well, you seem pretty bright!" he says as he is leaving. "Good luck. It's your problem now!"

Indeed it is.

You have the Excel spreadsheet but the columns that will receive the cash flows from the loan portfolio are blank. You have a data file from the client with the proposed initial loan portfolio information. You know from other deals done by the department what output reports are needed for this deal.

You also have this book. This book will walk you through, on a step-by-step basis, the construction of a robust, flexible, and easy-to-run model. It will teach you how to wrap the Excel model in a series of menus to bring in information. It will teach you how to read data from other Excel files and how to write reports from the results produced by the model. It will help you build a valid, working model that will accomplish more in a single afternoon than your predecessor was able to accomplish in a month using Excel alone. The model you will build will allow you to answer a wide Range of questions and to adroitly manage the risk assessment and structuring requirements of the deal. You will look like a star to the other members of the deal team and the management of your department. You will create an analytics engine that will describe the financial risk of the deal, serve the client, and answer the questions of the rating agencies.

After the deal has been created you will now embark on an equally important activity, measuring its performance! We will walk through the process of converting your newly created structuring model into a monitoring, surveillance, and valuation model. Once we have this monitoring model in hand we will examine the performance of the deal at quarterly intervals for the first two years of its life. We will look at the performance of the collateral performance and the debt structure and see how they weather the current credit crisis.

When you have completed this process you will have made a significant step forward in your professional development.

This is your chance to make your predecessor's problems your opportunities!

STRUCTURE OF THE BOOK

The book is comprised of seven parts and a number of technical appendices.

Part One is the Introduction and Chapter 2 deals with concepts of modeling in general.

Part Two consists of Chapter 3 and describes the asset securitization process and the business case study we will model.

Part Three focuses on model design. Chapter 4 deals with understanding the structure of the Excel Waterfall spreadsheet of our predecessor, and Chapter 5 the design of the VBA code we will place around it.

Part Four consists of six chapters that begin to teach you the VBA language. We start, in Chapter 6, by creating the internal structure of the model in the form of VBA modules and its external structure in the form of specially named directories to hold the model and its files. Chapter 7 introduces you to VBA code that is generated from simple recorded macros. Here we will use the VBA editor for the first time and look at recompiling our edited code. You will learn how to compile code and run a short macro. In a rudimentary way, this will be your first experience programming. This chapter will lead directly to Chapter 8, where we discuss VBA data, arrays, Ranges, and objects. You will learn what objects and methods are and will experiment with the Range function. In this chapter you will begin to implement simple menus. In Chapter 9, we will address the VBA statements that allow you to control the flow of the model. Here you will learn how to have the code make decisions, assign values to variables, and perform calculations. The next chapter, Chapter 10, introduces you to the concept of VBA code output and shows you how to produce error and progress messages for the user. Chapter 11 finishes the section by describing the reporting function.

Part Five focuses on writing VBA code—lots of it. Chapter 12 tackles the main program and the declaration of a host of global variables. These variables will hold all of the input information about the portfolio and intermediate calculation results. They will also hold results from the model run, the portfolio level cash flows. Chapter 13 will take you through the process of writing a collateral selection methodology. Chapter 14 calculates the cash flows on a loan-by-loan, period-by-period basis. Here you may wish to detour to the two Appendices at the back of the book on Mortgage and Bond mathematics and concepts. We will also introduce the concept of calculation optimization. Chapter 15 will teach you how to transfer the VBA results back out to the Excel waterfall, load it, and calculate it. We will also write the code to capture the results of the Excel waterfall and transfer them back to VBA variables for later output. The last chapter of the section, Chapter 16, will teach you how to use the debugger program to detect and correct different types of errors in the code you have written.

Part Six deals with the initial deployment of the model. Chapter 17 will discuss validation techniques and testing. We will want to be sure the model is correct before we use it on a real deal. In Chapter 18 we get to run the complete model for the first time and come up with the securities structure that will meet the requirements of all of the interested parties. These Range from our own internal constituencies to investors, rating agencies, and regulatory groups. Possible solutions to different problems we encounter will mirror what can happen in a live deal. After we have run a number of scenario sets, we will move on to improving the model. Chapter 19 describes the process of expanding the model with new inputs, calculation methodologies, and reports.

Part Seven addresses what happens after the model is deployed. In Chapter 20, we will discuss the subject of documentation: how much, what, and for whom. Chapter 21 describes how you protect and grow your model so that it can continue to create value for the business unit.

Part Eight concerns the fate of the deal once it has been launched. In Chapter 22, "Building a Portfolio Monitoring Model," we will do just that, drawing heavily off of the code and reports we created for the structuring model. This will allow us to put this model in place in a fraction of the time it took us to develop our first model. In Chapter 23, "Valuation Techniques: How Do We Determine Price?" we will look at the fundamentals of valuing the deal after it has been issued. In Chapter 24, "Challenging Times for the Deal," we will analyze the progress of the deal over the first two years of its life. We will employ our newly developed monitoring model to project the cash flows based on the empirical performance of the collateral to date. We will apply these cash flows to the deal's structure along with default and prepayment projections and other assumptions about the market to arrive at a series of pricing benchmarks for the notes.

Part Nine contains a single chapter, Chapter 25, "Parting Admonitions," which gives you some last words of advice, consolation, and appreciation, and caps the entire process you have undergone.

The book closes with a pair of technical appendices. These sections include a mathematical discussion of mortgage and bond math used in the model.

PUTTING THE DELIVERABLES "ON THE TARGET"

Emphasis on Deliverables in a Business Context

Every chapter starts with an **"Overview."**

The next section is named **"Deliverables."** This is what you should have achieved by the end of the chapter.

These deliverables are broken down into knowledge goals and production goals.

The **"Modeling Knowledge"** goals will relate to concepts and terms in finance, modeling, and programming. The **"VBA Programming"** goals will be the elements of the VBA language, VBA commands, logic structures, and code deliverables in the form of subroutines and functions you have written.

At the end of each chapter you will have a **"Deliverables Checklist"** section that will test you on the contents of the chapter you have just completed tied directly to the items in the **"Deliverables"** section.

In this way the completion of every chapter will add to a list of your intellectual and product development accomplishments. You will have a detailed list of specific goals to meet, and a checklist at the end of the chapter that tells you if you have met them.

Another section that will regularly, but not always, appear in the chapters is the **"Under Construction"** section. In this section anything that is being build, new template files, additions to the model, menus, new calculation capabilities, actions buttons, or even standalone programs will be described.

The next to last section will be entitled **"Next Steps."** This section contains a brief review of the chapter you have just completed and how it connects with the next two or three chapters. This section is designed to provide you with the perspective of how the material is integrated over a three-to-four-chapter span of ideas and techniques.

The last section of most chapters will be **"On the Web Site"** and will hold a description of the material related to the chapter that is available on the Web site of the book.

There is an ancient Roman saying, "Familiarity breeds contempt." From an intellectual perspective, this concept can be dangerous. As you progress through this book you will be learning something on almost every page. You may not be aware of the amount of knowledge and skill that you are accumulating. This is particularly true in some of the introductory chapters, for example Chapter 7, "Recorded Macros: A First Look at the VBA Language." This chapter seems a little passive in nature. We record a macro and then look at it. This is a simple macro that prints a column of numbers, sums them, and changes their font color and bold settings. Amazingly, this example introduces you to almost everything you need to build a simple model. It introduces objects and methods, variable assignments, looping structure, and output manipulation. It is the first concrete link you will see of the direct interaction between VBA and Excel. It actually contains about 80% of all the concepts we need to design models in VBA. In addition to all the VBA features of this example, we also are exposed to the VBA Editor and the VBA Debugger for the first time.

The ironic thing is that if you do not realize how much you have learned, you may feel as if you have hardly learned anything at all! The Deliverables section therefore is designed to give you a line-by-line list of your accomplishments. This is important, because the ultimate deliverable, a working model, can appear to be a large and distant goal for the beginner.

I want to re-emphasize that the way to succeed in this endeavor is to reduce this large task to bite-size entities and master them one-by-one in easy, incremental steps.

Development of Your Human Capital

There are seven major reasons why a person should learn to model using VBA/Excel:

1. Career development and enrichment
2. Managerial and peer recognition
3. Significantly increased responsibility, recognition, and reward
4. Broadening your business knowledge and perspectives

5. Potential for substantially more responsibility, exposure, experience, recognition, promotion, and reward than indicated in item 3
6. Intellectual stimulation, feelings of accomplishment, and the satisfaction of having added to your personal growth
7. Very much more responsibility (Oh! The responsibility is killing me!), promotion (Call me SIR!), and rewards (we hope!)

So take your pick of odds or evens, or even better, a mixture of both. Whatever your reasons, I hope you enjoy what is to come.

## CHAPTER 2

Common Sense

OVERVIEW

This chapter is without a doubt one of the shortest chapters in the book. This is not because there is little common sense to dispense when it comes to talking about the modeling process. It is because a little common sense can go a long way. Some of the subjects that we will talk about here will be touched upon in much greater detail in latter chapters. Some guidelines are so general that I hope that, when you hear them once, they will stick with you for a long time.

I would hope that eventually you would regard this collection of advice and admonition in the same way you would all the unheeded parental discussions you ever had. Mark Twain once said that when he left home at the age of 17, he did so because he could not stand how stupid his parents were. On returning 10 years later he was amazed at how smart they had become.

DELIVERABLES

The deliverable of this chapter is a good dose of common sense. We will look at four basic precepts of modeling and tell you why each is vitally important in its own way. The purpose of these admonishments is to help you deliver a complete, comprehensible, effective, and efficient product in a timely manner. More importantly, each contains a grain of wisdom in regards to self-preservation. Guard against over confidence and over promising. Remember to keep the perspective that this activity is only one piece of the greater effort to meet the requirements of the business and the clients. Take this advice as you would that of a solicitous aunt, uncle, or grandparent, offering it with your best interests at heart.

DO NOT EAT ANYTHING BIGGER THAN YOUR HEAD

As you progress through this book you will be presented with many new concepts and perspectives. Some of you will have never programmed before, some will have a modest amount of experience programming, and some of you may be experts. In this book you will grasp the concepts of program organization and design, how to write clear, concise, and efficient VBA code, and learn to combine VBA with Excel to optimize the properties of both. This will allow you tackle a whole set of problems in a way unavailable to you up until now.

Walk before you run.

One of the most common pitfalls for new model developers is to "bite off more than you can chew." I am assuming that the people who buy a book of this nature are mentally and intellectually aggressive. You want to try new things and learn new skills. The creative urge is closely associated with these drives. Be careful that you do not over-commit yourself in the early going.

Be prudent. Plan you first projects carefully and allow extra time. Manage the expectations of your target audiences. Do not over-promise.

Actively engage the people who will use the model to clearly identify the most critical functions needed before you start development. Assume nothing. Once you have all reached a consensus as to what needs to be done, get a concrete agreement as to timing and deliverables of the model. This does not need to be a 20-page-long planning document, usually just a 10-sentence-long e-mail reconfirming the priorities is sufficient.

If you are developing the model for yourself, be clear as to what the core requirements are. Write them down and stick with that list until the first version of the model is written, debugged, tested, and released. This will give you a base from which to build. To that base add all the bright ideas that occurred to you as you were writing the first version. This practice will allow you to develop and deliver the first cut of the model on time and hopefully, without too much pain and suffering on your part. It will also avoid the danger that the implementation of successive incremental ideas will delay or confuse the initial development effort.

Above all, especially if you are not going to be the only one using the model, communicate frequently with the parties involved in the process. Make them feel like partners in the development process, because they are. Convey to them that their cooperation is vital and that your success is their success. This is no more that the application of the Golden Rule. Imagine yourself in their positions and give them the communication and involvement they need so that both you and they achieve the stated objectives.

The first time one of your models works as planned and is critical to the success of the business is a thrilling time. Enjoy the feeling but stay focused. Keep the development effort focused on a defined and manageable set of objectives and work to achieve them. Guard against over-confidence and over-commitment.

YOU ONLY HURT THE ONE YOU LOVE

Who do you love? Yourself! Do not hurt the one you love!

Protect yourself! Remember that upon completion of the model, no matter how many other people eventually change it and use it, it will always be considered to be *your model*. It will be personally and directly associated with you and will be considered a reflection of your judgment, hard work, and professional standards.

This book will present very specific guidelines as to how to build the framework of your model. Follow them religiously until you have enough experience and success to deviate from them. These ideas have been tested and they work! Follow the organizational principals as to how to segregate your VBA code into appropriately separate modules that are easy to find and repurpose. Keep your subroutines short and to the point.

Later in the book you will learn that a comment is a particular type of notation that you can insert into a VBA program. **Comments are statements that are ignored by the computer; you create them only for the benefit and information of yourself, future developers, and the users of the model.** Use comments liberally. Unless you have a photographic memory, they will be worth their weight in gold if you return to the model after some time away from it. They will also be a roadmap that others will bless you for when you have been promoted and are no longer around to help. They can also free you to work on other opportunities by helping you train and leverage up the value of others. One other point should be mentioned. What may be clear to you may not be clear to the next person to look at the code. Comments can be a terrific help in guiding someone over the "hard parts" of the model. Comments may also provide that little extra piece of information to trigger the "Ah-ha!" of understanding for the next reader. That's a win-win for everyone!

One last thing. Above all else, *be neat*! Look at the VBA code examples and actively try to emulate their physical appearance. I refer specifically to **indentation and spacing**. While it seems trivial now, this can help immensely. It will allow your and others to implicitly grasp the chain of events that the VBA code is trying to perform. It will also help you find errors more quickly by giving you clues as to what part of the VBA code is doing what.

IT IS OK TO BE RIGHT; JUST DO NOT BE DEAD-RIGHT

Guess what? You *do not* know it all! Even though you have this wonderful, wonderful book to draw upon! (Just kidding.)

Be aware that modeling, while a valuable skill, is only one piece of what will become the completed business solution. Learn from the other members of your team. Learn the legal and regulatory environment of your business. Learn the concepts of risk analysis and credit assessment. Know the strategies of your firm and their product offerings. Understand your divisional and corporation marketing objectives and your model development policies

Above all, know your customers. In the process of building the model, seek out their knowledge and experience about what you are modeling. In an environment of clear and willing communication, this will always produce better models. Sometimes the smallest things can make a big difference. Many business processes and relationships have synergistic components to them. These relationships can at times, if ignored or unknown, cause significant deviations between the model predictions and the real-world behavior.

You cannot be an expert on everything. You can, however, actively avail yourself of the advice and knowledge of the people who *are* collectively the experts on everything!

The old saw of "don't be afraid to ask stupid questions" applies in spades here. No matter how august the personage you are questioning, they were not born with the knowledge of the issues in which they are now expert. They themselves had to learn what they know in one way or another, and somewhere along the way they no doubt had to ask "stupid" questions, too. Asking questions also helps in establishing the communication channels we spoke of above.

KNOW WHEN TO HOLD 'EM

Know when to fold them, know when to walk away, and know when to run. More specifically, know when "Enough is enough!"

For instance, you should be aware of the limitations of your model—it helps in determining what activities it is appropriate for and which not. Just because a model spits out a number does not mean that its analysis is the most appropriate one for the problem at hand. Put everything in context. Do not delude yourself that the numbers are the be-all and end-all of the business decision.

Modeling and analytics can only supply a part of the business solution. Do not become either myopic or self-delusional as to the primacy of computational analysis. Stay attuned to the business problem and the broader context of the business environment, and the solutions it demands.

Never knowingly allow your models to be used for morally questionable or fraudulent purposes. Remember that your work is a direct extension of your personal professional standards and will be viewed as such. Don't lose your good reputation; once lost, it is difficult or impossible to salvage.

NEXT STEPS

We are now ready to start with the real stuff.

In the next chapter we will examine the business problem we are going to model.

I hope that all of you find the exercises to follow as interesting as I did in my first trip down the Yellow Brick Road of modeling. It can be a bit foreboding, but quite an adventure, too.

The Securitization Process

## CHAPTER 3

Securitizing a Loan Portfolio

OVERVIEW

This chapter will describe the process we are going to model, the securitization of a loan portfolio. What is meant by "securitization"? In general, there are three ways by which a firm can access the capital markets; issuing debt, selling equity in the firm, or securitizing the cash flows from an asset pool.

This chapter will describe one of many structures that are used by banks, savings and loans, finance companies, insurance companies, and many others to raise capital. This is done through an asset-backed securitization, where many loans are pooled and their cash flows—the principal repayments and interest payments due from the loan holders—are bundled together to repay debt securities sold to investors.

Investors find these securities attractive for several reasons. Most attractive of these is the fact that the assets are diversified across many loan holders thereby potentially lessening the risk of the securities defaulting.

These securities can take a variety of forms, ranging from securities that are backed by the asset collateral as well as the issuer's credit, to non-recourse notes, where investors only look to the asset collateral for repayment. The most common debt securitizations are either public or private placement of notes. Another security that is widely used to finance asset securitization is commercial paper that is issued by a special purpose vehicle (SPV).

The payment of the principal and interest portions of the debt is solely predicated on the collateral cash flows and other funded reserves of the deal structure. If the cash flows generated by these assets are not sufficient to pay off the issued debt, the investors will suffer losses. It is therefore vitally important to correctly estimate the Range of possible cash flows that an asset pool can produce, and to issue an amount of debt consistent with this Range of possibilities and the credit ratings desired. As one might imagine, the cash flows from a given pool of assets can vary depending upon the Obligors' creditworthiness and their ability to negotiate changing micro- and macroeconomic conditions.

For our purposes, we will focus on non-recourse securitization, where just about any type of asset pool that produces cash flows can be securitized. The trick, so to speak, to any asset securitization is to understand the characteristics of the cash flows and then prudently match a debt structure to them.

This book is primarily a text in modeling, not a text in financial structuring methodology. As such, I have selected the simplest form of asset-backed securitization (ABS) as the example for the Excel model "waterfall." (A term you will hear many times in this book, waterfall refers to cash payments from the loans as a stream of water that sequentially fills a series of buckets that are the expenses and debt repayments of the deal.) It is the securitization of a pool of loans made to small businesses.

We will build a model to select collateral from a pool of candidates, project the cash flows of the selected collateral over its contractual life, and lastly, apply these cash flows to a financing structure to defease a debt issuance.

In this chapter we will present you with an overview of the securitization process and the role of modeling within that process. We will acquaint you with a number of terms and concepts that you see in both the Excel model of the debt structure and the VBA code that will generate and apply the collateral cash flows.

This is a brief and deliberately constrained description of the concepts of securitization finance. To catalog and describe all the types of ABS collateral that have been securitized and all the debt structures that have been developed in the last twenty years would call for ten books this size!

You need to focus on the business application just enough to understand it. The main emphasis of this book is to teach you how to model *any* kind of business application, not just a structured finance deal. To understand why and how the model is developed in the book you will need to understand what is being modeled.

Do not stop there!

Think about how you can apply the principles presented here to help you with your own specific applications. Having said that, let us talk about securitization.

DELIVERABLES

The following are the key deliverables for this chapter:

- An overview of what an asset-backed securitization (ABS) is
- A description of the role of modeling in the securitization decision
- The functions the model will need to perform and why

FINANCING A LOAN PORTFOLIO

The Concept of Securitization

Let us begin by identifying the typical parties to a securitization of a loan portfolio:

Obligor. The borrower, who has agreed to repay the loan over time at the stated interest rate and loan tenor (time remaining until loan comes due).

Originator/Seller/Transferor. The entity that extends the loan to the Obligor. This entity will bundle the loan together with similar loans to create a loan pool that is then transferred to another entity, which will in turn issue securities, typically notes, representing ownership rights to the loan pool and its cash flow. The Originator typically retains a residual interest in the cash flows generated by the assets; that is, the Originator will receive any cash flows in excess of those needed to repay the Note Holders.

Issuer/Conduit. The entity that issues securities backed by the cash flows of the collateral pool transferred by the Seller/Transferor. The Issuer is often a "bankruptcy-remote" special purpose vehicle established by the Seller/Transferor.

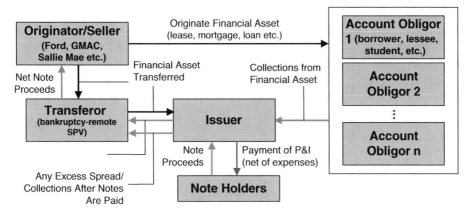

EXHIBIT 3.1   Schematic of a generic consumer asset securitization

Note Holders. Investors who buy the notes issued by the Issuer.

Servicer. The entity that agrees to service the assets while the notes issued are outstanding. Servicing typically includes ensuring that payments from the Obligors are properly paid and transferred to the proper bank accounts for payment to the Note Holders, following up on delinquent accounts, and pursuing appropriate remedies upon default by the Obligors. The Servicer can be the Originator or a third-party whose primary business is servicing asset pools.

Exhibit 3.1 is a schematic of a generic consumer asset securitization.

Advantages/Disadvantages of Securitization to the Seller

Advantages

- The Seller may be able to remove assets from its balance sheet; if so, the Seller also may be able to manage to targeted financial ratios, especially the debt/equity ratio.
- Securitization monetizes future cash flow earnings, accelerating the recognition of earnings.
- In non-recourse securitization, the risk of creditor default transfers from the Seller to Note Holders.
- Securitization may diversify risk by allowing the Seller to remove or limit over-concentrations of particular asset types from its holdings.
- Securitization facilitates the sale of nonessential, concentrated, undesirable, or excess assets; this often occurs immediately after a merger or acquisition has taken place.
- The Seller may be able to raise funds in the capital markets without impacting borrowing limits.
- The Seller may be able to retain servicing income or other fee streams from the assets.
- The Seller may benefit from improved brand recognition.
- The Seller may be able to access lower funding rates.
- Many assets that are candidates for securitization have long lives, so the Seller may be able to access longer-term funding than is possible through other means.

Disadvantages

- Securitization requires a "critical mass" to be economical. Some Seller portfolios will not have sufficient eligible collateral to justify the fixed expenses of the deal.
- If this is its first experience with securitization, the Seller will find a somewhat steep operational learning curve.
- If this is a first-time securitization, transaction costs may be high due to the need to modify accounting and servicing systems.
- The Seller may lack staffing to undertake a securitization or not have the right kind of staff available—these are especially important investments if securitization will be an ongoing activity.
- It is difficult or impossible to restructure securitizations once launched without retiring the existing debt. This leads to some degree of inflexibility and constraint.
- The Seller may be unable or unwilling to provide past performance due to the relative youth of the assets or to failure to retain necessary historical time series information on delinquencies, defaults, and recoveries. They may be unable to comply with rating agency or investor requests for this information.
- The Seller will have to disclose significant information about its underwriting criteria and practices, and its organization policies.
- The Seller may not be able to include in the securitization process assets that do not conform to standard payment features and protections that are representative of the type of collateral being securitized.

Importance of Due Diligence

Due diligence is the process of becoming familiar with all of the factors that can materially impact the cash flows that are expected to repay the securitized notes. These factors would typically include:

- The ability and willingness of Obligors to make timely payment on their loans:
  - Originator's underwriting criteria; target credit/Fair Isaacs and Company (FICO®) scores, employment history, documentation requirements, and so on
  - Actual asset pool characteristics; credit/FICO scores, documentation provided, and so on
  - Environmental factors that may cause the Obligors to default or prepay (e.g., rising or falling interest rates or asset values)
- Structure of the loans:
  - Coupon, tenor, prepayment options, and so on
  - Delinquency and default provisions and remedies
- Experience/motivation of the Originator—the entity as well as key individuals:
  - Why does the Originator want to do a securitization—exiting business, diversify funding sources, monetize future cash flows due to cash flow problems, and so on
  - Historical performance of assets originated by the Originator
- Experience/capabilities of the Servicer:
  - Financial strength of the Servicer and ability to withstand business cycles over life of securitization

- Servicer's systems and policies—especially with collecting on delinquent or defaulted accounts
- Historical performance of the Servicer—especially with collecting on delinquent or defaulted accounts

Since the purpose of modeling is to project future asset pool cash flows and note performance as accurately as possible, the modeler should be a part of, or at least thoroughly review, the results of the due diligence process. In the following sections, we assume that the due diligence process has been completed and we begin to build the model that will reflect what we know about the asset pool, the structure of the securitization transaction, and projected securitization cash flows and note performance. Recall that for illustrative purposes we are focusing on a non-recourse ABS, where the Note Holders can only look to the cash flows from the asset pool and any reserves or other sources that may be a part of the securitization structure.

Role of Modeling in the Securitization Task

The role of modeling will be focused on the following:

- Test the eligibility of the offered collateral in the proposed asset pool. Each loan must meet specific criteria for inclusion in the securitized pool.
- After the selection process is complete, produce a listing of all ineligible collateral for the Seller and the Issuer.
- From the eligible collateral pool, produce the necessary demographic and stratification reports concerning its composition.
- Amortize the assets of the pool in regard to various expected prepayment, delinquency, and default conditions. These scenarios will also need to cover stress tests from the rating agencies and investors.
- Use the results of these amortization runs to determine the issuance amount of the deal. That is, capture the debt structure performance results and determine the debt issuance amounts congruent with expected or desired risk ratings.
- Perform sensitivity analysis on critical model inputs to determine the possible Range of outcomes should economic conditions or Obligor performance change over time.

DESCRIPTION OF THE COLLATERAL

The Loans

In our example, the asset pool is a collection of small business loans. The loans were acquired by the Seller as part of a larger portfolio of mortgage, automobile, manufactured housing, and recreational vehicle loans. While the Seller is and expects to be a continuing buyer of these types of loans, it does not have a lending activity dedicated to commercial lending nor does it wish to develop one. It anticipates acquiring other portfolios of this type through activities such as mergers or acquisitions, and

EXHIBIT 3.2   Basic demographics of the loan portfolio

	Minimum	Maximum
Spread over Prime Rate	1.50%	5.75%
Gross Coupon	6.75%	11.00%
Original Terms (months)	55	309
Remaining Terms (months)	20	306
Seasoning (months)	1	64
Original Balance	$20,000	$2,340,000
Current Balance	$10,400	$1,648,800
Remaining Balance	$6,838	$1,640,244

already owns three smaller portfolios in addition to this one. It would like to realize an absolute minimum sale of $450 million's worth of loans.

The loan portfolio consists of approximately 2,500 loans with a $552 million original balance, and a $462 million remaining balance. These loans are all floating rate notes, whose index is the prime rate. The basic financial characteristics of the portfolio are outlined in Exhibit 3.2.

All loans reset both their coupons and payments quarterly. All loans use the 30/360-day count convention. Day count conventions govern how many days of interest must be paid on a monthly and annual basis by the loan or Note Holder. The portfolio is geographically diversified across all 50 states, with current balance concentrations in the states of New York, California, New Jersey, Florida, and Colorado.

The Seller has as an information services group backing up its portfolio management and servicing efforts. The group has been able to produce a data file that profiles the proposed collateral, and that contains everything we need to conduct a basic securitization modeling exercise. The information about each loan in the portfolio consists of 26 pieces of information. This information falls into four broad categories, as displayed in Exhibit 3.3:

1. **Balance Information.** The original and remaining balance of the loan, and the original and current equity positions relative to the current appraisal balances that are also supplied.
2. **Tenor Information.** The original and remaining term of the notes in months, from which we can calculate the seasoning of the loan. The origination and expected maturity dates are provided in year and month formats.
3. **Amortization Information.** Whether the loan is a fixed- or floating-rate loan, and its current coupon level. If it is a floating-rate loan, the terms of the floating-rate agreement are also included, citing the current coupon level, the index, the spread to the index, the reset periods and frequencies, the periodic and lifetime coupon floors and caps, and the day count convention of the loan.
4. **Demographic Information.** The state and ZIP code of the business location.

We will read this information into the model to determine how many of the loans are suitable for inclusion in the securitization. After the selection process has

EXHIBIT 3.3 Contents and information formats of the collateral data file

#	Item Name	Form
1	Original Balance	$
2	Current Balance	$
3	Current Coupon	% 3 digits
4	Original Term	#
5	Remaining Term	#
6	Seasoning	#
7	Fixed or Floating Coupon	1 = Fix, 2 = Float
8	Floating Rate Index	Alpha
9	Spread to Index	% 3 digits
10	Coupon Reset Frequency	#
11	Payment Reset Frequency	#
12	Lifetime Coupon Floor	% 3 digits
13	Lifetime Coupon Cap	% 3 digits
14	Coupon Reset Cap	% 3 digits
15	Coupon Reset Floor	% 3 digits
16	Day Count Method	# code 1-3
17	Stated Monthly Payment	$
18	Appraisal Value	$
19	Original Equity	$
20	Current Equity	$
21	Business Location State	2 digit Alpha Postal
22	Business Location ZIP Code	#
23	Origination Date—Year	YY
24	Origination Date—Month	MM
25	Maturity Date—Year	YY
26	Maturity Date—Month	MM

been completed, we will again use the information to produce stratification and demographic reports about the collateral. Finally, we will crunch it to calculate the cash flow generating potential of the loans.

COLLATERAL CASH FLOWS

Basic Cash Flow Components

The portfolio as a whole will generate either four or five cash flow components on a monthly basis. These components are:

1. **Coupon Payments.** The interest component of the securitized loan's monthly payment to investors.
2. **Scheduled Amortization of Principal.** The principal component of the loan's monthly payment to investors.

3. **Prepayments of Principal.** Additional payments of principal received after the regular monthly payment has been made. Usually this is in the form of a complete principal retirement of the loan balance.
4. **Defaults of Principal.** Permanent Obligor non-payment resulting in foreclosure and sale of the property or assets.
5. **Recoveries of Defaulted Principal.** Proceeds from the sale of the assets after liquidation costs.

Prepayment and Default Activity

As you might imagine, the accelerated prepayment of principal and default activity both reduce the total amount of cash flows available from the collateral pool.

Prepayments truncate coupon payments by immediately retiring the principal balance of the loan that would have continued to generate coupon income in the absence of such activity. Defaults dilute the cash flows by eliminating both future coupon income and receipt of principal.

The extent to which Obligors engage in either behavior will reduce the total cash flows of the collateral pool. If these cash flows are so attenuated as to be insufficient to cover the debt service and the retirement of the principal, losses will occur. The Issuer can build certain safeguards into the deal, such as default reserve funds. These reserve funds will hold monies that can then be used to make good on some or all of the lost cash flows. If these reserves prove insufficient to cover the lost revenue, the structure may experience loses.

Recoveries of Defaulted Principal

Typically, recoveries of defaulted principal occur many months after the Obligor defaults on the loan. A lender usually will not begin legal proceedings until the Obligor is three months or more in arrears in his payments. If the Obligor contests the seizure of the property and forces the lender to go through a full foreclosure, another year may be added to the time line. Once the lender has repossessed the property, it may need to bring the property up to marketable condition prior to a sale. The lender then disposes of the property through a negotiated sale or auction.

Any money received from the sale, less the selling expenses, is applied against the interest in arrears and the unpaid principal of the loan.

The difference between the economic value of the property at the time of the default and the value at the time of the sale is called the Market Value Decline (MVD) Factor, and is expressed as a percentage of the original appraisal of the property. Thus a property with an appraisal value of $1,000,000 at the time of default that realizes a recovery of $600,000 has experienced a 40% MVD. The time between the event of default and the receipt of the recovery monies is called the Recovery Lag (RL). In the above case, the Obligor was three months in arrears at the time of the initiation of foreclosure action. The foreclosure action took 12 months and the repair and sale activities took another three months. The RL in this case would be 18 months.

Exhibits 3.4 and 3.5 illustrate the effects that differing levels of MVD and current equity positions have on the expected Severity of Loss for the loan.

Loan Balance Recovery Examples Under Different Market Value Decline Assumptions

EXHIBIT 3.4 Recovery calculation for two loans with the same equity position and different MVDs

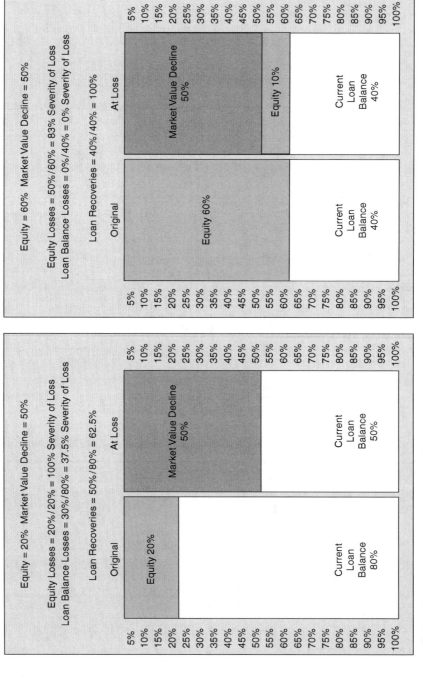

EXHIBIT 3.5 Recovery calculation for two loans with different equity positions and the same MVD

EXPENSE AND LIABILITY STRUCTURE

The following are terms that relate to the liability side of the securitization. Liabilities are the assignments of the funds realized from the sale of the collateral pool and the repayment of the indebtedness. The funds are used to pay fees and expenses, fund reserve accounts, pay debt service, retire outstanding principal, and provide excess servicing.

That is to say, every dollar of the cash flows from the asset side of the deal will end up in one of the liability categories on the debt side of the deal. It is everyone's hope that when the smoke clears, all expenses and fees, all debt service of the notes, and all repayment of note principal will be made in full, with a little excess servicing left over.

Advance Rates and Seller Interest

The advance rate is the percentage of notes sold in relationship to the beginning balance of the collateral pool. If our structure is going to issue \$450 million in notes, all supported by the cash flows of a collateral pool with a current balance of \$500 million, then the advance rate is \$450/\$500 = 90%.

The part of the advance rate for which no money is lent, the 100% − 90% = 10% in the example above, is called the Seller Interest. This is the liability retained by the Seller of the collateral. If the loans perform badly and the cash flows are insufficient to retire all of the money lent to the Seller by the Conduit, the Seller will not receive any cash flows from this 10% of the loans.

If, however, the loans perform well and the financing provided by the Conduit could be repaid in full, perhaps even ahead of schedule, then the cash flows, net of deal expenses and the debt service and principal retirement of the Conduit financing, belong solely to the Seller. The 10% Seller Interest can therefore be considered to be somewhat of a second financing in the deal. If the portfolio is \$500 million with a 10% Seller Interest, then the Seller has \$50 million at risk. If the collateral fails to retire the outstanding balance of the Conduit financing, the loss to the Seller Interest may well be 100% of the \$50 million. If the Conduit financing is repaid and there are still cash flows left over, this is referred to as excess servicing. The excess servicing may be less than, equal to, or greater than the original Seller Interest. If they totaled \$25 million, the loss to the Seller Interest would be 50%. If the excess cash flows were \$50 million, exactly the size of the Seller Interest, then the loss to the Seller Interest would be 0% and its coverage ratio would be 0%. If the excess cash flows were \$75 million, the loss to the Seller Interest would be 0% and the Seller Interest coverage ratio would be 50%.

Deal Expenses

Deal expenses can be many or few depending on the complexity of the deal structure. The major deal expenses are usually connected with servicing the collateral portfolio and running the Trustee services of the deal. There is any number of other expenses, but these two are in every deal.

Servicing fees are paid to the servicer to monitor the portfolio. They include but are not limited to monitoring the condition of the assets, payments processing, tax reporting, collection activities, arrears workout plans, legal actions such as fore-closure, property seizure and repair, and property resale.

Program fees are charged by the party providing the financing (the Conduit), for providing the program under which the securitization is funded.

Structural Triggers

Everyone hopes that things will go as planned when the deal is launched, but this is not always the case. It is commonly necessary to employ "triggers." Triggers are predefined tests which, when met or exceeded, automatically cause the deal to dynamically restructure itself to meet the changed conditions.

Many triggers relate to default conditions. For instance, we may determine that a certain level of defaults will attenuate the cash flows from the assets to such an extent that losses to the Note Holders become possible or probable. The trigger might be set to activate when a rolling-month average of defaults or delinquencies is reached, or a cumulative default level is reached. In most cases, triggers are designed to deploy should the full repayment of the notes appear to be in jeopardy: All available monies generated by the collateral pool are then directed to the repayment of the indebtedness and all payments to the Seller cease. This redirection of the collateral cash flows will serve to accelerate the repayment of the outstanding note balances. Little or no cash will be released to the Seller. Funds might flow from a default reserve account to the bondholders to retire principal.

Triggers can also be used for other than cash flow emergencies, however. They can be used to "clean up" the deal at the end of its life by forcing an accelerated retirement of the note principal when only a few of the notes remain. Most clean-up triggers are set at either 5% or 10% of the original balance of the notes.

Another type of trigger may be built into the deal to activate when the cash flows from the collateral pool are insufficient to pay the deal expenses and debt service of the notes. This is commonly referred to as a negative spread condition. If a negative spread condition occurs, various rerouting of cash flows may happen.

Yet another type of trigger may function if a non-financial or non-credit event occurs. This is called a qualitative trigger. In modeling, these triggers can be activated to observe the effects of rerouting more cash flows to the notes' principal payments. The increases are merely assumed to have occurred; they need not be based on a specific condition applying to either the collateral or the cash flows.

The deal in this book will have a qualitative trigger, a rolling three-month delinquency trigger, and a clean-up trigger set at 10% of the remaining notes.

Reserve Funds

Reserve funds can be thought of as blocks of money, designated for any number of nasty eventualities. John Milton (author of *Paradise Lost*) once said, "They also serve who only stand and wait." This is especially true of reserve funds, which are created in the hope that they will never be used.

Reserve funds can be created for general purposes, held at the ready to remedy any deal deficiencies. Or they can be set aside for very specific purposes, accessible only under very limited and special conditions. They can be fully funded, partially funded, or even unfunded at the beginning of the deal. In the latter two cases, there will be conditions in the deal agreements that will allow money to be diverted from excess servicing payments to increase the balance of the reserve funds over time. These monies will come from what is left over after all expenses, debt service, and principal have been paid.

Common practice releases all unapplied reserve fund balances to the Seller upon the final retirement of the indebtedness of the deal.

MEASURING THE PERFORMANCE OF THE STRUCTURE

Measuring the Performance of the Collateral

The description and measurement of the performance of the collateral cash flows is of paramount importance. It is the overwhelming determinate of how the structure will perform. "You can't make a silk purse from a sow's ear," goes the old adage. If the cash flows are regular and robust in regards to the deal expenses and the debt service, the note principal will be repaid in a timely manner.

If prepayments and defaults in the collateral pool dilute and diminish the cash flows, these shortfalls may not be covered by features of the structure, reserves, and so forth. In this case the repayment of the principal will at best be delayed or the cash flows will prove insufficient to fully retire the debt and losses will occur.

We must be able to describe in detail, based on model runs, where these breaking points are along the continuum of prepayment and default rate interactions. We must be able to confidently point to those conditions under which the structure will fail and make sure that the client and the investors are comfortable with the risk.

Lastly, we must be able to convince other parties, our own credit people, and/or rating agency personnel that the combination of the structure and the expected payment characteristics of the collateral are appropriate to the credit rating the structure will receive.

Measuring the Liability Structure Performance

We will need to measure the effects of prepayments, defaults, and recoveries on the collateral cash flows and the subsequent performance of the notes. How quickly will the note principal be repaid and what will be the timing of these repayments? What is the expected coupon income and how does that coupon income translate into a financial return to the investor?

To what extent will the structure mitigate losses? Under what circumstances will the structure fail and losses be incurred? What is the Range of these conditions, and how severe might the losses be?

We will need to capture this information not only for one scenario, but probably for many.

Role of Expenses

We will want to understand the timing and magnitude of the expenses. How much cash will they draw away from the repayment of the notes? What percentage of the total cash flows will the expected expenses represent? Expenses such as amounts paid to the servicer are expenses to the deal but income to the parties performing the functions. We will need to be able to tell these service providers what their expected fee streams will look like.

Reserve Fund Performance

We will want to monitor the adequacy of the delinquency reserve fund to determine what Ranges of interest shortfalls it can defease before becoming exhausted. This will be determined not only by the initial size of the reserve fund, but also by the timing of the draws made upon it.

FUNCTIONAL REQUIREMENTS OF THE MODEL

Data Sufficiency

The first and most important consideration in designing the model is to ascertain that all relevant information about the modeled process can be accommodated by the model. In the case of this model, it means not only the information on the collateral, but that all structural features of the liabilities are represented correctly in the Excel waterfall spreadsheet.

In addition to the above, the model must be able to make all critical calculations, both in the collateral amortization process and in the liability performance measurements. These calculations would include the Internal Rate of Return (IRR), average life, final maturity, and duration statistics of the debt.

Flexibility

We must design the model from the very start with the viewpoint of change. It can be taken as a given that there will be unforeseen circumstances that will alter our perception of the "necessary tasks" that the model will need to perform.

We need to design the structure of the model to be clear and receptive to changes. We must clearly segregate the functionality of the different processes the model must perform to accomplish our goals. Our structural design must allow for the quick and concise identification of the parts of the model that will need to be altered to effect changes.

The menu and reporting structures must allow additions and deletions to accommodate changing input and output requirements. The model should be designed so that only the minimum amount of work needs to be done to achieve a goal; that is, we should try to make the model as responsive and efficient as possible.

Clear and Concise Reporting

The report package of the model must be able to clearly state results in the form required by each constituent in the structuring process.

The Seller will need to understand the methodology and results of the collateral selection process—as applied to our model and must be able to translate the collateral pool into accurate cash flow estimates using accepted methodologies and then accurately report the flows' timing and magnitude. The Seller must also be able to clearly measure the economic advantages of the deal from the costs and returns presented in the reports.

The Issuer will need to be able to gauge the sensitivity to risk involved in the expected case (EC) assumptions, and how that risk affects the deal's economics.

The rating agencies must have the reports they need to make their credit assessment. This would include performance under extreme conditions.

Lastly we must anticipate and make digestible information that will be required by potential investors.

THE ROLE OF THE MODEL IN THE PROCESS OF SECURITIZATION

Collateral Proposal and Selection

The first step in the process of structuring the deal is to get as complete and accurate description of the collateral as possible. You will need to know the mechanical aspects of the payment characteristics of the obligations, such as payment frequency, day-count convention, coupon resets, and the like. You will also need to be up to speed on any other legal agreements that may govern the relationship between the lender and the borrower regarding rights of repayment.

You will need to understand the underwriting standards of the lender. How do they solicit and qualify their prospective borrowers? Are they clients with whom the lender has an ongoing relationship and whose credit histories are therefore known?

How much collateral is proposed for inclusion in the deal? Remember that some collateral of every proposed pool may be unsuitable. You will need to work closely with the client to determine what collateral the model will have to reject and for what reasons. You will also need to work closely with the client to insure that collateral is not deemed ineligible simply because of data errors as to its terms, composition or credit history. If this process of discovery is not rigorous you will end up with worse than nothing. You will end up with a model that is producing results you think are valid but in reality are both misleading and dangerous.

Running the Numbers

Armed with all the basic information about the collateral, the rating agency structuring criteria, the department risk and return guidelines, and the financial objectives of the client, we are ready to build a structure and run the numbers.

Later, in Chapter 17, we will discuss in more detail the act of validating the model. For the moment, let us assume that we are assured of the completeness and accuracy of the model calculation and reporting sequences. What needs to be done?

The model will need to produce, at a minimum, the following:

- **The Expected Case.** This is our best estimate of what we think will happen in the real world. It consists of a set of inputs for a single case that we think is the most likely scenario.

- **Sensitivity Analysis of the Expected Case.** Here we will take the collateral and the structure and perturb our original inputs across Ranges of possible values. For example, we may try a Range of prepayment speeds that are faster or slower than the EC, combined with a set of default rates faster or slower than the EC. We may vary the recovery rates or the recovery lag times, or both. We may vary the Seller Interest percentage to see how it attenuates losses across a Range of default scenarios.
- **Credit Approval Tests.** These are scenarios required to get the deal approved by the internal credit function.
- **Rating Agency Stress Tests.** These are a set of specified or negotiated stress tests in which the deal is "tested to destruction." Extreme conditions are modeled to see how the deal would respond.
- **Investor-requested Reports.** If there are investors interested in the deal, they may request that specific economic scenarios be evaluated to help them compare this deal to others and to ensure that the securitized notes meet the criteria for inclusion in their portfolios.

Structural Proposal

Once we have arrived at a structure we can propose it to the client. The proposal must include at a minimum:

- An analysis of the collateral pool (e.g., what was selected from the originally proposed pool and what was deemed unacceptable for inclusion and why)
- The proposed liability structure to include the advance rate and all costs
- The accounting and/or balance sheet benefits of doing the deal
- The rating agency criteria, how well the deal conforms to them, and the targeted credit rating
- The pricing of the notes in the market

Approval of the Structure

At this point all parties involved in the process must sign off on the proposed structure. These constituencies include but are not limited to the following:

Internal
- Department business head
- Credit committees
- Legal department
- Syndicate and sales personnel
- Trading desks of the security

External
- The Seller
- Rating Agencies (if necessary)

- External counsel (if necessary)
- Credit insurance providers (if necessary)

If all parties are in agreement, the deal will proceed.

DELIVERABLES CHECKLIST

These are the modeling and VBA language concepts you should take away from this chapter.

Model Knowledge Checklist
- An overview of the asset securitization process
- The role of modeling in developing an ABS structure
- The basic functional requirements of the model

NEXT STEPS

Armed with the broad outlines of the financing process, we can begin to develop a model. Fortunately in our case, we have a basic Excel spreadsheet with the deal structure and the waterfall correctly implemented from which to work.

In Chapter 4, "Understanding the Excel Waterfall," we will examine the waterfall in detail, column by column. First we will "get the view from 100,000 feet" by looking at the waterfall's major functional divisions. Next we will review each column to understand its contribution to the whole. Once we understand its functionality, we can begin to wrap the spreadsheet in menus and trigger its operations from a VBA program. We will begin the transformation of the spreadsheet into a true model. We will undertake those tasks in Chapters 5 and 6, "Designing the VBA Model" and "Laying the Model Groundwork," respectively.

ON THE WEB SITE

The Chapter 3 Web site material consists of the portfolio data file named "portfolio_orig.xls."

This data file consists of a total of 2,255 loans. Each loan is represented by a single row of data. The information of the loan is displayed across 26 columns. Using this information, we will later perform a collateral selection process to determine which loans we can place in the securitization. After we have selected the collateral for inclusion in our deal, we will then use the information in the file to produce the cash flows of each of the loans.

You can visually compare the contents of the file to the list of datum contained in Exhibit 3.3 to familiarize yourself with the type of collateral we are going to work with. This is our first piece of concrete information. In the next chapter we will see the Excel Waterfall model left by our predecessor.

Designing the Model

Understanding the Excel Waterfall

OVERVIEW

In Chapter 3, we got our first look at what securitization is and what our deal is all about. We are now about to move from the theoretical to the very concrete. Before us lies the Excel spreadsheet of our immediate predecessor in this position. We are expected to turn the Excel spreadsheet into a full-blown Excel/VBA model in the course of two months. We know what the collateral pool looks like. We know how many loans the Seller thinks he will offer in the first deal. The part of the model that stopped the previous analyst dead in his tracks was how to compute the amortization and cash flows of the collateral. We will do this later in the VBA chapters ahead of us. We cannot do it now. That is a task for VBA code and we do not know the first thing about VBA at this point in time.

Before we start down the road to VBA competency, we need to pause and take a moment to assess the hand that we have been dealt in this game. The Excel spreadsheet we have in front of us will be the core of our model. Around it we will build a hard framework of VBA. This framework will consist of a set of menus, the ability to read data files, a collateral cash flow generator, and a variety of report and other output mechanisms.

One inescapable fact remains, however. All of this framework, every last piece of it, will be built to service the Excel spreadsheet. All of the efforts and focus of the VBA will devolve upon the needs of this Excel spreadsheet waterfall.

"Before beginning operations establish a secure base from which to operate," has been a military axiom from at least the early fifth century BCE, and it is especially applicable in our situation.

We cannot begin to build the VBA model framework around this spreadsheet until we understand the spreadsheet itself. To this end we will now examine the spreadsheet on a column-by-column basis. We will look at the groupings of the columns and functionality. We will try to identify the key outputs that it will produce as we feed the various scenarios of collateral cash flows through the financing structure.

The spreadsheet will be the framework we will use to measure the ability of the collateral cash flows to repay the liabilities of the structure. Those liabilities will consist of the indebtedness of the Seller to the Issuer. The Issuer will finance some portion of the collateral principal based on the collateral's anticipated performance. The magnitude and the timing of the cash flows will determine the repayment characteristics of this indebtedness.

One of the goals of the modeling exercise will be to determine the amount of the deal's indebtedness based on an advance rate of 90 percent and a Seller Interest of 10 percent, as described in Chapter 3. We will seek to determine under what Range of conditions the collateral will generate sufficient cash flows to retire various amounts of financing based on appropriate advance rates.

DELIVERABLES

Modeling Knowledge Deliverables

The modeling deliverables for this chapter are:

- The overall schema of the model
- What a cash flow waterfall is and why we need it
- The overall design of an Excel structured finance deal waterfall
- The components of that waterfall
- The elements of the deal structure, such as expenses, fees, and reserves
- Commonly used debt performance measures, such as average life, final maturity, duration, yield, internal rate of return (IRR), and severity of loss

UNDER CONSTRUCTION

In this chapter we will introduce the Excel waterfall worksheet left to us by our predecessor. We won't have to do any work on this file, as it is complete and tested. We should, however, study it closely and start to develop our first ideas of how we will employ our VBA code. We will need to generate a series of cash flows and then populate the waterfall. After the waterfall has calculated we will need to capture its results and then transfer them to our VBA arrays for use in the output reports we will generate.

WATERFALLS

By the time you finish this book you will have heard the term "waterfall" mentioned hundreds of times. When we say the "deal waterfall," or simply "the waterfall," what do we mean?

The analogy of a waterfall in structured finance has been employed since at least the 1970s. It seeks to convey the picture of water, flowing from a high place, into a series of buckets. After each bucket fills up, the excess overflows, traveling downward to another bucket that then begins to fill to capacity, and so forth.

The water is the funds of the deal. The buckets are the various uses of all the funds from the very first, to the very last. Our deal is very typical of a simple structured finance waterfall. It starts at the faucet at the top of the deal, the source of the funds—that is, the collateral pool. The faucet is turned on and money, in the form of interest and principal payments from the small business loan debtors begins to flow into the deal. For those of you who have grown up without automatic icemakers in their refrigerators and had to fill a 20-count cube ice tray by hand, the image is immediate. The best way to fill such a tray is to tilt it at a 30-degree angle and let the water flow into the upper end of the tray, filling each section in turn and then spilling over to the next. Hold it under the tap until the last section fills and then bring it level. Behold! An evenly filled tray!

The first buckets of the waterfall are a series of expenses. Most of these expenses are being paid to people who help manage and monitor the deal. These fees pay the Master Servicer and the Trustee of the deal. The Master Servicer performs an important function in that it is responsible for the management of the collateral, while the Trustee has the responsibility of overseeing that all the legal stipulations of the deal are carried out. The next bucket is the payment of coupon interest to the Conduit for the money the Conduit has lent the Seller. The next bucket is the repayment to the Conduit by the Seller of some portion of the principal balance of indebtedness. The next bucket may need to add money to a reserve account. This is an account that serves as a form of self-funded insurance in case of future losses to the deal. The final bucket is any money left over that can be returned to the Seller after all the servicing expenses, coupon expense, and principal has been repaid. This payment pattern is run through the deal, each month, over and over again, until the Conduit is repaid or the collateral runs out of cash, or certain other events happen to stop the deal.

STRUCTURE OF THE CASH FLOW WATERFALL

Unlike Julius Caesar's Gaul, which was divided into three parts, the Excel waterfall is divided into 11 subsections. Each section is a functional division that performs and presents a specific task.

This is a simplified waterfall. There are, for example, only two expenses and three principal payment triggers. A typical deal might have as many as four to nine expenses and any number of triggers. The object of this exercise is to present the reader with an easily digested waterfall but one that still retains all of the basic features that will be present in even the most complex structures.

The sections of the waterfall named from left to right are:

1. **Collateral Cash Flows (ten columns).** These columns delineate the components of the collateral cash flows and combined represent the total amount of cash available to the structure.
2. **Expenses (eight columns).** The two deal expenses in the model are the Program Fees and the Servicing Fees.
3. **Conduit Interest (six columns).** The payment of the interest due the Issuer on the indebtedness.
4. **Conduit Principal (three columns).** The repayment of the Issuer's principal.
5. **Excess Cash Treatment (three columns).** The use of cash that is in excess of the amounts needed to pay Issuer interest and repay principal.

6. **Conduit Summary (five columns).** A summary section of Issuer coupon income and principal repayment.
7. **Delinquent Reserve Activity (six columns).** Payouts from the delinquent reserve account that is used to cover Issuer Interest payment shortfalls.
8. **Triggers (four columns).** Events that will direct all payments to the Issuer indebtedness bucket.
9. **Debt Costs (one column).** The per-period Issuer coupon rate.
10. **Default Tests (two columns).** The default rate calculations used in two of the triggers.
11. **Debt Performance Calculations (five columns).** Information used to calculate Issuer debt performance statistics.

We will now examine each of the components of these sections and the role they play in the deal structure. The number in parentheses before the title of the columns below is the spreadsheet waterfall reference number. This means that (2) is the second column of the waterfall, NOT necessarily column "B" of the Excel spreadsheet.

COLLATERAL CASH FLOWS SECTION

The Collateral Cash Flows section shown in Exhibit 4.1 consists of 10 columns:

(2) **Beginning Principal Balance.** Column K. The beginning principal balance of the collateral is the balance from the previous period. The formula is "=P(period before)."

Microsoft Excel - MODEL_BASE.xls

File Edit View Insert Format Tools Data Window Help

Times New Roman 10

K15 = =P14

	J	K	L	M	N	O	P	Q	R	S	T	U	V
5	1	2	3	4	5	6	7	8	9	10	11	12	13
6		Collateral Cashflows											
7–11		Beginning Principal Balance	Pool Factor	Regular Amort Principal	Prepaid Principal	Defaulted Principal	Ending Principal Balance Outstanding	Total Principal Retired	Coupon Income	Recoveries of Principal		Total Cash Available For Waterfall	
12				305,611,089	173,668,115	12,141,174		479,279,203	237,462,260	10,378,710		732,661,304	
13													
14	1	491,420,377	1.00000	1,869,776	81,646	124,057	489,344,899	1,951,422	2,458,405	-	1	4,409,827	1
15	2	489,344,899	0.99578	1,978,655	162,710	130,401	487,073,132	2,141,366	2,615,410	-	2	4,756,776	2
16	3	487,073,132	0.99115	2,066,372	243,104	136,523	484,627,133	2,309,476	2,720,175	-	3	5,029,651	3
17	4	484,627,133	0.98618	2,155,067	322,738	142,450	482,006,879	2,477,805	2,826,673	-	4	5,304,478	4
18	5	482,006,879	0.98084	2,165,486	401,588	148,183	479,291,621	2,567,074	2,811,348	-	5	5,378,422	5
19	6	479,291,621	0.97532	2,175,562	479,606	153,710	476,482,743	2,655,168	2,795,469	-	6	5,450,637	6
20	7	476,482,743	0.96960	2,185,290	556,743	159,040	473,581,670	2,742,033	2,779,046	-	7	5,521,079	7
21	8	473,581,670	0.96370	2,194,665	632,952	164,092	470,589,961	2,827,617	2,762,086	-	8	5,589,703	8
22	9	470,589,961	0.95761	2,203,681	708,188	168,928	467,509,163	2,911,869	2,744,598	-	9	5,690,915	9
23	10	467,509,163	0.95134	2,212,335	782,404	173,503	464,340,922	2,994,739	2,726,592	-	10	5,756,824	10
24	11	464,340,922	0.94490	2,220,621	855,556	177,808	461,086,936	3,076,177	2,708,078	-	11	5,820,775	11
25	12	461,086,936	0.93827	2,228,536	927,602	181,782	457,749,017	3,156,138	2,689,065	-	12	5,882,730	12
26	13	457,749,017	0.93148	2,236,076	998,498	185,450	454,328,992	3,234,575	2,669,565	111,954	13	6,054,606	13
27	14	454,328,992	0.92452	2,243,238	1,068,205	188,656	450,828,893	3,311,443	2,649,588	117,202	14	6,117,711	14
28	15	450,828,893	0.91740	2,250,017	1,136,684	191,573	447,250,619	3,386,701	2,629,145	122,249	15	6,178,515	15

EXHIBIT 4.1 Collateral Cash Flows section

(3) **Pool Factor.** Column L. The amount of original collateral principal remaining in the deal. A pool factor of 0.97565 is equal to 97.565% of the original collateral principal. The formula is: "=K15/$K$15," the current period balance K15 divided by the first period balance K$15.

(4) **Regular Amortized Principal.** Column M. The amount of principal that is contractually due in the period from the Obligor. This is an input from the VBA amortization module.

(5) **Prepaid Principal.** Column N. The amount of principal prepaid by the Obligors in that period. Prepayments are non-scheduled accelerated payments of principal. They have the effect of lowering future receipts of coupon income from the collateral pool. This is an input from the VBA amortization module.

(6) **Defaulted Principal.** Column O. The amount of defaulted principal in the period, principal that will remain unpaid by the Obligor. Some of this principal eventually may be recovered through the repossession and sale of the asset secured by the loan agreement. Defaults deprive the deal structure of both principal and future coupon payments. This is an input from the VBA amortization module.

(7) **Ending Principal Balance Outstanding.** Column P. The previous beginning period balance less defaulted principal, regular scheduled amortization of principal, and principal repayments. The formula is: "=IF((K15-SUM(M15:O15))>0.01,(K15-SUM(M15:O15)),0)."

(8) **Total Principal Retired.** Column Q. The sum of scheduled amortization of principal payments and prepayments of principal. The formula is "=M15+N15."

(9) **Coupon Income.** Column R. The interest payments of the collateral pool. This is an input from the VBA amortization module.

(10) **Recoveries of Principal.** Column S. Recoveries are the sums realized from the repossession and sale of the assets secured by the loan. It is dependent on the market value decline percentage (MVDP), the percentage of value of the original asset appraisal that is realized in the sale. If the current loan-to-value ratio of the defaulted collateral was 60% and the MVDP was 25%, for example, the loan would experience 100% recoveries. A total of 75% of the original value of the property would be realized in the recovery, more than enough to repay the 60% LTV loan. However, if the current LTV had been 90% and the MVDP was 55%, only 45% of the original appraisal value would be recovered. This would result in a 45%/90% = 50% loss severity on the loan. The receipt of the recoveries does not occur in the month of default. Most recovery assumptions lag the receipt of the proceeds by anywhere from 12 to 18 months. This is an input from the VBA amortization module.

(12) **Total Cash Available for Waterfall.** Column U. The sum of Regular Amortized Principal, Prepaid Principal, Coupon Income, Recoveries of Principal, and Releases from the Delinquent Reserve Account (in the previous period). The formula is: "=M15+N15+R15+S15+AR14."

	V	W	X	Y	Z	AA	AB	AC	AD	AE
5	13	14	15	16	17	18	19	20	21	22
6					Expenses					
7										
8		Program	Program	Program	Cash	Servicing	Servicing	Servicing	Cash	
9		Fees	Fees	Fees	Available	Fee	Fee	Fee	Available	
10		Due	Paid	Unpaid		Due	Paid	Unpaid		
11										
12		6,390,472	6,390,472	-		25,530,249	25,530,249	-	700,740,583	
13										
14	1	77,808	77,808	-	4,332,019	307,138	307,138	-	4,024,881	1
15	2	77,480	77,480	-	4,679,296	305,841	305,841	-	4,373,456	2
16	3	77,120	77,120	-	4,952,531	304,421	304,421	-	4,648,111	3
17	4	76,733	76,733	-	5,227,745	302,892	302,892	-	4,924,853	4
18	5	76,318	76,318	-	5,302,104	301,254	301,254	-	5,000,850	5
19	6	75,888	75,888	-	5,374,750	299,557	299,557	-	5,075,192	6
20	7	75,443	75,443	-	5,445,636	297,802	297,802	-	5,147,834	7
21	8	74,984	74,984	-	5,514,719	295,989	295,989	-	5,218,731	8
22	9	74,510	74,510	-	5,616,405	294,119	294,119	-	5,322,286	9
23	10	74,022	74,022	-	5,682,802	292,193	292,193	-	5,390,609	10
24	11	73,521	73,521	-	5,747,255	290,213	290,213	-	5,457,042	11
25	12	73,005	73,005	-	5,809,725	288,179	288,179	-	5,521,546	12

EXHIBIT 4.2   Deal Expenses section

DEAL EXPENSES SECTION

The section of the waterfall shown in Exhibit 4.2 calculates the two deal expenses and determines if there are funds available to pay them in the period. The following are a detailed description of its columns:

1. **(14) Program Fees Due.** Column W. The Program Deal Fees Due are the product of the Program expenses rate that was input on the Program Costs Menu and the Current Balance of the Conduit financing, plus any previously unpaid Program Deal Fees from a prior period. The formula is: "=m2ProgramExpenses*CFWaterfall!AU15/12+Y14."
2. **(15) Program Fees Paid.** Column X. The amount of the Program Fees Due paid in the period. If the amount of waterfall column (12), the Total Cash Available for Waterfall, is greater than or equal to (14) the Program Fees Due, all fees are paid. The formula is: "=MIN(W15,U15)."
3. **(16) Program Fees Unpaid.** Column Y. The shortfall in payment, if any, of (15) above. The formula is: "=W15-X15."
4. **(17) Cash Available.** Column Z. The amount of cash available to the waterfall after the payment of the program fees. The formula is: "=U15-X15."
5. **(18) Servicing Fee Due.** Column AA, this is the amount of Servicing Fees due in the period, based on the servicing fee rate input into the model on the Program Costs Menu and the current balance of the collateral pool. This fee is paid as compensation for the performance of portfolio servicing activities, collection activity, legal activity, repossession, managing property repairs and sales, and so

on. In most cases the Seller retains the servicing function and receives these fees. The formula is: "=m2ServicerExp*K15/12+AC14."

6. **(19) Servicing Fee Paid.** Column AB. The payment of the servicing fees due (18) from the cash available after the program fees have been paid (17). The formula is: "=MIN(AA15,Z15)."

7. **(20) Servicing Fee Unpaid.** Column AC. The deficiencies in payment of the servicing fees from available cash flows. The formula is: "=AA15-AB15."

8. **(21) Cash Available.** Column AD. All cash remaining after the payment of the Deal Program and Servicing fees. The formula is: "=Z15-AB15."

CONDUIT INTEREST SECTION

This section of the Waterfall Spreadsheet shown in Exhibit 4.3 relates to the payment of the interest charges on the Conduit indebtedness.

1. **(23) Interest Due.** Column AF. Total debt service due on the Issuer (Conduit) principal balance. This is the product of the Conduit Funding Coupon Rate (56) and the Conduit Beginning Principal Balance (38) plus any unpaid Interest Due from the previous period. The formula is: "=BM15/12*AU15+AJ14."

		Microsoft Excel - MODEL_BASE.xls						
		File Edit View Insert Format Tools Data Window Help						
					Times New Roman ▾ 10 ▾ **B**			
	AF15	= =IF(BV14=FALSE, IF(K15>0.01, BM15/12*AU15+AJ14, 0),0)						
	AE	AF	AG	AH	AI	AJ	AK	AL
5	22	23	24	25	26	27	28	29
6		**Conduit Interest**						
7			Interest		Interest			
8		Interest	Covered	Interest	Covered	Interest	Cash	
9		Due	By	Due	By	Unpaid	Available	
10			Available		Delinquency			
11			Cash		Reserve			
12		119,821,358	119,821,358		-	-		
13								
14	1	1,458,904	1,458,904	-	-	-	2,565,977	1
15	2	1,452,743	1,452,743	-	-	-	2,920,713	2
16	3	1,445,998	1,445,998	-	-	-	3,202,112	3
17	4	1,438,737	1,438,737	-	-	-	3,486,117	4
18	5	1,430,958	1,430,958	-	-	-	3,569,892	5
19	6	1,422,897	1,422,897	-	-	-	3,652,295	6
20	7	1,414,558	1,414,558	-	-	-	3,733,276	7
21	8	1,405,946	1,405,946	-	-	-	3,812,785	8
22	9	1,397,064	1,397,064	-	-	-	3,925,222	9
23	10	1,387,918	1,387,918	-	-	-	4,002,691	10
24	11	1,378,512	1,378,512	-	-	-	4,078,530	11
25	12	1,368,852	1,368,852	-	-	-	4,152,694	12

EXHIBIT 4.3 Conduit Interest section

2. **(24) Interest Covered by Available Cash.** – Column AG. The amount of debt service paid by the Cash Available (21). The formula is: "=MIN(AF15,AD15)."
3. **(25) Interest Due.** Column AH. Any shortfall in the payment of the Interest Due (23) above. The formula is: "=AF15-AG15."
4. **(26) Interest Covered by the Delinquency Reserve.** Column AI, if there is any Interest Due from (25) it may be paid from the balance of the Delinquency Reserve Fund provided the fund has any money available for that purpose. The formula is: "=MIN(AH15,BB15)."
5. **(27) Interest Unpaid.** Column AJ. Any continuing shortfall of interest after the payment from (26) above, (if any). The formula is: "=AH15-AI15."
6. **(28) Cash Available.** Column AK. Any remaining cash available after all payments of the Interest Due (23). The formula is: "=AD15-AG15."

CONDUIT PRINCIPAL SECTION

Exhibit 4.4 displays the section of the Waterfall Spreadsheet that relates to the repayment of the Conduit principal outstanding. The list below details each of the columns of the Conduit Principal Section.

1. **(30) Principal Due.** Column AM. If the trigger to give ALL payments to the principal balance outstanding of the Conduit indebtedness is TRUE, then all cash available will be used to pay down the Conduit balance. If the triggers are not TRUE, then the principal balance due will be the product of the Beginning Conduit Principal Balance (38) and (1.00- the Conduit Advance Rate in Cell AU12. The formula is: "=IF(BK15,MIN(AK15,AU15),AU15-CFWConduitPct*P15)."
2. **(31) Principal Paid.** Column AN. The minimum of the Cash Available (28) and the Principal Due (30). The formula is: "=MIN(AK15,AM15)."
3. **(32) Cash Available.** Column AO. This is the difference between (28) and (30) above. The formula is: "=AK15-AN15."

EXCESS CASH TREATMENT SECTION

Exhibit 4.5 displays the section of the Waterfall Spreadsheet that relates to the use of the cash that remains after the payment of the Conduit principal. This cash can be used to fund the Delinquent Reserve Account or it call be released to the Seller. The list below details the columns of the Excess Cash Treatment section of the spreadsheet.

1. **(34) Funding of the Delinquent Reserve Balance.** Column AQ. The formula for funding the Delinquent Account Reserve is: "=MAX(MIN(AO15, BA15-BB15),0)," where AO15 is the Cash Available After Principal Payment (32), BA15 is the Reserve Fund Cap, and BB15 is the Reserve Fund Balance.
2. **(35) Release of Delinquent Reserve.** Column AR. The formula is "=MAX(BB15-BA15,0)," which is to say the greater of either the Reserve Fund Balance − the Reserve Fund Cap, or zero.

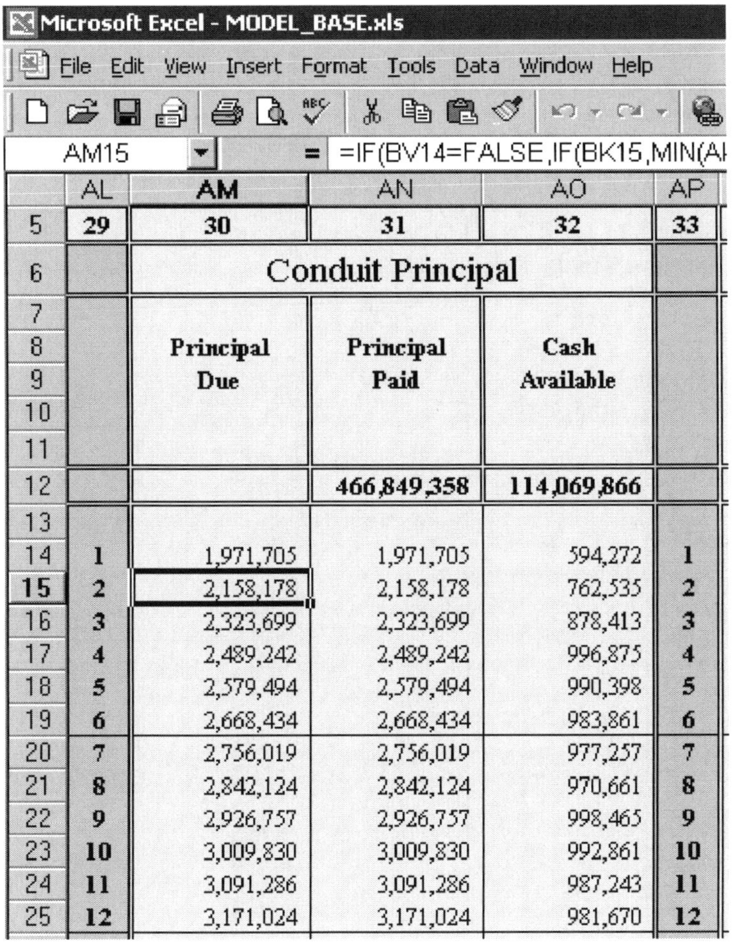

	AL	AM	AN	AO	AP
5	29	30	31	32	33
6		Conduit Principal			
7					
8		Principal	Principal	Cash	
9		Due	Paid	Available	
10					
11					
12			466,849,358	114,069,866	
13					
14	1	1,971,705	1,971,705	594,272	1
15	2	2,158,178	2,158,178	762,535	2
16	3	2,323,699	2,323,699	878,413	3
17	4	2,489,242	2,489,242	996,875	4
18	5	2,579,494	2,579,494	990,398	5
19	6	2,668,434	2,668,434	983,861	6
20	7	2,756,019	2,756,019	977,257	7
21	8	2,842,124	2,842,124	970,661	8
22	9	2,926,757	2,926,757	998,465	9
23	10	3,009,830	3,009,830	992,861	10
24	11	3,091,286	3,091,286	987,243	11
25	12	3,171,024	3,171,024	981,670	12

Cell reference: AM15 = =IF(BV14=FALSE,IF(BK15,MIN(A...

Title bar: Microsoft Excel - MODEL_BASE.xls

EXHIBIT 4.4   Conduit Principal section

3. **(36) Cash Released to Seller.** Column AS. That is to say, however much cash is available after funding the Reserve. This is Cash Available after Payment of Principal (32) – Funding of the Delinquent Reserve Balance (34).

CONDUIT SUMMARY SECTION

Exhibit 4.6 displays the section of the Waterfall Spreadsheet that summarizes the activity surrounding the Issuer indebtedness. The list below is a detailed description of the columns of the Conduit Summary section:

1. **(38) Conduit Beginning Balance.** Column AU. The beginning balance of the Conduit financing amount for the period. The formula for the first period is "=IF(K15 > 0, $K15*AU12, 0)"; if the collateral pool balance > 0, then

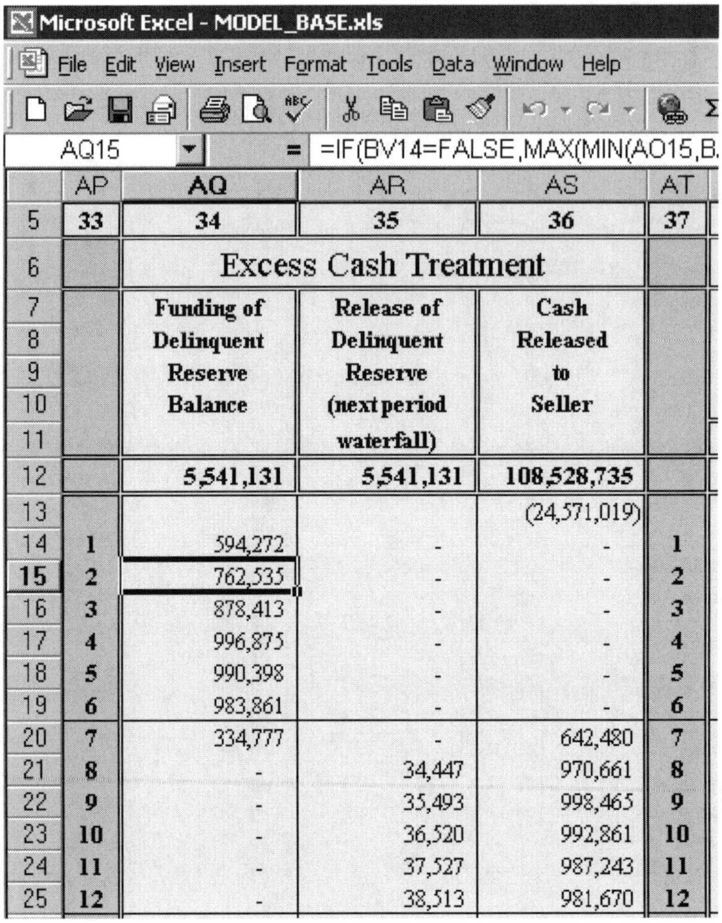

	AP	AQ	AR	AS	AT
5	33	34	35	36	37
6		**Excess Cash Treatment**			
7		**Funding of**	**Release of**	**Cash**	
8		**Delinquent**	**Delinquent**	**Released**	
9		**Reserve**	**Reserve**	**to**	
10		**Balance**	**(next period**	**Seller**	
11			**waterfall)**		
12		**5,541,131**	**5,541,131**	**108,528,735**	
13				(24,571,019)	
14	1	594,272	-	-	1
15	2	762,535	-	-	2
16	3	878,413	-	-	3
17	4	996,875	-	-	4
18	5	990,398	-	-	5
19	6	983,861	-	-	6
20	7	334,777	-	642,480	7
21	8	-	34,447	970,661	8
22	9	-	35,493	998,465	9
23	10	-	36,520	992,861	10
24	11	-	37,527	987,243	11
25	12	-	38,513	981,670	12

EXHIBIT 4.5 Excess Cash Treatment section

collateral pool balance times the advance rate, or 0. From the first period on, it is the balance of the preceding period minus any principal payments received in the prior period.

2. (39) **Conduit Position as Percentage of Original Balance.** Column AV. To determine this percentage, we simply divide the current balance of the Conduit financing by the original collateral principal balance. The formula is "=AU15/TotalBeginPrincipal." The result will serve as the basis for the clean-up trigger in (52), which we will address later.

3. (40) **Conduit Position as Percentage Current Balance.** Column AW. This is the percentage derived by dividing the current balance of the Conduit financing by the current collateral principal balances. The formula is "=IF(ISERROR(AU15/K15),0,AU15/K15)," which is to say that if the current balance of the Conduit financing/beginning current asset balance results in an error (division by 0), then use 0%, else do the calculation.

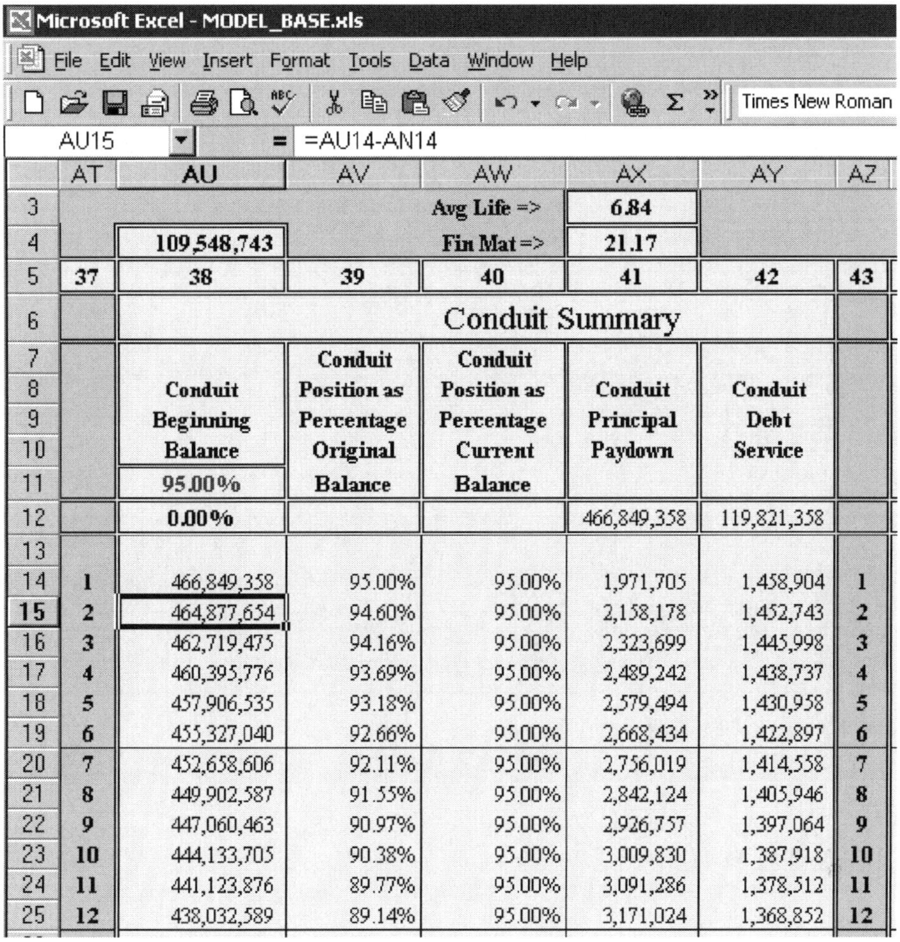

	AT	AU	AV	AW	AX	AY	AZ
3				Avg Life =>	6.84		
4		109,548,743		Fin Mat=>	21.17		
5	37	38	39	40	41	42	43
6		Conduit Summary					
7–11		Conduit Beginning Balance 95.00%	Conduit Position as Percentage Original Balance	Conduit Position as Percentage Current Balance	Conduit Principal Paydown	Conduit Debt Service	
12		0.00%			466,849,358	119,821,358	
13							
14	1	466,849,358	95.00%	95.00%	1,971,705	1,458,904	1
15	2	464,877,654	94.60%	95.00%	2,158,178	1,452,743	2
16	3	462,719,475	94.16%	95.00%	2,323,699	1,445,998	3
17	4	460,395,776	93.69%	95.00%	2,489,242	1,438,737	4
18	5	457,906,535	93.18%	95.00%	2,579,494	1,430,958	5
19	6	455,327,040	92.66%	95.00%	2,668,434	1,422,897	6
20	7	452,658,606	92.11%	95.00%	2,756,019	1,414,558	7
21	8	449,902,587	91.55%	95.00%	2,842,124	1,405,946	8
22	9	447,060,463	90.97%	95.00%	2,926,757	1,397,064	9
23	10	444,133,705	90.38%	95.00%	3,009,830	1,387,918	10
24	11	441,123,876	89.77%	95.00%	3,091,286	1,378,512	11
25	12	438,032,589	89.14%	95.00%	3,171,024	1,368,852	12

EXHIBIT 4.6 Conduit Summary section

4. (41) **Conduit Principal Paydown.** Column AX. This is the amount of principal paid to the Note Holders this period. The formula is "=AN15," a reference to (31) Principal Paid.
5. (42) **Conduit Debt Service.** Column AY. The amount of Conduit Interest paid in the period. The formula is (24) Interest Covered by Available Cash + (26) Interest Covered by Delinquency Reserve. The formula is: "=AG15+AI15."

DELINQUENCY RESERVE SECTION

Exhibit 4.7 displays the portion of the Waterfall Spreadsheet that outlines the activities of the Delinquent Reserve Account that is used as a back stop to pay Conduit Debt Service if the monthly cash flows from the collateral pool prove inadequate.

Microsoft Excel - MODEL_BASE.xls

BA15 = =IF(K15>0, SUMIF(J15:J16,">0",R15:R16),0)

	AZ	BA	BB	BC	BD	BE	BF	BG
5	43	44	45	46	47	48	49	50
6		Delinquent Reserve Activity						
7–11		Delinquent Account Reserve Cap	Beginning Delinquent Account Reserve Balance	Draws to Delinquent Reserve Account	Deposits to Delinquent Reserve Balance	Delinquent Reserve Account Release	Ending Delinquenct Account Reserve Balance	
12				-	5,541,131	5,541,131		
13								
14	1	5,073,815	-	-	594,272	-	594,272	1
15	2	5,335,585	594,272	-	762,535	-	1,356,807	2
16	3	5,546,848	1,356,807	-	878,413	-	2,235,220	3
17	4	5,638,021	2,235,220	-	996,875	-	3,232,095	4
18	5	5,606,817	3,232,095	-	990,398	-	4,222,493	5
19	6	5,574,515	4,222,493	-	983,861	-	5,206,354	6
20	7	5,541,131	5,206,354	-	334,777	-	5,541,131	7
21	8	5,506,684	5,541,131	-	-	34,447	5,506,684	8
22	9	5,471,190	5,506,684	-	-	35,493	5,471,190	9
23	10	5,434,670	5,471,190	-	-	36,520	5,434,670	10
24	11	5,397,143	5,434,670	-	-	37,527	5,397,143	11
25	12	5,358,630	5,397,143	-	-	38,513	5,358,630	12

EXHIBIT 4.7 Delinquency Reserve section

The list below is a detailed explanation of the columns of the Delinquency Reserve Activity section.

1. (44) **Delinquent Account Reserve Cap.** Column BA. The Delinquent Reserve Fund Cap is set to the sum of the next two months of Coupon Income from the collateral pool. If the balance of the collateral pool is zero, or if the sum of the next two months of Coupon Income is zero, the Reserve Cap is zero: "=IF(K15>0, SUMIF(J15:J16,">0",R15:R16),0)."
2. (45) **Beginning Delinquent Account Reserve Balance.** Column BB, the Delinquent Reserve Fund is not pre-funded at the inception of the deal. Instead, it is funded over time by excess cash flows, should they materialize. The first period balance is $0, the subsequent period balances are (49) the Delinquent Reserve Account Ending Balance. The formula is: "=BF15."
3. (46) **Draws to Delinquent Reserve Account.** Column BC. The draws to the reserve are (26) Interest Covered by Delinquency Reserve. The formula is: "=AI15."
4. (47) **Deposits to Delinquent Reserve Account.** Column BD. The deposits to the reserve are (34) Funding of the Delinquent Reserve Balance. The formula is: "=AQ15."
5. (48) **Delinquent Reserve Account Release.** Column BE. The release of funds from the reserve is (35) Release of Delinquent Reserve. The formula is: "=AR15."

6. **(49) Ending Delinquent Account Reserve Balance.** Column BF. This figure is arrived at by taking (45) Beginning Delinquent Account Reserve Balance – (46) Draws to Delinquent Reserve Account + (47) Deposits to Delinquent Reserve Balance – (48) Delinquent Reserve Account Release. The formula is: "=BB15-BC15+BD15-BE15."

DEAL TRIGGERS SECTION

Exhibit 4.8 displays the Deal Triggers section of the Waterfall Spreadsheet. The deal has three different triggers. The first relates to non-credit events, such as a breach in a contractual arrangement or a servicer default. The second is the clean-up trigger that applies all cash flows to the outstanding Conduit balance when it reaches 10% of its original amount. The third is a rolling three-month default rate trigger that applies all cash flows to the principal if the defaults in any three-month period exceed 5%.

1. **(51) Event Trigger.** Column BH. This is a non-financial condition event trigger; an event that is *not* related to the creditworthiness of the deal yet that imperils

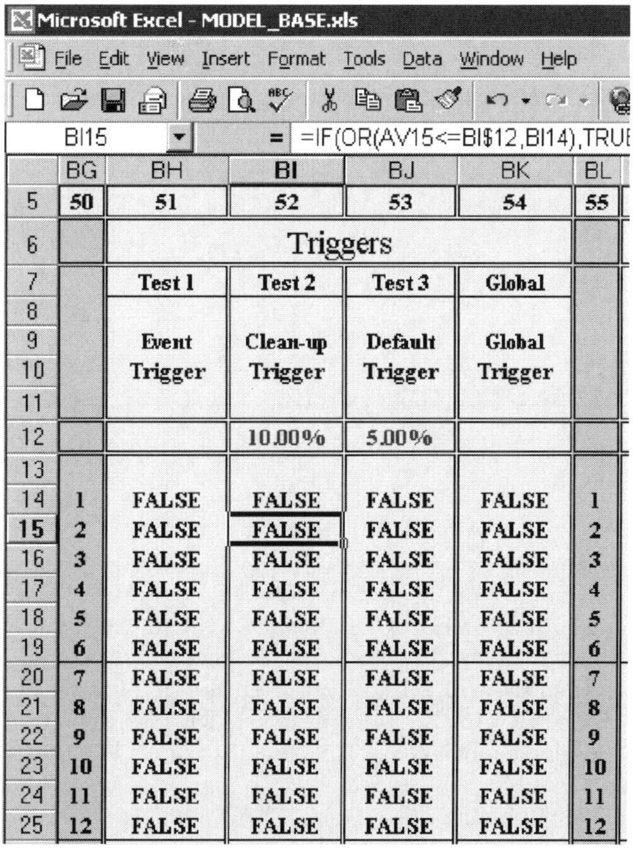

	BG	BH	BI	BJ	BK	BL
5	50	51	52	53	54	55
6		Triggers				
7		Test 1	Test 2	Test 3	Global	
8–11		Event Trigger	Clean-up Trigger	Default Trigger	Global Trigger	
12			10.00%	5.00%		
13						
14	1	FALSE	FALSE	FALSE	FALSE	1
15	2	FALSE	FALSE	FALSE	FALSE	2
16	3	FALSE	FALSE	FALSE	FALSE	3
17	4	FALSE	FALSE	FALSE	FALSE	4
18	5	FALSE	FALSE	FALSE	FALSE	5
19	6	FALSE	FALSE	FALSE	FALSE	6
20	7	FALSE	FALSE	FALSE	FALSE	7
21	8	FALSE	FALSE	FALSE	FALSE	8
22	9	FALSE	FALSE	FALSE	FALSE	9
23	10	FALSE	FALSE	FALSE	FALSE	10
24	11	FALSE	FALSE	FALSE	FALSE	11
25	12	FALSE	FALSE	FALSE	FALSE	12

EXHIBIT 4.8 Deal Triggers section

the deal structure has occurred. At this point, as with the other triggers, 100% of all cash flows are applied to the Conduit principal balance outstanding after the payment of fees and expenses.

2. **(52) Clean-up Trigger.** Column BI. This is the clean-up trigger. If the remaining principal balance of the Conduit financing goes below 10% of the original balance, the trigger is set to TRUE; also, if the trigger has been set to TRUE in the prior period, the trigger is set to TRUE in the current period. This feature assures that once the trigger is set it stays set. The formula is: "=IF(OR(AV15<=0.1,BI14),TRUE,FALSE)."

3. **(53) Default Trigger.** Column BJ. This trigger measures the rolling three-month default rate in any given month against a 5% limit. If the limit of 5% is reached in any monthly period from that time forward, the trigger is switched on and stays on for the remaining term of the deal. The formula is: "=IF(BO15>0.05,TRUE, FALSE)."

4. **(54) Global Trigger.** Column BK. If any of the triggers in (51), (52), or (53) is set to True, the Global Trigger is set to TRUE, allocating all cash flows to the Conduit Principal. The formula is: "=OR(BH15:BJ15)."

DEBT COSTS SECTION

Exhibit 4.9 displays the one-column section of the Waterfall Spreadsheet that contains the Conduit Funding Coupon Rate for the period.

1. **(56) Conduit Funding Coupon Rate.** Column BM. This is the projected coupon schedule for the remainder of the deal. It is taken into the spreadsheet from the Program Costs Menu. It is used to calculate the Interest Due column (23). The formula is: "='Defaults Menu'!V6."

DEFAULT TESTS SECTION

Exhibit 4.10 displays the portion of the Waterfall Spreadsheet that calculates the three-month rolling default rate and the cumulative lifetime default rate of the structure.

1. **(58) Rolling Three Month Default Rate.** Column BO. This is the average of the last three months of defaults. The default rate is calculated: "=IF(K15>0,SUM(O15:O17)/$K15,0)." If the current balance of the collateral pool is greater than $0, take the last three months of the Defaulted Principal and divide that sum by the Beginning Principal Balance of three months prior. If the Beginning Principal Balance of three months prior is $0 then the three-month rate is set to 0%.

2. **(59) Lifetime Default Rate.** Column BP. This is the sum of all prior months' Defaulted Principal, divided by the first period's Beginning Principal Balance. The formula for the cell is: "=SUM($O$15:O15)/TotalBeginPrincipal."

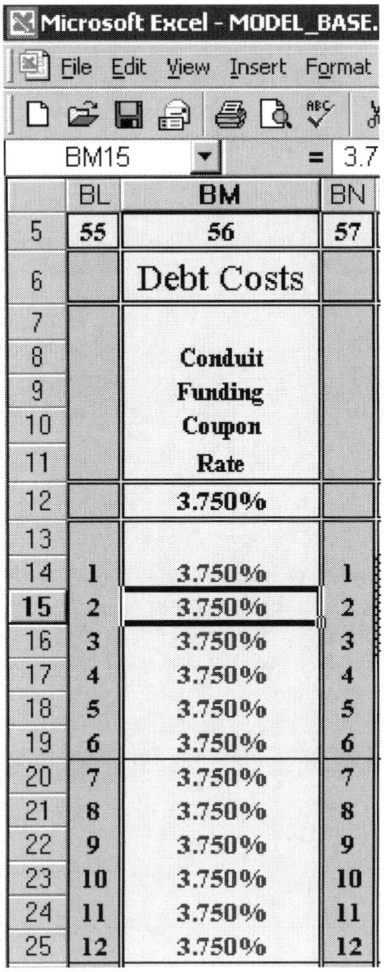

EXHIBIT 4.9   Debt Costs section

DEBT PERFORMANCE CALCULATIONS SUPPORT SECTION

Exhibit 4.11 displays the section of the cash flow waterfall spreadsheet which contains five columns that are used to calculate several performance criteria: average life, yield IRR, final maturity, and two measures of duration. The abbreviation in column BQ, "PV" stands for Present Value. The abbreviation in column BR, "Cum PV" stands for Cumulative Present Value. The abbreviation "CFs" in columns BS and BT stands for Cash Flows.

1. **(60) Conduit Funding Period PV Factor.** Column BQ. This is the PV factor based on the Conduit Funding Coupon Rate (56), which is equal to PVn = 1/(1+r)nth, where n=period, r=period adjusted Conduit Funding Rate. The formula for the cell is: "=1/(1+(BM14/12))."

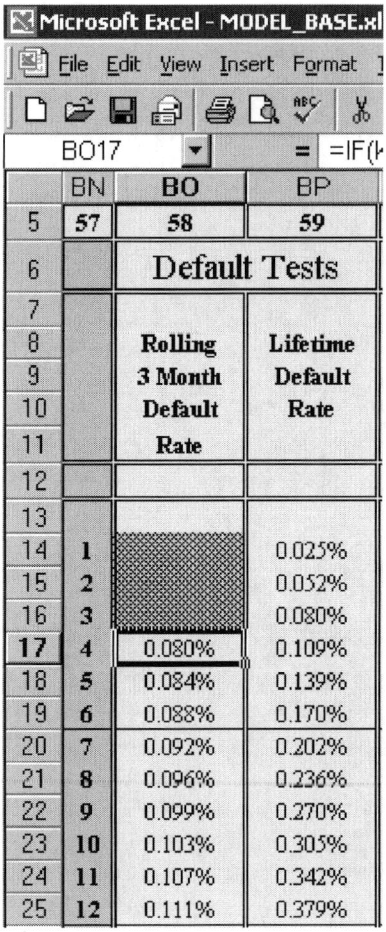

	BN	BO	BP
5	57	58	59
6		Default Tests	
7–11		Rolling 3 Month Default Rate	Lifetime Default Rate
12			
13			
14	1		0.025%
15	2		0.052%
16	3		0.080%
17	4	0.080%	0.109%
18	5	0.084%	0.139%
19	6	0.088%	0.170%
20	7	0.092%	0.202%
21	8	0.096%	0.236%
22	9	0.099%	0.270%
23	10	0.103%	0.305%
24	11	0.107%	0.342%
25	12	0.111%	0.379%

EXHIBIT 4.10 Default Tests section

2. (61) **Conduit Funding Cumulative PV Factor.** Column BR. This is the product of previous period PV factor, multiplied by the current period PV factor. The formula for the cell is: "=PRODUCT($BQ$14:BQ14)."
3. (62) **Total Conduit Cash Flows.** Column BS. The sum of (41) Conduit Principal Paydown + (42) Conduit Debt Service. The formula for the cell is: "=AY14+AX14."
4. (63) **NPV of Conduit Cash Flows.** Column BT. The Net Present Value (NPV) of the Conduit Cash Flows is equal to (62) Total Conduit Cash Flows times (61) Conduit Funding Cumulative PV Factor. The formula for the cell is: "=BS14*BR14."

DEAL WIND-DOWN TRIGGER

Exhibit 4.12 displays the column "Wind-down Triggers Activated." This column is used to determine if there is a negligible amount of cash flow left in the deal, and

	BQ	BR	BS	BT	BU
	Microsoft Excel - MODEL_BASE.xls				
	File Edit View Insert Format Tools Data Window Help				
	BQ15		=	=1/(1+(BM15/12))	
	BQ	**BR**	**BS**	**BT**	**BU**
5	**60**	**61**	**62**	**63**	**64**
6					
7					
8	**Conduit**	**Conduit**	**Total**	**NPV**	
9	**Funding**	**Funding**	**Conduit**	**Conduit**	
10	**Period PV**	**Cum PV**	**CFs**	**CFs**	
11	**Factor**	**Factor**			
12			586,670,716	466,849,358	
13			(466,849,358)		
14	0.996885	0.996885	3,430,609	3,419,922	1
15	0.996885	0.993779	3,610,921	3,588,458	2
16	0.996885	0.990683	3,769,697	3,734,576	3
17	0.996885	0.987597	3,927,979	3,879,260	4
18	0.996885	0.984520	4,010,452	3,948,372	5
19	0.996885	0.981453	4,091,331	4,015,451	6
20	0.996885	0.978396	4,170,577	4,080,476	7
21	0.996885	0.975348	4,248,070	4,143,346	8
22	0.996885	0.972309	4,323,821	4,204,092	9
23	0.996885	0.969280	4,397,747	4,262,651	10
24	0.996885	0.966261	4,469,798	4,318,991	11
25	0.996885	0.963251	4,539,875	4,373,038	12

EXHIBIT 4.11 Debt Performance Calculations Support section

signals whether to terminate the waterfall. If the value is "False" the deal continues to run, if "True" the waterfall calculations are halted.

1. **(65) Wind-down Triggers Activated.** Column BV. If for the immediate period, this condition was "True," the waterfall is in wind-down mode, and so the current period is "True" also. Once the wind-down starts, it is irreversible (since the deal has run out of money). If the value of the previous period is "False," then the spreadsheet checks to see if the sum of the Unpaid Program Fees, the Unpaid Servicing Fees, and the Unpaid Conduit Interest is greater than $0.01. If it is, the current period is set to "True," and a deal wind-down is commenced due to the inability to pay necessary fees. If the sum is equal to or less than $0.01, the current period maintains the condition as "False," and the deal continues as before.

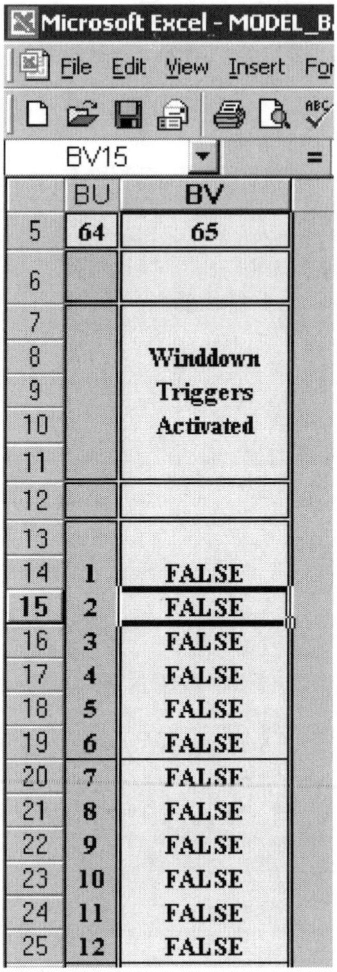

EXHIBIT 4.12   Deal Wind-down Trigger

CASH FLOW WATERFALL "BOX SCORE" SECTION

The Cash Flow Waterfall Box Score section shown in Exhibit 4.13 is a condensed representation of the results of a single scenario result. It spans Columns B through H on the spreadsheet and fills lines 6 through 41, inclusive. It contains three sections:

1. **Cash Flow Sources and Uses Section.** Lines 8 to 22. This section allows users to see at a glance the major sources and uses of funds for the deal. The sources are listed by the now-familiar components of the collateral cash flows. In addition to the dollar amounts of each of these flows, we have the total prepayment and defaults percentages of original collateral principal. In addition, we have the percentage of defaulted principal that was recovered over the life of the deal.

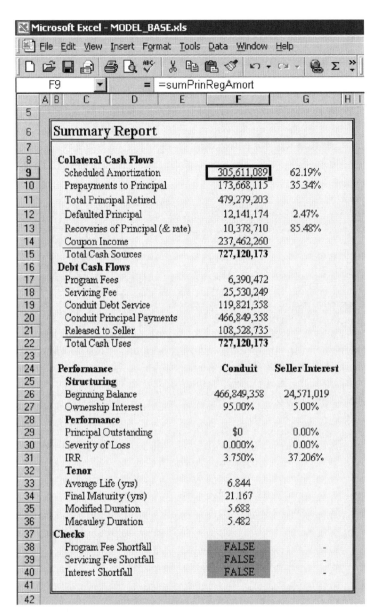

EXHIBIT 4.13   Cash Flow Waterfall Box Score section

2. **Performance Section.** Lines 24 to 36. This section lists the major bond performance statistics for the Conduit Financing performance: the advance rate, the Seller Interest rate, and the original dollar balances of the Conduit and Seller Interests. It also lists the severity of loss (if any) for the repayment of the Conduit financing.

3. **Checks Section.** Lines 37 to 40. This section flags three deal conditions, shortfalls in the payment of the Program Fee, the Servicing Fee, and the Interest.

DELIVERABLES CHECKLIST

Following are the modeling knowledge takeaways for this chapter.

Model Knowledge Checklist

- How to structure a basic Cash Flow Waterfall spreadsheet for a Conduit financing
- An explanation of the components of the deal
- A useable and valid Excel model that we can now develop further with the use of VBA

NEXT STEPS

We now have a working Excel waterfall. We can proceed immediately with the next step in the modeling process, the design of the VBA program. We will wrap this Excel spreadsheet with a VBA program that will control the input and output functions based on instructions entered through its menu interface.

We will design a program that will serve two functions:

- Allow us to select loans from the proposed collateral pool based on a number of financial and demographic features. This function will produce detailed reports of the composition of both the ineligible collateral deselected and the collateral that will be included in the deal.
- Automatically amortize these loans across a Range of assumptions. The model will have the ability to produce both detailed individual waterfall reports and multiple scenario summary reports. These summary reports will be designed to display the results of up to 100 scenarios.

We will now begin to tremendously leverage the functionality of this Excel waterfall with the automating power of VBA.

ON THE WEB SITE

The Web site material for this chapter consists of the Excel file named **"MODEL_BASE_Chap4.xls."** As noted above, this file contains the Excel Waterfall Worksheet that was developed and tested by our predecessor. It contains no VBA code or even any VBA modules to place the code in, even if we had any.

For now the model is a simple Excel spreadsheet. Soon we will change that. In Chapter 5 we will begin to develop the beginnings of a VBA infrastructure that will be the foundation structure of the model.

Designing the VBA Model

OVERVIEW

In this chapter we will begin to design the VBA model. We will first develop an understanding of the various processes that the model will need to perform from start to finish. From there we will be in position to outline the information needed by the model to perform these steps.

Some of this information will be input at the time that we run the model. Some of it will be read from the collateral file supplied to us by the client. Much of this last information will be conditional in nature. This conditionality is based on the character of the collateral itself. The model will use the collateral only if it passes a series of eligibility tests.

All the rest of the inputs, such as prepayment rates and default levels, are, in a sense, unconditional. The model will take these factors as "givens" in the environment and use them as they are presented.

The focus will be to organize and build the first and most basic framework of menus to allow for the transmittal of this information from the environment into the model. We will layout a series of menus that will allow us to direct the model to the data, and then prepare to move the data into the model. We will also design the report package that the model will produce.

To do this we will think of the highest-level processes the model must perform. We will examine the elements of information needed by the model to perform these processes and list where the data are to come from. We will design menus to allow us to input or access this information.

We must always remember that the design of the model is driven by the need to answer certain basic questions. The report package of the model serves to answer the following questions:

- What is the composition of the collateral pool?
- How much of the collateral pool can be used in the deal?
- Of the portion that is deemed ineligible, what are the causes of the ineligibility?
- What are the characteristics of the eligible collateral as measured by tenor (time remaining), geographic distribution, industrial distribution, loan-to-value ratios, coupon distribution, and balance distribution?
- What cash flows will this collateral pool produce under differing prepayment and default assumptions?

- What is the anticipated performance of the note structure given these cash flows?
- How do the results compare across various scenarios?
- How will the structure perform under extreme conditions, or "shock tests"?
- Does the performance of the structure meet the criteria imposed by all parties, such as rating agencies, credit insurance providers, investors, and the internal credit guidelines of the lender?

We will need reports to account for the disposition of every piece of proposed collateral. If a loan is ineligible, we must be able to identify it and explain why.

When the collateral selection process is complete, we must have a clear picture of the remaining risk elements of the eligible collateral. Remember, just because each piece of collateral is eligible on an individual basis does not mean that the collective portfolio will be free from risk. Many types of risk can arise simply from the phenomena of concentration. Too many loans in a particular industry or state (or both jointly), can represent a portfolio level risk exposure. Concentrations of large balance loans increase the risk of spikes in defaults or prepayments. A concentration of loans at certain coupon levels can make the portfolio more susceptible to interest-rate-driven prepayment activity. The presence of adjustable rate loans may induce risk based on "payment shock," triggered by coupon and payment level resets.

Once we have sifted through the collateral we will amortize it under various conditions. We will want to be able to examine the structure's waterfall performance in detail. We will also have to be able to see the big picture, across many scenarios. This will require a completely different set of reports.

At the end of the chapter we will have laid the groundwork for the functionality of the model by specifying its report package requirement. From this functionality we can design the menus the model will need to gather all the information it needs to perform its analytical tasks.

Successive chapters will then focus on how to implement these processes in Excel and VBA to produce a robust, valid, and flexible model.

DELIVERABLES

The modeling knowledge deliverables for this chapter are:

- Understanding that the process of designing a model starts with its report package. From the information requirements of the final reports, the process moves backward through the model calculations to the beginning requirements of collateral data and user inputs.
- An overall view of the model processes that need to be developed. These are collateral selection and reporting, cash flow generation, waterfall spreadsheet management, and finally, generation of the cash flow performance reports.
- What template files are, how they are used to build report packages, and their advantages and disadvantages.
- The steps the model needs to perform to turn a template file into a finished report.

- What the collateral selection process is. A brief overview of the computational method to identify and report ineligible collateral.
- The Collateral Selection Report package and how to read it.
- What a stratification report of eligible collateral is, and how to read it.
- What concentration risk is, and how to use stratification reports to identify possible portfolio level concentration risks.
- The steps in planning and implementing a Cash Flow Waterfall Report package.
- The form and function of a Cash Flow Matrix Report package that reports on up to 100 scenarios in a single report.
- The input that the model menus will require, and a layout of each.

UNDER CONSTRUCTION

The boss has given us a day off! In this chapter we will conceptualize only. Let's concentrate on thinking about what our report package will look like, what information it will contain, and what each report will tell its audience.

That should be more than enough to keep us busy.

WHAT ARE THE DESIRED RESULTS?

We will now talk about how to design an application. The most important thing to remember is the motto:

"Last things first, first things last"

The model is being built to provide the analyst with information upon which he or she can, with other considerations, make a decision about financial risk. It is the production of this information, its form, scope, detail, and content, that the entire model-building activity is about.

Do not become so enamored of the process that you forget the goal, a completed model! How you get there is important, but getting there is what matters most!

Do not confuse the process with the deliverable objective.

Too many novice modelers get so focused on the work of building the model itself that they lose sight of the fact that the model is a vehicle with which to perform the analysis, not an end in and of itself.

The last thing that is produced in a model run is the output. Start with the requirements of the decision-making process, design the output, and then build the model to produce it.

Having said this, what are we trying to measure, and how will we measure it?

In a word, we are trying to measure financial risk. What is the expectation that we, as the securitizing entity of the loans, will be paid back? How will the financing perform? How will the timing of our receipts affect our returns? What Range of unexpected or abnormal conditions will cause losses? How will these losses be absorbed? What will happen to the Seller Interest? Is a credit backstop in the form of a credit insurance policy economically feasible? Is the proposed structure sufficiently robust to satisfy our concerns as an investor?

WHAT PROCESSES MUST THE MODEL PERFORM?

Steps the Model Must Perform

To arrive at the final answers to the above questions we will need to complete the following tasks:

1. Examine the collateral that makes up the portfolio and determine how much of it is appropriate for inclusion in the deal structure. We can do this by applying the collateral exception criteria from the menu.
2. Print out the two collateral sets, eligible and ineligible. It is particularly important to be able to identify the specific conditions which render each piece of collateral ineligible. Many Sellers think of their collateral in the same light that they think of their children, everyone is at least "above average." If sizable portions of the collateral pool are rejected, an explanation of the conditions that rendered the collateral ineligible will be critical. Knowing what was wrong may allow the client to add incremental collateral to the deal, or to identify and correct data issues in the portfolio (some collateral may be fine, the data is just incorrect.)
3. Examine the configuration of the portfolio of eligible collateral for concentration risks across such issues as geography, coupon distribution, distribution by original and remaining term, seasoning, balances, and payment conditions. For floating rate collateral, you will want to also examine its benchmark index distribution.
4. Eliminate any collateral that is in violation of concentration risk guidelines.
5. Amortize the remaining eligible collateral and determine the component principal, interest, and defaults expected.
6. Enter the collateral cash flows into the Excel spreadsheet model we have built for the waterfall of the deal.
7. Capture the results of the structure's performance from the waterfall spreadsheet and store the results, for a single case or multiple cases.
8. Present these results in a set of reports that contain the requested performance measures and collateral information.

Basic Outline of the Reports Package

To be able to examine the interim results of these processes we will need a minimum of the following reports:

- A set of exception reports to tell us which loans have failed particular criteria, and how many have failed each particular criterion. This report set would include a summary of all eligible/ineligible loans that shows the ineligibility conditions. The summary will provide an overview of the distribution of collateral principal by ineligibility conditions and will also be helpful in spotting data errors in the preliminary analysis phase.
- A set of reports that list all the eligible collateral. In addition to an exhaustive list, this report package would include stratification reports to help identify concentration risk across various collateral features.

- A deal cash flow waterfall report. This report should show the monthly deal activity based on the collateral cash flow assumptions, the deal expenses, reserve account activity, and financing repayment.
- A summary of multiple-scenario runs. These results will be critical and should be grouped into major categories such as debt performance, tenor, returns, Seller Interest performance, and collateral loss defeasance. Displaying these results in a matrix format organized by prepayment/default scenarios will help us to more clearly compare the results and quickly identify soft spots in the performance of the proposed structure.

Template Files

With all of this said, a collateral exception report will look nothing like a deal waterfall report, which in turn will bear little resemblance to a scenario-level results report. Therefore, to meet all the goals set forth above, we are going to have a variety of reports and each will have a format different from the others. In addition, it is more likely than not that the format of the individual reports will tend to be complex rather than simplistic.

As all Excel users know, it is possible to record VBA macros and run them to format reports. Unfortunately, as we will see in Chapter 7, "Recorded Macros: A First Look at the VBA Language," recorded macros are not efficient. When a recorded macro is used to change the appearance of an individual cell, say its background color, it may well record many other cell objects and their properties that are totally unrelated to the desired color change. This can create quite a bit of extraneous code. To build report formatting code into our model would be a waste of time and space. It would also create hundreds (or maybe even thousands) of additional lines of code to maintain. To avoid these burdens we will make use of template files.

What are template files?

INTRODUCTION TO TEMPLATE FILES

A template file is essentially a preformatted blank form. All the characteristics of the report that will not change, such as header information, the number of columns, the display form of the information, and any presentation aspects such as colors and font enhancement, is fixed in place. It has been created so that all that needs to be done is to fill the template with a set of results from the model.

Why Use Template Files?

Template files generally stand apart from the model file, which is generating the data. This separateness helps to facilitate the management of multiple sets of reports. As we run the model, we may wish to evaluate tens or even hundreds of combinations of collateral selection and structuring assumptions. Each model run may produce up to 100 scenarios based on combinations of prepayment and default speeds. In addition to the basic structuring run, there will also be runs for other interested parties, such as the client, internal credit personnel, rating agencies, investors, and bond insurers.

By separating the template files from the model we are able to copy them, rename them, and then save them separately from the model itself.

This has two immediate advantages. The first is that the use of template files keeps the size of the model constant because the report package is separate from the model's Excel workbook. The second is that it allows you to produce almost unlimited numbers of output scenarios without the need to overwrite or manage the model file.

Template files are best kept in their own separate and clearly labeled directory, away from the location of the model file. We will revisit this issue in Chapter 6, when we set up the environment of the model and the directory structure we will use to organize its various components.

Turning a Template File into a Report File

Template files may contain spreadsheets with formulas, graphs, charts, table objects, or any other special features. These features are activated when the model populates the template file with data during the report-writing phase of the model run. Template files can also be constructed such that activities contained within them are triggered before, during, or after the entire model results have been written. The model transforms a blank template file into a fully populated report file by performing a simple series of actions. The usual sequence of activities in this process is typically:

1. Open the template file.
2. Immediately rename the template file to a pre-selected or user-designated name.
3. Save the renamed file to an output directory separate from the directory that contains the model.
4. Write the data from the model into the saved and renamed file.
5. At any time during Step 4, the data will trigger any worksheet methods such as "Calculate," as prescribed by the template.
6. Save and close the file.

Example of a Template File

Exhibits 5.1 and 5.2 show the change from a base template file to a fully populated report file.

Advantages of Template File Use

Template files have a number of advantages:

- They are *extensible*; it is easy to add new reports. This is especially true of cases when many of the reports have very similar formats.
- They are *easily edited* because they are away from the model proper. Changes to the template files do not necessitate changes to the model. Additional capabilities can be built into the template files by simply using the data already supplied by the model in different ways.

Collateral Selection Portfolio Exception Report
INELIGIBLE-4 Minimum/Maximum Current Loan Balance

Loan Number	Selection Criteria	Obligor Number	Obligor Name	Current Yield	Current Loan Balance	Current LTV	Current Equity Balance	Current Equity LTV	Original Appraisal Value
0			Averages/Totals		–	#DIV/0!	–	#DIV/0!	–

EXHIBIT 5.1   Blank template report with headers and colors in place

Collateral Selection Portfolio Exception Report
INELIGIBLE-4 Minimum/Maximum Current Balance

Loan Number	Selection Criteria	Obligor Number	Obligor Name	Current Yield	Current Loan Balance	Current LTV	Current Equity Balance	Current Equity LTV	Original Appraisal Value
52			Averages/Totals		976,754	52.500%	1,183,246	63.598%	1,860,500
1	3	11,617		10.500%	11,617	48.40%	18,383	76.60%	24,000
2	58	19,859		10.500%	19,859	58.41%	20,141	59.24%	34,000
3	61	17,476		10.500%	17,476	54.61%	22,524	70.39%	32,000
4	76	20,587		10.500%	20,587	60.55%	19,413	57.10%	34,000
5	175	22,014		10.500%	22,014	55.03%	17,986	44.97%	40,000
6	196	20,136		10.500%	20,136	59.22%	19,864	58.42%	34,000
7	222	21,094		10.500%	21,094	49.63%	28,906	68.01%	42,500
8	224	22,931		10.500%	22,931	57.33%	17,069	42.67%	40,000
9	230	20,826		10.500%	20,826	52.07%	19,174	47.93%	40,000
10	240	18,704		10.500%	18,704	55.01%	21,296	62.64%	34,000
11	268	17,402		11.500%	17,402	68.24%	12,598	49.40%	25,500
12	283	24,306		9.500%	24,306	43.40%	45,694	81.60%	56,000
13	308	21,742		10.500%	21,742	63.95%	18,258	53.70%	34,000
14	375	19,064		10.500%	19,064	56.07%	20,936	61.58%	34,000
15	453	11,273		11.500%	11,273	66.31%	8,727	51.34%	17,000

EXHIBIT 5.2   Template file in Exhibit 5.1 has now been populated by the program

- Because they are not part of the model file proper, *template files do not consume resources in the model file,* nor necessitate the model's expansion if additional reports are required. This especially true of the use of *pre-configured graphics.* The model developer can write very complex graphs and charts once. Each time the program writes to the template file, the graphic is immediately updated.
- Template files allow *more extensive mechanization of the output and report generation process.* Carried to an extreme case, the entire model may be put into another VBA program (a shell). The shell then populates all the menus and simulates the actions of the analyst. The shell then can be placed inside another VBA program that contains a looping structure. Multiple runs can then be generated, with their resultant *output files all individually stored and named.*
- The use of template files for *multiple runs of the model will, over time, create a collection of identically formatted output files.* In that these files will have a standardized format, it will be possible to write other programs to easily access the results of the output files en masse for use in other databases and other applications.
- Template files contain most of their own formatting, which *eliminates the use of long formatting macros in the model file.* Formatting macros for reports of even moderate complexity can run into hundreds of statements. The more code your model processes, the greater the draw on system resources.
- Template files make *model validation and back testing of new model versions much easier.* With identical formats you can develop programs to automatically compare actual model results with expected or previous model results in other file sets. Any differences between the two sets of files can be immediately determined without having to compare them manually.

Disadvantages of Template File Use

Template files also have some disadvantages:

- You have to be careful *not to lose the output* because it is stored away from and outside of the model itself. Analysts using a sophisticated model to structure a typical ABS transaction generally have to make dozens of runs to answer all the questions. It is necessary to segregate and clearly label each set of output reports so that it can be quickly located. It is extremely frustrating to lose output by misplacing it away from the model.
- You have to keep the *model and the template file "in sync"* so that changes to one are reflected in the other. Every time there is a change to the model one must be careful to reflect these changes in the template files. This especially relates to reports containing inputs to the model. If additional inputs are introduced you need to update the template files to contain them. Additionally, changes to the model may require changes or additions to the template files to accommodate new information.
- If you are going to do analysis across sets of results *you will have to look at different sets of files* to do so. This can be considered both an advantage and a disadvantage as was alluded to in the sixth bullet in the preceding **"Advantages"** section. One way to nullify this disadvantage is to write a VBA program that can search a list of output files that you have designated, extract specific information

from each, and prepare a summary report of the results contained in all of them on a single new report. We will, in fact, do just this in Chapter 18, "Running the Model."

■ You have to *be careful not to overwrite or destroy existing output* when you generate new output. It is quite easy in the course of running the model four times quickly to forget to change the name that you want the template file renamed to, and thus overwrite the previous run's results. You will learn how to build error messages that can mimic those in Excel and tell you if you are about to overwrite an existing file. This is much easier to avoid when you are keeping all the output in the model file itself.

Template File Sets Required by the Model

We will need at least four sets of different reports in at least two template files (maybe more later) to produce the output to understand this deal and facilitate the needs of all the parties (ourselves, clients, credit surety providers, and rating agencies).

They are, in order of use, the following:

1. Ineligible collateral reports, both for single- and multiple-ineligibility conditions
2. Eligible collateral reports, both itemized and stratified
3. Individual scenario cash flow waterfall reports showing detailed monthly activity
4. Summary matrix reports of multiple-scenario runs

COLLATERAL SELECTION REPORTS

These reports are designed to inform the user if a particular loan has passed or failed a specific collateral test. Collateral tests are designed to weed out collateral that has unsuitable credit or cash flow characteristics.

As we examine the contents of the collateral information file we will apply various tests to each of the collateral on an individual basis. It will be useful to be able to specifically identify each ineligible piece of collateral by cause, and to get a total of all such ineligible loans.

Of additional interest would be a report of the ineligible loans by their payment and credit characteristics. This will allow us to quickly assess the scope of any problems with the eligibility of the collateral, report to the client, and see if replacement collateral is available, or whether a remedy can be negotiated. Lastly, it will tell us if the model is performing the task properly in that we will have a listing of all ineligible loans to visually compare against the original collateral file.

Templates for the Collateral Selection Reports

The model has a total of 11 collateral tests. We will look at each in Chapter 11 when we design the VBA code to perform the selection criteria testing. There are clearly many, many possible tests that can be employed to weed out unsuitable collateral. We will start with these tests to demonstrate the concept and the basic approach to designing a multi-condition screening process. Once you understand one or two of them, the rest can be fitted into the existing framework without a lot of difficulty.

The key to collateral selection is to remain flexible in your approach and tailor the selection process to the characteristics of the collateral you are working on.

As you gain experience you will develop a sixth sense on how to conduct this process, but for now we will start simply.

Example of a Collateral Screening Exercise

For example, we may apply the following test against the portfolio as initial screening of the collateral:

- No loans from the state of Connecticut

We would load these selection criteria into the geographic menu. The model would perform the selection process tagging the loans that violated our criteria.

If there were ineligible loans in any of the particular categories, it would populate that specific report. If not, that worksheet of the file would be deleted because it was not used. At the end of the single cause ineligibility, a comprehensive loan-by-loan listing and a summary report would be generated. We would now have all the information we needed to talk to the client about the suitability of the proposed portfolio.

INELIGIBLE COLLATERAL REPORTS

Exhibit 5.3 is an example of the typical layout for an ineligible collateral report.

A Sample Ineligibility Report
(Ineligibility by Geographic Region)

We know the following things about this set of ineligible loans from this report:

- A total of 99 loans are ineligible due to unsuitable geographic codes.
- They can be identified specifically from their place in the data file by the Loan Number value.
- They comprised $17.718 million of current loan balances.
- The state that caused their ineligibility from the portfolio is identified.
- The ineligible loans collectively represent $13.967 million in equity.
- Their average Loan-to-Value (LTV) ratio is 55.918%.
- Their average equity position is 44.082% of the total appraisal value of the portfolio.
- Their aggregate appraisal value is $31.686 million.
- We can identify them individually, by their client names (scrubbed for this example).

Summary Ineligibility Reports

To gain a more comprehensive view of the eligible vs. ineligible collateral, we will need to complement these ineligibility reports with summary information reports, which will provide an overview of the results of the entire selection process at the portfolio level.

Collateral Selection Portfolio Exception Report
INELIGIBLE-7 Excluded State Codes

	Loan Number	Selection Criteria	Obligor Number	Obligor Name	Current Yield	Current Loan Balance	Current LTV	Current Equity Balance	Current Equity LTV	Original Appraisal Value
99				Averages/Totals		17,718,260	55.918%	13,967,740	44.082%	31,686,000
1	1	Connecticut			9.000%	29,569	42.24%	40,431	57.76%	70,000
2	2	Connecticut			9.000%	50,137	41.78%	69,863	58.22%	120,000
3	113	Connecticut			9.000%	70,541	58.78%	49,459	41.22%	120,000
4	122	Connecticut			9.000%	43,057	61.51%	26,943	38.49%	70,000
5	205	Connecticut			9.000%	48,384	53.76%	41,616	46.24%	90,000
6	217	Connecticut			9.000%	93,294	71.76%	36,706	28.24%	130,000
7	275	Connecticut			9.000%	55,834	46.53%	64,166	53.47%	120,000
8	302	Connecticut			9.000%	73,089	73.09%	26,911	26.91%	100,000
9	339	Connecticut			9.000%	67,085	47.92%	72,915	52.08%	140,000
10	341	Connecticut			8.000%	618,634	52.87%	551,366	47.13%	1,170,000
11	432	Connecticut			8.250%	89,907	59.94%	60,093	40.06%	150,000
12	438	Connecticut			8.750%	350,173	72.95%	129,827	27.05%	480,000
13	455	Connecticut			9.000%	73,554	56.58%	56,446	43.42%	130,000
14	514	Connecticut			8.250%	102,881	46.76%	117,119	53.24%	220,000
15	547	Connecticut			9.000%	63,659	53.05%	56,341	46.95%	120,000
16	564	Connecticut			9.000%	61,984	68.87%	28,016	31.13%	90,000
17	648	Connecticut			8.500%	369,552	65.99%	190,448	34.01%	560,000
18	654	Connecticut			8.750%	227,576	58.35%	162,424	41.65%	390,000
19	684	Connecticut			9.000%	78,205	60.16%	51,795	39.84%	130,000
20	686	Connecticut			9.000%	53,897	59.89%	36,103	40.11%	90,000

EXHIBIT 5.3   Geographic Selection ineligible loans report

The first of these summary reports will tell us how many loans are ineligible based upon each of the test conditions. It will, in essence, be the summary statistics of the entire set of individual ineligibility reports we looked at above. This will not, however, complete the picture. A loan may be ineligible for two or more reasons simultaneously. In that case its balance will be counted in this report once for each ineligibility condition that it triggered. We would therefore overstate the aggregate amount of ineligible collateral balances.

The second summary report will tell us how many loans were ineligible that had the same unique pattern of ineligibility criteria. This second summary report will give us a picture of the "severity" of the ineligible collateral. We will be able to tell at a glance if most of the loans are ineligible for combinations of failures, rather than for a single cause of failure. We will build-in ineligibility codes to represent all the compound ineligibility conditions possible.

Ineligible Loan Listing

If we had run a different set of multiple-selection criteria against the portfolio, we might have derived the results illustrated in Exhibit 5.4. The program lists each of the ineligible loans and puts a tick mark in the column of any failed eligibility test.

Loan Listing Exception Report
Individual Loan Ineligibility Conditions

Ineligibility Condition Reference

1 = Min/Max Remaining Term	7 = Excluded State or Geographic Region
2 = Min/Max Original Term	8 = Inconsistent Original vs Remaining Term
3 = Min Max Original Balance	9 = Inconsistent Original vs Remaining Balance
4 = Min/Max Current Balance	10 = Calculated vs. Stated Payment Differences
5 = Exceeds Maximum LTV	11 = Unacceptable Gross Coupon
6 = Unacceptable Floater Indice/Spread	

Total Loans Rejected	Loan Number	Ineligibility Condition											Loan Yield	Current Balance
		1	2	3	4	5	6	7	8	9	10	11		
56		0	0	24	52	0	4	0	0	0	0	1	7.940%	3,024,285
1	3			1	1								10.000%	11,617
2	58			1	1								10.000%	19,859
3	61			1	1								10.000%	17,476
4	76				1								10.000%	20,587
5	175				1								10.000%	22,014
6	196				1								10.000%	20,136
7	222				1								10.000%	21,094
8	224				1								10.000%	22,931
9	230				1								10.000%	20,826
10	240	1			1								10.000%	18,704

EXHIBIT 5.4　Individual Loan Ineligibility Condition report (partial)

It identifies the loan by its number and provides a count of all the loans that failed each test in the header. It displays the sum of the current balances. It also shows the current coupon of each individual loan and the dollar weighted average coupon (WAC) of all of the ineligibles. The loans of the portfolio failed four tests, the most failed was test #4, the Minimum/Maximum Current Balance test.

Unique Combination Ineligibility Report

This second summary report, shown in Exhibit 5.5, lists the unique permutations of ineligible criteria for the entire set of ineligible loans in the portfolio. This report uses a scoring system to identify unique ineligibility conditions. The system is described in detail in Chapter 13, "Writing the Collateral Selection Code." The score is then used to group the loans by this failure pattern.

The scoring methodology is as follows:

- The ineligibility conditions are ordered sequentially 1 through 11 (one for each test).
- Each ineligibility condition is assigned a numeric value that is the base of 2 raised to an exponent. The exponent is determined by subtracting 1 from the number of the ineligibility test. Thus, if the loan failed the third eligibility test it would be assigned a value of 2 to the (3-1) power, or 2^2, or ultimately, 4.
- These values are then summed and the result is the error code.
- Example: A loan fails tests 1, 4, and 6. The exponent values of the failed tests minus one each are 0, 3, and 5, respectively.

Summary Exception Report
Contracts Grouped By Unique Ineligibility Combinations

Ineligibility Condition Reference

1 = Min/Max Remaining Term	7 = Excluded State or Geographic Region
2 = Min/Max Original Term	8 = Inconsistent Original vs Remaining Term
3 = Min Max Original Balance	9 = Inconsistent Original vs Remaining Balance
4 = Min/Max Current Balance	10 = Calculated vs. Stated Payment Differences
5 = Exceeds Maximum LTV	11 = Unacceptable Gross Coupon
6 = Unacceptable Floater Indice/Spread	

Unique Ineligibility Code	Ineligibility Condition											Number of Loans	Total Current Balance	Total Equity Position
	1	2	3	4	5	6	7	8	9	10	11			
	0	0	1	2	0	2	0	0	0	0	1	56	3,024,285	646,065
8				1								28	620,496	25,150
12			1	1								24	356,258	10,582
32						1						3	1,618,184	69,679
1056						1					1	1	429,347	540,653

EXHIBIT 5.5 Unique Ineligibility Combinations report (full)

The sums of the values are:

$$(2 \text{ to 0th}) + (2 \text{ to 3rd})) + (2 \text{ to 5th}) = 1 + 8 + 32 = 41 \text{ total ineligibility score}$$

It is important to note that the magnitude of any particular score does not at all mean that a loan is *more ineligible* than a loan with a lower score. If a loan fails a test, then it is ineligible, period. In the sample report below, for example, there are four unique scores, 8, 12, 32, and 1056. None of the four combinations is more ineligible than the others.

ELIGIBLE COLLATERAL REPORTS

Concentration Risks at the Portfolio Level

Having now purged the portfolio of ineligible collateral, what do we have left? What we have is a collection of loans that individually meet all of the selection criteria tests. A loan portfolio that has passed each of the *individual* selection criteria tests on a loan-by-loan basis should not be confused with having a risk-free portfolio. There is the question of collective or systemic risk.

Systemic or collective risk arises from the combination of the collateral characteristics, rather than from risk associated with an individual item of collateral. The most commonly recognizable form of collective portfolio risk is concentration risk. Concentration risk is the risk of having "too many of your eggs in a single basket."

Geographic Concentration Risk

Concentration risk is the opposite of diversification. An example of concentration risk would be abnormally large numbers of loans originated in a geographic area, industry, or over a brief period of time by a single issuer.

The following is an example of geographic risk. A client presents us with a portfolio that is purportedly a nationally diverse set of loans. We find, however, that 55% of the total number of loans and 62% of the current balance of the portfolio is concentrated in three states, California, Michigan, and Florida. After running two stratification reports on geographic characteristics, we find that 35% of the total portfolio is from California alone and that 80% of those balances are in four ZIP codes in southern California. A total of 28% of the principal balance of 28% (35%*80%), is extremely concentrated. If there were a local economic event in the form of weather or seismic activity, losses would be immediate and severe.

Prepayment Risk Based on Coupon Concentration

The previous examples have all concentrated on dilution of the portfolio cash flows through default. Prepayment risk can also be accentuated or triggered by coupon concentrations in the portfolio. Let us assume that we have three portfolios. The distribution of their current balances by coupon is shown in Exhibit 5.6.

These three portfolios all have the same weighted average coupon of 8.00%.

The prepayment risk of each is very different based on the distribution of the balances by coupon. The current rate environment is 9.00%. The benchmark index falls over a one-year period by 150 basis points to 7.50%. The results are displayed in Exhibit 5.7.

Portfolio 1 experiences modest prepayment activity or none at all. The rate change between 8.00% and 7.50% is not substantial enough to make a refinancing economically attractive. Portfolios 2 and 3 experience selective heavy prepayment among the 10.00 to 11.00% loans, and modest prepayment activity in the 9.00% loans.

The coupon-generating ability of Portfolio 1 is only slightly impaired. It still has 95% of its principal outstanding and a WAC of 8.00%. Portfolio 2 is doing less well, with 74.6% of its principal outstanding and a WAC of 7.75%. Portfolio 3 has 75% of its principal outstanding, but its WAC has fallen to 7.40%, a decline of 60 basis points!

Now let us say that an additional 1.5% decline in the benchmark rate takes place over the next year. The results are detailed in Exhibit 5.8.

EXHIBIT 5.6 Initial distribution of coupons and balances

Coupon	Portfolio 1	Portfolio 2	Portfolio 3
5%		$10,000,000	
6%		$20,000,000	$100,000,000
7%		$50,000,000	$50,000,000
8%	$300,000,000	$100,000,000	
9%		$50,000,000	$50,000,000
10%		$20,000,000	$100,000,000
11%		$10,000,000	
WAC	8.00%	8.00%	8.00%

EXHIBIT 5.7   Distribution of balances by coupon at one year

One Year Later—Benchmark Rate has fallen from 9% to 7.5%			
Coupon	Portfolio 1	Portfolio 2	Portfolio 3
5%		$10,000,000	
6%		$20,000,000	$100,000,000
7%		$50,000,000	$50,000,000
8%	$285,000,000	$95,000,000	
9%		$35,000,000	$35,000,000
10%		$12,000,000	$40,000,000
11%		$2,000,000	
Total	$285,000,000	$224,000,000	$225,000,000
WAC	8.00%	7.75%	7.40%

As we can see in Exhibit 5.8, the prepayment behaviors of these three portfolios are markedly different. The WAC of Portfolio 2 has fallen further to 7.18%. The WAC on Portfolio 3 has all but collapsed; it now stands at 6.32% due to catastrophic prepayments in the loans with an original coupon level of 9.00–10.00%! Without a stratification report on coupon, we would not be aware of the potential divergence from a homogeneous 8.00% coupon pool.

Basic Stratification Report Package

The basic stratification report package will consist of the 11 reports, three stratify the portfolio by tenor, one each by coupon or spread, two by loan-to-value ratios, two by balances, and two by geography.

Each report will consist of the stratification levels displayed in columns 1 to 3 of the report and a report body in columns 4 to 18. The report columns will be identical across all reports. A typical report is shown in Exhibit 5.9.

EXHIBIT 5.8   Distribution of balances by coupon after two years

Two Years Later—Benchmark Rate has fallen from 9% to 6%			
Coupon	Portfolio 1	Portfolio 2	Portfolio 3
5%		$10,000,000	
6%		$20,000,000	$100,000,000
7%		$47,500,000	$47,500,000
8%	$199,500,000	$66,500,000	
9%			
10%			
11%			
Total	$199,500,000	$144,000,000	$147,000,000
WAC	8.00%	7.18%	6.32%

Eligible Collateral Report #1
Current Balances Distribution by Original Terms

	4	5	6	7	8	9	10	11	12	13	14	15	16
Original Term Range	Number of Loans	Current Loan Balance	Current Loan LTV	% Current Balances	Cum % Current Balances	Average Loan Balance	WtAvg Current Yield	WtAvg Original Term	WtAvg Remain Term	WtAvg Current Seasoning	Equity Balance	Equity % Appraisal	Total Appraisal
	2,199	458,874,175									362,915,825		821,790,000
49 to 60	4	734,222	57.361%	0.160%	0.160%	183,555	8.562%	58.97	41.25	17.72	545,778	42.639%	1,280,000
73 to 84	486	36,419,710	55.994%	7.937%	8.097%	74,938	8.930%	83.67	66.13	17.54	29,090,290	44.406%	65,510,000
85 to 96	33	3,478,211	51.301%	0.758%	8.855%	105,400	8.772%	94.81	75.00	19.81	3,301,789	48.699%	6,780,000
97 to 108	69	11,442,952	56.314%	2.494%	11.348%	165,840	8.754%	107.13	90.91	16.22	8,877,048	43.686%	20,320,000
109 to 120	686	118,638,872	58.351%	25.854%	37.203%	172,943	8.684%	119.54	107.11	12.43	84,681,128	41.649%	203,320,000
121 to 132	33	5,936,513	58.144%	1.294%	38.496%	179,894	8.582%	126.38	116.45	9.93	4,273,487	41.856%	10,210,000
133 to 144	15	4,731,780	57.425%	1.031%	39.528%	315,452	8.537%	143.02	133.06	9.96	3,308,220	42.575%	8,240,000
145 to 156	15	5,254,515	61.385%	1.145%	40.673%	350,301	8.426%	154.93	143.31	11.62	3,305,485	38.615%	8,560,000
157 to 168	9	4,062,798	60.012%	0.885%	41.558%	451,422	8.623%	166.90	152.56	14.34	2,707,202	39.983%	6,770,000
169 to 180	59	19,193,303	52.860%	4.183%	45.741%	325,310	8.593%	179.25	160.16	19.09	17,116,697	47.140%	36,310,000
181 to 192	12	4,070,650	53.703%	0.887%	46.628%	339,221	8.494%	191.61	170.79	20.83	3,509,350	46.297%	7,580,000
193 to 204	18	6,674,044	55.897%	1.454%	48.082%	370,780	8.396%	203.13	187.93	15.20	5,265,956	44.103%	11,940,000
205 to 216	25	8,199,965	52.631%	1.787%	49.869%	327,999	8.388%	215.68	196.11	19.57	7,380,035	47.369%	15,580,000
217 to 228	17	4,583,747	48.919%	0.999%	50.868%	269,632	8.502%	227.38	204.94	22.44	4,786,253	51.081%	9,370,000
229 to 240	184	49,619,995	51.388%	10.813%	61.682%	269,674	8.465%	239.58	218.93	20.65	46,940,005	48.612%	96,560,000
241 to 252	40	12,367,793	56.192%	2.695%	64.377%	309,195	8.311%	250.17	236.59	13.58	9,642,207	43.808%	22,010,000
253 to 264	40	10,640,199	56.960%	2.319%	66.696%	266,005	8.375%	262.39	250.17	12.22	8,039,801	43.040%	18,680,000
265 to 276	54	18,482,716	58.956%	4.028%	70.724%	342,273	8.308%	274.85	262.04	12.81	12,867,284	41.044%	31,350,000
277 to 288	69	27,794,273	58.539%	6.057%	76.781%	402,816	8.335%	287.24	274.93	12.31	19,685,727	41.461%	47,480,000
289 to 300	326	104,477,384	54.884%	22.768%	99.549%	320,483	8.294%	299.27	282.98	16.29	85,882,616	45.116%	190,360,000
301 to 312	5	2,070,533	57.836%	0.451%	100.000%	414,107	8.233%	305.00	298.69	6.32	1,509,467	42.164%	3,580,000

EXHIBIT 5.9 Current balances by original term eligible collateral report (full)

88

CASH FLOW WATERFALL REPORTS

Having arrived at the eligible loan selection, our next step is to calculate the cash flows of the loans and determine the effects of running them through the proposed structure.

In Chapter 4 we designed a cash flow waterfall for the deal. We will still need to produce a set of collateral cash flows for each of the prepayment/default scenario combinations we want to explore. After computing the collateral cash flows in the VBA model, we will populate the appropriate columns of the Excel model. We will trigger a calculation of the waterfall and capture the results. It would be very helpful to have a complete copy of the waterfall for each of the scenarios we run. We would be in a position to closely scrutinize the results, and the waterfalls themselves would be immediately available for inclusion in reports, presentations, and for model validation purposes (see Chapter 17, "Validating the Results").

To capture the information from the individual waterfall worksheets, we will create a template file with a single copy of the worksheet, but without any of the formulas in the report layout.

CASH FLOW MATRIX REPORTS

To complement the cash flow waterfall report, we need a report that can display the results of multiple model runs. The basic format for this report can be seen in Exhibit 5.10.

Four divisions of information seem to make the most sense. The first of these is tenor, how long it will take for the notes to be repaid. The second is the magnitude of the collateral cash flows by component. The next is the timing and magnitude of defaults and their impact on note performance. The fourth is the passive credit enhancement and cash flow shortfalls, if any.

The basic report package will look like this:

- Tenor measurements of the Conduit financing
- Collateral cash flow components
- Conduit note performance
- Seller Interest performance

DESIGNING THE MENUS

Having laid out what we want the model to produce, we now have to provide the model with the information it needs to do the job. We will need to specify the following:

- Input file information. What is the name of the collateral file and what directory is it in?
- What are the names of the template files and what directory are they in?
- What name do we want to give to this scenario and subsequent report set?

Summary Matrix Report #2
Collateral Cash Flow Report

Total Scheduled Amortization
Total Prepayment to Principal
Total Principal Retired
Total Defaults of Principal
Total Recoveries of Principal
Total Coupon Cashflows

Default Levels	PSA Prepayment Methodology				
	1	2	3	4	5
	100.00%	125.00%	150.00%	175.00%	200.00%
1	305,611,089	278,134,403	254,692,895	234,565,599	217,171,836
	173,668,115	201,541,716	225,358,804	245,842,068	263,573,700
100.00% PSA	479,279,203	479,676,119	480,051,699	480,407,666	480,745,535
	12,141,174	11,744,258	11,368,678	11,012,711	10,674,842
	10,378,710	10,044,703	9,728,578	9,428,888	9,144,361
	237,462,260	221,851,254	208,071,926	195,858,979	184,989,584
2	301,788,990	274,779,344	251,730,701	231,935,753	214,824,781
	171,536,413	199,134,678	222,740,410	243,063,456	260,675,768
150.00% PSA	473,325,403	473,914,022	474,471,111	474,999,209	475,500,549
	18,094,974	17,506,355	16,949,266	16,421,168	15,919,828
	15,469,001	14,973,664	14,504,754	14,060,138	13,637,939
	234,955,170	219,596,597	206,036,858	194,015,595	183,314,115
3	298,017,063	271,467,280	248,805,541	229,337,968	212,505,616

EXHIBIT 5.10 Collateral cash flow components

- Which selection criteria are active, and what are the values we are to select against?
- What are the various structural considerations? The floors, caps, triggers, model costs, and so forth.
- How are we going to specify the collateral behavior, including prepayment and default methodology and levels, the recovery rate, and the recovery time lag?

We will also need to make these items easy for the user to manipulate. To do this we will design and use menus. Menus are the points of access that a modeler designs, so that running the model will be a controlled and orderly progress. Some considerations in designing menus are:

- Menus guide the user to perform preset actions.
- Menus limit the accessibility of the user to the code.
- Menus allow for the specification of directory and file locations.
- Menus allow the user to specify modifications to the runtime options of the model, utilizing or ignoring computational or operational branching as the model runs.
- Menus allow the immediate display of the assumptions to be used in the model, and a place to display input error messages.
- Lastly, menus can display progress and error messages, and display intermediate results that inform the user of the stage of completion of the model.

We will be using menus to accomplish the following things

- Start the model running.
- Specify the location of output template files.
- Display the assumptions of the model in such a way that they are accessible to the user for examination and/or change.
- Serve as a backdrop for error messages.
- Display progress messages.
- Display partial or interim results of the execution of the model while it is running.
- Designate the number and types of reports.

Designing the Input Menus

To accomplish the goals on the preceding page we will need the following five menus:

1. Main Menu
2. Collateral Selection Criteria Menu
3. Prepayments and Default Assumptions Menu
4. Geographic Selection Criteria Menu
5. Report Selections Menu

We will also have a menu to display intermediate results to the analyst:

6. Selection Results Menu. This is a portfolio-level summary of the eligible/ineligible loans.

In Chapter 8 we will learn how to create menus and how to link them to the VBA code of the models. In that chapter we also will learn the basic building blocks of a simple menu. We need to look at the information requirements of the model and design the menus to provide an entry point into the program for that information. To accomplish that, we will examine each of the functional requirements of the menu set one-by-one, starting with the primary entry gate into the model, the Main Menu.

Main Menu

The Main Menu, whose layout can be seen in Exhibit 5.11, is the primary entry point into the model. It contains the highest level of inputs. These include the run options of the model that serve as the program flow control switches. These switches turn on and off the major functional blocks of the code. We need to specify the directory pathways the model will use to locate various files. We are using template files for the reporting mechanism of the model. The model must also include a field to specify the directory that contains the set of template files. The last input field block will take the names of the output file names and the designated template files that will be populated to produce these reports.

Reports Selection Menu

The Reports Selection Menu allows the user to individually select each of the eleven collateral stratification reports and each of the four cash flow matrix reports.

Loan Securitization Model Main Menu

Program Execution Options   (Y=YES; N=NO)

Y	Perform the Collateral Eligibility Test?
Y	Write out Ineligible Collateral Reports?
Y	Write out Eligible Collateral Reports?
Y	Write out Eligible Collateral Loan File?
Y	Write out Cash Flow Waterfall Reports?
Y	Write out Matrix Summary Reports?
N	Write out Cash Flow Trace files? (*Caution: can generate VERY LENGTHY run times!*)

Run the Model

Input File Information

C:\VBA_Class\AnalystProgram\	
CombinedCollatSprd.xls	Collateral Data File Name
0	# of Loans *Enter "0" to read all available, otherwise enter the number of loans that you want to have read from the top of the file.*

	Report Group Prefix (attached to alll output files)		Template File Names
TestRun_01_	Report Group Prefix (attached to alll output files)		
Ineligibles.xls	Ineligible Collateral Reports File Name	<=====	inelig_template.xls
Collateral.xls	Eligible Collateral Reports File Name	<=====	collat_template.xls
Waterfall.xls	Cash Flow Waterfalls Report File Name	<=====	waterfall_template.xls
Matrix.xls	Summary Matrix Reports Files	<=====	matrix_template.xls
CombinesCollat.xls	Eligible Collateral File	<=====	datafile_template.xls

EXHIBIT 5.11   Main Menu of the model

Geographic Selection Menu

This menu allows us to select or deselect loans based on their geographic characteristics. Users can select a single state or region, or multiple states or regions, or all states.

When selecting or deselecting a region, we can link a button on the menu to a small VBA subroutine that will place an "X" in the input cells in each of the states in that region.

Prepayments and Default Rate Menu

The left side of this menu displays the default information to be used in amortizing the collateral, while the right side displays the prepayment information.

Default and Prepayment Rate Sections

Default Speed Methodologies   There are two methodologies that can be used for specifying either default or prepayment rates built into the model. These are:

1. CPR—Constant Prepayment Rate
2. PSA—Public Securities Association

We need to be able to specify a Range of default rates. We can do this by establishing a base rate, an incremental rate, and the number of increments. This will produce a ladder of default rates.

If we set the default rate to 10%, with a step of 2% and the number of steps at 7, the model will evaluate default rates of 10%, 12%, 14%, 16%, 18%, 20%, and 22%.

User-defined Default Distributions   User-defined default rates allow the entry of any distribution of annual default proportions across annual periods.

Other Information

Market Value Decline and Recovery Lag   The remaining inputs on this menu are the Market Value Decline (MVD) percentage experienced by defaulted property, and the recovery lag. The MVD is used as a proxy for the severity of loss (SOL) percentage for a project. Since the order of liquidation is equity first, then loans, then if the (1.00-SOL) >= LTV, there is no loss. If the SOL is greater than the equity position, the loan will suffer a loss equal to:

$$\text{Current Loan Balance}^*(1.00 - ((1.00\text{-SOL})/\text{loan LTV}))$$

The recovery lag is the delay of the receipt of the recovered principal from a default and is measured in months. Due to the lag in receipt of these recoveries, it is important to provide time periods in the waterfall well past the final maturity of the longest loan.

Day-Count Conventions   This menu can also include a table of the day-count conventions for the three most widely used day-count methodologies. The first is 30/360, wherein each month has 30 days and the year has 360 days. The second is Actual/360, in which each month has 30 days and the year has 365 or 366 days. The last methodology is Actual/Actual, which calculates the actual day count per month, with actual year length of 365 or 366 days.

Interest Rate Benchmark Index Tables   These tables allow the user to enter a movement pattern for up to three benchmark rates. The benchmark levels will be applied to all loans whose reset coupons are tied to that particular benchmark.

Collateral Selection Criteria Menu

This menu sets the minimum and maximum for the selection of eligible collateral. One input block allows selections to be made using tenor, balance, coupon, LTV, and payment information criteria. Another block allows collateral to be selected based on the combination of its underlying index and the minimum spread.

Program Costs and Principal Repayment Trigger Menu

The expense block of this menu would list any ongoing monthly expenses of the waterfall. The second block would be used to specify conditions where there is increased risk to the Conduit financing repayment, and where additional repayments to principal need to be applied.

DESIGNING THE COLLATERAL SELECTION OUTPUT SCREEN

The following menu is different from the others in that it is a menu for outputs, not inputs. This screen displays the selection results. We may need to try a number of selection criteria combinations before we proceed to amortize the portfolio. If we allow the user to screen collateral without running the cash flow generator and the waterfall, the user can get a series of snapshots of the results of the selection processes much sooner.

We would want to see how many and what amount of loans were ineligible, and how many were fully eligible. A display that shows the failures by criteria also would be very useful.

IT SHOULD LOOK LIKE THIS

The framework of the complete model will look like Exhibit 5.12.

DELIVERABLES CHECKLIST

The modeling concepts that are the takeaways for this chapter are:

- The concept of "Last Things First, First Things Last" in report and menu design
- The concept and use of template files
- The Ineligible Collateral Report package
- Looking at the portfolio as a whole to determine potential concentration risk
- How to use stratification reports to identify concentration risk
- The form and content of the Eligible Collateral Report package
- Basic framework of the cash flow waterfall report
- Basic framework of the summary matrix reports
- Screen layout of the Main Menu

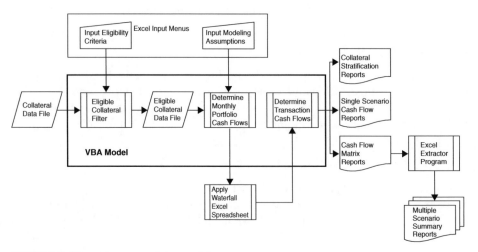

EXHIBIT 5.12   Schematic of the model

NEXT STEPS

We have now completed the design phase! We cannot do anything more until we become more familiar with the VBA Editor and Debugger and learn how to write code in the VBA language.

In Chapter 6 we will set up a working environment into which we will write our VBA code. We will create an Excel file and populate it with worksheets to accommodate the menus we have examined here. We will also create all the VBA modules that we will need to hold the VBA code and that will become the body of the model. Some of the code that we will write will specifically manage the movement of data from the menus of the models. The menus will take the information from the model user and the VBA code will transfer it into VBA variables and arrays. We can then use it in the collateral selection process and then later, in the calculation of the portfolio cash flows and their application to the structure waterfall.

We will have created the bare bones of the model in Chapter 6. In Chapter 7, we will have our first brush with VBA code in the form of recorded macros. We will take a look at the code the recording process produces. We will then apply some judicious editing to improve this code and allow it to perform the same functionality, but with far fewer statements.

In Chapter 8, we will return to the menus we designed here and link them to the model. We will build the VBA bridges that will take the information from the collateral files and the input menus and make it available to the model.

In Chapter 9, we will begin to learn the building blocks of the language itself.

ON THE WEB SITE

There is no material on the Web site related to this chapter.

Learning the VBA Language

## CHAPTER 6

Laying the Model Groundwork

OVERVIEW

In Chapter 5 we began the process of translating our conception of the model into reality. We thought about what output we would want to see and how we will display it. We also started to write the menus for the model and assign some of the Excel features, such as Range names, to them.

External Environment

Before we go any further in the development of the model we need to create an operating environment for it. We will need to have a directory system in place to store and manage the client information, the model itself, and the various sets of output that we will produce. We need to create a structural support for the model outside of the model, where we can position the template files that the model will use to produce the output, and later in the model development process, a place for the model documentation and validation material.

When we are finished with this task we will begin work on the model itself.

Up until this time we have, in a sense, been working on the "surface" of the model. We have laid out the designs for the menus and many of the results reports. All of this work is in the Excel region of the model. These are the parts that are seen by others.

Internal Environment

Now we will develop the skeletal structure of the model. This skeleton is a series of buckets into which we will place the groups of functionally related VBA code subroutines and functions. We will group the VBA code by its functional role in the model. We will place these collections of VBA code into the modules and label the modules with related names. This will help us immediately locate where code that performs a specific task resides. For example, all menu support code will be collocated in a module whose name might begin with the word "Read." After the model has finished its calculations, we will need to produce the various reports. The VBA subroutines that will perform this role will be in modules that start with the word "Write." Following this pattern, all of the VBA modules that contain subroutines that calculate collateral cash flows will be prefaced by the label "Calc." We will therefore be able to tell at a glance which modules contain the subroutines that are reading information, calculating information, and writing out the results of the model.

If we further differentiate the names of the modules by identifying what subtask of "Read" is occurring, such as a module with the name **"Read_Main_Menu,"** or "Write," such as **"Write_Matrix_Reports,"** we will improve the clarity of the module organization. Why is this important? As the model grows, there will be more and more functionality. We will need to make it as easy as possible to be able to zero in on any particular part of the model that we need to examine or work on. The use of functional module names act like ZIP codes in a modern large city. They will not put us directly in front of the house we want to visit, but they will certainly get us into the immediate neighborhood! We can proceed from there, knowing at least that we do not have to search the rest of the city!

Once we have created these modules, we can begin the task of writing the model.

These modules will serve as concrete organizational elements into which we can write the VBA code. By the end of this chapter, we will have both the exterior and interior framework in place to start writing the model.

Writing Out the Functional Outline of the Model

Having created the organizational framework, we will now create an outline of the functional framework of the model. We do not know how to write VBA code just yet (although we are all eager to start!). We can, however, write the next best thing—"pseudo code." Pseudo code is very much like the preliminary outline of the model. It is not written in VBA code, it is written in your own words. We will write the Main Program subroutine in this manner inside one of the modules. It is in the form of a "comment" statement. Comment statements are ignored by the computer. They were designed so developers could write notes and explanations of the function of the program directly in the program itself. Thus, when you are looking at someone else's VBA code (or your own after an absence from it), you can more easily understand what the program was designed to do. The VBA Editor and Debugger will ignore this statement—it is not visible even to them—and therefore will not try to treat it as a line of VBA code.

Each comment line we write will describe a functional unit of the model.

The following is representative of a piece of pseudo code:

```
! Read the inputs from the Prepayments/Defaults Menu
```

When we actually write the VBA code to transfer the user inputs from the Prepayment and Defaults Menu into the VBA program itself, we will have to perform several, much more detailed steps. We will write VBA code to access the Range names of the menu and then read the data into VBA variables that we have previously declared. As a "placeholder" for these steps in the model, this is enough for now. It tells us where this activity will occur in the sequence of steps the model will take to run, and describes in the most general terms what has to be done at that point. We can add additional comment lines of this type before and after this statement until we have a complete functional description of the model, from its first task to its last.

DELIVERABLES

The deliverables for this chapter are:

VBA Language Knowledge Deliverables
- How to enter the VBA Editor and insert a blank module into the program
- How to use the **View=>Properties Window** in the VBA Editor to name or rename a module

Modeling Knowledge Deliverables
- The concepts behind creating an external environment for the model
- The creation of the external environment for the model, which will include directories for the client data, the model itself, any reporting template files necessary to run the model, the output directory to hold the model run results, a validation directory to hold back test results, and a documentation directory
- Why you should use modules to segregate, organize, and identify the VBA code of your module
- How to develop a naming system for the modules of a multiple module model by basing the names on the functionality of the VBA code the module will hold
- What pseudo code is and how to use it to organize your thoughts in regard to the steps and sequence of operations you need to later write in VBA code

UNDER CONSTRUCTION

After our day off in Chapter 5, we should be rested and ready to go. We will therefore be eager to tackle the task of designing a series of VBA modules within the model file that will serve as the future home and infrastructure for all the VBA code we are about to write.

Following the instructions in this chapter and a set on naming conventions to make finding everything easier, we will begin out first foray into the territory of VBA. When we are finished we will have planned and set up a list of names for the VBA modules of the program. This skeletal structure of our model and will provide us with a designated, convenient, and easily identifiable set of locations to begin writing our VBA code.

This planning will serve us in good stead as we begin to build the model. First we will build code to support the menus of the models. We will then develop VBA code to read the inputs once they are error checked. The next step will be to filter the collateral according to the selection criteria and produce the appropriate reports. Once we have the collateral, we can calculate the cash flows and run them through the waterfall. The last steps will be to aggregate the results and produce the reports detailing the performance of the structure.

At each of these development steps we will create additional modules to segregate and organize the code. You will see the list of VBA modules grow with each stage of model development. In the finished model it will fully assume the numbers and structure of the module list at the end of this chapter.

CREATING THE EXTERNAL MODEL ENVIRONMENT

Before we do anything else in the way of creating the model from the design characteristics discussed above, we must first create the external environment of the model. Many models that are used as examples in Excel/VBA programming books are viewed as existing in a vacuum. The inputs are entered on one worksheet of the model. Many times, all of the results are also written to the same worksheet or another worksheet in the same Excel workbook. In the real world, especially the world of structured finance, this is quite atypical.

One of the first tasks in a structured finance is the collateral selection process. This process involves the examination of every single piece of collateral that is proposed for inclusion in the deal. If the portfolio consists of only several thousand loans, it may well be possible to have the data located in the model on a separate spreadsheet. When the portfolio size moves into the tens of thousands or hundreds of thousands of loans, this becomes problematic. File sizes can become quite large and, if you are constantly saving newly developed incremental versions of the model, terribly cumbersome. The data should therefore be separated from the model.

The same is true for the results of the model runs. If the model is writing the results of its calculations to the same workbook that serves as its residence, we have a similar problem. The only way to save successive model runs is to copy the results worksheets over and over inside the model, or make multiple copies of the model, each of which contains a single result set within the same workbook. Neither of these solutions is feasible if several or many reports are required to complete the analysis. This method of preserving the various sets of results can quickly become unmanageable.

At this point the age old strategy of "Divide and conquer!" becomes the rule of the day. By positioning the data and results files externally, away from the model file, we can gain several immediate advantages. In regard to collateral files they are, at a minimum, the following:

1. The collateral file can be very large and will not increase the size of the model file at all.
2. The collateral file can be reconfigured without modifications to the model. What do we mean by this? In the collateral selection process, it is very unusual to include into the deal all of the initially offered collateral. Collateral can become ineligible for inclusion for a number of reasons that we will examine later. In some cases, as much as 50% of the collateral may be excluded from the deal for one reason or another. For example, a portfolio that originally consisted of 225,000 loans might have 75,000 of them deemed ineligible. Once the selection process has been completed, the data file could be reconfigured to include only eligible collateral. (In fact we will do just this later in Chapter 13, "Writing the Collateral Selection Code.") When the model can produce a data file containing only the eligible collateral, each successive run thereafter only needs to run a portfolio of 150,000 loans instead of 225,000, a time savings of 33%.
3. Along the lines of (2) above, the collateral files can be divided or recombined into many different sub-portfolios. These reconstituted portfolios can either be run separately or combined as needed.

4. If you need to clean up or reconfigure the original information in the collateral file, the task is much easier to do outside the model.

5. If the collateral file is separate from the model file, you can make copies of the collateral file without making copies of the model. This is especially important if the model file and the data sets are changing at the same time. The more copies and versions of the model that are floating around, the more difficult it is to keep track of the changes you made to each. I will teach you how to manage this process so that you can significantly decrease the chances of accidents happening, but it is a serious concern when you are writing your first applications. We will revisit this subject in Chapter 18, "Running the Model," and in Chapter 21, "Managing the Growth of the Model."

We can achieve many of the same advantages by segregating the output of the model to a separate Excel workbook. Excel is the easiest medium in which to create reports; essentially you are limited only by your imagination. It is an extremely flexible tool to use and can combine all manner of graphic presentation features. By separating the reports file from the model, we can achieve the following advantages:

■ The report file can be very, very large and not affect the size of the model. A particularly striking example of this is when it is necessary or desirable to replicate in a report file **the entire waterfall** of the deal. This separation can be a godsend if the model is running a group of scenarios, say 40 combinations of prepayment and default scenarios, through 25 stress runs for a rating agency. You can use VBA to have the model open an Excel workbook that is the output file, create a blank worksheet for each scenario you have run, and copy into each of these separate worksheets the results of an individual scenario.

■ If there is a need for a large number of complex reports, the output reports template file can be extensively preconfigured. Upon completion of the model run, the model opens the output template file, copies it, and writes the scenario results into the appropriate worksheets. The model can then trigger a "Calculate" sequence and any formulas, graphics, or other features based on the data will be activated and completed. Again, the development of a complicated or voluminous report file does not impact the file that the model resides in.

■ The approach allows a very manageable way to create a specific results file for each model run without destroying any information from previous model runs. Unlike a model that overwrites the previous results with the current results, VBA can allow us to rename each model run and create a separate identifiable, preserved record of the results.

■ Using external results template files allows us to annotate each results file with all the conditions and assumptions of the model run. For example, we can create a separate worksheet in the results file to list a complete set of model run assumptions. This page would then be populated as the results file was produced, giving us an audit track. These can then be used for a variety of purposes, including back testing of newer versions of the model. We will design specific reports to accomplish just this in Chapter 11, "Designing the Model's Reports."

```
Sample directory structure
C:\VBA_Class
        \AnalystProgram
                \data
                \documentation
                \model
                \output
                \templates
                \validation
```

EXHIBIT 6.1 Directory structure of the model environment

By now I hope you are fully convinced of all the advantages that derive from the segregation of the data files and report files from the model file itself. To implement this strategy, we will set up a master directory in the name of the project and then create a series of special purpose subdirectories to hold the collateral data and the report files.

In the broadest sweep, the purpose of these additional subdirectories will be to hold the inputs to the model, the model itself, and the results of the model runs.

We will organize these directories as shown in Exhibit 6.1. We will establish:

- The overall project directory under which all the other directories will list. In that we do not have a client name associated with the deal, we will simply call this directory "**AnalystProgram.**"
- A subdirectory "**data**" to hold the collateral data file from the client. This directory will have a subdirectory named "**backup**" to save a copy of the data file (which copy we will make as soon as we get the data file, and before we do anything else!). We can also create other subdirectories with date stamps, if we receive subsequent collateral files.
- A subdirectory "**model**" to hold the model code. We will need a "**backup**" subdirectory here also, so that we can keep older versions of the model. We can reasonably expect the model to change over the life of the deal as new requirements, information, or risk analysis ideas emerge from the deal structuring process. We will save working versions of the model in the "**backup**" subdirectory. Stable versions of the model will be assigned their own subdirectories.
- A subdirectory named "**templates,**" to hold all of the report template files. We currently have four template files, but that could change. In Chapter 19, "Building Additional Capabilities," we will introduce additional reports. Once the template files have been created, we will also make copies of them and immediately place them in a "**backup**" subdirectory. We will end up saving them as sets that are cross-referenced to the model version that they were created under. In that case, we will probably need to also add subdirectories under the named "**template_set_0001,**" "**template_set_0002,**" and so on.
- A subdirectory named "**output**" to hold the results of the model runs. The primary division of this directory will be split between model runs generated for internal constituencies and runs generated for external constituencies. The former would be reports for us in the business units, internal credit approval, and such groups as audit and financial control. Each of these subdirectories may have numerous subdirectories for each of the case sets required by the groups. For sizing and structuring purposes, we will store the output in related

sets, grouped by the major analytical study patterns they were created under. An example of such a subdirectory might be one that looks at various Seller Interest-level sensitivities. As for the external groups, we will also need subdirectories to hold output for rating agency runs, investor runs, and maybe even program validation runs if third parties audit the model. The final structure of this directory can be seen in Chapter 18, "Running the Model."

- A subdirectory named **"validation"** to hold benchmark runs of the model. As the model is developed over time, you will need to be assured that it is still performing its early functions in an accurate manner. This subdirectory will hold earlier version model runs against which you can benchmark the newest versions of the model before making them available for use. This is especially true when it comes to the issue of back testing. You should make every effort to plan for the model to be backward-compatible with its earlier versions. Obviously, weeding out errors in the earlier model versions should not get in the way of this process. Nevertheless, back testing can provide a broad-based validation assurance. The key concern to address is that incremental changes to the model have not affected any of the core features of an earlier version that they should not have.
- A subdirectory named **"documentation,"** in which we will place the following sub-subdirectories:
  - **Product** documentation. Information about the product, industry information.
  - **Regulatory** information. Financial and regulatory documents from the Securities and Exchange Commission (SEC), or Financial Accounting Standards Board (FASB), or other outside regulatory bodies.
  - **Research** documentation. Internal and external research reports.
  - **Technical** documentation. Outside of the model, documentation for audit and control purposes.
  - **User** documentation Copies of our model Standard Operating Procedures (SOPs) and copies of a user manual if we choose to develop one. This would also include such things as case studies if the model becomes part of a multiple-year product development effort.

Having the program environment well in hand, we can now take our first steps in creating the model.

CREATING THE INTERNAL MODEL ENVIRONMENT

Advantages of Using VBA Modules to Organize the Model

Before we start creating these modules to hold our code we should ask ourselves the question, "Why are we doing this?" Properly employed VBA modules can be powerful organizational tools. They should serve the following roles in organizing the VBA code of the model:

- Each module should represent a major functional block of the model's VBA code; the module should be named after that function so that it is readily identifiable to anyone working on the model.

- All the subroutines and functions (i.e., the smaller specialty blocks of code we will learn to write) should be grouped in these modules based on their functional contribution to the overall task of the module. This will make it much, much easier to quickly locate a particular VBA subroutine when we have to fix the model or make changes to it.
- A separate module should be created to hold the declarations of all the global variables of the model. We have not yet talked about variables, much less global variables. These are names and data sets created by you to hold the information of the model. They are very powerful because they make the information placed in them available to every part of the model. As a result, they are the variables that carry the critical information. Placing them in one location allows us to see them collectively and modify them quickly if needed. We will discuss this in much more detail in Chapter 8, "Writing Menus: An Introduction to Data, Ranges, Arrays, and Objects."
- A separate module should be created to hold all of the constants of the model. Constants are given a value and that value cannot be altered, neither by calculation nor reassignment, during the run of the model. They are extremely useful for a number of very important roles in controlling the operation of the model. Constants are also discussed in Chapter 8 mentioned above.
- A separate module should be created to hold the Main Program, from which all the other VBA code is controlled.
- There is an additional set of tasks of the model, aside from those mentioned above, that will require their own modules. These are:
  - Reading the collateral selection and structuring constraint information from the menus
  - Reading the collateral data from the file
  - Performing the collateral selection process
  - Reporting the eligible/ineligible collateral based on the selection process
  - Calculating each component of the collateral cash flows
  - Loading the Excel spreadsheet with the collateral cash flows
  - Reading the results from the Excel spreadsheet waterfall and storing them
  - Writing the individual scenario reports
  - Writing the summary reports

Creating a Main Program Module

We will now open an Excel file. When the file is open in Excel, press the **"Alt"** key and the **"F11"** key simultaneously to display the VBA Editor. Pull down the editor's Insert Menu and click on the "Module" option. This will insert a new and unnamed module into your program. (See Exhibit 6.2.)

We now need to name the module that we created in Exhibit 6.3. We will do this by dropping down the View Menu and clicking on the Project Explorer option, as shown in Exhibit 6.4.

From the View Menu we will select the Properties Window option. We will now see the Properties Window, as displayed in Exhibit 6.5a. We will use the Properties Editor to access and change the properties of the module we have just created. The module has a "Name" property, as you can see in Exhibit 6.5a. When we first enter the Properties Editor this name is "Module1," the default name for a newly created

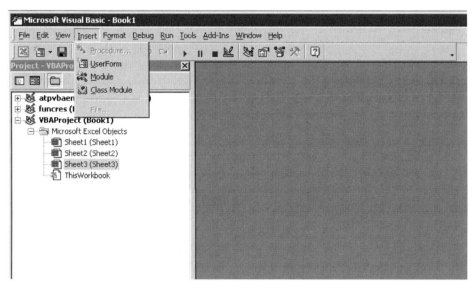

EXHIBIT 6.2   Step 1 in creating a VBA module: Select "Module" from the Insert Menu

module. Using the Properties Editor, we can modify this default name and insert the name we wish to label this module, "A_Main_Program." We enter the new name for this module, "A_Main_Program," in the Properties Editor, as shown in Exhibit 6.5b.

After entering the name in the Properties Editor line and hitting return, we can see the renamed module listed in Exhibit 6.6: The name "Module1" has been replaced by the name "A_Main_Program." This name also appears on the tree structure diagram

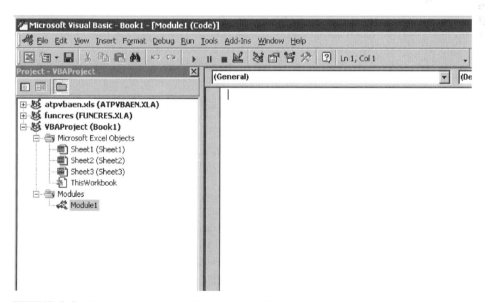

EXHIBIT 6.3   Step 2 in creating a VBA module: The module appears to the right of the screen and a Module icon appears in the "Project – VBAProject" window

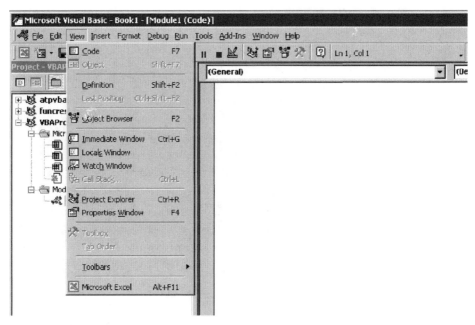

EXHIBIT 6.4   Use the View Menu to access the Properties Window

of the modules of the project in the VBA-Project window above the Properties Editor window.

Creating the Remaining Modules

The model will need more than a single module to hold the code we will write. We earlier listed a number of functions, such as "reading information from menus," as a reason for creating a module to hold related pieces of VBA code.

Now we need to step back and think of the model again in more detail. We have six major tasks:

1. Create a Main Model of VBA code that will manage all the others.
2. Manage the menus of the model, to include:
   a. Reading the menu inputs.
   b. Error checking the inputs.
3. Manage the collateral of the portfolio:
   a. Read the contents of the collateral data file.
   b. Perform the collateral selection process.
   c. Generate cash flows from the eligible collateral.
   d. Generate prepayment and default rate calculations.
   e. Load the cash flows into the waterfall and run it.
4. Manage the output of the model, in this order:
   a. Write out the ineligible collateral reports.
   b. Write out the eligible collateral reports.
   c. Write a collateral data file of the eligible loans.

(a)

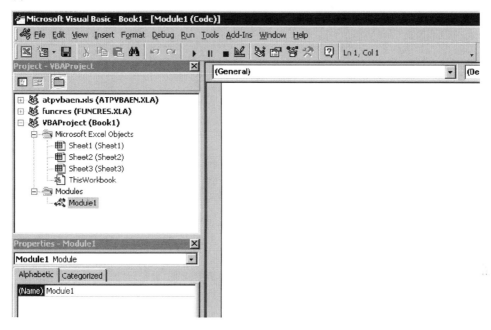

(b)

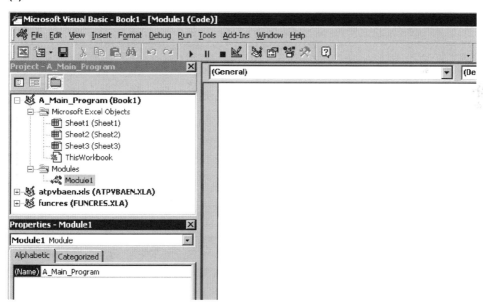

EXHIBIT 6.5   Properties Editor for the module that we have just created

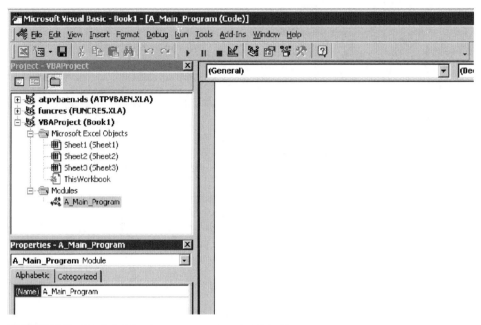

EXHIBIT 6.6   Module1 has been renamed to A_Main_Program

    d. Write the model assumptions.
    e. Write the cash flow waterfall report package.
    f. Write the summary matrix reports.
  5. Create other miscellaneous modules:
    a. A module for "utility" code (housekeeping functions).
    b. A module for menu buttons (more on this later).
    c. A module to produce a log of the changes we have made to the model.
  6. Create modules to hold data and control variables:
    a. Global variables (variables that will hold the bulk of the model information).
    b. Constants (conditions that will help us control the flow of the model).

This leaves us with a total of 19 modules.

This sounds like a lot of modules! A moment ago we only had one! The advantage to having modules that are specialized, sometimes highly so, is that you, and others who will work on the model after you, will be able to rapidly focus on various segments of the VBA code based on the way the modules are grouped and named.

For example, if there is a question in regards to the **selection processing** of ineligible and eligible collateral, which of the following modules should we look in first?

    Module 1 – CollateralReadDataFile

    Module 2 – CollateralSelectionSubs

    Module 3 – WriteCollateralFiles

    Module 4 – MenusReadInputs

    Module 5 – CollateralCFGenerator

The answer is, I hope, obvious. Module 2 most likely contains the code that we should look at first. That is not to say that it is always this simple to find the source of coding problems. A change could have been made that affected how the selection criteria used in the collateral eligibility test was read from the menu into the VBA code. If we suspected that, then Module 4 would be our first choice.

Nevertheless, the modules will allow us to both segregate and group our VBA code at the same time. If in the future we design an entirely different functionality into the model we may well create additional modules to hold and identify that code. For now, filling up the list of modules in Exhibit 6.7 with VBA code as we build up the model will keep us busy, safely off the streets, for some time in the future! Exhibit 6.7 contains all the modules we need to immediately create, grouped by their functional roles.

In Exhibit 6.8, Project Menu showing all the modules needed by the program, the prefix "A_" is used in front of the modules that hold the constants, Global Variable declarations, and the Main Program in order to position these modules at the top of the list (the window lists all modules in alphabetical order). Related modules have similar names. All output function modules have the word "write" in their names. This is also true of all menu-handling modules whose names start with the word "Menu." Modules prefixed with "Z_" are all utility modules and are listed last, as they serve to perform general functionalities used by several of the other modules.

EXHIBIT 6.7 List of modules we will create as we build the model

Name Prefix	Core Name	Function
A_	Constants	Holds all the constants variables declarations
A_	Globals	Holds all the Global variables declarations
A_	MainProgram	The Main Program of the model
Collateral	CFGenerator	Calculates collateral cash flows
Collateral	PreDefCals	Performs specialty prepayment and default calculations
Collateral	ReadDataFile	Finds, opens, and reads collateral data file contents into VBA
Collateral	SelectionSubs	Performs the collateral eligibility selection process
LoadRun	CaptureResults	Loads the cash flows in the spreadsheet, captures results
Menus	ErrorChecking	Performs all menu input error checking, prints error messages
Menus	ReadInputs	Reads all menu inputs of the model into VBA variables
Menus	PrepayDefault	Reads the prepayment and default menu
Write	AssumptReport	Outputs a set of assumptions pages into other reports
Write	CollateralReports	Outputs eligible collateral report package
Write	EligCollatFile	Outputs a file that contains eligible collateral only
Write	IneligibleReports	Outputs ineligible collateral reports
Write	MatrixReports	Outputs summary reports of multiple scenario model runs
Write	WaterfallReports	Outputs the complete waterfalls of all scenarios
Z_	ButtonSubs	Code that controls macro buttons on the menus
Z_	ChangeLog	Module to hold comments of changes over time
Z_	UtilitySubroutines	Code that performs various non-calculation functions

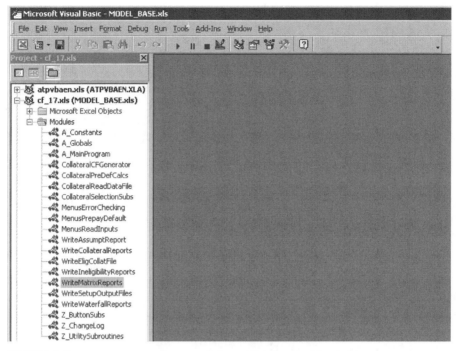

EXHIBIT 6.8   Project Menu showing all the modules needed by the program

WRITING THE MAIN PROGRAM IN PSEUDO CODE

We are now ready to write pseudo code into the Main Program module. This is much like building a provisional outline for the steps the model will take to complete its run. We are going to have to perform the following activity "blocks:"

- Read the menu information.
- Perform the collateral selection process (if required).
- If we performed the collateral selection process, and we want to see the disposition reports, write the Eligible and Ineligible Collateral Report Package.
- Generate the cash flows for the accepted collateral, based on the prepayment and default criteria.
- Paste the results into the waterfall and calculate the waterfall worksheet.
- Record the results at whatever level of detail is desired.
- Write either the Waterfall Report Package or the Summary Matrix Report, or both.

What Is Pseudo Code?

"Pseudo" is defined as "false, deceptive, sham." Pseudo code is not VBA or any other kind of code. Pseudo code is a method that persons new to the science and art of modeling can employ to organize their thoughts regardless of which kind of programming language they will eventually use.

It allows one to construct the basic underpinnings of a model without knowing anything about the language at all! You should write pseudo code so you can get your thoughts down into the editor for the first time, and then play around with them. The model will be a model with a few loops, prefaced by some inputs and error checking, and followed by output routines.

We are now ready to begin to construct an outline of the model. We are going to place this outline in the Main Module.

Outlining the Model in Pseudo Code

In Exhibit 6.9 we have written the highest level of the program in pseudo code. This pseudo code will be our first rough-draft at organizing the model. As we proceed to build the model, we may well have second thoughts or inspirations that change the layout we have proposed here. This pseudo code is, however, a good way to start.

```
'================================================================================
'  BUSINESS LOAN CONDUIT FINANCING MODEL
'  Author:   Your Name        Contact Info:   Telephone number, email address
'  Date:     When you began work
'  Purpose:  Description of the model
'================================================================================
Sub Loan_Financing_Model
'
'      Read all Menu Information
'      Error Check all Menu Inputs, produce Error Messages by Menu
'      Read the Collateral File
'
'      If (we want to apply selection criteria) Then Perform Collateral
'          Selection Process
'      If (we want to write out selection results) Then
'              Output the Ineligible Collateral Reports
'              Output the Eligible Collateral Stratification Reports
'      End If
'
'      For (number of Prepayment & Default rate combinations) Loop
'              Compute the Portfolio Cash Flows
'                    Calculate Defaulted Principal
'                    Calculate Coupon Income
'                    Calculate Scheduled Principal Amortization
'                    Calculate Prepayments of Principal
'                    Calculate Recoveries of Defaulted Principal
'              Paste the Finished Cash Flows into the Waterfall Spreadsheet
'              Read the Waterfall Results and store in VBA variables
'      End Loop
'
'      If (write Waterfall Reports or Summary Matrix Reports) Then
'              If (write Waterfall Reports) Then Write Waterfall
'                  Reports Package
'              If (write Matrix Reports) Then Write Summary Matrix
'                  Reports Package
'      End If
'
End Sub
```

EXHIBIT 6.9   Main Program written in pseudo code

We will place the pseudo code in the **"A_Main_Program"** module. Remember, none of this is VBA code. If the first character of the line begins with a "ı" character, the line is turned to green by the VBA Editor and is ignored.

Note that **all the lines of the listing are green** because we have put the "ı" symbol in front of each line, which designates each as a comment. Comments are lines we can enter into a VBA program that are ignored by the computer. They only serve to inform the person looking at the VBA code what is going on or to offer advice or guidance. We can see them, the computer cannot!

With this pseudo code in place we now have a functional outline of the entire model. As we construct the model, we will replace these general comment statements one by one with valid VBA subroutines.

DELIVERABLES CHECKLIST

The following is the VBA knowledge checklist for this chapter:

- How to enter the VBA Editor and use it to create an unnamed module
- How to name (or rename) a VBA module

The following are the modeling knowledge checklist points for this chapter:

- Learning the concepts behind creating an orderly external environment for the model
- Creation of a directory structure to organize and manage the model data, program, results, validation, and documentation files
- Use of modules to internally organize your VBA code in functional groupings
- How to develop a naming system for your modules
- How to use pseudo code to design and outline the functional and procedural steps of your code

NEXT STEPS

We have now created the basic environment in which to house the program. We have also opened an Excel workbook and populated it with VBA modules that will serve as functional containers for our future model code.

We cannot do anything more until we learn the VBA language. Chapter 7 will give us a first look at the VBA language as it is produced when we record a macro. We will get a chance to edit this code and improve its clarity and speed. Chapters 8 and 9 will introduce us to the language itself.

ON THE WEB SITE

On the Web site you will find the completed first steps in development of our VBA model. Our next step in model development is the version **"Model_Base_**

Chap06.xls." If we open this file we can examine the effects of our work in this chapter.

Using "Alt+F11" we can enter the VBA Editor and view the modules we created. If we pull down the "View" option and select "Project Explorer" we will see an icon named "Modules." Clicking on this icon will display a list of the 20 modules we created. If we double click on any of this we will display its contents in the right side of the screen. All will be blank, as we have not begun to write our VBA program just yet.

After we learn the syntax of VBA and how to use its various features, we will fill each of these modules up one after the other as we sink our teeth into the work ahead of us!

As we start to build the model we will add all these modules one by one as we need them. This will make the incremental steps of building the model clearer. You will see the specific functionality of the VBA code added one or two modules at a time in many of the upcoming chapters. This process will continue until the model is complete.

## CHAPTER 7

Recorded Macros: A First Look at the VBA Language

OVERVIEW

In this chapter we will dip our toes into the VBA language ocean. Our approach will be to use the Record New Macro facility of Excel to record a simple macro. Once we have familiarized ourselves with this code, we will try to write a "proto" model in VBA code that builds on the functionality of the recorded macros.

First Exercise: Record a Macro and Edit It

We will use the VBA Editor to examine the VBA code that was generated by the program when we recorded the macro. The next step will be to learn how to read this code with the idea of streamlining it. Along the way, we will see how VBA can be used to modify the Excel environment. This ability will be crucial when we start to develop the reporting package of the model. It will also suggest ways of running the model in a repeated manner without human intervention. This last feature is one that you will find to have the greatest leverage in using VBA over Excel. After we have finished examining and editing the recorded macro, we will write a simple looping structure to improve its performance.

Second Exercise: Build a "Proto" Model

The second subject of this chapter will be to construct a "proto" model, a primitive precursor to the model that we will be building throughout the rest of the book. The comparison of a Devonian Age armored fish of 400 million years ago and a salmon is apt here. Both are clearly fish. Both have scales and gills, a head at one end and a tail at the other. Each has a mouth, eyes, nostrils for scent detection, and a lateral line. After that the similarities become more blurred because of the degree of sophistication and specialization of the modern form over the more primitive. Nevertheless, all the things that elicit the response "fish" when we see either of them are present.

So it is with the proto model. It has a menu that contains information the program needs to run. Using the menu information, the model opens a data file and reads the file's information into the computer's memory. The model uses this information to perform a simple set of spreadsheet calculations. Next it opens an output file that contains a simple report and populates the output file with the results of the computation. The file is closed and saved. The model ends.

To create this model we will use the concepts that will be introduced to us in the first exercise. We will learn to use Excel's Record Macro facility to generate the code we need to build the model. For example, we will obtain macro-generated code for the opening, saving, and closing of a of specific file. In the process, we will learn several basic elements of the VBA language:

- How to declare a VBA variable
- How to assign a value to a variable
- How to make a choice between two alternatives if a condition is True
- How to build a simple loop that can cause a set of VBA statements to repeat a fixed number of times

DELIVERABLES

VBA Language

- How to recognize a set of VBA statements as a program. The use of the **Sub** and **End Sub** restricted words
- How VBA represents cell locations in the Excel worksheet, either with the Range or Cells statement
- How to assign a value to an Excel worksheet location using VBA statements
- How to read information from an Excel worksheet using VBA statements
- How to modify the appearance of an Excel cell using VBA statements
- How to declare a VBA variable using the reserved word Dim
- How to declare the vector and array forms of a variable
- Understanding the types of VBA variables: Integer, Double, and String
- How to open, save, and close Excel files using VBA commands
- How to build a simple looping structure that will repeat a collection of VBA commands over a predetermined number of times
- How to use a variable index in an array in a loop, the For . . . Next loop
- How to use the If . . . Then . . . Else . . . EndIf statement to make choices between two alternatives
- What a comment statement is, why it is important, and how to enter it into an Excel program
- How to set the color of an Excel cell font and other appearance properties of the **cell** by using VBA commands

VBA Editor and Debugger

- How to open and enter the VBA Editor using the "Alt + F11" key combination
- How to create and name a VBA code module
- How to name and record a VBA macro from Excel
- How to select, delete, copy, and paste VBA statements
- How to use the VBA Record Macro function to record code for operations you don't know how to perform

- How to use the recorded code in another module or program
- How to compile and then run a VBA program using the "F5" key, how to reset the program after it is run, and why you need to do this
- How to set and clear VBA breakpoints. These stop a program at a predetermined point
- How to advance through a program one line at a time using the "F8" key
- How to examine the value of a variable

Modeling Knowledge Deliverables

- Create a model file that has a single worksheet that serves as the menu for the program
- Create a data file and fill it with data
- Create a results file and place inside of it a preconfigured report template
- Run the model and produce preliminary results
- Run the model and produce a targeted result

UNDER CONSTRUCTION

In this chapter we will first encounter VBA code itself. We will use the "Record Macro" feature to generate most of this code for us, (especially the tricky parts, like opening and saving files).

We will not be working directly with the model itself. Rather we will use these two exercises to increase our familiarity and comfort levels with VBA code in any form before we begin writing it ourselves. We will be able to observe the form of the code and to just get used to looking at VBA in general.

In the first exercise we will record a macro and then edit it.

In the second exercise, this one contained entirely on the Web site, we will piece together a simple VBA model. To do this we will first write an outline of the steps we want the program to take and then, using samples of recorded macros, finish a simple "proto-model."

RECORDING VBA CODE

One of the easiest and fastest ways to get a feel for VBA code is to use the Excel recorder feature. You activate it by choosing the "Tools" menu, then "Macro," then "Record New Macro." The screen should look like Exhibit 7.1.

```
Tools -> Macro -> Record New Macro
```

Not only will this procedure produce pieces of error-free VBA code, but it serves as an excellent way to learn how VBA accomplishes specific tasks. Later in this chapter we will use recorded code to augment the code that we are writing. *One tip on recorded code!* Once you have selected the recording option **every single thing** you do will be recorded. To avoid unnecessary confusion, it is best to practice what

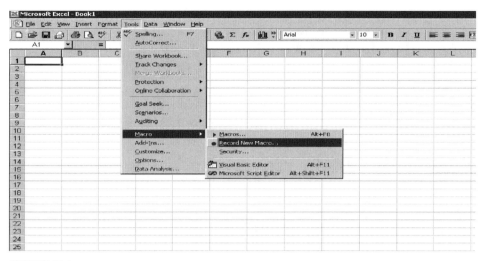

EXHIBIT 7.1 How to turn on macro recording

you want to record once or twice before you turn the recorder on. This will keep the
recorded code to a minimum and make it easier to read.

After you select "Record New Macro," a pop-up window will appear: It should
look like the dialog box displayed in Exhibit 7.2. Note that it shows that name of
the recorder, the date, and a default name, "Macro1," for the VBA code that the
process will capture. We will give the macro a meaningful name.

After you select the "**OK**" button, a small button icon will appear (usually in
Excel's title bar). This indicates the recorder is on; when we are finished, we will
click this button to stop the recording process. We can now perform the actions we
intend. In this case we will enter a series of numbers in a column. If the number is
greater than 5, we will set the font to red and then change the entry in the cell to
bold. If the number is less than 5, we will set the cell background to yellow. Lastly,
we will take the sum of the numbers and enter it at the bottom of the column.

After we have finished the aforementioned operations in Excel we should have
a worksheet with the display shown in Exhibit 7.3.

Record Macro	? ✕		Record Macro	? ✕
Macro name:			Macro name:	
Macro1			NumberListWithColors	
Shortcut key:	Store macro in:		Shortcut key:	Store macro in:
Ctrl+	This Workbook ▼		Ctrl+	This Workbook ▼
Description:			Description:	
Macro recorded 9/25/2006 by William H Preinitz			Macro recorded 9/25/2006 by William H Preinitz	
	OK	Cancel		OK	Cancel

EXHIBIT 7.2 How to name the recorded macro

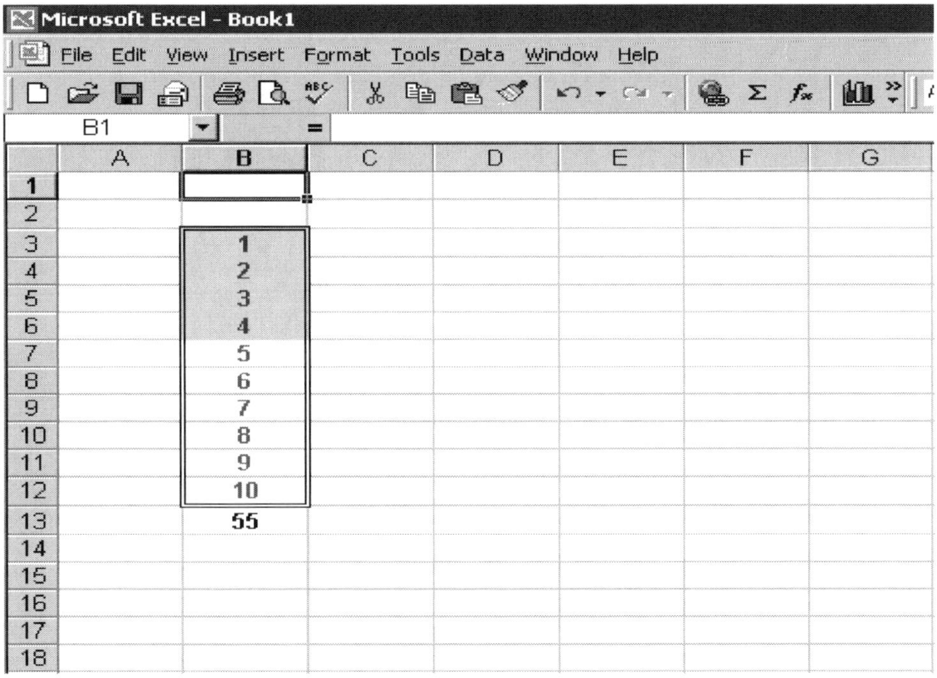

EXHIBIT 7.3   End of the process

Looking at the Recorded Code

To view the results we need to enter the VBA editor, press the keys "Alt" and "F11" simultaneously. The screen will now look like Exhibit 7.4.

If we click on the "Modules" icon on the left side of the screen, we will see a subordinate icon named "Module01." This is the module that we have just recorded. Because the projects that we will learn to build will probably have more than one module—in fact, our application will require 10 modules—we need to rename this module to a title something more meaningful than the rather non-descriptive name it now has. To do this, we will pull down the "Properties Window" from the VBA Editor toolbar. This will allow us to rename "Module1." See Exhibits 7.5 and 7.6 for these steps.

Stepping through the Recorded Macro

We are now ready to display the VBA code. Double click on the name of the module and the right-hand side of the screen will now display the code, looking something like Exhibit 7.7. This is the VBA code that is needed to perform the operations of creating and modifying the list. Each step we took has a corresponding set of VBA instructions that produced the result in the Excel worksheet. Each line of the listing you see on the right-hand side of the screen is a single statement of code. This piece of code, while apparently indecipherable, will give us a surprisingly complete beginning example from which to study the elements of the VBA language.

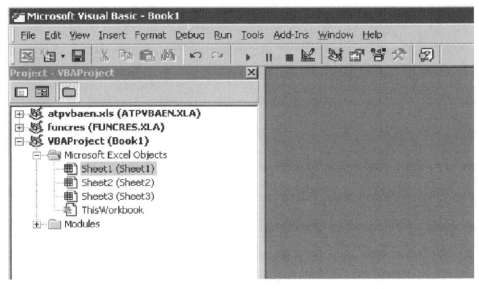

EXHIBIT 7.4   Opening the VBA Editor to view the recorded macro

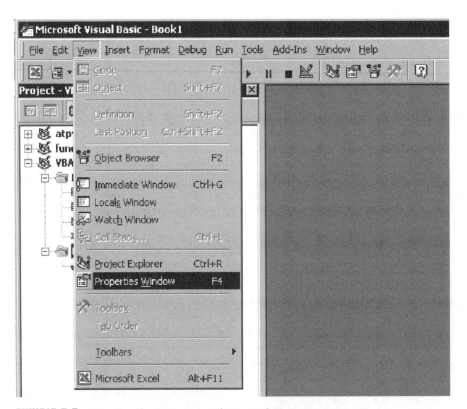

EXHIBIT 7.5   Opening the Properties Editor window

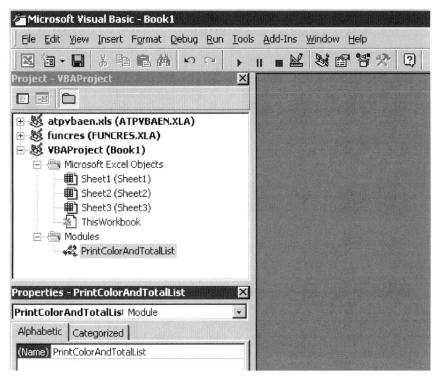

EXHIBIT 7.6   Assigning a name to the module that contains the recorded macro

The first thing that we see is a pair of boxes in the upper-right corner of the screen. These contain the words "General" and "NumberListWithColors." The first refers to the type of module we have built, while the second box tells us the name of the subroutine or function that we are currently in. (Some subroutines can be long and you can display only part of the code in the window. This feature is designed so

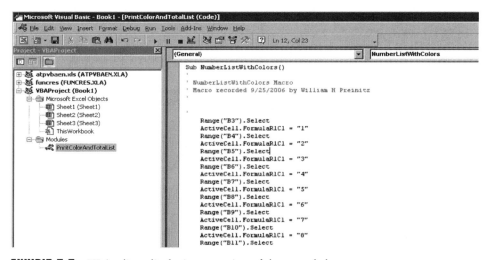

EXHIBIT 7.7   VBA editor displaying a portion of the recorded macro

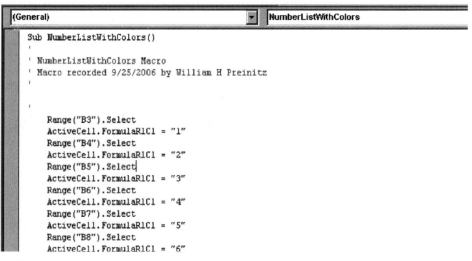

EXHIBIT 7.8   Header and first lines of the recorded macro

you can tell at a glance where you are.) The next thing you will see is that some of the words are in different colors, specifically blue, green, and black.

- Green = Comment lines. Ignored by the computer, comment lines are helpers to inform the person reading the code what is happening, or intended to happen.
- Blue = Reserved words. Parts of the VBA language that cannot be used by the programmer for any but their special purpose.
- Black = VBA Programmer code. Commands you enter.

Exhibit 7.8 displays the beginning of the recorded macro. The first line of code starts with the reserved word Sub, which means subroutine. A subroutine is a block of related statements that perform a task. Following Sub is its name "NumberList-WithColors" in black with the symbols "()" at its end. If there is no text between the parentheses at the end of the subroutine, the subroutine is not expecting to receive any data from any other place in the model. The green lines are comments. These lines are invisible to the computer and only serve to tell you and other humans what is happening in the code. The black lines are the first model statements. They start the process of building the list by putting numeric values in specific Excel cells that are designated by the Range command.

Scroll down the entire length of the recorded macro and look at the VBA statements. Think of them as a quasi-human language in an alpha-numeric code.

The French Egyptologist, Jean Francois Champoillon, who was the first to decipher hieroglyphics, did so by finding keys in the repetitions of the names of certain rulers in the text of the Rosetta Stone (Cleopatra was one of those most frequently recurring). We can immediately spot obvious characteristics and repetitions in the recorded code sample we have before us.

- The word "Range" appears 18 times. It is always followed by a cell notation grouping in brackets and ends with ".Select."
- The words "With Selection" and "End With" are grouped and all statements in between are indented.

```
(General)                                            ▼    NumberListWithCo

Sub NumberListWithColors()
'
' NumberListWithColors Macro
' Macro recorded 9/25/2006 by William H Preinitz
'
    'Enter the numbers in each of the cells in a column
    Range("B3").Select:    ActiveCell.FormulaR1C1 = "1"
    Range("B4").Select:    ActiveCell.FormulaR1C1 = "2"
    Range("B5").Select:    ActiveCell.FormulaR1C1 = "3"
    Range("B6").Select:    ActiveCell.FormulaR1C1 = "4"
    Range("B7").Select:    ActiveCell.FormulaR1C1 = "5"
    Range("B8").Select:    ActiveCell.FormulaR1C1 = "6"
    Range("B9").Select:    ActiveCell.FormulaR1C1 = "7"
    Range("B10").Select:   ActiveCell.FormulaR1C1 = "8"
    Range("B11").Select:   ActiveCell.FormulaR1C1 = "9"
    Range("B12").Select:   ActiveCell.FormulaR1C1 = "10"
    'Center all the numbers on the column
    Range("B3:B12").Select
    With Selection
        .HorizontalAlignment = xlCenter
        .VerticalAlignment = xlBottom
        .WrapText = False
        .Orientation = 0
        .AddIndent = False
        .ShrinkToFit = False
        .MergeCells = False
    End With
```

EXHIBIT 7.9   Add two comment lines and move some of the lines to the ends of others

- We see certain words always in blue—"With," "End With," and "False."
- There are a very large number of "=" signs.
- There seem to be an awfully large number of lines of code for what would be a relatively simple task.

Let us add some to the VBA code comments, and do some minor editing to improve readability. When we are done the program will look like Exhibit 7.9.

All the commands in the VBA editor are identical to those in Microsoft Word, including drag and drop of text, and the "Ctrl-C," "Ctrl-V" keystroke combinations, for "Cut" and "Paste," respectively. Backspace will delete. If we move the lines beginning with **ActiveCell.Formula ...**" to the end of the lines just before them, we immediately get a one-to-one correspondence with the Range("B?").Select statements.

Now the function and relationship between these pairs is quite apparent, the first statement identifies for the model where the value is to be placed and the second statement of the pair assigns the value to the selected cell location. Notice in each of these statements that the Range command is designating a single cell; later in this chapter we will see it used to designate collections of cells.

The first step in the process is now completed and we will now arrange to center the numbers that we have input within their respective cells. To do this, we will select all the numbers in their respective cells with the command: Range("B3:B12").Select. This then allows us to operate on this selection as a single entity. We will do this using the With Selection command, which will apply the same effect(s) to each item contained in the Range specified. The change we will make is to center the number horizontally in each of the cells of the Range. Every statement that is indented

```
          As Recorded                            After Editing
'Center all the numbers on the column   'Center all the numbers on the column
Range("B7:B12").Select                   Range("B7:B12").Select
With Selection                           Selection.Font.FontStyle = "Bold"
    .HorizontalAlignment = xlCenter      Selection.HorizontalAlignment = xlCenter
    .VerticalAlignment = xlBottom
    .WrapText = False
    .Orientation = 0
    .AddIndent = False
    .ShrinkToFit = False
    .MergeCells = FalseEnd With
```

EXHIBIT 7.10   Simplifying the centering code of the macro

between the With . . . End With statement block will assign values to other settings of these cells. With the exception of "xlCenter," all of these values are the standard default values of the cell. Only "xlCenter" makes a change to the selected cell Range.

This editing process can be seen in Exhibit 7.10.

Simplifying the Code

This section illustrates the code reduction for the actions changing the text in the first Range of cells to the color red (code 3) and bold. Since the With . . . End With statement is designed to accommodate a number of actions, we can carry the process one step further. The With and End With statements can themselves be eliminated because we are only setting a single property of the cells in the Range. Look at the next Range statement selection and you will see that it is slightly different in that we are now selecting to work on only the font characteristics, by changing the font style to bold and the color to red (color code 3). Using the same approach we did with the previous editing we can eliminate many unnecessary lines in the next three With . . . End With blocks, resulting in the reconfigured code in Exhibit 7.11.

```
          As Recorded                            After Editing
'Cells > 5 = font red and bold          'Cells > 5 = font red and bold
Range("B7:B12").Select                   Range("B7:B12").Select
With Selection.Font                      Selection.Font.FontStyle = "Bold"
    .Name = "Arial"                      Selection.Font.ColorIndex = 3 !Red
    .FontStyle = "Bold"
    .Size = 10
    .Strikethrough = False
    .Superscript = False
    .Subscript = False
    .OutlineFont = False
    .Shadow = False
    .Underline = xlUnderlineStyleNone
    .ColorIndex = 3
End With
```

EXHIBIT 7.11   Keeping only the code that turns the text both bold and red

```
            As Recorded                           After Editing
'Cells < 5 = yellow interior        'Cells < 5 = yellow interior
Range("B3:B6").Select               Range("B3:B6").Select
With Selection.Font                 Selection.Font.ColorIndex = 5        !Blue
    .Name = "Arial"                 Selection.Interior.ColorIndex = 19 !Yellow
    .FontStyle = "Bold"             Selection.Interior.Pattern = "xlSolid"
    .Size = 10
    .Strikethrough = False
    .Superscript = False
    .Subscript = False
    .OutlineFont = False
    .Shadow = False
    .Underline = xlUnderlineStyleNone
    .ColorIndex = 5     !Blue
End With
With Selection.Interior
    .ColorIndex = 19        'Yellow
    .Pattern = "xlSolid"
    .PatternColorIndex = xlAutomatic
End With
```

EXHIBIT 7.12   Recorded code to change the cell pattern background to yellow

This example shows the editing reductions for the next sequence, in which the remaining cells are changed to a bold, blue font with a yellow interior. Streamlining this code results in Exhibit 7.12.

The last piece of the recorded VBA code is the assignment of the sum function to the bottom of the column and the formatting of the result. The function call cannot be simplified, but the formatting can. This edit is displayed in Exhibit 7.13.

Making the Code More Efficient

There still remains a troublesome piece of code at the top of the subroutine. Over and over, a pair of statements is repeated. Can this be simplified? It can! However, it will require us to make the first use of variables in the subroutine, and to employ a looping structure called a For...Next loop. You will notice that all the paired

```
            As Recorded                           After Editing
'Sum the column, center and bold font  'Sum the column, center and bold font
Range("B13").Select                  Range("B13").Select
Selection.FormulaR1C1 =              Selection.FormulaR1C1 =
        "=SUM(R[-10]C:R[-1]C)"              "=SUM(R[-10]C:R[-1]C)"
With Selection                       Selection.HorizontalAlignment = xlCenter
    .HorizontalAlignment = xlCenter  Selection.Font.Bold = True
    .VerticalAlignment = xl Bottom   Range("B1").Select
    .WrapText = False
    .Orientation = 0
    .AddIndent = False
    .ShrinkToFit = False
    .MergeCells = False
End With
Selection.Font.Bold = True
Range("B1").Select
```

EXHIBIT 7.13   Taking the column sum, centering the number, and making the font bold

```
                    As Recorded                                              After Editing
Sub NumbersListWithColors()                                 Sub NumberListWithColors2()
'                                                           'Macro edited 4/25/2008
' NumberListWith Colors Macro                               Dim i     As Integer loop counter
' Macro recorded 4/25/2008 by Wm Preinitz                   Dim cell_name As String cell name
'Enter the numbers in the cells                             Enter the numbers in the cells
Range("B3").Select: ActiveCell.FormulaRC1 = "1"             For i = 1 to 10
Range("B4").Select: ActiveCell.FormulaRC1 = "2"                 cell_name = "B" & (I+2)
Range("B5").Select: ActiveCell.FormulaRC1 = "3"                 Range(cell_name) = i
Range("B6").Select: ActiveCell.FormulaRC1 = "4"             Next i
Range("B7").Select: ActiveCell.FormulaRC1 = "5"
Range("B8").Select: ActiveCell.FormulaRC1 = "6"
Range("B9").Select: ActiveCell.FormulaRC1 = "7"
Range("B10").Select: ActiveCell.FormulaRC1 = "8"
Range("B11").Select: ActiveCell.FormulaRC1 = "9"
Range("B12").Select: ActiveCell.FormulaRC1 = "10"
```

EXHIBIT 7.14   Simplifying the code that inserts the numbers

statements begin by using a Range statement to select a worksheet cell, and then an ActiveCell statement to assign the numeric value to that cell. Ten pairs of statements are enough, but what would happen if we had to populate a column 50,000 cells long? There, a loop would be critical. We will now write our first piece of VBA code.

To do this, we will use a For . . . Next statement. A For . . . Next has a loop, which repeats a process for the number of times that we specify before the beginning of the loop operation. It needs a variable to count by and a variable or constant to set the number of loops. It increments the counter variable by 1 (default) each time the loop is executed; when the limit of the loop iterations is reached, it stops. The before and after editing are shown in Exhibit 7.14.

The fully edited recorded VBA macro is now shown in Exhibit 7.15.

RUNNING THE EDITED CODE

We will now run the rewritten VBA code to see if the compressed and edited version gives the same results. In addition to running the code, we are going to have our first lesson in the use of the VBA Debugger. The role of the debugger is to compile the code, checking for syntax errors, and then allowing the author to execute the code in a controlled manner. This means that you can watch blocks of code or even individual statements execute one at a time. What we will now do is enter the debugger and then watch the code execute a block at a time. To do this, we will need to learn a few simple commands and set up the code so it can be stopped and started under user control and not simply run from beginning to end. To accomplish this, we need to enter the VBA Editor and set breakpoints in the lines of code. Breakpoints are most easily set by clicking on the left-hand margin of the editor window. Breakpoints can only be set on lines of code, not comments or blank lines. When the model reaches the breakpoint it stops, without executing that statement. We will set breakpoints in front of each of the major blocks of code in the model. This will also give us a chance to see the For . . . Next loop in action, and how variable values are assigned.

```
Sub NumberListWithColors2()
'Macro edited 4/25/2008  Author: W. Preinitz

Dim i            As Integer            'loop counter
Dim cell_name    As String             'cell name

    'Enter the numbers in the cells
    For i = 1 to 10
        cell_name = "B" & (I+2)
        Range(cell_name) = i
    Next i
    'Center all the numbers in the column
    Range("B3:B12").Select
    Selection.HorizontalAlignment = xlCenter

    'Cells > 5 = font red and bold
    Range("B7:B12").Select
    Selection.Font.FontStyle = "Bold"
    Selection.Font.ColorIndex = 3   !Red

    'Cells < 5 = yellow interior
    Range("B3:B6").Select
    Selection.Font.ColorIndex = 19 !Yellow
    Selection.Interior.Pattern = "xlSolid"

    'Sum the column, center and bold font
    Range("B13").Select
    Selection.FormulaR1C1 =   "=SUM(R[-10]C:R[-1]C)"
    Selection.HorizontalAlignment = xlCenter
    Selection.Font.Bold = True
    Range("B1").Select

End Sub
```

EXHIBIT 7.15   Fully edited macro, reduced from 62 to 17 lines of code

Breakpoint lines are highlighted in red. We can go step-by-step one line of code at a time using the "F8" key, or we can jump from one breakpoint to the by next using "F5" key. The location of the breakpoints is shown in Exhibit 7.16.

Stepping through the Code

First close the Project Explorer window, then move the VBA Editor window to the right of the screen. This will allow us to see the changes to the worksheet as they occur. Your screen should now look like Exhibit 7.17.

To run the code, pull down the Run menu and select "Run Sub/User Form" or just press the "F5" key. See Exhibit 7.18.

We are now running the model! The current line we are on is highlighted in yellow. We have stopped at the first breakpoint. The Debugger Window should now look like Exhibit 7.19.

Press the "F8" key three times. This will advance the model three lines of code. We see that the first cell of the column has been populated. See Exhibit 7.20.

As we entered the first loop, several things happened. In the three statements above the loop, VBA created two variables named "i" and cell_name. The variable "i" is an integer; its value can be a whole number (1, 2, 3 . . .)—but no decimals.

```
Sub NumberListWithColors2()
'Macro edited 4/25/2008
Dim i           As Integer        'loop counter
Dim cell_name   As String         'cell name
'Enter the numbers in the cells
    For i = 1 to 10                                  <=Breakpoint Set
      cell_name = "B" & (I+2)
      Range(cell_name) = i
    Next i
    'Center all the numbers in the column
    Range("B3:B12").Select                           <=Breakpoint Set
    Selection.HorizontalAlignment = xlCenter
    'Cells > 5 = font red and bold
    Range("B7:B12").Select                           <=Breakpoint Set
    Selection.Font.FontStyle = "Bold"
    Selection.Font.ColorIndex = 3   !Red
    'Cells < 5 = yellow interior
    Range("B3:B6").Select                            <=Breakpoint Set
    Selection.Font.ColorIndex = 19
    Selection.Interior.Pattern = "xlSolid"
    'Sum the column, center and bold font
    Range("B13").Select                              <=Breakpoint Set
    Selection.FormulaR1C1 =  "=SUM(R[-10]C:R[-1]C)"
    Selection.HorizontalAlignment = xlCenter
    Selection.Font.Bold = True
    Range("B1").Select

End Sub
```

EXHIBIT 7.16   Setting breakpoints to monitor the progress of the code

The variable cell_name is a string. Strings can contain numbers and letters (and some special characters that are neither).

The variable "i" is a loop control variable. Later in the book we will give loop control variables meaningful names that will identify their functions; for now, in this small loop "i" is sufficient. It will increment across the values set in the loop For...Next statement. It will start at 1 and go to 10. When the value of the variable equals 10, the loop will stop and the model will continue. By advancing three lines of code we have completed one loop and caused the model to perform four operations. The first two operations were generated by the line of code that creates

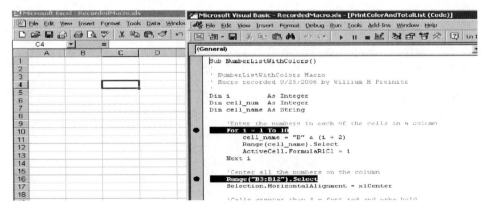

EXHIBIT 7.17   Entering the VBA Debugger in Break mode

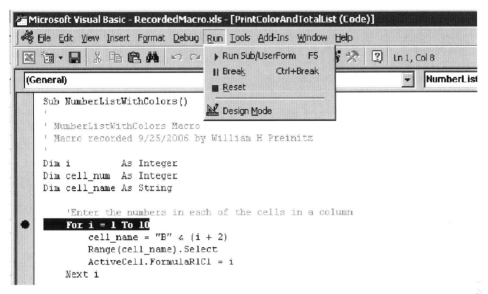

EXHIBIT 7.18   Run command

and assigns the value for the variable cell_name. In this line of code, the literal "B" was concatenated (using the & sign) to the value of "i+2." Concatenation is the operation that combines the contents of two or more String variables into a single String variable. If the variable being concatenated is not a String variable to start out with, VBA expresses its value as a String variable of the same value and then pastes the two terms together. The "i" variable began with a value of 1 in that it is the first time the loop is executed, and the Range of the loop counters starts at 1 and stops at 10. That makes the value of cell_name the first time that the loop operates the equal

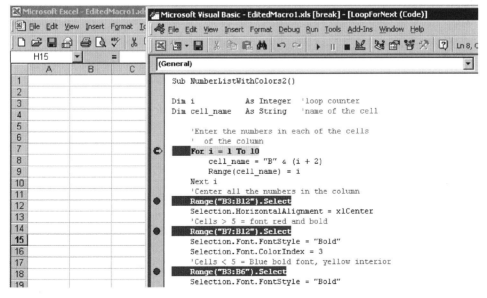

EXHIBIT 7.19   Hitting the first break point

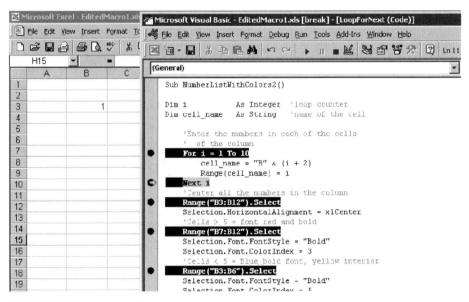

EXHIBIT 7.20 Moving through a For…Next loop

to "B" pasted together with ("1," the value of "i")+2; or a finished "B3." The value "B3" is then put into the variable cell_name.

To make this assignment, the variable name is on the left side of an equal sign and the value to be placed in it is on the left. What the equals sign means here is, "put the result "B3" inside of variable cell_name." The next line sets the Range to be "B3," the value of cell_name, and selects it. The third and final line of the loop puts the value of "i" into the Range. If we press the "F5" button, the model completes nine more loops and stops at the next breakpoint. See Exhibit 7.21.

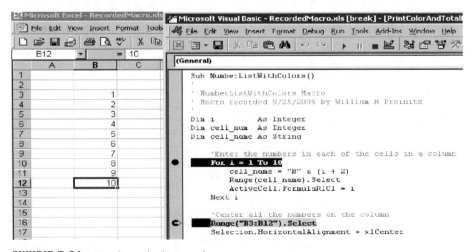

EXHIBIT 7.21 Finishing the loop code

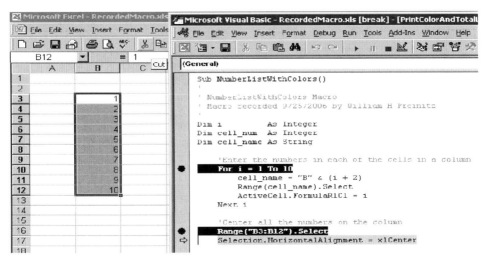

EXHIBIT 7.22   Moving forward one statement at a time

If we press "F8" to advance by one statement, the model now selects the entire Range of output numbers and sets the Range up for formatting. See Exhibit 7.22.

Press "F5." The model has now centered the selected Range. See Exhibit 7.23.

Press "F5." The model selected the Range of cells B7 to B12, and made the font red and bold

Press "F5." Cells B3 to B6 are selected, their respective fonts set to bold, their font color to blue (which is 5), their background to yellow, and solid which is 6, xSolid from the regular color selection palette xlAutomatic.

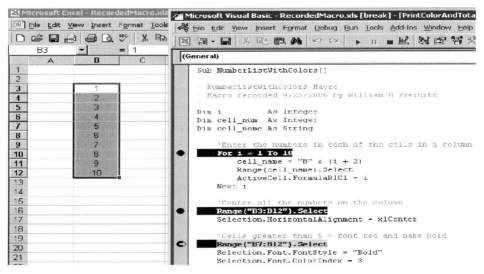

EXHIBIT 7.23   Cell value test

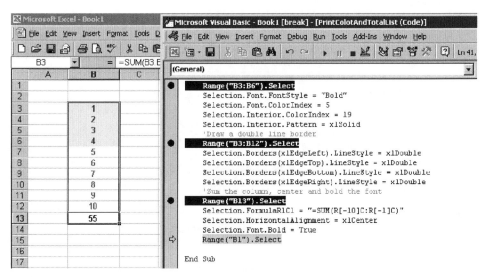

EXHIBIT 7.24 Inserting the Sum function at the base of the column

Press "F5." The next four lines draw a "xlDouble" line style around the left, top, bottom, and right of the Range B3 to B12. See Exhibit 7.24.

Press "F5." The Range of a single cell, B13, is selected, the SUM function is inserted, the results are centered and made bold. The yellow line has disappeared. The macro has finished.

Having satisfied ourselves that the model works, we can remove the breakpoints. Select from the menu

```
Debug => Clear All Breakpoints
```

or use a three-keystroke combination.

```
Ctrl+Shft+F9
```

USING RECORDED MACROS TO BUILD A SIMPLE MODEL

The Web site that accompanies this book contains an exercise that uses recorded macros to build and run a small model. This model has all the gross functionality of the structured finance model we will build in the book. It opens a data file, reads the information from it, stores the information, reads it into the model file, processes the information, generates a result, opens up a report template file, renames the template file, writes the results into the renamed file, and then saves the file. Having completed those tasks, the model stops.

I highly recommend that you take the time to study this example closely. If you can grasp the basic fundamentals of this small model, it will greatly improve your chances of understanding the content and organization of the larger model.

DELIVERABLES CHECKLIST

The VBA Knowledge Checklist for this chapter is:

- The use of the **Sub** and **End Sub** restricted words
- Understanding the use of the Range and Cells statements to access the Excel worksheet
- How to use VBA to assign a value to an Excel spreadsheet cell or Range
- How to use VBA to read a value from an Excel spreadsheet cell or Range
- How to use VBA to change the appearance of an Excel spreadsheet cell by changing its font color, background color, or "bold" font setting
- How to declare a VBA variable using the reserved word Dim
- How to declare the vector or array forms of a variable using subscripts for multiple individual data. Examples are averages (5), numbers (5,3)
- What the VBA variable types—Integer, Double, and String—represent
- How to Open, Save, and Close an Excel workbook using VBA commands
- How to build a simple looping structure using the For . . . Next statement
- How to build a simple choice structure using the If . . . Then . . . Else . . . EndIf statement
- What a comment statement is, how to create a comment statement, and why they are important. Example: **!Comments are important, as they may save you lots of embarrassment some day**
- How to open the VBA Editor using the "Alt+F11" keystroke combination
- How to create and name a VBA code module
- How to record a VBA macro from Excel, and how to name the VBA code module in which the code resides
- How to compile a VBA program
- How to run a VBA program from inside the VBA Editor using the "F5" key command
- How to set a breakpoint by using either the "F9" key or the cursor
- How to remove all breakpoints in the program by using the "Ctl+Shift+F9" keystroke combination
- How to move line by line through a VBA program by using the "F8" command
- How to reset a VBA program after it has run, and why you need to do this
- How to examine the value of a variable by placing it over the variable while the VBA program is active

The Modeling Knowledge Checklist for this chapter is:

- Creating a model file with a menu
- Creating a data file that holds the information for the model run
- Creating a results file that holds a template for an output report
- Running the proto-model to achieve an initial result
- Running the proto model to achieve a targeted result. This result was one of the adjusted averages exceeding the 20-point cutoff score. The model then recast one of the output records in red

NEXT STEPS

Congratulations! You have built your first model!

Believe it or not, you have now mastered at least 75% of the basic concepts that you will need to build a much more elaborate and productive model. You have gotten you toes wet in the VBA Editor and Debugger. (Do not worry, Chapter 16, "Debugging the Model," is devoted to the use of the debugger!).

You have declared variables, used a simple decision choice statement, and witnessed a loop in action.

More importantly you have performed the following tasks:

- Opened files
- Read information from them
- Stored the information in VBA variables
- Used that information to perform calculations
- Opened a reporting file
- Found and populated a template report
- Changed the appearance of the report based on the input to it
- Closed and saved the file

That list is the list of tasks that you must perform to run *any model*.

Now you, like the Devonian fish, are ready to engage in some serious evolution!

In Chapter 8 we will enlarge on what you have learned here to design and build the menu interface for the model.

ON THE WEB SITE

The Web site material for chapter 7 contains three sets of files.

The *first* set relates to the first exercise of the chapter in which we recorded a macro and then edited it into a more efficient form. The original recorded macro is contained in the file **"RecordedMacro1.xls."** After we have read and understood what was in this file we modified it to reduce the total number of lines of VBA code while preserving all of its functionality. The resultant file is named **"Edited-Macro1.xls."**

The *second* set of files relate to the Proto Model project. In this project we have a collection of three files: the model is named, appropriately, **"Proto-Model_WebSite.xls"**; the data file is named **"DataFile.xls"**; and the output file is named **"ResultsFile.xls."** You can run the proto model using these three files. By using the VBA Debugger and setting breakpoints you can alternatively run the model step by step using the **"F8"** button to advance line-by-line as the program executes.

While these two files are not part of our modeling effort they are very instructive of how VBA operates. They are also an excellent first look at the form and function of a simple VBA program.

The third set of files are the Proto Model project rewritten but now incorporating many of the VBA language features and modeling techniques that you will learn from the later chapters of the book. This revamped model is named **"Proto-Model_Advanced.xls."** It uses the same supporting **"Data.xls"** and **"Results.xls"** but has some added features. I thought that it would be an interesting additional piece of VBA for you to look at, especially in comparison with the first version of the model.

## CHAPTER 8

Writing Menus: An Introduction to Data, Ranges, Arrays, and Objects

OVERVIEW

Menus are one of the most critical components of a successful model. This is especially true if the model is to be used repeatedly over a long period of time, or over a series of similar or identical deals. Menus should be designed to facilitate the use of the application, not put a barrier between the analyst and the goal of solving the problem.

The menu is the transition boundary between the visible world of the Excel worksheet at the surface of the model and the hidden (although not to us!), VBA language portion of the model. As such, it is the first arbiter of the model inputs.

All well-designed models have common menu features. They use headers to announce their purpose in the general schema of the model's organization. They contain fields for input and output, and explanatory text to tell the user what can be input and how to input it. They may contain display messages to inform the user of the model's progress or of error conditions. They may use action buttons to help the user select options or set of options for the model's performance.

Remember, no matter how simple or sophisticated the model, its menu interface is the first thing the user sees. This chapter is designed to help you make a good first impression!

DELIVERABLES

This is a very "dense" chapter. We are going to cover *a lot* of ground. A clear understanding of the use of the most common forms of VBA language—variables, Ranges, and objects—is absolutely critical to powerful modeling techniques. This chapter will give you probably 75% of the nitty-gritty of VBA development.

Pay attention to detail. This is **not** a view from 100,000 feet. It is **not** a conceptual chapter. You need to know every one of the concepts presented here to succeed in the upcoming code development activities. If you do not understand a concept, review it until you do. The deliverables in this section are numerous, but vital.

VBA Language Knowledge Deliverables

- What is a variable type, and how variable types determine what information can be stored in them. The major types are Integer, Long, Double, String, and Boolean.
- How to declare variables and define their scope. This scope has three levels of increasing availability: Local, Module, and Global.
- How to name variables and comment variables.
- How to assign values to variables and use those values in various tasks and activities.
- What a constant is.
- What the Option Explicit statement is, and how to use it.
- What a Range statement is, and how to use it to move data between Excel and VBA.
- How to create, name, select, edit, and reference a Range of cells on an Excel worksheet.
- How to read data from and write data to a Range of cells on an Excel worksheet from VBA.
- What is a VBA object? What are methods and properties of objects?

Modeling Knowledge Deliverables

- The role of menus in planning, developing, and running models
- The three tenants of model development: clarity, simplicity, and specificity
- The components of a well-designed menu: header, body, input/output fields, explanatory text, message fields, and action buttons

UNDER CONSTRUCTION

In this chapter we will add the menus the model needs to allow us to enter our model run specifications into the program. We will also create Range names in the menus to allow us to more efficiently transfer information from the menus to the VBA code.

Now we will begin to fill the some of the previously created VBA modules with our first model code. The following modules will be the first we will use to begin the construction of the VBA portions of the model:

"**A_Constants**" will contain a set of public constant variables we will use to manage the menus of the model.

"**A_Globals**" will contain all the global variables we will need to support the menus we are building in this chapter. There will be one group of global variables declared for each of the menus of the model. Each section will contain the individual variables for every field on each menu. These variables will hold all the user-entered information of the model after we have error checked it for form, consistency, reasonableness and completeness. This module will also contain a long list of global variables that we will use to store the data from the loan portfolio file. We do not as yet have any VBA code to read the portfolio data from the file but we can name and declare the variables in anticipation of this information. The collateral file we will read into the model is named "**portfolio_orig.xls.**"

"**A_MainProgram**" will contain the highest level subroutine calls that will be later developed to perform all the menu functions. For now we will content ourselves with simply naming the major functional block subroutines that we will later develop in much more detail. We will therefore content ourselves with setting these subroutines up in a main program context. We will need the following functional units to complete the run of the model:

1. "ErrCheck_All_Menu"—Error check the user inputs from the menu.
2. "Read_All_Menu_Information"—Read the contents of the menus.
3. "Read_Portfolio_Data_File"—Read the collateral information.
4. "Compute_Collateral_CashFlows"—Amortize the collateral.
5. "Load_and_Run_the_Waterfall"—Apply the computed cash flows above the waterfall structure and capture the results.
6. "Write_the_Waterfall_Report_Package"—Produce a detailed report of each waterfall run in the analysis.
7. "Write_Matrix_Report_Package"—Produce the summary matrix report package.

The subroutine structure of the main program, which we have named "Loan_Financing_Model" is shown in Exhibit 8.1.

ROLE OF THE MENU

Historically, most people have thought of menus as simply a way of getting information from the outside, the environment, of the model to the inside, the computational or processing part of the model. But the role that the menu serves should be considered in broader terms.

A model with a well-designed menu structure serves many other functions than simply that of data transfer. If well-designed and customized to the analytical task that the model is designed to address, menus also serve:

- To provide a checklist for all the information required to run the model
- As the first error detection point in the model
- As a reinforcement of a preferred sequence of events in running the model
- As powerful tools in organizing the data of the model
- As allowing flexibility in managing the production and form of model results
- To focus the thoughts of the analyst on the framework of the problem

Each Menu Should Have a Clear and Distinct Function

Each menu should have a clear and distinct function. This function should be segregated from the functions performed by the other menus of the model. It should also serve to reinforce the overall menu structure of the model. Try not to mix unrelated information together in the same menu. Clearly differentiate between those menus that provide input to the model or control its flow, and those that provide

Hierarchy for Loan_Financing_Model Main Program in Module "A_MainProgram"

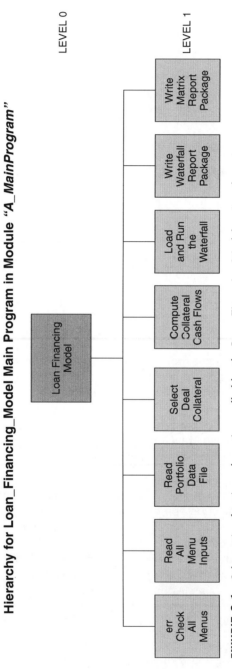

EXHIBIT 8.1 Schematic of major subroutines called by the Loan Financing Model main subroutine

a view of the model results. The functional roles of the menus of the model are the following:

- Establish the location of all files (and their directories) needed to run the model.
- Set collateral selection parameters.
- Display the collateral selection results.
- Generate a table of default and prepayment assumptions, to be used in the collateral amortization calculations.
- Present collateral selection criteria based on geographic location.
- Generate a table of all deal expenses and amortization triggers.
- Generate a table to select output reports.
- Generate a table to display selected results without producing a report package.

Menus Should Help Present and Organize Assumptions

Menus should provide a framework for checking for the completeness of all the information required to run the model. This information can take the form of data from files, feeds from other programs or external products, and user keyboard input. Menus are a powerful tool in organizing and segregating the various inputs of the model, contributing to the control process by ensuring that all the necessary information is available to the model *before* it is run. Use models to tell the intended users what information they need to know, and to what level of detail the data must conform.

Menus Should Help the User Run the Model Correctly

By clearly structuring the use of action buttons on the menu, the model designer can lay out for the model user the correct sequence of events required to run the model in a valid form.

The designer can also allow for partial model function. For example, the overall model will perform five major operational blocks of work to complete its analytical task. It may be that the model can allow the analyst to bifurcate the operation of steps 1 and 2 from that of steps 3, 4, and 5, allowing these latter tasks to be run later at your leisure. Action buttons can control the flow of the model code in this matter, avoiding additional, unnecessary work.

Menus Should Help Screen the Assumptions and Inputs

Menus provide the ideal place for the first screening of the data. This can be done in several different ways. The first is to explicitly error-check menu information immediately as it "crosses the border" into the model. This error checking can take the form of value checks (is this a reasonable input for the parameter being measured), type checks (did the user enter a date into a dollar amount column), or cross-checking (do the requested model operations match the assumptions of the content of the data input?). Error, warning, and informational messages can be linked directly to the VBA code that specifically supports a given menu. This code can then be used to perform immediate error checks before the program begins to run with information that will invalidate the results.

Menus Are Very Useful in Documenting a Program

"One picture is worth a thousand words." This is especially true of the use of menus in the documentation process. The picture of a menu in an offline documentation piece can be used to reinforce many elements of the process. It first shows the reader exactly what the visible front end of the model looked like at the time of the documentation. If it is annotated with explanatory text, it may go some distance in explaining the function and sequence of the model operation. The menu can be the focal point of the descriptive sections of the documentation, and visually guide the audience through a step-by-step account of a typical session of model use.

Menus Should Substantially Increase the Model's Ease of Use

Menus should directly contribute to the ease of use of the model. They should form an accessible medium between the model user and the rest of the model. It is much easier to enter assumptions and file names into Excel worksheet fields than it is to integrate this information directly into the VBA code of the program itself.

Menus can in this way directly facilitate thinking about the analytical problem; they free the model user from a burdensome task and allow him to think about what he is doing, instead of how he needs to do something. The menus should invite the user into the model, and also protect him from the most obvious and damaging errors.

Menus Document the Input Assumptions Used

If you want to have a record of the inputs that were used to generate a particular model run, the input menus that contained the run's parameters can be copied from the model into the output report package. This not only preserves the contents of all of the input data and assumptions, but also presents an exact picture of the menu configurations used at the time the run was produced. This practice is implemented in this book when we design the output report package in Chapter 11.

Another vital contribution of menus is in the activity of back testing new versions of the model to make sure they are compatible with older runs and analyses. Reproductions of the menus from one version to the next, when saved with the older versions of the model, allow a quick, clear, and visually compelling check of the assumptions that produced the earlier run. You are not faced with the problem of having to hunt for the assumptions used in the prior run, because they are in a concentrated form, contained in the older menu layouts.

Menus Help in Debugging

Lastly, menus can help in the debugging process. As we will see later in the section entitled "Building a Menu from Scratch," the use of various VBA programming techniques can help the model developer clearly understand where the model data came from, in what form it is expected to arrive, and the pathway it took into the model. This can be invaluable when it comes to getting the model to run from a syntactical standpoint as well as understanding the data flow though the model for finding logical errors.

STRUCTURAL ELEMENTS OF A MENU

An often overlooked aspect of menu design is that menus have recognizable structural elements. These elements help the model user learn how to use the model, how to know where they are in the model, and what they need to do before and after they have run the model.

Menu Title

Believe it or not, many people simply do not title their menus.

Menus should be titled both at the top of the Excel sheet and on the Excel worksheet tab at the bottom of the page. The title at the top of the Main Menu announces the name of the model to the user, or, if it is a supporting menu, the function of the menu. The menu title should relate directly to the function or contents of the menu. The menu title on the Excel worksheet tab should be brief but clear. It may be necessary to refer to the model in the online documentation or to programmatically direct the user to the spreadsheet containing the menu in the course of running the program. In either case, brevity is the key!

Entry and/or Display Fields

The most important parts of the menu are the fields for the entry or display of information.

These fields should be clearly displayed. Where there is related data they should be grouped, and, if necessary, a border or some other visual demarcation should be placed around them. The fields should, if possible, be colored in a different manner from the background of the menu. Do not use high-contrast colors, in that they will induce eyestrain and drowsiness with repeated long-term usage. It is highly recommended that the font of all menu fields that receive input be of a uniform color. Blue is the color used by most people, and allows the user at a glance to understand that these fields contain inputs not results. Green is frequently used when the input is from another program or electronic data feed. **Black should be used exclusively for output and results**. The data fields of the menu should accept their entries only in the form that you want the data to be available in. This leads to less confusion, and enforces a basic level of first-degree data integrity. See Exhibit 8.2.

Entry and display fields also form the natural attachment point for the origination of user-directed messages from the model, and of warning and error messages as well. It is at this point that you want to head trouble off at the pass, before it can get any further into the model run. Conversely, display fields can be used to highlight unusual or anomalous results and to immediately alert the analyst to a problem.

Loan Securitization Model Main Menu

Program Execution Option	(Y=YES; N=NO)	
Y	Perform the Collateral Eligibility Test?	
Y	Write out Ineligible Collateral Reports?	*Run the*
Y	Write out Eligible Collateral Reports?	*Model*
Y	Write out Eligible Collateral Loan File?	
Y	Write out Cash Flow Waterfall Reports?	
Y	Write out Matrix Summary Reports?	
N	Write out Cash Flow Trace files? *(Caution: can generate VERY LENGTHY run times)*	

Input File Information

C:\VBA_Class\AnalystProgram\		
CombinedCollatSprd.xls	Collateral Data File Name	
0	# of Loans *Enter "0" to read all available, otherwise enter the number of loans that you want to have read from the top of the file.*	

		Template File Names
TestRun_01_	Report Group Prefix (attached to all output files)	
Ineligibles.xls	Ineligible Collateral Reports File Name <======	inelig_template.xls
Collateral.xls	Eligible Collateral Reports File Name <======	collat_template.xls
Waterfall.xls	Cash Flow Waterfalls Report File Name <======	waterfall_template.xls
Matrix.xls	Summary Matrix Reports Files <======	matrix_template.xls
CombinedCollat.xls	Eligible Collateral File <======	datafile_template.xls

EXHIBIT 8.2   Main Menu of the loan financing model

Explanatory Text

This text can serve several purposes and can come in several forms depending on the complexity of the menu function. The developer may want to put a piece of explanatory text at the top or the bottom of the menu to convey an overall sense of what the menu is trying to accomplish. Text blocks can also spell out run options, or the restrictions of use of the data, or of action buttons on the menu.

Each input or display field should have an accompanying label identifying its contents. As before, clarity with brevity is the key here. If there are restrictions on what can go into the fields, this is a good place to cite those restrictions.

Group your input and display fields if the data is similar and related. If there is a large collection of related fields, you may wish to have VBA outline the group using the "Format => Cells => Border" menu command in Excel.

Explanatory text can also contain the version number of the model or any other help feature, such as the name and telephone number of the developer (if you are kind).

Action Buttons

These are the buttons that allow you to activate the program to perform specific functions.

The most common uses of action buttons are:

- Locate and load input data files.
- Trigger error-checking VBA code to scan the menu for mistakes and omissions.

- Run the program.
- Display results to output menus containing tables or graphs.
- Manipulate the appearance of the program or the menu itself.
- Quickly add or remove selection choices from the menu.

Tying the Menus to the Model

We will revisit error checking in the design of menus in Chapter 10, "Building Messaging Capabilities." Next, however, we will address how we get the menus we have designed to interact with the rest of the model. To do that, we will need to start learning about data and how it is represented in VBA. We will then link the menus into the model and create the mechanism to make our inputs to the menu available to the model's calculation subroutines.

INTRODUCTION TO VBA VARIABLES

To be able to build our menus, we will need to learn about the use (and abuse) of data in VBA. It is the VBA language that will be the workhorse in moving our specified inputs, whether they are numbers, dates, schedules, or filenames, into the model.

Therefore, in this section we will cover the following topics:

- The basic data types that can be used by the VBA language
- How to declare variables and arrays
- How to interactively change the size of arrays
- Variable scope—where and to what degree a variable is active
- Constants—elements whose value does not change
- How to assign values to variables
- Calculation rules of variables
- The Range command and how to use it to move information

VARIABLE TYPES

Before we can start running our model, we will need to get the data inside it, in a form that it can use. VBA has a number of data types from which we can choose when we want to make our information available for computation. All of these types have limitations, not only on the Range of values that they can assume (greater than X but less than Y), but also in terms of what types of computational operations can be performed upon them.

All data types have different degrees of specificity or accuracy. Using them incorrectly can lead to unintended results, some of which can be quite subtle. Data is assigned to variables. A variable is a unit that can change as the value or form of the data inside it changes.

There are 11 data types supported by VBA, these are:

1. Array	7. Long
2. Boolean	8. Object
3. Currency	9. Single
4. Date	10. String
5. Double	11. Variant
6. Integer	

To specify a data type include the **As** keyword followed by the desired data type in the **Dim** (as in dimension) statement:

```
Dim number_of_loans As Integer
```

Data types were designed so that the computer could efficiently allocate scarce storage capacity.

Each data type is optimal for a specific type of data storage. The main types we will concentrate on are **Boolean, Date, Double, Integer, Long,** and **String.**

- **Boolean** can assume the value of either **TRUE** or **FALSE.**
- **Date** variables hold date information. Input may Range from 1/1/0100 to 12/31/9999.
- **Double** holds floating point real numbers. Input may Range from $-1.8E308$ to $1.8E308$ (E = power of 10).
- **Integer** is designed to hold small integer values. Input may Range from $-32,768$ to 32,767.
- **Long** is designed to hold large integer values. Input may Range from $-2.147E9$ to 2.147E9.
- **String** variables hold alphanumeric information up to 64,000 characters long.

So when would we be most likely to use these various data types?

- **Boolean** for a choice or to indicate a condition (e.g., whether a process is complete).
- **Date** for calendar dates, monthly start dates.
- **Double** for any type of computation, especially financial, compounding sequences, very small or very large amounts, and numbers that require decimal precision.
- **Integer** for small counting values and loop counters.
- **Long** for large counting values, large data sets, and large loop counters.
- **String** for any data not purely a number, an address, a name, a label, a directory or filename, workbook, worksheet, or Range name.

HOW TO CREATE AND USE VARIABLES

Variables are labels that the developer assigns to collections of data. Variables can be scalars, vectors, or arrays. A **scalar** is a single piece of information. A **vector** is

```
'MAIN MENU VARIABLES
Public gfn_collateral_file    As String    'Name of the INPUT collateral data file
Public g_run_exceptions       As Boolean   'Run the selection criteria exceptions report
Public g_pathway              As String    'Directory level pathway
Public g_pathway_template     As String    'Report templates directory pathway
Public g_pathway_output       As String    'Outputs directory pathway
```

EXHIBIT 8.3   A set of variables

a list of information that has one dimension. An example would be a single row or column on an Excel worksheet. An **array** is a table of data, with two or more dimensions. An example of a two-dimensional array is an Excel table 10 rows by 20 columns.

A variable also has scope. **Scope** determines when and where a variable is active, and for how long it should hold its value. Variables, as their name implies, change value. They change value when we or the model assigns a different value to them.

Declaring Variables

Variables are declared (created) by the use of the Dim statement. Dim is a reserved word and will appear in blue. Follow the word Dim with the variable name you have selected, and finish with the word "As" and the data type you want the variable to have. You should always follow a variable declaration with a comment that advises the reader what the variable denotes. Notice that in Exhibit 8.3, all in-line comments explaining the variables start with an apostrophe.

They are specified as to type by using the As statement. The notation at the right side of the example is a developer comment. It tells us what the variable represents and constitutes an indispensable element of in-model documentation.

Forms of Variables

In Exhibit 8.4, we have examples of each of the forms a variable can take—scalar, vector, or array. The first declaration is a scalar, a single piece of information. The second is a vector, a list of up to six values. The third is an array, a table, 6 rows deep and 360 columns wide

Another way to visualize variables is as shown in Exhibit 8.5.

```
'Sample Variable Declarations
Dim i_row                     As Integer 'scalar, row counter
Dim loan_types(1 to 6)        As Integer 'vector, numeric codes for the loan
                                          types
Dim amort_prin(1 to 6, 1 to 360)  As Double '2 dimensional array, cash flows from
                                              6 loans
```

EXHIBIT 8.4   Example of the declaration of a scalar, vector, and an array. The first two are of type Integer, and the third is of type Double

Arrays from 0 to 4 Dimensions

Scalar

1

1 Dimensional Array (3 rows)

1
2
3

2 Dimensional Array (5 rows, 3 columns)

(1,1)	(1,2)	(1,3)
(2,1)	(2,2)	(2,3)
(3,1)	(3,2)	(3,3)
(4,1)	(4,2)	(4,3)
(5,1)	(5,2)	(5,3)

3 Dimensional Array (5 rows, 3 columns, 2 tables)

Table 1:

(1,1,1)	(1,2,1)	(1,3,1)
(2,1,1)	(2,2,1)	(2,3,1)
(3,1,1)	(3,2,1)	(3,3,1)
(4,1,1)	(4,2,1)	(4,3,1)
(5,1,1)	(5,2,1)	(5,3,1)

Table 2:

(1,1,2)	(1,2,2)	(1,3,2)
		(2,3,2)
		(3,3,2)
		(4,3,2)
		(5,3,2)

Table 3:

(1,1,3)	(1,2,3)	(1,3,3)
		(2,3,3)
		(3,3,3)
		(4,3,3)
		(5,3,3)

4 Dimensional Arrays (5 rows, 3 columns, 2 tables, 2 sets of tables)

Set 1, Table 1:

(1,1,1,1)	(1,2,1,1)	(1,3,1,1)
(2,1,1,1)	(2,2,1,1)	(2,3,1,1)
(3,1,1,1)	(3,2,1,1)	(3,3,1,1)
(4,1,1,1)	(4,2,1,1)	(4,3,1,1)
(5,1,1,1)	(5,2,1,1)	(5,3,1,1)

Set 1, Table 2:

(1,1,2,1)	(1,2,2,1)	(1,3,2,1)
		(2,3,2,1)
		(3,3,2,1)
		(4,3,2,1)
		(5,3,2,1)

Set 1, Table 3:

(1,1,3,1)	(1,2,3,1)	(1,3,3,1)
		(2,3,3,1)
		(3,3,3,1)
		(4,3,3,1)
		(5,3,3,1)

Set 2, Table 1:

(1,1,1,2)	(1,2,1,2)	(1,3,1,2)
(2,1,1,2)	(2,2,1,2)	(2,3,1,2)
(3,1,1,2)	(3,2,1,2)	(3,3,1,2)
(4,1,1,2)	(4,2,1,2)	(4,3,1,2)
(5,1,1,2)	(5,2,1,2)	(5,3,1,2)

Set 2, Table 2:

(1,1,2,2)	(1,2,2,2)	(1,3,2,2)
		(2,3,2,2)
		(3,3,2,2)
		(4,3,2,2)
		(5,3,2,2)

Set 2, Table 3:

(1,1,3,2)	(1,2,3,2)	(1,3,3,2)
		(2,3,3,2)
		(3,3,3,2)
		(4,3,3,2)
		(5,3,3,2)

EXHIBIT 8.5 Representation of a scalar, and 1-, 2-, 3-, and 4-dimensional arrays

```
'Cashflow components
Public g_prepay_prin()      As Double    'per period prepayments of principal
Public g_default_prin()     As Double    'per period defaulted principal
Public g_amort_prin()       As Double    'per period amortized principal
Public g_coupon()           As Double    'per period coupon payments
Public g_recover_prin()     As Double    'per period recoveries of defaulted
                                             principal
```

EXHIBIT 8.6 Declarations of arrays that have yet to be given a dimension

How to Dynamically Dimension Arrays

There are occasions when the size requirement of a vector or array will not be known at the start of a model. Sometimes, we will know the size of the array, such as the maximum statutory term for the longest loans in months, 360 (e.g., 30 years). Conversely, the initial size of the array may be known but we may want to resize it subsequently, after the model has begun to run. For example, we may start with a portfolio of 2,500 loans and need to read information into the model about each of them. During the course of the collateral selection process we may find that 20% of the portfolio is ineligible; we need only retain the information on 2,000 loans in total. In this case we would need to pare our original array of 2,500 loans down to an array of only 2,000 loans. VBA has a command to allow us to do just that.

To declare a flexibly dimensioned array, we would still use the VBA keyword **Dim** or **Public**, but instead of declaring a fixed size to the array, we would leave the size specification blank. The VBA model will now recognize the name g_prepay_prin as a valid variable in the model. It will not, however, allocate any storage space for its contents. In the model we may run any number of prepayment and default scenarios. The number of prepayments and default scenarios are entirely left to the analyst. In that case we would assign the array size after we obtain the number, as input by the user into a menu.

The variable declarations in Exhibit 8.6 create a variable, but do not allocate any storage memory for it. We need to tell the model how large these vectors or arrays will be before we use them. We will do that in Exhibit 8.7.

We know before we make this declaration how many prepayment and default scenarios the model is going to evaluate. We have also set a constant (an element whose value never changes), named "PAY_DATES," to a value that it will hold throughout the model run. In a typical model run, the number of prepayment scenarios may be 5, the default scenarios 2, and the number of payment dates 360.

```
'cash flow components variables
ReDim g_prepay_prin(1 To g_prepay_levels, 1 To g_default_levels, 1 To PAY_DATES)
  As Double
ReDim g_default_prin(1 To g_prepay_levels, 1 To g_default_levels, 1 To PAY_DATES)
  As Double
ReDim g_amort_prin(1 To g_prepay_levels, 1 To g_default_levels, 1 To PAY_DATES)
  As Double
ReDim g_coupon(1 To g_prepay_levels, 1 To g_default_levels, 1 To PAY_DATES)
  As Double
ReDim g_recover_prin(1 To g_prepay_levels, 1 To g_default_levels, 1 To PAY_DATES)
  As Double
```

EXHIBIT 8.7 The arrays now have a fixed size

All told, the number of storage locations required would therefore be 5 times 2 times 360, or 3,600. The data for the variables is now ready to pour into the model!

SCOPE OF VARIABLES

"Scope" refers to how long a variable holds its value, and where in the model it holds its value. When you declare a variable inside of a subroutine or function, its value is held only as long as the model is working on that portion of the VBA code. To make variable values available to different parts of the model, you can change the form and location of their declaration statements.

Types of Scope

Local variables are available only to the procedure in which they are declared. **Module** variables (which you may elect to be prefixed later by assigning an "m") have the scope of all procedures contained in the VBA module in which they are declared. **Global** variables (prefixed later with a "g") are available to all procedures in all modules in the application you are running, (and any other applications you have open at the same time).

Local Variables

Local variables are active only in the subroutine or function in which they are declared:

```
Sub Run_Selection_Criteria()
Dim i                As Integer    'loop counter
Dim iloan            As Integer    'loop counter for loans in portfolio
Dim ok               As Boolean    'logic test, ok=TRUE continue

End Sub
```

Module Variables

The scope of module variables is declared prior to the first subroutine or function in a module. The variables are created when the code in the module is being used, and they cease to exist when the model leaves the module to continue running elsewhere. Some VBA modules can be very large. Such a module may contain hundreds or, in some cases, thousands of lines of VBA code in numerous subroutines and functions. In this situation you may want to prefix all module level variables with the symbol "m_." This tells the person reading the code that the variable is a module variable available to all the subroutines and functions of the module. Exhibit 8.7 is the declaration statements for a set of two vectors "all_zip" and "all_zip_state." They each declare arrays that are now available to every subroutine and function in the VBA module. If this was a particularly large or complex VBA module, we could change the names to m_all_zip" and "m_all_zip_state," respectively, if we felt it would improve the clarity of the code.

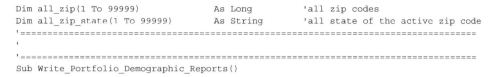

```
Dim all_zip(1 To 99999)          As Long        'all zip codes
Dim all_zip_state(1 To 99999)    As String      'all state of the active zip code
'=================================================================================
'
'=================================================================================
Sub Write_Portfolio_Demographic_Reports()
```

EXHIBIT 8.8   Declaration of a module variable

The variables declared in Exhibit 8.8 are all used to build ZIP code, state code, and index-exception reports. All the VBA code that produces those reports is contained in this module. It therefore makes sense to assign these variables as "module variables" because of the limited scope of their use.

Global Variables

Global variables are given their scope by being declared outside any procedure of the VBA module. They use the keyword **Public** instead of **Dim**.

It is an ***extremely good idea*** to keep the declarations of global variables away from the rest of your code modules. Earlier we created a separate module for them called "A_GlobalVariables." An example of global variable declaration is shown in Exhibit 8.9.

These variables contain the original and remaining terms of the loans, as well as their original and remaining balances. As a result, they will be used not only in the portions of the model that will select the eligible collateral, but in the cash flow amortization portion as well. By declaring them as "public" they will be global variables, available to all portions of the model code. (Note the use of the g_ suffix in the names of the variables; more on this in the very next section.)

Naming Conventions for Variables

Required rules for naming variables and arrays are:

- The name must begin with an alphabetic symbol.
- The name cannot be longer than 255 characters.
- The name cannot be the same as any of the Excel or VBA keywords or their built-in function names.
- The name cannot contain a space or any of the following characters: . ! # $ % & @

Recommended guidelines for naming variables and arrays are:

- *ALWAYS* prefix global variables with "g_," or "G_," or just "G," to distinguish them from module variables and local variables.
- You may wish to prefix module variables with "m_," or "M_," or just "M," although this is not as helpful, as it might seem (except in the case of very large and complicated modules).

```
'SELECTION CRITERIA MENU VARIABLES
Public g_crit_min_orig_term              As Double       'Min original term in months
Public g_crit_max_orig_term              As Double       'Max original term in months
Public g_crit_min_rem_term               As Double       'Min remaining term in months
Public g_crit_max_rem_term               As Double       'Max remaining term in months
Public g_crit_min_orig_bal               As Double       'Min original balance
Public g_crit_max_orig_bal               As Double       'Max original balance
Public g_crit_min_rem_bal                As Double       'Min remaining balance
Public g_crit_max_rem_bal                As Double       'Max remaining balance
Public g_crit_max_del                    As Double       'Max times delinquent ever
Public g_crit_max_loan                   As Double       'Max loan LTV
Public g_crit_min_spread(1 To SEL_CRIT_INDEX_SPREADS)    As Double       'Min spread to floating rate index
Public g_crit_acc_index(1 To SEL_CRIT_INDEX_SPREADS)     As String       'Min spread to floating rate index
Public g_crit_max_spread                 As Double       'Min spread to floating rate index
Public g_crit_min_coupon                 As Double       'Min current yield
Public g_crit_max_coupon                 As Double       'Max current yield
Public g_crit_pay_diff                   As Double       'Max diff stated/calculated pmt
```

EXHIBIT 8.9   Declarations of global variables that are used to store information for the collateral selection process

- Try to use prefix codes to group menu inputs, such as "mm_" for information read-in from the main menu, or "pdm_" for the prepayment and default rates menu. Alternatively, you could set up a numbering scheme by giving each menu a number and assigning prefixes to the variables based on the inputs of each menu by using "m1_," "m2_," and so on, for each menu.

- Try to use prefix codes to group related information, such as "g_client" for individual information, or "g_sum" for totaled information. For example, if the client has address and corporate name information in the data file, we might capture it in the variables g_client_address and g_client_cname, respectively. If we were taking the sum of all prepayments of principal we might use a variable with g_sum_prepayments.

- If a number of related variables are used to store the model results from interim calculations, and these variables will be used in the production of a report or a set of related reports, then prefixing the output variables with an abbreviation of the report name may be useful. We are going to put the following information on a report named "Cash Flow Waterfall":g_waterfall_name, g_waterfall_method.

A Note on Variable Naming Conventions

Some people use mixed case lettering when declaring variable names and some do not.

In practice, everyone can agree that the names of all constants (elements whose value is set and will remain unchangeable for the remainder of the model run) should be in all upper case. An example in this model is the constant named PAY_DATES, which is set to a value of 360, the maximum number of months on the longest loan.

In the case of global or local variables, there is very little difference in using all lower case letters, or a mixture of upper and lower case letters, to compose your variable names. The one advantage to mixed case is this, however: If you have declared a variable with the name of "G_xyz" and you type in that variable name in as "g_xyz"a place in the model where the variable is active, the VBA editor will automatically correct "g_xyz" to "G_xyz." This is a wonderful thing because it prevents an all-too-common type of error, the misspelling of a variable. If you have declared "g_xyz" and you type in the name "g_xyy" someplace instead of the correct name the VBA program will not know what you are talking about. If you used mixed case the "g" would remain lower case and you might well notice the misspelling more readily.

This model uses lower case names for all variables. It is, unfortunately, a proclivity of the author and you, dear reader, are sort of stuck with it (sorry). Feel free to use mixed case if you wish, I will not be offended; in fact it could be better if you do!

Commenting on Variable Declarations

You will have noticed that all the code examples shown so far have comments that identify the contents of the variable. These comment lines are what are known as "in-line" comments and occur on the same line as the variable declaration.

It is vitally important that developers do this while they are writing the code. It is a laborious task, but if done in an incremental manner, an entirely manageable one. It is particularly important that *all global variables* be commented immediately upon creation. These variables carry their values across the entire width and breadth of the model, and their use therefore needs to be clearly understood.

In Chapter 6 we created a VBA module to hold all of the global variables. This module, named **"A_Globals,"** will serve as a central repository for the globally available information in the model. It will be your first point of reference if you have questions about a global variable. It needs to be as informative and complete as you can make it.

It also serves as a form of insurance, not only for the firm you work for, but for you as well. It is entirely possible that you will be called on to run the model, or teach others how to run and support it after you have been away from it for some time. Given the complexity of many structured finance models, and the fact that you will have worked on others in the intervening time, it is highly unlikely that the schema of the model will immediately leap to mind! (It may, but the odds are against you. . . .) Meaningful, careful, and utilitarian commenting will be worth its weight in diamonds. The time pressures of a development schedule often preclude doing everything we can in this regard, but it is a very dangerous, irresponsible, and *unprofessional* behavior not to give others the best chance they have to understand your work.

ASSIGNING VALUES TO VARIABLES

Now that your variables have been declared, how do you assign values to them?

Values are assigned by the use of the "=" symbol. Unlike algebraic operations, the symbol "=" does not have the meaning of "equal to" instead it means "read into." When a new value is read into a variable, the old value is overwritten and discarded. For example, to assign the value of 50,000 to the variable g_port_total we write:

```
g_port_total = 50000
```

One variable can also be assigned into another variable. The first variable is assigned the value of the second:

```
value_b = value_a
```

In the previous example we assigned the value of 50,000 to the g_port_total variable. If we wanted to add an additional 10,000 to the value of the variable we would do it in the following manner:

```
g_port_total = g_port_total + 10000
```

This statement in effect says:

Take the existing value that was in the variable, add 10,000, and make that sum the new value for the variable. This is mostly used when summing a series of variables (usually within a loop) into a variable designed to hold a total.

```
port_total = 0#  'get the total accepted remaining balances
For iloan = 1 To g_total_loans
  If g_loan_ok(iloan) Then
     port_total = port_total + g_bank_cur_bal(iloan)
  End If
Next iloan
```

EXHIBIT 8.10   Example of incremental assignment

The value of the portfolio total balance variable—port_tot—is initially set to zero outside of a loop. Then each of the loans, from the first to the last loan contained in the g_total_loans variable, has its current loan balance accumulated into the value of the variable portfolio total. See Exhibit 8.10.

Limits to Assignments

- You can only assign data of one variable to another variable of appropriate types.
- All smaller numerical data will go into larger data types with greater precision. Thus Reals will go into Doubles, Integers will go into Longs, and Integers into Reals and Doubles. But Reals and Doubles can never go into Integers or Longs, because the latter do not provision for decimal values. You cannot put ten pounds of concrete into a five-pound bag!
- Likewise String, Date, and Boolean are non-numeric and cannot go into any other variable type but themselves.
- Reals, Doubles, Integers, and Longs can go into strings, but become non-numeric when they do so. The value of numeric 3 is not the same as the symbol "3."
- If you violate one of these rules, you will get the message shown in Exhibit 8.11.

The program in Exhibit 8.11 is inexplicably trying to put the contents of a street address variable that is declared as a String into a variable designed to hold the total payment amount that is declared as a Double.

The limitations of the Range of values that can be stored in the receiving variable can also result in an error even in the case of otherwise compatible data types. When you exceed the value that a variable can handle, you get an "Overflow" error message as seen in Exhibit 8.12. Overflow means too big!

In Exhibit 8.12, the magnitude of the value of the total_payments variable is far too large for the storage capacity of the small_change variable.

CONSTANTS

Constants are special elements that are not variable. Just because it cannot be changed does not mean it cannot be very useful to the VBA modeler. A constant is declared once, has its value set, and then, is, well, constant! Constants can be of any

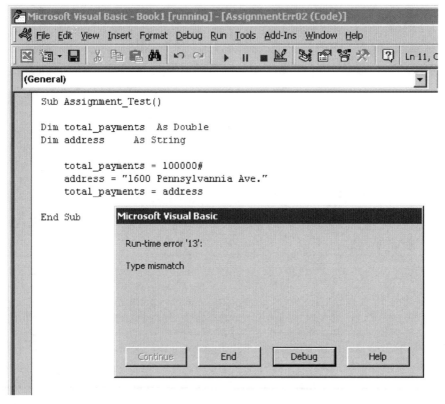

EXHIBIT 8.11   The dreaded "Type Mismatch" message!

scope, global, module, or local. Here are some guidelines concerning constants and their uses:

- Constants should be declared in all capital letters. This allows them to be immediately distinguished from all other element types. Earlier in this chapter we saw an example of a constant named TOTAL_ZIP_CODES. The value of this constant was set to 99999 to allow for that many individual ZIP codes to be represented in a report listing.
- Constants are useful to pin down the value of something that is not going to change during the course of running the model. This is especially true of structural limitations of the model, such as the number of time periods. An earlier constant that we saw was named PAY_DATES and represented the maximum number of cash flow periods in the model.
- They are declared by the reserved word Const, as shown in Exhibit 8.13. Here we are declaring a series of identification numbers that we will use in the collateral selection process. These numbers will not change over the course of the model run. Indeed, it is *vitally important that they do not change* as they will form part of a unique labeling system that identifies the conditions under which a loan may be excluded from the deal!

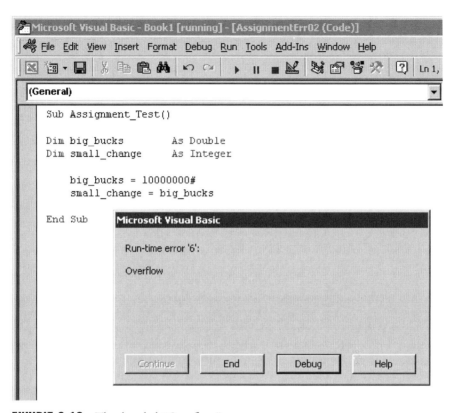

EXHIBIT 8.12 The dreaded "Overflow" message

The constants in Exhibit 8.13 are used in the production of the reports that describe the rejected collateral. The first constant at the top, named INELIGIBLE_REPORTS sets the number of reports in the ineligible collateral reports package. The others (which are ordered in powers of 2) are identifier tags for each selection criterion, values that will not change during the course of the model operation.

IT IS HIGHLY RECOMMENDED THAT ALL CONSTANTS BE DECLARED AS GLOBAL IN SCOPE AND BE PLACED IN THE SAME MODULE AS OTHER CONSTANT VARIABLES.

```
Public Const INELIGIBLE_REPORTS = 11          'Number of exception reports
Public Const EXCEPT_REMAINING_TERM = 1        'Over/Under remaining term range
Public Const EXCEPT_ORIGINAL_TERM = 2         'Over/Under original term range
Public Const EXCEPT_ORIGINAL_BALANCE = 4      'Over/Under original balance range
Public Const EXCEPT_CURRENT_BALANCE = 8       'Over/Under remaining balance range
Public Const EXCEPT_MAX_LTV = 16              'Exceeds maximum LTV
Public Const EXCEPT_INDEX = 32                'Under minimum spread
Public Const EXCEPT_STATE_CODE = 64           'Excluded state code
Public Const EXCEPT_TENOR_TEST = 128          'Orig Term / Rem Term Relationship
Public Const EXCEPT_BAL_TEST = 256            'Orig Bal / Rem Bal Relationship
Public Const EXCEPT_PMT_TEST = 512            'Calculated Pmt vs. Stated Pmt
Public Const EXCEPT_COUPON_TEST = 1024        'Acceptable gross coupon
```

EXHIBIT 8.13 The typical form of a constant declaration

If you have a large number of constants you may wish to create a separate module to hold them, as was done in this model. An exception to this is if the constants are specific to a particular process that was segregated in a single module. Then it would make much more sense to declare them at the top of that module, isolating them from the remainder of the modules of the model. An example of this type of declaration will be seen when we write the code for the module that produces the collateral reports in Chapter 13, "Writing the Collateral Selection Code."

Constants have several important uses, as follows:

- **Constants are extremely useful in establishing limits for the model.** These limits can take the form of maximum time periods, maximum number of portfolios, maximum number of loans in a portfolio, maximum number of portfolios in a deal.
- **Constants are a way to attach an alphanumerical label** to an unchanging numerical amount. What do we mean by this? Later, we will learn to write a statement that allows us to pick out a value from a Range of values. If you have three different reports and want to produce them sequentially in some cases but individually in others, you would use this type of Select statement. If in the second choice you wanted to produce a report summarizing the conduit financing performance results, you can create a constant with a value of two, and a name of MATRIX_CONDUIT_REPORT. If you want to test against a set of four possible types of matrix reports, and produce only the second one, it is much clearer in your code to say "Case Is = MATRIX_CONDUIT_REPORT," instead of this, "Case Is = 2." The value "2" could mean anything, but there isn't much doubt now as to which report this selection will point!
- **Constants are a way to set limits on groups of items.** Several vectors and/or arrays in the model have columns and rows corresponding in a one-to-one relationship to the members of some set. An example of this is the number of states in the United States. At the time of this writing the United States consists of 50 states. We could therefore declare the constant STATES and set it equal to 50. We could then use it in the model to dimension arrays holding information by state, or set flow control statement loop counters to run from 1 to STATES. But let us say we wanted to add several U.S. territories to the state listing. We could simply change the number in the constant STATES to the new number of states + territories, and all the array dimensions and loop counters would also change.

Exhibit 8.14 displays some VBA code fragments as examples of the use of constants.

In Exhibit 8.15, the constant named STATES is used to declare the dimensions of a number of related arrays. If the number of states in the United States changes, all one would have to do is change the constant declaration to the one below the declaration box, from 50 to, say, 54.

```
'cash flow components variables
ReDim g_prepay_prin(1 To g_prepay_levels, 1 To g_default_levels,
  1 To PAY_DATES)As Double
```

EXHIBIT 8.14   Constant PAY_DATES specifies the maximum number of payment dates that cash flows are computed against

```
Public Const STATES = 50                    'Number of states and territories

Public g_state_select(1 To STATES)   As Boolean  'Array of which states are selected

Public Const STATES = 54                    'Number of states and territories
```

EXHIBIT 8.15   Use of the constant STATES

In Exhibit 8.16, the constant STATES is being used to control a looping action. If the change shown above in the immediately preceding example were made, the number of loops this loop would perform would automatically change also, as would the number of loops any other loop in the program would perform. This saves time: The developer does not need to try to run down and change all references to the numeric literal "50."

OPTION EXPLICIT STATEMENT

The Option Explicit statement is a statement, that, when inserted into the top of your model, forces you to use the Dim or Public statement to declare all variables. One of the most common mistakes is to misspell a variable name somewhere in the model. When this happens, the model identifies it as a new variable, and initializes it with a default value. The model will then use the default value from that point forward, the model producing incorrect results if it doesn't crash first.

Here is a parting remonstrative related to declaring variables (please take it to heart!):

- Always, always, always use the Option Explicit statement.
- Make variable names meaningful.
- Keep names short, but not so short you forget what they mean.
- Preface global variables with "g_," or "G_," or "G," so they can be identified at a glance.
- Always, always, always declare constants in uppercase.
- Write a **comment** at the end of each line where you declare a variable or a constant. Be sure to enter a clear and meaningful description of what the element is. This goes double (or maybe even triple) for all global elements!

PERFORMING CALCULATIONS WITH VARIABLES

Arithmetic operators are provided in VBA to build in-line calculation sequences. We have already seen the use of the "+" operator in the section on assignments

```
For i_state = 1 To STATES
  If state_id = g_state_postal(i_state) Then
    Assign_State_Number = i_state
    Exit For
  End If
Next i_state
```

EXHIBIT 8.16   Using the constant STATES to control a loop

EXHIBIT 8.17   Table of numeric operators for VBA data

Operator	Name	Example	Result
"+"	Addition	=10+5	15
"−"	Subtraction	=10−5	5
"−"	Negation	=−10	−10
"*"	Multiplication	=10*5	50
"/"	Division	=10/5	2
"%"	Percentage	=10%	0.10
"^"	Exponentiation	=10^5	100,000

to variables. This set of operations has an order of precedence for action. This precedence of operation is used when more than one operator is present in a formula. See Exhibit 8.17 for a list of the most common numeric VBA operators.

The set of operations in Exhibit 8.17 has an order of precedence of action: Negation, Percentage, Exponentiation, Multiplication and Division, Addition and Subtraction, Concatenation.

The order of precedence can be modified or controlled by the use of parentheses. In Exhibit 8.18, we can see three vary different results when different (or no) parentheses are applied to the same equation.

With no parentheses at all, the order of operation is: exponentiation, division and multiplication, and subtraction. We see the results of the default order of operational precedence in the lower example of Exhibit 8.18.

The use of parentheses to control the order of calculation is the same as that used in standard algebraic notation. If there is more than one set of operations taking place in a formula, parentheses should be used to visually clarify the code.

For example:

```
profit = units_sold * gross_margin - fixed_costs + overhead
```

With parentheses:

```
profit = (units_sold * gross_margin) - (fixed_costs + overhead)
```

EXHIBIT 8.18   How the use of parentheses affects the calculation order and outcomes

Formula	Step 1	Step 2	Step 3	Result
3^(15/5)*2−5	3^3*2−5	27*2−5	54−5	49
3^((15/5)*2−5)	3^(3*2−5)	3^(6−5)	3^1	3

Formula	Step 1	Step 2	Result
3^15/5*2−5	14.348,907/5*2−5	2,869,781*2−5	5,739,558

RANGES

No discussion of VBA variables and data can be complete without an examination of the Range command. From the standpoint of moving data into and out of the menus of the model, the Range command is indispensable! We will use the Range command many times in our modeling exercise and the sooner you get comfortable with it, the better. The Range command allows the developer to label a portion of any Excel worksheet and to refer to this region by name. The most appealing aspect of this is that, if you need to redesign any of your Excel worksheets, you can cut and paste a Range and the name you've assigned it will go with it. The model then knows where to input or output data with any other modification. The general form of the Range command is fairly straightforward and we have already seen it in the section of recorded VBA code we edited back in Chapter 6

In Exhibit 8.19, the Range command has a block of cells inside of it. It has been used to select the set of cells "B3:B6." As we see in the latter lines of this code fragment, it will perform various operations on the properties of these cell objects. Instead of referring to this set of cells by notation, we could have assigned them a name and referred to them by that name.

Naming a Range

We can assign Range names by selecting a portion of a worksheet and entering the name in the window at the upper left-hand corner of the worksheet. Here we name the outlined cells "m20Coupons" (see Exhibit 8.20).

Selecting a Range

In Exhibit 8.21, we have selected a field that specifies the minimum gross coupon for any loan selected into the portfolio. We have typed the name in the Range window and pressed **"Enter."** The Range name has now been added into a list of Range names for the workbook. If we want to confirm the extent of the Range, all we have to do is pulled down the Range Name Window, find the Range name on the list and press "Enter." The Range will then be selected automatically.

In Exhibit 8.21, the Range named "m5MinGrossCoupon" is displayed. Note how the last part of the name is displayed in the window box, while the first part of the name is displayed in the drop-down menu. This allows viewing a name that is too long to fit in the window box alone.

Editing a Range

You can also define, edit, or delete Ranges using the **"Insert => Name => Define"** menu. This menu will display a dialog box containing the current, selected portion

```
'Cells less than 5 = font blue, bold,
Range("B3:B36").Select
Selection.Font.FontStyle = "Bold"
Selection.Font.ColorIndex = 19
```

EXHIBIT 8.19   A very simple Range command that accesses Cells B3 to B6 in a column

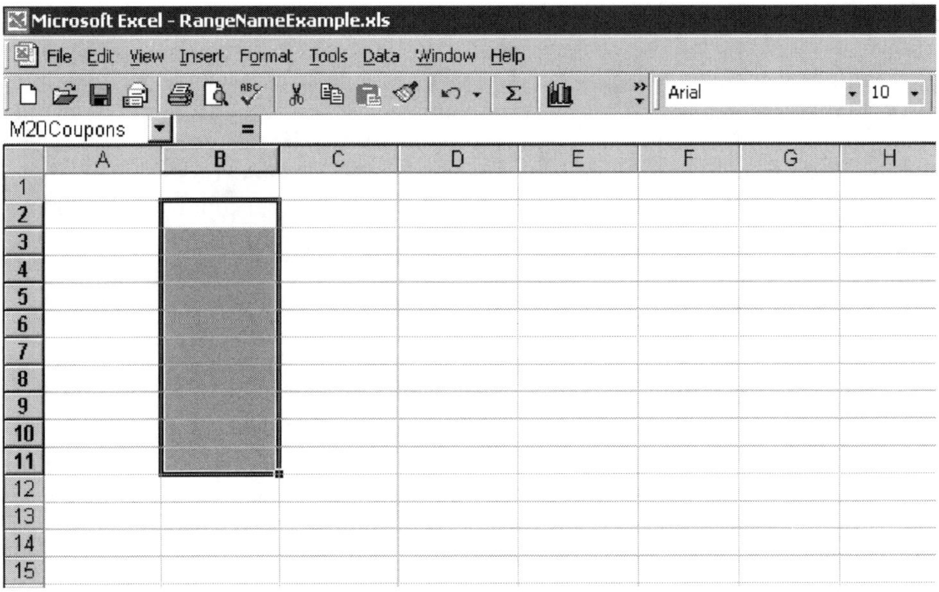

EXHIBIT 8.20   How to name a Range "m20Coupons"

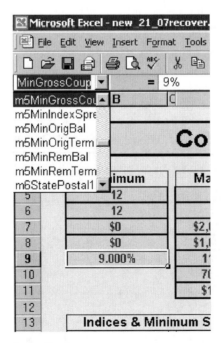

EXHIBIT 8.21   How to select a Range

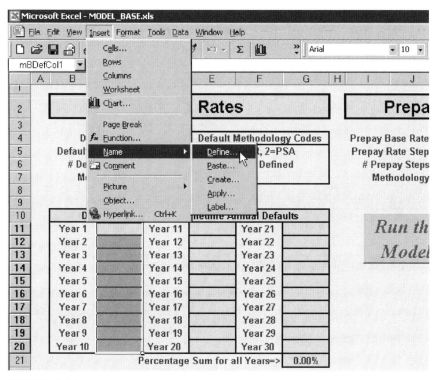

EXHIBIT 8.22 How to edit a Range

of the worksheet you are in, a list of all the Range names in the workbook, a line to enter a Range name, and a window to edit the currently selected cells. (See Exhibit 8.22.)

In Exhibit 8.23, the upper box is the initial appearance of the menu. The lower box indicates that a Range name has been selected and its reference location ID is shown below. You can now delete this Range by pressing **"Delete,"** modify it, or create a new Range by selecting **"Add."**

Referencing the Range

We can read the Range's information as in Exhibit 8.24, but we can also just as easily read the contents of the Range command in variables using a set of loops. This loop is set by a global **Const** to the dimensions of the Range and arrays.

In Exhibit 8.24 the constant named PAY_DATES controls how many times the loop will operate. Each time it does, it will select a value from one of the arrays and place it into an Excel cell that is part of the described Range.

This process can read-in scalars, vectors, or arrays.

Remember this is a two-way street. The process can also be reversed when we want to put the results of the model out to a file, or to a worksheet elsewhere in the model.

In Exhibit 8.25, the model is reading information into elements of an array from a variety of Ranges in the waterfall worksheet.

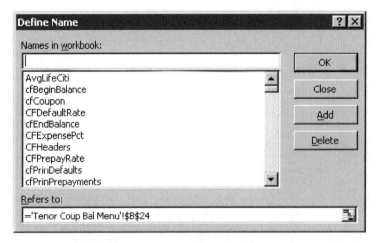

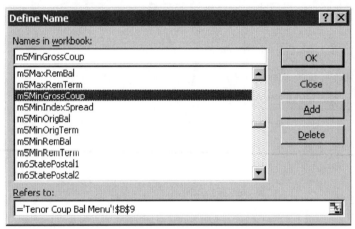

EXHIBIT 8.23   Selecting the Range name for editing

```
Range("TotalBeginPrincipal") = g_beg_collateral
For irow = 1 To PAY_DATES
    Range("cfPrinRegAmort").Cells(irow) = g_amort_prin(i_p, i_d, irow)
    Range("cfPrinPrepayments").Cells(irow) = g_prepay_prin(i_p, i_d, irow)
    Range("cfPrinDefaults").Cells(irow) = g_default_prin(i_p, i_d, irow)
    Range("cfPrinRecoveries").Cells(irow) = g_recover_prin(i_p, i_d, irow)
    Range("cfCoupon").Cells(irow) = g_coupon(i_p, i_d, irow)
Next irow
```

EXHIBIT 8.24   Using a constant to read the contents of a Range

```
'prepayment and default headers
    g_waterfall_misc(s, 1) = Range("CFDefaultRate")          'prepayment rate
    g_waterfall_misc(s, 2) = Range("CFPrepayRate")           'default rate
```

EXHIBIT 8.25   A number of values from single cells are being read into a number of array locations

```
Sub Update_Totals_Columns()

        Range("m3TotalNumLoans") = iloan
        Range("m3TotalCurBals") = grand_total
        Range("m3NumLoansRejected") = number_rejected
        Range("m3CurBalRejected") = rej_cur_bal
        Range("m3CurBalRejPct") = pct_rejected
        Range("m3NumLoansOK") = number_accepted
        Range("m3CurBalOK") = acc_cur_bal
        Range("m3CurBalOKPct") = pct_accepted
        Range("m3LoansOKWAC") = sum_wac_1
        Range("m3LoansOKWART") = sum_rem_1
        Range("m3LoansOKWASeason") = sum_sea_1

End Sub
```

EXHIBIT 8.26 Reading results out to a menu. In this case, menu "m3," the menu that displays the results of the collateral selection process

In Exhibit 8.26, the Range is used to write the value of a variable to a location on a menu.

You should note the fact that all of the Range names in this example start with the prefix "m3." In this designation, the "m" identifies them as Ranges on a menu, and the 3 stands for the Selection Progress Menu. These numbers are not specific to any menu order. You can assign them as you create each of the menus in turn. Just be orderly and consistent. The prefix "m#" is designed to help you, and anyone else looking at your code, quickly identify all the Ranges that belong to the same menu. You might alternatively use an abbreviation which is a combination of the letters making up the menu title. For example "mm" might prefix all Ranges on the main menu while "pcm" might be used for the Ranges of the Program Costs Menu.

As you will see in Chapter 12, "Main Program and Menus," as we build the model we will use a common prefix in all the names of the Ranges that relate to menu inputs. This prefix will take the form of "m#" where the "#" is a number specific to the menu that contains the Range name.

In Exhibit 8.27, the Range is used to read the value from a location on a menu into a variable. This is the exact reverse of the operation performed in Exhibit 8.26, the transfer of the value of a variable to a Range on a menu.

```
Sub Read_Program_Costs_Menu()

 Sheets("Program Costs Menu").Select
 Range("A1").Select

 'Read program costs section of the menu
 g_exp_service = Range("m2ServicerExp")/12#       'servicing fee
 g_exp_program = Range("m2ProgramExpenses")/12#   'program expenses
 g_trig_cleanup = Range("m2TrigCleanUpPct")       'principal reallocation trigger
 g_trig_3M_delinq = Range("m2Trig3MDelRate")      'principal reallocation trigger
 g_advance_rate = Range("m2AdvanceRate")          'conduit advance rate
 g_conduit_spread = Range("m2ConduitSpread")      'conduit financing spread

End Sub
```

EXHIBIT 8.27 Example of a VBA subroutine that reads Range values from a menu. In this case, menu "m2," a menu containing deal fee and expense rates

Using Ranges and Loops

Exhibit 8.28 provides an example of reading a menu with a list in a column format. Here the Range is not a single cell on the menu, as it was in the VBA code we saw in Exhibits 8.26 and 8.27. The constant named PORTFOLIO_REPORTS has a value of 11. The subroutine begins by selecting the worksheet "Reports Menu." This is the menu that contains the listing of the eligible collateral stratification reports and the cash flow summary matrix reports. The Ranges on this menu are prefixed with the designator "m4." The For . . . Next loop uses the variable i_rep as a counter. The value of i_rep will start at 1 and progress through 11, and then the loop will cease functioning. Inside the loop an array named g_report, which is a Boolean data type, will be initially assigned a value of "False." This means that unless the value is changed we will not produce that stratification report. The model now reads the Range. As we have outlined, the Range is not a single cell on the worksheet, but is instead a collection of cells. We will need to tell the model *which one* of the cells of the Range we are interested in reading! We do this by appending the suffix ".Cells(i_rep)" to the end of the Range command.

If the value of i_rep is 1, as it will be on the first iteration of the loop, the model will read the value that is in the first cell in the Range named "m4ReportsSelected." If that cell has an "X" in it, then the If . . . Then statement is "True" and we execute the next statement down. This next VBA statement sets the g_report array position of "1" to "True," meaning that the stratification report associated with this cell has been selected for production in the eligible Collateral Reports package. We then have completed the test and fall to the bottom of the loop. This operation will continue ten more times until all the cells that are contained in the Range named "m4ReportsSelected" have had their values checked, and the corresponding values of the g_report have been assigned as either "True" or "False."

Ranges are particularly helpful when the model needs to write a series of columnar results out to the Excel worksheet environment. In Exhibits 8.29, 8.30, and 8.31, you will see the VBA code that populates the Ranges of the waterfall spreadsheet.

```
Sub Read_Report_Selection_Menu()

    Sheets("Reports Menu").Select
    Range("A1").Select

    'collateral reports
    For i_rep = 1 To PORTFOLIO_REPORTS
        g_report(i_rep) = False
        If Range("m4ReportsSelected").Cells(i_rep) = "X" Then _
                g_report(i_rep) = True
    Next i_rep

    'matrix summary reports
    For i_rep = 1 To MATRIX_REPORTS
        g_matrix_report(i_rep) = False
        If Range("m4MatrixRepsSelected").Cells(i_rep) = "X" Then _
                g_matrix_report(i_rep) = True
    Next i_rep

End Sub
```

EXHIBIT 8.28   Using a loop to read a Range on a menu

This subroutine makes extensive use of the Range command. If fact, it uses little other than the Range command to perform its three functions. These functions are:

- Fill in the speeds and methodologies of the prepayment and default assumptions.
- Clear the contents of the five collateral cash flow vectors from the previous run of the model.
- Write the five collateral cash flow vectors for the current scenario now being run by the model.

We have already seen examples in Exhibits 8.26 and 8.28 that use the same form of Range command to perform the first and third functions.

With regard to the second function, "ClearContents," we should mention that a Range is a VBA object. Objects are elements in VBA that have special characteristics called "properties." The properties of objects can be acted upon by things called methods. Not all methods can act on all objects. The method named

```
Sub Load_Collateral_Cashflows(i_p, i_d)

    Application.Calculation = xlCalculationManual
    Sheets("CFWaterfall").Select

    'Fill in the prepayment and default speeds and methodologies in the header
    Range("CFDefaultRate") = g_default_rate(i_d)
    Range("CFPrepayRate") = g_prepay_rate(i_p)
    Select Case g_default_method
      Case Is = 1: Range("CFDefaultMethod") = "CPR"
      Case Is = 2: Range("CFDefaultMethod") = "PSA"
      Case Is = 3: Range("CFDefaultMethod") = "USR"
    End Select
    Select Case g_prepay_method
      Case Is = 1: Range("CFPrepayMethod") = "CPR"
      Case Is = 2: Range("CFPrepayMethod") = "PSA"
    End Select

    'Clear the contents of the spreadsheet columns that hold the collateral
       cash flows
    Range("cfPrinRegAmort").ClearContents
    Range("cfPrinPrepayments").ClearContents
    Range("cfPrinDefaults").ClearContents
    Range("cfPrinRecoveries").ClearContents
    Range("cfCoupon").ClearContents

    'Enter the beginning collateral balances and the cash flow components by period
    Range("TotalBeginPrincipal") = g_beg_collateral
    For irow = 1 To PAY_DATES
      Range("cfPrinRegAmort").Cells(irow) = g_amort_prin(i_p, i_d, irow)
      Range("cfPrinPrepayments").Cells(irow) = g_prepay_prin(i_p, i_d, irow)
      Range("cfPrinDefaults").Cells(irow) = g_default_prin(i_p, i_d, irow)
      Range("cfPrinRecoveries").Cells(irow) = g_recover_prin(i_p, i_d, irow)
      Range("cfCoupon").Cells(irow) = g_coupon(i_p, i_d, irow)
    Next irow

End Sub
```

EXHIBIT 8.29 The subroutine that populates the waterfall spreadsheet with the collateral cash flows for each scenario that was run by the model

Single Scenario Cash Flow Waterfall Report

		<= Default Rate
		<= Prepayment Rate

Summary Report	
Collateral Cash Flows	
Scheduled Amortization	
Prepayments to Principal	
Total Principal Retired	
Defaulted Principal	
Recoveries of Principal (& rate)	
Coupon Income	
Total Cash Sources	
Debt Cash Flows	
Program Fees	
Servicing Fee	
Conduit Debt Service	
Conduit Principal Payments	
Released to Seller	
Total Cash Uses	

1	2	3	4	5	6	7
	Collateral Cashflows					
	Beginning Principal Balance	**Pool Factor**	**Regular Amort Principal**	**Prepaid Principal**	**Defaulted Principal**	**Ending Principal Balance Outstanding**
			-	-	-	
1						
2						
3						
4						
5						
6						
7						
8						
9						
10						

Single Scenario Cash Flow Waterfall Report

500%	**PSA**	*<= Default Rate*
300%	**PSA**	*<= Prepayment Rate*

Summary Report		
Collateral Cash Flows		
Scheduled Amortization	148,766,543	
Prepayments to Principal	296,681,396	60.37%
Total Principal Retired	445,447,939	
Defaulted Principal	45,972,438	9.36%
Recoveries of Principal (& rate)	39,468,894	85.85%
Coupon Income	175,641,977	
Total Cash Sources	**660,558,809**	
Debt Cash Flows		
Program Fees	3,833,751	
Servicing Fee	15,594,605	
Conduit Debt Service	71,882,833	
Conduit Principal Payments	466,849,358	
Released to Seller	102,398,261	
Total Cash Uses	**660,558,809**	

1	2	3	4	5	6	7
	Collateral Cashflows					
	Beginning Principal Balance	**Pool Factor**	**Regular Amort Principal**	**Prepaid Principal**	**Defaulted Principal**	**Ending Principal Balance Outstanding**
			148,766,543	**296,681,396**	**45,972,438**	
1	491,420,377	1.00000	1,922,577	245,111	625,070	488,627,619
2	488,627,619	0.99432	1,932,678	488,733	655,909	485,550,299
3	485,550,299	0.98805	1,941,720	730,431	685,446	482,192,702
4	482,192,702	0.98122	1,949,686	969,773	713,779	478,559,465
5	478,559,465	0.97383	1,956,557	1,206,333	740,894	474,655,681
6	474,655,681	0.96589	1,962,318	1,439,693	766,589	470,487,082
7	470,487,082	0.95740	1,966,956	1,669,438	790,885	466,059,803
8	466,059,803	0.94839	1,970,462	1,895,168	813,360	461,380,813
9	461,380,813	0.93887	1,972,826	2,116,490	834,295	456,457,202

EXHIBIT 8.30 Cash flow waterfall worksheet before and after read to Range action

"ClearContents," however, is a very useful one when you need to clear the values and formulas out of the set of cells that are contained in a Range. If we attach this method to a Range object, as in the VBA subroutine in Exhibit 8.29, VBA immediately blanks all values and formulas in every cell in the Range specified. One command, BANG!, and they are all gone! In the case of one of the Ranges, the "cfCoupon" Range, all 360 cells of it, are immediately set to "," or NULL.

There are many interesting methods that can be used with Ranges, but the use of the "ClearContents" is one of the easiest to understand. These methods are what make Ranges very useful to the VBA modeler seeking to manage the appearance and functionality of the Excel portions of the model.

Exhibits 8.30 and 8.31 display the appearance of the cash flow waterfall before and after the action of this subroutine.

OBJECTS

In addition to performing calculations and manipulating data within VBA, you will need to modify the Excel environment to successfully complete the model.

Excel is organized into groups of objects. Some are familiar to you already, a few may be new to you. Common Excel objects are:

- **Application.** The global environment of the model
- **Workbook.** A collection of worksheet objects
- **Worksheet.** A collection of cells and Ranges
- **Range.** Collections of one or more cells
- **Cells.** One of the most basic objects, a place for performing formatting, data, and calculation actions

What Is an Object?

For VBA, an Excel object is something that you can see and manipulate in some way. Objects are described and manipulated by changing the characteristics of their properties. You can change their physical appearances, enter data into them, sort their contents, and change their fonts and font sizes, among other things. In addition, most properties of commonplace objects can easily be changed through simple assignment statements, much as we would assign values to any other variable.

Properties of Objects

If VBA recognized a "human" as an object, here are some of the object properties it might see:

- Height
- Weight
- Hair color
- Eye color
- Gender
- Marital status
- Employment status
- Highest educational level attained
- Voter registration status

Then you might see VBA code such as the one shown in Exhibit 8.31.

Using Recorded VBA Code to Examine Object Properties

One of the easiest ways to examine the most commonly used objects is to read the code generated by recorded macros. As you make changes to the properties of an object while you are recording VBA code, the recorder function will generally list all properties that can be edited for the object you are working on, whether you have actively edited them or not.

```
Range("Humanity").Human(individual).Select
With Selection
    .Height = 65                    'inches
    .Weight = 110                   'pounds
    .HairColor = 3                  'red
    .EyeColor=24                    'green
    .Gender = xlFemale              'also xlMale
    .MaritalStaus = xlMarried       'or xlSingle,xlSeperated,xlDivorced,xlWidowed
    .Employed = True                'also False
    .Education = xlGradSchool       'also xlHSchool, xlCollege, xlPhD, xlpostDoc
    .VoterRegistered = True         'also False
Selection End
```

EXHIBIT 8.31   What a "human" object might look like to VBA

While this feature has the drawback of producing large amounts of code that does not do anything, it is informative as to the underlying structure of the object and the hierarchy of the property levels.

Every object has properties. These properties are its defining characteristics, and they control the object's position and appearance in the application. We can employ VBA to initialize or dynamically change the appearance of most object properties while a model is running. For example, we may have a large report and wish to draw the reader's attention to a particular set of numbers. However, we may wish to do this only when the numbers exceed a specific value. An example would be losses to the Seller Interest greater than zero, or perhaps losses to the conduit financing position greater than zero. We could even use a program logic statement to apply a color to the object based on a particular value, say the level of the severity of the loss.

Assigning Values to Objects

If we use the code in Exhibit 8.32, we can change the font color of an Excel cell to red (3 is the color code for red) whenever the value of the cell is greater than zero.

We first recorded a macro in which a series of cells were colored-in by using the "Format =>Cells" menu in Excel.

In these samples of recorded VBA code, we will see a more complete listing of the **Cell.Font** properties. It is interesting to note that each of these properties has a one-to-one correspondence with the items on the "**Format=>Cells=>Font**" submenu in the Excel editor. The block in Exhibit 8.33 is a list of general properties of cells, the upper-right a listing of cell borders, and the lower-right of display formats.

Two code fragments in Exhibit 8.33 display the method of assigning values to objects. The first example is the formatting command for the font of a single cell, the second is that of formatting a three-digit number in a cell or Range.

```
If Cells(irow,icol).value > 0.0 Then
    Cells(irow,icol).Font.ColorIndex = 3
End If
```

EXHIBIT 8.32   Call this the "In the RED" macro. Example of displaying an Excel font in red when the dollar amount displayed is less than zero

```
Range("DG8").Select
With Selection.Font
     .Name = "Arial"
     .Size = 10
     .Strikethrough = False
     .Superscript = False
     .Subscript = False
     .OutlineFont = False
     .Shadow = False
     .Underline = xlUnderlineStyleNone
     .ColorIndex = xlAutomatic
End With

Selection.NumberFormat = "#,##0.000"
```

EXHIBIT 8.33   Assigning values to objects

Most if not all object properties can be set directly by the use of VBA commands. You just have to know the name of the object and the name of the property or properties you want to modify. Some properties have sub-properties. The font property of a cell object also has the sub-properties of background, bold, color, color index, font style, italic, name, size, strikethrough, subscript, superscript, and underline.

Methods of Objects

While properties describe what an object is, methods describe what an object does.

Most Excel objects have between 10 to 150 methods that can be applied against them. For the purposes of this instruction, we will use only a tiny fraction of the most common of them. An example of the methods that can be used with the workbook object are "Activate," "Close," "Protect," "Save," "Save As," and "Unprotect."

```
ActiveWorkbook.Save
ActiveWorkbook.Close
```

The above VBA statements will save and close a template file into which a series of reports have been written.

```
ActiveWorkbook.SaveAs Filename: = g_filename_output
```

The above statement will save the current file to the name of the value of the variable on the right of the equal sign.

BUILDING A MENU FROM SCRATCH

We now have all the information we need to build a working menu. So let us try to build one!

Geographic Selection Menu

One of the first menus we will have to build is a Geographic Selection Menu. This menu will allow us to select loans based on their geographic location. We can include or exclude loans in the portfolio by entering our intentions on this menu.

For example, there might be a prohibition about putting any loans from a particular region or state into the collateral portfolio. This may arise if a state has a particularly adverse delinquency or default history, or if the inclusion of loans from the state may trigger concentration issues. Whatever the reason, we need to design a menu that will allow us to do the following operations:

- Display a listing of all the states in alphabetical order, accompanied by their two letter postal codes.
  - Include a set of check boxes next to each loan name to allow us to either select it for inclusion in the portfolio or deselect it.
  - Feature action buttons that let us select/deselect loans by region. There will be two action buttons for selecting/deselecting at the National level and an additional two each for selecting/deselecting the New England, Mid-Atlantic, Southeast, Southwest, Midwest, and Northwest regions.
  - We also want an action button to run the model from this screen.
  - All of the data is to be identified by Range names so we can read it into the VBA.

After we have completed the design of the menu, we will then declare global variables to hold the following information:

- The selection status of the loans of each individual state. This will be a Boolean variable that can assume a value of either True or False, depending upon whether the state is selected for inclusion or exclusion from the portfolio.
- The name of the state.
- The postal code of the state.
- A constant for the number of states and territories.

We have a menu design criteria as follows: The background of the menus will be in light yellow. All explanatory text will be in black. The text for all input fields will be blue font, with a light-gray background. The font will be Arial. All menus will have a title block. Every effort will be made to have all the menu information immediately visible in a standard single screen. The text for the "Run the Model" action button will be in red.

If we follow these criteria, the first draft of the Geographic Selection Menu might look something like that shown in Exhibit 8.34.

The menu in Exhibit 8.34 meets all the general formatting and appearance specifications we set forth for the model, and can be constructed with no knowledge of VBA whatsoever. We have listed the regions at the right side of the menu. The states are displayed in three parallel columns so that they will be visible on a single screen. The "Run the Program" button is created, but not linked to a macro. The same is true for all the "Include" and "Exclude" buttons of the regions.

Geographic Selections Menu

X	AK	Alaska	X	MA	Massachusettes	X	OR	Oregon	National	Include	Exclude
X	AL	Alabama	X	MD	Maryland	X	PA	Pennsylvania	New England	Include	Exclude
X	AR	Arkansas		ME	Maine		RI	Rhode Island	Mid-Atlantic	Include	Exclude
X	AZ	Arizona	X	MI	Michigan	X	SC	South Carolina	South East	Include	Exclude
X	CA	California	X	MN	Minnesota	X	SD	South Dakota	Midwest	Include	Exclude
X	CO	Colorado	X	MO	Missouri	X	TN	Tennessee	South West	Include	Exclude
X	CT	Connecticut	X	MS	Mississippi	X	TX	Texas	North West	Include	Exclude
X	DE	Delaware	X	MT	Montana		UT	Utah			
X	FL	Florida	X	NC	North Carolina	X	VA	Virginia	*Run the*		
X	GA	Georgia	X	ND	North Dakota		VT	Vermont	*Program*		
X	HI	Hawaii	X	NE	Nebraska	X	WA	Washington			
X	IA	Iowa		NH	New Hampshire	X	WI	Wisconsin			
X	ID	Idaho	X	NJ	New Jersey	X	WV	West Virginia			
X	IL	Illinois	X	NM	New Mexico	X	WY	Wyoming			
X	IN	Indiana	X	NV	Nevada	X	DC	Dist of Col			
X	KS	Kansas	X	NY	New York	X	VI	US Virgin Is			
X	KY	Kentucky	X	OH	Ohio	X	GM	US Marians Is			
X	LA	Louisana	X	OK	Oklahoma	X	PR	Puerto Rico			

EXHIBIT 8.34 Basic Geographic Selection Menu

Building the Ranges into the Menu

The next step is to designate the Ranges we will use on the menu to access the data. We will use the following Ranges:

- Cells B4:B21, cells F4:F21, and cells J4:J21 will be given the Range names of "m6States1," "m6States2," and "m6States3," respectively.
- Cells C4:C21, cells E4:E21, and cells K4:K21 will be given the Range names of "m6StatesPostal1," "m6_StatesPostal2," "m6StatesPostal3," respectively.
- Cells D4:D21, cells G4:G21, and cells L4:L21 will be given the Range names of "m6StatesName1," "m6StatesName2," and "m6StatesName3," respectively.

Each of the above Ranges is eighteen cells long. This is due to the fact that in addition to the fifty states we also have to include some of the territories of the United Sates, namely the Virgin Islands, the Mariana Islands, Puerto Rico, and the District of Columbia, for a total of fifty-four. It also conveniently puts everything we need to see and do on a single page. You will also notice that each of the Range names is prefixed with the alphanumeric "m6_" which will serve to immediately identify it as belonging to this menu when we see it referenced inside the VBA code.

Setting Up the Global Variables and Constants

Declaring Constants to Help Read the Menu Contents

There are a total of fifty states and four territories in the Geographic Menu listing that we can select from. When we read the information from this menu, we will probably use the For . . . Next looping structure that we saw in the "Using Ranges and Loops" section earlier. We will probably have several loops in the program that will want to examine the entire list of geographic entries. If we declare a constant in the name STATES, we can use it as a loop terminus, and if we declare a constant of STATES_PER_COL we can use that to peruse each of the columns of the menu. We will add these declarations to the **"A_Constants"** VBA Module we created in Chapter 6.

```
Public Const STATES = 54
Public Const STATES_PER_COL = 18
```

Once these are declared, we can use them to build the code and dimension the arrays we will use to hold the geographic data.

Declaring the Global Variables that Support the Geographic Menu   We will need to declare global variables for the following three sets of information contained in this menu: the selection status of the state, the postal code of the state, and the name of the state.

We need to create three names for the arrays and we have to decide on what type of variable we will declare them to be. Based on the type of data involved the following declarations are appropriate:

Array Contents	Array Name	Variable Type
Selection status (selected/not selected)	g_state_select	Boolean
Postal code of the state	g_state_postal	String
Full name of the state	g_state_name	String

We will place these declarations in the **"A_Global"** Module of the model. Since we know that the size of the arrays will not change during the run of the program and the number of STATES (54) is fixed, we will use the constant STATES to dimension them.

```
Public g_state_select(1 to STATES) as Boolean  !selection status for individual states
Public g_state_postal(1 to STATES) as String   !postal codes of individual states
Public g_state_name(1 to STATES) as String      !names of individual states
```

We now have all the variables we need to declare to support the model.

Reading the Data into the Variables

We have the layout of the menu complete. Range names are attached to all of the input fields. We have declared the variable arrays we are going to put the menu information into. Lastly we have created a pair of constants to help us dimension the arrays.

Now is the time to link the menu to the VBA code.

```
Sub Read_Geographic_Menu()

    Sheets("Geographic Menu").Select
    Range("A1").Select
    i_state = 0
    g_num_select_states = 0
    For icol = 1 To 3
      For irow = 1 To STATES_PER_COL
        i_state = i_state + 1
        g_state_select(i_state) = False
        g_state_postal(i_state) = Range("m6StatePostal" & icol).Cells(irow)
        g_state_name(i_state) = Range("m6StatesNames" & icol).Cells(irow)
        g_state_id_number(i_state) = i_state
        If Range("m6States" & icol).Cells(irow) <> "" Then
          g_state_select(i_state) = True
          g_num_select_states = g_num_select_states + 1
        End If
      Next irow
    Next icol

End Sub
```

EXHIBIT 8.35   Subroutine to read the contents of the Geographic Menu

The first thing we will do is to create a subroutine whose task is to read the contents of this menu and name it "Read_Geographic_Menu." As we develop the model we will have a separate VBA subroutine for each menu. These subroutines will read whatever input information is contained in the menu.

We will place this subroutine in the VBA code module named **"Menus_Read_Inputs."**

The information is in three columns. The three columns on the menu are each 18 cells long. We have created a constant named STATES_PER_COL. We will use this to read each of the three columns and store the contents of those columns in the global arrays.

The code for that functionality is shown in Exhibit 8.35.

The subroutine performs the following:

Step 1. Finds the "Geographic Menu" worksheet and displays it. It selects the cell A1, which places the cursor in the uppermost left hand corner of the displayed menu area, so that the maximum amount of the menu is visible on the screen. It sets a counter variable, "i_state = 0." (We will discuss the use of "i_state" in Step 3). Note that by giving the spreadsheet that contains the menu a clearly identifying name "Geographic Menu," we can immediately understand what is happening in this phase of the VBA code operation.

Step 2. Starts a set of loops. The overall structure of the subroutine is a pair of nested For...Next loops. The outermost loop will loop three times and stop, one for each of the columns on the Geographic Menu. The counter for this loop is the variable "icol." The second loop inside the first loop will loop 18 times, the value of the STATES_PER_COL constant for each time that the outer loop executes. The counter for this loop is the variable "irow." This means that whatever code is in the middle of these two loops will be executed (3∗18) or 54 times, the number of states and territories on the menu.

Step 3. Each time we are in the inner loop we must determine which column we are in and which row of that column we are in. Each row in each column is therefore a separate and distinct entity. We have one complicating factor and that is to load our arrays in order from three groups of 18 items each to one group numbering 1 to 54. The way we will do this is to keep count of each time we read information from the Ranges into the global arrays. We will use the variable "i_state." Each time an operation is performed in the innermost loop, the value of the variable i_state will increase by one: "i_state = i_state+1." In this way the variable i_state is keeping track of the number of states and their position in the overall array without regard to their position in the columns of the menu. The first state in the second column will be correctly put into the nineteenth position of each of the global variables.

Step 4. We must also remember that we are reading from three different Ranges when we read the data. In the first column of the menu, all of the Ranges end in the number "1," in the second column "2," and in the third column "3." Therefore we can just append these numbers to the base name of the Range to read the contents of the correct column. The operator that concatenates this is the "&" sign. Therefore "m6States & 1" gives the results of "m6States1." Also remember how we read multiple cells in a Range. If we wanted to read the sixth cell in the Range XYZ, then we would use the statement of Range("XYZ").Cells(6).

Step 5. Each time the inner loop executes it will combine the number of the column of the outer loop with the name of the Range and read the current row of that particular Range. It will then place the information in the i_state slot in the global data array.

Hooking Up the Include/Exclude Regional Action Buttons

We want to provide the user with the ability to include or exclude sets of states by region. The easiest way to do this is to write a small macro that turns the selection switch for each state in the region either on or off based on the action desired.

We can then use the **"Tools=>Macro=>Assign Macro"** menu to link the button with the macro.

For now, the macro can simple put an "X" in the state location of each state of the region by its cell location in the menu, or exclude it by putting in a blank "." See Exhibit 8.36.

Now all we have to do is link up each of the subroutines with the appropriate button. To do this we click on the button with the right mouse button and select **"Assign Macro,"** just as we would do in Excel if we wanted to connect a button to a recorded macro instead of a subroutine we had written. A small window appears named **"Assign Macro."** Scroll down until we find the subroutine we want to link to the button, select it, and select the **"OK"** button. You have linked the button to the subroutine and are finished! This is button support code, so we will place this code in the module **"Z_Button_Subs."**

```
Sub Include_New_England()
    Cells(10, 2).Value = "X"        'Connecticut
    Cells(4, 6).Value = "X"         'Massachusetts
    Cells(6, 6).Value = "X"         'Maine
    Cells(15, 6).Value = "X"        'New Hampshire
    Cells(6, 10).Value = "X"        'Rhode Island
    Cells(13, 10).Value = "X"       'Vermont
End Sub
Sub Exclude_New_England()
    Cells(10, 2).Value = ""         'Connecticut
    Cells(4, 6).Value = ""          'Massachusetts
    Cells(6, 6).Value = ""          'Maine
    Cells(15, 6).Value = ""         'New Hampshire
    Cells(6, 10).Value = ""         'Rhode Island
    Cells(13, 10).Value = ""        'Vermont
End Sub
```

EXHIBIT 8.36   Button support VBA subroutines for the Geographic Menu

Hooking Up the "Run the Model" Action Button

The subroutine that we need to hook the "Run the Model" button up to is not created yet. We will call the subroutine "Loan_Financing_Model."

It does not exist yet, so we will need to create it. We will place this subroutine in the "**A_Main_Program**" module that we created back in Chapter 5. Then it will be ready when we start to develop the model in later chapters. By hooking this action button to the module, we will have finished the implementation of the menu.

Until we develop the model further we cannot do anything more.

You have created your first menu from scratch!

Congratulations!

DELIVERABLES CHECKLIST

The VBA Knowledge Checklist for this chapter is:

- The six most commonly used variable types: Integer, Date, Long, Double, String, and Boolean.
- How to declare variables, how to comment them, and how to assign values and data to them.
- How to use variables in calculations.
- The three types of scope for VBA variables; local, module, and global.
- How to name variables. The suggested naming conventions for global scope variables.
- Use of constants to dimension arrays and control loops across the model.
- Use of the Option Explicit statement to force the declaration and type of all variables in the model.
- What a Range on an Excel worksheet is. How Ranges are used to design menus.
- How to create, name, select, edit, and reference a Range location from Excel.
- How to transfer data from a Range in an Excel worksheet to a VBA variable in a VBA module.

- How to use Ranges in combinations with loops to read columns or tables of data into VBA variables.
- What an object is. That all objects have properties that describe their characteristics.
- That all objects have methods that allow you to modify them or trigger them to perform operations.

The Model Knowledge Checklist for this chapter is:

- The seven roles that menus play in models and model development
- The structural elements of a well-designed model; the header, the body, the fields, the explanatory text, action buttons, and message windows
- Three basic tenets of menu design: clarity, simplicity, and specificity

NEXT STEPS

We have now learned about the most common and useful forms of variables. We have learned how to write calculations using variables, and what Ranges are.

We have created a menu, and provided VBA code to transfer the information from the Excel interface to the VBA variables.

In Chapter 9, we will learn how to control the flow of the VBA code. We will cover some items that we have seen before, specifically how to create subroutines, and how to use the For ... Next type of loop, and If ... Then ... Else ... End If statements to make decisions between various alternatives. We will also learn various other flow control constructs that you have yet to see.

ON THE WEB SITE

One the Web site we will find the model in progress file named "MODEL_BASE_Chap08.xls."

This model is immediately different from its immediate predecessor in the Chapter 6 Web site materials in that it now contains no less than seven new worksheets. Six of these are menus. They are the Main, Program Cost, Defaults, Collateral Criteria, Geographic, and Reports Selection menus. The seventh worksheet is not a menu at all but instead it is a screen that will display the results of the collateral selection process. In back of these menus we have taken our first concrete steps in building the model.

If we enter the VBA Editor, we will find, in addition to the new menus, the model contains three new VBA modules. The contents of these modules support the menus that we have just created. In them we will declare the constants and global variables that we will use to capture the information input by the model user into the menu screens.

The first of these new modules, **"A_Constants"** contains a set of constants that we have declared to help us later on when we seek to read the inputs from the various menus we have created. The second named **"A_Globals"** contains a long list of global variables. We can see by the comments we placed there that these variables serve two purposes.

The first list corresponds to all menu entries. The second grouping refers to all the data we will read, on a loan-by-loan basis, from the portfolio information file, **"portfolio_orig.xls."**

With the foundation of these constants and Public variables we are ready to begin writing several core pieces of VBA code for the model. These are the error checking subroutines for each of the menus, the input reading subroutines for these same menus once the data has been checked and approved, and the code to read the contents of the collateral data file.

In addition we find an additional module **"A_MainProgram."** This module contains our first attempt at outlining the master subroutine of the model. This is the subroutine that will call all others but be called in turn by none. In it we can see the basic framework of high-level tasks that we will need to complete during a model run.

We will have to error check the inputs from the menus, read the checked inputs from the menus into the model, read the contents of the portfolio data file, select the eligible collateral, produce collateral reports, produce cash flows, run the cash flows through the waterfall, and print the output reports.

This first attempt at the Main Program gives us the broad outlines of the model. In successive chapters we will fill in the blanks and bring our model to completion.

## CHAPTER 9

Controlling the Flow of the Model

OVERVIEW

Models and stories have three things in common, a beginning, middle, and an end. Models usually start by reading data and collecting additional information from their users and other sources. The middle part of a model's story is processing that data into the desired results, and monitoring itself so it knows when to stop. The end is the output of the results in the expected formats to the user. Obviously this is the theory at the highest level of abstraction. The hard part is getting the model to perform the above steps in a correct, efficient, and intelligible manner.

To that end, we need to lay out the sequence of operations the model needs to perform, and then control the operation of the model so that it completes its work in accordance with our wishes. VBA provides the developer with several different ways of controlling the flow of the model.

These fall into two main groups:

1. **Decision Structures.** Code that performs a test on its environment and then decides what to do next based on the results of the test
2. **Looping Structures.** Code that executes a set of statements inside the bounds of a loop for a fixed or variable number of iterations

We have already seen one of each of these structures:

```
Typical Decision Structure --  If...Then...Else Statement
Typical Looping Structure --  For...Next  Statement
```

We will now reexamine these two statements and show you others.

DELIVERABLES

The VBA Language Knowledge deliverables for this chapter are:

- The types of Decision Structures in the VBA language that allow the modeler to make choices between alternatives based on either simple or compound test conditions.
- The types of Looping Structures in the VBA language that allow the user to repeat groups of statements for either a fixed or variable number of repetitions.

- The six basic logical operators for Decision Statements, "<" less than, "<=" less than or equal to, ">" greater than, ">=" greater than or equal to, "<>" not equal to, and "=" equal to.
- How to set up simple and compound decision tests for use in decision statements.
- How to use variables, constants, and numerical values in decision testing.
- The use of the reserved words .AND. and .OR. to link simple decision tests into compound decision tests.
- The use of the If...Then...Else statement to make one or two alternative decision tests. The use of nested statements of this type to make 3-choice or 4-choice decision statements.
- Use of the Select...Case decision statement to make decisions between three or more choices. This is also the preferred statement to use when you want to make a series of sequential choices.
- Use of the For...Next looping structure to repeatedly execute a series of VBA statements a pre-determined number of times.
- How to nest For...Next loops, and some possible pitfalls that can degrade your model's performance.
- The use of the Exit For statement to end a For...Next looping structure before the number of pre-determined repetitions have completed.
- The use of the Do...While and Do...Until looping structures to repeatedly execute a set of VBA statements an indeterminate number of times, based on satisfying decision test criteria.
- What a VBA subroutine is and how subroutines are used to construct models.
- How the program uses subroutines to perform its tasks.
- What a VBA function is, and how its functions differ from subroutines.

The Modeling Knowledge deliverables of this chapter are:

- Examples of how to use simple and complex decision structures to route the model code.
- Practical examples of simple and nested If...Then...Else decision structures.
- Various uses of the Select...Case statement to route output, select among calculation methodologies, assign selection criteria values, control report formatting, construct error messages, and control subroutine call selections.
- How to use simple and nested looping structures, especially nested For...Next statements.
- The combination of using For...Next and Select...Case statements to sequentially execute a series of ordered choices.
- The dangers of using nested looping structures. This can lead to unnecessary work by the model.
- The use of conditional looping structures such as Do...While and Do...Until statements.
- How to design efficient subroutines that have a clear, specialized, and distinct purpose.
- How to decide between the use of a function or a subroutine to perform a specialized task.
- Examples of subroutine hierarchies and how to think about building effective subroutine hierarchies in the model.

UNDER CONSTRUCTION

We have another day off!

Although we will look at a lot of code and learn some of the most important commands of the VBA language in this chapter, we will not add anything else to the model at this time.

DECISION STRUCTURES

Logical Operators

In an earlier part of the presentation we examined arithmetic operators used in calculations. We will now examine logical operators used to construct decision tests. You will note that many of the expressions listed in Exhibit 9.1 are identical to their common use in algebra. We will use these six operators to describe a particular condition. Based on the Boolean result of the condition (either TRUE or FALSE), the model will typically decide between two or more alternatives and execute a set of VBA statements. A simple example is "a<b." If a=1 and b=3 then the Boolean value of "a<b" is TRUE. If "a" has a value of 5 instead, the value of the expression "a<b" would be FALSE. Exhibit 9.1 lists all logical operators.

Using Logical Operators to Build Tests

Logical operators can be used to design a wide variety of tests. They can be used to construct very simple two-element comparisons ("a to b"), or much more complex combinations of computed or multiple-condition compound tests. The following example illustrates the Range of simple comparisons that can be constructed. We will first look at a series of paring between a variable named "large_account" and "small_account." The next section will then show examples of using variables, numerical values, and constants in decision tests.

Exhibit 9.2 lists all the resultant Boolean values of a test between two variables, named small_acccout and large_account. The value of the variable large_account is $175,000 and the value of the variable small_account is $20,000.

EXHIBIT 9.1   VBA logical operators

	Logical Evaluation
=	Equal To
<	Less Than
<=	Less Than or Equal To
>	Greater Than
>=	Greater Than or Equal To
<>	Not Equal To

EXHIBIT 9.2   Tests between two variables

Symbol	Logical Evaluation
account_large = account_small	FALSE
account_large < account_small	FALSE
account_large <= account_small	FALSE
account_large > account_small	TRUE
account_large >= account_small	TRUE
account_large <> account_small	TRUE

Building Decision Tests

Decision tests can be constructed between any combination of variables, constants, numbers or computed values. Exhibit 9.3 displays a variety of these examples:

Using AND or OR to Build Logical Tests

The logical operators .AND. and .OR. are used to build compound decision tests.

```
                    condition01 .AND. condition02
If condition01 is True and condition02 is True then the entire test is True.
If either condition01 or condition02 is False the combined condition is False.
If both condition01 and condition02 is False then the combined condition is False.


                    condition01 .OR. condition02
If condition01 is True or condition02 is True then the combined condition is True.
If both condition01 and condition02 is True, then the combined condition is True.
If both condition01 and condition02 are False then the combined condition is False.
```

These operators can also be combined in a variety of ways, much like you would use them in Excel statements in the cell of a worksheet:

```
( (Condition01 AND Condition02) AND (Condition03 OR Condition04) )
```

The If . . . Then . . . Else Statement

Now that we have seen how to use the logical operators of VBA and how to set up both simple and compound decision conditions, we can put these features to work.

The If . . . Then . . . Else statement is possibly the most ubiquitous statement in any VBA model. It is the elementary building block for creating the ability to make simple "this or that" choices based on almost any condition imaginable. In addition, this statement can be embedded within itself to construct ladders of simple decisions, one dependent upon the next.

```
                    account_small <= 175000
                account_small <= (175000 * owner_pct)
          account_small  =  (account_large / FED_RES_PCT)
          account_small  <> account_large + (down_pay * min_rate)
(account_small * pay_down)    <    (account_large + (a_bal * b_pct))
```

EXHIBIT 9.3   Use of logical operators to construct decision tests

The most simple form of this statement is the test of a condition, which, if TRUE, leads to an action and, if FALSE, leads to no action.

```
If condition Then execute this VBA statement
```

The next simplest form of the statement leads to a choice of actions. In this form, if the condition is TRUE execute one set of VBA statements; if it is FALSE execute another, different, set of VBA statements.

```
If condition1 Then
      VBA statements executed if condition1 is True
Else
      VBA statements executed if condition1 is False
End If
```

As shown in Exhibit 9.4, it is also possible to nest If . . . Then . . . Else statements within each other. This occurs when it is necessary to make a decision based on a sequence of conditions.

An example of a nested If . . . Then . . . Else statement can be seen in Exhibit 9.5. Here the program checks the setting of a Boolean variable named go_ok. If the value of go_ok is True, it means that all the checking done in the subroutine "ErrCheck_ALL_Menus" has not turned up any problems. All of our inputs are valid and we can proceed. In this case, the program will run until it meets another If . . . Then statement, which tests to see if we are asking to have the two sets of cash flow reports—the Cash Flow Waterfall Report package and/or the Summary Matrix Report package—printed out.

The test, shown in Exhibit 9.5, checks to see if the value of the Boolean variable go_ok is TRUE. If it is TRUE, then there are no menu data errors. The program proceeds to call a series of subroutines that selects the collateral and loads the cash flow calculation assumptions. A second nested If . . . Then . . . Else statement checks the values of g_out_matrix to determine if is TRUE (do we print Summary Matrix Report package) or if g_out_cfdetail is TRUE (do we print the Waterfall Report package).

As pointed out before, this is one of the most widely used decision statements. The completed model has over 500 of them! There is one problem with the

```
If condition1 Then
    If condition2 Then
        Statements executed if condition1 is True and condition2 is True
    Else
        Statements executed if condition1 is True and condition2 is False
    End If
Else
    If condition3 Then
        Statements executed if condition1 is False and condition3 is True
    Else
      Statements executed if condition1 is False and condition3 is False
    End If
End If
```

EXHIBIT 9.4   An example of nested If . . . Then . . . Else statements

```
If(g_loan_season(iloan)+im-1) Mod g_loan_reset_rate(iloan)=0 Then 'its a reset month

    now_rate = g_index_levels(im, ifloat) + g_loan_spread(iloan)

    'two checks for limits on periodic resets
    If now_rate >= g_Joan_reset_cap(iloan) + beg_rate Then
       now_rate = beg_rate + g_loan_reset_cap(iloan)
    End If
    If now_rate <= beg_rate - g_loan_reset_floor(iloan) Then
       now_rate = beg_rate - g_loan_reset_floor(iloan)
    End If

    'check results against the lifetime cap and floor for the loan
    If now_rate >= g_loan_life_cap(iloan) Then now_rate = g_loan_life_cap(iloan)
    If now_rate <= g_loan_life_floor(iloan) Then now_rate = g_loan_life_floor(iloan)

    'reset the beginning rate to this rate
    g_loan_coupon(iloan, im) = now_rate
    beg_rate = now_rate

Else

    g _loan_coupon(iloan, im) = beg_rate

End If
```

EXHIBIT 9.5   An If...Then...Else and If...Then statement that set the coupon rate for a floating rate note for a given month

If...Then...Else statement. It can become confusing if the statements are nested more than three layers deep. This is especially the case if each of the layers contains compound conditions. Always try to keep your If...Then...Else statements simple and concise. Avoid the use of compound or multiple-compound conditions wherever possible. Instead of nesting If...Then...Else statements to make choices between multiple alternatives, there is another decision statement that we can use.

Select...Case Statement

Sometimes it is necessary to choose a single option out of a list of options. When you are faced with selecting one alternative from among three or more possible alternatives, you will find that the Select...Case statement is your best bet. The Select...Case statement is more efficient and much easier to read and understand than a series of nested If...Then...Else statements. It allows you to set out a hierarchical list of conditions and, working from top to bottom, select the first condition that meets the requirements; it then executes a block of statements based on that choice. Each test can be individually tailored to the decision at hand. If all preceding tests fail, you can designate an additional default condition test called a Case Else choice. This default clause is placed at the end of the statement block. The default case action will activate after all other cases fail. It is especially useful when it is built into the structure as a catchall or error-trapping feature.

Each option of the Select...Case statement can contain a block of VBA statements within it. The statement ends with the reserved words End Select. The syntax of the statement is given in Exhibit 9.6.

```
Select Case condition
   Case test_1
          VBA statement(s) executed if test_1 is True
   Case test_2
          VBA statement(s) executed if test_2 is True
   Case Else
          neither test_1 or test_2 is True
End Select
```

EXHIBIT 9.6 An example of a Select . . . Case statement that has two tested choices and a default choice

The tests can be either variables or calculated amounts. This structure is especially useful inside of looping structures for accumulating totals or sorting out varied responses.

Uses of the Select . . . Case Statement The Select . . . Case statement is very versatile and can be used to build powerful and efficient code blocks when decisions among three or more alternatives need to be made. It is particularly useful in the following roles:

- To make choices based on the values of calculated values.
- To specify a choice of worksheet or file into which to direct output.
- To specify a choice of formatting alternatives (color, font, etc.).
- To choose among report titles or headers based on variable values or the number of a report inside a multiple report package.
- To allow the identification of unique error conditions and be able to respond with a wide variety of message responses based on the specific content of the error.
- To set a variable to a certain value or set of values based on a test condition.
- To branch between a series of options based on a calculation methodology or collateral characteristic. An example would be to select one of the six possible default calculation methodologies based on a menu input.
- To branch among a series of stratification values to aggregate collateral or some other form of information. For example, there are 50 state codes and we need to sum the original and remaining balances of all loans by state.

In Exhibit 9.7, we need to establish the test variable for a collateral selection test. Based on the test that is currently being performed (the constants used as the test criteria have sequential numbers), the value of the variable test_value is assigned from the appropriate test parameter variable. In the case of ORIG_TERM, a constant with a value of 1, the Select . . . Case statement will assign the value of the original term of the loan currently stored in the variable g_orig_term to the variable test_value. Note that by placing a semicolon after the test in the "Case Is =" line it is possible to place the action code for that choice on the same line. In VBA a ":" (colon) symbol indicates a new line of code on the same line in the VBA Editor. Use of the ":" makes the Select . . . Cases statements more compact and in many ways easier to read. An example of this format is shown in Exhibit 9.7.

```
'for the numeric interval tests set the test criteria, interval tests only
'single test criteria will be set in the loop
        Select Case test_criteria
          Case Is = ORIG_TERM:     test_value = g_loan_orig_term(iloan)
          Case Is = REM_TERM:      test_value = g_loan_rem_term(iloan)
          Case Is = SEASONING:     test_value = g_loan_season(iloan)
          Case Is = CUR_COUPON:    test_value = g_loan_coup(iloan)
          Case Is = SPREAD:        test_value = g_loan_spread(iloan)
          Case Is = EQUITY_PCT:    test_value = g_loan_cur_equity(iloan)/_
                                     g_loan_appraisal(iloan)
          Case Is = MAX_LTV:       test_value = g_loan_cur_bal(iloan)/_
                                     g_loan_appraisal(iloan)
          Case Is = CURR_BALANCE: test_value = g_loan_cur_bal(iloan)
          Case Is = ORIG_BALANCE: test_value = g_loan_orig_bal(iloan)
        End Select
```

EXHIBIT 9.7   A Select . . . Case statement is used to test criteria based on a constant

Use of the Select . . . Case Statement in Report Formatting   The entire subroutine shown in Exhibit 9.8 is essentially a single Select . . . Case statement. The subroutine takes as an input value the variable named data_type.

This variable can assume a Range of values from 1 to 11, each value of which corresponds to a particular collateral stratification report. Each of these values has a constant assigned to it to allow for more clarity in the code. Each of the constant names corresponds to a stratification statistic for an individual stratification report. For example, the first report stratifies the collateral by its original term in months at three-month intervals. The constant name for that report is declared as: "Const ORIG_TERM = 1"

The values of each of these constants are declared at the top of the "Write Collateral Reports" VBA module. The first nine reports all have numeric Ranges as their sorting criteria. Each of the intervals has a low value and a high value. The next interval low is the previous interval high. The tenth report in the sequence is sorted by original balance and the value of the constant named ORIGINAL_BAL is 9.

```
Sub Print_Interval_Test(data_type)

    Select Case data_type
        Case Is <= ORIG_BALANCE
          For interval = 1 To total_intervals
              Cells(irow, 2).Value = low(interval)
              Cells(irow, 4).Value = high(interval)
              irow = irow + 1
          Next interval
        Case Is = STATE_CODE
          For interval = 1 To total_intervals
              Cells(irow, 2).Value = g_state_id_number(interval)
              Cells(irow, 3).Value = g_state_name(interval)
              Cells(irow, 4).Value = g_state_postal(interval)
              irow = irow + 1
          Next interval
    End Select

End Sub
```

EXHIBIT 9.8   A Select . . . Case statement is used to determine what type of selection criteria to print in the first two or three columns of each collateral stratification report

If this does not sound familiar, refer to Chapter 5, "Designing the VBA Model," in which we discuss the composition and use of the stratification report package.

The subroutine will print the low and high interval values for the first 9 reports. If the variable data_type has a value of less than or equal to 9 (the value of the constant named ORIGINAL_BAL), the Select . . . Case statement will execute the statement block under the first case condition.

The tenth report is a stratification code that uses the postal state code, NY for New York, as the stratification item. Here, the model must print out a completely different sort of criteria line than for the first nine reports. It will produce a number that is the nth position of the state in an alphabetical listing of the selected states, then the full state name, and then the state postal code. Here the Select . . . Case code is triggered by the value of the variable data_type when it matches the constant named STATE_CODE.

The final case of the Select . . . Case statement is activated when the value of data_type is equal to the value of the constant named ZIP_CODE. This option prints the number of the active ZIP code and the corresponding state that the Zip code is in. These are the stratification parameters for the report, "Balances by ZIP Code." Exhibit 9.8 illustrates the use of the statement to determine the contents of the first three columns of information printed in the eligible collateral reports.

Using a Select . . . Case Statement to Choose the Correct Default Methodology Calculation Exhibit 9.9 displays the use of the Select . . . Case statement as it compares the value of the variable g_default_method with three different constant values. Each of these constants represents different default methodology calculation options of the model. When the Select . . . Case statement finds a match, it calls the appropriate subroutine to calculate the defaults under the assumptions entered in the "Defaults and Prepayments Menu."

In Exhibit 9.9 you will notice a small change in the appearance of the Select . . . Case statement. If the case statement is activated, for example, and the value of the decision variable "g_default method" is the value of the selection option "DEF_PSA," the Select . . . Case statement will call the subroutine "Get_PSA_Factors." Usually the action taken by a selection choice is on the next line and indented, but here it is not. Why?

By using a ":" symbol at the end of the selection choice portion of the Select . . . Case statement, we indicate to the VBA compiler that we have started a new line. The new line is, of course, the call to the "Get_PSA_Factors" subroutine. It is often very convenient and also very orderly to use the semicolon symbol followed by the action you want the Select . . . Case statement to take in a particular case. This notation should be used if there is only one line of code as the response to the choice. We see the case condition test followed immediately by the action to be taken. The cause and effect relationship is very clear!

```
Select Case g_default_method
    Case Is = DEF_CPR:  Call Get_CPR_Factors(DEFAULTS)   'constant prepay rate
    Case Is = DEF_PSA:  Call Get_PSA_Factors(DEFAULTS)   'public sec admin rate
    Case Is = DEF_USR:  Call Get_USR_Factors            'user input prorata
End Select
```

EXHIBIT 9.9 Selection of the desired defaults calculation methods

```
Select Case test_score
        Case >= 90%: letter_grade = "A"
            Select Case test_score
                Case >= 98%: letter_grade = letter_grade & "+"
                Case <= 92%: letter_grade = letter_grade & "-"
            End Select
        Case >= 80%: letter_grade = "B"
        Case >= 70%: letter_grade = "C"
        Case >= 60%: letter_grade = "D"
        Case Else:   letter_grade = "F"
End Select
```

EXHIBIT 9.10   A nested Select...Case statement assigns a "+" or "−" to an "A" grade

Nesting Select . . . Case Statements

The Select...Case statement can be nested within other Select...Case statements. This is similar to earlier in the chapter, when we looked at nesting If...Then...Else statements.

A Select...Case structure can be inserted into any of the existing Case tests. Below is an example that assigns a grade and an accompanying "+" or "−" to it based on a test score. The nested Select...Case will assign a grade of "A" to any score above 90%. An "A−" to a score of 90% to 92%, an "A" to a score of 93% to 97%, and an "A+" to a score greater than or equal to 98%. Example 9.10 demonstrates how to accomplish this.

LOOPING STRUCTURES

For . . . Next and Do . . . While or Do . . . Until

The ability to repeatedly execute portions of the model is a powerful and necessary feature of the VBA (and all other) programming languages. Looping code in models is used for many purposes. The most common of these are:

- **Repeated operations over time.** In structured finance applications, these are commonly a long series of monthly intervals. This is especially true when we are amortizing collateral, or testing for a repeated monthly condition such as a deal trigger event.
- **Repeated operations over a related series of conditions.** An example of this would be applying a sequence of distinct and ordered prepayment rates or default rates to a set of scenarios. The user inputs a base prepayment rate and a step increase of the rate. A total of 10 steps in the rate are to be calculated. A looping structure would start with the first rate, run the model, increment the rate by the step increase, run the model, and so on until all of the ten steps had been calculated.
- **Causing a series of related events to happen.** A looping routine could be designed to print out 15 different reports one after another by sequentially calling a series of report-writing modules.

- **Performing a series of mathematical or logical operations on data held in vectors and arrays.** A simple example of this would be summing all elements in a given column or row of an array.
- **Input or output the contents of a Range that is used in a menu or output report.** For example, say there is a column of information on a menu 360 cells long, all of it pertaining to a monthly interest rate scenario over the 30-year life of the deal. A looping structure could sequentially read this information from the menu and assign it to an array.

When we perform looping operations in the model we will find that they are naturally divided into two broad classes. The first class comprises those conditions in which we know exactly how many times the loop will be repeated. The second class comprises those conditions where we don't! In this case the number of loops is dependent on some criteria being satisfied. What could be simpler?

Fortunately, VBA provides us with several easily understood and mastered language features to accommodate both instances.

Fixed Repetition Looping   The For...Next statement is a looping structure that is used when you know exactly how many iterations of the loop you need to perform and that lets you specify that number at the beginning of the loop as a fixed count. The loop usually progresses by integer numbers and can start from any number and proceed to any number. The default is one unit at a time (i.e., 1, 2, 3, etc.), but can be specified to be a constant interval such as 2 (1, 3, 5, etc.). The loop also can be specified to count in a decreasing increment, 5, 4, 3, 2, 1, 0, −1, and so on.

The loop continues until the specified number of repetitions has been performed and then stops.

Variable Repetition Looping   The Do...Until/While statement is a looping structure that is used when you don't know in advance how many iterations of the loop you will need to perform. More specifically, Do...Until/While enables the effects of the actions inside the loop to determine when the loop will terminate itself.

The completion condition is specified at either the top or the bottom of the loop, and the loop continues until the condition is met or runaway looping generates an error condition in the program.

For . . . Next Loop

As we have mentioned previously the For...Next loop structure is the method of choice when we know exactly how many iterations of the loop are required.

In what type of situation would we favor the use of the For...Next loop structure?

- When examining data stored in an array where the dimensions of the array are constant and known
- When performing an operation across a fixed series of time intervals
- When we are operating on a set of objects (like clients) whose number is known
- When we are counting across a Range of numbers or cases (a predetermined number of reports, rows, or columns)

```
For counter = start To end  Step increment
    [VBA Statements]
Next counter
```

EXHIBIT 9.11   Basic form of the For...Next looping structure

Form of the For...Next Loop   The syntax of the For...Next loop structure is shown in Exhibit 9.11.

In Exhibit 9.11 the variable **counter** is an incremental numeric that tells the model how many times the loop has been repeated. The variables **start** and **end** represent the beginning and ending values of the loop. Start is usually either 0 or 1, however the beginning of the loop can be any value (including negatives) The variable **increment** is the increment that the loop steps through from the beginning (with the value of **start**) to the end (value of **end**). Increment is optional and defaults to 1 if not declared. It can be either positive or negative, but must be consistent with the loop start and loop end values. Exhibit 9.12 displays a For...Next loop that reads a Range in the Reports Selection Menu. If the element of the Range contains an "**X**," then the report will be included in the output.

Use of a Simple For...Next Loop

```
Sub Read_Report_Selection_Menu()

  Sheets("Reports Menu").Select
  Range("A1").Select

  'collateral reports
  For i_rep = 1 To PORTFOLIO_REPORTS
      g_report(i_rep) = False
      If Range("m4ReportsSelected").Cells(i_rep) = "X" Then g_report(i_rep) = True
  Next i_rep
  'summary reports
  For i_rep = 1 To MATRIX_REPORTS
      g_matrix_report(i_rep) = False
      If Range("m4MatrixRepsSelected").Cells(i_rep) = "X" Then g_matrix_
        report(i_rep) = True
  Next i_rep

End Sub
```

EXHIBIT 9.12   Use of a pair of simple For...Next loops to read the contents of a column of the Reports Selection Menu

Nested For...Next Loops

Exhibit 9.13 illustrates the use of nested For...Next loops, four of them to be exact, whose purpose is to produce the monthly cash flows for the loan portfolio. The outermost loop cycles through the number of prepayment rate levels that we have specified, one at a time, using the variable named i_prepay as a counter. Starting at 1, it steps by single-scenario increments to the terminal value of the loop g_prepay_levels. It encompasses all of the code in between the For statement and the statement at the bottom of the code, Next i_prepay. Inside of this loop are three other loops.

Example of Nested For...Next Statements

Values of the loop counters
g_prepay_levels = 5 g_default_levels = 7 g_total loans = 10
g_rem_term(1) = 240 g_rem_term(2) = 60 g_rem_term(3) = 123 g_rem_term(4) = 24 g_rem_term(5) = 333 g_rem_term(6) = 220 g_rem_term(7) = 36 g_rem_term(8) = 174 g_rem_term(9) = 72 g_rem_term(10) = 301
Total all g_rem_term = 1,583

```
*Amortization code for the collateral cash flows, reg amort,
*   prepayments, defaults, recoveries
    For i_prepay = 1 to g_prepay_levels
        Statement 1
        For i_defaults = 1 to g_default_levels
            Statement 2
            For i_loans = 1 to g_total_loans
                Statement 3
                For i_periods = g_rem_term(i_loan)
                    Statement 4
                Next i_period
            Next i_loans
        Next i_defaults
    Next i_prepays
```

Number of times each statement will be executed

	i_prepay Loop	i_defaults Loop	i_loans Loop	i_periods Loop	RESULT
Statement 1	5				5 times
Statement 2	5	7			35 times
Statement 3	5	7	10		350 times
Statement 4	5	7	10	1,503	554,050 times

EXHIBIT 9.13 How many times a VBA statement is called depends on where it is in the looping structure

They relate to the number of default levels, the number of loans in the portfolio, and the number of remaining months in the life of each loan. Each of these loops will individually execute to its terminal value before advancing to the next outer loop.

How the For . . . Next Loop Works   Here is the internal process that a For . . . Next loop goes through during its execution cycle:

- The value of the loop counter variable is initialized to the starting value of the loop Range. In the case of the prepayments loop, the Range is 1 to g_prepay_rates, or 5. So, the loop counter, i_prepay, will loop from 1 to 5, starting at one.
- The loop will execute all statements inside of it until it comes to its corresponding Next statement. When it gets to the Next statement, it jumps to the beginning of the loop, the For statement again.
- At the beginning of the loop it increments the loop counter variable i_prepay to the next step, in this case 2. It continues until the loop counter value is greater that the loop end value (5).
- When it exceeds the loop end value, it jumps to the "Next" at the bottom of the loop statement and continues from that point on.

A Cautionary Note Concerning Nesting   When For . . . Next loops are nested inside of each other, the inner loops need to cycle through each of the set of statements that are contained within their individual For . . . Next boundary. Thus, if the outer

```
For i_prepay = 1 to g_prepay_scen                  '10 scenarios
   For i_default = 1 to g_default_scen              '10 scenarios
      For i_loan = 1 to g_loan_num                  '2,500 loans
         For i_month = 1 to 360
            g_cf_sum = (A + B + (C * D)) * i_month
         Next i_month
      Next i_loan
   Next i_default
Next i_prepay
```

EXHIBIT 9.14   A nested loop structure guaranteed to produce an inefficient program

For...Next loop is scheduled to loop 10 times and contains an inner For...Next loop that is scheduled to loop 360 times, the inner loop will count from 1 to 360 for each increment of the outer loop. This means that any VBA statement inside the inner loop will be executed 3,600 times! When you are thinking about the flow of the model you need to be **VERY** careful not to place any code inside of loops that does not need to be there. However, nested For...Next loops are very powerful and can get a lot of work done in a small amount of space. One further thing, no matter how small the span of the loop is, *always* put the name of the loop counter variable at the Next statement, such as Next i_prepay. This greatly improves the clarity of the model, especially when there are more than 3 loops. Exhibits 9.14 and 9.15 are cautionary notes of how one must be careful with nested loops.

The formula at the middle of the code in Figure 9.14 inside of this set of four nested loops will execute 10*10*2500*360 times. That means that each run of the model will execute the calculation statement 90,000,000 times! There are five mathematical operations in the statement, therefore there will be 450,000,000 operations performed in the middle of these loops! You should also notice that the value of the variables A, B, C, and D do not change based on the action of the loops. Only the value of the variable i_month changes as the loops change. We can therefore calculate the sum of A+B+C*D outside the loops and only multiply it by the value of i_month inside the loop. We would rewrite the code as shown in Exhibit 9.15

The unchanging portion of the calculation is now outside the loops! We have reduced the number of mathematical operations from 450,000,000 to 180,000,000 a savings of 60%.

Exit...For Command   The Exit...For command is used when we want to immediately terminate the execution of a loop.

```
E = A + B + (C * D)
For i_prepay = 1 to g_prepay_scen                  '10 scenarios
   For i_default = 1 to g_default_scen              '10 scenarios
      For i_loan = 1 to g_loan_num                  '2,500 loans
         For i_month = 1 to 360
            g_cf_sum = E * i_month
         Next i_month
      Next i_loan
   Next i_default
Next i_prepay
```

EXHIBIT 9.15   The result is the same using the code in either Exhibit 9.14 or Exhibit 9.15, but the work is much reduced in the latter

```
Function Assign_State_Number(state_id)

    For i_state = 1 To STATES
        If state_id = g_state_postal(i_state) Then
            Assign_State_Number = i_state
            Exit For
        End If
    Next i_state

End Function
```

EXHIBIT 9.16 Using Exit...For statement to break out of a loop

Even though we think that we know how many times a For...Next loop is going to operate, a condition arising in the model may warrant early termination of the loop. For example:

- We are summing a series of numbers and need to stop when a total has been exceeded, even if the loop is not done, (might consider a Do...Until loop instead).
- A disastrous error condition has occurred, and to continue the operation of the model would corrupt the output results.
- An event has occurred that may or may not be singular, but is, in and of itself, grounds for stopping the loop.

In Exhibit 9.16, the Assign_State_Number function receives a value from the calling program that is a two-letter state postal code. It then searches an array of all possible postal codes until it finds a match. When the model has found a match, the loop has hit its stopping criteria. We do not need to continue to compare the state_id variable value to the g_state_postal array any longer since we have what we need. The model immediately exits the loop. The use of the Exit...For statement improves the efficiency of the model by avoiding unnecessary loop repetition.

Do...While Looping Command

The Do...While loop is the method of choice when the number of iterations the loop needs to perform is unknown or dynamic in nature. Examples are:

- When reading data in from a file where the number of records is unknown or when some may be rejected immediately at the time they are read.
- When a process is affecting its own ending point. In some simulations you may use a Do...While loop to continue a process where the ending point is influenced by what has happened before, e.g., loan amortization periods at high prepayment rates.

```
Do While condition
    [VBA statement block]
Loop
```

EXHIBIT 9.17 Looping structure checks to see it has completed the task before executing the statement block

```
Do condition
    [VBA statement block]
Loop While
```

EXHIBIT 9.18   Looping structure checks to see it has completed the task after executing the statement block

Form of the Do...While Looping Command   The Do... While looping structure syntax has two forms, as shown in Figures 9.17 and 9.18.

The form in Exhibit 9.18 checks the condition before executing the loop; it then executes the statements if the conditions are True.

Exhibit 9.18 shows the form of the Do... While statement that checks the completion condition after executing the loop.

In Exhibit 9.19 we have to open a file and read records from it, saving the record count. We need the record count because we will use it to **ReDim**, or redimension, the size of our loan information arrays. We have no idea how many loans are in the file, so we cannot use a For... Next looping structure with a fixed terminus. The Do... While runs until it hits an empty cell in the first column of the file, the principal balance column (this must be the end of the file, as all loans have a principal balance), and then gives us a row count. The value of the variable g_total_loans is then decreased by 1, because the top row of the Excel file is a set of column headers.

```
Sub Read_Portfolio_Data_File()

    Workbooks.Open Filename:=g_pathway & "data\" & gfn_collateral_file
    j = 1
    current_row = FIRST_DATA_ROW
    Sheets("LoanInformation").Select
    Range("A1").Select
    'if the number of loans in the portfolio is entered as 0 count the file
    'if a number greater than zero is entered read that number of records
    If g_total_loans = 0 Then
        Do While Cells(current_row, 1).Value <> ""
            current_row = current_row + 1
            g_total_loans = g_total_loans + 1
        Loop
        row_stop = current_row - 1
    Else
        row_stop = current_row + g_total_loans - 1
    End If

    'redimension the data arrays based on the number of total loans in the portfolio
    ReDim g_sel_tot(g_total_loans) As Double
    ReDim g_sel_tag(g_total_loans, INELIGIBLE_REPORTS) As Boolean
    Call ReDim_Portfolio_Data(g_total_loans)

    'read the loans data file based on the program count or the input count
    j = Read_Portfolio_Data(FIRST_DATA_ROW, row_stop, j)
    ActiveWorkbook.Close

End Sub
```

EXHIBIT 9.19   Use of a Do... While command to read collateral file records

```
Do Until condition
    [VBA statement block]
Loop
```

EXHIBIT 9.20   Checking for the completion condition before executing the statement block

```
Do condition
    [VBA statement block]
Loop Until
```

EXHIBIT 9.21   Checking for the completion condition after executing the statement block

Do . . . Until Looping Command

Form of the Do . . . Until Looping Command   The Do . . . Until looping structure syntax has two forms as shown in Exhibits 9.20 and 9.21.

This form checks the condition before executing the statements within the loop. If the conditions are False, it then executes the statements.

This form checks the condition after executing the loop. It will continue to loop if the test condition is False.

SUBROUTINES

All executable code in VBA is contained in subroutines and functions:

- Subroutines perform a task that modifies the environment of the model, but they cannot return a value to the model.
- Functions cannot modify the environment, but can return values to the calling procedures.

All VBA programs start as a single subroutine that calls other subordinate subroutines. A "master" or "main" subroutine may have several or many subroutines and functions contained within it; the "main" subroutine forms the framework of the model. The other subroutines and functions perform specific tasks to complete the work.

The Form of Subroutines

Exhibit 9.22 displays the general form of a VBA subroutine.

```
Sub Name of the Subroutine (argument1, argument2, ...)
[Variable declarations]
     [Sets of Visual Basic statements]
End Sub
```

EXHIBIT 9.22   The general form of a subroutine

```
Sub Loan_Financing_Model()

   Application.DisplayAlerts = False          'temporarily turn off the warning
                                                messages
   Call Display_PrepayDefault_ProgressMsg(99) 'display program progress msg (null)
   Call ErrCheck_All_Menus                    'error check all menu entries
   Call Read_All_Menu_Input                   'transfer the menu entries to variables
   Call Read_Portfolio_Data_File              'read in the loan information to
                                                variables
   Call Select_Deal_Collateral               'run the basic eligibility test or
                                                accept all
   g_main_filename = ActiveWorkbook.Name
   Call Compute_Collateral_Cashflows          'generating the cash flows
   Call Load_and_Run_thc_Waterfall            'loads scenario cfs and runs the
                                                waterfall
   Call Write_Waterfall_Report_Package        'write waterfall reports in detail
   Call Write_Matrix_Report_Package           'write matrix reports
   Sheets("Main Menu").Select
   Application.DisplayAlerts = True            'turn message displays back on
   Application.StatusBar = False

End Sub
```

EXHIBIT 9.23 A specific use of the subroutine form, the main program, the subroutine Loan_Financing_Model

Exhibit 9.23 displays the main model subroutine. From it all other subroutines of the model are called and no other subroutines call it. In our model, it calls only nine other subroutines. Each of these nine subroutines is a top subroutine in that it calls others, but each subroutine itself is not called by any other than the main model subroutine. A collection of many, many more subroutines are called on a procedural and hierarchical basis to complete the analysis of the portfolio and deal structure.

Characteristics of subroutines are:

- They begin with the reserved word Sub.
- They end with the reserved words End Sub.
- They can contain variable declarations that create variables of local scope, for use solely inside of the subroutine.
- They can use information passed in from the calling model to perform their task.
- They can call other subroutines and functions.
- They cannot return a value or result that is directly assigned to the calling routine (we will talk about this later).

Calling a Subroutine

To activate the VBA code within a subroutine, the subroutine must be called. All subroutines with the exception of the Main Program subroutines are called by other subroutines or button macros. Exhibit 9.24 is an example of one subroutine calling another. The subroutine "Master_Program" is calling two subroutines. The first subroutine to be called is "Read_All_Menu_Inputs," the second one is "Set_Starting_Collateral_File_Row." The first subroutine will run to completion before the second one is called. The second subroutine will then run to completion, and the program will end.

```
Sub Master_Program()

        Call Read_All_Menu_Input
        Call Set_Starting_Collateral_File_Row

End Sub
```

EXHIBIT 9.24   A specific use of the subroutine form, the main program

Advantages of Using Subroutines

We could write all of our code one line after another and it would still run. There
are a number of gigantic advantages to using subroutines. These are:

- **Subroutines allow us to use identical pieces of VBA code all over the program,
  yet only write it once.** The "Call" feature of subroutines allows us to enter the
  subroutine from anywhere in the model. If we need to use the functionality of
  the subroutine over and over, we only need to write it once. We then call it from
  wherever we need it in the model.
- **Subroutines make it very efficient to change and modify code.** When you use
  a subroutine in a model, you will sooner or later need to correct or expand its
  VBA code. You will need to make changes only to that subroutine once to effect
  the change throughout the entire program, everywhere the subroutine is called.
- **Subroutines allow us a way to hierarchically organize the sequence of events in
  the model's execution plan.** The model involves two distinct processes. The first
  is the selection of eligible collateral, and the second, the running of the financing
  structure. These processes are very different. Subroutines allow us to segregate
  the code that performs these different tasks and to segment it into separate,
  independent pieces. See Exhibit 9.25.
- **Subroutines also allow us to segregate specific tasks.** This allows the decomposition of very complex tasks into a series of smaller and smaller tasks. Each is
  more specific and concise than the previous one. It helps rationalize and organize
  the thought processes when building the model.
- **Subroutines help document and organize the model.** The name of each subroutine should reflect its functional purpose. By looking at the hierarchy of
  subroutines, we can see the major model task, the component sub-tasks, and so
  forth, down to the most specific operations needed to run the model.
- **Well-designed and structured subroutines aid in documentation.** Simply writing
  down the call structure of a model that has a well-designed subroutine calling
  pattern will be a huge help to you in training others on how to use the model,
  and to developers who will assume responsibility for the model after you.
- **The use of well-designed subroutines will greatly improve the efficiency of the
  debugging process.** Subroutines are modular in nature. If you have a bug in a
  particular task, say report writing, you will be able to locate it and isolate it
  much quicker. You should be able to go almost directly to the piece of code that
  generates the report and concentrate your energies there, instead of having to
  search all through the model.
- **Subroutines also help you more efficiently develop additional functionality in
  your model.** They do this in two different ways. If you wish to add features that

Typical Calling Hierarchy in a Complex Program

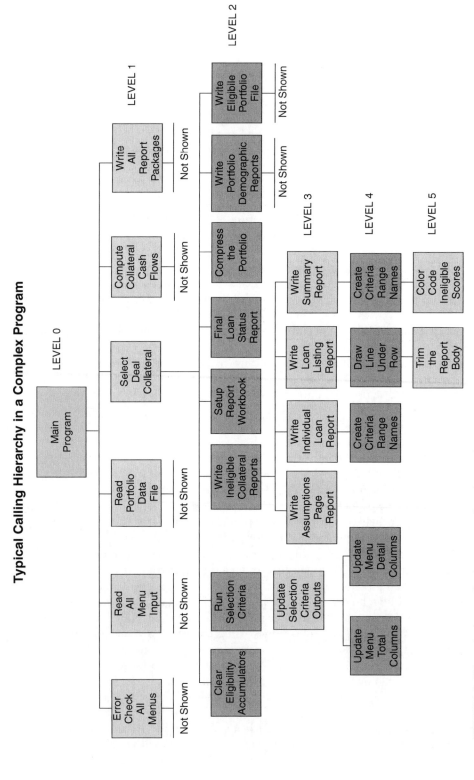

EXHIBIT 9.25 Schematic of subroutine calling hierarchy

are similar to the existing features of the model, you can call existing subroutines to help you. You will also find that it is easier to expand the model if it has a well-designed subroutine structure because you will now have a much better idea *where* to add the new code based on the existing structure of the model.

FUNCTIONS

Form of Functions

General Form

```
Function NameOfFunction ( argument1, argument2, ...)
[Variable declarations]
     [Sets of Visual Basic statements]
     NameOfFunction = returned_value
End Function
```

Example

```
Function CalcLoanSeasoning(orig_term, rem_term)
Dim seasoning as Integer
     seasoning = orig_term - rem_term
     CalcLoanSeasoning = seasoning
End Function
```

Things to note about functions:

- They begin with the reserved word Function.
- They end with the reserved words End Function.
- They may contain variable declarations, which are commands that create variables for use inside the subroutine.
- They can use information passed in from the calling code to perform their task.
- They can pass information out to any other function or subroutine.
- When called, they are called "in-line," as part of another statement, as if they were some kind of super-variable.
- They tend to be very, very specific as to their role and outputs.

Example of Function Use

In Exhibit 9.26 we will see a subroutine that calls two different functions that work together to translate a state postal code into the nth alphabetic rank of the state's name. The functions called are:

1. Assign_State_Number
2. Assign_State_Name

The "Fill_Test_Parameter" subroutine is used to place values in the left-most column of the set of eligible collateral stratification reports. The tenth report in this

```
Sub Fill_Test_Parameter(rep_num)

Dim x      As Integer   'state number
Dim y      As String    'state name

  Select Case rep_num
    Case Is = TEST_REM_TERM:  Range(r_name(3)).Cells(irow) = g_loan_rem_term(iloan)
    Case Is = TEST_ORIG_TERM: Range(r_name(3)).Cells(irow) = g_loan_orig_term(iloan)
    Case Is = TEST_ORIG_BAL:  Range(r_name(3)).Cells(irow) = g_loan_orig_bal(iloan)
    Case Is = TEST_REM_BAL:   Range(r_name(3)).Cells(irow) = g_loan_cur_bal(iloan)
    Case Is = TEST_MAX_LTV:
              Range(r_name(3)).Cells(irow) = g_loan_orig_bal(iloan) / g_loan_
                appraisal(iloan)
    Case Is = TEST_INDEX:     Range(r_name(3)).Cells(irow) = g_loan_spread(iloan)
    Case Is = TEST_STATE_CODE:
              x = Assign_State_Number(g_state(iloan))
              y = Assign_State_Name(x)
              Range(r_name(3)).Cells(irow) = y
    Case Is = TEST_TENOR_CODE: Range("D" & irow).Select: Selection.Interior.Pattern =
                               xlLightUp
    Case Is = TEST_BAL_CODE:   Range("D" & irow).Select: Selection.Interior.Pattern =
                               xlLightUp
    Case Is = TEST_PMT_CODE:   Range(r_name(3)).Cells(irow) = g_loan_calc_pmt(iloan)
  End Select

End Sub
```

EXHIBIT 9.26   The Fill_Test_Parameter subroutine

series lists the balances of the selected collateral by the state location of the loans. Each of the states is listed in alphabetical order.

The model has already read the names of the states and their two-letter postal codes from the Geographic Selection Menu. The names of the 54 state entities are stored in the array g_state_name and the postal codes are stored in the array g_state_postal. The model needs to find the number of the state in the list and then, using that number, return the name of the state. We have the two-letter postal code of the loan stored in the array g_state from reading the records of the data file.

The two functions shown in Exhibits 9.27 and 9.28 work together to translate the postal code. A state code, for example "NY," is accepted by the first function and is used to return the nth listing of the state code in the list of 1 to 54 postal codes. This number is the ordinal number of where the state falls on a list of all states in alphabetical order. The second function takes the state number supplied by the first function and returns the common name for the state.

```
Function Assign_State_Number(state_id)
      For i_state = 1 to STATES
          If state_id = g_state_postal(i_state) Then
                Assign_State_Number = i_state
                Exit For
          End If
      Next i_state
End Function
```

EXHIBIT 9.27   This function accepts the variable state_id, which is the two-letter postal code for state location of the business. It then runs down the list of all postal codes, and when it finds a match it exits the For . . . Next loop

```
Function Assign_State_Name(i)

    Assign_State_Name = g_state_name(i)

End Function
```

EXHIBIT 9.28   The Assign_State_Name function

DELIVERABLES CHECKLIST

The following are the VBA Knowledge Checklist items for this chapter:

- What the major decision structures of the VBA language are
- What the major looping structures of the VBA language are
- The six logical operators of the VBA language, " <," " <=," " <>," " =," " >=," and " >"
- How to write simple and compound decision tests
- How to use variables, constants, and numerical amounts in constructing decision tests
- The use of the reserved words ".AND." and ".OR." to build compound decision tests
- What an If...Then...Else statement is, and when to use it
- The Select...Case statement and when to use it (three or more alternatives)
- How to nest If...Then...Else and Select...Case statements
- What a For...Next loop is, a looping structure when the number of repetitions is known
- How to use the Exit...For statement to break out of a For...Next loop
- Use of the Do...While and Do...Until looping statements. Looping an indeterminate number of times
- What subroutines and functions are, and how they differ
- The advantages to using subroutines and functions in VBA modeling
- How to wrap Select...Case statements inside of For...Next loops to execute or check for a series of sequential choices

The following are the Modeling Knowledge Checklist items for this chapter:

- How to use constants in conjunction with Select...Case statements to select a single option from a list
- How to use constants and Select...Case statements to run down a series of values and execute each one in sequence
- How to use For...Next loops to move through an array and operate on each of its elements
- The dangers of putting statements inside nested loops if the number of iterations is high
- Using the Exit...For statement to break out of a loop once a condition has been met
- How to nest subroutine and function calls
- How to design subroutines to decompose complex tasks into simple ones, and segregate functionality

NEXT STEPS

Having mastered flow control statements in this chapter we can begin to put them to use in Chapter 10, "Building Messaging Capabilities." In that chapter we will make use of flow control statements and some of the other features of the VBA language to build message generating capabilities into the program. These messages will fall into two broad categories, progress messages and error messages. We will begin to construct the menu error-checking code that we alluded to in Chapter 8. We will also write a series of messages that will inform the model user of the progress of the model during its run cycle.

ON THE WEB SITE

There is no material on the Web site for this chapter.

## CHAPTER 10

Building Messaging Capabilities

OVERVIEW

In this chapter, we will learn how to build a messaging facility into the model. These messages will help the model perform its task, will help us spot trouble, and will inform us of the progress of the model as it performs its various tasks.

Messages are an often-overlooked part of modeling. This does not mean that they are unimportant. Quite to the contrary! As anyone who has ever sat watching music download over the Internet, progress messages can mean the difference between knowing that something is happening and not having a clue in the world what is going on!

Every model should be able to generate error messages to keep us informed of potentially harmful situations. Just as important are progress messages, which keep us informed of the work the model is performing. In this chapter we will learn how to create both of these types of messages and the proper places to employ them. The error-checking subroutines we will write in this chapter will all reside in the VBA module named "**MenuErrorChecking.**"

DELIVERABLES

VBA Language Knowledge Deliverables
- How to design and implement progress and error messages using existing VBA objects and methods
- How to direct progress messages to the Application Status Bar area of an Excel worksheet
- How to build complex messages from program output and smaller, component message units
- How to use VBA functions such as IsNumerics in data-checking activities
- How to display these error messages in message box objects that feature action buttons

Modeling Knowledge Deliverables
- Learn the roles of progress and error messages in a model
- How to combine various forms of error checking with error messaging capabilities

- The five types of error checking—Data Type, Value, Cross-checking, File Checking, and Run Options—are useful in all models
- How to design and build each error-checking mechanism, and attach them to the menus of our model

UNDER CONSTRUCTION

In this chapter we will see many lines of the type of VBA code that we will be writing in Chapter 12 when we begin to develop the menu support subroutines that will first error check and then read the information input on the menus.

For the moment we will not add any code to the small amount already in the model. Take this time to look at the VBA code samples here, including some complete subroutines. Study the use of the variables, the flow control statements, and how they accomplish their tasks.

PROGRESS MESSAGES

Progress messages are a daily fact of life for every computer user. Simple messages are relatively easy to construct and can tell the user a lot about what is going on. Progress messages also serve a crucial psychological need; they reassure the user that the model is indeed running. They are also useful for the designer. This is especially true during the development phase of the model, where progress messages can confirm that you are on the right path to achieving the desired results.

Most programs will take some time to run. Usually we do not have a clear idea of how much time until we have experienced running the model repeatedly. This applies especially to programs with large data files or complex calculations. In this model, there are two very obvious places where we should give the user ongoing updates as to the progress that the model is making.

The Collateral Selection Process

The first of these is in the collateral selection process. Although our original portfolio is not large, the next portfolio might be one of 250,000 loans! In that case the selection process might take over an hour. To have the user stare at an unchanging screen for an hour and take it on faith that the model is busy in the background (instead of stopped, or uselessly looping) is asking a lot of anyone. Additionally, progress messages can actually improve efficiency by displaying interim results. If it looks like the run is not headed in the right direction the model run can be interrupted and another avenue of analysis can be explored instead.

The Cash Flow Calculation Process

The second place a progress message would be useful is during the calculation of the various prepayment/default/recovery scenarios. Here, seeing how many of the amortization sets have been completed confirms for the user that the model is,

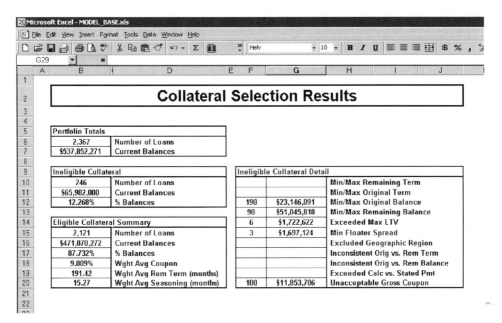

EXHIBIT 10.1 Loan Selection Results screen

indeed, running. It also gives the user a rough estimate of the time remaining. This can be a simple message. The absolute minimum content would be the number of prepayment and default scenario combinations completed so far.

Earlier in the Chapter 5, "Designing the VBA Model," we built a menu display to tell the user how much of the collateral was eligible under the selection criteria specified. This screen was a simple display and only differentiated between eligible and ineligible. It was updated on a loan-by-loan basis as the selection process was performed. As such, it can also serve as a progress message. Well, all done with that problem! We don't need to write another line of code other than what we were going to do anyway to give the user a real-time summary of the results. This screen is shown in Exhibit 10.1.

The second progress message, the one dealing with the completion of the collateral amortization calculations, does not need to be as elaborate as the screen we just saw.

It needs only to report the number of scenarios completed, the total number to complete, and maybe some information as to the scenario it is working on.

Succinctly it might say:

```
Prepay 1 of 5, Default 3 of 5, Completed 3 of 25,    % Completed = 12%%
```

Since this is such a concise message, we may want to place it in the application message bar area at the lower right of the screen, where is immediately available and easily visible. The subroutine builds a text message and then sets the value of the "Application.StatusBar," which is the VBA object in the Excel worksheet that

```
Sub Display_Amortization_ProgressMsg(i_pre as Integer, i_def as Integer)

Dim pct_done      As Double    'percentage of cash flow scenarios completed
Dim num_total     As Integer   'total number of cash flow scenarios this model run

  m_complete = m_complete + 1                    'running total of completed
                                                  scenarios
  num_total = g_prepay_levels * g_default_levels 'total number of scenarios
  pct_done = m_complete / num_total              'percentage scenarios completed

  'Print the message to the status bar
  Application.StatusBar = "Prepayments = " & i_pre & " of " & g_prepay_levels & _
    " Defaults = " & i_def & " of " & g_default_levels & _
    " Scenarios Completed " & m_complete & " of " & num_total & _
    " % Complete = " & Format(pct_done, "0.0%")

End Sub
```

EXHIBIT 10.2   VBA code to produce a progress message in Excel's Application Status Bar

will display it. The VBA subroutine that builds and displays this message is shown in Exhibit 10.2.

The message will be displayed in the lower-right of the screen. See Exhibit 10.3.

General Program Execution Progress Messages

Lastly, it is always a good idea to intersperse progress messages throughout the program if the model run is either long or complicated. The important concept here is that the user, *and that may often be yourself,* needs to be keep informed of what is going on at all times. Remember, you are going to be the person with whom this model will be associated. If the model is confusing, difficult to understand, and

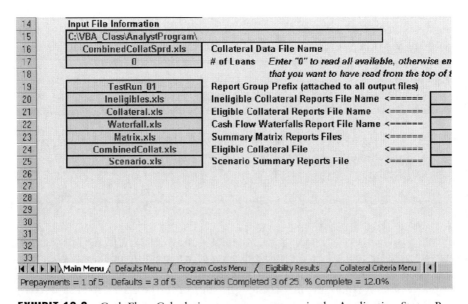

EXHIBIT 10.3   Cash Flow Calculation progress message in the Application Status Bar

stress-producing to work with, you have not done yourself or your reputation any favors.

All of us need to step back from our models from time to time and see the model as others see it. Is it a tool that is informative and easy to use? Can you tell what is happening and therefore avoid problems before they occur? Can you confidently tell someone else how long a particular type of analysis should take? Progress messages are useful in dealing with all of these concerns.

ERROR MESSAGES

The second type of message output is error messages. Surprisingly, many models do not have any error messages at all. Writing error message VBA code is a skill that many modelers feel they need not take the time to develop. Time spent on this task takes them away from what is viewed as the main activity, the development of the core functionality of the model. There is also the feeling that error messages are unnecessary. Complex models are often used by a limited number of people, who become quite familiar with the model. "Expert users don't need error messages, they don't make mistakes! They are experts!" This is a very amateurish position and one that can be used to distinguish the "hackers" from the professionals. These objections limit the ability to leverage the model's use across a larger number of people. It is a sound programming practice to learn how to write error-trapping routines and error messages in your code.

Error messages require thought to be effective. They also come in a variety of flavors:

- **Data type checking.** Do not put letters in places for numbers, or vice versa.
- **Value checking.** Inputs must fall between specified Ranges, especially non-zero entries and non-negative entries.
- **Cross-checking.** Related entries that are inconsistent across two or more fields.
- **File checking.** Determining the existence (or non-existence) of files before you try to use them.
- **Inconsistent Run Options.** Asking the model to perform a secondary analysis when the primary analysis has not been selected.

While this may appear a bit daunting at first blush, it is not. It is a little painstaking, but generally quite straightforward and most importantly a prudent thing to do.

Data Type Checking

Data type checking is the most simple of all the kinds of error messages. The wrong type of data is entered into a menu field of variable input. What does this mean? Mostly it means String data (mixes of numbers and letters) are in a purely number field. On the surface this seems like an abysmally stupid thing to do—and it is, most of the time. The exceptions come when a person is entering a long stream of numbers and mistypes a character by error or, more frequently, if the inputs for the model are file-driven. In this case, a change in the input file could result in a miscue of all of

```
'set all IsNumeric tests to OK
For itest = 1  to ISNUMERIC_TESTS_PROG_COSTS
    err_result(itest) = False      'False means that no error is detected
Next itest

'check each of the fields for non numerics
err_result(1) = (IsNumeric(Range("m2ServicerExp")) = False)
err_result(2) = (IsNumeric(Range("m2ProgramExpenses")) = False)
err_result(3) = (IsNumeric(Range("m2TrigCleanUpPct")) = False)
err_result(4) = (IsNumeric(Range("m2Trig3MDelRate")) = False)
err_result(5) = (IsNumeric(Range("m2AdvanceRate")) = False)
err_result(6) = (IsNumeric(Range("m2ConduitSpread")) = False)
```

EXHIBIT 10.4   Data Type checking code for entries to the Deal Expenses Menu

the subsequent inputs (a shift in one field), for example. The code to check whether a field has a numeric input is easy to implement and also has the benefit of being reasonably compact. See Exhibit 10.4.

The example in Exhibit 10.4 populates an array named err_result, which is six elements long, of type Boolean. If an error is detected in the inputs, the value of the array element will be changed to the value True. Each of the elements corresponds to a single field on the Program Costs Menu. The line of code tests the value of the Range name variable using the function IsNumeric. If the value in the menu field is a non-numeric entry, then the value the function returns is False. The return value of the function is compared to the value, hard-coded in as False, and since False = False is the value True, an error has occurred. Now we have an array filled with a collection of either True or False values for each of the six positions. How do we turn this into an error message the user can see?

To display an error message we must first build a String variable that we can use in a VBA message box subroutine. The subroutine "MsgBox" will display anything you put into it, in a box, on the active worksheet screen. This is exactly the type of box you see when you try to exit a file without saving it. The subroutine takes three arguments, in this order:

1. The message to be displayed
2. A code for action buttons to be displayed in the box
3. A title for the error message box

The call that produces the message box for the non-numeric inputs is shown in Exhibit 10.5.

The code for the For...Next loop at the top of this subroutine initially sets all three positions of the menu_case array to False. The menu case variable is a Boolean array of three elements. Each element of the array corresponds to one of the menus we are now about to error check. An initial setting of False means that there are no errors as yet detected. The loop, using a Select...Case statement, then calls three different subroutines. Each of these subroutines error checks the numeric inputs of a specific menu. The menus are, in order: the Program Costs Menu, the Collateral Criteria Menu, and the Default and Prepayment Menus. As each of these three subroutines compares the inputs, the subroutine that finds a non-numeric value will set the corresponding menu_case variable to True. Each time one of the elements

```
Sub errAllMenus_for_IsNumerics()

    'error checks fields for the Program Costs, Selection Criteria and Prepay/
       Defaults menus
    Call IsNumeric_ProgramCostsInfo        'populates msgInfo(1) & errcase(1) variable
    Call IsNumeric_CriteriaInfo            'populates msgInfo(2) & errcase(2) variable
    Call IsNumeric_DefaultPrepayInfo       'populates msgInfo(3) & errcase(3) variable

    'If err_total greater than zero there are errors to print -- print them!
    err_total = errcase(1) + errcase(2) + errcase(3)
    If err_total > 0 Then
        'Error box title -- displayed above any errors
        msgTotal = "Non-numeric inputs for the following Tables" & Chr(13) & Chr(13)
        'Print the combination of errors based on the error code value
        If errcase(1) > 0 Then msgTotal = msgTotal & msgInfo(1)   'program costs
                                                                     menu errors
        If errcase(2) > 0 Then msgTotal = msgTotal & msgInfo(2)   'selection criteria
                                                                     menu errors
        If errcase(3) > 0 Then msgTotal = msgTotal & msgInfo(3)   'default/prepay
                                                                     menu errors
        msgPrompt = msgTotal
        msgResult = MsgBox(msgPrompt, cMsgButtonCode1, msgTitle)
        End
    End If

End Sub
```

EXHIBIT 10.5   VBA code to generate an error for non-numeric data in a numeric menu field

of the menu_case array assumes a value of True, the subroutine will concatenate an error statement to the msgTotal variable. Each one of the elements of the msgInfo array contains a specific error message related to the menu that generated it.

To illustrate this process, Exhibit 10.6 displays the Program Costs Menu prior to error check. There is an extraneous character "/" in the "Clean Up Call Level" field.

Program Costs Menu		

Program Expenses

0.75%	Servicer Fee (off of Asset Balance)
0.20%	Program Fees (off of Note Balance)

Run the Model

Principal Reallocation Triggers

10%/	Clean Up Call Level
5.00%	Rolling 3 Month Default Rate

Advance Rate

95.00%	Conduit Percentage

2.00%	Conduit Spread

EXHIBIT 10.6   Program Costs Menu

```
Sub IsNumeric_ProgramCostsInfo()

    msgInfo(1) = "Program Cost Menu   => non-numeric entry in inputs" & Chr(13)
    msgComp(1) = "    Servicing Expense rate" & Chr(13)
    msgComp(2) = "    Program Expense charge rate" & Chr(13)
    msgComp(3) = "    Note Clean Up Trigger Percentage" & Chr(13)
    msgComp(4) = "    3 Month Rolling Delinquency Rate" & Chr(13)
    msgComp(5) = "    Conduit Advance Rate" & Chr(13)
    msgComp(6) = "    Conduit Financing Spread Rate" & Chr(13)
```

EXHIBIT 10.7 Listing of data entry items as String variables for use in an error message box

Exhibit 10.7 is the declaration for msgComp, a six-element String array, each element of which is an error message for a single field on the menu. In addition, the base message, the variable named msgInfo, is populated with a string telling the user which menu is being checked. If no errors are found, this will never be printed, but for now it is the base and foundation message upon which we will concatenate additional error messages containing more specific information if needed. The symbol Chr(13) calls for a new line, as if we had created a carriage return by placing it at the beginning or end of a string. This produces a line-by-line effect for the combined message. The next block of code in Exhibit 10.8 we have seen before: it checks each of the Range names to see if the data input is numeric. If the data is not numeric, a value of False is returned. When compared with the False of the statement, a True is generated (an error is found).

If the code is working correctly err_result element 3 will have a True value.

We can check this by using the debugger and putting a watch on err_result.

The code will now test each of the elements of the err_result array. If that array element is True, it will append a specific error message for that test onto the base msgInfo message. See Exhibit 10.9.

The variable msgInfo will grow longer as each new error condition is detected and appended. This is the starting value for the variable msgInfo as the loop begins to operate.

```
"Program Cost Menu   => non-numeric entry in inputs"
```

The value of menu_case(1) is True, so the subroutine appends the error message to msgInfo.

```
"Program Cost Menu   => non-numeric entry in inputs"
"    Note Cleanup Trigger Percentage "
```

```
'set all IsNumeric tests to OK
For itest = 1 To ISNUMERIC_TESTS_PROG_COSTS
    err_result(itest) = False     'False means that no error is detected
Next itest

'check each of the fields for non numerics
err_result(1) = (IsNumeric(Range("m2ServicerExp")) = False)
err_result(2) = (IsNumeric(Range("m2ProgramExpenses")) = False)
err_result(3) = (IsNumeric(Range("m2TrigCleanUpPct")) = False)
err_result(4) = (IsNumeric(Range("m2Trig3MDelRate")) = False)
err_result(5) = (IsNumeric(Range("m2AdvanceRate")) = False)
err_result(6) = (IsNumeric(Range("m2ConduitSpread")) = False)
```

EXHIBIT 10.8 VBA code that checks for numeric data in each of the menu fields

```
'combine any or all of the above messages into a compound message
  'the compound message will be sent to the calling sub for display
  errcase(1) = False    'no non numerics detected
  For itest = 1 To ISNUMERIC_TESTS_PROG_COSTS
    If err_result(itest) = True Then  'got one!
        errcase(1) = errcase(1) + 1   'tell calling sub there are errors on
                                             this menu
        msgInfo(1) = msgInfo(1) & msgComp(itest)  'add detail msg to general
                                                     header msg

    End If
  Next itest

End Sub
```

EXHIBIT 10.9 Loop assembles each of the component messages into a single, long message

The subroutine named "IsNumeric_ProgramCostsInfo" is now complete. The program returns to the calling subroutine, "errAllMenu_is_ForNumerics." The upper loop now completes and the other two menus are checked in turn. Neither the Collateral Criteria Menu or the Defaults and Prepayment Menu have any numeric errors. As such, when we complete the loop the value of the errcase array is True in position 1 and False in positions 2 and 3, corresponding to the results across the three menus checked. Given these values then, only the msgInfo(1) variable value will be concatenated to the msgTotal variable. See Exhibit 10.10.

At this point we have the completed error message and have stored it in the msgTotal variable. We now write it into the msgPrompt variable and the first argument of the MsgBox function is complete! The second argument of the function is an indication of what buttons and controls we want to go within the window. We need to specify what combinations of buttons and icon marking we want the message box to display, and whether there is to be an action button in the box. This can be accomplished by combining a number of VBA-supplied values into a single variable, and passing that value as the second argument of the msgBox function. See Exhibit 10.11.

```
'If there are errors to print -- print them!

  err_total = errcase(1) + errcase(2) + errcase(3)
  If err_total > 0 Then
     'Error box title -- displayed above any errors
     msgTotal = "Non-numeric Inputs for the following Tables" & Chr(13) & Chr(13)
     'Print the combination of errors based on the error code value
     If errcase(1) > 0 Then msgTotal = msgTotal & msgInfo(1)  'program costs menu
     If errcase(2) > 0 Then msgTotal = msgTotal & msgInfo(2)  'selection criteria
                                                                 menu
     If errcase(3) > 0 Then msgTotal = msgTotal & msgInfo(3)  'prepay/deault menu
     msgPrompt = msgTotal
     msgResult = MsgBox(msgPrompt, cMsgButtonCode1, msgTitle)
     End
  End If

End Sub
```

EXHIBIT 10.10 We have returned to the "errAllMenus_for_IsNumerics" subroutine. Only errcase(1) has a value greater than 0. We will therefore append the value of msgInfo(1) to msgTotal

```
Const cMsgButtonCode1        As Integer = vbOKOnly + vbCritical
Const cMsgButtonCode2        As Integer = vbOKOnly + vbExclamation
```

EXHIBIT 10.11   Assigning values at the declarations for button code variables

Earlier we declared an Integer variable by the name of cMsgButtonCode01. This button combined the "vb" display codes of vbOKOnly and vbCritical. The combination will produce a single "OK" button, with a "Critical" warning icon in the form of a red circle enclosing a white cross. When constructing error message boxes, you can combine one button, one default button, and one icon message into a single message box. The complete listing of these is shown in Exhibit 10.12.

The final element is the title for the error message box. All the error checking is concerned with is the contents of the menus. It does not worry about anything that occurs while the model is running, or the reasonableness of the outputs, or anything else at all for that matter. We can therefore assign a simple and direct title for all the input checking error message boxes. It is a common message for all error checking, whether checking data types, values, reasonableness, files, and so forth. We can assign this value as we enter the topmost function, which will then make it available to all the other functions. See Exhibit 10.13.

With all the pieces in place we get the call to the msgBox function, as shown in Exhibit 10.14.

Value Checking

The preceding example of an error-checking and -messaging subroutine has 99% of what you need to know. Thankfully, the following examples of different types of

EXHIBIT 10.12   Table of button code constants and their display effects

Table of MsgBox Button Constants

Button Constant Label	What It Does
VbOKOnly	1 Button – OK
VbOKCancel	2 Buttons – OK & Cancel
VbYesNoOnly	2 Buttons – Yes & No
VbYesNoCancel	3 Buttons – Yes, No, & Cancel
VbRetryCancel	2 Buttons – Retry & Cancel
VbAbortRetryIgnore	3 Buttons – Abort, Retry, & Ignore
Default Button Identifiers	**What It Does**
vbDefaultButton1	Highlights 1st from left Button
vbDefaultButton2	Highlights 2nd or middle Button
vbDefaultButton3	Highlights rightmost Button
Icon Identifiers	**What It Does**
VbCritical	Displays a Critical Icon
VbExclamation	Displays a Exclamation Icon
VbInformation	Displays a Information Icon
VbQuestion	Displays a Question Icon

```
'===========================================================================
' This is the overall error checking subroutine. With the exception of the subroutine
'  "errAllMenus_for_IsNumerics" each subroutine error checks a specific menu. The
'  errAllMenus_for_IsNumerics' subroutine checks for non-numeric information in the
'  fields of the Selection Criteria, the Program Costs, and the Default Prepayment
'  menu. That subroutine returns a compound message for the numeric checks of all of
'  the error conditions of the three menus in one box.
'===========================================================================
Sub ErrCheck_All_Menus()

    'Set up of message title
    msgTitle = "MODEL MENUs Input Error"
    Call errAllMenus_for_IsNumerics  'IsNumerics check for 3 menus
    Call errMainMenu                 'error check Main menu
    Call errProgramCostsMenu         'error check Program Costs menu
    Call errReportsMenu              'error check Report Election menu
    Call errGeographicMenu           'error check Geographic Selection menu
    Call errSelectionCriteriaMenu    'error check Selection Criteria menu
    Call errDefaultsMenu             'error check Default/Prepay menu

End Sub
```

EXHIBIT 10.13 Subroutine to check all menu inputs

error checking will be much more succinct. Error checking for values is primarily focused on preventing someone from putting in what is obviously an outrageously egregious value, a negative original balance, say. Again, these errors are often the result of naive users or bad data transfers, but better to catch them before you run the model for 20 minutes and it blows up! Exhibit 10.15 is an example for the fields in the Collateral Criteria Menu. The first step is to declare the set of error messages we could possibly produce based on the tests we are to perform.

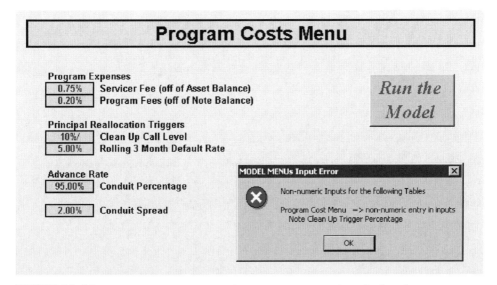

EXHIBIT 10.14 Program Costs Menu with error message window displayed

```
Sub errSelectionCriteriaMenu()

Dim err_sum    As Integer  'check sum to see if ANY errors are present

  msgTotal = "Collateral Selection Criteria Menu => " & Chr(13)

  msgInfo(1) = "Failed Test = Value must be Greater Than Zero" & Chr(13)
  msgInfo(2) = "Failed Test = Minimum value must be less than Maximum value " &
    Chr(13)
  msgInfo(3) = "Failed Test = Value must be less than 25%" & Chr(13)
  msgInfo(4) = "Failed Test = Value must be less than 100%" & Chr(13)

  'detailed error messages for individual input fields
  msgComp(1)  = " minimum orig term,"
  msgComp(2)  = " maximum orig term,"
  msgComp(3)  = " minimum rem term,":
  msgComp(4)  = " maximum rem term,"
  msgComp(5)  = " minimum orig balance,":
  msgComp(6)  = " maximum orig balance,"
  msgComp(7)  = " minimum rem balance,":
  msgComp(8)  = " maximum rem balance,"
  msgComp(9)  = " minimum gross coupon,":
  msgComp(10) = " maximum gross coupon,"
  msgComp(11) = " maximum LTV"
```

EXHIBIT 10.15   Components of possible error messages for the values of the collateral selection criteria tests

We can see that we are going to test: entry > 0, minimum < maximum, some entries < 25%, and some entries < 100%.

In Exhibit 10.16, there are 11 tests in total. If the menu input is to be tested against lower and upper bounds, both x and y are assigned a value.

The main testing loop is going to apply the four tests cited in Exhibit 10.15. Inside of the outer loop, the next loop will be of the data elements we are inputting into the menu. When we are testing whether a minimum/maximum pair is OK, we will need to load the data for both. If we are only going to test for a single condition,

```
'The outer loop will apply each of the 4 tests described in the MsgInfo variables
'above. The inner loop will cycle through each of the 11 variables on the Selection
'Criteria Menu. We are using the variables x and y for brevity.
  For icondition = 1 To VALUE_TESTS_SEL_CRIT
    For itest = 1 To SEL_CRIT_FIELDS
      err_result(itest) = False
      y = 0#
      Select Case itest
          Case Is = 1: x = Range("m5MinOrigTerm"): y = Range("m5MaxOrigTerm")
            Case Is = 2: x = Range("m5MaxOrigTerm")
            Case Is = 3: x = Range("m5MinRemTerm"): y = Range("m5MaxRemTerm")
            Case Is = 4: x = Range("m5MaxRemTerm")
            Case Is = 5: x = Range("m5MinOrigBal"): y = Range("m5MaxOrigBal")
            Case Is = 6: x = Range("m5MaxOrigBal")
            Case Is = 7: x = Range("m5MinRemBal"): y = Range("m5MaxRemBal")
            Case Is = 8: x = Range("m5MaxRemBal")
            Case Is = 9: x = Range("m5MinGrossCoup"): y = Range("m5MaxGrossCoup")
            Case Is = 10: x = Range("m5MaxGrossCoup")
          Case Is = 11: x = Range("m5MaxLTV")
      End Select
```

EXHIBIT 10.16   Select...Case statement for the collateral eligibility tests

```
Select Case icondition   'build the messages
    Case Is = 1:      'test for > 0
       If x < 0# Or y < 0# Then
           errcase(icondition) = errcase(icondition) + 1
           If errcase(icondition) >= 4 Then msgInfo(1) = msgInfo(1) & Chr(13)
           msgInfo(1) = msgInfo(1) & msgComp(itest)
       End If
    Case Is = 2:      'test minimum and maximum range input
       If itest = 1 Or itest = 3 Or itest = 5 Or itest = 7 Or itest = 9 Then
           If x >= y Then
               errcase(icondition) = errcase(icondition) + 1
               If errcase(icondition) >= 2 Then msgInfo(2) = msgInfo(2) & Chr(13)
               msgInfo(2) = msgInfo(2) & msgComp(itest) & msgComp(itest + 1)
           End If
       End If
    Case Is = 3:      'test that the value is less than 25%
       If itest = 9 Or itest = 10 Then
           If x >= 0.25 Then
               errcase(icondition) = errcase(icondition) + 1
               msgInfo(3) = msgInfo(3) & msgComp(itest)
           End If
       End If

    Case Is = 4:      'test that the value input is less than 100%
       If itest = 11 Then
           If x > 1# Then
               errcase(icondition) = errcase(icondition) + 1
               msgInfo(4) = msgInfo(4) & msgComp(itest)
           End If
       End If

    End Select
  Next itest
 Next icondition
```

EXHIBIT 10.17   Testing for values

we only need the value of a single menu field. The Select . . . Case statement will read in information from the Ranges on the menu and assign them to working variables. We will then use these variables to conduct the tests. Dependent on which variable is in use, specific tests will be applied to that variable will be applied. See Exhibits 10.16 and 10.17.

All inputs to the menu have Test 1 (non-Negativity) applied. Variables 1, 3, 5, 7, and 9, which are all the minimums, have the "minimum must be less than maximum" test applied. Variables 9 and 10, the minimum and maximum gross coupon, are tested against 25%. Variable 11, the maximum Loan-to-Value (LTV) ratio, is tested against 100%.

At each test point, an appropriate error message is appended to the master base message and a trigger to concatenate the message to the main message is set. In the end, the tests with the positive triggers are appended to the base message to produce the final compound messages summarizing all the error conditions of the page. See Exhibit 10.18.

In Exhibit 10.18, if the model determines that any of the elements of the errcase variable are True, their sum will be greater that zero. If the sum is greater than zero, some of the variables have failed some of the tests. The model then tests each variable and writes out the error messages generated.

```
'Print the combination of errors based on the error code value
For itest = 1 To VALUE_TESTS_SEL_CRIT
     err_sum = err_sum + errcase(itest)
Next itest
If err_sum > 0 Then
     Sheets("Collateral Criteria Menu").Select
     For itest = 1 To VALUE_TESTS_SEL_CRIT
          If errcase(itest) > 0 Then msgTotal = msgTotal & Chr(13) & msgInfo(itest)
     Next itest
     msgPrompt = msgTotal
     msgResult = MsgBox(msgPrompt, cMsgButtonCode1, msgTitle)
     End
End If
```

EXHIBIT 10.18   Testing if any error conditions are True

See Exhibit 10.19 for an example of the Collateral Selection Criteria Menu that produced this error message box.

Cross-checking of Inputs

An example of cross-checking can be as simple as the following: The user indicates that collateral selection is to be performed. On the Geographic Menu, the user meant to select only the loans from the state of California to isolate the characteristics of that geographic population. The easiest way to do this is to click the "Exclude" button for

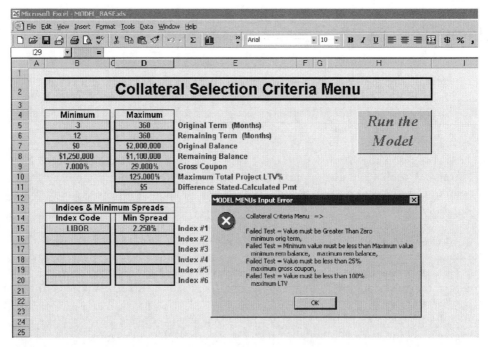

EXHIBIT 10.19   Collateral Selection Criteria Menu showing incorrect entries and the error message box displayed

```
Sub errGeographicMenu()

    msgTotal = "Geographic Selection Menu " & Chr(13)
    msgInfo(1) = " Failed Test = No States are selected" & Chr(13)
    If Range("m1CollatElig") Then
        For itest = 1 To STATES_PER_COL
            If Range("m6States1").Cells(irow) <> "" Then Exit Sub
            If Range("m6States2").Cells(irow) <> "" Then Exit Sub
            If Range("m6States3").Cells(irow) <> "" Then Exit Sub
        Next itest
        Sheets("Geographic Menu").Select
        msgTotal = msgTotal & msgInfo(1)
        msgPrompt = msgTotal
        msgResult = MsgBox(msgPrompt, cMsgButtonCode1, msgTitle)
        End
    End If

End Sub
```

EXHIBIT 10.20   Cross-checking between menus

the National category that will deselect all the states. Then simply select California by placing an "X" in the state box. However, the fateful "X" was not entered, (the user being distracted at the time), and the model is run with no geographic regions selected at all. The code that performs this check is in Exhibit 10.20. The subroutine will use a For . . . Next loop to test each row of the three column Ranges of the menu for *anything* other than a blank cell. If it finds even one of the cells in a non-blank configuration, it immediately exits the subroutine using the "Exit Sub" command. However, if it does not exit the subroutine by the end of the loop, there have been no states selected, and an error message is issued to that effect. Take a minute to study Exhibit 10.20 again. This is a simple way to approach the task of validating lists on menus if you only need to find a single item checked to pass the test. A similar approach would work equally well on the Reports Selection Menu, for example.

With all states unselected, every loan in the portfolio would be eliminated in the collateral selection process!

File Specification Error Checking

All of the reports that we wish to produce are based on a set of template files. At various points, the model will try to locate and open these template files to recopy them to the names of the output files. The model will crash looking for a misspelled template file name if we fail to detect this before we start the run. A good error-checking routine will first confirm that the template file exists, and second, confirm that the file is not protected from writing activity from the model or a user (e.g., that the file is not already in use and thus unavailable). The subroutine featured in Exhibits 10.21 and 10.22 accomplishes both ends.

Here we first build the file pathway, then try to open it. If we get an error when we try to open the template file, we will jump to a special block of code, out of sequence from the subroutine. This block of code tests the error code that we get from the attempt to open the file. If the error code is **52, 53, 75, or 76**, then the file either does not exist, the pathway does not exist, or the file or its directory cannot

```
Sub errMainMenu_FilesCheckTemplate()

Dim iblock                     As Integer        'counter for number of file checks
Dim errFileMissing(1 To MAIN_MENU_
  TEMPLATE_FILE_NAMES)         As Boolean        'code for missing file by file
Dim a                          As String         'abbreviation for pathway
Dim template_pathway           As String         'pathway to the template directory
Dim template_file_name         As String         'current file being tested
Dim template_file_target       As String         'expected file name
Dim output_pathway             As String         'pathway to the results directory
Dim output_file_name           As String         'current output file being tested
Dim output_file_target         As String         'expected output file name
Dim iFileNumber                As Integer        'error code number from Excel
Dim count_miss                 As Integer        'how many files are missing?
Dim go_ok_03                   As Boolean        'trigger that a file is missing

     msgTotal = "MAIN MENU INPUT ERROR MESSAGES " & Chr(13) & Chr(13)
     'Missing template filename entry error messages
     msgInfo(1) = "  OUTPUT TEMPLATE FILES are missing" & Chr(13)
     msgInfo(2) = "    Collateral Report template file missing" & Chr(13)
     msgInfo(3) = "    Exceptions Report template file missing" & Chr(13)
     msgInfo(4) = "    Cash Flow Waterfall template file missing" & Chr(13)
     msgInfo(5) = "    Matrix Summary template file missing" & Chr(13)
     msgInfo(6) = "    Single Scenario template file missing" & Chr(13)
     'set up the pathway to the template directory
     a = Range("m1DirectoryPath")
     template_pathway = a & "template\"
     count_miss = 0    'number of missing template files
```

EXHIBIT 10.21   Checking for existence of the Report Packages template files

be written to. We therefore record the template file as missing (= True) and set the switch to produce the error message later. See Exhibit 10.23.

The VBA code in Exhibit 10.24 builds the error message based on the missing template files. Then because we have set the local go_ok_03 to True (something is wrong, the template file cannot be located), we display the message box. Normally this would be the end of the subroutine, but with the file opening error code displaying, we need to exit the subroutine before we get to the **End Sub** statement. **Exit Sub** will do just as well, and we use it here. We can also use the mirror version of this statement to check that the designated output files names *are not already there*, so that the model does not overwrite them.

```
go_ok_03 = True
For iblock = 1 To 5
   Select Case iblock
         Case Is = 1:   template_file_name = Range("templateCollat")
         Case Is = 2:   template_file_name = Range("templateIneligible")
         Case Is = 3:   template_file_name = Range("templateWaterfall")
         Case Is = 4:   template_file_name = Range("templateMatrix")
         Case Is = 5:   template_file_name = Range("templateScenario")
   End Select
   template_file_target = template_pathway & template_file_name
   'open template file and set err message
   errFileMissing(iblock) = False
   On Error GoTo TemplateFileErr
   iFileNumber = FreeFile()
   Open template_file_target For Input As iFileNumber
Next iblock
```

EXHIBIT 10.22   Checking each of the template file name fields

```
TemplateFileErr:
    Select Case Err
        Case Is = 52, 53, 75, 76
            errFileMissing(iblock) = True
            count_miss = count_miss + 1
    End Select
    Resume Next
```

EXHIBIT 10.23   Missing file error message code

```
'based on the number of missing files write the compound error message
    If count_miss > 0 Then
        go_ok_03 = False
        If count_miss > 0 Then msgTotal = msgTotal & msgInfo(1)
        For itest = 2 To MAIN_MENU_TEMPLATE_FILE_NAMES + 1
            If errFileMissing(itest - 1) Then msgTotal = msgTotal & msgInfo(itest)
        Next itest
    End If

    'Print out the results of the error scan
    If go_ok_03 = False Then
        Sheets("Main Menu").Select
        msgPrompt = msgTotal
        msgResult = MsgBox(msgPrompt, cMsgButtonCode1, msgTitle)
        End
    End If
    On Error GoTo 0
Exit Sub
```

EXHIBIT 10.24   Building a compound error message

RUNTIME OPTION ERROR CHECKING

The last type of error checking is for inconsistent run options. The user wants a collateral selection exceptions report, but does not specify the collateral to be screened. Running the matrix summary reports is indicated, but either the output file name or the template file name for the matrix report is missing. These are simple subroutines to write. Exhibit 10.25 displays a subroutine that checks to see if any of the constituent matrix summary reports are selected, and if the overall matrix

```
Sub errMatrixReports()
    msgTotal = "Report Selection Menu -- Summary Reports " & Chr(13)
    msgInfo(1) = " Summary Matrix Writing Selected = No Matrix Reports selected" &
Chr(13)
    test_sum = 0
    If Range("m1WriteCFSummary") Then              'print out the matrix reports
        For itest = 1 To MATRIX_REPORTS
            If Range("m4MatrixRepsSelected").Cells(irow) <> "" Then Exit Sub
        Next itest
        Sheets("Reports Menu").Select
        msgPrompt = msgTotal & msgInfo(1)         'no reports selected message
        msgResult = MsgBox(msgPrompt, cMsgButtonCode1, msgTitle)
        End
    End If
End Sub
```

EXHIBIT 10.25   Runtime option error-checking code—no matrix reports selected

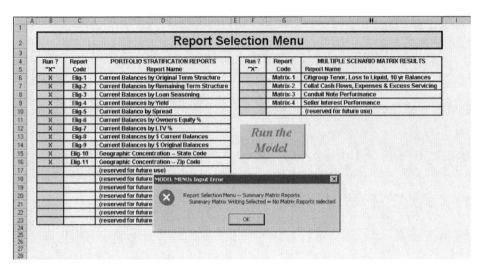

EXHIBIT 10.26   Runtime option error-checking code

analysis has been selected. An example of the resulting error message is displayed in Exhibit 10.26.

In Exhibit 10.26, the person running the model has indicated that he wishes to produce the Matrix Report package by entering their selection from the Main Menu. No individual matrix reports were selected from the Report Selection Menu. In this case, the model would have performed all the requisite calculations to populate the reports, and then simply not have produced any matrix report output!

DELIVERABLES CHECKLIST

The VBA Knowledge Checklist items for this chapter are:

- How to display progress messages on the Application Status Bar of an Excel worksheet
- How to use the IsNumeric function in error-checking subroutines
- How to write a general purpose error-checking subroutine
- How to associate a series of error tests with a particular menu
- How to use Select…Case and For…Next statements to construct complex error messages
- How to declare constant variables and set them to different button code actions
- The set of most commonly used button, icon, and default button code
- How to program a missing file error-checking subroutine

The Model Knowledge Checklist items for this chapter are:

- The roles of progress and error messages in a model
- The five types of error checks: Data Type, Value, Cross-check, File check, Run Option
- How to design each type of error check

NEXT STEPS

So far we have been concentrating on the front end of the model, its menus, and how to check the information they will channel into the model. We have also learned the rudiments of the VBA language.

In Chapter 11, "Designing the Model's Reports," we are going to jump to the back of the model. We will design a series of report packages. Two of these packages will be used to report on the disposition of the collateral of the deal after the selection process has been completed. The first will support the selection process by giving us a listing of all the ineligible loans in the portfolio. These are loans that for one reason or another are not suitable for inclusion in the proposed structure. The second set of reports will display the demographics of the loans that were accepted for inclusion in the deal.

Lastly, we will layout the formats for the report files that will relate the performance of the financial structure itself. It will tell us the behavior of the collateral cash flows under various combinations of prepayment and default conditions. We will be able to review in detail the month-by-month performance of the proposed structure. In addition, we will design high-level deal performance summary reports that allow us to compare large sets of model runs (up to 100 scenarios) in a single report.

The report package will clearly define the goals of the program design that we will now undertake. They will provide specific requirements as to the scope, quantity, and detail of the results we must produce and display.

Using this roadmap, we can then aggressively tackle the task of building our model.

ON THE WEB SITE

There is no Web site material for Chapter 10.

## CHAPTER 11

Designing the Model's Reports

OVERVIEW

In Chapter 10, we concentrated on messaging and output that informs model users about the model's progress and runtime errors. Specifically, error checking was incorporated to validate the information coming from the menus in order to proactively avert problems during model runs.

We are now going to turn our attention to designing the report package that we will produce from the model runs.

These reports will fall into four major groups:

1. The Ineligible Collateral Report Package
2. The Eligible Collateral Report Package
3. The Cash Flow Waterfall Report Package
4. The Deal Summary Matrix Report Package

Each of these report sets is very different from the others. All provide important information. We will consider them in the above order.

DELIVERABLES

Modeling Deliverables

- The modeling deliverable for this chapter is to design the report packages for the collateral selection process and the cash flow waterfall performance.

UNDER CONSTRUCTION

In this chapter we will design and create a set of four template files. They will contain the two sets of collateral selection results, the Ineligible Collateral Reports and the Eligible Collateral Demographic Reports. In addition we will design the templates for the Cash Flow Waterfall Report and the Summary Matrix Report.

None of these reports will have any VBA in them. Nor will we do any further development on the model.

This chapter and the reports we will design here are critical to the overall development of the model. It is these reports that will drive all of our subsequent VBA development. It will be the sole purpose of the model to produce the information to populate these reports in a meaningful way.

In the next chapter we will start writing VBA code in earnest. We will be able to do that because in this chapter we will have firmly established our goals through the design of these reports.

COLLATERAL REPORTING ACTIVITY

The production of the collateral selection reports is the first instance of output from the model. These reports will serve to tell us:

- How much collateral can be included in the deal. What was eligible as opposed to what was ineligible, and, more importantly, a detailed explanation of why it was ineligible.
- Of the collateral deemed to be ineligible:
  - All loans which have failed a particular test
  - Which criteria were failed by each loan
  - The number of loans that failed unique combinations of criteria
- What are the characteristics of the eligible collateral across a number of criteria such as:
  - Balance information
  - Loan-to-value statistics
  - Tenor characteristics
  - Geographic dispersion
  - Coupon levels

It is fairly certain that the form of the report packages will be constant while we deploy the model, though as we use the model, we may find that our initial report package has some holes in it. We may find that certain reports that are helpful in other situations are not so critical in this deal. If the product line is active and the model is robust, the report package will probably be central to the business. In this case the model and reporting package grow in size and complexity. At this point in time, the initial design phase of the model, we will lock the report package into this first configuration and freeze it. This will allow us to keep our development goals firm and to hone in on exactly what we will report. It is important to develop these specific goals early in the design and development process, so that time and effort are not spent chasing moving targets!

Using Template files

Once we set up the form of the reports, we will be building the model around them (not vice versa). This process will make use of the template files that we designed in Chapter 5. The design process will explicitly set up each of the reports with its own template file. Once these formats are described and "locked down," it is merely a matter of writing the VBA code to "fill-in-the-blanks." From that point onward, all the results of the model will go into template files in one form or another.

We now need to focus on specifying each of the report packages, what types of reports we want in them, and the content of those reports, down to the last detail. In Chapters 12 through 15 we will develop the VBA program to populate these reports. We will assume for the moment that we can find, copy, rename, and populate various report packages at will. *What, however, will we put in them?*

INELIGIBLE COLLATERAL REPORTING

The first step in the process of putting the deal together is to qualify the building blocks of the process, the loans in the portfolio. To do this, we will have built a menu into which the analyst can enter his selection criteria. These criteria define those characteristics that would render a loan ineligible for inclusion in the deal. Each loan in the portfolio will be individually selected for or against these criteria. Only those loans that pass all criteria will be considered for inclusion in the securitization.

We must develop a methodology that allows us to report on the ineligible collateral as distinct from the eligible collateral. This methodology must capture enough information about the causes of the disqualifying conditions of the rejected loan so that we are able to identify the specific ineligible loans and analyze any systemic causes of the ineligibility. It would also be useful if we could come up with a way to present both the uniqueness of the causes of the ineligibility condition and its "severity." What is meant by ineligible "severity"? It is both the number and types of ineligible conditions present for a given piece of collateral, and then, in a broader sense, for the portfolio as a whole.

There will be four basic types of reports in the ineligible collateral report package:

1. The **Single Criteria Exceptions Report.** A listing of all loans that failed a particular eligibility test. Since there are 11 individual selection criteria, there will be one report for each of the 11 tests.
2. The **Loan Listing Exception Report.** A listing of the loan-by-loan results, each ineligible loan listed in portfolio order, along with its respective failed eligibility criteria.
3. The **Summary Exception Report.** This report aggregates ineligible loans by the unique set of ineligibility conditions that they collectively failed. That is to say, all loans that failed the first and third eligibility tests only, and so on.
4. The **Assumptions Report.** This reports all assumptions, including the selection criteria used, so that we can replicate or modify this selection process later if we need to. This report will also contain the name of the collateral file containing the loan-by-loan information.

Single Criteria Ineligibility Report

Our first set of reports is the Single Criteria Ineligibility Report Package. This report set is a group of single-page reports that list all loans that were deemed ineligible due to a specific selection criteria test. The report lists the value of the eligibility test

Collateral Selection Portfolio Exception Report
INELIGIBLE-4 Minimum/Maximum Current Loan Balance

	Loan Number	Selection Criteria	Obligor Number	Obligor Name	Current Yield	Current Loan Balance	Current LTV	Current Equity Balance	Current Equity LTV	Original Appraisal Value
0				Averages/Totals		-	#DIV/0!	-	#DIV/0!	-

EXHIBIT 11.1   Template file format for the Single Criteria Ineligibility Report

criteria so that the reason the loan failed is immediately apparent. The information regarding the loan is displayed and the loans are aggregated as a group. It should be noted that an individual loan may appear on more than one or all of the Single Criteria Ineligibility Reports depending on how many of its characteristics fail the selection process. The template file version of such a report is found in Exhibit 11.1.

How do we determine that a loan is ineligible for inclusion in the portfolio? On the Collateral Criteria Menu, we have a number of parameters entered in regard to tests on balances, terms, coupon levels, loan-to-value (LTV) ratios, payments, and spread. The model will transfer these inputs from the menu into the model and employ them in a collateral screening process. We will need to compare each characteristic of the loan to the selection criteria to determine if it passes the test for inclusion. When it does not pass, we will need to record the cause or causes of its ineligibility, whether a single or multiple fail. This information will be stored so as to be useable when the time comes to write the ineligible collateral reports.

We will first need to get the data off the Collateral Criteria Menu and into the VBA variables. Then we can manipulate the data to use it as the selection basis for determining loan eligibility. When we get to the point of writing the VBA code, we will create a block of global variables to collectively hold these criteria.

Individual Condition Selection Criteria   There will be a total of 11 eligibility tests. They are:

1. Minimum and maximum remaining term
2. Minimum and maximum original term
3. Minimum and maximum original balance
4. Minimum and maximum remaining balance
5. Maximum LTV

6. Minimum spread for floating-rate loans
7. Eligible geographic code (state level)
8. Original must be greater than remaining term test
9. Original balance must be greater than remaining balance test
10. Stated payment must match calculated payment
11. Minimum or maximum gross coupon

It should be noted that this is a fairly simple and straightforward list of criteria. Depending upon the idiosyncrasies of the portfolio, you may end up having to apply much more complex selection criteria.

Selection Methodology   Once we have the selection criteria information ready to use, it will be applied to the proposed portfolio on a loan-by-loan basis to determine eligibility. To do this, we will design a subroutine to perform a series of tests on the values of criteria characteristics. That is the easy part. The comparisons will be mostly Range tests, in which we will see if the value of the loan datum is within the Range of the selection criteria minimum or maximum.

A typical test is applied against the remaining term of the loan. Deals normally take two to three months to put together. Loans that will be paid off by the time we are closing the deal are not suitable collateral. The test is a simple If . . . Then . . . Else statement. If the remaining term of the loan (in months) is less than or equal to the minimum selection criteria hurdle, the loan is ineligible.

Once we have developed the ineligibility patterns for each of the loans, we have all the data we need to produce all of the single-test ineligibility reports.

There is one other issue that we should mention at this point. Just because a piece of collateral passes all of the selection criteria does not mean that it will ultimately be included in the deal. In Chapter 18, "Running the Model," we will see that there are also collective selection tests that relate to concentration issues. Concentration issues result when there are too many pieces of collateral with similar or identical characteristics. These similarities can make the entire portfolio subject to specialized risk. For example, a portfolio with loans concentrated in a few adjoining ZIP codes may be vulnerable to localized economic or physical risk. An example would be the localized effects visited upon New Orleans by Hurricane Katrina.

Writing the Single Criteria Ineligibility Report   The program will now run through the portfolio, testing each loan successively, to see if it has failed the current single criteria test that the report displays. If it finds a match for the ineligibility condition, it adds the loan to the report. In the process of printing out the individual loan, it also prints out the test parameter value that caused the test to fail. These criteria will be different for each report. Most will be numeric, but some will not, such as two-letter postal codes on the Geographic Selection Report. When completed, a typical report will look like the one in Exhibit 11.2.

Writing the Loan Listing Exception Report   The next step in reporting the composition of the ineligible collateral is to produce a report that simply lists all ineligible loans. As noted earlier, the Single Criteria Ineligibility Report only reports those loans that are ineligible for one specific cause. A loan may appear on one, several, or

Collateral Selection Portfolio Exception Report
INELIGIBLE-4 Minimum/Maximum Current Balance

	Loan Number	Selection Criteria	Obligor Number	Obligor Name	Current Yield	Current Loan Balance	Current LTV	Current Equity Balance	Current Equity LTV	Original Appraisal Value
52				Averages/Totals		976,754	52.500%	1,183,246	63.598%	1,860,500
1	3	11,617			10.500%	11,617	48.40%	18,383	76.60%	24,000
2	58	19,859			10.500%	19,859	58.41%	20,141	59.24%	34,000
3	61	17,476			10.500%	17,476	54.61%	22,524	70.39%	32,000
4	76	20,587			10.500%	20,587	60.55%	19,413	57.10%	34,000
5	175	22,014			10.500%	22,014	55.03%	17,986	44.97%	40,000
6	196	20,136			10.500%	20,136	59.22%	19,864	58.42%	34,000
7	222	21,094			10.500%	21,094	49.63%	28,906	68.01%	42,500
8	224	22,931			10.500%	22,931	57.33%	17,069	42.67%	40,000
9	230	20,826			10.500%	20,826	52.07%	19,174	47.93%	40,000
10	240	18,704			10.500%	18,704	55.01%	21,296	62.64%	34,000
11	268	17,402			11.500%	17,402	68.24%	12,598	49.40%	25,500
12	283	24,306			9.500%	24,306	43.40%	45,694	81.60%	56,000
13	308	21,742			10.500%	21,742	63.95%	18,258	53.70%	34,000
14	375	19,064			10.500%	19,064	56.07%	20,936	61.58%	34,000
15	453	11,273			11.500%	11,273	66.31%	8,727	51.34%	17,000

EXHIBIT 11.2　Sample of the Single Criteria Ineligibility Report

all of these reports. Without this report there is no way to tell how many ineligible loans there are in total, short of laboriously cross-tabulating each of the 11 reports. The Loan-by-Loan Report addresses this problem by listing and then summarizing the disposition of all of the ineligible loans. The report provides an overview of the portfolio and also a laundry list of each loan, along with each loan's attendant rejection criteria. The report lists an abbreviated set of information concerning the loan, and then has a grid to display the single (or multiple) rejection criteria. See Exhibit 11.3.

Writing the Summary Exception Report　The last report of the Ineligible Collateral Report Package is the Summary Exception Report. This report lists the total number of ineligible loans and their aggregate balance, organized by their unique combination of eligibility test failures.

This report is particularly useful in trying to determine the basic feasibility of using the proposed collateral in the deal. If the analysis turns up many, many loans, each with multiple ineligible conditions, you may have to start from scratch with a different portfolio (assuming one is available). If, however, there are few ineligible loans and each is ineligible for a single reason, the viability of the portfolio may be fine. Collateral can be substituted, purchased, or future conforming production can be pledged to the deal. This report is also particularly valuable for detecting systemic data errors. An example is where a particular data field was incorrectly formatted, or where the data from one field is erroneously placed in another. See Exhibit 11.4.

To produce this report we will have to efficiently identify each of the unique ineligibility patterns in the portfolio. All the loans bearing that pattern would then

Loan Listing Exception Report
Individual Loan Ineligibility Conditions

Ineligibility Condition Reference

1 = Min/Max Remaining Term
2 = Min/Max Original Term
3 = Min Max Original Balance
4 = Min/Max Current Balance
5 = Exceeds Maximum LTV
6 = Unacceptable Floater Indice/Spread

7 = Excluded State or Geographic Region
8 = Inconsistent Original vs Remaining Term
9 = Inconsistent Original vs Remaining Balance
10 = Calculated vs. Stated Payment Differences
11 = Unacceptable Gross Coupon

Total Loans Rejected	Loan Number	Ineligibility Condition											Loan Yield	Current Balance
		1	2	3	4	5	6	7	8	9	10	11		
0		0	0	0	0	0	0	0	0	0	0	0	#DIV/0!	-

Loan Listing Exception Report
Individual Loan Ineligibility Conditions

Ineligibility Condition Reference

1 = Min/Max Remaining Term
2 = Min/Max Original Term
3 = Min Max Original Balance
4 = Min/Max Current Balance
5 = Exceeds Maximum LTV
6 = Unacceptable Floater Indice/Spread

7 = Excluded State or Geographic Region
8 = Inconsistent Original vs Remaining Term
9 = Inconsistent Original vs Remaining Balance
10 = Calculated vs. Stated Payment Differences
11 = Unacceptable Gross Coupon

Total Loans Rejected	Loan Number	Ineligibility Condition											Loan Yield	Current Balance
		1	2	3	4	5	6	7	8	9	10	11		
56		0	0	24	52	0	4	0	0	0	0	1	7.940%	3,024,285
1	3			1	1								10.000%	11,617
2	58			1	1								10.000%	19,859
3	61			1	1								10.000%	17,476
4	76				1								10.000%	20,587
5	175				1								10.000%	22,014
6	196				1								10.000%	20,136
7	222				1								10.000%	21,094
8	224				1								10.000%	22,931
9	230				1								10.000%	20,826
10	240			1	1								10.000%	18,704

EXHIBIT 11.3 From blank template file to populated report

be located and summed into a group total. We will tackle that problem with some very interesting VBA code later in Chapter 13, "Writing the Collateral Selection Code!" When completed it will look like Exhibit 11.5.

Writing the Complete Ineligible Collateral Report Package Having completed the formatting of each of these reports, it would not be a bad idea to review the steps

Summary Exception Report
Contracts Grouped By Unique Ineligibility Combinations

Ineligibility Condition Reference

1 = Min/Max Remaining Term
2 = Min/Max Original Term
3 = Min Max Original Balance
4 = Min/Max Current Balance
5 = Exceeds Maximum LTV
6 = Unacceptable Floater Indice/Spread
7 = Excluded State or Geographic Region
8 = Inconsistent Original vs Remaining Term
9 = Inconsistent Original vs Remaining Balance
10 = Calculated vs. Stated Payment Differences
11 = Unacceptable Gross Coupon

Unique Ineligibility Code	Ineligibility Condition											Number of Loans	Total Current Balance	Total Equity Position
	1	2	3	4	5	6	7	8	9	10	11			
	0	0	0	0	0	0	0	0	0	0	0	0	0	0

EXHIBIT 11.4 Template for the Summary Exception Report

that the model will need to perform to produce the package from start to finish. They are, in order:

1. Open the Ineligible Collateral template file.
2. Rename the template file to the name of the desired output file.
3. Use the ActiveWorkbook.SaveAs command to save the copy of the template file to the new filename.
4. Write the Assumptions Page so we know the selection criteria used for the reports.
5. Write Single Criteria Eligibility reports; if no loans are ineligible for a particular criteria, delete the report from the file.

Summary Exception Report
Contracts Grouped By Unique Ineligibility Combinations

Ineligibility Condition Reference

1 = Min/Max Remaining Term
2 = Min/Max Original Term
3 = Min Max Original Balance
4 = Min/Max Current Balance
5 = Exceeds Maximum LTV
6 = Unacceptable Floater Indice/Spread
7 = Excluded State or Geographic Region
8 = Inconsistent Original vs Remaining Term
9 = Inconsistent Original vs Remaining Balance
10 = Calculated vs. Stated Payment Differences
11 = Unacceptable Gross Coupon

Unique Ineligibility Code	Ineligibility Condition											Number of Loans	Total Current Balance	Total Equity Position
	1	2	3	4	5	6	7	8	9	10	11			
	0	0	1	2	0	2	0	0	0	0	1	56	3,024,285	646,065
8				1								28	620,496	25,150
12			1	1								24	356,258	10,582
32						1						3	1,618,184	69,679
1056						1					1	1	429,347	540,653

EXHIBIT 11.5 Summary Exception Report fully populated

6. Write the Loan Listing Exception Report.
7. Write the Summary Exception Report.
8. Save and close the file.

ELIGIBLE COLLATERAL REPORTING

Having determined what collateral is ineligible, then, by definition, everything that remains is eligible collateral! We can now produce reports concerning the eligible portfolio's composition.

These reports will be the standard, "slice and dice," reports.

Slice and dice reports stratify the portfolio by a number of different variables, mainly:

- Balance information—both original and current, and equity component
- Coupon information—especially useful for prepayment analysis
- Tenor information—original and remaining term
- LTV statistics—for both static and dynamic loss protection
- Geographic information—for concentration risk studies
- Borrower demographics–for economic demographics

Exhibit 11.6 displays the format of a typical stratification report.

Eligible Collateral Report #10
Current Balances Distribution by State or Territory

			4	5	6	7	8
			Number of Loans	Current Loan Balance	Current Loan LTV	% Current Balances	Cum % Current Balances
#	Name	Postal	0	-			

EXHIBIT 11.6 Typical Eligible Collateral stratification report

Eligible Collateral Report #10
Current Balances Distribution by State or Territory

			4	5	6	7	8	9	10
			Number of Loans	Current Loan Balance	Current Loan LTV	% Current Balances	Cum % Current Balances	Average Loan Balance	WtAvg Current Yield
#	Name	Postal	2,194	457,622,420					
1	California	CA	214	37,271,893	61.816%	8.145%	8.145%	174,168	9.139%
2	New Jersey	NJ	175	37,056,278	62.263%	8.098%	16.242%	211,750	9.105%
3	New York	NY	123	32,415,152	59.913%	7.083%	23.326%	263,538	9.038%
4	Texas	TX	95	28,574,832	65.460%	6.244%	29.570%	300,788	8.803%
5	Florida	FL	90	23,638,608	62.540%	5.166%	34.735%	262,651	8.988%
6	Georgia	GA	133	22,745,780	60.213%	4.970%	39.706%	171,021	9.002%
7	Colorado	CO	110	21,793,819	57.499%	4.762%	44.468%	198,126	9.109%
8	Arizona	AZ	90	21,114,531	64.638%	4.614%	49.082%	234,606	9.109%
9	Connecticut	CT	96	16,945,735	61.698%	3.703%	52.785%	176,518	9.005%
10	Pennsylvania	PA	91	16,798,410	59.025%	3.671%	56.456%	184,598	9.198%
12	Illinois	IL	80	15,020,312	63.120%	3.282%	59.738%	187,754	9.005%
13	Oregon	OR	68	14,827,009	61.724%	3.240%	62.978%	218,044	8.966%
14	Alabama	AL	59	14,536,326	60.323%	3.176%	66.155%	246,378	8.809%
15	Washington	WA	58	13,208,142	61.654%	2.886%	69.041%	227,727	8.892%

EXHIBIT 11.7   Completed collateral stratification report

This format is broadly similar to what every stratification or "strat" report looks like. It is a summary of all eligible collateral, their respective balances, tenors, dollar-weighted average coupon (WAC), and LTVs.

Each report will be different because of the type of sorting parameter used. Some reports will sort their information into numeric Ranges, a Distribution of Current Balances Report, for example. Here the stratifications will be a balance number with an interval, say $100,000 to $200,000. A second type of stratification report is based on a single criterion—state, ZIP code, industry, dwelling type, occupation, ethnicity, gender, and so on.

The sample report in Exhibit 11.7 is a stratification report based on geographical location. The geographical strats are the states and territories of the United States. Each cut of the report will be the number of loans and their collective information for all loans that are for business based in the state. The report would be produced for all geographic entities selected from the Geographic Menu. See Exhibit 11.7 for a populated report.

CASH FLOW WATERFALL REPORT

The third set of reports is a collection of detailed cash flow waterfalls. There will be a report for each unique combination of prepayment and default scenarios that we have specified to be run. This report is a full representation of the Cash Flow Waterfall Excel spreadsheet. We will see in a detailed, month-to-month schedule, the effects of the application of the cash flows from the eligible collateral pool and the resultant performance of the proposed deal structure. This report will be invaluable when we turn to the task of validating the operations of the model in Chapter 17.

The inputs to the waterfall are monthly cash flows containing:

- Scheduled amortization of principal
- Prepayments to principal
- Defaulted principal
- Recoveries of defaulted principal (after lag effects)
- Coupon income
- Beginning and ending collateral balances

The format of this report is, as mentioned above, identical to the waterfall contained in the Excel spreadsheet that we set up in Chapter 4, "Understanding the Excel Waterfall."

The amortization activity will be performed entirely in VBA. The waterfall then receives the cash flows as the model transfers the information from VBA arrays that hold the results of the number of prepayment/default scenario combinations specified. There is one set of vectors for each scenario. A scenario is defined as a unique combination of a prepayment speed and default rate level. The scenario specific cash flows are written into the Excel worksheet. The worksheet calculation network is then triggered with a "Calculate" command from the VBA program. The worksheet calculates the results, the VBA code extracts the scenario performance information, and the worksheet is copied, in its entirety, into another VBA array. It is stored there until it is written to an output file that, like the collateral eligibility reports previously discussed, was created from a template file.

In that the report will be identical to the waterfall worksheet itself, we have completed the design and layout of this report by designing the waterfall! All we need to do is copy the complete waterfall to the output file. This will then allow us to examine, in complete detail, all the spreadsheet numbers for each scenario. It will allow us to compare the dynamics of the differing prepayment and default scenarios, and their effects on the timing and performance of the financing repayment.

DEAL SUMMARY MATRIX REPORTS

While there is a lot of information about the behavior of the structure in the cash flow waterfall file, quite frankly, it can be **too much information** (TMI!). Twenty or 30 worksheets, each with 65 columns of numbers covering as many as 300 months, can be stupefying! After we have run the model a number of times and have satisfied ourselves that the waterfall is correct and the cash flow components are being correctly calculated, we can dispense with that level of detail in the reports. Now we are interested in looking at sets of scenarios, not individual cases. We want to see the **BIG PICTURE**. To this end we will generate the final level of model output, the Summary Matrix Report.

The matrix reports are a series of reports that present only summary information across the collective set of scenarios. Each of these reports look at related results and group four, five, or six performance measurements into a single cell that represents the output of an individual scenario. These reports will display the results of the

Summary Matrix Report #1
Conduit Financing Tenor Report

Average Life
Final Maturity
Macauley Duration
Modified Duration
Conduit $ Principal Outstanding 10 Yrs
Conduit % of Orig Bal Outstanding 10 Yrs

Default Levels	PSA Prepayment Methodology					
	1	2	3	4	5	6
	100.00%	125.00%	150.00%	175.00%	200.00%	225.00%
1 100.00% PSA	6.844 21.167 5.688 5.482 109,548,743 22.29%	6.380 20.417 5.364 5.171 95,273,736 19.39%	5.971 19.583 5.076 4.892 82,679,064 16.82%	5.611 18.750 4.817 4.643 71,588,603 14.57%	5.292 17.917 4.584 4.419 61,842,367 12.58%	5.009 17.167 4.375 4.217 53,295,247 10.85%
2 150.00% PSA	6.772 21.083 5.633 5.430 107,606,846 21.90%	6.315 20.333 5.315 5.123 93,584,882 19.04%	5.913 19.500 5.031 4.849 81,213,467 16.53%	5.558 18.667 4.776 4.603 70,319,599 14.31%	5.244 17.833 4.547 4.382 60,746,129 12.36%	4.965 17.083 4.340 4.183 52,350,517 10.65%

EXHIBIT 11.8 Sample Matrix Summary report displaying the results of 12 scenarios

scenarios in the model on a single page. They allow us to see trends and variance across as many as 100 scenarios at a time. One example of this is the Conduit Note Paydown Report. A key at the top of the page lists the information by position in the cell. Each individual cell holds the representative corresponding information for each scenario.

In Exhibit 11.8 we can see a portion of a populated Matrix Report. This segment displays twelve scenarios, the combination of two default levels of 100% and 150% PSA, and six prepayment rate levels of 100%, 125%, 150%, 175%, 200%, and 225%.

The maximum capacity of a single Matrix Report template is 100 scenarios—up to 10 prepayment speeds displayed in columns, and up to 10 default speeds displayed in rows.

There are four reports in the Summary Matrix Report Package. The template file has a single worksheet for each of the reports. The sample portion of the report shown in Exhibit 11.8 covers 5 prepay by 2 default scenarios, a total of 10 model runs.

If the matrix reports are to be run, the model will run the cash flow waterfalls one after another to produce the summary information needed by the reports. This will occur whether or not the waterfalls themselves are to be saved and output to a separate file. As each of the waterfall reports are run, a subroutine will capture the summary information from selected fields on the waterfall. As stated before, all of the information is in the form of individual datum, single numbers (average life, total defaulted principal, total releases from Seller Interest, etc.). We can

EXHIBIT 11.9   Contents of the Summary Matrix Reports

Conduit Financing Tenor Report	Conduit Note Paydown Report
1 Average Life	Total P&I Payments
2 Final Maturity	Principal Repayments
3 Macauley Duration	Debt Service Paid
4 Modified Duration	Severity of Principal Loss
5 Conduit $ Balance Outstanding 10 yrs	Coverage Ratio
6 Conduit % Balance Outstanding 10 yrs	Internal Rate of Return
Seller Interest Performance	**Collateral Cash Flow Components**
1 Seller Interest Internal Rates of Return	Total Scheduled Amortization
2 Excess Servicing Released to Seller	Total Prepayments to Principal
3 Seller Interest Coverage (or Loss)	Total Principal Retired
4 Program Fee Shortfall	Total Defaults of Principal
5 Servicing Fee Shortfall	Total Recoveries of Principal
6 Interest Shortfall	Total Coupon Cash Flows

capture this information in a two-dimensional array that is ordered by prepayment speed and default speed. These arrays will be later used to populate the reports. See Exhibit 11.9 for a listing of the fields of each report.

MATRIX REPORT PACKAGE

Exhibit 11.9 shows the reports that will comprise this report package.

ASSUMPTIONS REPORT

Another type of output that is particularly useful is a listing of the assumptions used to generate the output. This is even more useful when it is included in the output report itself. This is a direct expression of the principle discussed in Chapter 2, "Common Sense," which as you may recall goes, "You always hurt the one you love!" By including an Assumption Report with every report file you have immediately included what is in effect a *mega* comment. If there are questions about the results produced by that model run versus others, or if you wish to replicate the model run for validation purposes, you have all the information you need at your finger tips. It is such a wonderful idea to include the assumption information with each of the output files, so we will standardize the Assumption Report's form so we can easily drop it into whatever output file we are generating.

In addition to being useful, it also has the advantage of being simple to construct and write.

We already have menu examples of all of the inputs, and the variables into which they are being stored. We only need to reverse the process of reading them from the menu screen to write them into an output template.

Assumptions Page

Program Expenses	
	Servicer Expense
	Program Expenses
	Conduit Spread
Seller Interest	
	Initial Seller Interest
Principal Acceleration Triggers	
	Rolling 3-Month Deliquency Rate
	Cumulative Default Trigger
	Clean-Up Call Level

Collateral Selection Criteria		
Minimum	**Maximum**	
		Original Term (Months)
		Remaining Term (Months)
		Original Balance
		Remaining Balance
		Gross Coupon
		Maximum Total Project LTV%
		Difference Stated-Calculated Pmt

Indices & Minimum Spreads		
Index Code	**Min Spread**	
		Index #1 and Minimum Spread
		Index #2 and Minimum Spread
		Index #3 and Minimum Spread
		Index #4 and Minimum Spread
		Index #5 and Minimum Spread
		Index #6 and Minimum Spread

Geographic Selection		
	AK	Alaska
	AL	Alabama
	AR	Arkansas
	AZ	Arizona
	CA	California
	CO	Colorado
	CT	Connecticut
	DE	Delaware
	FL	Florida
	GA	Georgia
	HI	Hawaii
	IA	Iowa
	ID	Idaho
	IL	Illinois

Collateral Data File	
Default Sensitivity	
	Base Portfolio Default Rate
	Scenario Default Rate Step Increase
	Scenarios
	Default Methodology 1=CPR, 2=PSA, 3=User Defined
Prepayment Sensitivity	
	Base Prepayment Rate Rate
	Scenario Prepayment Rate Step Increase
	Scenarios
	Prepayment Methodology 1=CPR, 2=PSA
Loss & Recovery	
	Market Value Decline
	Recovery Period (months)

Distribution of Defaulted Principal					
Year 1		Year 11		Year 21	
Year 2		Year 12		Year 22	
Year 3		Year 13		Year 23	
Year 4		Year 14		Year 24	
Year 5		Year 15		Year 25	
Year 6		Year 16		Year 26	
Year 7		Year 17		Year 27	
Year 8		Year 18		Year 28	
Year 9		Year 19		Year 29	
Year 10		Year 20		Year 30	

EXHIBIT 11.10 Assumption Report, which accompanies each of the report packages to provide a clear guide to the criteria used in the analysis

The asssumptions files will also serve as a "living history" of the various model runs we will make over the course of the project. If we save and protect them, they will be available for model validation and documentation efforts later on in the life of the model. See Exhibit 11.10.

DELIVERABLES CHECKLIST

The Model Knowledge Checklist items for this chapter are:

- The four report packages are now completely specified.

NEXT STEPS

This completes the design process of the report packages.

Now that we know the content of the output files that we are responsible to produce, we can immediately begin to develop the model. In the next chapter, Chapter 12, "Main Program and Menus," we will begin to write the framework of the model.

We will start by laying out the Main Program and creating subroutine names for the major activities that we need to perform in the course of running the model.

The rest of the chapter will be spent on developing VBA subroutines that read the information from the modes and error-check the data, producing error messages if necessary.

In Chapters 13, 14, and 15, we will tackle, respectively, the tasks of writing the collateral selection code, calculating the collateral cash flows, and applying those cash flows to the Excel waterfall model.

ON THE WEB SITE

The Web site for this chapter contains the four template files that will comprise the complete report package for the model. The reports are contained in the following template files.

The file **"inelig_template.xls"** contains the eleven reports that list individual ineligible conditions for the collateral followed by the two summary level reports, the loan listing of each ineligible loan, and the summary report showing the loans grouped by unique ineligibility code.

The file **"collat_template.xls"** contains the demographic, balance, tenor, and coupon stratification reports of the eligible collateral.

The file **"waterfall_template.xls"** contains the single worksheet waterfall report. A copy of this sheet is propagated by the Main Program for the number of scenarios needed to be displayed based on the product of the number of prepayment and default speed assumptions.

The file **"matrix_template.xls"** contains the four Matrix Summary Reports for tenor, cash flows, Conduit Financing performance and Seller Interest performance.

Writing the Model

Main Program and Menus

OVERVIEW

Development of the Main Program

The Main Program is the brain and spinal cord of the model. It is the highest-level subroutine in the entire application. From it, all other calls to subroutines are made. No other subroutine calls it. A well-designed Main Program is generally brief. It should block out the major functionality of the model in less than a dozen calls to other high-level subroutines. The processes the model will perform as it runs should be evident in a glance at the subroutine calls of the Main Program. This will certainly be the case with the Main Program that you will build for this model! This model needs to accomplish the following:

- Accept and verify information entries input from the menus
- Open and read the contents of the proposed collateral file
- Perform a selection of collateral, eliminating ineligible collateral from the deal
- Produce reports on the eligible and ineligible collateral
- Amortize the collateral under specified prepayment and default assumptions
- Apply the cash flows to the structure waterfall and record the performance of the deal
- Produce reports displaying the deal performance

The structure of the Main Program will directly follow the steps outlined above.

The next three chapters, 13, "Writing the Collateral Selection Code"; 14, "Calculating the Cash Flows"; and 15, "Running the Waterfall: Producing Initial Results," will build the core of the model one step at a time. Working from the framework of the Main Program, we will move from general tasks to more and more specific tasks. Chapter 13 will focus on writing the subroutines to implement the collateral selection process and its reports. Chapter 14 will focus on the amortization of the eligible collateral and calculating the cash flows that will be transferred to the waterfall spreadsheet. In Chapter 15 we will develop the functionality that will manage the placement of these cash flows into the waterfall spreadsheet, trigger its calculation, and save the structural performance results.

Now we begin the heavy lifting of building the model. You will need to understand each of these processes in turn before moving on to the next. What we build in the next three chapters will be an ever-increasing elaboration of the framework of the Main Program we create here. A few, very few, high-level subroutine calls will trigger a cascade of ever more detailed operations. The Main Program code should be clear, precise, and ruthlessly logical. It is the framework upon which every other piece of VBA code will depend.

The Main Program is the central position from which all actions and subroutines/functions are subordinate. It is the ultimate senior subroutine, from which all other subroutines are called, and which is called by none. If it is not correctly and clearly constructed we will be building our castle on a base of sand. This chapter will also create the framework that will lie under the Main Program and that will guide us through the construction of the code in the succeeding chapters. The VBA code for the Main Program will be placed in a module named **"A_MainModel."** All the modules we create are listed in the VBA Editor window in alphabetical order, and we will use the "A_" prefix to position it at the top of the module list. This will position it with the **"A_Constants"** and **"A_Globals"** modules in the top of the Project Explorer window so we can readily identify it as a senior and critical module.

Integration of the Menus into the Model

The second focus of this chapter is to develop the Menu input activity. In Chapter 5 we designed the menus. As part of that process, Range names were assigned to each of the fields of the menus. In Chapter 6, "Laying the Model Groundwork," we created a series of VBA Modules to hold the code that will be written for all parts of the model. In Chapter 8, "Writing Menus: An Introduction to Data Ranges, Arrays, and Objects," the different types of VBA variables were listed and discussed. The type of information that was appropriate for each variable class and the different scopes that variables could assume were examined. These three components, the menus themselves, the Ranges of the menu spreadsheets, and the VBA variables are now combined. This chapter will focus on the process of moving data from the menus to the VBA arrays of the model where it can be used to direct the function of the model.

DELIVERABLES

The following are the VBA Language Deliverables for the chapter:

- How to structure a Main Program subroutine. How to create and use very high-level subroutines call that encompass the major functional blocks of the model. How to arrange this subroutine call into a clear and concise piece of code that serves as the foundation of the model.
- Looking at the subroutine structure under one of the high-level subroutines called from the Main Program. The subroutine will be the "Select_Deal_Collateral" subroutine. It performs the eligibility tests on the portfolio collateral. It also produces two report packages on the ineligible and the eligible collateral.
- How to use Ranges on the menus to efficiently error check and load the menu information into the VBA variables of the model. How to build a model wide menu errorchecking capability in the model.
- How to use the IsNumeric function in error checking.
- How to identify individual error conditions. How to associate specific error messages with those conditions, and how to use these component error messages to build more complex error box messages.

The following are the Modeling Deliverables for the chapter:

- What is a Main Program, what are its general characteristics, and how to write it
- How to design subroutines to error check the information input from the menus of the model
- Using the calling structure of the "Select_Deal_Collateral" subroutine as an example; getting familiar with nesting subroutine calls to perform ever more specific tasks
- Building all menu error checking subroutines
- Building subroutines to transfer the information from the menus to the VBA arrays of the model
- Declaring variables and constants to support the data moving into the model from the menus

UNDER CONSTRUCTION

In this chapter, we will add the menus the model needs to allow us to enter our model run specifications into the program. We will also create Range names in the models to allow us to more efficiently transfer information from the model to the VBA code.

Now we will begin to fill some of the previously created VBA modules with our first model code. The following modules will be the first we will use to begin the construction of the VBA portions of the model:

"A_Constants" will contain a set of public constant variables we will use to manage the menus of the model.

"A_Globals" will contain all the global variables we will need to support the menus we are building in this chapter. There will be one for every field on each menu. This module will also contain the data on the loan portfolio file we will read into the model named "portfolio_orig.xls."

"A_MainProgram" will contain the highest-level subroutine calls that will later be developed to perform all the menu functions. For now we will content ourselves with error checking the information input into the menus, if the inputs pass inspection reading them from the menus in VBA variables, and reading the contents of the collateral file.

Exhibit 12.1 "Hierarchy for Loan_Financing_Model Main Program in Module 'A_MainProgram'" will contain the highest level subroutines in the model. Each of these subroutines executes a major functional phase of the model

Exhibit 12.2 "Hierarchy for Read_Portfolio_Data_Files subroutine in Module 'CollateralReadDataFile'" will contain the subroutines that read the contents of the "portfolio_orig.xls" file.

Exhibit 12.3 "Hierarchy for error checking subroutines in Module 'Menus-ErrorChecking'" will contain a total of 17 subroutines that check all the input fields on every model.

Exhibit 12.4 "Hierarchy for Read_All_Menu_Inputs subroutine in Module 'MenusReadInputs' and hierarchy for Read_Prepay_Default_Menu subroutine in Module 'MenusPrepayDefault'" contains seven subroutines that read all the information from the menu once it has passed through the error checking process.

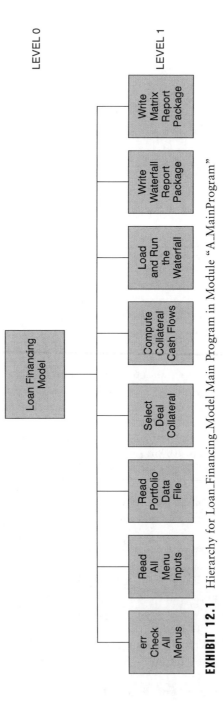

LEVEL 0

LEVEL 1

EXHIBIT 12.1 Hierarchy for Loan_Financing_Model Main Program in Module "A_MainProgram"

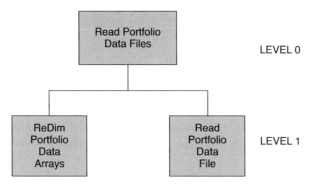

EXHIBIT 12.2 Hierarchy for Read_Portfolio_Data_Files subroutine in Module "CollateralReadDataFile"

MAIN PROGRAM

Well-designed Main Programs are brief. Let me repeat that.

Well-designed Main Programs are brief. Do we need to repeat it again? I think not.

The real question is "*Why* are they so brief?"

They are brief because they contain only the highest-level subroutine calls of the program. There may be only a dozen calls in the Main Program, but any one of them, or all or them, may have extensive and extremely detailed sets of other subroutines underneath them. A subroutine called from the Main Program is almost another Main Program in and of itself.

An example of this is the Collateral Selection and Reporting Process VBA code. This set of subroutines could be lifted completely out of the model and it would still function perfectly. (As the model matures you may elect to split this function out of the model and use it as a separate piece of software! In fact we will discuss just that in Chapter 21, "Managing the Growth of the Model.") The same would also be true for the reporting functionality of the model. Once the results have been captured from the waterfall spreadsheet, they could be written to files and the reporting software could be run against them without reference to the VBA code that created the results in the first place.

Keeping the above in mind, the number of subroutine and function calls from the Main Program is usually less than twenty, and can sometimes be as few as five or less. The subroutines called directly from the Main Program tend to be umbrella subroutines that in turn may have tens, or in the case of large models, hundreds of subroutines beneath them. This Main Program code in Exhibit 12.5 calls nine subroutines.

From the Main Program we cannot see any of the detail under these nine subroutine calls. However, the name of each of these subroutines (with one exception) indicates a wide scope of activity.

The *first* subroutine call, "Call PrepayDefault_ProgressMsg," simply clears the Application Status Bar of any existing messages. This "clearing the decks" is always a good thing to do so any messages that were there prior to start of the model are erased, preventing confusion.

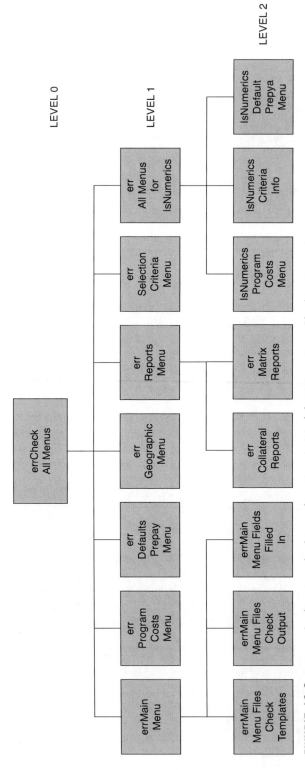

EXHIBIT 12.3   Hierarchy for error checking subroutines in Module "MenusErrorChecking"

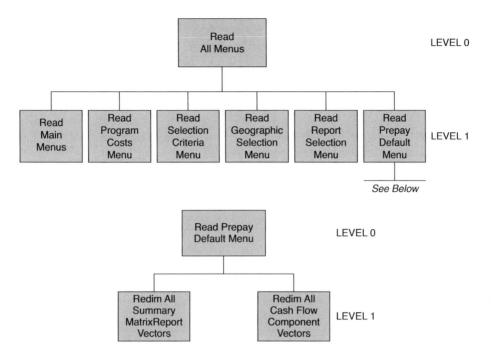

EXHIBIT 12.4 Hierarchy for Read_All_Menu_Inputs subroutine in Module "MenusReadInputs" and hierarchy for Read_Prepay_Default_Menu subroutine in Module "MenusPrepayDefault"

The *second* subroutine call, "Call ErrCheck_All_Menus" initiates error checking on all the inputs from the menus. It will make sure they are in the proper data form and that there is consistency between menus and requested actions

If all menu input is error free **the program will continue to run. If there are errors present the error checking subroutine will print the error message and end the program.**

```
Sub Loan_Financing_Model()

    Application.DisplayAlerts = False        'temporarily turn off the warning messages
    Call Display_PrepayDefault_              'display program progress msg (null)
      ProgressMsg(99)
    Call ErrCheck_All_Menus                  'error check all menu entries
    Call Read_All_Menu_Input                 'transfer the menu entries to variables
    Call Read_Portfolio_Data_File            'read in the loan information to variables
    Call Select_Deal_Collateral              'run the basic eligibility test or accept all
    Call Compute_Collateral_Cashflows        'generating the cash flows
    Call Load_and_Run_the_Waterfall          'runs the waterfall
    Call Write_Waterfall_Report_Package      'package of waterfall reports in detail
    Call Write_Matrix_Report_Package         'package of matrix reports
    Sheets("Main Menu").Select
    Application.DisplayAlerts = True          'turn message displays back on

End Sub
```

EXHIBIT 12.5 Code of the Main Model, which is named Loan_Financing_Model

The *third* subroutine call, "Call Read_All_Menu_Input," will now read in the verified data for the menu.

The *fourth* subroutine call, "Call Read_Portfolio_Data_File," will open the collateral file and read its contents. This will transfer all of the loan data from the collateral file and place the information in VBA arrays. It is this data that will form the basis for the eligibility testing and cash flow amortization that will follow later.

The *fifth* subroutine call, "Call Select_Deal_Collateral," performs the collateral selection process and writes the reports for both the ineligible and the eligible collateral.

The *sixth* subroutine call, "Call Compute_Collateral_Cashflows,"amortizes the cash flows of the collateral portfolio on a loan-by-loan basis.

The *seventh* subroutine call, "Call Load_and_Run_the_Waterfall,"populates the EXCEL waterfall model with the results and captures the structural performance accumulating both detailed and summary information.

The *eighth* subroutine call, "Call Write_Waterfall_Report_Package," produces the detailed waterfall report package.

The *ninth* subroutine call, "Call Write_Matrix_Report_Package,"produces the summary matrix report package.

This Main Program is a clear and concise expression of the steps we need to perform the analysis. A person with no knowledge of VBA would be able to look at the model steps that we laid out in the **"Overview"** section and trace the process step by step from beginning to end.

TYPICAL SUBROUTINE CALLED BY THE MAIN PROGRAM

One of the Main Program subroutine calls is the "Select_Deal_Collateral" subroutine. This high-level subroutine initiates the collateral selection process. It must make use of the entries from the Collateral Selection Criteria Menu to sort through the initially proposed loan portfolio and test each of the loans against a series of eleven tests. The outcome of these tests will determine which of the loans are eligible for inclusion in the deal.

Moving from its first call to its last, this subroutine makes a total of 46 subroutine and function calls to complete its tasks.

THREE SUBROUTINE CALLS FROM THE MAIN PROGRAM

The remainder of this chapter will look at the VBA code we will need to implement the first three high-level subroutines of the Main Program. These are:

1. **ErrCheck_AllMenus.** This subroutine moves from one menu to the next and reads the inputs from the model. It then error checks them for correct form, type, value Range, and reasonableness.
2. **Read_All_Menu_Input.** Once the "ErrCheck_AllMenus" subroutine has done its work, we know that the information contained on the menus can be used by the model. We now move the information from the Ranges of the menus into sets of global variables we will declare to receive them.

3. **Read_Portfolio_Data_File.** This subroutine locates, opens, and reads the loan portfolio information into a collection of global variables for later use in the collateral selection and cash flow amortization process.

We will now start at the beginning of this process and review what we will need to complete each of these steps. We will look at the structure of the model, and the structure of the subroutine trees that branch off the Main Program code. We will be adding code to the model and declaring variables and constants. These we will add to the appropriate modules as we progress.

We will build the model from the top down, declaring subroutines and functions by name in higher-level pseudo code before we write the VBA code for them. To repeat, much of this code you have already seen, especially the error checking and selection code; now we will simply put it all together. We will start with the subroutine "ErrCheck_AllMenus," the second executable statement of the model. This is the subroutine that initiates the error checking process for all the menu inputs prior to their use.

BUILDING MENU ERROR CHECKING

In Chapter 10, we first looked at the task of creating error messages to report various problems that could arise in the contents of the data and the function of the model. The process of error checking can take a variety of forms. The subroutine, shown in Exhibit 12.6, which initiates this activity is one of the nine high-level subroutines in the model and draws on a number of other calls immediately upon beginning its execution. Each of the subordinate subroutines called performs either an error checking or menu support function. High-level subroutines have a general form, mostly being composed of a laundry list of calls to their subordinates; this is the most prevalent organization for a model of this nature. See Exhibit 12.2.

This subroutine, like the other eight highest-level subroutines, has a very simple, if not stark appearance. It is a series of Call statements to other subroutines to perform a set of sequential tasks. The first task is to check that all data that needs to be in a numeric form is in that form. This screening process is important because if the model attempts to perform arithmetic operations on nonnumeric data, it will stop dead in its tracks. Once this task has been accomplished the model will need to check the contents of each of the other menus in turn. It will look at their inputs singularly,

```
Sub ErrCheck_All_Menus()
    'Set up of message title
    msgTitle = "MODEL MENUs Input Error"
    Call errAllMenus_for_IsNumerics
    Call errMainMenu
    Call errProgramCostsMenu
    Call errReportsMenu
    Call errGeographicMenu
    Call errCriteriaMenu
    Call errDefaultsMenu
End Sub
```

EXHIBIT 12.6 ErrCheck_All_Menus subroutine code

and then as they refer to related inputs across the other menus. This subroutine and all other menu error checking code will reside in the module "**MenuErrorChecking.**"

Error Checking All Menus for Correct Numeric Entries

Exhibit 12.7 contains the VBA code needed to error check the three menus that carry the numeric data of the model, the Program Costs Menu, the Collateral Selection Criteria Menu, and the Default and Prepayment Menu. At the top of the subroutine there is a small For…Next loop that will iterate three times, calling subroutines specifically designed to error check each of the aforementioned menus.

Each of these three subroutines will create a compound error message from any error conditions that are found in the menu inputs. If an error condition is detected, the value of the variable errcase will be incremented for each error that is detected on the menu. If we sum all three values of errcase together and the total is greater than 0, at least one of the error checking subroutines has found an error.

The variable msgTotal is then initialized to the value of the String "Non-numeric Inputs for the following Menus" and a pair of line returns are inserted. If subsequently the value of the variable errcase(1) is greater than 0, the "IsNumeric_ProgramCostsInfo" subroutine has found a problem and created an error message in the variable msgInfo101. Each of the other two elements of the errcase array are also tested and if msgInfo102 or msgInfo103 is greater than 0 the error messages they contain will also be added to the error message box.

```
'==============================================================================
' errProbMenu_for_IsNumerics
'   This subroutine checks for non-numeric entry errors in each of the tables of all
'   of the menus.  This subroutine must run first or you will be unable to test for
'   the reasonableness of the data, or load it into the declared numeric arrays.
'==============================================================================
Sub errAllMenus_for_IsNumerics()

    'error checks fields for the Program Costs, Selection Criteria and
    ' Prepay/Defaults menus
    Call IsNumeric_ProgramCostsInfo      'populates msgInfo(1) & errcase
    Call IsNumeric_CriteriaInfo          'populates msgInfo(2) & errcase
    Call IsNumeric_DefaultPrepayInfo     'populates msgInfo(3) & errcase

    'If err_total greater than zero there are errors to print -- print them!
    err_total = errcase(1) + errcase(2) + errcase(3)
    If err_total > 0 Then
        'Error box title -- displayed above any errors
        msgTotal = "Non-numeric Inputs for the following Tables" & Chr(13) & Chr(13)
        'Print the combination of errors based on the error code value
        If errcase(1) > 0 Then msgTotal = msgTotal & msgInfo(1) 'program costs menu
        If errcase(2) > 0 Then msgTotal = msgTotal & msgInfo(2) 'selection criteria menu
        If errcase(3) > 0 Then msgTotal = msgTotal & msgInfo(3) 'default/prepay menu
        msgPrompt = msgTotal
        msgResult = MsgBox(msgPrompt, cMsgButtonCode1, msgTitle)
        End
    End If

End Sub
```

EXHIBIT 12.7   errAllMenus_for_IsNumerics subroutine

```
Sub IsNumeric_DefaultPrepayInfo()

Const ISNUMERIC_TESTS = 8

    msgInfo(3) = "Prepayment, Defaults, & Losses Menu   => non-numeric entry in
                                                           inputs" & Chr(13)
    msgComp(1) = "    Base Default Rate" & Chr(13)
    msgComp(2) = "    Default Rate Increment" & Chr(13)
    msgComp(3) = "    Number of Default Increments" & Chr(13)
    msgComp(4) = "    Base Prepayment Rate" & Chr(13)
    msgComp(5) = "    Prepayment Rate Increment" & Chr(13)
    msgComp(6) = "    Number of Prepayment Increments" & Chr(13)
    msgComp(7) = "    Recovery Lag in Months" & Chr(13)
    msgComp(8) = "    Market Value Decline in Foreclosure" & Chr(13)
    'set all IsNumeric tests to OK
    For itest = 1 To ISNUMERIC_TESTS
          err_result(itest) = False
    Next itest
    'check each of the fields for non numerics
    err_result(1) = (IsNumeric(Range("m8DefBaseRate")) = False)
    err_result(2) = (IsNumeric(Range("m8DefIncrement")) = False)
    err_result(3) = (IsNumeric(Range("m8DefNumLevels")) = False)
    err_result(4) = (IsNumeric(Range("m8PreBaseRate")) = False)
    err_result(5) = (IsNumeric(Range("m8PreIncrement")) = False)
    err_result(6) = (IsNumeric(Range("m8PreNumLevels")) = False)
    err_result(7) = (IsNumeric(Range("m8RecoveryLag")) = False)
    err_result(8) = (IsNumeric(Range("m8MarketValDecline")) = False)
    'combine any or all of the above messages into a compound message
    'the compound message will be sent to the calling sub for display
    errcase(3) = False          'no non numerics detected
    For itest = 1 To ISNUMERIC_TESTS
        If err_result(itest) = True Then        'got one!
            errcase(3) = errcase(3) + 1         'tell calling sub to print out
            msgInfo(3) = msgInfo(3) & msgComp(itest)  'add detail msg to
               general header msg
        End If
    Next itest
End Sub
```

EXHIBIT 12.8   IsNumeric_DefaultPrepayInfo subroutine

If each of the variables msgInfo101, msgInfo102, and msgInfo3 are all equal to "1" the subroutine will simply sequentially concatenate the appropriate additional error messages onto the variable msgTotal. Thus the message in msgTotal will sequentially grow larger and larger until each of the variables is tested and later display it in the error message box.

The next step, shown in Exhibit 12.8, is to go one step deeper into the code and see how the values of msgInfo(1), msgInfo(2), and msgInfo(3) are constructed. In that the three subroutines that check for "IsNumeric" conditions are broadly similar we can look at just one. The subroutine that checks for numeric input on the Prepayment and Default Menu is shown in Exhibit 12.8.

The role of this subroutine is to check a total of eight different fields that contain Prepayment and Default speed information, the value of the Market Value Decline (MVD) percentage and the Recovery Lag (RL) in months from the time of the default.

The subroutine begins by declaring the base value of msgInfo(3) that identifies which menu the error message is being generated from. The next eight statements assign values to the array msg, one for each of the possible component error conditions. Once these declarations are in place, we have all the component parts of an all-inclusive error message. We just need to test the values of the Ranges on the menu to see if any of the values input are nonnumeric in nature.

The next step of the subroutine is to set all values of the err_result array to "False." This condition indicates that no errors have yet been detected. Testing of the values entered into the Ranges of the menu can now begin. The test is conducted with the following type of statement:

```
err_result(n) = (IsNumeric(Range("SomeRangeName")) = False)
```

How does this statement work?

If the contents of the Range *is* numeric then err_result in the following test will be set to True:

```
err_result(n) = IsNumeric(Range("SomeRangeName"))
```

The first test condition would then be equal to "True." If the second part of the test is now added, "= False" the test could be rewritten in the following form:

```
err_result(n) = (True = False)
```

True does not equal False (unless you are a politician). In that "True" does not equal "False" and the whole statement to the right of the "=" sign must be now "False." If, however, *the value in the Range is not numeric* in form, the statement will be evaluated as the following:

```
err_result(n) = (False = False)
```

The statement "False=False" is of course True! A value of "True" in this case means that there is an error present!

Confused? I certainly was the first time I saw this! I, however, wisely refrained from throttling the person who wrote the test and looked at it again a second time. It is quite clever! If you do not quite get it the first time, review the above until you do. It is a marvelous way to structure a one-line test to detect errors from a Range menu input.

Once we have the results of these tests we can move on to the next step—which is pasting all the sub messages together into one long message and displaying it in the message box. Remember that even though this composite message is growing longer and longer as each successive error condition is detected, it will appear as a series of short one-line messages to the user of the model. Why? We are able use the "Chr(13)" to introduce carriage returns into the body of the text that we will eventually print in the message box. See Exhibit 12.8.

The final portion of the subroutine sequentially tests each of the values of the err_result array. If any of the values of the array have changed from "False," their initial condition, to "True," then an error has been detected! The value of errcase(3) gets incremented by 1 to show that there is at least one error on the menu and the

```
Sub errCollateralReports()
    msgTotal = "Report Selection Menu -- Collateral Reports " & Chr(13)
    msgInfo(1) = "Collateral Report Writing Selected = No Reports selected" & Chr(13)
    If UCase(Range("m1WritePortReps")) = "Y" Then ' print out the matrix reports
        For itest = 1 To PORTFOLIO_REPORTS
            If Range("m4ReportsSelected").Cells(irow) <> "" Then Exit Sub
        Next itest
        Sheets("Reports Menu").Select
        msgTotal = msgTotal & msgInfo(1)      ' none selected
        msgPrompt = msgTotal
        msgResult = MsgBox(msgPrompt, cMsgButtonCode1, msgTitle)
        End
    End If
End Sub
```

EXHIBIT 12.9   errCollateralReports subroutine

variable msgInfo103 has the description of the error concatenated to its value. Again you should notice that each of the individual error conditions has Chr(13) at the end of it to start a new line. This will allow users to display the collective errors as a list inside of the message box under the separate headers for each individual menu in which they were detected.

Error Checking the Reports Menu

The subroutine in Exhibit 12.9 is an example of a simple error checking subroutine that tests if the user has selected any collateral reports. This error check is performed only if the user has selected to produce the collateral stratification reports. Once *any* selected report is found, everything is all right! If even a single report has been selected, it means that there is no error condition present for this portion of the menu. The subroutine would then branch to the command Exit Sub and immediately leave the subroutine. If the model fails to find a single selected field, the subroutine steps through the logic block and straight into the error message code. The code then displays the message at the top of the function. This general form of error checker is also found in the Geographic and Matrix Reports error subroutines.

READING THE CONTENTS OF ALL THE MENUS

Having verified that the data in the Ranges of the menus is in an acceptable form and has no detectable internal inconsistencies, we now need to move it from the menus into the model. We will do this with menu specific transfer subroutines that will load the data into VBA variables and arrays. Exhibit 12.10 contains the "Read_Menu_Inputs" subroutine that will oversee this task. We can tell at once that this is a very high-level subroutine in that it does nothing other than to call six other subroutines. Even if we did not have the in-line comments to the right of each of the calls, we would know by the look of the subroutine names, as each of them would call a specific menu and read the information we have entered into it.

```
Sub Read_All_Menu_Input()

    Call Read_Main_Menu                   ' Read Main Menu -- set program run options
    Call Read_Program_Costs_Menu          ' Reads the program costs
    Call Read_Selection_Criteria_Menu     ' Read tenor, coupon & balance selection criteria
    Call Read_Report_Selection_Menu       ' Read menu for report selections
    Call Read_Geographic_Menu             ' Read state code geographic selection criteria
    Call Read_Prepay_Defaults_Menu        ' Read prepayment and default schedule to apply

End Sub
```

EXHIBIT 12.10   Read_All_Menu_Input subroutine

Declaration of Variables to Hold Menu Inputs

Having error checked all of this menu information, we need to move the information from the menus into the body of the model and begin to use it. To this end, a variable will have to be created for each of the menu fields that we are going to read into the model.

We now need to declare variables, and *lots of them*! We will transfer the information from the screen using the Range statements the same way we read it into the error checking subroutines. Some of these inputs will require the model to perform rudimentary calculations to expand what we have input into a more usable form. This specifically relates to the extension of the prepayment and default speeds.

All of these variables will be global in scope and as such will all start with the prefix "g." If they are input variables that will be initialized by Range values from a menu screen, their declarations will be grouped by the menu into which the model's user entered the information. Exhibit 12.11 lists the variable declarations for the Program Costs Menu.

Each of the menus has a separate block of variables declared under a comment that is all in capital letters to identify the menus from which the information is entered into the model.

```
'MAIN MENU VARIABLES


    The Main Menu.


' SELECTION CRITERIA MENU VARIABLES




' PROGRAM COSTS MENU VARIABLES
Public g_exp_service      As Double    'Percentage rate for servicing
Public g_exp_program      As Double    'Percentage for program expense fees
Public g_trig_cleanup     As Double    'percentage for clean up call of notes
Public g_trig_3M_delinq   As Double    'percentage of rolling 3 month delinquencies
Public g_advance_rate     As Double    'conduit advance rate
```

EXHIBIT 12.11   Declaration of the VBA global variables that will hold the inputs from the Program Costs Menu

```
Public very_important_array()    as Double      !redimension later
```

EXHIBIT 12.12 Declaration of a global variable that has no fixed dimensions as yet

These global variables will support the Collateral Selection Criteria Menu.

```
' REPORT SELECTION MENU
```

These support the Report Package Selection Menu

```
' GEOGRAPHIC REGION SELECTION MENU
```

These support the Geographic and Report Selection Menus.

Although we have not produced any output yet, once we have named the prepayment and default variables, we can now also declare the variables of some of the reports. In particular, all the output to the Summary Matrix Reports is dimensioned as rows = default levels, and columns = prepayment levels. Thus for each of the reports of the Matrix Workbook we can declare the arrays now, and immediately redimension them once we have the information from the Prepayments and Defaults Menu. To declare an array without currently knowing the dimension you simply leave the dimension information in the parenthesis blank. Exhibit 12.12 displays an example of this type of declaration. We can then later in the program use the Redim statement to specify the dimensions of the array when we know what they need to be. If you need to remind yourself about the use of the Redim statement take a quick peek at Chapter 8, "Writing Menus: An Introduction to Data, Ranges, Arrays, and Objects." It is an important concept and we will use it a number of times at various locations in the model's code.

Reading the Main Menu

As we read the menus of the model we will transfer the information from the Excel worksheet menus into the VBA variables, vectors, and arrays. Exhibit 12.13 contains the code for the subroutine that reads the contents of the Main Menu. By the time we are finished reading the contents of all of the Ranges on each of the menus we will have all the information we need to run the model with the exception of the collateral characteristics contained in the collateral data file.

The subroutine "Read_Main_Menu" in Exhibit 12.13 reads all entries specified by the user into different sets of VBA variables. Each of these sets of variables are grouped under different comment lines telling us which part of the Main Menu the information is coming from.

The first section contains the program runtime options that tells the model which operations it is to perform. There are five Ranges and each of them has a particular form of test for the value of the Range field. The line of code to read the value entered into the Range says "Ucase." This command changes whatever is inside the parenthesis immediately following the word "Ucase" into upper case. In the example of the first line, the item inside of the parenthesis is Range("m1CollatElig"), which is the choice to run collateral selection code. If the user entered a "y" in the Range, it

```vba
'==============================================================================
'
' Read the Main Menu Screen
'
'==============================================================================
Sub Read_Main_Menu()

    Sheets("Main Menu").Select
    Range("A1").Select

    'Read the program runtime options selections
    g_run_exceptions = UCase(Trim(Range("m1CollatElig"))) = "Y"
                                            'run except process?
    g_write_exceptions = UCase(Trim(Range("m1WriteCollatInelig"))) = "Y"
                                            'write out except reports?
    g_write_reports = UCase(Trim(Range("m1WritePortReps"))) = "Y"
                                            'write out portfolio reports?
    g_out_matrix = UCase(Trim(Range("m1WriteCFSummary"))) = "Y"
                                            'write out matrix reports?
    g_out_cfdetail = UCase(Trim(Range("m1WriteCFDetail"))) = "Y"
                                            'write out cashflow reports?
    g_out_collat_file = UCase(Trim(Range("m1WriteEligCollatFile"))) = "Y"
                                            'write out eligible collateral?


    'Read deal name and number of loans in the collateral file
    g_pathway = Trim(Range("m1DirectoryPath"))
                                    'name of root directory for the code
    g_pathway_template = g_pathway & "template\"
                                    'complete for the template directory
    g_pathway_output = g_pathway & "output\"
                                    'complete for the output file directory
    g_total_loans = Range("m1CollatNumLoans")
                                    'total loans in the portfolio


    'names of the output report files
    gfn_output_prefix = Trim(Range("m1FilePrefix"))
                                    'output files prefix
    gfn_collateral_file = Trim(Range("m1CollatRepName"))
                                    'data file of collateral information
    gfn_accepted_loans_file = Trim(Range("m1CollatFileName"))
                                    'output file for collateral reports
    gfn_waterfall_cfs_file = Trim(Range("m1CFFileName"))
                                    'output file for cashflow reports
    gfn_exceptions_file = Trim(Range("m1ExceptRepName"))
                                    'output file for ineligible collateral
    gfn_matrix_file = Trim(Range("m1MatrixRepName"))
                                    'output file for matrix report package
    'names of the template files
    g_template_collateral = Trim(Range("templateCollat"))
                                    'template file collateral selected
    g_template_waterfall = Trim(Range("templateWaterfall"))
                                    'template file cash flow waterfall
    g_template_ineligible = Trim(Range("templateIneligible"))
                                    'template file ineligible collateral
    g_template_matrix = Trim(Range("templateMatrix"))
                                    'template file summary matrix reports
    g_template_elig_file = Trim(Range("templateEligCollat"))
                                    'template for the eligible collateral file

End Sub
```

EXHIBIT 12.13   Subroutine that reads the contents of the Main Menu of the model

is converted to "Y." This converted value is then compared to the second part of the statement " = 'Y'. "If the two values match (in this case they would be "Y"="Y"), then the statement is True. The variable to the left of the statement g_run_exceptions is then assigned this value. The g_run_exceptions variable is a Boolean and we will later test it to see if we need to run the collateral selection process. If any value other than "y" or "Y" is entered in the field (say "n"), this test will evaluate to "False" and the collateral selection process will be bypassed.

The second section of the subroutine reads all of the file pathway information. It first reads the main pathway, which is the one from which we set up all the sub-directories back in Chapter 6, "Laying the Model Groundwork." It next concatenates (meaning it joins two or more string variables together) each of the sub-directory names to the pathway of the main directory. If the value of "g_pathway" was "C:\VBA_Class\AnalystProgram\" then the value of "g_pathway_template" now becomes "C:\VBA_Class\AnalystProgram\templates." The third section of the subroutine reads two Ranges. The first is a file prefix that the model will add to each report file it generates to help us keep everything together and organized. The second is the name of the data file containing the collateral information.

The fourth and last section of the subroutine read a block of Ranges containing the names of all of the report files we want the model to produce and place in the "\output" sub-directory.

One of the Ranges in the Main Menu accepts an entry for the number of loans in the collateral file.

We have two methods to determine how many loans we will read from the portfolio. If the user enters a "0" the model will read the file, starting at the top, and keep a count of each loan record encountered. If the user enters any number other than "0," for example "500," the model will take this as the number of loans in the portfolio as a whole. Later, after we have left this subroutine, the program will redimension the arrays that will hold the loan data. These arrays will have their dimensions set to either the number of records found or to a number input by the user. You will note these declarations, like those we have mentioned earlier in this chapter, all have long descriptive comments to the right of their declarations. This is absolutely critical for any model that will be used by more than one person over some period of time. Please refer back to the section "You Only Hurt the One You Love" in Chapter 2, "Common Sense," to refresh yourself as to the value of comments. You must always leave yourself and those that will follow you in the code the maximum help you can give to understanding what you did and why you did it. Exhibit 12.14 is a portion of the list of variables we will use to read in the contents of the collateral data file.

We can now redimension the variables we have previously declared in the "A_Globals" Module. The value of the g_total_loans variable represents the initial number of loans in the file. (Remember that this total count of the loans in the portfolio may be later reduced by action of the collateral selection process, which may rule some of them ineligible.)

Reading the Program Costs Menu

Smaller menus can have very simple subroutines to transfer the information from the menu to the model. In Exhibit 12.15 we can see the VBA code

```
'----------------------------------------------------------------------------
'Portfolio data in the data file
'   This data is, with a very few exceptions read into the program from the
'   "Loan Information" worksheet of the data file.  The exceptions are:
'       state_code      Mapped to a numeric from the 2 alpha postal abbreviation
'       obligor_code    Assigned to track multiple loans to the same obligor
'----------------------------------------------------------------------------
Public g_loan_ok()          As Boolean      'Loan accepted for securitization?
                                                (0=yes,1=no)
Public g_loan_num()         As String       'Loan number
Public g_loan_orig_bal()    As Double       'Original loan balance
Public g_loan_cur_bal()     As Double       'Current loan balance
Public g_loan_coup()        As Double       'Implicit yield of the loan
Public g_loan_orig_term()   As Integer      'Original term of the loan (months)
Public g_loan_rem_term()    As Integer      'Remaining term of the loan (months)
Public g_loan_season()      As Integer      'Seasoning
```

EXHIBIT 12.14   Variables declaration block in the "A_Globals" module to hold loan collateral information

that reads the contents of the Program Costs Menu, a menu that has only five inputs.

This subroutine reads each of the five Ranges of the menu with very simple, one-to-one assignment statements corresponding each Range to each VBA variable in the transfer.

Reading the Geographic Menu

The Geographic Menu contains three separate columns of 18 fields each. Exhibit 12.16 contains the subroutine that reads this menu. This subroutine will read the entries in the menu fields that indicate that the loan is eligible if it is from a selected state or territory. It will also read the two letter postal codes and names from the menu. The outer loop reads the columns one by one; the inner loop reads the rows in the columns.

Reading the Prepayments and Default Menu

The subroutine in Exhibit 12.17 will tackle the Defaults and Prepayment Menu. This is the first menu in which, having once read the data, we will perform some quick calculations using the menu information.


```
Sub Read_Program_Costs_Menu()

    Sheets("Program Costs Menu").Select
    Range("A1").Select

    'Read program costs section of the menu
    g_exp_service = Range("m2ServicerExp")/12#        'servicing fee
    g_exp_program = Range("m2ProgramExpenses")/12#    'program expenses
    g_trig_cleanup = Range("m2TrigCleanUpPct")        'principal reallocation trigger
    g_trig_3M_delinq = Range("m2Trig3MDelRate")       '3 month delinquency  trigger
    g_advance_rate = Range("m2AdvanceRate")           'conduit advance rate

End Sub
```

EXHIBIT 12.15   Subroutine that reads the contents of the Program Costs Menu

```
Sub Read_Geographic_Menu()

    Sheets("Geographic Menu").Select
    Range("A1").Select
    i_state = 0
    g_num_select_states = 0

    For icol = 1 To 3
        For irow = 1 To STATES_PER_COL
            i_state = i_state + 1
            g_state_select(i_state) = False
            g_state_postal(i_state) = Range("m6StatePostal" & icol).Cells(irow)
            g_state_name(i_state) = Range("m6StatesNames" & icol).Cells(irow)
            g_state_id_number(i_state) = i_state
            If Range("m6States" & icol).Cells(irow) <> "" Then
                    g_state_select(i_state) = True
                    g_num_select_states = g_num_select_states + 1
            End If
        Next irow
    Next icol

End Sub
```

EXHIBIT 12.16 Reads the Geographic Selection Menu

```
Sub Redim_All_SummaryMatrixReport_Vectors()

  'If we are going to produce the summary matrix cashflows
  If g_out_matrix Then
    'tenor report arrays
    ReDim g_out_avg_life(1 To g_prepay_levels, 1 To g_default_levels) As Double
    ReDim g_out_fin_mat(1 To g_prepay_levels, 1 To g_default_levels) As Double
    ReDim g_out_mod_durat(1 To g_prepay_levels, 1 To g_default_levels) As Double
    ReDim g_out_mac_durat(1 To g_prepay_levels, 1 To g_default_levels) As Double
    ReDim g_out_amt_10yr(1 To g_prepay_levels, 1 To g_default_levels) As Double
    'csh flow report arrays
    ReDim g_out_tot_defaults(1 To g_prepay_levels, 1 To g_default_levels) As Double
    ReDim g_out_recoveries(1 To g_prepay_levels, 1 To g_default_levels) As Double
    ReDim g_out_pct_pd_excess(1 To g_prepay_levels, 1 To g_default_levels) As Double
    ReDim g_out_pct_pd_seller(1 To g_prepay_levels, 1 To g_default_levels) As Double
    ReDim g_out_tot_sch_amort(1 To g_prepay_levels, 1 To g_default_levels) As Double
    ReDim g_out_tot_prepaid(1 To g_prepay_levels, 1 To g_default_levels) As Double
    ReDim g_out_tot_coupon(1 To g_prepay_levels, 1 To g_default_levels) As Double
    'conduit performance arrays
    ReDim g_out_cond_repay(1 To g_prepay_levels, 1 To g_default_levels) As Double
    ReDim g_out_cond_debt_service(1 To g_prepay_levels, 1 To g_default_levels)
      As Double
    ReDim g_out_cond_sol(1 To g_prepay_levels, 1 To g_default_levels) As Double
    ReDim g_out_cond_cover(1 To g_prepay_levels, 1 To g_default_levels) As Double
    ReDim g_out_cond_irr(1 To g_prepay_levels, 1 To g_default_levels) As Double
    'seller interest arrays
    ReDim g_out_si_irr(1 To g_prepay_levels, 1 To g_default_levels) As Double
    ReDim g_out_rel_ex_sprd(1 To g_prepay_levels, 1 To g_default_levels) As Double
    ReDim g_out_sel_coverage(1 To g_prepay_levels, 1 To g_default_levels) As Double
    ReDim g_out_program_short(1 To g_prepay_levels, 1 To g_default_levels) As Double
    ReDim g_out_servicer_short(1 To g_prepay_levels, 1 To g_default_levels) As Double
    ReDim g_out_coupon_short(1 To g_prepay_levels, 1 To g_default_levels) As Double
  End If

End Sub
```

EXHIBIT 12.17 Subroutine that redimensions all the variables used in the Matrix Summary Reports

In this case we will do a very straightforward read of the data in a Variable = Range assignment on a line-by-line basis. Once we have the default rates, however, we have to take the annual rates and create a series of monthly vectors from them. This is because when we come to calculate the collateral cash flows, these rates will be applied on a monthly periodicity (the minimum time frame of the model).

At the end of the subroutine there are two calls.

Since we now know from the number of prepayment speeds and the number of default speeds how many scenarios the model will produce, we can use this information to redimension the arrays that will hold information for the matrix reports. Alternatively we can also dimension the arrays, which will hold, on a scenario-by-scenario basis, the results of the collateral cash flow calculations that we will send to the Excel Waterfall worksheet.

Redimensioning the Matrix Report Variables

Now that we have the number of prepayment and default scenarios in hand, we can redimension all the variables, especially reporting variables that depend on them. The subroutine in Exhibit 12.17 sets up all the Output Matrix Report variables.

Having arrived at the end of this subroutine, we have not only read all the information from the menus, but have also declared and populated all of the VBA arrays the model will use to store the information. The last pieces of information we need to read into the model are the datum of the loans in the collateral portfolio. When we have that information in hand and in its proper place in the model, we will have everything we need to begin calculations.

READING THE CONTENTS OF THE COLLATERAL FILE

Now we need to get the collateral portfolio information on the loans. In the real world these data files will consist of anywhere from 15 to 100 pieces of data fields on each loan, depending on the particular type of asset.

The subroutine in Exhibit 12.18 will open the collateral data file based on the pathway and file information entered on the Main Menu. The first column of the collateral file contains the loan number. The subroutine reads this cell and, if it is not blank, increments the read position, drops through the loop, and repeats the process. The first time it hits a blank cell it drops through the loop, and, since we know that that row of the file does not contain a loan record, immediately decrements the loan counter by one, in the very next statement. The loan count is then assigned to the variable g_total_loans. Using g_total_loans, the function Read_Portfolio_Data reads the file into a series of global variable arrays that record the characteristics of each loan.

We now know the number of loans in the collateral data file. Before we can read the contents of the collateral file into the model, we will need to have variables previously declared and then properly dimensioned available to receive the information. We will declare these as global variables in the "**A_Globals**" module as shown in Exhibit 12.19.

```
Sub Read_Portfolio_Data_File()

   Workbooks.Open Filename:=g_pathway & "data\" & gfn_collateral_file
   j = 1                        'starting record position
   current_row = FIRST_DATA_ROW
   Sheets("LoanInformation").Select
   Range("A1").Select

   'if the number of loans in the portfolio is entered as 0 count the file
   'if a number greater than zero is entered read that number of records
   If g_total_loans = 0 Then
       Do While Cells(current_row, 1).Value <> ""
           current_row = current_row + 1
           g_total_loans = g_total_loans + 1
       Loop
       row_stop = current_row - 1
   Else
       row_stop = current_row + g_total_loans - 1
   End If

   'redimension the data arrays based on the number of total loans in the portfolio
   ReDim g_sel_tot(g_total_loans) As Double
   ReDim g_sel_tag(g_total_loans, INELIGIBLE_REPORTS) As Boolean
   Call ReDim_Portfolio_Data(g_total_loans)
   'read the loans data file based on the program count or the input count
   j = Read_Portfolio_Data(FIRST_DATA_ROW, row_stop, j)
   ' Total lines read minus one = number of collateral pieces
   ActiveWorkbook.Close

End Sub
```

EXHIBIT 12.18   Read_Portfolio_Data_File subroutine that is the high-level subroutine to read the collateral data file information into the model

With the variables in place, we can redimension the arrays and read the information. Note that it is always a good thing to use comments to fill in the columns that are not being read. It is a lot easier to keep track of the column counts, especially in large files. All the data arrays need to be redimensioned to the value of **g_total_loans** before we can read any information from the file into these arrays. With the arrays ready to receive the data, we will begin to read the now opened collateral data file. As before with the inputs from the various menu screens, it would be a good idea to perform some rudimentary error checking. In this case we will simply check that all data that we expect to be in numeric format is. This would include all term, rate, balance, and type information. IsNumeric will not allow anything other than a numeric value to read into the arrays. The subroutine that reads the data file is in Exhibit 12.20. Near the end of the subroutine there is an inline comment. The comment says "columns 24, 25, 26, 27 not read." This comment tells us that the model will not need the information in these columns of the data file. These placeholders are very, very useful things to place in your code when reading large files, especially when you have over 20 pieces of information. In files where there are hundreds of columns, and you may be reading or extracting only a small portion of the total, these comments are virtually mandatory. These comments help to keep track of the contents of the file and allow anyone to quickly see the overall file layout even if the model is not using all of it.

```
'----------------------------------------------------------------------------------
'Portfolio data in the data file
'  This data is, with a very few exceptions read into the program from the "Loan
'  Information" worksheet of the data file.  The exceptions are:
'       state_code     Mapped to a numeric from the 2 alpha postal abbreviation
'       obligor_code   Assigned to track multiple loans to the same obligor
'----------------------------------------------------------------------------------
Public g_loan_ok()            As Boolean   'Loan accepted for securitization?
                                                (0=yes,1=no)
Public g_loan_num()           As String    'Loan number
Public g_loan_orig_bal()      As Double    'Original loan balance
Public g_loan_cur_bal()       As Double    'Current loan balance
Public g_loan_coup()          As Double    'Implicit yield of the loan
Public g_loan_orig_term()     As Integer   'Original term of the loan (months)
Public g_loan_rem_term()      As Integer   'Remaining term of the loan (months)
Public g_loan_season()        As Integer   'Seasoning
Public g_loan_fixed_float()   As Integer   'Fixed or floating rate 1=Fixed, 2=Float
Public g_loan_index()         As String    'Floater underlying index for variable
                                                pay loans
Public g_loan_floater_code()  As Integer   'numeric code 1=prime, 2=LIBOR, 3=10yrTSY
Public g_loan_spread()        As Double    'Floater spread
Public g_loan_reset_rate()    As String    'Frequency of coupon adjustment
Public g_loan_reset_pmt()     As String    'Frequency of payment adjustment
Public g_loan_life_cap()      As Double    'Lifetime interest rate cap
Public g_loan_life_floor()    As Double    'Lifetime interest rate floor
Public g_loan_reset_cap()     As Double    'Quarterly interest rate reset cap
Public g_loan_reset_floor()   As Double    'Quarterly interest rate reset floor
Public g_loan_day_count()     As Integer   'Day count convention
Public g_loan_calc_pmt()      As Double    'Calculated loan payment
Public g_loan_stated_pmt()    As Double    'Stated payment
'Project Information & Demographics
Public g_loan_appraisal()     As Double    'Appraisal value of project
Public g_loan_orig_equity()   As Double    'Original owners equity
Public g_loan_cur_equity()    As Double    'Current owners equity (estimated)
Public g_state()              As String    '2 letter state postal code
Public g_state_code()         As Integer   'Numeric state code for reporting
Public g_zip_code()           As Double    'Zip code
Public g_obligor_code()       As Integer   'lender assigned obligor code number
```

EXHIBIT 12.19   Declarations of the variables needed to store the collateral file information

This chapter is now complete. We have all the information available checked and squirreled away in the VBA arrays of the model. We are now ready to write the VBA code to put it to use.

DELIVERABLES CHECKLIST

The VBA Knowledge Checklist items for this chapter are:

- What a Main Program subroutine looks like (brief) and how to construct one
- Getting some exposure to developing a large collection of task related subroutines
- Using Range names and VBA arrays to transfer the inputs from menus into the model

```
Function Read_Portfolio_Data(row_start, row_stop, j)

 For i2 = row_start To row_stop
  g_loan_ok(j) = True
  'Loan information
  g_loan_num(j) = Trim(Cells(i2, 1).Value)
  If (isNumeric(Trim(Cells(i2, 2).Value)) Then g_loan_orig_bal(j) = Cells(i2, 2).Value
  If (isNumeric(Trim(Cells(i2, 3).Value)) Then g_loan_cur_bal(j) = Cells(i2, 3).Value
  If (isNumeric(Trim(Cells(i2, 4).Value)) Then g_loan_coup(j) = Cells(i2, 4).Value
  If (isNumeric(Trim(Cells(i2, 5).Value)) Then g_loan_orig_term(j) = Cells(i2, 5).Value
  If (isNumeric(Trim(Cells(i2, 6).Value)) Then g_loan_rem_term(j) = Cells(i2, 6).Value
  If (isNumeric(Trim(Cells(i2, 7).Value)) Then g_loan_season(j) = Cells(i2, 7).Value
  If (isNumeric(Trim(Cells(i2, 8).Value)) Then g_loan_fixed_float(j) = Cells(i2, 8).Value
  g_loan_index(j) = UCase(Trim(Cells(i2, 9).Value))
     Select Case g_loan_index(j)
        Case Is = "PRIME":     g_loan_floater_code(j) = 1
        Case Is = "LIBOR":     g_loan_floater_code(j) = 2
        Case Is = "10YRTSY":   g_loan_floater_code(j) = 3
     End Select
  If (isNumeric(Trim(Cells(i2, 10).Value)) Then g_loan_spread(j) = Cells(i2, 10).Value
  If (isNumeric(Trim(Cells(i2, 11).Value)) Then g_loan_reset_rate(j) = Cells(i2, 11).Value
  If (isNumeric(Trim(Cells(i2, 12).Value)) Then g_loan_reset_pmt(j) = Cells(i2, 12).Value
  If (isNumeric(Trim(Cells(i2, 13).Value)) Then g_loan_life_floor(j) = Cells(i2, 13).Value
  If (isNumeric(Trim(Cells(i2, 14).Value)) Then g_loan_life_cap(j) = Cells(i2, 14).Value
  If (isNumeric(Trim(Cells(i2, 15).Value)) Then g_loan_reset_cap(j) = Cells(i2, 15).Value
  If (isNumeric(Trim(Cells(i2, 16).Value)) Then g_loan_reset_floor(j) = Cells(i2, 16).Value
  If (isNumeric(Trim(Cells(i2, 17).Value)) Then g_loan_day_count(j) = Cells(i2, 17).Value
  If (isNumeric(Trim(Cells(i2, 18).Value)) Then g_loan_calc_pmt(j) = Cells(i2, 18).Value
  'Project Information (non-loan demographics)
  If (isNumeric(Trim(Cells(i2, 19).Value)) Then g_loan_appraisal(j) = Cells(i2, 19).Value
  If (isNumeric(Trim(Cells(i2, 20).Value)) Then g_loan_orig_equity(j) = Cells(i2
  If (isNumeric(Trim(Cells(i2, 21).Value)) Then g_loan_cur_equity(j) = Cells(i2, 21).Value
  g_state(j) = Trim(Cells(i2, 22).Value)
  g_state_code(j) = Assign_State_Number(g_state(j))
  If (isNumeric(Trim(Cells(i2, 23).Value)) Then g_zip_code(j) = Cells(i2, 23).Value

  'columns 24, 25, 26, 27 not read
  If (isNumeric(Trim(Cells(i2, 28).Value)) Then g_loan_stated_pmt(j) = Cells(i2, 28).Value
  Cells(1, 1).Value = j
  j = j + 1
 Next

 Read_Portfolio_Data = j - 1

End Function
```

EXHIBIT 12.20   Subroutine that reads the data files from the file

- How to declare detailed error messages and then assemble them into complex messages
- Use of IsNumeric function for error checking subroutines

The Model Knowledge Checklist items for this chapter are:

- Designing and programming the Main Program
- Building the menu error checking and input reading functionality
- Building the functionality to open a collateral data file, count its records, and read the contents

NEXT STEPS

This chapter is a big step in the creation and framework of the model.

All the menu inputs have been error checked and read into VBA arrays. They are now available for use by the model. The contents of the Collateral File are also accessible to the model.

In Chapter 13, "Writing the Collateral Selection Code," and Chapter 14, "Calculating the Cash Flows," we will take the next steps in model development.

Once we have the eligible collateral segregated from the rest, we can amortize each of the loans of the selected portfolio according to the set of specified prepayment and default assumptions. This will determine the timing and magnitude of the cash flows

We will then apply these available cash flows to the cash flow waterfall Excel spreadsheet and begin to structure the deal.

We are on our way!

ON THE WEB SITE

You will find an under development version of the model named **"Base_Model_Chap12.xls."**

It has all the subroutines needed and in place to run the menu error checking code, to read the user inputs from all of the menus, and to read the collateral portfolio information file.

When you open this model and enter the VBA Editor, you will immediately see that some of the modules that were there before have changed and that there are several new modules present that were not there before. Let us start at the top and work our way down.

The module **"A_Constants"** contains a single new declaration, a global constant named "MATRIX_REPORTS" and set to the value of 4.

To the module **"A_Globals"** we have added a block of variables to accommodate the default and prepayment information we will later use to produce the header information for the Waterfall and Matrix reports. We have also added two other large blocks of variables that will hold the Matrix Report information and the Waterfall Report information.

The module **"A_MainProgram"** now has a number of lines that have changed from comments to actual VBA subroutine calls. We have done this because these major subroutine calls and all the VBA code beneath them is now active. The calls are "ErrCheck_All_Menus," "Read_All_Menu_Input," and "Read_Portfolio_Data_File." If we set breakpoints and run the model, it will function up to the limits of the installed code.

In order that they are called from the "Loan_Financing_Model" subroutine, the main program, the following modules are now complete:

The **"MenusErrorChecking"** module contains all the error checking code needed to test all menu inputs.

The **"MenusReadInputs"** module contains all the VBA code to read all the menus.

The **"MenusPrepayDefault"** module contains the code to read the Defaults Menu and redimension all the waterfall and summary matrix variables based on the inputs to that menu.

The **"CollateralReadDataFile"** module contains all the VBA code necessary to read the collateral data file and store the information in the appropriate arrays.

The **"Z_ButtonSubs"** module contains the utility code to support the Geographic Selection Menu.

The **"Z_UtilitySubs"** module contains a series of miscellaneous subroutines that help the program map geographic codes or format reports.

Just remember you can read all the code you want but there is no substitute for writing code. Start from scratch and see if you can replicate both a subroutine that reads information from the menus and one that error checks the same information. Even if you just mirror the functionality of one of the these sets of subroutines, you will get a lot out of the experience. Open an Excel file and create a small menu with two or three fields. Insert Range names into the input fields of the menu. Open up the VBA Editor and create a single module. Into it place two subroutines named "Read_Menu" and "Error_Check_Menu." Follow the general formats for menu reading and error-checking you have seen in this chapter. Don't hesitate to cut and paste code from the model to help you along. Don't stop until you have created a small but working menu. There is no substitute for doing!

## CHAPTER 13

Writing the Collateral Selection Code

OVERVIEW

We are now going to turn our attention to creating the VBA code that will test each piece of collateral against a series of selection criteria. This process will identify the ineligible collateral and report on it separately. In addition, we will create summary reports to help us understand the distribution of ineligible collateral across each of its individual disqualifying conditions. Lastly, we will produce a series of reports on the collateral that has passed all the selection criteria and can be included in the securitization.

These reports will take four forms:

1. Single Criteria Ineligibility Reports
2. Unique Ineligibility Combination Reports
3. Ineligibility Summary Reports
4. Eligible Collateral Reports

Each of these sets of reports is very different from the others. All provide important information.

The subroutines that we will develop to perform these functions will be placed in the following VBA modules:

- Performing the Collateral Selection Process = "**CollateralSelectionSubs**"
- Writing the Ineligible Collateral Reports = "**WriteIneligibleReports**"
- Writing the Eligible Collateral Reports = "**WriteCollateralReports**"
- Writing the Eligible Collateral File = "**WriteEligCollatFile**"
- Writing the Assumptions Report = "**WriteModelAssumptions**"

DELIVERABLES

VBA Language Knowledge Deliverables
- How to locate, open, and save template files
- How to construct file pathways from a combination of menu inputs and use these pathways to populate report template files
- How to use the Workbooks.Open, the ActiveWorkbook.SaveAs, and the ActiveWorkbook.Close commands

- How to set up a group of global variables to hold the values used as criteria in the collateral selection process
- How to populate these variables using the Range objects of the menus
- How to set up a group of constant variables to list all the collateral selection criteria failure conditions and to establish unique ineligibility codes for use in the selection process
- How to use a series of nested If...Then...Else statements inside of a For...Next loop to sequentially test the eligibility of the collateral
- How to use a Select...Case statement to populate the selection criteria columns of a report
- How to write a subroutine that will condense the total listing of all collateral failure codes into a single ordered list
- How to create a list of Range names to simplify writing out the eligible collateral reports

Modeling Knowledge Deliverables

- How to integrate a set of report template files into a model.
- How to populate and save these reports.
- How to produce a set of Eligible Collateral Reports.
- How to create a set of Assumption Reports in both the ineligible and the eligible report packages to allow the user to view the selection criteria used in the screening process.

UNDER CONSTRUCTION

To create the collateral selection and reporting portion of the model, we will need to make several additions to the model. These additions can be seen in "Model_Base_Chap13.xls" on the Web site.

We will add VBA code to some of the existing modules and create several new modules and populate them with the specialized subroutines we need to perform these incremental tasks.

Let's start at the top and work our way down.

In the "A_Constants" module, we will add two blocks of global constant variables to help us keep track of the various types of collateral eligibility tests and the values that we are going to assign to each.

In the "A_Globals" module, we will need to add only a few variables to what is there already. In Chapter 12, when we added all the variables to support the Selection Criteria Menu we declared everything we needed to move the inputs from the menu into the program. Now that we are going to employ these variables in the collateral selection process we will need somewhere to store the results. Two variables will play a central role in the process. The first is g_sel_tag, an array that will hold each loan's eligibility test results on a test-by-test basis. The second is g_sel_tot, which will assign a single unique numeric value to the combination of failed eligibility tests for each loan.

In "A_MainProgram" we will uncomment the call to the subroutine "Select_Deal_Collateral." We will then write this high-level subroutine in the module immediately below the main program, "Loan_Financing_Model." This subroutine will call all the rest of the code we need to both perform the collateral eligibility selection process and to write both the Eligible and Ineligible Collateral Report Packages. The tree structure for all the subroutines in this part of the model are shown in Exhibit 13.1 and 13.2.

The "CollateralReadDataFile" module is unchanged.

The "CollateralSelectionSubs" module will contain the code needed to determine the eligibility/ineligibility of each loan in the portfolio. These subroutines will test each loan individually against the selection criteria and assign a number of values to various arrays so that we can identify the unique combination of failed criteria tests (if any) for each loan.

The modules "MenusErrorChecking," "MenusPrepayDefault," and "Menus-ReadInputs" will require no additional code.

We will add the module "WriteAssumptionsReport." This module will contain the code that will generate the Assumptions Report that we add to every one of our report packages.

We will add the module "WriteCollateralReports," which will produce the stratification and demographic reports of the eligible collateral.

We will add the module "WriteCollatFile," which will produce a collateral portfolio file of only the eligible collateral.

We will add the module "WriteIneligibleReports," which will produce the various reports listing the ineligible collateral and the unique patterns of the ineligibility conditions of the loans.

We will add the module "SetupOutputFiles," which selects the proper template file for a requested report package and saves the template file to the requested file name.

We will add the module "Z_ChangeLog" to record future changes to the model after its initial release.

The modules "Z_ButtonSubs" and "Z_UtilitySubroutines" will require no additional code.

When all this work is finished, we should be able to run the first half of the model, reading the collateral file and menus, applying the eligibility selection criteria, and printing the collateral reports for both eligible and ineligible collateral.

THE COLLATERAL REPORTING PACKAGE

Using Template Files

This chapter will walk us through the process of creating and populating the Collateral Selection Report Package. To produce these reports, we will use the template files that we designed in Chapter 11. We will specify to the program the names to be used when the files are produced and sent to the output directory. We entered this information on the Main Menu in Exhibit 13.3.

The two template files that will concern us in this chapter are "ineligibles_template.xls" and "collateral_template.xls." These template files are for the Ineligible and Eligible Collateral Report Packages, respectively. When the selection process is finished, we will have populated the component reports of each of the files and saved them in the output directory under the names of "Test_Ineligibles.xls" and

Hierarchy for Select_Deal_Collateral in the Module "CollateralSelectionSubs"

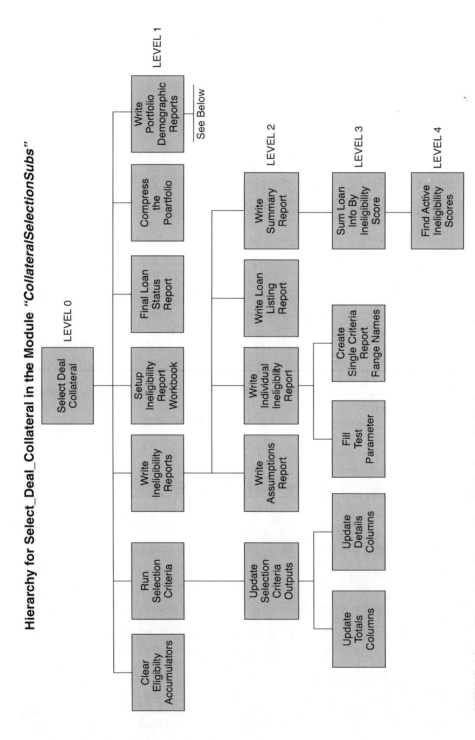

EXHIBIT 13.1 The subroutine tree for the Collateral Selection process code

Hierarchy for Write_Portfolio_Demographic_Reports in the Module "*WriteCollateralReports*"

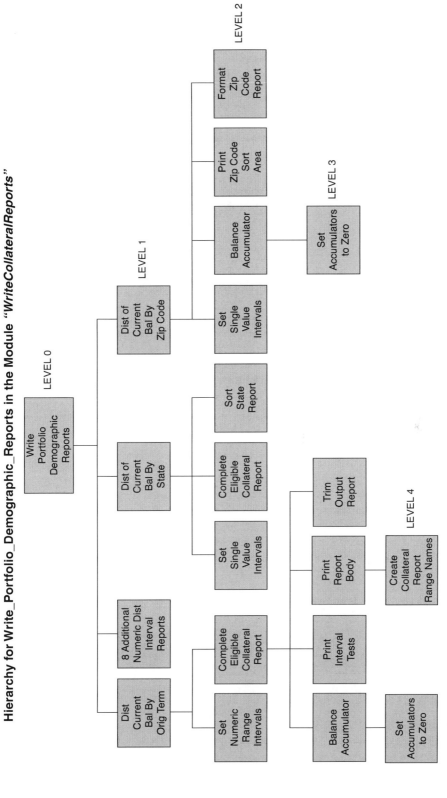

EXHIBIT 13.2 The subroutine tree of the code that produces the Eligible Collateral Report Package

Loan Securitization Model Main Menu

Program Execution Options   (Y=YES; N=NO)

Y	Perform the Collateral Eligibility Test?
Y	Write out Ineligible Collateral Reports?
Y	Write out Eligible Collateral Reports?
Y	Write out Eligible Collateral Loan File?
Y	Write out Cash Flow Waterfall Reports?
Y	Write out Matrix Summary Reports?
N	Write out Cash Flow Trace files? (*Caution: can generate VERY LENGTHY run times!*)

Run the Model

Input File Information

C:\VBA_Class\AnalystProgram\	
CombinedCollatSprd.xls	Collateral Data File Name
0	# of Loans *Enter "0" to read all available, otherwise enter the number of loans that you want to have read from the top of the file.*

	Report Group Prefix (attached to alll output files)		Template File Names
TestRun_01_			
Ineligibles.xls	Ineligible Collateral Reports File Name	<=======	inelig_template.xls
Collateral.xls	Eligible Collateral Reports File Name	<=======	collat_template.xls
Waterfall.xls	Cash Flow Waterfalls Report File Name	<=======	waterfall_template.xls
Matrix.xls	Summary Matrix Reports Files	<=======	matrix_template.xls
CombinedCollat.xls	Eligible Collateral File	<=======	datafile_template.xls

EXHIBIT 13.3   Designation of template and output file names on the Main Menu

"Test_Collateral.xls," respectively. The prefix "Test_" is designed to help the user more easily assign a label to various sets of collateral files if more than one selection criteria run is performed on the portfolio. The following pages will illustrate these steps.

In Chapter 12, "Main Program and Menus," we declared a large collection of global variables to accept the Main Menu information from Excel and store it in VBA arrays where the model can make use of it.

The pathway information is available for us to use, as are the names of the input files.

With these variables declared, we can now read into them the names of the template files and output files specified on the menu. See Exhibit 13.4.

We will now use the filenames stored in the global variables to find and open the template files and then save them to the names we designated for the output report files. The name of the template file we are going to use for the collateral reporting is "collateral_template.xls." The name of the output file we want to create using this template file is "Collateral.xls." We are also going to prefix the file with "Test_."

The steps of the process are:

1. Find the template file and open it.
2. Save the opened template file, using the ActiveWorkbook.SaveAs command to the name of the output filename.
3. Close the file using the ActiveWokbook.close command. It is now saved under the output filename and is ready for use.

```
'Read deal name and number of loans in the collateral file
g_pathway = Range("m1DirectoryPath")          'name of root directory for the code
g_pathway_template = g_pathway & "template\"  'complete for the template directory
g_pathway_output = g_pathway & "output\"       'complete for the output file directory
```

EXHIBIT 13.4   Steps in building directory pathways in VBA

```
Sub Setup_Report_Workbook()

    Workbooks.Open Filename:=g_pathway_template & g_template_collateral
    ActiveWorkbook.SaveAs Filename:=g_pathway_output & gfn_output_prefix & _
            gfn_accepted_loans_file
    ActiveWorkbook.Close

End Sub
```

EXHIBIT 13.5   Opening a template and saving it to the name of the Collateral

Earlier we created a module name **"WriteSetupOutputFiles."** This seems the perfect place to write the first subroutines of the process. These subroutines will open the Ineligible Collateral Reports template file and the Eligible Collateral Reports template files. Remember when we use any method such as SaveAs, Open, or Close, on the ActiveWorkbook object, we will affect the Excel workbook currently displayed on the screen at the time the command is issued. See Exhibit 13.5.

The Workbooks.Open opens up the file that is the combination of the two String variables g_pathway_template and g_template_collateral. The combined string is:

```
C:\VBA_Class\AnalystProgram\template\collateral_template.xls
```

Next we will use the ActiveWorkbook.SaveAs command to save the now opened template file to the combination of the g_pathway_output variable, the gfn_output_prefix variable, and the gfn_accepted_loan_file variable.

```
C:\VBA_Class\AnalystProgram \output\Test_Collateral.xls
```

This file, with the template worksheets within it, is now waiting to be written to by the model, and then saved in the output directory we also entered in the Main Menu. We will repeat this process when setting up the template file that we will use for the Eligible Collateral Reports as well.

It is relatively simple to use these template files, *if one is careful.* The only serious problem with the systemic use of template files is the effort required to keep them synchronized with the Main Program. We also need to manage the contents of these report files. For example, the template file may contain 15 worksheets, each being a separate report. We may not need, or want, to produce all of these reports even if they are available. For example, Ineligible Collateral Reports that list loans that have failed specific selection criteria will not be produced unless there are loans ineligible under those particular selection criteria; later we will learn to use VBA to actively manage the composition of the collateral report outputs by deleting unneeded files.

The use of template files will become a bit more complicated when we look at the template file for the Cash Flow Waterfall results, and even more so when we look at the templates for the Matrix Summary Reports. However, all that lies in the future!

We have now opened, renamed, and saved a template file to a name and in the form of the output file we need. The next step is to write to it. We will start with the output file for the ineligible collateral.

INELIGIBLE COLLATERAL REPORT PACKAGE

This package is a series of reports that itemize each of the loans that failed the individual test of the report. There is also an additional report that shows each loan that failed and the number of eligibility conditions under which it failed. Lastly, there is a report that shows the sum of all ineligible loans that failed a unique set of multiple criteria. We will start simply with the individual failure condition reports.

There are four basic types of reports in the Ineligible Collateral Report Package:

1. **The Assumptions Report.** All assumptions including the selection criteria used
2. **The Single Criteria Ineligibility Report.** Single-test ineligible collateral listings
3. **The Loan Listing Report.** The loan-by-loan results
4. **The Summary Report.** The unique set of ineligibility combinations

We are going to look at the Assumptions Report last, after we finish the discussion of the eligible collateral reports.

Single Criteria Ineligibility Report

Our first set of reports is the collection of Single Criteria Ineligibility Reports. These reports are a series of single-page reports that list each loan that is ineligible for a specific reason. Each report lists the individual characteristics for each of the ineligible loans and then sums the group collectively. It should be noted that an individual loan may appear on more than one, in fact several, or all, of the Single Criteria Ineligibility Reports depending on how many of its characteristics fail the selection process. The template file version of such a report is found in Exhibit 13.6.

Collateral Selection Portfolio Exception Report
INELIGIBLE-4 Minimum/Maximum Current Loan Balance

	Loan Number	Selection Criteria	Obligor Number	Obligor Name	Current Yield	Current Loan Balance	Current LTV	Current Equity Balance	Current Equity LTV	Original Appraisal Value
0				Averages/Totals		-	#DIV/0!	-	#DIV/0!	-

EXHIBIT 13.6   Typical collateral template file

Overview of the Selection Process

How do we determine that a loan is ineligible for inclusion in the portfolio?

On the Collateral Criteria Menu we have a number of parameters entered in regard to balances, terms, coupons, Loan-to-Value ratios (LTV), payments, and spreads. We need to transfer these inputs from the menu into the model and employ them in a collateral screening process. We will need to compare each characteristic of the loan to the selection criteria to determine if it passes the test for inclusion. If it does not, we will need to record the cause of its ineligibility, either a single or multiple criteria failure. We will need to store this information in such a way as to be useable when the time comes to write the Ineligible Collateral Reports.

However, before we begin any selection process, we will need to know what the selection criteria are. To read the criteria into the model, we will need to get the selection criteria from the Collateral Criteria Menu and into VBA variables so we can use them. Fortunately, we have already done this in Chapter 12. In that chapter we wrote the error checking VBA subroutines for each of the menus of the model. We also declared the VBA variables we would need to store the information from the menus after we had completed the error checking process.

In that the information contained in these variables is critical to many of the functions of the model, we declared them as global variables. To review, the reserved VBA word **Public** in their declaration statements will make them available to all the modules of the program. All the declarations of these variables were placed with our other global variables in the module "**A_Globals.**" We gave them a type declaration and an in-line comment to identify them. All the variables begin with the prefix **g_** (for global) and **crit_** (for selection criteria). A complete listing of these variables is shown in Exhibit 13.7. Once the contents of the Ranges in the Selection Criteria Menu were verified we wrote the code in the module "**ReadAllMenus**" to transfer the information from the menu using Range names. The next step in the collateral selection process will be to apply these criteria to the collateral information on a loan-by-loan basis.

```
' SELECTION CRITERIA MENU VARIABLES
Public g_crit_min_orig_term    As Double    'Min original term in months
Public g_crit_max_orig_term    As Double    'Max original term in months
Public g_crit_min_rem_term     As Double    'Min remaining term in months
Public g_crit_max_rem_term     As Double    'Max remaining term in months
Public g_crit_min_orig_bal     As Double    'Min original balance
Public g_crit_max_orig_bal     As Double    'Max original balance
Public g_crit_min_rem_bal      As Double    'Min remaining balance
Public g_crit_max_rem_bal      As Double    'Max remaining balance
Public g_crit_max_del          As Double    'Max times delinquent ever
Public g_crit_max_loan         As Double    'Max loan LTV
Public g_crit_min_spread(1 To SEL_CRIT_INDEX_SPREADS) As Double
                               'Min spread to floating rate index
Public g_crit_acc_index(1 To SEL_CRIT_INDEX_SPREADS) As String
                               'Min spread to floating rate index
Public g_crit_max_spread       As Double    'Min spread to floating rate index
Public g_crit_min_coupon       As Double    'Min current yield
Public g_crit_max_coupon       As Double    'Max current yield
Public g_crit_pay_diff         As Double    'Max diff between stated/calculated pmt
```

EXHIBIT 13.7 Declaration of selection criteria variables

```
'===============================================================================
' Read the tenor and coupon selection criteria menu
'===============================================================================
Sub Read_Selection_Criteria_Menu()

  Sheets("Collateral Criteria Menu").Select
  Range("A1").Select
  'Read the collateral selection criteria; if collateral screening is to be performed
  If g_run_exceptions Then
      g_crit_min_orig_term = Range("m5MinOrigTerm")    'Min original term in months
      g_crit_max_orig_term = Range("m5MaxOrigTerm")    'Max original term in months
      g_crit_min_rem_term = Range("m5MinRemTerm")      'Min remaining term in months
      g_crit_max_rem_term = Range("m5MaxRemTerm")      'Max remaining term in months
      g_crit_min_orig_bal = Range("m5MinOrigBal")      'Min original balance
      g_crit_max_orig_bal = Range("m5MaxOrigBal")      'Max original balance
      g_crit_min_rem_bal = Range("m5MinRemBal")        'Min remaining balance
      g_crit_max_rem_bal = Range("m5MaxRemBal")        'Max remaining balance
      g_crit_min_coupon = Range("m5MinGrossCoup")      'Min gross coupon
      g_crit_max_coupon = Range("m5MaxGrossCoup")      'Max gross coupon
      g_crit_max_loan = Range("m5MaxLTV")              'Max LTV ratio
      g_crit_pay_diff = Range("m5MaxPayDiff")          'Difference stated/calc pmt
      For irow = 1 To SEL_CRIT_INDEX_SPREADS
          g_crit_acc_index(irow) = Trim(Range("m5IndexCode").Cells(irow))
          g_crit_min_spread(irow) = Range("m5MinIndexSpread").Cells(irow)
      Next irow
  End If

End Sub
```

EXHIBIT 13.8   Reading the values of the Collateral Selection Menu into the global variables we declared in Exhibit 13.5

In Exhibit 13.8, the "Read_Selection_Criteria_Menu" subroutine selects the worksheet that is the Collateral Criteria Menu. If the option to run these criteria against the portfolio of loans is selected, the value of the Boolean variable g_run_exceptions, is True and the model will read the values from the Ranges on the Selection Criteria Menu into the VBA variables.

Reading the Selection Criteria from the Menu

We now need to read the selection criteria from the Collateral Criteria Menu. The code in Exhibit 13.8 will allow us to do just that. The steps in writing the above subroutine are:

1. Create a variable name for each of the selection criteria in the tests and declare them in the **"A_Globals"** module. (We have already done this!)
2. Select the module into which this subroutine is to reside. The most suitable module is **"MenusReadInputs."**
3. Enter the reserved word Sub, followed by the name of the subroutine we are about to create. The name of the subroutine should be descriptive of its action but not overly long. The name "Read_Selection_Criteria_Menu" is both descriptive and reasonably concise. The VBA editor will automatically enter an End Sub statement.

4. Select the menu. We can accomplish this with the Sheets(name).Select command. After the Excel worksheet has been selected, position the upper-left cell so that we maximize the visible portion of the menu. Selecting the "A1" cell will accomplish this.

5. We will next check the value of the global variable g_run_exceptions to see if the model is to perform eligibility testing. Using an If . . . Then statement, we will read the selection criteria only if the variable g_run_exceptions is True.

6. Range commands read the contents of the menu into the VBA variables. For the single value variables this is very straightforward. In the case of the small table we will use a looping structure.

7. Since the number of rows in the small table of indices and spreads is known and fixed, we will use a For . . . Next statement to loop through the Range that the table is contained within. Note that the index of the For . . . Next loop picks each cell of the table in a row-by-row manner.

The selection criteria has now been read from the menu and stored in a set of global variables where the VBA code can use it. We will want to apply the values contained in these variables to the eligibility tests on a loan-by-loan basis. To do this, we will design a subroutine to perform a series of tests on the values of criteria characteristics.

These tests are straightforward. The comparisons generally test whether or not the value of the loan data point fails within an acceptable Range of values and is in the correct format. Let us assume for a moment that we can apply the selection criteria to the portfolio and obtain a result from each test. How will we make use of the information?

We will need to store the results of each of the eligibility tests for each loan and quickly and clearly represent and use the results. To help us do this, we will create two arrays. One will store single criteria test results, the other the sum of the tests.

Storing the Results of the Ineligibility Testing Process

As we test these loans against the 11 tests, some will pass all of them, some will fail one, and some will fail more than one. Hopefully none will fail *all* of them! The first array that we will create to hold the results will be the **g_sel_tag** array. The name **g_sel_tag** is short for selection_tag or the record of the selection activity performed on the loan. It is a two dimensional array of type Boolean, in which the first dimension is the number of loans, while the second dimension is the number of eligibility tests. As we subject each of the loans to the ineligibility test, we will record its test outcome. If it is ineligible under the test conditions, we will make it True, if it is eligible, False. If we have 2,255 loans in the initial portfolio, and 11 eligibility tests, the array will be dimensioned to g_sel_tag(2255, 11). See Exhibit 13.9.

Since this is a very important part of the model, I think that we will step back at this point and consider exactly what we are about to do. Once we have our plan in hand it will be much easier for us to figure out how to implement it.

What we need to do is to test each of the loans in our portfolio against a set of selection criteria. We need to record what the outcome of each of the eligibility tests were for each of the loans in the portfolio on an individual basis. We need to do this

```
'-----------------------------------------------------------------------------------
' Collateral Selection Results variables
'-----------------------------------------------------------------------------------
Public g_sel_tag()      As Boolean    'Vector of 1s and 0s indicating pass/fail
                                        of eligibility tests
Public g_sel_tot()      As Double     'Expression of g_sel_tag binary code in
                                        base 10 math
Public g_sel_max_combo  As Double     'Value of the highest score ineligible
                                        combination
Public g_except_report(INELIG_SINGLE_REPS) As Boolean
                        'checks if there are ANY exceptions in this category
```

EXHIBIT 13.9   Declaration of ineligibility tracking arrays and variables

on an individual basis because at this point in the process we will be either accepting or rejecting them for inclusion into our deal on their standalone merits.

When we report the final selection status of the loans, they will fall into one of two categories: eligible (having passed all the tests), or ineligible (having failed one or more of the tests). We will then generate a series of demographic and financial stratification reports on the eligible loans as a whole. The ineligible loans will be reported in three ways. We described these presentations in Chapter 11, "Designing the Model's Reports." There will be a set of eleven reports that will list each individual loan that failed a particular test. There will be a listing of all individual loans that failed any of the tests, and the report will indicate which test or tests the loan failed. The final report will group all loans that failed the same pattern of tests and list each of these unique combinations.

To do this we will need some way of identifying not only the individual performance of the loan in the selection process but also, if it fails, a unique label for the pattern of the failure.

As we discussed above we will use the array **g_sel_tag** to keep track of the individual selection test results for each of the loans.

We will also create an array named **g_sel_tot.** The purpose of this array is to hold a single number that will serve to identify the unique pattern of loan ineligibility for each loan (if the loan fails any of the tests). The value stored in this array should clearly and indisputably be absolutely unique to a given test failure pattern and no other. We clearly do not want to have a value of "43," for instance, relate to two different failure patterns! We would then find ourselves aggregating loans with different ineligibility issues into the same category. This will not help us when we sit with the client and try to resolve differences about what collateral can and cannot be included in the deal. (This pattern analysis is also very useful in spotting data issues with the client that may make collateral appear ineligible when it is not, a situation no one wants.)

So the problem we are faced with is how to change the contents of the **g_sel_tag** array (results of individual tests), into a unique identifier value in the **g_sel_tot** array for use in the combination reporting we need to do.

As with many complex problems, a good way to figure out what we need to do is to start with a much simpler example and use it to develop our strategy. Instead of starting out with 2,255 loans and eleven selection criteria tests we will reduce the portfolio to only 20 loans and five tests.

Loan Number	Criteria Test Results by Test (1Failed Test)					# Tests Failed	"g_sel_tag" array
	Test 5	Test 4	Test 3	Test 2	Test 1		

Initial Results
Twenty Loans, Each Subjected to Five Eligibility Tests

Loan Number	Test 5	Test 4	Test 3	Test 2	Test 1	# Tests Failed	"g_sel_tag" array
1	0	0	0	0	0	0	00000
2	0	0	1	1	0	2	00110
3	0	0	0	0	0	0	00000
4	0	0	0	0	0	0	00000
5	0	0	0	1	1	2	00011
6	0	1	0	1	0	2	01010
7	0	0	0	0	0	0	00000
8	0	0	0	0	1	1	00011
9	0	0	0	0	0	0	00000
10	0	0	0	0	0	0	00000
11	0	0	0	0	0	0	00000
12	1	0	0	0	0	1	10000
13	0	0	0	0	0	0	00000
14	0	0	0	0	0	0	00000
15	0	0	0	0	0	0	00000
16	0	0	0	0	0	0	00000
17	0	0	0	0	0	0	00000
18	0	0	0	0	1	1	00001
19	0	1	0	1	0	2	01010
20	0	1	0	1	0	2	01010
Totals	1	3	1	5	3		

EXHIBIT 13.10 Results of the initial selection process against our portfolio of 20 loans

For our thought experiment it really does not matter what the tests themselves represent, only that they exist and the loans have been subjected to them. After running each of the twenty loans through the testing pattern, we have arrived at the results shown in Exhibit 13.10.

Looking at Exhibit 13.10 we can see that the initial selection process has yielded the following results:

1. Twelve loans passed all tests, eight loans failed at least one test.
2. Of the eight loans that are ineligible, three loans failed one test, and five loans failed two tests. No loan failed more than two tests.
3. From the perspective of the tests, five loans failed Test #2, three loans failed Test #1, three failed Test #4, and one loan each failed Test #3, and Test #5.
4. If we look at the rightmost column of the report we can see that the pattern of failures is clustered. There are five unique patterns of failure. If we assign a "0" for a "Pass" and a "1" for a "Fail," and read the "Pass/Fail" pattern from right to left as it is represented in the body of the table, we have the following five patterns: 00001, 00011, 00110, 01010, and 10000.
5. In regards to the failure pattern, the patterns **00001**, **00110**, and **10000** had one loan each. The pattern **00011** had a total of two loans, and the pattern **01010** had three loans.

Loan Number	Value of Each Failed Criteria Test					"g_sel_tot" array value	Loan Staus
	16	8	4	2	1		
	Test 5	Test 4	Test 3	Test 2	Test 1		
1	0	0	0	0	0	0	Eligible
2	0	0	4	2	0	6	Ineligible
3	0	0	0	0	0	0	Eligible
4	0	0	0	0	0	0	Eligible
5	0	0	0	2	1	3	Ineligible
6	0	8	0	2	0	10	Ineligible
7	0	0	0	0	0	0	Eligible
8	0	0	0	0	1	1	Ineligible
9	0	0	0	0	0	0	Eligible
10	0	0	0	0	0	0	Eligible
11	0	0	0	0	0	0	Eligible
12	16	0	0	0	0	16	Ineligible
13	0	0	0	0	0	0	Eligible
14	0	0	0	0	0	0	Eligible
15	0	0	0	0	0	0	Eligible
16	0	0	0	0	0	0	Eligible
17	0	0	0	0	0	0	Eligible
18	0	0	0	0	1	1	Ineligible
19	0	8	0	2	0	10	Ineligible
20	0	8	0	2	0	10	Ineligible

Value of the Initial Result
Twenty Loans, Each Subjected to Five Eligibility Tests

EXHIBIT 13.11 Assigning values to the various test failure conditions

What other information can we glean from this report?

In that the loans are listed in order of their loan numbers, 1–20, we can identify the individual loans that failed and the failure conditions of each.

As many of you have realized by now, the body of this report is such that the **"g_sel_tag"** array is merely a shorthand method of representing the detailed results of the selection process on a loan-by-loan level.

While we see that we have a fair amount of information captured in the **"g_sel_tag"** array, we are still lacking one important result. We still do not have a unique identifier of the failure pattern. Let us now develop one! See Exhibit 13.11.

Now this is quite a different story!

We have five tests. If we assign the following numbers to each of the five tests, 1, 2, 4, 8, 16, we can develop a unique score for each of the failure patterns of the portfolio.

For example, Loan #2 has a pattern of **00110** which results in a **"g_sel_tot"** score of "6." Why? The formula is as follows, reading the individual tests and their weightings from right to left:

$$\text{Test 5} \quad \text{Test 4} \quad \text{Test 3} \quad \text{Test 2} \quad \text{Test 1} = \text{Total Score}$$
$$(0*16) + (0*8) + (1*4) + (1*2) + (0*1) = \text{Total Score}$$
$$0 \quad + \quad 0 \quad + \quad 4 \quad + \quad 2 \quad + \quad 0 = 6$$

There you have it!

Not only that, but each total number will be unique to the particular pattern that generated it. Best of all, we can reduce this representation to a single base 10 number! Instead of having to deal with a number such as **00011,** we now have a unique number "3." The differences of the patterns are now visible at a glance.

Any loan with a score of greater than "0" is Ineligible. Loans with scores of "0" are Eligible for inclusion in the deal. We can now store the results of these calculations into the array "g_sel_tot" and we have what we wanted in the first place. The array "g_sel_tag" now holds the detailed information while the array "g_sel_tot" holds the unique failure pattern in an easy to use number.

Using Constants to Assign Ineligibility Value to the Collateral   To test the collateral and record the results we will need to assign a number of values using constants. We will need to assign one constant for each test and we will need to assign the corresponding binary number value for the test. Thus the first test will be assigned "1," the first binary number, the second test "2,"the third test "4," the fourth test "8," and so on.

We will place both sets of these declarations in the module **"A_Constants."** The declarations in Exhibit 13.7 will handle the first set of these constants, one number for each of the successive tests. The value of each of the constants in Exhibit 13.12 correspond to the sequence of the individual test and its column location in the sel_tag array. If, for example, a loan fails the test for maximum LTV, the fifth column of the loan record in the **sel_tag** array would be assigned a value of "1."

In Exhibit 13.12, note the explanatory comment at the top of the declaration block. This is critical in that we don't want to confuse the role of these constants with those in Exhibit 13.13 that assign a numeric penalty weight to the test. These are the weights that will be used to construct the decimal equivalent of the binary failure pattern. The names of the constants are all self-explanatory in that they correspond

```
'============================================================================
' EXCEPTION REPORTING CONSTANTS
' Number of individual test exception reports
' Note: should be equal to the maximum number of TEST_????? constants below
'============================================================================
Public Const INELIGIBLE_REPORTS = 11    'Number of exception reports
'============================================================================
' Loan selection criteria test conditions
Public Const TEST_REM_TERM = 1
Public Const TEST_ORIG_TERM = 2
Public Const TEST_ORIG_BAL = 3
Public Const TEST_REM_BAL = 4
Public Const TEST_MAX_LTV = 5
Public Const TEST_INDEX = 6
Public Const TEST_STATE_CODE = 7
Public Const TEST_TENOR_CODE = 8
Public Const TEST_BAL_CODE = 9
Public Const TEST_PMT_CODE = 10
Public Const TEST_COUPON_CODE = 11
```

EXHIBIT 13.12   Declaring the constants to map the locations of the eligibility test result within the sel_tag array

```
' Loan selection criteria test conditions
Public Const EXCEPT_REMAINING_TERM = 1        'Over/Under remaining term range
Public Const EXCEPT_ORIGINAL_TERM = 2         'Over/Under original term range
Public Const EXCEPT_ORIGINAL_BALANCE = 4      'Over/Under original balance range
Public Const EXCEPT_CURRENT_BALANCE = 8       'Over/Under remaining balance range
Public Const EXCEPT_MAX_LTV = 16              'Exceeds original loan-to-value ratio
Public Const EXCEPT_INDEX = 32               'Under minimum spread
Public Const EXCEPT_STATE_CODE = 64          'Excluded state code
Public Const EXCEPT_TENOR_TEST = 128         'Orig Term / Rem Term Relationship
Public Const EXCEPT_BAL_TEST = 256           'Orig Bal / Rem Bal Relationship
Public Const EXCEPT_PMT_TEST = 512           'Calculated Payment vs. Stated Payment
Public Const EXCEPT_COUPON = 1024            'Acceptable gross coupon
```

EXHIBIT 13.13   Declaring the constants to hold the numerical values for the failure codes

on a one-to-one basis with the eligibility tests. Notice that all have in-line comments linking them to the specific test nevertheless! See Exhibit 13.13.

Building the Collateral Testing Code

Each piece of collateral can be tested in a direct manner. One, or at most two blocks of VBA code will be enough to perform each of the tests. The individual loan characteristic is tested against a Range (such as a minimum and maximum acceptable value) or against a single value (state code or ZIP code). If the loan fails the test we assign the appropriate array element in the **g_sel_tag** array the value of "True" and we increase the decimal score of the **g_sel_tot** array by the value associated with that particular test. If we were testing the 100th loan of the portfolio and it failed the 5th selection criteria test we would assign **g_sel_tag(100,5)**=1 and increment the value of **g_sel_tot(100)** by 16. At the end of the process, loans with scores with a **g_sel_tot** equal to zero will have passed all of the criteria and the ineligible loans will have a decimal score reflecting their unique failure pattern. On to the testing code! We will place this subroutine in the **"CollateralSelectionSubs"** module.

We will need some working variables to handle the Range boundaries and a couple for the single test stuff such as geographic areas. See Exhibit 13.14.

In Exhibit 13.14, the subroutine "Run_Selection_Criteria" begins by declaring a series of local variables. These will hold values that we will use for each loan or test, and then generally discard or overwrite. These are generally called working or utility variables.

The subroutine then starts with a For...Next loop that runs from the value 1 to the number of INELIGIBLE_REPORTS that we know to be 11 in that we earlier assigned the variable to that constant. It sets the value of each member of the **"g_except_report"** array, a Boolean type variable to "False." Each element of this array will later be tested. If any of the elements have to be changed to "True" by the operation of this subroutine, it means that there is at least one loan that is ineligible in that category. Specifically if all the loans, except one loan, were eligible, and the single loan that was ineligible had failed the 5th test, then the first four values of the array **g_except_report** would remain "False" as would the 6th to the 11th values. Only the 5th value of **g_except_report** would be "True" indicating that we would need to print an Ineligible Loan Report for this selection criteria (exceeding the maximum LTV).

```
Sub Run_Selection_Criteria()

Dim i            As Integer  'loop counter
Dim iloan        As Integer  'portfolio loan by loan counter
Dim ok           As Integer  'counter for index and spread table
Dim low_range    As Double   'low end of selection range
Dim high_range   As Double   'high end of selection range
Dim state_code_ok As Integer 'is state code found

  'initialize all ineligibility reports to FALSE, there are no loans found for
  ' these ineligibility conditions.  If the array location remains with a
  ' value of FALSE at the end of the subroutine run we do not have to produce
  ' the corresponding single criteria ineligibility report
  For i = 1 To INELIG_SINGLE_REPS
      g_except_report(i) = False
  Next i
  'set the maximum ineligibility score recorder to zero, as this subroutine finds
  ' ineligible loans we will compare the ineligibility combination score with the
  ' current running maximum and update the variable's value if the current
  ' ineligible score is greater.
  g_sel_max_combo = 0

  For iloan = 1 To g_total_loans

    ' Test #1  Minimum and maximum remaining term
    If g_rem_term(iloan) ≤ g_crit_min_rem_term Or _
       g_rem_term(iloan) > g_crit_max_rem_term Then
               g_sel_tag(iloan, TEST_REM_TERM) = True
               g_sel_tot(iloan) = g_sel_tot(iloan) + EXCEPT_REMAINING_TERM
               g_except_report(TEST_REM_TERM) = True
    End If
```

EXHIBIT 13.14 VBA code to perform the first selection tests

The next section of the subroutine establishes a For . . . Next loop that will cycle through each loan of the portfolio (1 to **g_total_loans**), and begin the testing process.

The first test is a two value Range test in which the remaining term of the loan being tested must fall between the two values of the selection variables of "**g_crit_min_rem_term**" and "**g_crit_max_rem_term.**" This is, of course, the test for remaining term, in months, of the loan. If the value falls within the test the loan passes. If it does not the loan is rejected.

If the loan fails the test three things happen. The first is that the position of the test, as determined by the value of the constant named TEST_REM_TERM in the "**g_sel_tag**" array is set to "True." Thus the configuration of the "**g_sel_tag**" array for this loan has gone from **00000000000** to **0000000001**. The second VBA statement inside the If . . . Then statement now records the test failure in the "**g_sel_tot**" array. If this is the first loan in the portfolio, the **g_sel_tot(1)** array location value is increased by the value of the EXCEPT_REMANING_TERM constant which we earlier set to "1." This gives the loan a total current ineligibility score of "1," and tells us immediately that it is ineligible no matter what else happens. Lastly, the third statement sets the value of the first array location in the **g_except_report** array value to "True" indicating that there is at least one loan that failed this test. This means that no matter what else happens with the selection process across the rest of the portfolio

```
' Test #7  Acceptable state code
state_code_ok = False          'there must be an explicit match or remains FALSE
For i = 1 To STATES
    ' If it matches any of the selected state codes it is OK
    If g_state(iloan) = g_state_postal(i) Then
        If g_state_select(i) Then
            state_code_ok = True
            Exit For
        End If
    End If
Next
If state_code_ok = False Then
    g_sel_tag(iloan, TEST_STATE_CODE) = True
    g_sel_tot(iloan) = g_sel_tot(iloan) + EXCEPT_STATE_CODE
    g_except_report(TEST_STATE_CODE) = True
End If
```

EXHIBIT 13.15   Eligibility Test #7 for geographic codes

we will be printing the first Ineligible Loan Report, the report that list loans that have failed the minimum or maximum remaining term test.

In Exhibit 13.15, we can see a different form of selection testing. The test begins by declaring a variable to hold the initial status of the test condition. The initial condition of the test is again set to "False," meaning that the assumption is that the loan will fail the test. In the course of this test, we must explicitly set the value of the variable to "True" by finding a match for the geographic code of the loan from a list of valid geographic codes we have read from the menu. Upon finding such a match the loan will then be eligible under this test.

This test first uses a For...Next loop that runs from 1 to a number of valid geographic codes. These geographic regions number a total of 54 entities, 50 states, and 4 territories.

The For...Next loop now moves through the set of eligible codes looking for a match. When it finds one, the condition of the test variable state_code_ok is set to "True." Once this action is taken, the next statement is an "Exit For" statement. This statement immediately terminates the action of the "For...Next" loop, stopping the comparison procedure dead in its tracks. It also exits the loop structure.

Upon leaving the loop structure, the next statement to be encountered tests the condition of the g_state_ok variable with the condition "False." If the g_state_ok variable is "False" (meaning a match between the state code of the loan and the list of valid sate codes read from the menu was NOT found) the test condition of the If...Then statement is "True." This is because "False=False" is "True!"

If the test is "True," (no match), then the same three actions that we observed in the remaining term code of Exhibit 13.14 will occur. The only difference is that now, in the first statement, the 7th column position of the **"g_sel_tag"** array is changed from 0 to 1. If this was the loan we tested in Exhibit 13.13, the change in the **"g_sel_tag"** array would be from

00000000001   to   00001000001

The value of the **"g_sel_tot"** array for this loan would increase from 1 to 65, an increase of 64, the value of constant EXCEPT_STATE_CODE (see Exhibit 3.12).

```
'If the sum total of all the exception codes is zero the loan has passed all tests
If g_sel_tot(iloan) > 0 Then
     g_loan_ok(iloan) = False
     'if the current ineligibility combination score is greater
     ' than the current maximum reset the maximum value
     If g_sel_tot(iloan) > g_sel_max_combo Then
         g_sel_max_combo = g_sel_tot(iloan)
     End If
End If
```

EXHIBIT 13.16   At the end of the 10 tests the value of g_sel_tot is tested

Lastly we would set the 7th position of the g_except_report to "True." This action would eventually trigger the production of the 7th Ineligible Collateral Report that pertains to ineligibility due to geographic code.

Lastly, in Exhibit 13.16, we test if the sum of the g_sel_tot variable for the loan is greater than 0. If it is, then the loan has failed at least one eligibility test. It is therefore marked as "False" in the **"g_loan_ok"** array.

PRODUCING THE INELIGIBILITY REPORT PACKAGE

Now that we have made the eligibility determination for each of the loans we can begin to produce the report package. We will need to perform the following operations. We have previously created a module name **"WriteExceptionReports."** This is the location for all the code that we will use to produce the Ineligible Collateral Reports Package. We have already read the name for the template of this report package from the Main Menu and stored it in the variable g_template_ineligible. The structure of this file consists of 13 reports that fall into the following categories.

1. **Single Criteria Reports.** Which loans failed an individual test. There is one report for each of the 11 tests.
2. **Loan Listing Report.** This report lists all loans that are ineligible, individually, and, in a column format indicates which test the loan failed.
3. **Summary Report.** This report groups loans by the unique combinations of their ineligibility conditions.

When we want to produce this report package, we will first design a subroutine that will address the entire process from a higher level. This subroutine will loop through each of these 13 possible reports, 11 Individual Criteria, 1 Loan Listing, and 1 Summary Report. Based on which iteration of the loop the program is in it will call a specialized subroutine to produce each of the individual reports as needed.

In that the formats for the first 11 Individual Criteria Reports are either broadly similar or in some cases almost identical, we should be able to design a general-purpose subroutine that we can use to populate all of them.

The Loan Listing and Summary Reports are different from the first 11 reports. They are also different from each other. They will require different logic and contain very different sets of information in their formats. These two reports will be produced by two separate subroutines.

Master Subroutine for the Ineligible Collateral Report Package

The tasks that this subroutine must perform are:

1. Open the correct template file, rename the file based on the name we entered on the Main Menu, and save it.
2. Find the Assumptions Report worksheet and write the Assumptions Report.
3. Find the correct template worksheet for each report and write the 13 reports (or as many as are needed). If there are no loans ineligible under a given report condition, the report worksheet is deleted from the workbook.
4. Save the file and close it.

We will now look at the VBA code necessary to perform the actions displayed in Exhibit 13.17.

```vba
Sub Write_Ineligibility_Reports()

Dim i_sheet          As Integer     'generic loop counter for worksheets
Dim sheet_name       As String      'name of sheet created or renamed

  'open the ineligible report template file and save it to the user designated name
  Workbooks.Open Filename:=g_pathway_template & g_template_ineligible
  ActiveWorkbook.SaveAs Filename:=q_pathway_output & gfn_output_prefix & gfn_
exceptions_file

  Call Write_Assumptions_Page
  For i_sheet = 1 To INELIG_SUMMARY_REP
      'get to the correct page of the target workbook
      If i_sheet ≤ INELIG_SINGLE_REPS Then
          sheet_name = "Inelig" & i_sheet
          If g_except_report(i_sheet) Then
              Sheets(sheet_name).Select    'there are exceptions, print report
              Range("A1").Select
          Else
              Sheets(sheet_name).Delete    'there are no exceptions of this type
          End If
      Else
         If i_sheet = INELIG_LISTING_REP Then Sheets("IneligALL").Select
         If i_sheet = INELIG_SUMMARY_REP Then Sheets("IneligSUM").Select
      End If
      'output the report
      Select Case i_sheet
           Case Is ≤ INELIG_SINGLE_REPS:
              If g_except_report(i_sheet) Then Call Write_Individual_Report(i_sheet)
           Case Is ≤ INELIG_LISTING_REP:   Call Write_Loan_Listing_Report
           Case Is ≤ INELIG_SUMMARY_REP:   Call Write_Summary_Report
      End Select
      Range("A1").Select
  Next i_sheet
  ActiveWorkbook.Save
  ActiveWorkbook.Close

End Sub
```

EXHIBIT 13.17   Ineligible Collateral Report Package master subroutine

Setting up the Ineligible Collateral Reports File The name of the subroutine is short and to the point. "Write Ineligibility Reports" says exactly what is about to happen. We use the Workbooks.Open statement to open the template file. Next we save the opened file to the name designated as a combination of the file prefix, the name of the output file and the output directory pathway. We now have an open, renamed, and saved report file into which we can write the ineligibility reports. The next thing to do is to call a subroutine to populate the Assumptions Report page that is in the file. We will not look at this subroutine at this time, but will return to it later.

The Structure of the Subroutine We have earlier declared a public constant with the name INELIG_SINGLE_REPS and assigned it a value of 11. We next set up a loop that will go through each of the reports in turn. As earlier noted, we have 13 reports to produce, not 11. We will therefore set the loop counter to INELIG_SUMMARY_REP the last report we will write in the loop.

The Excel worksheets in the template file are named Inelig1 to Inelig10 for the individual reports, and IneligALL and IneligSUM for the two summary reports. We need to be sure that we are going to write the correct information into each of these reports. The next step, therefore, is to direct the program to the correct sheet at the correct time. We do not, however, want to produce any blank reports, so we will delete any reports that have no loans ineligible for the selection criteria of that particular report.

To accomplish this we will use an If...Then...Else statement that will first test if the loop is on one of the first 11 individual reports. The steps in the process are as follows:

1. If the loop has a value of INELIG_SINGLE_REPS or less, we are writing an individual report. It will construct a worksheet name from the literal "Inelig" and the number of the loop.
2. Next it will check the array **g_except_report** to see if the value for this report is "True." If it is then there are ineligible loans to write to the report.
3. If the result is "True" for the test, it will use the Sheets().Select commands to move to that sheet and position the cursor in Cell A1. If the test fails and the report is not required, it will use the Sheets().Delete command to delete from the workbook eliminating the report from the package.
4. If the loop value is greater than INELIG_SNGLE_REPS we are now producing a Loan Listing Report or a Summary Report. These reports are produced under all circumstances. All we have to determine is which report we are about to produce. If the loop is equal to INELIG_LISTING_REP, a value of 12, we are writing the Loan Listing Report. If the loop value is equal to INELIG_SUMMARY_REP, a value of 13, we are writing the Summary Report. Based on the loop value we select the appropriate worksheet, either EligALL or EligSUM.

Writing Out the Ineligibilty Report We now have built the workbook and selected the correct report worksheet to populate with the selection results. The final part of the master subroutine is below. We will now create the logic to write each type of report.

Collateral Selection Portfolio Exception Report
INELIGIBLE-4 Minimum/Maximum Current Loan Balance

	Loan Number	Selection Criteria	Obligor Number	Obligor Name	Current Yield	Current Loan Balance	Current LTV	Current Equity Balance	Current Equity LTV	Original Appraisal Value
0				Averages/Totals		-	#DIV/0!	-	#DIV/0!	-

EXHIBIT 13.18   Individual Ineligibility Criteria Report layout

We will use a Select...Case statement to do this. If you remember from Chapter 9, "Controlling the Flow of the Model," this statement is the one of choice when we have three or more alternatives to select from.

If the value of the loop is INELIG_SINGLE_REPS or less, the program will call the subroutine that will produce the Individual Ineligibility Reports. If it is INELIG_LISTING_REP, it will call the subroutine that prints the Listing Report. Finally, if the value of the loop is INELIG_SUMMARY_REP, it will call the subroutine to produce the Summary Report.

After *each* of the reports is written to the appropriate Worksheet it will save the Workbook. Why? If the report writer code fails, we will at least have all the reports up until the point of failure. When all the reports are written and the loop is complete, the subroutine will close the Workbook and we are finished.

Individual Ineligibility Reports

Before we do anything we should refresh our memories as to what the template file form for these reports look like. See Exhibit 13.18.

The report begins on the eleventh row of the worksheet. It spans the columns "B" through "L." The first column numbers each of the ineligible loans of the report so that we may refer to them more easily. The remaining fields of the report display the characteristics of the loan in regard to balances, coupon, Obligor, and LTV criteria. We need to write a VBA subroutine to populate a series of 11 of these reports, each with a separate ineligible condition.

We will start out by creating a subroutine with the name of "Write_Individual_Reports." This subroutine will be used to populate all 11 of the Individual Ineligible Condition Reports. See Exhibit 13.19.

```
'=========================================================================
'  Single Test Exception Report
'  This subroutine produces a list of each piece of collateral that failed a
'        single test
'  It produces a set of reports that list each piece of collateral that failed a
'        specific one time test such as minimum remaining term, maximum remaining
'        balance, minimum coupon etc.
'  If the piece of collateral fails more than one test it will be listed on each of
'        the single test exception reports.
'=========================================================================
Sub Write_Individual_Report(rep_num As Integer)

    irow = 1                      'print position in the range
    col1 = "B": col2 = "L"        'beg/end column to draw guideline

    Call Create_SingleCriteriaReport_RangeNames(rep_num)
    'Run through the portfolio for the exceptions
    For iloan = 1 To g_total_loans
        If g_loan_ok(iloan) = False Then        'if the loan is OK ignore it
            If g_sel_tag(iloan, rep_num) Then   'read the sel_tag for a match
                Range(r_name(1)).Cells(irow) = irow
                Range(r_name(2)).Cells(irow) = g_loan_num(iloan)
                'based on the particular report list the ineligible value in column 3
                Call Fill_Test_Parameter(rep_num)
                'loan descriptive information
                'Range(r_name(4)).Cells(irow) = g_obligor_code(iloan)
                'Range("F" & irow + 10).Select: Selection.Interior.Pattern = xlLightUp
                Range(r_name(6)).Cells(irow) = g_loan_coup(iloan)
                Range(r_name(7)).Cells(irow) = g_loan_cur_bal(iloan)
                Range(r_name(8)).Cells(irow) = g_loan_cur_bal(iloan) / g_loan_
appraisal(iloan)
                Range(r_name(9)).Cells(irow) = g_loan_cur_equity(iloan)
                Range(r_name(10)).Cells(irow) = g_loan_cur_equity(iloan) / g_loan_
appraisal(iloan)
                Range(r_name(11)).Cells(irow) = g_loan_appraisal(iloan)
                If irow Mod 5 = 0 Then Call Draw_Line_Under_Row(col1, col2, irow + 10)
                irow = irow + 1
            End If
        End If
    Next iloan

End Sub
```

EXHIBIT 13.19   VBA code to write the Individual Report for ineligible loans

To write this report we will need to perform the following steps:

1. Find the correct starting print position in the template file.
2. Set the width of the output area in columns (first column to last column).
3. Set an initial counter for the number of this type of ineligible loan.
4. Loop through all the loans in the portfolio.
5. Test each to see if they are ineligible for this test condition.
6. If the loan is ineligible, write out value of the loan characteristic that caused it to fail and other balance, LTV ratio, and coupon specifics as per the template report layout.
7. For every fifth ineligible loan of the report, draw a sight guideline across the bottom of the report.

Stepping through the Write_Individual_Report Subroutine   We will start by typing the reserved word Sub and then stating the name of the subroutine as above. The irow variable is used as a counter for which line of the report we are currently writing to. As we are just starting out and no loans have been written to the report, the starting position is 11 (the first row of the body of the template form).

Set the two columns that determine the width of the report. We are doing this because we said that we would be drawing a sight line for every fifth line of the body of the report. These column labels will tell us where to start and finish that line.

Set a counter variable that will keep track of the number of ineligible loans we will write into the report. Again, as we are just beginning, we set this counter to 1. When we find the first ineligible loan this will be its ordinal position in the report. We will enter this into the first column of the report.

We now need to go through each of the loans of the portfolio and find out which of them are ineligible for this condition. To do this we will use a For...Next loop and loop through it the number of times that there are loans in the portfolio. We know how many loans there are and have stored this information in the global variable g_total_loans, so we will set the loop counter to that terminus. **Note: It is an** *excellent* **idea that as soon as you write the For...Next statement you immediately write the Next statement at the bottom and annotate it with the loop counter value.** In this case the statement would be Next iloan. This eliminates errors later, especially in nested loops, and guarantees you will put all the code inside the loop.

Now we have all the initial counters and the main loop of the subroutine established. We now need to write the statements to fill in the body of the subroutine and draw the sight lines if necessary. We only want to print out those loans that have failed this criteria test. How do we determine if a loan is ineligible for the reason specific to this report? Back in the testing process we established and populated an array with the name "**g_sel_tag.**" Each loan has a row in this array and the array has a column location for each of the criteria tests. All we need to do is to test the column location of the array for each loan to determine whether or not it failed. This we will now do.

We use an If...Then...End If statement to do so and test the value of **g_sel_tag**(iloan, rep_num) where iloan is the loop counter for the loan and rep_num is the number of the report we are writing which we received from the calling subroutine. If the test is positive, the loan is ineligible for this condition. If the test is negative the loan passed this condition, we can move on to the next loan. For the loans that test positive we will now fill in a line of the report with the characteristics of that particular loan. For the loans that test negative, that passed this test, we fall immediately to the bottom of the test and proceed to examine the next loan.

Populating the Body of the Report   The first column of the report receives the nth number of the ineligible loan, if it is the third loan we have found, a "3" will go into the column. The second column of the report gets the loan number that is used in the data file to identify the loan. The third column of the report is more difficult to fill. We need to find the value of the loan characteristic that caused the ineligibility condition and place it there. In that each of the reports is different, each of these criteria may be different. We will need to have a method in place to find the correct criteria based on the particular test. Putting this aside for the moment we will move on.

The fifth and the seventh through the fourteenth columns of the report can all be filled with the information we have placed into these global variables from reading the portfolio file. The sixth column presents a problem, however.

The client has asked that we suppress the borrower identities on the reports until the finalization of the deal. To replace this information, we will simply create the cell location by concatenation of the letter designation of the column "F" and the irow counter. We will then fill that cell using a Range command with a cross hatch effectively blanking it out.

Filing in the Selection Criteria Value in Column 3   Now let us return to the problem of filling the third column of the report with the selection criteria.

The value in this column depends on the test that is being currently performed. Therefore the VBA code that fills that column must be specific to the test and fill the value that triggered the ineligibility condition of this particular loan. Let us look at Exhibit 13.20 to see how we are going to accomplish this!

The entire subroutine is contained inside a single large Select...Case statement. Using the list of constants we declared earlier, the subroutine selects the loan datum to print on the report based on the value of the report number being printed. This number is received by the subroutine as an argument from the calling subroutine.

Based on the value of the rep_num variable the Select...Case makes its choice from among the 11 possible reports and prints the appropriate value of the loan datum that triggered the ineligibility condition.

```
Sub Fill_Test_Parameter(rep_num)

Dim x        As Integer     'state number
Dim y        As String      'state name

    Select Case rep_num
        Case Is = TEST_REM_TERM:  Range(r_name(3)).Cells(irow) = g_loan_rem_term(iloan)
        Case Is = TEST_ORIG_TERM: Range(r_name(3)).Cells(irow) = g_loan_orig_term(iloan)
        Case Is = TEST_ORIG_BAL:  Range(r_name(3)).Cells(irow) = g_loan_orig_bal(iloan)
        Case Is = TEST_REM_BAL:   Range(r_name(3)).Cells(irow) = g_loan_cur_bal(iloan)
        Case Is = TEST_MAX_LTV:
            Range(r_name(3)).Cells(irow) = g_loan_orig_bal(iloan) / g_loan_
                appraisal(iloan)
        Case Is = TEST_INDEX:     Range(r_name(3)).Cells(irow) = g_loan_spread(iloan)
        Case Is = TEST_STATE_CODE:
            x = Assign_State_Number(g_state(iloan))
            y = Assign_State_Name(x)
            Range(r_name(3)).Cells(irow) = y
        Case Is = TEST_TENOR_CODE:
            Range("D" & irow).Select: Selection.Interior.Pattern = xlLightUp
        Case Is = TEST_BAL_CODE:
            Range("D" & irow).Select: Selection.Interior.Pattern = xlLightUp
        Case Is = TEST_PMT_CODE: Range(r_name(3)).Cells(irow) = g_loan_calc_pmt(iloan)
    End Select

End Sub
```

EXHIBIT 13.20   Fill_test_parameter subroutine

Ineligible Loan Listing Report

The next step is to display the disposition of all of the ineligible loans, so that we have a laundry list of each with its attendant rejection criteria. We would not have this information by viewing each of the Individual Selection Criteria Reports in isolation. A loan may be ineligible under several criteria. It would therefore be listed on several of the Single Criteria Reports. Without a laborious cross-tabulation of the results, we would not be able to produce a single definitive list of ineligibles. The VBA code for this report is contained in Exhibit 13.21.

To write this report we will need to perform the following steps:

1. Find the correct starting print position in the template file.
2. Set the width of the output area in columns (first column to last column).
3. Set an initial counter for the number of loans with this type of ineligible condition.
4. Loop through all the loans in the portfolio.
5. Test each to see if they are ineligible for any of the criteria test conditions.
6. If the loan is ineligible, write out the ID number of the loan, and the "**g_sel_tag**" array contents (which will tell us the tests the loan failed), its current coupon, and its current balance.
7. For every fifth ineligible loan of the report, draw a guideline across the bottom of the report.

The VBA code for this subroutine (Exhibit 13.21) is virtually identical to that of the Individual Criteria Reports. The first statement of the subroutine sets the listing

```
Sub Write_Loan_Listing_Report()

Dim inelig_loan          As Long      'nth ineligible loan on report

    inelig_loan = 1             'starting loan listing number for report
    col1 = "B":  col2 = "P"         'report width in columns, used to draw sight lines
    irow = 1                'inital print position inside the ranges

    ' Run through the portfolio for the exceptions
    For iloan = 1 To g_total_loans
        If g_loan_ok(iloan) = False Then
            Range("IneligALL_Count").Cells(irow) = inelig_loan
            Range("IneligALL_LoanNum").Cells(irow) = g_loan_num(iloan)
            For icol = 1 To INELIGIBLE_REPORTS
                If g_sel_tag(iloan, icol) Then
                    Range("IneligALL_Grid").Cells(irow, icol) = 1
                End If
            Next icol
            Range("IneligALL_Yield").Cells(irow) = g_loan_coup(iloan)
            Range("IneligALL_BankBal").Cells(irow) = g_loan_cur_bal(iloan)
            inelig_loan = inelig_loan + 1
            If irow Mod 5 = 0 Then Call Draw_Line_Under_Row(col1, col2, irow + 15)
            irow = irow + 1
        End If
    Next iloan

End Sub
```

EXHIBIT 13.21   Write_Loan_Listing_Report subroutine

number of the next loan to be printed. Since we are just starting out this number is of course "1." The next statement establishes the beginning and ending columns of the report, and the third statement the row, inside of the Ranges in which we will print the results. This last number, set to one, should not in any way be confused with the 1st row of the Excel worksheet itself.

As with the prior subroutine, we will be using a For...Next loop to examine each of the loans of the portfolio in turn and determine which of them are ineligible and need to be printed out to this report. The test we will make is against the value of the "g_loan_ok" array. If the value of the loan's "g_loan_ok" is False, it is an ineligible loan and should be added to the report. We will then write the listing number in the first report column and the loan ID number in the second column of the report.

For the third through the twelfth columns, we will write out the contents of the "g_sel_tag" array for this loan. To do this we will use another nested For...Next loop. It will loop through each of the 11 array positions of the criteria tests and print a "1" in each of the columns of the Range that indicate a failed criteria test.

Following that, we will add the yield and current balances of the loan to the thirteenth and fourteenth column of the report. Lastly, we will increment the loan counter by one and draw a sight line if the number of the loans we have added to the report is an even multiple of five. We can determine this by testing the value of the irow variable using the Modular function. This function tells us the remainder of dividing one number by another. In the If...Then test the "Mod 5 = 0" divides the value of irow by five. If the remainder, or Mod, is equal to 0, it is a multiple of five and we need to draw a sight line on the report.

When completed the report should look like Exhibit 13.22.

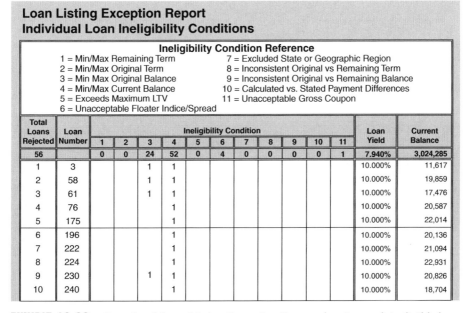

EXHIBIT 13.22 Completed Loan Listing Exception Report showing each ineligible loan and its condition

The Summary Exception Report

The purpose of the Summary Exception Report is to present a report of all the unique combinations of ineligibility conditions found in the portfolio by the selection process. All loans that have a common specific pattern are aggregated and the pattern is displayed.

The loans are displayed in the ranking of the ineligibility score, that is, the sum of the scores of each of their individual ineligibility scores. The pattern is displayed by ticking off a series of test boxes as was done in the Loan Listing Exception Report. The number of loans with the pattern is displayed along with the sum of their current balances, and the sum of the owner's equity positions.

This report is particularly valuable for detecting systemic data errors. An example is when a particular data field was incorrectly formatted, or where the data from one field is erroneously placed in another field. In a specific instance, wrong data was placed in a data field entitled "Times Repossessed,"in the data file of an auto loan securitization. Most fields in the file were therefore 0, but some were –1 (impossible) and others as high as 4, (suspiciously high!). The result was that about 25% of the portfolio was rejected for this reason alone. See Exhibit 13.23.

This is the most complex report that we have had to write so far. This is the first report in which the template report will not produce certain totals simply because we write the loans into the report and then compute the summary statistics by using Excel spreadsheet features. We cannot total the number of loans, the loan balances, and the equity balances of the loans in any one of the combination groups by using the spreadsheet functions built into the template file.

We will have to set up a series of local variables to hold the totals. We will also have to build each of the lines of this report before we are able to print them. That means that we will have to identify the total ineligibility score of each of the combinations in advance of accumulating them.

Summary Exception Report
Contracts Grouped By Unique Ineligibility Combinations

Ineligibility Condition Reference	
1 = Min/Max Remaining Term	7 = Excluded State or Geographic Region
2 = Min/Max Original Term	8 = Inconsistent Original vs Remaining Term
3 = Min Max Original Balance	9 = Inconsistent Original vs Remaining Balance
4 = Min/Max Current Balance	10 = Calculated vs. Stated Payment Differences
5 = Exceeds Maximum LTV	11 = Unacceptable Gross Coupon
6 = Unacceptable Floater Indice/Spread	

Unique Ineligibility Code	Ineligibility Condition											Number of Loans	Total Current Balance	Total Equity Position
	1	2	3	4	5	6	7	8	9	10	11			
	0	0	0	0	0	0	0	0	0	0	0	0	0	0

EXHIBIT 13.23   Template for the Summary Exception Report

To write this report we will need to perform the following steps:

1. Find the number of unique ineligibility combination scores and how many loans are in each category. (We will use a special purpose subroutine to do this.)
2. Loop through a list of all the unique combinations and check for the loans having that score.
3. Total the number of loans, their balances, and their equity positions by their shared combination score.
4. Write out the set of unique scores to the report.

Finding the Set of Unique Ineligibility Scores   To be able to produce this report in its finished configuration, we are going to have to find every one of the unique ineligibility codes in the portfolio. Next we will have to find each loan with a matching code and combine its balances into the total line for the report.

One obvious way to do this is to simply have an outer For...Next loop that searches each of the ineligibility codes one by one and then an inner For...Next loop that searches each of the loans to see if it is a match to the ineligibility code of the outer loop. If the subroutine finds a match, it sums the information of the loan to that particular ineligibility score set. Unfortunately, this could take a lot of time and effort on the part of the computer. This approach is barely acceptable for the size of the portfolio we have and the number of ineligibility codes. It will not work well for larger portfolios. The current portfolio is comprised of approximately 2,200 loans. There are 2nd to 11th power −1 possible error codes; or 2,047 codes by 2,200 loans. The statements within the inner loop would execute 4,503,400 times. That is too many times!

Besides, what happens next month when we get a portfolio of 53,450 loans and 17 component ineligibility codes? That would be $53,450^{*}((2\hat{}17)\text{-}1)$ loops, or slightly over seven billion loops, a far bigger number!

There must be a better way! You will learn from experience that ineligibility conditions in portfolios tend to be grouped, usually because of failures in the underwriting processes or unavoidable concentration issues. We can alleviate much of this frenzied looping with a little careful preparatory work. This is the type of professional foresight that one needs to develop and that distinguishes the programmers who know what they are doing from those who do not.

Finding the Active Ineligibility Combinations   We suspect, but cannot know for sure, that the ineligibility combinations are probably clumped up. This is to say many of the loans will be ineligible for the same combination or similar combinations of criteria due to underwriting practices or economic conditions at the time of issuance. It is also highly unlikely that there is an ineligible loan for each of the possible ineligibility combinations. We simply do not have enough loans! If there are enough component tests, there will simply be far more combinations than there will be loans to fill them (even if the entire portfolio starts out ineligible!). We need to trim down the number of possible ineligibility combinations we are going to examine for this report and determine how many loans are in each. This is a little tricky, but it can be done.

Let us return to our earlier example of the simple portfolio of twenty loans against which was applied five collateral selection tests. The test values for a failed test are 1, 2, 4, 8, and 16 for Test #1 through Test #5, respectively. There are

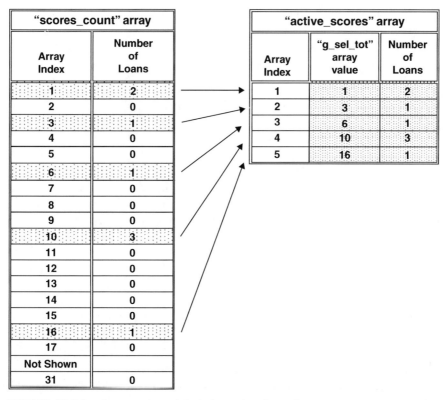

EXHIBIT 13.24   Compression of the information from the scores_count array to the active_scores array (scores_count array locations 18–30 are excluded for brevity)

therefore $(2^5)-1$ or 31 unique ineligibility pattern combinations possible. As stated, the portfolio consists of 20 loans, and we know that eight of them will be ineligible. Under these criteria, if we use the exhaustive method we will loop a total of 620 times, (20 loans multiplied by 31 combinations), to find the unique ineligible combinations and group the 20 loans into them. See Exhibit 13.24.

We can build a subroutine that will help us limit this looping by doing the following:

- Create two arrays:
  - The array **"scores_count"** that has one dimension, the size of the theoretical limit of the number of combinations. In our sample case with four ineligibility conditions this would be 31, or ((2 to the 5th power) −1)
  - The array **"active_scores"** that has two dimensions, a combination score, and the number of loans with that particular ineligibility score
- Loop through the portfolio one time, loan-by-loan. Increment the value of the array position equal to the ineligibility score every time we find an ineligible loan. For example, if a loan had a **g_sel_tot** value of 9 then

$$scores\_count(9) = score\_count(9) + 1$$

When the portfolio loop is finished, loop through the score_count array. Starting at 1 in the active_scores array, place the index of any occupied score_count cell into the first dimension of the active_scores array, and the number of loans with that unique combination into the second array position.

Now we know for certain that there are only five unique combinations of ineligibility scores and we know how many loans are in each category. Let's look at the VBA subroutine that performs this task. The VBA function in Exhibit 13.25 searches the **scores_count** array that was populated by reading the values of the **"g_sel_tot"** array. Fortunately, we may not need to search all the way to the largest possible combination. When the model was performing the eligibility testing we kept track of the maximum value of the **g_sel_tot** array and stored it in the global variable **g_sel_max_combo**.

```
Function Find_Active_Ineligibily_Scores()

Dim active_index    As Long      'index to load active scores in order
Dim index       As Long      'index value for array incrementation

  'set up a vector with one position for any possible ineligibility score
  '    the index position of the array in the g_sel_tot value for the loan
  '    and the value of the position is the number of loans with that value.
  ReDim scores_count(1 To g_sel_max_combo) As Long

  'we want to fill this array sequentially with the active cells of the
  '    scores_count array above.
  ReDim active_scores(1 To g_sel_max_combo, 2) As Long

  'this loop increments the nth slot of the array scores_count when
  '  it finds a loan that is ineligible with a combined score equal
  '  to the nth slot
  For iloan = 1 To g_total_loans
      If g_sel_tot(iloan) > 0 Then
          'assign the ineligibile combination score to be the array
          '  index, increment the index location of the array by one
          '  to get the total loan count for that unique score
          index = g_sel_tot(iloan)
          scores_count(index) = scores_count(index) + 1
      End If
  Next iloan

  'this for loop populates the active_scores array with the indexes
  '    of the scores_count array that have a non-zero balance
  active_index = 1
  For iscore = 1 To g_sel_max_combo
      If scores_count(iscore) > 0 Then
          'there is at least one loan with this score combination
          active_scores(active_index, 1) = iscore
          active_scores(active_index, 2) = scores_count(iscore)
          max_inelig = active_index  'number of unique conbinations present
          'increment to the next write location in the active_scores array
          active_index = active_index + 1
      End If
  Next iscore

End Function
```

EXHIBIT 13.25 The Find_Active_Ineligibily_Scores function

```
Sub Sum_Loan_Info_By_Ineligibility_Score()

    'sum the components of the ineligible loans by their shared error codes
    Call Find_Active_Ineligibily_Scores
    ReDim total_bal(1 To max_inelig, 1 To 3) As Double
    ReDim total_loans(1 To max_inelig) As Long
    ReDim total_tag(1 To max_inelig, 1 To 11) As Boolean

    For iscore = 1 To max_inelig
        For iloan = 1 To g_total_loans
            'test to see if the loan has the same score as the one we are now
            '  actively looking for
            If g_sel_tot(iloan) = active_scores(iscore, 1) Then
                total_loans(iscore) = total_loans(iscore) + 1
                total_bal(iscore, 1) = total_bal(iscore, 1) + g_loan_cur_bal(iloan)
                total_bal(iscore, 3) = total_bal(iscore, 2) + g_loan_cur_equity(iloan)
                For icol = 1 To INELIG_SINGLE_REPS
                    total_tag(iscore, icol) = g_sel_tag(iloan, icol)
                Next icol
                'if we have found all the ineligibles with this unique score exit the loop
                If total_loans(iscore) = active_scores(iscore, 2) Then Exit For
            End If
        Next iloan
    Next iscore

End Sub
```

EXHIBIT 13.26   The Sum_Loan_Info_By_Ineligibility_Score subroutine

We now have a much-reduced array, **active_scores,** that contains two very important piece of information. The first is a list of all the unique ineligibility combination scores. The second is the total number of ineligible loans with that particular score.

We now have everything we need to move to the next step of the process of writing the Ineligibility Summary Report. With a list of the unique ineligibility scores in hand, we need to comb the portfolio and find the loans, by score, and aggregate their financial information for the report.

The subroutine "Sum_Loan_Info_By_Ineligibility_Score" will perform this task for us. See Exhibit 13.26.

We now have all the balances that we need to produce the Summary Ineligibility Report. See Exhibit 13.27.

We have now finished the Ineligible Collateral Report Package.

Use of Module Variables

In this subroutine, we will begin by declaring a number of module level variables. If this were a large module with 10+ subroutines and hundreds and hundreds of lines of VBA code we would probably use the "m_" naming convention. Fortunately for us, this module will comprise less than 300 lines of VBA code and only 10 subroutines, (several of them very brief). As a result, we will forgo the "m_" prefix naming convention and continue on our way. The first variable, icnt, will be used as a loop counter for the number of lines of the report. The next three variables,

```
Sub Write_Summary_Report()

  'sum the components of the ineligible loans by their shared error codes
  Call Sum_Loan_Info_By_Ineligibility_Score

  'go forward to the max score find all loans with this unique score
  irow = 1              'initial print position in the ranges
  col1 = "B":  col2 = "Q"    'beginning and ending columns of the report

  For iscore = 1 To max_inelig
     Range("IneligSUM_Code").Cells(irow) = active_scores(iscore, 1) 'sum of codes
     For icol = 1 To INELIGIBLE_REPORTS              'grid of failure codes
        If total_tag(iscore, icol) Then Range("IneligSUM_Grid").Cells(irow, icol) = 1
     Next icol
     Range("IneligSUM_NumLoans").Cells(irow) = total_loans(iscore)'number of loans
     Range("IneligSUM_BankBal").Cells(irow) = total_bal(iscore, 1)'current bank bals
     Range("IneligSUM_EqBal").Cells(irow) = total_bal(iscore, 3)'current equity bals
     If irow Mod 1 = 0 Then Call Draw_Line_Under_Row(col1, col2, irow + 15)
     irow = irow + 1
  Next iscore

End Sub
```

EXHIBIT 13.27 Write_Summary_Report subroutine

total_bal, total_loans, and total_tag are used to accumulate balance information for each unique ineligibility condition combination. Remember each combination can have one, several, or many loans in it. The variables col_start and col_stop will hold the beginning and ending columns of the section of the report where we list the individual ineligibility conditions of the loan. Lastly the variable i3 is a counting variable that we will use to loop through the individual ineligibility conditions of the loan.

Writing Out the Unique Combination Information

We have now accumulated all the information into the unique ineligibility scores. All we have to do is print them out. These are the steps inside of the For...Next loop that run through the number of combinations that were returned by the "Find_Active_Ineligibilty_Codes" subroutine.

1. We print the active_score(record,1) into the first column of the report. This is the unique score for this combination of ineligible conditions.
2. The components of the score are then placed in the next 11 cells from the contents of the total_tag array.
3. The loan count for the combination goes into the fourteenth column of the Worksheet, and the three aggregated balances are placed in the fifteenth to the seventeenth columns.
4. If we have printed out five lines on the page, we draw a sight line.

See Exhibit 13.28 for an example of the completed report.

Summary Exception Report
Contracts Grouped By Unique Ineligibility Combinations

Ineligibility Condition Reference

1 = Min/Max Remaining Term	7 = Excluded State or Geographic Region
2 = Min/Max Original Term	8 = Inconsistent Original vs Remaining Term
3 = Min Max Original Balance	9 = Inconsistent Original vs Remaining Balance
4 = Min/Max Current Balance	10 = Calculated vs. Stated Payment Differences
5 = Exceeds Maximum LTV	11 = Unacceptable Gross Coupon
6 = Unacceptable Floater Indice/Spread	

Unique Ineligibility Code	Ineligibility Condition											Number of Loans	Total Current Balance	Total Equity Position
	1	2	3	4	5	6	7	8	9	10	11			
	0	0	1	2	0	2	0	0	0	0	1	56	3,024,285	646,065
8				1								28	620,496	25,150
12			1	1								24	356,258	10,582
32						1						3	1,618,184	69,679
1056						1					1	1	429,347	540,653

EXHIBIT 13.28   Summary Exception Report

HELPING MAKE IT ALL HAPPEN

Module Variables

In order to get the preceding set of subroutines to work, we made use of several variables that we did not declare locally. Remember our earlier discussions on the subject of the scope of variables? Variables inside a subroutine are local and exist only as long as the code execution is occurring in that subroutine. Module variables exist as long as the code is running in any subroutine in the module. Global variables exist as long as the program is running—period. We needed to declare a few variables as being module in scope. These variables were declared to be modular in scope for one of two reasons:

First, they were used in two or more subroutines within the module and needed to transfer between these subroutines intact and to carry their values.

Second, they were used for simple utilitarian work across many subroutines (such as loop counters), and we did not want to declare them locally over and over and over again.

The variables declared at the module level are in the model and on the Web site.

The variables iloan, iscore, icol, and irow are all loop counters. The variables col1 and col2 are used to delineate the width of the reports so that sight lines can be drawn.

The arrays total_bal, total_loans, and total_tag are used in the Summary Report to hold the row totals for all loans that have identical ineligibility criteria scores. These cross subroutine lines in that they are computed in "Sum_Loan_Info_By_Ineligibility_Score" that sums the balances and passes them to the subroutine "Write_Summary_Report."

The max_inelig scalar and the active_scores array are computed in the subroutine "Find_Active_Error_Codes" and then passed to the "Write_Summary_Report" subroutine.

The **r_name** array is used to hold the list of unique Range names in each of the Single Criteria reports. The names are generated in the "Create_SingleCriteriaReport_RangeNames" subroutine and then passed to the "Write_Individual_Report" subroutine each time a new report is about to be written.

Generating Range Names to Simplify Report Writing

The Excel product does not allow a Range name to be used in a workbook in more than one place. This limitation precludes our creating and using a set of identical Range names across worksheets on a single Workbook.

The Single Criteria Ineligibility Reports all have the same number of columns. From the fourth column of the report onward, all columns hold exactly the same data. We cannot, however, assign each column of successive reports with the same Range name. We must therefore assign each of the sheets a similar but unique Range name. As the program runs and we are in a position to begin putting our results into the reports, we need to correctly identify where this data is to be written. The easiest way to solve this problem is to assign the reports a Range name consisting of two distinct elements. The first is the name of the report and the second is the name of the column in the report. There are 11 Single Criteria Ineligibility Reports. We will therefore assign a Range name for each of the report columns as follows: "Inelig" & report# & column name. The program can then generate an array of these names as we progress from report to report and properly write the data to the appropriate Ranges of the reports. It needs only the report number to construct a series of Range names and pass them back to the calling program so they can be used to direct each of our sets of report information to the proper place in the report. The code that performs this task can be seen on the Web site. This code is contained in the subroutine "Create_SingleCriteriaReport_RangeNames," which resides in the **"WriteIneligibilityReports"** module.

Why go through all this trouble? Why not use the "Cell(irow).Value = output" notation to write the values?

Just because the reports have identical formats *now* does not mean that this will always be the case. A decision might be made in six months time to eliminate six of the columns and then reshuffle the remaining columns. *If the Cells approach was used this would take a long and time-consuming rewrite of the output code.* Using Range names would dramatically cut the time needed to make changes.

Using our method we would only need to delete the columns from the reports, adjust the code in the writing output subroutine, and eliminate the unused names from the above subroutine and the task would be done.

ELIGIBLE COLLATERAL REPORT PACKAGE

Stratification Reports

General Form of a Stratification Report   Having determined the eligible portfolio, we can now produce reports concerning its composition.

These reports will be the standard, "slice and dice" reports, with one exception: a static loss report. Slice and dice reports stratify the portfolio by a number of different

Eligible Collateral Report #10
Current Balances Distribution by State or Territory

			4	5	6	7	8	9
			Number of Loans	Current Loan Balance	Current Loan LTV	% Current Balances	Cum % Current Balances	Average Loan Balance
#	Name	Postal	0	-				

EXHIBIT 13.29   Typical Eligible Collateral stratification report

variables. Mainly, these reports stratify data across balance information, coupon distribution information, tenor information, LTV statistics, geographic distribution, and borrower demographics.

This layout is typical of the standard stratification report. The left-most column will contain the information to which the stratification will be applied. The columns to the right will contain the sums of that particular sub cut of the portfolio. See Exhibit 13.29.

The task of producing the collateral demographic reports is a major functionality of the model. As such it is called from the "Select_Deal_Collateral" subroutine, which is itself a call from the Main Program.

The "Write_Portfolio_Demographic_Reports" subroutine writes all the eligible collateral reports. These are what are commonly referred to as "Strat" reports. The present information across a series of rows that stratify the data of the report across a series of fixed intervals. The bodies of the reports are identical: loan counts, their balances, tenors, WACs, and LTVs. Some of these reports stratify their information on numeric Ranges, others on alphabetic codes. For balance and numeric reports, the stratifications will employ an interval such as $100,000 to $200,000. A second type of common stratification report is based on a single criteria, state, ZIP code, industry, dwelling type, occupation, ethnicity, gender, marital status, and so on.

The report that we will trace over the next several pages is a stratification report based on the loan's geographical location. This geographical report breaks out the eligible collateral of the portfolio by locations across the states and territories of the United States. Each cut of the report will have an individual line containing the number of loans and their collective information for all loans that in an individual state. The report will be produced for all geographic entities selected from the Geographic

```
Sub Write_Portfolio_Demographic_Reports()

  Workbooks.Open Filename:=g_pathway_output & gfn_output_prefix & gfn_accepted_loans_
                     file

  Call Write_Assumptions_Page

  For irep = 1 To PORTFOLIO_REPORTS
      If g_report(irep) Then
          Select Case irep
              Case Is = ORIG_TERM:        Call Dist_Current_Bal_by_Orig_Term
              Case Is = REM_TERM:         Call Dist_Current_Bal_by_Rem_Term
              Case Is = SEASONING:        Call Dist_Current_Bal_by_Seasoning
              Case Is = CUR_COUPON:       Call Dist_Current_Bal_by_Current_Coupon
              Case Is = SPREAD:           Call Dist_Current_Bal_by_Spread
              Case Is = EQUITY_PCT:       Call Dist_Current_Bal_by_Equity
              Case Is = MAX_LTV:          Call Dist_Current_Bal_by_LTV
              Case Is = CURR_BALANCE:     Call Dist_Current_Bal_by_Current_Balance
              Case Is = ORIG_BALANCE:     Call Dist_Current_Bal_by_Original_Balance
              Case Is = STATE_CODE:       Call Dist_Current_Bal_by_State
              Case Is = ZIP_CODE:         Call Dist_Current_Bal_by_Zip_Code
          End Select
      End If
  Next irep


  ActiveWorkbook.Save
  ActiveWorkbook.Close

End Sub
```

EXHIBIT 13.30 VBA subroutine that calls each of the Eligible Collateral Report writing subroutines based on the user's entries in the Reports Selection Menu

Criteria Menu. Geographic regions with no eligible loans will not be printed in the report.

The form of the subroutine is very typical of what you can expect to see of a master subroutine that produces a report package consisting of similar or related reports. For the VBA code, see Exhibit 13.30.

Steps in Producing a Eligible Collateral Report To produce the Eligible Collateral Report Package we must perform the following tasks:

- Have a portfolio of eligible collateral that has passed the selection process.
- Open the Eligible Collateral Report template file and save it to the output file name.
- Read the contents of the eligible collateral file into the model.
- Populate the Assumptions Report so we have a record of the selection criteria.
- The model calls a series of report specific subroutines, one for each selected report.
- Save the reports as they are created, then close the file, saving it in the output directory.

Stepping through the Subroutine The first task this subroutine performs is to open the output file that was created earlier in the process of running the model. Once the output file is open, the second task is to write the Assumptions Report page into the

```
'======================================================================
'   Distribution of Current Balances By Original Term
'======================================================================
Sub Dist_Current_Bal_by_Orig_Term()

  Sheets("Elig1").Select 'select the correct worksheet
  begin_intervals = 0      'set the stratification intervals
  total_intervals = 30
  step_up = 12
  offset = 1
  Call Set_Numeric_Range_Intervals(begin_intervals, step_up, offset)
  Call Complete_Eligible_Collateral_Report(ORIG_TERM, TEST_INTERVAL)

End Sub
```

EXHIBIT 13.31   From blank template file to populated report

file. Next the subroutine will execute the For . . . Next loop of the subroutine once for each of the eligible collateral reports.

If the report has been selected for production, that is, the value of the Boolean variable g_report(loop_counter) is "True," a subroutine specific to that report is called.

This subroutine will call others to perform the tasks of sorting the collateral along the stratification lines and then writing the results to the report. At the conclusion of writing the report it may also reformat the length of the report to eliminate vacant brackets. Each report is in a separate worksheet in the output file workbook. This is the subroutine that is called on the eleventh loop of the subroutine loop. It has a total of eight lines of code and six of them are calls to other subroutines. See Exhibit 13.31.

Writing the Geographic Distribution Report   The subroutine Dist_Current_Bal_by_State first selects the appropriate worksheet within the Eligible Collateral Report Template Workbook. It knows where to look because when we developed the report package back in Chapter 5 we made a list of the required stratification reports and assigned numbers to them. The Geographic Concentration Report was the 11th of the package. This worksheet has its headings filled in and has Excel functions to produce totals in a number of its columns. Its initial state can be seen in Exhibit 13.32.

```
Sub Set_Single_Value_Intervals(data_type)

    For interval = 1 To total_intervals
      Select Case data_type
        Case Is = STATE_CODE:  state_test_value(interval) = g_state_postal(interval)
        Case Is = ZIP_CODE:    zip_test_value(interval) = active_zips(interval)
        Case Is = INDEX_CODE:  index_test_value(interval) = 1
      End Select
    Next interval

End Sub
```

EXHIBIT 13.32   VBA code that fills in the selection criteria in the report

The second task will be to set the number of rows in the report. This is not a simple balance stratification where we can start at a given base number and increase each interval by a fixed amount. We are basing the stratification of the report on a two-letter alphabetic code. The information we are sorting the loans against will come from a list. Clearly, something more complicated in the way of VBA code is needed to accomplish this. We have one piece of information that will make our task here easier. We know all the elements of the state and territory list and we know how many there are in total. We can therefore immediately populate the selection portion of the report with their names and codes. The total number of intervals is set in the constant variable called STATES. Its value is 54. Again remember this is the sum of 50 states and 4 U.S. territories.

To prepare for the selection process we will set to zero the accumulation variables of the report. We will then sort and accumulate the loans of the portfolio across the selection criteria. Once we have collected all the collateral data by the appropriate groups, we will print the results to the report. The final task is to "clean up" the report by eliminating any of the stratification rows that do not contain information.

Setting the Sorting Interval for the Report   This is the first subroutine called by the geographic report subroutine and its role in the overall process is to address the task of setting the intervals. We have four reports in the Eligible Collateral Report Package that will not use either a percentage or dollar amount numeric interval. For these reports, we will have to establish how many sorting and accumulating levels there are. From a design standpoint, it would be better if we consolidated this function in a single subroutine that encompassed all the nonnumeric reports. We can write special purpose subroutines to be called from that subroutine as each of the nonnumeric reports are called. All we need is to supply each of them with the expected number of intervals. The subroutine in Exhibit 13.32 will serve just this purpose.

Setting Up the Interval Values of the Report   We will differentiate this subroutine from others that set numeric intervals by naming it the "Set_Single_Value_Intervals." We will pass it the **"data_type"** of the selection criteria. The subroutine will handle reports that deal with states, ZIP codes, and interest rate indexes. Each report will have a different number of sorting/accumulating factors so we will have to make this determination of how many intervals there are for the report we are about to write and pass that information to the subroutine. We will use the variables total_intervals to hold the stratification marks. The total_intervals variable will be declared as a module variable. We will use it as an outer For...Next loop counter to assign each of the selection values for the various intervals of the reports. A Select...Case statement is used to branch to the appropriate report type. In the case of this report, the subroutine will then fill in the array **"state_test_values"** with each of the state and territory codes. We now have a complete list of selection criteria for the report.

Setting the Accumulator Variables to Zero   We now have to prepare to do the sorting and accumulation activity. First we need to set to zero any values in the accumulator values. This sounds like such a simple and mundane activity but it is absolutely critical to the process. Writing the VBA code to perform this activity is an

```
Const MAX_INTERVALS = 5000              'maximum selection

Dim cum_pct                             As Double    'cumulative pct
Dim total_curr_bal                      As Double    'total current balances
Dim loan_count(1 To MAX_INTERVALS)      As Double    '# of loans in group
Dim loan_balance(1 To MAX_INTERVALS)    As Double    'sum of balances
Dim equity_balance(1 To MAX_INTERVALS)  As Double    'sum of equity balances
Dim tot_appraisal(1 To MAX_INTERVALS)   As Double    'sum of appraisal values
Dim wac_sum(1 To MAX_INTERVALS)         As Double    'weighted average coupon
Dim was_sum(1 To MAX_INTERVALS)         As Double    'weighted average seasoning
Dim waom_sum(1 To MAX_INTERVALS)        As Double    'weighted average original
                                                       maturity
Dim warm_sum(1 To MAX_INTERVALS)        As Double    'weighted average remaining term
```

EXHIBIT 13.33 Declaration of the accumulator variables

often and inadvertently overlooked task. The result is that on each successive model run, the numbers in the accumulator variables just get larger and larger, producing erroneous results. The next subroutine, which is named "Set_Accumulators_To_Zero" does just that. The VBA code is simple. The accumulator variables are used by all of the stratification reports and are therefore declared at the module level. The list of their declarations can be seen in Exhibit 13.33. Each of the accumulators relate to one of the columns of the stratification report. The VBA code that initializes these variables to zero is shown in Exhibit 13.34.

In the subroutine, "Set_Accumulators_to_Zero," shown in Exhibit 13.27 we will use the VBA reserved word Erase to clear each of the arrays. Erase is a VBA statement that sets a variable or all members of an array to a null condition. In this case, all members of each of these arrays are set to zero. We will then refill them as the report is run. The names of the first five variables inside are descriptive of their function; the last four variables are dollar-weighted averages of coupon, seasoning, original maturity, and remaining maturity, respectively. Having set the accumulator variable balances to zero, we can begin to build the information that we need for this report.

Accumulating the Loan Information Into the Correct Interval   To accumulate the stratification totals for all the intervals of the report, we will need to complete the

```
Sub Set_Accumulators_to_Zero()

    cum_pct = 0#
    total_curr_bal = 0#
    Erase loan_count
    Erase loan_balance
    Erase equity_balance
    Erase tot_appraisal
    Erase wac_sum
    Erase was_sum
    Erase waom_sum
    Erase warm_sum

End Sub
```

EXHIBIT 13.34 The Set_Accumulators_to_Zero subroutine

```
Sub Balance_Accumulator(test_criteria, test_type)

Dim accumulate As Boolean

  For iloan = 1 To g_total_loans

    ' for the numeric interval tests set the test criteria, interval tests only
    ' single test criteria will be set in the loop
    Select Case test_criteria
       Case Is = ORIG_TERM:     test_value = g_loan_orig_term(iloan)
       Case Is = REM_TERM:      test_value = g_loan_rem_term(iloan)
       Case Is = SEASONING:     test_value = g_loan_season(iloan)
       Case Is = CUR_COUPON:    test_value = g_loan_coup(iloan)
       Case Is = SPREAD:        test_value = g_loan_spread(iloan)
       Case Is = EQUITY_PCT:    test_value = g_loan_cur_equity(iloan) / g_loan_
                                                appraisal(iloan)
       Case Is = MAX_LTV:       test_value = g_loan_cur_bal(iloan) / g_loan_
                                                appraisal(iloan)
       Case Is = CURR_BALANCE:  test_value = g_loan_cur_bal(iloan)
       Case Is = ORIG_BALANCE:  test_value = g_loan_orig_bal(iloan)
    End Select
```

EXHIBIT 13.35 Subroutine Balance Accumulator that sets up the test values for the interval of the stratification report

following tasks. The VBA code to do this for the eligible collateral reports is shown in Exhibit 13.35.

- Read each loan in sequence and select from the loan record that particular piece of information that we will use to test against whatever intervals we have established for the report. In this example it will be the geographic code of the loan.
- Compare the loan test criteria information in one of two ways to determine what interval of the report into which it will be accumulated. If it is a numeric interval test, determine which interval of the report the test value of the loan falls within. If it is a single criteria report (state, ZIP, or index), find the interval that matches the loan criteria.
- Accumulate the individual loan information into the interval information.

Setting the Test Value for the Interval Testing If the stratification report is designed using numeric intervals, we will need to identify the loan datum that we will use as a comparison value and assign its value to the test_value variable. The test_value variable will serve equally well for any type of numeric data that we want to sort into the Ranges of the stratification reports, regardless of whether it represents dollar amounts, original term, remaining term and loan seasoning values, and LTV or equity ownership percentages. Ten of the stratification reports accumulate their information by testing the loan datum across intervals specified with numeric values. The test_value variable will be compared to each of the stratification intervals until it finds a fit in the appropriate interval and then its balances will be accumulated.

A Select . . . Case statement will be the best way to make the assignment of the loan datum to the test_value variable. In the top of the module we will declare each of these test items as a constant. They will have a one-to-one correspondence with the stratification reports we are going to produce. We deliberately numbered them in this manner so we can use them for the Select . . . Case statement labels. If the test is a numeric test, we are now all set to go on to the portion of the subroutine that conducts the interval testing.

If the comparison value from the loan is not a numeric value, we need to determine what the equivalent of the above numeric "**test_value**" will be. To make this assignment we do not have to set up the equivalent of a "**test_value**," we can instead use the test criteria itself.

Our outer For . . . Next loop of the subroutine ran from 1 to value of "**g_total_loans**," checking each loan of the portfolio from first to last. We will now need to set up an inner For . . . Next loop for the 1 to "intervals" (the number of stratification levels of the report, however many there will be), to complete the sorting and accumulation process. The combination of these two loops will pass each loan over each sorting interval of the stratification report. A Boolean variable named accumulate will tell us when we have found a match between the loan datum and the appropriate interval and set a signal to accumulate the loan information into that specific interval. It will be declared at the module level and when its value becomes "True" we know that we have found the interval match.

We will set the initial value of the accumulate variable to "False" initializing the state of the loan to a condition where no interval match has been found as yet.

Returning to Exhibit 13.35 for the moment we can see that if the test is not a test of a numeric value against a set of numeric value intervals, none of the cases in the first Select Case will be triggered. If it *is* a numeric test, one of the cases will be correct and the value of "**test_value**" will be assigned the appropriate loan datum.

For stratification reports that use nonnumeric interval testing, the logic of the Select . . . Case will test each case in turn, and finding no match, will drop through the test criteria and the variable "test_value" will not be assigned a value. This is perfectly okay because we will be comparing the postal code of the loan or its ZIP code, which are nonnumeric test values. By the time we finish with the upper Select . . . Case statement of this subroutine, we will have assigned a numeric value to the variable test_value or if the test criteria are nonnumeric, we will not have made an assignment here.

We now need to actually match the test_value variable to an interval on a report and accumulate the information. This code is shown in Exhibit 13.36.

Sorting and Accumulating the Loan Information to the Interval First we set the value of the accumulate variable to "False." We are now ready to enter the For . . . Next loop that runs from 1 to total_intervals and that is nested inside the outermost For . . . Next loop that runs 1 to g_total_loans.

The first test inside this loop is to determine if the loan criteria being tested is a single value test or a numeric test against an interval. We have two tests that are single criteria tests. They are by state or by ZIP code. If the report is a single-test criteria report, then we can immediately assign the value from the information of the loan record. If we get a match we can set the value of the "accumulate" variable to "True."

If the loan criteria test is against a Range, we will then compare the value of the test_value variable against the low and high values of the stratification report intervals. When we find the appropriate interval match we will set the value of the accumulate variable to "True."

```
'Accumulate the individual loans into the appropriate report intervals
  accumulate = False
  For interval = 1 To total_intervals
      'Find the type of match we need for this report, either a exact match, or a
      ' match in which the value falls inside of an interval range on a report.
      Select Case test_type
          'We are testing against an exact match, either state code or a zip code
          Case Is = TEST_SINGLE
              Select Case test_criteria
                  Case Is = STATE_CODE:
                      If g_state(iloan) = state_test_value(interval) Then_
                              accumulate = True
                  Case Is = ZIP_CODE:
                      If g_zip_code(iloan) = zip_test_value(interval) Then_
                                accumulate = True
              End Select
              'All other tests that have numeric intervals are tested here
              Case Is = TEST_INTERVAL
                  If test_value >= low(interval) And test_value <= high(interval) Then_
                      accumulate = True
      End Select
      'The variable "Accumulate" is now tested, if it has been set to TRUE above we have
      ' found the correct state, zip code, or value interval match and need to add its
      ' balances to that interval.
      If accumulate Then
          loan_count(interval) = loan_count(interval) + 1
          loan_balance(interval) = loan_balance(interval) + g_loan_cur_bal(iloan)
          equity_balance(interval) = equity_balance(interval) + g_loan_cur_equity(iloan)
          tot_appraisal(interval) = tot_appraisal(interval) + g_loan_appraisal(iloan)
          wac_sum(interval) =
              wac_sum(interval) + (g_loan_cur_bal(iloan) * g_loan_coup(iloan))
          was_sum(interval) =
              was_sum(interval) + (g_loan_cur_bal(iloan) * g_loan_season(iloan))
          waom_sum(interval) =
              waom_sum(interval) + (g_loan_cur_bal(iloan) * g_loan_orig_term(iloan))
          warm_sum(interval) =
              warm_sum(interval) + (g_loan_cur_bal(iloan) * g_loan_rem_term(iloan))
          total_curr_bal = total_curr_bal + g_loan_cur_bal(iloan)
          Exit For
      End If

  Next interval

 Next iloan

End Sub
```

EXHIBIT 13.36 VBA code that adds the values of the rejected loans to the report column totals

We are ready for the final step in the report preparation process. Now that we have a match with the interval (whether it is a single or interval test), we can accumulate the loan information into the appropriate holding variables. First we increase the loan counter for the interval by 1 (this displays the number of loans in the interval). Next we accumulate the current balance, the current equity balance, and the property appraisal value into separate accumulator variables. We then add the dollar weighted coupon, seasoning, original term, and remaining term to their separate accumulators.

Lastly we will add the current balance to the report total current balance. This is a critical number for all of these reports. We need to keep track of the sum of current balances for all the loans in the report. We will need to use this number repeatedly later as the denominator for the calculation of the last four dollar weighted average statistics of the report.

Writing the Eligible Collateral Reports

Writing the Interval Information to the Template File The first step in the process of populating a report in the Eligible Collateral Report Package is to set forth the selection criteria for the stratification intervals of the report in the leftmost columns of the report. In ten of the reports, this will be a set of numeric intervals. A typical stratification interval entry might be "$100,000 to $200,000" where the $100,000 will be the low value of the Range and the $200,000 will be the high value of the Range. The noted first 10 reports are numeric interval codes, hence any report that has a ranking of ten or less is different from the remaining two nonnumerically sorted reports. In the subroutine the test for <= ORIG_BALANCE captures this feature as the value of the constant ORIG_BALANCE is "10."

The remaining two tests are for state and ZIP codes that are single- entry tests.

The subroutine that prints these stratification intervals in each of the reports is named **"Print_Interval_Test"** and is found in the **"WriteCollateralReports"** module.

Writing the Report Body to the Template File We are now ready to fill the body of the template report with the information stored in the accumulator variables. The VBA subroutine to perform this task is shown in Exhibit 13.37. We know how many intervals there are on each of the reports because we have either set them or calculated them before the accumulation process.

We can therefore use a For... Next loop which will fill the report in on a line-by-line basis. Inside the loop we place an If... Then statement to test if the loan count for the interval is greater than zero. If the loan count is zero, we do not print the interval because there is no information to print. There are some things that we need to be careful of. A number of the line items need to have some finishing calculations made to them before they can be printed. These are:

- In the third column of the report we need to divide the total loan balance for the interval by the total appraisal values for the interval to arrive at the interval Loan-To-Value ratio.
- In the fourth and fifth columns we need to compute what the percentage of the loan balance is of the total portfolio and then what is the cumulative percentage of the interval on the report. In the cumulative percentage column we calculate the interval percentage and add it to the running cumulative balance. In the next line of VBA code we then increment the cumulative percentage by the interval percentage we have just calculated.
- In the sixth column we find the average loan balance for the interval by dividing the sum of the interval loan balances by the number of loans of the interval.
- In the seventh to the tenth columns we finish the calculation to produce the dollar weighted coupon, seasoning, original, and remaining balance statistics.
- In the eleventh and thirteenth columns of the report we find the equity and equity LTV percentage.

```
Sub Print_Report_Body(rep_num)

    Call Create_CollateralReport_RangeNames(rep_num)

    For interval = 1 To total_intervals

        ' Print out only the active ranges
        If loan_count(interval) > 0 Then
            Range(r_name(1)).Cells(irow) = loan_count(interval)
            Range(r_name(2)).Cells(irow) = loan_balance(interval)
            Range(r_name(3)).Cells(irow) = loan_balance(interval) / tot_
                                           appraisal(interval)
            Range(r_name(4)).Cells(irow) = loan_balance(interval) / total_curr_bal
            Range(r_name(5)).Cells(irow) = cum_pct + (loan_balance(interval) / total_
                                           curr_bal)
            cum_pct = cum_pct + (loan_balance(interval) / total_curr_bal)
            Range(r_name(6)).Cells(irow) = loan_balance(interval) / loan_count(interval)
            Range(r_name(7)).Cells(irow) = wac_sum(interval) / loan_balance(interval)
            Range(r_name(8)).Cells(irow) = waom_sum(interval) / loan_balance(interval)
            Range(r_name(9)).Cells(irow) = warm_sum(interval) / loan_balance(interval)
            Range(r_name(10)).Cells(irow) = was_sum(interval) / loan_balance(interval)
            Range(r_name(11)).Cells(irow) = equity_balance(interval)
            Range(r_name(12)).Cells(irow) = equity_balance(interval) / tot_
                                            appraisal(interval)
            Range(r_name(13)).Cells(irow) = tot_appraisal(interval)
        End If
        irow = irow + 1

    Next interval

    irow = 0

End Sub
```

EXHIBIT 13.37   Subroutine that populates the Eligible Collateral Report

Complete the Report, Clean-Up Formatting   After we have finished populating the stratification Ranges of the report body, the last thing we need to accomplish to complete the report is to clean up the format of the template report.

To do this we will do two things:

1. Delete any unused lines from the last active line of the report to the bottom of the template file.
2. Draw a double line across the bottom of the last printed line to "box-out" the report for presentation (if needed).

This subroutine consists of two sequential For...Next loops.

The first For...Next loop is somewhat unusual in that it has a Step command in the loop line. The Step command is used in For...Next loops when you want to have the loop advance by any value other that 1. In this case we want the loop to work its way upward from the bottom of the report and delete any line that has a loan count of less than 1.

Each time the subroutine finds a line in the report that meets this test it uses the Select command to select the current line and then the Delete command to delete it. When this For...Next loop completes its run there should be only active lines in the report.

The second For . . . Next loop now starts and runs from the top of the report to the final row. At each line of the report it tests for a value in the fifth column of the Worksheet. The first time it finds a zero value, it is at the end of the report; it then drops back one line and draws a double weight line across the bottom of the columns of the report.

When finished the report should look like the one in Exhibit 13.38.

WRITING OUT THE ASSUMPTIONS OF THE MODEL RUN

An often overlooked, but vital, report is a listing of the assumptions used to generate the output. It is best when included in the output report itself. We can standardize the form of the report and just drop it into whatever output file we are generating. In addition to being useful it is also simple to write. We only need to reverse the process of reading from the menu screen to writing them into an output template file. We will create a separate subroutine to produce this report. This will allow us to easily add it to any report package.

The Assumptions Report will be set up as a template Worksheet in the report package. The subroutine uses a series of assignment statements to transfer the information from global variables to the report itself. A series of For . . . Next loops copies the geographic and default sections. This code can be found in the model in the **"WriteModelAssumptions"** module.

The subroutine that writes the Assumption Report is probably one of the most straightforward of any we will see in the model. It simply takes the values of all the variables that we have either entered into the various menus of the model or read from the collateral file, and prints them to a template worksheet inside the report package. Again, it should be noted that although this is a very simple report to produce, it is one that you may find absolutely critical. Here is one reason why: A year after the deal closes, you are asked to produce a series of runs similar to the ones we will produce in Chapter 18, "Running the Model." If you have this file you will know exactly what menu entries you need to replicate the original model runs. Once you have the original model runs replicated, you can proceed with the newly requested runs knowing that you are working off the very same set of criteria you used originally. Whatever happens with the new runs, you will at least know that you are on an "apples-to-apples" basis (without an orange in sight!).

The VBA code that produces the Assumptions Report is in Exhibit 13.39. An example of the template for this report can be seen in Exhibit 11.10.

This subroutine is broken down into three very distinct portions. The first writes the contents of the program costs assumptions, collateral selection criteria, and the spread selection criteria. The second section displays the collateral amortization assumptions of default and prepayment rates. The third and last section outlines the geographic selection criteria for the portfolio. As you can see, the entire subroutine consists of a large number of simple VBA statements that write the assumptions of the model run that were used to produce the report spreadsheet.

Eligible Collateral Report #10
Current Balances Distribution by State or Territory

#	Name	Postal	Number of Loans	Current Loan Balance	Current Loan LTV	% Current Balances	Cum % Current Balances	Average Loan Balances
			4	5	6	7	8	9
			2,178	436,877,281				
1	California	CA	213	36,008,866	61.527%	8.242%	8.242%	169,056
2	New Jersey	NJ	174	35,816,526	62.036%	8.198%	16.441%	205,842
3	New York	NY	121	29,689,706	59.405%	6.796%	23.237%	245,369
4	Texas	TX	93	26,016,517	64.702%	5.955%	29.192%	279,747
5	Georgia	GA	133	22,745,780	60.213%	5.206%	34.398%	171,021
6	Colorado	CO	109	20,676,177	57.045%	4.733%	39.131%	189,690
7	Florida	FL	87	19,949,392	61.369%	4.566%	43.697%	229,303
8	Arizona	AZ	89	19,886,802	64.388%	4.552%	48.249%	223,447
9	Connecticut	CT	96	16,945,735	61.698%	3.879%	52.128%	176,518
10	Pennsylvania	PA	91	16,798,410	59.025%	3.845%	55.973%	184,598
11	Illinois	IL	80	15,020,312	63.120%	3.438%	59.411%	187,754
12	Oregon	OR	68	14,827,009	61.724%	3.394%	62.805%	218,044
13	Washington	WA	58	13,208,142	61.654%	3.023%	65.828%	227,727
14	Alabama	AL	58	13,134,919	59.161%	3.007%	68.835%	226,464

EXHIBIT 13.38 Completed collateral stratification report

DELIVERABLES CHECKLIST

The VBA Knowledge Checklist items for this chapter are:

- How to open, rename, populate, and save template files.
- How to use the concatenation operator with menu inputs to construct directory and filename
- How to use the SaveAs and Close methods on the ActiveWorkbook object.
- How to transfer the collateral selection criteria from the model menus to global variables.
- How to use a For . . . Next loop and a list of constant variables to sequentially produce reports.
- How to use a set of constant variables to establish a set of uniquely weighted error codes.
- How to create a list of Range names specific to each of the ineligible/eligible collateral reports.

The Model Knowledge Checklist items for this chapter are:

- How to integrate a set of reports into a model.
- How to manage the creation of a multiple report package.
- The importance of including an Assumptions Report with major report packages so that they can be replicated, if need be, at a later date using the identical conditions.

NEXT STEPS

We now have a portfolio of eligible collateral to work with.

The next steps will be to take this portfolio and calculate its cash flows under a Range of prepayment and default assumptions. To accomplish this task we will examine each of the loans, note its payment characteristics, compute its cash flows, and sum them for transfer to the Excel waterfall spreadsheet. These calculations will be the real "number crunching" of the model. We will go over this process in excruciating detail in Chapter 14, "Calculating the Cash Flows."

In Chapter 15, "Running the Waterfall: Producing Initial Results," we will see how the timing and magnitude of these cash flows, along with their constituent components of defaulted principal, amortized principal, prepaid principal, coupon income, and loss recovery principal affect the retirement of the deal's indebtedness.

ON THE WEB SITE

The Web site will contain the model version containing the newly added collateral selection code. The **"MODEL_BASE_Chap13.xls"** file shows the incremental changes from the version of **"MODEL_BASE"** in the previous chapter.

```
Sub Write_Assumptions_Page()

    Sheets("Assumptions").Select

    'SECTION I - Program Costs, Selection Criteria, Spread Information
    'load the program costs section
    Cells(4, 2).Value = g_exp_service * 12#          'servicing fee
    Cells(5, 2).Value = g_exp_program * 12#          'program expenses
    Cells(6, 2).Value = g_conduit_spread             'condit financing spread
    Cells(8, 2).Value = 1 - g_advance_rate           'seller interest percentage
    Cells(10, 2).Value = g_trig_3M_delinq            'principal reallocation trigger
    Cells(12, 2).Value = g_trig_cleanup              'principal reallocation trigger

    'load the collateral selection criteria
    Cells(15, 2).Value = g_crit_min_orig_term        'min original term in months
    Cells(15, 4).Value = g_crit_max_orig_term        'max original term in months
    Cells(16, 2).Value = g_crit_min_rem_term         'min remaining term in months
    Cells(16, 4).Value = g_crit_max_rem_term         'max remaining term in months
    Cells(17, 2).Value = g_crit_min_orig_bal         'min original balance
    Cells(17, 4).Value = g_crit_max_orig_bal         'max original balance
    Cells(18, 2).Value = g_crit_min_rem_bal          'min remaining balance
    Cells(18, 4).Value = g_crit_max_rem_bal          'max remaining balance
    Cells(19, 2).Value = g_crit_min_coupon           'min gross coupon
    Cells(19, 4).Value = g_crit_max_coupon           'max gross coupon
    Cells(20, 4).Value = g_crit_max_loan             'max LTV ratio
    Cells(21, 4).Value = g_crit_pay_diff             'difference stated/calc pmt

    'write the spread information
    i_count = 1
    For irow = 24 To 29
      Cells(irow, 2).Value = g_crit_acc_index(i_count)
      Cells(irow, 4).Value = g_crit_min_spread(i_count)
      i_count = i_count + 1
    Next irow

    'SECTION II - Prepayment and default assumptions
    'collateral file information
    Cells(4, 9).Value = g_pathway & "data\" & gfn_collateral_file
    'load default information
    Cells(6, 9).Value = g_default_base_rate
    Cells(7, 9).Value = g_default_increment
    Cells(8, 9).Value = g_default_levels
    Cells(9, 9).Value = g_default_method
    'load repayment levels
    Cells(11, 9).Value = g_prepay_base_rate
    Cells(12, 9).Value = g_prepay_increment
    Cells(13, 9).Value = g_prepay_levels
    Cells(14, 9).Value = g_prepay_method
    'load market value information
    Cells(16, 9).Value = g_loss_sever_pct
    Cells(17, 9).Value = g_recovery_lag
    ' Read the annual default distribution schedule and set up the default_factor vector
    i_count = 1
    For icol = 10 To 14 Step 2
      For irow = 19 To 28
        If g_ann_defdist(i_count) > 0# Then
           Cells(irow, icol).Value = g_ann_defdist(i_count)
           i_count = i_count + 1
        End If
      Next
    Next

    'SECTION III - Geographic Selection Parameters
    'load the state and territory selections
    For irow = 1 To 54
      Cells(4 + irow - 1, 16) = g_state_select(irow)
    Next irow

End Sub
```

EXHIBIT 13.39   Write_Assumptions_Report subroutine

To review all of these changes go back and reread the "Under Construction" section of his chapter.

The model is compiled and will run. The model can perform all the steps from reading the menus, reading the data file, performing the eligibility tests and printing the eligibility reports.

## CHAPTER 14

Calculating the Cash Flows

OVERVIEW

We are now ready to produce the cash flow streams that we will need to drive the Excel cash flow waterfall spreadsheet model. For each of the combinations of prepayment and default rates, we will produce the principal and coupon cash flows and the amount of prepaid, defaulted, and recovered principal. We will save these results in a series of arrays and then load them sequentially into the Excel model. There are a number of vacant columns of the spreadsheet that are designed to receive these precomputed cash flows. The spreadsheet will then activate, the waterfall will calculate, and we will be able to read the results. We will, in turn, store these results and display them later in the Cash Flow Waterfall Reports Package and the Matrix Report Package. The location of the code for the cash flow generator can be seen in Exhibit 14.1.

DELIVERABLES

The deliverable for this chapter is to write the VBA code that will take the information that we have about the collateral, combine it with our prepayment, default, recovery rate, and interest rate environment assumptions and produce the monthly cash flows. These cash flows will have five components: (1) defaulted principal, (2) coupon payments, (3) scheduled amortization of principal, (4) prepayments of principal, and (5) recoveries of defaulted principal.

We will compute these cash flows for each loan monthly and aggregate them at the portfolio level. We will store them in a three-dimensional array by time period, prepayment scenario, and default scenario. We are also going to write a trace function so that we can validate the cash flow calculations on a loan-by-loan basis if need be.

When we are finished, we will have the completed array available to be read into the Cash Flow Waterfall spreadsheet on a scenario-by-scenario basis.

```
Sub Loan_Financing_Model()

    Application.DisplayAlerts = False          'temporarily turn off the warning
                                                messages
    Call Display_PrepayDefault_ProgressMsg(99) 'display program progress msg (null)
    Call ErrCheck_All_Menus                    'error check all menu entries
    Call Read_All_Menu_Input                   'transfer the menu entries to
                                                variables
    Call Read_Portfolio_Data_File              'read in the loan information to
                                                variables
    Call Select_Deal_Collateral                'run the basic eligibility test or
                                                accept all
    Call Compute_Collateral_Cashflows          'generating the cash flows
    Call Load_and_Run_the_Waterfall            'runs the waterfall
    Call Write_Waterfall_Report_Package        'package of waterfall reports in
                                                detail
    Call Write_Matrix_Report_Package           'package of 9 matrix reports
    Sheets("Main Menu").Select
    Application.DisplayAlerts = True           'turn message displays back on

End Sub
```

EXHIBIT 14.1 Main Program calling to the Compute_Collateral_Cashflows subroutine

VBA Language Knowledge Goals

The VBA language and programming goals are focused on producing the aggregated portfolio cash flows for each of the pairings of prepayment and default rates scenarios.

- Get your first experience in programming a computationally intensive program. You will see how to segregate calculation sequences and even parts of formulas that can be calculated in nonrepetitive code and then used elsewhere.
- You will gain experience writing a fairly serious trace function that will allow us to verify the calculation accuracy of the portfolio on an individual loan basis.
- You will learn how to reformat template file configurations on the fly because of the need to limit the storage size of the trace file.
- You will get a lot of experience with the implications of nested looping structures. The master subroutine will have a calculation structure that is four nested loops deep.
- You will learn how to program prepayment and default methodologies.

Model Production Goals

The goals for the model production are:

- Develop a schematic of how you are going to build the cash flows generator. This schematic should include at minimum a separate subroutine for calculating each of the five components of the cash flows. It should also help you lay out which calculation functions must be placed inside the looping structure you will write and which can be moved outside of it.
- After you have written the pseudo code schema, determine how much or what portions of the calculations can be moved outside of the inner loops. This is your first experience in program optimization.

- Learn the bond math for the two prepayments methodologies and the three default methodologies.
- Learn how to set up coupon levels for a floating rate loan.
- Learn how loan amortization is calculated.
- Declare all the variables needed to calculate and store the cash flows.
- Create the master subroutine for the cash flow calculations.
- Create the supporting calculation subroutines that deal with setting the scenario prepayment and default speeds.
- Create the subroutines that calculate the monthly default and prepayment attrition factors.
- Create the subroutines that set the floating rate coupon levels for the loans.
- Create the subroutines that calculate the scheduled amortization factors for the loans.
- Create the subroutines that calculate each of the five components of the cash flow streams.
- Create the subroutines that accumulate the cash flows to the portfolio level.
- Create a set of subroutines to allow us to write out and save all of the periodic cash flows that we calculate by loan. This will be critical in the validation process of the model.

UNDER CONSTRUCTION

In this chapter we will add all the VBA code necessary to perform the cash flow calculations for the model. In order from the top of the Project Explorer window of the model "**Model_Base_Chap14.xls**" we will see the following changes:

The "**A_Constants**" module contains some additional declarations. These declarations are listed under the "Modeling Inputs" section, sub-section "Prepayment and Default Level Constants." They serve to define the two prepayment and three default methodologies used in the model.

The "**A_Globals**" module contains a new group of public variable declarations at the bottom of the module. These arrays and vectors hold the various intermediate and final results of the cash flow calculation process.

The "**CollateralCFGenerator**" module is new and contains the overall organizational code that will drive the cash flow generation. It consists of twenty-one subroutines that produce the monthly component cash flows of the collateral pool. See the subroutine tree diagram for this module in Exhibit 14.2.

The "**CollaterPreDefCalcs**" module is new and contains the subroutines that specifically focused on the calculation of the prepayment and the default cash flows. This module contains eight subroutines that serve to create the prepayment and default factors on a monthly basis for two prepayment and three default methodologies. See the subroutine tree diagram for this module in Exhibit 14.2.

PAUSE AWHILE AND REFLECT

Before we plunge right into feverishly writing VBA statements, we should pause and consider what we are about to do at this point in the model. A common saying in

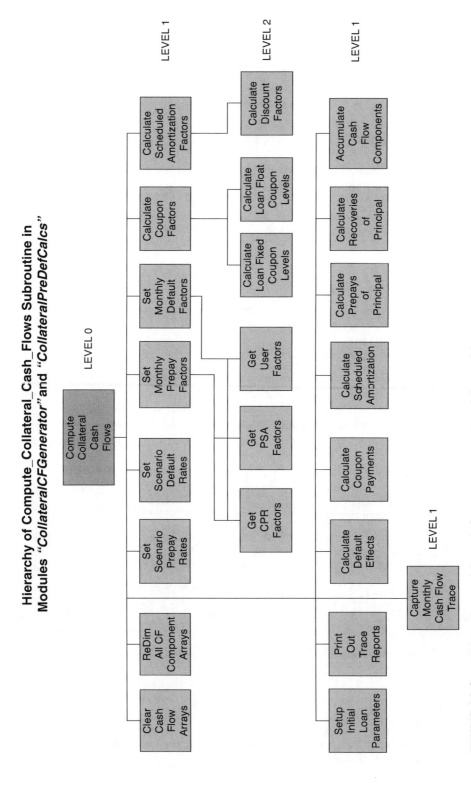

Hierarchy of Compute_Collateral_Cash_Flows Subroutine in Modules "CollateralCFGenerator" and "CollateralPreDefCalcs"

EXHIBIT 14.2 Subroutine tree of the cash flow generator engine of the model

carpentry is "measure twice, cut once." So before we dive boldly (or foolhardily) into one of the most complex portions of the model, we should break down the process into more manageable pieces.

It is abundantly clear at the offset that we need to, at a minimum, accomplish the following tasks:

- Amortize each individual loan of the portfolio generating its component cash flows of defaulted principal, coupon income, scheduled amortization of principal, prepayments of principal, and finally recoveries.
- Know what the loan looks like from the standpoint of balances, tenor, and coupon characteristics.
- Apply the principal default assumptions to each loan.
- Apply principal prepayment assumptions to each loan.

We also want to do this so that we are not doing any extra work that we can avoid. The portfolio is relatively small, only 2,200 loans, but we do not know that small portfolios are the only ones in our future. We need to design the program to be as efficient as possible. We want to be ready for the day when a 220,000-loan portfolio walks through the door. Then we will have an optimally configured model ready to deal with the situation. We will look like a miracle worker with the structuring team, the managers, and everyone else! In addition we will be seen as critical to the business and be rewarded for our efforts!

One of the best ways to set about organizing one's thoughts when faced with this complex task (especially for the first time) is to think about it as one would if peeling an onion. The structure of an onion is a series of encompassing layers, one on top of the other from the core outward.

This programming problem, like many other programming problems, is like an onion. There is an identifiable basic core requirement and essentially most if not all of the rest of the requirements for solving the problem follow directly from the requirements of solving the core task. The core task in this instance is the amortization of the portfolio. More than that, the immediate task is simply to get the program to amortize a single loan much less the whole portfolio! After we get one of the loans correctly amortized, the rest should hopefully fall right into line. This portfolio is fairly homogeneous. We can be reasonably sure that this expectation will be met if we are careful.

Thinking About the Amortization Process

The key drivers in estimating the amount and timing of the cash flows from the portfolio are defaults and prepayments. Defaults are deleterious to the portfolio because they deprive it of two streams of future cash flows, principal, and interest income. The defaulted principal will never be paid back, although we may get something in recoveries. We will additionally lose all the coupon interest we would have gotten from the borrower from the point of default across the remaining life of the loan. Plus there is no free lunch. The defaulted principal will have to be made up from somewhere. We can set up a Seller Interest, or a reserve account, or both. We may wish to hold back any excess income that the issuer might have gotten. Nevertheless, it is still an annoying thing to have to deal with.

Prepayments are only slightly better. Prepayments provide the deal structure with additional principal cash flows faster than they would have been available. Prepayments deprive the structure of all future coupon income attributable to the prepaid principal amounts. The upside of prepayments is the old saw "Prepaid principal can't default later." The effects of prepayments are mixed at best.

The next thing we need to ask ourselves (as all good modelers should) is what is happening in the real world.

Out There: The Real World

In the real world, the following behavior is almost universally observed with loan portfolios:

- If the borrower is going to default, they default. That is it. After some period of time, usually preceded by a period of delinquency, the payments simply stop coming. In most cases that is the end of it. There are no further payments to be made and the lender begins to apply legal remedies to perfect their claim on the remaining value of the assets. At some point in the future, depending mostly on what type of a business it was, a recovery is realized. Some lenders can realize larger recoveries sooner if the property and chattel are in a high demand or if it is a single-purpose facility such as a service station or a general warehouse. In most cases, however, the recovery will take more than a year to effect and will be a fraction of the value of the original property.
- The borrower makes a payment. Most of the time the payment is the scheduled payment but sometimes it is less and sometimes more. When the payment is received, the first dollars are applied against any delinquent interest, and the second dollars are applied to the current interest.
- After the coupon has been subtracted from the payment, the next item to receive dollars is the scheduled amortization. This is usually the end of the story and next month the cycle begins again.
- In some cases, however, there are additional remittances available after all coupon and scheduled principal has been paid. If these extra dollars are enough to retire the principal balance of the loan, it is a full prepayment. If these dollars are a significant but nontrivial amount, it is called a partial prepayment. If the amount is small it is termed a curtailment prepayment. Curtailments may seem irrelevant but they can have significant long-term effects. These can, over a longer tenor note, say 25 or 30 years, measurably reduce the coupon by systemically retiring the principal earlier than scheduled. That in turn allows more dollars to be paid against the outstanding balance in the next and all subsequent payments.

Thus the sequence in a nutshell is:

1. Defaulted Principal first
2. Coupon Income next
3. Scheduled Principal next
4. Prepayments next
5. Recoveries (if any) last

```
Call Calculate_Defaults
Call Calculate_Coupon_Payments
Call Calculate_Scheduled_Principal
Call Calculate_Prepaid_Principal
Call Calculate_Recoveries_of_Defaulted_Principal
```

EXHIBIT 14.3   Payment activity subroutines

It Is An Onion: Building The Cash Flow Generator

One Month of Payment Activity   To start, the cash flow generator onion will have at its heart the functionality listed above and the task will be performed in that order. Each of these calculations is different enough that we should put them in different subroutines. This is what will happen for a single monthly payment. We can write them in pseudo code as seen in Exhibit 14.3.

Adding This Month to Others   We may wish to add an additional subroutine call at this time. In Exhibit 14.3 we are talking about the cash flows of a single loan for one month. We need to come up with a portfolio total so we had better find a way to aggregate the cash flows from each month of each loan. In addition to just recording the cash flows, we are going to need some way to check whether they are correct. We will write a subroutine to dump the results to an output file where we can assure ourselves of their accuracy. We will need a variable to trigger this trace function, so let's create one called g_out_cftrace and make it a Boolean. If we want to trace the cash flows, we will set it to "True," if not to "False." To effect this we will add the code in Exhibit 14.4.

Extending the Amortization Process over the Life of the Loan   We need to perform this process for more than one month; in fact, we need to do it for as long as the loan has an outstanding principal balance. To do this we will need to have the whole process put in a loop so that we can repeat it on a monthly basis. The limit of the contractual obligation is the remaining term of the loan. It is a fixed time period (and therefore a fixed number of loops), so we can use a For...Next loop as in Exhibit 14.5.

From One Loan to the Entire Portfolio   The above commands will provide a sufficient process to amortize a single loan, but we need to do more than that. We need to amortize an entire portfolio. To accurately perform the amortization of the portfolio, it will be necessary the have all the relevant information about each loan in the portfolio we are amortizing. So the next thing we must add is a loop to go through the portfolio on a loan-by-loan basis. Each time this loop operates, it will

```
Call Calculate_Defaults
Call Calculate_Coupon_Payments
Call Calculate_Scheduled_Principal
Call Calculate_Prepaid_Principal
Call Calculate_Recoveries_of_Defaulted_Principal
Call Accumulate_the_Cash_Flows
If g_out_cftrace Then Call Capture_Monthly_CF_Trace
```

EXHIBIT 14.4   Adding the accumulator and trace capabilities for one period

```
For iperiod = 1 to g_rem_term(iloan)
    Call Calculate_Defaults
    Call Calculate_Coupon_Payments
    Call Calculate_Scheduled_Principal
    Call Calculate_Prepaid_Principal
    Call Calculate_Recoveries_of_Defaulted_Principal
    Call Accumulate_the_Cash_Flows
    If g_out_cftrace Then Call Capture_Monthly_CF_Trace
Next iperiod
```

EXHIBIT 14.5   Adding the code to run the accumulator and trace capabilities for all periods

call a subroutine to supply the model with all the amortization information needed to produce the cash flows for that particular loan. If we are in the validation process of the model, or if we need to monitor loans specifically, this is an excellent time to display the calculation results. If the period-by-period cash flows of the loan need to be looked at, they are complete at the end of the iperiod loop and we can print them out to another workbook if we so desire. See Exhibit 14.6.

Applying the Default Scenarios   We now have the model running through each month of every loan, and every loan in the portfolio. We now need to introduce a mechanism to make our default assumptions available to the model as it calculates the monthly results. We have designed the model to have a maximum capacity of ten default scenarios. On any given model run, we may or may not choose to enter the maximum number of scenarios. We should, more to the point, run only the number of scenarios that are entered by the model user. This we have captured in the variable g_default_levels from where it was entered on the Prepayment and Defaults Menu.

We will now add another layer to the onion by wrapping it in a loop that will cycle through each of the specified default scenarios until it has exhausted them. You will note that we are not including a call to any subroutine to compute default factors in between the default loop and the loans loop. Why? We will let the reader ponder that for a short while. Hint: Go back to Chapter 9, "Controlling the Flow of the Model," and look at Exhibits 9.14 and 9.15! In the interim we will add the loop. See Exhibit 14.7.

```
For iloan = 1 to g_total_loans
    Call Setup_Initial_Loan_Parameters
    For iperiod = 1 to g_rem_term(iloan)
        Call Calculate_Defaults
        Call Calculate_Coupon_Payments
        Call Calculate_Scheduled_Principal
        Call Calculate_Prepaid_Principal
        Call Calculate_Recoveries_of_Defaulted_Principal
        Call Accumulate_the_Cash_Flows
        If g_out_cftrace Then Call Capture_Monthly_CF_Trace
    Next iperiod
    If g_out_cftrace Then Call Print_Out_Trace_Report
Next iloan
```

EXHIBIT 14.6   Adding the loan information setup subroutine and wrapping the loan-by-loan loop around all the calls

```
For idefault = 1 to g_default_levels
     For iloan = 1 to g_total_loans
           Call Setup_Initial_Loan_Parameters
           For iperiod = 1 to g_rem_term(iloan)
                 Call Calculate_Defaults
                 Call Calculate_Coupon_Payments
                 Call Calculate_Scheduled_Principal
                 Call Calculate_Prepaid_Principal
                 Call Calculate_Recoveries_of_Defaulted_Principal
                 Call Accumulate_the_Cash_Flows
                 If g_out_cftrace Then Call Capture_Monthly_CF_Trace
           Next iperiod
     Next iloan
Next i_default
```

EXHIBIT 14.7   Adding the default scenarios loop

Applying the Prepayment Scenarios   We now call the reader back from their ruminations upon the question we asked mere seconds ago. The answer is this: If we can figure out a way to precompute the information necessary to perform the default calculations outside of the default loop, we should by all means do so. The same is also true of the prepayments of principal.

Speaking of prepayments to principal, and we *were* just speaking of prepayments, we now need a way to cycle through the prepayment scenarios. As with the default scenarios we know that this model has a maximum capacity to handle ten prepayment scenarios. Again, as with the defaults, we also suspect that the model will probably not be run with ten prepayment scenarios all the time. We therefore want to add a looping mechanism to cycle through the number of specified prepayment scenarios one at a time. Each time we select a prepayment scenario, we will run each of the default scenarios with it. Upon exhaustion of the default scenarios we will advance to the next prepayment scenario and run through the attendant default scenarios again. We will repeat this process until we have evaluated each of the prepayment scenarios in conjunction with each of the default scenarios.

To this end, we will now add a prepayment loop to the outmost layer of the cash flow calculation onion. See Exhibit 14.8.

This will accomplish what we desire, a fully amortized portfolio.

```
For iprepay = 1 to g_prepay_levels
     For idefault = 1 to g_default_levels
        For iloan = 1 to g_total_loans
              Call Setup_Initial_Loan_Parameters
              For iperiod = 1 to g_rem_term(iloan)
                    Call Calculate_Defaults
                    Call Calculate_Coupon_Payments
                    Call Calculate_Scheduled_Principal
                    Call Calculate_Prepaid_Principal
                    Call Calculate_Recoveries_of_Defaulted_Principal
                    Call Accumulate_the_Cash_Flows
                    If g_out_cftrace Then Call Capture_Monthly_CF_Trace
              Next iperiod
              If g_out_cftrace Then Call Print_Out_Trace_Report
        Next iloan
     Next i_default
  Next iprepay
```

EXHIBIT 14.8   Adding the prepayment scenarios loop

Two Last Things: Prepayment and Default Attrition Only two things are now missing. The first is the calculation of the prepayment attrition factors that will be applied to the portfolio balances, and the second is the default attrition factors. We would like to put these activities outside of the four loops of the subroutine so that we are not calling them repeatedly.

Is this possible? Yes.

We will see that it is certainly the case with the prepayment factors. What we would ideally like to end up with is a set of percentage factors that tell us, in no uncertain terms, what percentage of the current outstanding loan balance is going to prepay in any given month. It would then be very simple to perform the calculation. The balance would be multiplied by the percentage rate and the resultant amount of principal would be regarded as having prepaid. We will start with prepayments and then move on to the slightly more complicated situation of defaults.

Calculating Prepayment Attrition Both prepayment methodologies in this model use a fractional prepayment method. This is to say that if a prepayment method is specified, a slice of every loan in the portfolio is considered to have partially prepaid. This is not the only way to perform prepayment analysis. An alternative method is to employ Monte Carlo techniques where entire loans are selected and their full remaining balance is prepaid in a single month.

The format of this model is a continuous partial prepayment activity. Both methods that the model employs, constant prepayment rate (CPR) and Public Securities Association (PSA), employ a form of monthly attrition factor. These factors are easily translated into a stream of monthly attrition rates. Only the PSA method is sensitive to the age of the assets. As we have seen, the PSA method has a ramping period and changes its monthly rate for the first 30 months of the model. The CPR method produces rates that are constant over the life of the loan. The methodology is applied to all loans in the portfolio.

We can therefore create the prepayment attrition rates and place them in arrays for later use. We never have to compute them inside the looping structures of the subroutine at all.

To accomplish this we need to do several things:

- Take the information input from the Prepayment and Defaults Menu and use it to construct however many base prepayment speeds there are. For example, the method selected was CPR, the base rate was entered as 6%, with eight incremental steps of 0.5%. Expanded, this will yield a vector of ten prepayment scenarios with the rate 6%, 6.5%, 7%, 7.5%, 8%, 8.5%, 9%, and 9.5%.
- Once we have these rates, we can expand them into a series of monthly prepayment attrition rates. We will place these factors in an array named **"g_monthly_prate."** The array will have two dimensions. The first will be the number of prepayment scenarios requested by the user. In the example above the array would have six rows. The number of columns will be the number of months in the model, **PAY_DATES**, or 360.
- Using the base rates, we will then loop through the prepayment algorithms to fill the monthly columns. We could then apply the precalculated monthly factors if

using the CPR method. If using the PSA method, we would need to check the age of the loan and then find the correct monthly rate to use based on whether the loan was on or off the ramp.

Calculating Default Attrition

CPR and PSA   The first two default methodologies are the familiar CPR and PSA. As we have seen above, these can be precomputed and subsequently applied without difficulty.

User Defined Distribution   The third default methodology allows the user to specify any timing pattern for any Base Rate of default. The loans are applied based on the seasoning of the loans. That is to say that a loan that is 48 months old will have the fifth year of the timing table applied to the first year of its amortization.

Computing the Coupon and Payment Resets

Coupon Resets   There is one last task that we need to finish outside of the loop. All of the loans in the portfolio are floating rate notes. As is the case with floating rate notes, their future coupon levels are determined by the following factors:

- Current level of the reference index, the loans in the portfolio float off of the prime index
- Spread to the index
- Coupon rate reset frequency
- Payment rate reset frequency
- Reset interval cap and floor limits
- Lifetime cap and floor limits

We have read the above information into the global arrays from the data file. We have a table of projected index coupon levels.

We therefore have everything we need to construct the anticipated coupon level of each of the loans. All we have to do is match the projected level of the index and the spread of the loan and we will have the provisional gross coupon at each of the reset events. We can then compare the gross rate prior to the reset event to the current rate to determine if any of the restrictions apply.

If the current month is a reset period, we will know we need to calculate the new coupon level and compare it to the existing coupon level of the loan.

- If the coupon has increased at this reset period, test it against the reset increase limit. If the change exceeds the reset limit, increase the coupon to the reset limit only.
- If the coupon has decreased this reset period, test it against the reset decline limit. If the change exceeds the reset limit, decrease the coupon to the reset limit only.
- If the new coupon exceeds the lifetime cap, reduce it to the lifetime cap.
- If the new coupon is below the lifetime floor, raise it to the lifetime floor.

Why do we want to do this at this point in the model?

We want to do it now to avoid doing it within the heart of the onion. A common beginning mistake would be to place these calculations in the subroutine that computes the monthly coupon income. That subroutine is in the exact middle of the loops. Again refer to the concept in Chapter 9, and look at the example in Exhibits 9.14, and 9.15. If we can calculate the coupon levels once for each loan in the portfolio outside of the prepayment and default loops, we can save an immense number of calculations. Let us assume on average there are 60 reset calculations per loan over its life and each requires ten steps. Performing these calculations outside the prepayment and default loops for each of the 2,200 loans of the portfolio takes (2,200 * 60 * 10 = 1,320,000) operations. If the typical model run has six prepayment speeds and six default speeds, the equation now becomes (6 * 6 * 2,200 * 60 * 10 = 36 * 1,320,000 = 47,520,000)!

Prepayment levels and default levels have absolutely no impact on coupon reset mechanics. (The opposite is *not* true, however.)

Payment Level Resets   As we are working through the coupon resets for the loan, we can also save ourselves a lot of time and headache by calculating the payment reset factors at the same time.

We know that every time the coupon rate of the floating loan resets, we must also reset the monthly payment. The monthly payment is dependent on three things only:

1. The current coupon level
2. The amount of principal balance outstanding at the beginning of the period
3. The remaining term of the loan in months (payment periods)

At each of the reset dates, two out of three of these things are known. We know the coupon level because we just reset it. We know the remaining term of the loan. What we do not know is the outstanding principal balance of the loan. We do not know this outside the loop because we have not yet begun to apply the prepayment and default attrition.

This does not mean the exercise is not worth doing!

Recall for a moment the formula for the level monthly payment of a loan. It consists of the principal balance to be retired divided by the sum of the time weighted discount factors of the coupon at each payment date. The bulk of the work is the calculation of the series of time weighted present value terms.

We have the ability to calculate these discount factors once the coupon reset has occurred! We must assume at the point of the coupon reset that the newest reset coupon level will be constant across the remaining life of the loan. We have to assume this because we have no way of knowing what the succeeding coupon levels for the loan will be (we cannot look into the future!). We know the remaining term. Therefore, if we know the remaining term and the coupon level for the loan we can compute the monthly discount factors without any other information! The rest is just a matter of putting the calculation inside of a For...Next loop and letting it run.

Once we have the sum of the remaining Present Value factors, we can store them in an array specific to that individual loan

```
Dim g_pmt_reset(1 to g_total_loans, 1 to PAY_DATES) as double
```

When we arrive at a reset date in the inner loop, all we need to do is divide the outstanding principal balance by the factor in the array. This simple operation will produce the amount of the new fully amortizing payment level, (until the coupon resets itself again).

One further consideration is very important. Most of the loans in our portfolio reset on a quarterly basis. It is highly probable that the loan will experience prepayment and default attrition between one payment reset date and the next. This will serve to reduce the amount of monthly payments received, as a portion of the collateral balance represented by the prepaid or default loan will now be nonperforming. We must therefore keep track of the nonperforming balances and fractionally decrease the amount of the originally reset monthly payment accordingly. To state this more clearly, consider the following example. There are three loans in a portfolio. One has a current balance of $100,000 and the other two have a current balance of $50,000. Their amortization characteristics in regard to term and coupon mechanics are identical. The payment for the first loan is obviously exactly twice that of the second and third loans. If either of the second or third loans were to fully prepay or default, the monthly payments of the three-loan portfolio would be reduced by 25%. This is because 25% of the portfolio is now not making payments. The exact effect would happen if there was a single loan in the portfolio with a balance of $200,000, ($100,000+$50,000+$50,000), and the model were to apply a 25% one-month prepayment or default incident. The monthly cash flows from the one loan portfolio would decrease by 25%!

Finishing Off the Onion   We will now add the finishing touches to the cash flow onion. The first two calls will take the Base Rate input by the analyst and expand it to however many scenario rates are requested. The second pair of calls will use the expanded Base Rates and produce a series of monthly prepayment and default vectors from them. See Exhibit 14.9.

These last additions complete the process. Now let us take a look at the VBA code we can now write to actualize this plan.

OVERVIEW OF THE CASH FLOW GENERATOR

The "Compute_Collateral_Cashflows" is the master cash flow generating subroutine. It is the top-dog subroutine of the cash flow generation process, the subroutine that controls and sequences all other subroutines involved in the calculation of the collateral cash flows of the portfolio. We will put all the code that performs the collateral amortization in the VBA module "CollateralCFGenerator." The one exception to this will be the specialized prepayment and default calculation

```
Call Clear_CashFlow_Arrays
Call Set_Scenario_Prepayment_Rates
Call Set_Scenario_Default_Rates
Call Set_Monthly_Prepayment_Factors
Call Set_Monthly_Default_Factors
Call Calc_Coupon_Factors
Call Calc_SchAmortization_Factors

For iprepay = 1 to g_prepay_levels
    For idefault = 1 to g_default_levels
        For iloan = 1 to g_total_loans
                Call Setup_Initial_Loan_Parameters
                For iperiod = 1 to g_rem_term(iloan)
                        Call Calculate_Defaults
                        Call Calculate_Coupon_Payments
                        Call Calculate_Scheduled_Principal
                        Call Calculate_Prepaid_Principal
                        Call Calculate_Recoveries_of_Defaulted_Principal
                        Call Accumulate_the_Cash_Flows
                        If g_out_cftrace Then Call Capture_Monthly_CF_Trace
                Next iperiod
                If g_out_cftrace Then Call Print_Out_Trace_Report
        Next iloan
        Call Display_Amortization_Progress_Message
    Next i_default
Next iprepay
```

EXHIBIT 14.9   Final form of the cash flow computation subroutine

subroutines, which will reside in the VBA module "CollateralPreDefCalcs." See Exhibit 14.10.

You Look Familiar! Haven't We Met Somewhere Before?

The code in Exhibit 14.10 is the basic outline of the Cash Flow Generator transformed on an almost line-by-line translation of our earlier schematic as we constructed the onion on a step-by-step basis earlier in this chapter!

We have the basic calculation engines in the center of the set of four nested For...Next loops.

The group of subroutine calls at the top of Exhibit 14.10 are the ones that perform all the set up for the analytics. We have successfully moved these away from the calculation engines and out of the innermost loop to improve model efficiency. At the very beginning of the subroutine we have added an initialization subroutine. This subroutine clears the results from the previous model run.

Splitting the VBA Code between Two Modules

The subroutines that comprise the VBA code of the "Calculate_Collateral_CashFlows" master subroutine have been segregated between two different VBA modules. The reason this was done was to more clearly differentiate their function in the cash flow generation process. The first set of subroutines deal with the process in a more general way; the second focus exclusively on prepayment and default calculations. This separation also allows for the isolation of various constant and

```
'================================================================================
' Perform the amortization of the portfolios
' We will amortize the cashflows over 100 combinations of default and prepayment
' levels.  These cashflows will be stored and then sequentially run through a
' separate spreadsheet.
'================================================================================
Sub Compute_Collateral_Cashflows()

    Call Clear_Cashflow_Arrays                  'zero out the payment components
    Call Redim_All_CashFlowComponent_Vectors    'redimensions the cash flow vectors
    Sheets("Main Menu").Select                  'display the progress counter on Main Menu
    m_complete = 0                              'amortization progress counter
    Call Set_Scenario_Prepay_Rate              'expand the Base Prepayment Rate scenarios
    Call Set_Scenario_Default_Rate             'expand the Base Default Rate scenarios
    Call Set_Monthly_Prepay_Factors            'calc monthly prepayments factors for
                                                 each loan
    Call Set_Monthly_Default_Factors           'calc monthly defaults factors for
                                                 each loan
    Call Calc_Coupon_Factors                   'set coupon and payment resets by loan
    Call Calc_SchAmortization_Factors          'set principal amortization by period

    For iprepay = 1 To g_prepay_levels         'loop through the Base Prepayment Rates
        For idefault = 1 To g_default_levels   'loop through the Base Default Rates
            For iloan = 1 To g_total_loans     'loop loan-by-loan
                Call Setup_Initial_Loan_Parameters
                For iperiod = 1 To g_rem_term(iloan)
                    Call Calculate_Default_Effects
                    Call Calculate_Coupon_Payments
                    Call Calculate_Scheduled_Amortization
                    Call Calculate_Prepayments_of_Principal
                    Call Calculate_Recoveries
                    Call Accumulate_CF_Components
                    If g_out_cftrace Then Call Capture_Monthly_CF_Trace
                Next iperiod
                 If g_out_cftrace Then Call Print_Out_Trace_Report
            Next iloan
            Call Display_Amortization_ProgressMsg(iprepay, idefault)
        Next idefault
    Next iprepay

End Sub
```

EXHIBIT 14.10   Compute_Collateral_Cashflows subroutine

module level variables. Those variables used in the prepayment and default calculations are more narrowly focused and more numerous. The combined set would be cumbersome if the code was not split.

CollateralCFGenerator Module   The subroutines that comprise the core of the cash flow generation activity will reside in this module. They are:

```
Setup_Initial_Loan_Parameters
Calculate_Defaults
Calculate_Coupon_Payments
Calculate_Scheduled_Principal
Calculate_Prepaid_Principal
Calculate_Recoveries_of_Defaulted_Principal
Accumulate_the_Cash_Flows
```

We will also position any of the code that we use in the validation process here.

```
Capture_Monthly_CF_Trace
Print_Out_Trace_Report
```

All of the above subroutines encompass the cash flow mechanisms of the portfolio as a whole and allow us to check out calculations to make sure that they are accurate. They will, however, use the results of other more specialized subroutines that will construct sets of intermediate prepayment and default data. These are subroutines that we will most definitely NOT want inside of the major loops.

The master subroutine "Compute_Collateral_CashFlows" is in this module.

CollateralPreDefCalc Module   The below-listed subroutines are the specialists of the prepayment and default calculation portion of the cash flow generation process.

```
Set_Scenario_Prepayment_Rates
Set_Scenario_Default_Rates
Set_Monthly_Prepayment_Factors
Set_Monthly_Default_Factors
Calc_Coupon_Factors
Calc_SchAmortization_Factors
```

These subroutines provide much of the intermediate calculation results that allow the cash flow calculation subroutines inside of the loop to function more efficiently. In fact, without the intermediate results produced by these subroutines, the cash flow calculations inside the loops could not occur at all. They calculate a myriad of preparatory information that otherwise would have to be included inside the looping structure. This tremendously simplifies the calculations inside the loop and results in considerable speed savings to the model.

WRITING THE VBA CODE

With the overall view of the landscape in our minds we can now begin the process of writing the VBA code. We develop each of the subroutines in order and look at their functionality, contribution to the overall process, and their data and infrastructure requirements.

Set Scenario Prepayment Rates

The first task we will address is setting the prepayment rate for the scenario.

We need to establish the number and magnitude of the prepayment scenarios we will run.

Using the values entered into the Prepayments and Defaults Menu the subroutine in Exhibit 14.11 creates a series of Portfolio Base Rates from the **g_prepay_base_rate**, the number of incremental steps, and the increment we entered. The CPR and PSA methodologies will use these rates to calculate the period-by-period attrition from prepayments.

```
Sub Set_Scenario_Prepay_Rate()

    'Sets the gross prepayment levels for the model based on the base default rate
    'the number of increases and the size of the increase
    For iprepay = 1 To g_prepay_levels
        If iprepay = 1 Then
            'base rate for the initial scenario
            g_prepay_rate(1) = g_prepay_base_rate
        Else
            'incremental rates for additional scenarios
            g_prepay_rate(iprepay) = g_prepay_rate(iprepay - 1) + g_prepay_increment
        End If
    Next iprepay

End Sub
```

EXHIBIT 14.11   Using the menu entries to set the number and speeds of the prepayment scenarios

Set Scenario Default Rates

We now need to establish the number and magnitude of the default scenarios we will run. In conjunction with the prepayment rates we just established in the prior subroutine these levels will form the main loops of the cash flow calculation sequence.

Using the values entered into the Prepayments and Defaults Menu it creates a series of Portfolio Base Rates from the **g_default_base_rate**, the number of incremental steps and the increment we entered. The CPR and PSA methodologies will use these rates to establish an annual rate of principal attrition due to defaults. The User methodology applies these rates to establish a level of aggregate lifetime defaults. This approach then looks to the timing schedule to distribute the aggregate defaulted principal across the specified time Range. See Exhibit 14.12.

Calculate the Monthly Prepayment Factors

The subroutine shown in Exhibit 14.13 is the first step in developing a detailed set of monthly prepayment factors. A Select . . . Case statement is used to make a choice between the two available prepayment methodologies.

The calculation of each of these methods is different enough to warrant their positioning in separate subroutines. The use of the Select . . . Case statement also

```
Sub Set_Scenario_Default_Rate()

    'Sets the gross default levels for the model based on the base default rate
    'the number of increases and the size of the increase
    For idefault = 1 To g_default_levels
        If idefault = 1 Then
            g_default_rate(1) = g_default_base_rate
        Else
            g_default_rate(idefault) = g_default_rate(idefault - 1) + g_default_increment
        End If
    Next idefault

End Sub
```

EXHIBIT 14.12   Using the menu entries to set the number and speeds of the default scenarios

```
Sub Set_Monthly_Prepay_Factors()

    Call Display_PrepayDefault_ProgressMsg(2)
    Select Case g_prepay_method
        Case Is = PREPAY_CPR:      Call Get_CPR_Factors(PREPAYS)
        Case Is = PREPAY_PSA:      Call Get_PSA_Factors(PREPAYS)
    End Select

End Sub
```

EXHIBIT 14.13 Establishes the monthly prepayment factors in either the CPR or PSA methodology

allows a form that can be easily expanded to include additional methodologies. We will make use of constants to identify each of the approaches so that the VBA code is more easily understood.

Before we get too far along, we need to set up an array to hold the monthly factors we will be creating in these subroutines. We will call it "**g_monthly_prate**" and will declare it as a global variable. It will need to have two dimensions to accommodate multiple prepayment speeds and the time dimension. We know there is a design limit of ten prepayment scenarios that can be output to the Matrix Report Package. The second dimension will be that of time. We will declare this dimension equal to the constant PAY_DATES. This constant has a value of 360 (the maximum number of months we have designed for the model). It is likely that we will not be running the maximum number of prepayment scenarios each time we use the model. We will therefore dimension the array as follows in the "**Globals**" module:

```
Public g_monthly_prate() as Double
```

When we have read the inputs for the number of prepayment scenarios we will redimension the arrays as follows:

```
Redim g_monthly_prate(1 to g_prepay_levels, 1 to PAY_DATES) as Double
```

Get_CPR_Factors   The subroutine in Exhibit 14.14 will now compute the monthly factors of a Constant Percentage Rate (CPR) prepayment factors stream. These factors will be multiplied against the monthly current balance outstanding to determine the principal prepayment attrition each month.

The subroutine is generating a full stream of factors out to the last period of the deal as set by the constant variable PAY_DATES. When the factors are employed against any particular loan, only the periods one to the remaining term of the loan will be used in the calculations.

This stream is not dependent on the seasoning of the collateral.

The same is not true for the following methodology PSA.

Get_PSA_Factors   The second prepayment methodology is the Public Securities Administration method (PSA). It uses a ramp of 0.02% CPR in the first month of the loan, increasing by 0.02% for each month. This continues until the 30th month is reached. At that time the rate becomes constant at its then current level of 6.0%

```
Sub Get_CPR_Factors(f_type)

  'Since we are using CPR as the prepayment methodology the rate is constant
  Select Case f_type
    Case Is = PREPAYS
      For ip = 1 To g_prepay_levels
        For imonth = 1 To PAY_DATES
          g_monthly_prate(ip, imonth) = 1# - (1# - (g_prepay_rate(ip))) ^ (1 / 12)
        Next imonth
      Next ip
    Case Is = DEFAULTS
      For id = 1 To g_default_levels
        For imonth = 1 To PAY_DATES
          g_monthly_drate(id, imonth, 1) = 1# - (1# - (g_default_rate(id))) ^ (1 / 12)
        Next imonth
      Next id
  End Select  '

End Sub
```

EXHIBIT 14.14 Subroutine that computes the CPR monthly factors

CPR per annum for the remaining term of the loan. This pattern is called 100 PSA and is the base case for the method.

In the PSA prepayment method, rate multiples of this base curve are expressed in ratios of 100. Thus, a Base Rate of prepayment entered as 200 means that the prepayment speeds will start at 0.04% CPR, and ramp incrementally by that amount topping out at 12.0%.

After the **g_monthly_prate** number is calculated for the time period, it is then multiplied by the **g_prepay_rate** of the scenario. This is the scenario Base Rate.

The base pattern is constructed first. Since this methodology is also a default speed methodology, the subroutine looks to the value of the f_type variable to determine whether the results should be placed in the monthly prepayment factors array of the monthly default factors array. After the choice has been made, the base rate curve numbers are scaled up by multiplying each of them by the Base Rate/100. See Exhibit 14.15.

Set Monthly Default Factors

The subroutine in Exhibit 14.16 calls subroutines that will compute the monthly default factors.

Setting up an Array to Hold the Monthly Default Factors   We will name this variable in a similar manner to the prepayment variable g_monthly_drate. Like the prepayment array above, it will have a dimension for the number of default scenarios (a maximum of ten) and the number of months in the model PAY_DATES. We will however have to build-in a third dimension. Let us see why.

First, there are three different default methodologies the user can choose from. These are identical to the first two prepayment methodologies: CPR and PSA.

The third default method is the **User Specified** distribution. The default rate is for the total defaults over the life of the deal based on the original balance. The defaults are then distributed according to the annual timing table on the Prepayment and Defaults Menu.

```
'=====================================================================================
'PSA Standard Prepayment Model is 0.2% CPR from month one increasing monthly by
' 0.2% CPR to month 30 and then stable at 6% CPR thereafter. 400% PSA is 4x the
' base curve.
'PSA Standard Default Assumption (100% SDA) is 0.02% defaults (annualized) from
' month one increasing monthly by 0.02% to month 30, stable at 0.6% from month
' 30 to 60, and then decreasing by 0.0095% monthly to .3% in month 120 and thereafter.
'=====================================================================================
Sub Get_PSA_Factors(f_type)

Dim psa_factor(1 To PAY_DATES)  As Double        'monthly PSA factor

 Select Case f_type
   Case Is = PREPAYS
     For imonth = 1 To PAY_DATES
       If imonth <= 30 Then
          psa_factor(imonth) = imonth * 0.002
       Else
          psa_factor(imonth) = 0.06
       End If
     Next imonth
     For ip = 1 To g_prepay_levels
       For imonth = 1 To PAY_DATES
         g_monthly_prate(ip, imonth) = _
           1# - (1# - psa_factor(imonth) * g_prepay_rate(ip))^(1/12)
       Next imonth
     Next ip
   Case Is = DEFAULTS
     For imonth = 1 To PAY_DATES
       Select Case imonth
         Case Is <= 30:  psa_factor(imonth) = imonth * 0.0002
         Case Is <= 60:  psa_factor(imonth) = 0.006
         Case Is < 120:  psa_factor(imonth) = 0.006 - (imonth - 60) * 0.000095
         Case Else: psa_factor(imonth) = 0.0003
       End Select
     Next imonth
     For id = 1 To g_default_levels
       For imonth = 1 To PAY_DATES
         g_monthly_drate(id, imonth) = _
           1# - (1# - psa_factor(imonth) * g_default_rate(id))^(1/12)
       Next imonth
     Next id
 End Select

End Sub
```

EXHIBIT 14.15   Computation of the monthly PSA prepayment and default factors

```
Sub Set_Monthly_Default_Factors()

    'Read the annual default timing schedule
    Call Display_PrepayDefault_ProgressMsg(3)
    'Apply the selected methods
    Select Case g_default_method
        Case Is = DEFAULTS_CPR:
                Call Get_CPR_Factors(DEFAULTS)  'constant prepay rate
        Case Is = DEFAULTS_PSA:
                Call Get_PSA_Factors(DEFAULTS)  'public sec admin rate
        Case Is = DEFAULTS_USR:
                Call Get_USR_Factors            'user input proration
    End Select

End Sub
```

EXHIBIT 14.16   Subroutine that begins the computation of the monthly default factors

Structure of the Subroutine   The first thing we need to do is load the annual default distribution pattern from the Prepayments and Default Menu into a VBA array where we can make use of it. We do this in the For...Next loop that reads each of the three columns of default distributions.

The next thing we need to do is set up a mechanism to direct the code to the subroutine that will implement the default method of our choice. We will use a Select...Case statement to accomplish this. The test values are all constants, one per each method. The Select...Case statement will then channel the program flow to the appropriate calculation.

Get User Pattern Factors   We may well be faced with situations in which none of the standard default methodologies seem appropriate. It may also be the case that we may need to run default scenarios for others who wish to see absolute amounts of defaults rather than relative amounts of defaults. I use the term absolute as meaning an amount of defaulted principal that is expressed as a percentage of the original principal balance of the collateral pool rather than the ongoing (and therefore ***declining***) balance of the pool. In addition, these default patterns may have unusual, and most likely asymmetrical distributions of defaults over the life of the collateral. The most common characteristic of this pattern is that the losses are concentrated in the first few years of the deal to induce cash flow stress on the structure. These constituencies may need to qualify the deal structure against their own credit criteria. Research on the product line and testing of the deal may also require running unique default patterns. For these reasons, having the ability to create individually tailored default scenarios is critical. See the subroutine in Exhibit 14.17.

Fortunately, the systemic approaches we have used in the previous two methodologies are broadly similar to what we have to do here. We have the Base Rate(s) and what we need to do next is create a monthly sequence of default factors from the timing distribution.

This can be accomplished in two easy steps. First we set up the outer For...Next loop to cycle through the default levels specified. The Base Rate is divided by 12 to create a long-term monthly Base Rate. The inner loop moves across all the PAY_DATES, 360 months. Using the Mod 12 function, we increment the annual timing percentage index every year. The annual distribution percentage number for the year is prorated and multiplied by the monthly pro-rated Base Rate to arrive at the monthly default factor. See the subroutine in Exhibit 14.17.

```
Sub Get_USR_Factors()

  For idefault = 1 To g_default_levels
      dfactor = g_default_rate(idefault) / 12#
      iyear = 1
      For imonth = 1 To PAY_DATES
          If (imonth > 1 And (imonth - 1) Mod 12 = 0) Then iyear = iyear + 1
          g_monthly_drate(idefault, imonth) = dfactor * g_ann_defdist(iyear)
      Next imonth
  Next idefault

End Sub
```

EXHIBIT 14.17   Calculation of the monthly USER method default factors

Compute Monthly Coupon Levels

This subroutine and the two that it calls will establish a monthly coupon level schedule for each of the loans of the portfolio. It is especially important that we do these calculations outside of the looping part of the cash flow calculations. There are two reasons for this. The first is that they can be computationally burdensome, and the second is that *they can be done here,* thus saving us a lot of time and effort later on.

An added benefit of having a specific schedule of coupon rates for each loan is that we will be about to do most of the calculations that are necessary to determine the periodic monthly payment reset amounts. The payment amount for any loan, fixed or floating, can be calculated if one knows two things. The first is the balance of the loan at the time, and the second is the sum of the series of the terms $1/(1+r)$ Nth where r is the periodically adjusted coupon and n is the number of remaining periods.

By setting the coupon levels in this subroutine, we will provide ourselves with everything except the current balance of the loan at the time of the reset period. All we need to do at that point is to divide that sum of the discount factors into the current balance and we have our new payment level. See Exhibit 14.18.

The calculation of the coupon pattern for a fixed rate note is as simple as a task can be. Just take the current coupon level and fill every future monthly period with the identical rate until you reach the end of the remaining term of the loan.

For floating rate loans the coupon level is dependent upon a number of factors. To review, these are:

1. The current rate level of the index off of which the loan floats.
2. The spread to that reference index.
3. The frequency of the interest rate reset period.
4. The frequency of the payment reset period (especially if it is different from 3 above).
5. The lifetime floor rate of the loan (the lowest the coupon is *ever* allowed to be).
6. The lifetime cap rate of the loan (the highest the coupon is *ever* allowed to be).
7. The periodic reset cap (the largest increase allowed at the time a reset occurs).
8. The periodic reset floor (the largest decrease allowed at the time a reset occurs).

```
Sub Calc_Coupon_Factors(fin_type)

        Call Display_PrepayDefault_ProgressMsg(5)
        For iloan = 1 To g_total_loans
           dtype = g_loan_day_count(iloan)        ' day count convention 1, 2, or 3
           Select Case g_loan_fixed_float(iloan)
             Case Is = FIXED_RATE:  Call Calculate_Loan_Fixed_Coupon_Levels(iloan)
             Case Is = FLOAT_RATE: Call Calculate_Loan_Floater_Coupon_Levels(iloan)
           End Select
        Next iloan

End Sub
```

EXHIBIT 14.18 Subroutine that determines which coupon calculation subroutine to use for either fixed or floating rate loans

If there is a single set of assumptions that govern the behavior of the underlying index for the floating rate loans, then we can match that index to the loan terms and extrapolate its coupon level over the remaining life of the deal. By doing, this we are free of the burden of doing it each time the model is run. The model runs are differentiated by prepayment and default conditions, not interest rate scenarios.

Once we have the future interest rates established we could also prepare another series of factors that will be useful inside the loop structure.

All loans in this portfolio reset their payments when they reset their coupons. By knowing the coupon rate of the note at the reset event, we can sum the present value factors of the new rate from that point in time to the end of the loan's term. This will not give us the payment in and of itself. It will, however, give us the sum of the discount factors from that month to the remaining term of the loan. The current balance outstanding of the loan can then be divided by the sum of these factors to arrive at the current monthly payment amount necessary to fully amortize the loan. That will make the recalculation of the payment a single statement calculation instead of a multiperiod loop inside the larger loops that would need to be repeated for each default/prepayment scenario.

The goal of these two subroutines is to populate the array

```
g_coup(1 to g_total_loans, 1 to PAY_DATES)
```

with a series of monthly coupon level factors from period one to the remaining term of each loan.

Keeping all this firmly in mind, let us advance to the two coupon setting subroutines.

One final note, this code relates to subjects other than prepayment and default. As a result we will place it in the **"CollateralCFGenerator module,"** not the **"CollateralPreDefCalcs"** module.

Calculate the Fixed Coupon Factors   All we need to do is to fill the **"g_coup"** array row of the loan with a single fixed coupon level. We know that the number of periods to fill is the remaining term of the loan. We can therefore set up a For...Next loop to run from period one to the remaining term of the loan, and read into each array element the current coupon level.

There is one thing that we need to be careful about, which is to correct the coupon rate for the day count of the period. We have precomputed these day counts and stored them in the **"g_day_factors"** array. We just multiply the annual coupon rate by the decimal expression of the current month day count and we are done. See Exhibit 14.19.

```
Sub Calculate_Loan_Fixed_Coupon_Levels(iloan)

  For iperiod = 1 To g_rem_term(iloan)
    g_loan_coupon(iloan, iperiod) = _ g_loan_coup(iloan)*g_day_factors(iperiod, dtype)
  Next iperiod

End Sub
```

EXHIBIT 14.19   Subroutine that calculates the future coupon levels for a fixed rate note

Calculate the Floater Coupon Factors   The process of setting the coupons for a floating rate loan is obviously far more complex than that in the previous example with the fixed coupon loan. It is, however, not anything to be afraid of! We will simply break down the task into a series of easily digested pieces first.

We need to do the following:

- Establish for each loan what index the loan is floating over.
- Set the current rate to a variable that we can then use to compare to the new coupon level when a change occurs. This gives us a baseline to measure the proposed change against. We will call this variable beg_rate, meaning the period beginning coupon rate.
- Set up another variable that we will set to the provisional change. We will call this variable now_rate. Both now_rate and beg_rate will be declared as Doubles as they hold percentage numbers. The variable now_rate is assigned a coupon rate value at the time of the reset based on the level of the index and the floater spread.
- Adjust now_rate according to the rules of the floating rate agreement. The value of now_rate when it is first calculated is *provisional. It is subject to the terms and conditions pursuant to the floating rate loan contract.* We may need to adjust it according to four conditions. We must make sure that the reset rate is between the limits established by the lifetime cap and floor rates. We must also make sure that the amount of the adjustment in this reset period is between the periodic cap and floor reset rate limits of the this loan.
- After the value of now_rate has been subjected to the four tests in the paragraph above, it becomes the new loan coupon level until the next reset period. We also assign its value to the variable beg_rate making it the new ongoing coupon rate and the starting position we will use at the next reset exercise.
- Lastly, since we have just reset the coupon, we can use this opportunity to calculate the discount factors for the remaining term of the loan for future use in determining the payment resets.

Let us now implement these steps in VBA code.

The first task will be to declare a number of local variables. These will be ifloat, which will serve as the number of the base index interest rate schedule that the loan floats off of, beg_rate and now_rate, for the existing and provisional coupon rates and "im" a counter for the months of the loan.

Next we need to identify the index from which the note floats. We have this information stored in the array **"g_floater_code,"** by loan. We will read the value for the particular loan from the array **"g_floater_code"** into the variable ifloater.

We now set the period one coupon by adding the index coupon level to the loan's spread. This becomes our beginning rate and we assign it to the beg_rate variable. In that it is the existing coupon level, it is assumed to have passed all the criteria tests for floors and caps so we can also assign it to the first element of **"g_coup."**

We now will loop through the remaining term of the loan.

At each loop, we will determine if the period is a coupon/payment reset period. If it is, we will compute the new provisional coupon level and test it against the four criteria of caps and floors. If the period is not a reset period we will simple assign the value of beg_rate to the **"g_coup"** array as the current coupon level of the loan.

Entering the month-to-month loop, we first test to see if the loan is at a reset period. We can do this easily by employing the trusty Mod function. The current period of the loan since it was originated is the sum of its seasoning added to how many months we have looped already and decreased by one. This is the current age of the loan at the time of the test. We can Mod that against the loans reset frequency that is stored in "g_adjust_freq" array on a loan-by-loan basis. If the result is zero, then the current age is an exact multiple of the reset periodicity and we need to reset the coupon.

If we are in a reset period, we will compute the value of the provisional coupon rate. This is the current level of the index plus the spread for the individual loan. This new coupon level becomes the current value of now_rate. We must at this point put the now_rate value through a series of tests to see if it needs to be adjusted by the terms and conditions of the floating reset agreements.

The first test is the lifetime cap. If now_rate is higher that the cap, it is reduced to the cap.

The second test is the lifetime floor. If now_rate is lower than the floor, it is raised to the floor.

With these tests complete, we still have to verify that the change in the now_rate from the previous coupon level does not exceed the maximum increase or decrease over a single reset period. The next two tests do just that.

If now_rate has increased or decreased greater than the single reset interval limits, they are adjusted accordingly.

With the tests now complete, we can assign the value of now_rate to both the "g_coup" array element for the period and reset beg_rate to the value of now_rate as the rate to be used until the next reset period.

Since this is a reset period, we will now call the subroutine to compute the coupon discount factors that will determine the newly reset payment level. We will look at that subroutine in a moment. Lastly, if the period was not a reset period we can immediately, (and with no further ado) assign the value of beg_rate to the array "g_coup."

Calculate the Payment Reset Factor   Since we have already taken the trouble to determine the coupon levels for each of the loans we can further exploit this information to develop the sum of the coupon discount factors at each of the payment reset dates. This sum will be the sum of the familiar "$1/(1+r)$nth" series where r is the coupon rate adjusted to a monthly decimal equivalent of a year the series is one term per month for the remaining term of the loan. See Exhibit 14.20

EXHIBIT 14.20   Table of coupon rate and discount factors

Period	Coupon Rate	Day Count Factor (30/360)	Factor	Running Factor	Cumulative Sum of Running Factors
1	9.00%	.08333	.992556	.992556	0.992556
2	9.00%	.08333	.992556	.985167	1.977723
3	9.00%	.08333	.992556	.977833	2.955556
4	9.00%	.08333	.992556	.970554	3.926110
5	9.00%	.08333	.992556	.963329	4.889440
6	9.00%	.08333	.992556	.956158	5.845598

```
Sub Calculate_DiscountFactors(t_periods,)
Dim base_factor       As Double        'incremental period discount factor
Dim run_factor        As Double        'current period discount factor
Dim itime             As Integer       'loop counter for periods
  dfacts(0) = 1#
  run_factor = 1#
  For itime = 1 To t_periods
      base_factor = 1 + (g_loan_coupon(iloan, itime) * g_day_factors(itime, dtype))
      run_factor = run_factor * base_factor
      dfacts(itime) = run_factor
  Next itime

End Sub
```

EXHIBIT 14.21   Subroutine calculates the discount factors for the remaining life of the loan which will be used later to set the new payment level

for a tabular example of this calculation and Exhibit 14.21 for the VBA code to implement it.

   We will only need to create three local variables and a loop counter to facilitate this calculation. The first variable factor will hold the current period discount factor. The second variable, "run_factor," will hold the product of all preceding factors and the third variable will be the sum of all preceding "run_factors." The sum_factor will then be assigned to the array **"g_pmt_reset."** This array that is dimensioned "(1to g_total_loans, 1 to PAY_DATES)" will hold the sum_factor value at the period of the reset. All we need to do later is to divide this number into the current outstanding balance of the loan to determine the payment amount at the reset date. An example of this calculation follows. If the remaining balance of the loan was $10,000, with a remaining term of six months, then the monthly payment needed to fully amortize the loan would be $10,000/5.845598 or $1,710.69. See Exhibit 14.22.

Calculation of the Scheduled Amortization of Principal Factors

For each loan in the portfolio, once its coupon level and remaining term are known, we can calculate the fraction of scheduled amortization that will occur at any future period. See Exhibit 14.23.

EXHIBIT 14.22   Setting or resetting a payment

Period	Coupon Rate	Beginning Principal Balance	Coupon Expense	Principal Balance Amortized	Ending Principal Balance
1	9.00%	10,000.00	75.00	1,635.69	8,364.31
2	9.00%	8,364.31	62.73	1,647.96	6,716.35
3	9.00%	6,716.35	50.37	1,660.32	5,056.04
4	9.00%	5,056.04	37.92	1,672.77	3,383.27
5	9.00%	3,383.27	25.37	1,685.31	1,697.95
6	9.00%	1,697.95	12.73	1,697.95	0.00

```
Sub Calc_SchAmortization_Factors()
Dim base        As Double   'factor remaining term of the loan
Dim im          As Integer
ReDim g_loan_amort_factors(1 To g_total_loans, 1 To PAY_DATES) 'per period schamort

  Call Display_PrepayDefault_ProgressMsg(5)
  For iloan = 1 To g_total_loans
      Select Case g_loan_fixed_float(iloan)
          Case Is = FIXED_RATE
            For im = 1 To g_loan_rem_term(iloan)
                If im = 1 Then Call Calculate_DiscountFactors(g_loan_rem_term(iloan))
                base = dfacts(g_loan_rem_term(iloan))
                g_loan_amort_factors(iloan, im) = _
                    1 - ((base - dfacts(im)) / (base - dfacts(im - 1)))
            Next im
          Case Is = FLOAT_RATE
            For im = 1 To g_loan_rem_term(iloan)
                If im = 1 Then Call Calculate_DiscountFactors(g_loan_rem_term(iloan))
                'if its a reset period recalculate the factor sets
                If (g_loan_season(iloan) + im - 1) Mod g_loan_reset_rate(iloan) = 0 Then
                    Call Calculate_DiscountFactors(g_loan_rem_term(iloan) - im)
                End If
                base = dfacts(g_loan_rem_term(iloan))
                g_loan_amort_factors(iloan, im) = _
                    1 - ((base - dfacts(im)) / (base - dfacts(im - 1)))
            Next im
      End Select
  Next iloan
  Call Display_PrepayDefault_ProgressMsg(99)

End Sub
```

EXHIBIT 14.23   Once we have the coupon levels for each of the loans, we can use them to calculate the amount of principal that will be retired through periodic payment

The formula for the percentage of outstanding principal retired by scheduled payment activity in any given period is:

N = total number of remain term period

n = period of the principal retirement

n − 1 = period immediately prior to the retirement period

R = periodic coupon rate

Principal amortization of period $n = 1 - \{[(1 + R)^N - (1 + R)^n] / [(1+R)^N - (1+R)^{n-1}]\}$

For each loan, therefore, we will end up with a series of factors, one for each remaining month of the loan. The factor for the period, when multiplied by the current balance outstanding, will immediately produce the amount of scheduled amortization triggered by the receipt of the monthly payment.

To complete the calculation, we will need to compute the following three terms:

$$(1 + R)^N \qquad (1 + R)^n \qquad (1 + R)^{n-1}$$

The very convenient aspect to this calculation is that in the process of computing $(1+R)^N$, we will of necessity *have to compute* the other two terms as they are

```
Sub Calculate_DiscountFactors(t_periods, fin_type)

Dim base_factor      As Double       'incremental period discount factor
Dim run_factor       As Double       'current period discount factor
Dim itime            As Integer      'loop counter for periods

  dfacts(0) = 1#
  run_factor = 1#
  For itime = 1 To t_periods
      base_factor = 1 + (g_loan_coupon(iloan, itime) * g_day_factors(itime, dtype))
      run_factor = run_factor * base_factor
      dfacts(itime) = run_factor
  Next itime

End Sub
```

EXHIBIT 14.24   This subroutine calculates the discount factors needed to produce the periodic scheduled amortization percentages numbers by loan

part of the same geometric sequence. To perform these factor calculations, we can write a very brief little number crunching subroutine appropriately named "Calculate_DiscountFactors." See Exhibit 14.24.

The above calculations are triggered at the first period of the loan and at every coupon reset date. It fills the array **"dfact(1 to PAY_DATES)"** that we declared above as a module variable with a string of discount factors. We need the entire set of numbers to find the last term in the series, $(1+R)N$. Along the way we will have also computed all the intervening factors so we should be able to select those we need $(1+R)n$ and $(1+R)n-1$ for the calculation of the two monthly factors to complete the equation. The calculation for the actual principal retirement factor will be completed in the calling subroutine based on the contents of the "dfact" vector.

Fixed Rate Loan   In the case of fixed rate loans, we have a fairly straightforward solution. There is only one set of discount factors that will have to be constructed due to the fact that the coupon level for the loan never changes over its life.

A For...Next loop will generate the principal retirement percentage factors for the periods of the remaining life of the deal. It starts at time period one and runs to "g_rem_term(iloan)."

If the loop is in the first period of the remaining term, it calls "Calculate_DiscountFactors" that then computes the entire sequence of "dfacts" for the life of the loan. Upon return to the calling subroutine "Calc_SchAmortizaton_Factors," the "dfact" vector is complete.

The loop now simply picks the successive values of the "dfact" vector and uses the last term of the factor $(1+R)N$ to complete the calculation. These results are now stored in an array that is indexed by loans, **"g_loan_amort_factor."** It is from this array that we will read the percentage retirement numbers when we compute the scheduled amortization inside the loop. See Exhibit 14.25.

Floating Rate Notes   Floating rates notes require a bit more work because they float off of an index that can change in level and they have various triggers and conditions that will affect their coupon level at each of the reset dates.

Every time that the coupon changes on the floater, all the $(1+R)$ terms will change and need to be recalculated. If the loan is determined to be a floater, as with

EXHIBIT 14.25 Principal payment factors calculation for a 9% fixed rate loan

Fixed Rate Loan Example				
n	R	(1+R)	(1+R)n	Factor
0			1.0000000	
1	9.000%	1.00750	1.0075000	0.079951
2	9.000%	1.00750	1.0150563	0.087551
3	9.000%	1.00750	1.0226692	0.096671
4	9.000%	1.00750	1.0303392	0.107819
5	9.000%	1.00750	1.0380667	0.121756
6	9.000%	1.00750	1.0458522	0.139675
7	9.000%	1.00750	1.0536961	0.163569
8	9.000%	1.00750	1.0615988	0.197022
9	9.000%	1.00750	1.0695608	0.247205
10	9.000%	1.00750	1.0775825	0.330846
11	9.000%	1.00750	1.0856644	0.498132
12	9.000%	1.00750	1.0938069	1.000000

the fixed rate loans, the "Calculate_DiscountFactors" subroutine is called and the factors from now to the remaining term are calculated. If this were a fixed rate loan we would be done. All that would be left to do would be to plug the numbers into the successive time periods and we would have the factor sequence in hand. With a floating rate note, we must recalculate the factors at each of the reset dates if the coupon has changed at that time. The subroutine tests if the current period of the loop is a reset period by using the Mod function. For example:

Seasoning of the loan period 1 = 22

Reset periodicity = 3

Months into the loop (value of im loop counter) = 4

Formula test for reset:

If(g_seasoning(iloan) + im − 1 Mod g_reset_rate(iloan) = 0 Then
Current period evaluates to :   (22 + 4 − 1) = 25   25 Mod 3 = 2 **False**
Two months later :   (22 + 6 − 1) = 27   27 Mod 3 = 0 **True**

Two periods from now we will have to recalculate the discount factor array again using the new coupon rate. We would he have all the numbers we would need to set the percentage principal pay factors for the months between now and the next reset date. See Exhibit 14.26.

Exhibit 14.26 displays the calculation sequence for a floating rate note, which has a three-month reset frequency, and a 12-month remaining life in which four resets will occur. These resets will occur in months 3, 6, 9, and 12.

EXHIBIT 14.26 Initial factor calculation at month 1 through month 2 to first reset (left). First reset calculation from month 3 to month 6 (right)

Floating Rate Loan Example
From Period 1 to 1st Reset Period 3

n	R	(1+R)	(1+R)n	Factor
0			1.0000000	
1	9.000%	1.00750	1.0075000	**0.079951**
2	9.000%	1.00750	1.0150563	**0.087551**
3	9.000%	1.00750	1.0226692	0.096671
4	9.000%	1.00750	1.0303392	0.107819
5	9.000%	1.00750	1.0380667	0.121756
6	9.000%	1.00750	1.0458522	0.139675
7	9.000%	1.00750	1.0536961	0.163569
8	9.000%	1.00750	1.0615988	0.197022
9	9.000%	1.00750	1.0695608	0.247205
10	9.000%	1.00750	1.0775825	0.330846
11	9.000%	1.00750	1.0856644	0.498132
12	9.000%	1.00750	1.0938069	1.000000

Floating Rate Loan Example
From Period 3 to 2nd Reset Period 6

n	R	(1+R)	(1+R)n	Factor
				0.079951
0			1.0000000	**0.087551**
1	9.500%	1.00792	1.0079167	**0.096489**
2	9.500%	1.00792	1.0158960	**0.107639**
3	9.500%	1.00792	1.0239385	**0.121577**
4	9.500%	1.00792	1.0320447	0.139500
5	9.500%	1.00792	1.0402151	0.163398
6	9.500%	1.00792	1.0484501	0.196858
7	9.500%	1.00792	1.0567503	0.247051
8	9.500%	1.00792	1.0651163	0.330708
9	9.500%	1.00792	1.0735484	0.498029
10	9.500%	1.00792	1.0820474	1.000000

The loan has an initial 9% coupon that resets to 9.5% in period three, 10% in period six, 9.75% in period nine, and finally 9.5% in period twelve. See Exhibit 14.26 left side display for the calculation of the present value factors for months one and two.

At month three the first reset activity occurs. The new rate reset coupon rate for the loan is 9.5%. In that a 9.5% coupon rate will result in different present value discount factors, we need to calculate the present value factors for the new coupon rate from period three through the end of the loan in period twelve. This is accomplished in the right side of Exhibit 14.26. What was originally the third *remaining* period of the loan is now the first *remaining* period of the loan. The loan now has ten more periods to run including this one. We now compute the present value factors from the new month one to the end of the loan.

In the left side of Exhibit 14.27, we see the loan from its first period through its first reset to the verge of its second reset period, the original period six. The next reset now occurs in what was the original period six. The coupon rate resets from a level of 9.5% up to 10%. In that the coupon rate has changed again we now recalculate the discount factors out to the remaining term of the loan, now only seven periods more.

Time marches on!

In another three months, we arrive at the situation in the right hand side of Exhibit 14.27. We are now in what was originally the ninth *remaining* period of the original loan term. The coupon resets to 9.75%. (Thank goodness it finally went *down* for once!). We now recalculate the remaining term present value factors based on the 9.75% rate. This brings us to the last period of the loan.

We are now in the situation displayed in Exhibit 14.28. (We are nearly done!). With a single period remaining, the loan resets for a fourth time in its life. The coupon rate resets upwards from the existing 9.75% to 10.00%, (drats, another uptick in the payment). We calculate the last discount factor and we are done.

On to the Loops!

All the tasks that can be profitably accomplished outside of the looping structure are now finished. The next step is to build the code that will run inside of the loops and utilize the groundwork of calculations that we have performed to this point!

Declaring Cash Flow Calculation Variables

CollateralCFGenerator Module Variables Before we begin we must declare the variables that we will use in this process. We will need four groups of variables:

Group 1: Utilitarian working variables to control loops and to hold certain trigger values. These can be seen in Exhibit 14.29.

Group 2: Variables that will hold the interim values that are required to amortize the loan and account for the working balances that we will eventually accumulate and pass the Excel worksheet model. This will include the precomputed monthly prepayment and default attrition factors, the monthly coupon paths for the loans, and the information needed to recalculate the

EXHIBIT 14.27 Second reset calculation from month 6 to month 9 (left). Second reset calculation from month 9 to month 12 (right)

Floating Rate Loan Example
From Period 9 to 4th Reset Period 12

n	R	(1+R)	(1+R)n	Factor
				0.079951
				0.087551
				0.096489
				0.107639
				0.121577
				0.139325
				0.163228
0			1.0000000	0.196694
1	9.750%	1.00813	1.0081250	0.246974
2	9.750%	1.00813	1.0163160	0.330640
3	9.750%	1.00813	1.0245736	0.497977
4	9.750%	1.00813	1.0328982	1.000000

Floating Rate Loan Example
From Period 6 to 3rd Reset Period 8

n	R	(1+R)	(1+R)n	Factor
				0.079951
				0.087551
				0.096489
				0.107639
0			1.0000000	0.121577
1	10.000%	1.00833	1.0083333	0.139325
2	10.000%	1.00833	1.0167361	0.163228
3	10.000%	1.00833	1.0252089	0.196694
4	10.000%	1.00833	1.0337523	0.246897
5	10.000%	1.00833	1.0423669	0.330571
6	10.000%	1.00833	1.0510533	0.497925
7	10.000%	1.00833	1.0598121	1.000000

EXHIBIT 14.28 Final reset calculation from month 12

Floating Rate Loan Example				
Period 12				
n	R	(1+R)	(1+R)n	Factor
				0.079951
				0.087551
				0.096489
				0.107639
				0.121577
				0.139325
				0.163228
				0.196694
				0.246974
				0.330640
0			1.0000000	0.497977
1	10.000%	1.00833	1.0083333	1.000000

new monthly payments at the time of their resets. These can be seen in Exhibit 14.30.

Group 3: These variables will hold the sums of each component of the cash flows: the amortized principal, prepayments, defaults, recoveries, coupon income, and collateral beginning and ending balances. They also include the variables to keep track of the ongoing changes in the equity positions of the loan as the loan balances amortize over time. These variables are especially critical when we will come to the calculation of defaulted principal recovery amount. Remember the effects that different levels of equity had on loan losses in Exhibits 3.4 and 3.5.

The declarations of these variables can be seen in Exhibits 14.31 and 14.32.

Group 4: This last set of variables is used by the validation subroutines. These variables will contain the results of each individual amortization run in case we need to record the results using the "Capture_Monthly_CF_Trace" subroutine. These declarations are shown in Exhibit 14.33.

The first four of these variables in Exhibit 14.29 are the major loop counters of the master subroutine. The remaining four variables are used for utility purposes in several of the calculation subroutines. The variable named g_loan_coupon supports the calculation of the coupon resets and the payment resets. The variable dtype tells

```
Option Explicit

Dim iprepay      As Double    'Prepayments loop counter
Dim idefault     As Double    'Default level loop counter
Dim iloan             As Double    'Loan loop counter
Dim iperiod      As Double 'Payment periods loop counter
'Per period coupon level for each loan based on index and spread
Dim g_loan_coupon()    As Double          'monthly coupon level, index+spread
Dim dtype              As Double          'index number of day count convention
                                          'used for this loan
Dim sch_amort_fact(1 To PAY_DATES)            As Double
Dim dfacts(0 To PAY_DATES) As Double          'per period discount factors
```

EXHIBIT 14.29   Module level variables for the cash flow generator

us which day count convention the loan uses. The array **"sch_amort_factor"** holds
the sequence of principal amortization factors for a single loan. The array **"dfacts"**
holds the key information needed to recalculate the monthly payment. It is in the
form of the sum of the remaining discount factors based on the pattern of loan
coupon resets over the remaining period of the life of the loan.

We will use the variables in Exhibit 14.30 to keep track of the month-by-month
loan balance and cash flow calculation amounts as we amortize the loan.

Of the variables declared in Exhibit 14.31, the first, cur_project, tracks the
percentage of the original value of the collateral backing a loan over its lifetime.
This number will decrease as it is diluted by the accumulation of prepayments and
defaults that occur until the loan retires. The variable cur_ltv tracks the ratio between
the current balance of the loan and the cur_project value. The coup_income variable
captures the monthly coupon income. The last variable, m_complete tells us how
many of the scenarios of the model have been completed to date. This is the variable
that we use in the computational progress message on the Main Menu shown in
Exhibit 10.2 in Chapter 10, "Building Messaging Capabilities."

The variables in Exhibit 14.32 are used by the model to capture the dollar
balances of the components of the loan amortization activity if we elect to run the
Trace program for model validation processes.

```
'Loan amortization variables
Dim m_loan_cur_bal          As Double    'Current balance of the unguaranteed portion
Dim m_loan_ratio            As Double    'Ratio of the loan and total indebtness
Dim m_loan_prepays          As Double    'Prepayments of the loan
Dim m_loan_coup_income      As Double    'Loan coupon income
Dim m_loan_orig_bal         As Double    'Original loan balance
Dim m_loan_defaults         As Double    'Defaulted principal of loan
Dim m_loan_life_defaults    As Double    'Total defaults over life of loan
Dim m_loan_prin_ret         As Double    'Loan principal retired this month
```

EXHIBIT 14.30   Cash flow calculation variables to amortize the loan

```
Dim cur_project  As Double 'Current amount of original project appraisal value
                              outstanding
Dim cur_ltv      As Double 'instantaneous LTV
Dim coup_income  As Double 'Period coupon income
Dim m_complete   As Double 'progress message counter
```

EXHIBIT 14.31   These variables are working variables that hold intermediate results or totals

```
' 'Validation report variables
Dim row_num                         As Long      'validation report row number
Dim icol                            As Long      'validation report column number
Dim v_defaults(1 To PAY_DATES)      As Double    'total defaults by loan
Dim v_coup_income(1 To PAY_DATES)   As Double    'total coupon income by loan
Dim v_prin_ret(1 To PAY_DATES)      As Double    'total principal amortized by loan
Dim v_prepays(1 To PAY_DATES)       As Double    'toal prepayments by loan
Dim v_coup(1 To PAY_DATES)          As Double    'coupon rate per period
Dim cf_trace_col_num                As Integer   'current print col of cf trace report
```

EXHIBIT 14.32   Variables for the cash flow verification report

SETTING UP THE SCENARIO LOOPS

We now add the loops that will walk the model through the combinations of the prepayment and default rate conditions. See Exhibit 14.33.

The subroutine performs the following steps:

1. Enters the fourth outermost prepayment scenarios loop.
2. Enters the third outermost default scenarios loop.
3. Enters the second outermost loan-by-loan loop.
4. Calls the "SetUp_Initial_Loan_Parameters" subroutine. This subroutine reads all the information about the loan that we will need to compute its monthly cash flows.
5. Enters the innermost period-by-period loop.
6. Tests to see if the loan has a current balance greater than $ 0.01.
7. Calls a sequence of calculation subroutines that generate the cash flows:
   a. Defaults of principal
   b. Coupon income
   c. Scheduled amortization of principal
   d. Prepayments of principal

```
For iprepay = 1 To g_prepay_levels                  'loop through the Base Rates
    For idefault = 1 To g_default_levels            'loop through the Base rates
        For iloan = 1 To g_total_loans              'loop loan-by-loan
            Call Setup_Initial_Loan_Parameters
            For iperiod = 1 To g_rem_term(iloan)
                Call Calculate_Default_Effects(iloan)
                Call Calculate_Coupon_Payments
                Call Calculate_Scheduled_Amortization
                Call Calculate_Prepayments_of_Principal
                Call Calculate_Recoveries
                Call Accumulate_CF_Components
                If g_out_cftrace Then Call Capture_Monthly_CF_Trace
            Next iperiod
            If g_out_cftrace Then Call Print_Out_Trace_Report
        Next iloan
        Call Display_Amortization_ProgressMsg(iprepay, idefault)
    Next idefault
Next iprepay
```

EXHIBIT 14.33   The layout of the main looping structures for the cash flow calculation sequence

   e. Recoveries of principal
   f. Accumulate all the cash flows
8. Exits the innermost three loops.
9. Displays a progress message indicating which scenario has just completed.
10. Exits the prepayment scenarios loop, end the subroutine.

CASH FLOW CALCULATION SEQUENCE

Set Up the Initial Loan Parameters

The cash flow generator now needs information about various aspects of the loan. We will need to set up a few working variables before we start the amortization process.

   If we have elected to use a User Defined default methodology, we will need to determine the total amount of defaulted principal that we have specified will be attributed to this loan. We will calculate the amount from the current balance of the loan and scenario default rate.

   The next calculation will determine the initial loan financing Loan To Value ratio using the cur_project variable that holds the appraisal value of the collective collateral. The last assignment is the original balance of the loan. See Exhibit 14.34.

Calculate the Default Effects

The first cash flow component on our list is the calculation of defaulted principal. See Exhibit 14.35.

   We have already calculated the monthly default factors for each of the loans over their remaining lives. This factor will now be applied to calculate the amount of defaulted principal.

   Once the amount is determined we can make other adjustments, such as adjustments to the monthly payment factor to reflect this loss of the performing principal from the deal.

```
Sub Setup_Initial_Loan_Parameters()

  'project information
  cur_project = g_loan_appraisal(iloan) 'Portion of project not prepaid or defaulted
  'initialize loan information
  m_loan_cur_bal = g_loan_cur_bal(iloan)
  m_loan_orig_bal = g_loan_orig_bal(iloan)
  If g_default_method = DEF_USR Then
      m_loan_life_defaults = g_default_rate(idefault) * m_loan_orig_bal
  Else
      m_loan_life_defaults = 0#
  End If
  m_loan_ratio = m_loan_cur_bal / cur_project

End Sub
```

EXHIBIT 14.34   Establishing the initial information about a piece of loan collateral

```
Sub Calculate_Default_Effects()

  'beginning period cltv
  If cur_project > 0.01 Then
    cur_ltv = m_loan_cur_bal / cur_project
  Else
    cur_ltv = 0
  End If
  'calculate the loan defaults
  m_loan_defaults = 0#
  If m_loan_cur_bal > 1# Then
    Select Case g_default_method
      Case Is = DEF_CPR: m_loan_defaults = _
          m_loan_orig_bal * g_monthly_drate(idefault, iperiod + g_loan_season(iloan))
      Case Is = DEF_PSA: m_loan_defaults = _
          m_loan_cur_bal * g_monthly_drate(idefault, iperiod + g_loan_season(iloan))
      Case Is = DEF_USR: m_loan_defaults = _
          g_loan_cur_bal(iloan) * g_monthly_drate(idefault, iperiod)
    End Select
    If m_loan_defaults > m_loan_cur_bal Then m_loan_defaults = m_loan_cur_bal
    m_loan_cur_bal = m_loan_cur_bal - m_loan_defaults
  End If
  'Compute what portion of the appraised value these defaults represent and
  'subtract it from the beginning appraisal value of the entire project
  If cur_ltv > 0# Then
      cur_project = cur_project - (m_loan_defaults / cur_ltv)
  End If

End Sub
```

EXHIBIT 14.35 Calculation of the monthly defaulted amounts from a single piece of collateral

First we set the current Loan To Value ratio for the beginning of the period. This is the ratio between the current balance and the current value of the property the loan applies to.

Next we determine which default methodology is going to be applied against the pool.

In the cases of CPR and PSA, we need to match the default factor table with the original tenor of the loan. We can multiply the monthly default factor by the current balance of the loan. This is the calculation:

m_loan_defaults =
m_loan_orig_bal * g_monthly_drate(idefault, iperiod + g_loan_season(iloan))

If the default methodology selected is USER, the g_monthly_default factor is applied to the current balance of the loan at the beginning of the model run. Do not get confused here! Any loan that is seasoned when we put it into the deal will have a current balance different from its original balance at inception. For the purposes of the securitization however, the current balance at the time the loan becomes part of the deal is its original balance in relation to how much of the collateral it represents to the deal at the time of the origin of the deal. As such, when we say that the User Default method uses original balance upon which to base its defaulted principal amounts, we mean the unchanged and unchanging current balance of the loan at the time it enters the deal as a piece of eligible collateral. To clarify further because this is a really important distinction:

Original balance of loan at inception	$100,000
Current balance of loan in period #1 of the deal	$ 50,000
User Default rate (monthly, unchanging)	1%
Current balance of loan month #3	$ 49,900
Defaulted principal month #3	$ 500

The defaulted amount in period #3 is NOT (1% * 49,900) or $499, it is 1% times the current balance of the loan in period #1, $500.

$$m\_loan\_defaults = m\_loan\_orig\_bal * g\_monthly\_drate(idefault, iperiod)$$

We now have the amount of defaulted principal for the loan for that single month.

We now need to adjust several factors because of these defaults.

First, if the defaulted amount is greater than the remaining balance of the loan, it is set to the remaining balance of the loan. One cannot default principal one does not have!

Second, we decrease the outstanding current balance of the loan by the defaulted amount.

Third, we increment the amount of nonperforming principal by the amount of the default.

Fourth, we decrease the monthly payment by the percentage the defaulted principal was of the current outstanding balance.

Calculate Coupon Income

Outside of the loop, we have done almost all of the work necessary to calculate the coupon income for the period. Coupon income, or interest, from the loan is the product of the current balance, the contents of the "**g_loan_coupon**" array element for this loan in this period, and the day count for the period. See Exhibit 14.36.

```
Sub Calculate_Coupon_Payments()

  'Calculate the coupon income
  m_loan_coup_income = 0#
  m_loan_coup_income = _
      g_loan_coupon(iloan, iperiod) * m_loan_cur_bal * g_day_factors(iperiod, dtype)
  'Total income
  coup_income = m_loan_coup_income

End Sub
```

EXHIBIT 14.36   Calculation of the monthly coupon income

```
Sub Calculate_Scheduled_Amortization()

  m_loan_prin_ret = 0#
  If m_loan_cur_bal > 1# Then
     m_loan_prin_ret = m_loan_cur_bal * g_loan_amort_factors(iloan, iperiod)
     m_loan_cur_bal = m_loan_cur_bal - m_loan_prin_ret
     Else
     m_loan_prin_ret = m_loan_cur_bal
     m_loan_cur_bal = 0#
  End If

End Sub
```

EXHIBIT 14.37   Calculation of scheduled amortization of principal

Calculate Scheduled Amortization

Having determined the defaults of principal and subsequently calculated the coupon income, we can now calculate the scheduled amortization of principal! In each of the blocks, we are going to set the working variable loan_prin_ret to zero to prevent any carryover values from leaking into the calculation. Next, we check whether we should engage in this activity at all!

Is the loan active? If its balance is greater than $0.01, it is and we need to proceed.

Here is where the prior calculation of the principal retirement factors is so useful. We can simply multiply the remaining balance of the loan by the principal retirement factor and we are finished. See Exhibit 14.37.

We then subtract the principal retired from the current balance and we are done.

Calculate Prepayments of Principal

In prepayments of principal, as in the earlier sections, the calculations are almost anticlimactic. We have already calculated the prepayment factors. All we have to do is multiply the monthly factor of the loan by the current balance and we are done! All the heavy computational lifting was done outside the loops.

We will later use the cur_project variable to determine the LTV. This variable represents the amount of the original principal balance of all the loans that was neither prepaid nor defaulted. As such, it is the current outstanding balance of the indebtedness and can be used to calculate the equity portion of the project. This is an important piece of information when we evaluate the severity of loss of the project. See Exhibit 14.38.

Calculate Recoveries of Principal

Before you just plunge into this code, take a minute to review the two exhibits in Chapter 3, "Securitizing a Loan Portfolio," Exhibits 3.4 and 3.5. These exhibits graphically summarize the interplay between the effects of Market Value Decline and Loan To Value Ratio on the calculation of the recovery amount.

There are two possible situations relative to default. The first is that the severity of loss to the project is not sufficient to impact the level of financing. The second is that the severity of loss subsumes the entire equity position and then impacts on some or all of the loan position. See Exhibit 14.39.

```
Sub Calculate_Prepayments_of_Principal()

  'Compute prepayments on the loan and adjust balance
  m_loan_prepays = 0#
  If m_loan_cur_bal > 1# Then
      m_loan_prepays = m_loan_cur_bal * g_monthly_prate(iprepay, iperiod)
      m_loan_cur_bal = m_loan_cur_bal - m_loan_prepays
  End If
  'Compute what portion of the appraised value these prepayments represent and
  ' subtract it from the beginning appraisal value of the entire project.  This is
  ' later used to determine severity of loss.
  If cur_ltv > 0# Then
      cur_project = cur_project - (m_loan_prepays / cur_ltv)
  End If

End Sub
```

EXHIBIT 14.38   Calculation of prepayments to principal

Accumulate the Cash Flows of the Period

The subroutine in Exhibit 14.40 is the last subroutine in the inner loops of the cash flow calculation process. It aggregates the monthly results, loan by loan, and stores them in a series of arrays named after each of the components of the cash flows. Each of these arrays are dimensioned:

```
g_array_name(1 to g_prepay_levels, 1 to g_default_levels, 1 to PAY_DATES) as Double
```

It is this array that we will use to populate the waterfall spreadsheet.

```
Sub Calculate_Recoveries()
Dim loss_factor      As Double
  ' RECOVERIES CALCULATION SECTION
  ' If the severity of loss of the scenario is less than the current cltv of the loan
  '    to the project there are 100% recoveries
  ' Remember the severity of loss is on the entire project and will hit the equity
  '    first, and the loan position last.
  ' If there is a 70% MarketValueDecline (SOL) against a 20% LTV then the first
  '    expression will be true (1-.70)=.30 .30>=.20 recovery everything!
  ' If there is a 70 SOL against a 50% LTV then the second expression will be true:
  '    recovery_factor = (.70-.50)/.50 = .40
  '    recoveries      = total balance defaulted * (1.00-.40) or 60% of the position
  ' this is easy to check in that a $1,000,000 project with a 50% LTV suffering
  '    a 70% SOL will wipe out the $500,000 above the loan, and $200,000 of the
  '    loan position leaving the recovery of $500,000 (loan)- $200,000 loan
  '    loss = $300,000 loan recovery. $300,000 is 60% of the loan posi-
tion of $500,000
  ' Remember you can only recover the amount of the default, not more than the
  '    amount you have outstanding.
  If (1 - g_loss_sever_pct) >= m_loan_ratio Then
      recoveries = m_loan_defaults
  Else
      loss_factor = m_loan_ratio - (1# - g_loss_sever_pct)
      recoveries = m_loan_defaults * ((m_loan_ratio - loss_factor) / m_loan_ratio)
  End If
End Sub
```

EXHIBIT 14.39   The recoveries of principal calculation

```
Sub Accumulate_CF_Components()

  'Accumulate the cashflow components: prepayments, defaults, regular principal,
  ' coupon
  g_default_prin(iprepay, idefault, iperiod) = g_default_prin(iprepay, idefault, _
                                  iperiod) + m_loan_defaults
  g_prepay_prin(iprepay, idefault, iperiod) = g_prepay_prin(iprepay, idefault, _
                                  iperiod) + m_loan_prepays
  g_amort_prin(iprepay, idefault, iperiod) = g_amort_prin(iprepay, idefault, _
                                  iperiod)  + m_loan_prin_ret
  g_coupon(iprepay, idefault, iperiod) = g_coupon(iprepay, idefault, iperiod) _
                               + g_up_income

  ' Sum the recoveries, we are allowed to cover past the end of the deal so put those
  '  recoveries into the last period
  If iperiod + g_recovery_lag <= PAY_DATES Then
      g_recover_prin(iprepay, idefault, iperiod + g_recovery_lag) = _
                  g_recover_prin(iprepay, idefault, iperiod + g_recovery_lag) _
                  + recoveries
  Else
      g_recover_prin(iprepay, idefault, PAY_DATES) = _
                  g_recover_prin(iprepay, idefault, PAY_DATES) + recoveries
  End If

End Sub
```

EXHIBIT 14.40   Aggregating the monthly cash flows of each loan into the portfolio total

The one thing that we have to remember to do in this subroutine is to lag the receipt of the recovered principal by the value of the g_recovery_lag variable. All we have to do is offset the period the recoveries are recognized by adding the "g_recovery_lag" value to the current value of iperiod. If the recovery period would fall beyond the last period of the model, it is allowable to recognize the receipt of the recovered amount on the last date. In our model, the final date will be the constant PAY_DATES. If "iperiod+g_recovery_lag > PAY_DATES" we can recognize the recovery as having occurred on the PAY_DATES period. (In some securitizations where there are balloon payments expected on the last payment date, recoveries of defaulted principal are allowed to be recognized for up to 12 months after the original maturity date of the deal. Again, because this is an introductory book, we will assume the convention that all recoveries that would fall beyond the last period of the deal can be recognized on the last period of the deal.

We have now completed the calculation of the collateral cash flows and are ready to run them through the waterfall we created earlier.

BUILDING A CASH FLOW TRACE CAPABILITY

In a survey of U.S. drivers, 85% rated themselves "above average" or better. This is a curious phenomenon. While none of us will admit to being perfect, everyone tends to think of themselves as somewhat better than most people. The same is true of people who design models. It is therefore of some value to have a reality check from time to time. The cash flow trace feature is designed to provide that reality check. It would be a distressing thing indeed, not to mention acutely embarrassing, to have the model produce incorrect cash flows at this point. We are about to drive the waterfall with them and with that we will be able to assess the performance of the deal structure. If the cash flows are incorrect at this point, there can be severe business consequences. These risks can take two broad forms, franchise risk, that is to say, damage to the reputation of the firm, and secondly, financial liability.

Better to be safe than sorry. A stitch in time saves nine. A penny of prevention is worth a pound of cure. Need I go on?

What we now want to do is build a small piece of code to help us verify that the wonderful calculation engine that we have so painstakingly assembled above is actually doing the job. This is the trace function.

The trace function will print out the period-by-period cash flows of every one of the loans in the portfolio onto a single Excel worksheet. This worksheet will reside in a workbook that will be named after the combination of prepayment speed and default speed that was used to generate the flows. We will undertake this activity in Chapter 17, "Validating the Model."

CONCLUDING REMARKS

We now have a complete cash flow generator.

The next step will be to place the cash flows in the Excel waterfall spreadsheet and see how the structure performs against a Range of prepayment and default scenarios.

DELIVERABLES CHECKLIST

The VBA Knowledge Checklist items for this chapter are:

- Get experience in programming a computationally intense process, the amortization of the loan portfolio.
- Get your first experience in optimizing the performance of VBA code by separating certain functionalities from others to avoid performing unnecessary calculations inside of looping structures.
- Develop a computational structure that uses four nested loops.
- Develop a trace function to validate the cash flow calculation methodologies.
- Learn how to interactively reconfigure and format large files to minimize their size.
- Learn how to program loan amortization.
- Learn how to program default and prepayment methodologies.
- Learn how to use the Erase command to clear arrays.

The Model Production Checklist items for this chapter are:

- Write a schematic for the master subroutine to calculate the cash flows.
- Learn the bond math for the amortization of loans.
- Learn how to set up the monthly coupon levels for floating rate notes using their terms and conditions and a specified benchmark interest rate level.
- Declare all variables needed for the cash flow calculations.

- Declare constants labels for the prepayment and default methodologies.
- Translate the master subroutine schematic into a series of VBA subroutine calls.
- Create the supporting subroutines for the prepayment and default methodologies.
- Create the subroutines that create the monthly prepayment and default attrition factors.
- Create the subroutines to set the monthly coupon levels for floating rate loans.
- Create the subroutine to calculate the monthly retirement of scheduled amortization factors.
- Create the subroutines to calculate the five cash flow components for each of the loans.
- Create the subroutines that accumulate each of the five cash flow components at the portfolio level by monthly period.

NEXT STEPS

Since we have now gone through all the pain and suffering of computing this myriad of cash flows we probably should do something with them!

In Chapter 15, "Running the Waterfall: Producing Initial Results," we will develop a way to get these cash flows from the VBA arrays where they now reside to the Excel waterfall spreadsheet that we developed back in Chapter 4.

Once there we can power the waterfall with them and get some preliminary indications of how the model is working.

Chapter 16, "Debugging the Model," will step us through how to make sure the model is in working condition. But getting the model to simply work is not enough. It may be mechanically functional but be producing incorrect results.

As a result, Chapter 17, "Validating the Model," will help us make sure we have everything correct when we finally start to run the model for real.

Well, that is as far ahead as we should look now!

Let us take out cash flows on to the waterfall spreadsheet and see how we have done.

ON THE WEB SITE

The material on the Web site for this chapter is the model named **"MODEL_BASE_Chap14.xls."**

The difference between this model and that of Chapter 13 is the addition of the cash flow generating subroutines and their supporting global variables and constants.

There are two new modules in the model. They are the modules that contain all of the cash flow, prepayment, default, coupon, amortization, and recoveries calculation VBA code. They are specifically:

1. CollateralCFGenerator module
2. CollateralPreDefCalcs module

In addition to the VBA code in these modules, there have been additional variables added to the **"A_Globals"** modules and a number of constants added to **"A_Constants."**

As with the other partial models, **"MODEL_BASE_Chap14.xls.,"** is compiled and will perform all the model steps up to and including the calculation of the cash flows.

## CHAPTER 15

Running the Waterfall: Producing Initial Results

OVERVIEW

In Chapter 14, we computed the periodic cash flows for each of the cash flow components of the collateral pool. We now have the monthly streams of defaulted principal, coupon income, scheduled amortization of principal, prepayments of principal, and the recoveries of defaulted principal for each month of every loan, segregated by each combination of prepayment and default assumptions.

The collateral cash flow generation portion of the model is now complete.

Another way to look at it is that we have built the Mother of All Cash Flow Arrays, and now all we have to do is to feed it scenario-by-scenario to the Waterfall Spreadsheet. We will sequentially load these cash flows into the waterfall structure and calculate the spreadsheet. We can then record the performance of the proposed structure and proceed with the next two tasks, verifying the waterfall and generating the preliminary results.

This would probably be a good time to look at the listing of the Main Program, Exhibit 15.1. We can see that we have accomplished quite a lot so far. Specifically, we have completed VBA subroutines that perform the following tasks:

- Perform error checking on all the menus and alert the users to any potential problems with pop-up message boxes.
- After error checking, read all the information from the menus.
- Open and read the data file that contains all the loan information; Store this information in global variables and arrays.
- Perform the collateral selection process.
- Prepare collateral selection reports of ineligible and eligible collateral.
- Compute the collateral cash flows using the loan information and menu inputs.

We only need to accomplish three more tasks and we are done. These are:

- Load the cash flows into the Excel Waterfall Spreadsheet columns.
- Calculate the worksheet and extract the results from the Waterfall Spreadsheet, storing them in VBA arrays.
- Using these results, produce the reporting packages selected by the user.

We will build the sets of VBA subroutines (in Exhibit 15.1) to accomplish these ends.

```
Sub Loan_Financing_Model()

    Application.DisplayAlerts = False          'turn off the warning messages
    Call Display_PrepayDefault_ProgressMsg(99) 'display program progress msg (null)
    Call ErrCheck_All_Menus                    'error check all menu entries
    Call Read_All_Menu_Input                   'transfer the menu entries to
                                                variables
    Call Read_Portfolio_Data_File              'read in the loan information to
                                                variables
    Call Select_Deal_Collateral                'run the basic eligibility test or
                                                accept all
    Call Compute_Collateral_Cashflows          'generating the cash flows
    Call Load_and_Run_the_Waterfall            'runs the waterfall
    Call Write_Waterfall_Report_Package        'package of waterfall reports in
                                                detail
    Call Write_Matrix_Report_Package           'package of 9 matrix reports
    Sheets("Main Menu").Select
    Application.DisplayAlerts = True                'turn message displays back on

End Sub
```

EXHIBIT 15.1   Main Program showing the portions we will contrast in this chapter

DELIVERABLES

The deliverable for this chapter is the Waterfall Results Reporting Package. The VBA Language Knowledge Goals for this chapter are:

- How to implement a set of preformatted Excel Workbooks that each contain a collection of report templates.
- Most of the knowledge here will consist of reinforcing what you learned when we designed and coded the VBA that produced the Collateral Selection Reports. You should now feel much more comfortable with this approach and you will find this more of a mechanical exercise than a conceptual one.
- Using the "ClearContents" method with the Range command to clear the contents but not the formatting or formulas of a Range. Example: Range('cfCoupon").ClearContents.
- Learning how to set the Calculation method of the Application object (in this case a spreadsheet to manual). This means that the worksheet will not recalculate after every entry but only when the Calculate command is issued in the model. This command is Application.Calculate = xlCalculationManual.
- How to rename Excel worksheets in VBA code: Sheets("CF-1").Name = new_name.
- How to insert a new worksheet into an Excel workbook at a position immediately following another worksheet. Sheets(new_name).Copy After: Sheets("Sheet1").
- How to move a worksheet in front of an existing worksheet in an Excel workbook. Sheets(new_name).Move Before = Sheets("Sheet1").
- Using a Select Case statement inside of a For...Next statement to sequentially check if a given report of a multiple report package has been selected for

production. If it has, print the report, if not, delete the report template worksheet from the workbook.

- Using public constants to create a list of names for individual reports in a report workbook file. Example: Public Const MATRIX_CFS_REPORT = 4.
- As you are writing out a report, changing the appearance of an Excel Cell object based on the value of the output number you have just written to the Cell. Example that changes the font color to bright red: Cells(irow,icol).Font.ColorIndex = 3.
- Reading file names of template files and report files from the menus. Reading directory pathway files from the menus. Combining these into working pathways to specify individual files in directories separate from the models directory.
- Using the "Workbook.Open *filename:* =" statement to open template files.
- Using the "Workbook.SaveAs *filename* =" statement to save the opened template files to the designated output file name.

To deliver this reporting package we will need to write the VBA subroutines to perform the following for both the Cash Flow Waterfall Reports and the Matrix Reports:

- Sequentially load the Cash Flow Waterfall spreadsheet with the scenario specific cash flows we have generated, and calculate the worksheet, producing the scenario results.
- Find the respective template files, open them, and save them to the designated output file names in the output directory.
- Extract the scenario-by-scenario results from the Cash Flow Worksheet as needed by both sets of reports.
- Direct these results into the Waterfall Report Package on a scenario-by-scenario basis with one worksheet replicating the contents of each scenario.
- Populate the four Matrix Reports, or be able to delete the unselected reports from the Matrix Report Package.
- Trim both types of reports for unused report lines.
- Close and save both of the report packages.

When these deliverables are complete, we will be able to debug the model once more and begin running it. We will be very close to having a fully working version of the model. All that will be necessary is to validate the calculation accuracy and make sure the logical structures give us the results we want.

UNDER CONSTRUCTION

The portions of the model that we will build in this chapter will be focused on performing three general operations. These are, in order, loading the cash flows from the collateral into the Waterfall Spreadsheet and triggering its calculation; extracting the results from the Waterfall Spreadsheet and placing them into VBA

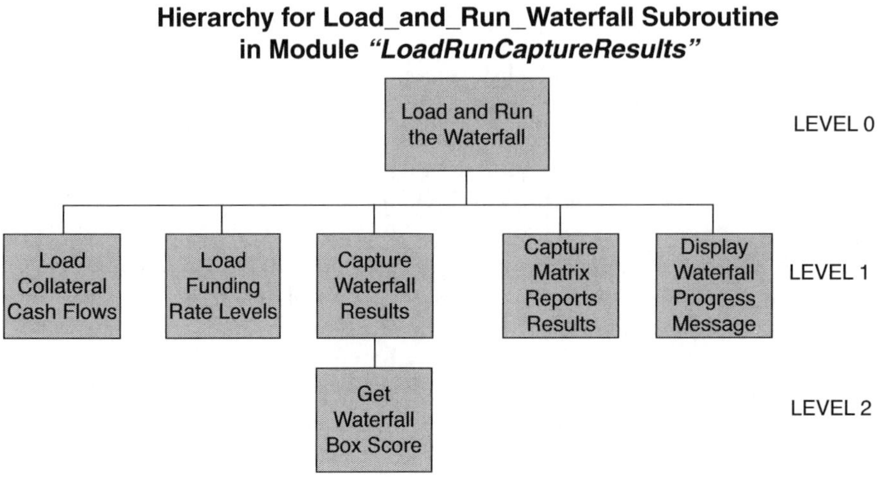

Hierarchy for Load_and_Run_Waterfall Subroutine
in Module *"LoadRunCaptureResults"*

EXHIBIT 15.2 Subroutine tree structure to load and run the Waterfall Spreadsheet

arrays; and using the information in the VBA arrays to produce first the Waterfall Reports Package and then the Summary Matrix Reports Package.

That being said, the lion's share of the new VBA code will be placed in one of three modules. These modules are the **"LoadRunCaptureResults"** module, and the two report generators, the **"WriteWaterfallReports"** module and the **"WriteMatrixReports"** module.

In addition, we will be declaring some additional global variables and constants.

Thus the changes to our prior version will be concentrated in the following VBA modules.

In the **"A_Constants"** module we will add two blocks of global constants. The first will be the single constant "MAX_SCEN" which is set to the product of the current limit of ten prepayment and ten default scenarios. The second is a set of constants for the Matrix Report Package that tells us the current number of reports in the package and an identified tag for each one.

In the **"A_Globals"** module we will add a block of global variables that will receive the contents of the calculated spreadsheet. All of these variables will be prefixed by the name g_waterfall_, and can be found at the bottom of the module under the subheading "Waterfall Variables."

In the **"LoadRunCaptureResults"** module we will build six subroutines to load the precalculated cash flows into the Waterfall Spreadsheet, run it, and capture the results in VBA arrays. See Exhibit 15.2.

In the **"WriteWaterfallReports"** module, we will build six subroutines that will open the Waterfall Report Package template file, populate it with one spreadsheet per scenario, write the contents of the waterfall itself, write the summary section of the report, fill in the header information, and save the report file. See Exhibit 15.3.

In the **"WriteMatrixReports"** module we will build ten subroutines that will write the four Summary Matrix Reports, populated by the results that have been saved in various VBA arrays. See Exhibit 15.4.

Hierarchy for Write_Waterfall_Report_Package Subroutine in Module *"WriteWaterfallReports"*

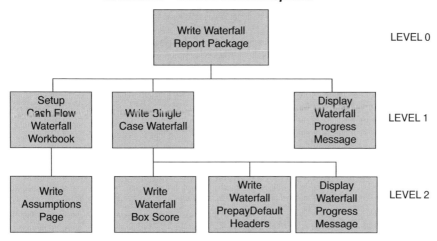

EXHIBIT 15.3 Subroutine tree structure to write Waterfall Report Package

Hierarchy for Write_Matrix_Report_Package Subroutine in Module *"WriteMatrixReports"*

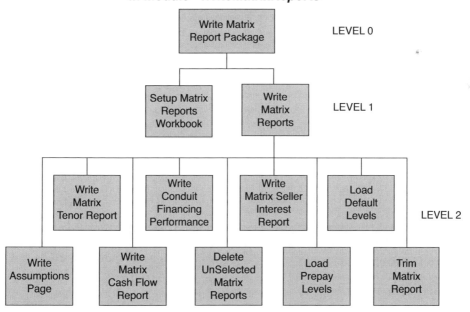

EXHIBIT 15.4 Subroutine tree structure to write Matrix Report Package

```
Sub Load_and_Run_the_Waterfall()

    i_scenario = 0
    For i_prepay = 1 To g_prepay_levels
        For i_default = 1 To g_default_levels
            i_scenario = i_scenario + 1
            Call Load_Collateral_Cashflows(i_prepay, i_default)
            Call Load_Funding_Rate_Levels
            Calculate
            If g_out_cfdetail Then Call Capture_Waterfall_Results(i_scenario)
            If g_out_matrix Then Call Capture_Matrix_Report_Results
            Call Display_Waterfall_ProgressMsg(i_scenario, 2)
        Next i_default
    Next i_prepay

End Sub
```

EXHIBIT 15.5   Subroutine loads the cash flows into the waterfall and captures the results

RUNNING THE WATERFALL SPREADSHEET

The purpose of this code is to load the collateral cash flows into the Waterfall Spreadsheet and the financing rate for the Conduit debt, calculate the Waterfall Spreadsheet, and then capture the results. We will place this code in the "**A_Main_Program**" module. We need to capture two sets of outputs from the Waterfall worksheet:

1. The first is the contents of the waterfall. This we will place in a series of arrays. Most of it will be placed in a very large array named "**g_waterfall_info**." This array is designed to take a snapshot of the entire contents of the waterfall (minus some of the header information). The dimensions of the array directly match those of the Waterfall Spreadsheet itself. It will serve as a place where we can store what is essentially a picture of each of the unique scenarios on a cell-by-cell basis. We will also capture the information in the Summary Information section on the same worksheet. It is in the region of the report underneath the report title on the far left of the spreadsheet.
2. The second set of information is stored in a series of arrays that will be written to the Matrix Reports that we designed in Chapter 5. The results are stored in arrays that begin with the prefix "g_out". Various combinations of these arrays will be used to write the four matrix reports.

Both of these results sets will be read from the spreadsheet and saved after each calculation sequence is complete. All the information will be stored in the arrays until it is required for the report writing function. Each set of reports has a separate template report. Each set of reports is written completely and finished before the model moves on to any other tasks. See Exhibit 15.5.

LOADING THE COLLATERAL CASHFLOWS

Having completed the task of computing the cash flows for all of the prepayment and default level combinations, we now want to put them to use.

```
Sub Load_Collateral_Cashflows(i_p As Integer, i_d As Integer)

    Application.Calculation = xlCalculationManual

    Sheets("CFWaterfall").Select
    Range("CFDefaultRate") = g_default_rate(i_d)
    Range("CFPrepayRate") = g_prepay_rate(i_p)
    Select Case g_default_method
        Case Is = 1: Range("CFDefaultMethod") = "CPR"
        Case Is = 2: Range("CFDefaultMethod") = "PSA"
        Case Is = 3: Range("CFDefaultMethod") = "USR"
    End Select
    Select Case g_prepay_method
        Case Is = 1: Range("CFPrepayMethod") = "CPR"
        Case Is = 2: Range("CFPrepayMethod") = "PSA"
    End Select

    Range("cfPrinRegAmort").ClearContents
    Range("cfPrinPrepayments").ClearContents
    Range("cfPrinDefaults").ClearContents
    Range("cfPrinRecoveries").ClearContents
    Range("cfCoupon").ClearContents

    Range("TotalBeginPrincipal") = g_beg_collateral
    For irow = 1 To PAY_DATES
        Range("cfPrinRegAmort").Cells(irow) = g_amort_prin(i_p, i_d, irow)
        Range("cfPrinPrepayments").Cells(irow) = g_prepay_prin(i_p, i_d, irow)
        Range("cfPrinDefaults").Cells(irow) = g_default_prin(i_p, i_d, irow)
        Range("cfPrinRecoveries").Cells(irow) = g_recover_prin(i_p, i_d, irow)
        Range("cfCoupon").Cells(irow) = g_coupon(i_p, i_d, irow)
    Next irow

    Calculate

End Sub
```

EXHIBIT 15.6 Subroutine that loads the collateral cash flows based on individual scenario conditions of prepayment and default rates

We have already prepared the waterfall worksheet, we will now sequentially load the cash flow vectors of each of the prepayment and default scenarios into it and capture the results.

The "Load_Collateral_Cashflows" subroutine will do just that. See Exhibit 15.6.

The "Load_Collateral_Cashflows" subroutine, in Exhibit 15.6, will write the contents of the "**g_amort_prin**," "**g_prepay_prin**," "**g_default_prin**," "**g_coupon**," and "**g_recover_prin**" arrays into the Waterfall Spreadsheet. It will do this based on the values of the arguments "i_p" and "i_d." The variable "i_p" is the number of prepayment scenario and the variable "i_d" is the number of the default scenario whose specific cash flows are to be read into the Waterfall Spreadsheet.

Before we proceed with this action, we need to take some precautionary steps first.

Setting the Application.Calculation Method to Manual from Automatic

When any value is changed on an Excel Spreadsheet and the value of the Calculation method of the Application is "xlCalculationAutomatic," the entire spreadsheet recalculates all formulas. **This is the last thing we want to have happen when we write the cash flows to the model.** If there are five cash flow components and 300 time periods to the model run, the waterfall will calculate 1,500 just to produce a single result. We can avoid this by setting the method of the Application.Calculation Object of the Waterfall Spreadsheet to the value "xlCalculationManual." If we do this we can write as many values as we want on to the Waterfall Spreadsheet and it will not calculate. It will only calculate when we tell it to by issuing the command Calculate.

We can now completely control the point in the model execution that the spreadsheet will recalculate based on the addition of the cash flows of the particular prepayment and default scenario we have loaded! The spreadsheet will calculate only once at the point that the model execution reaches this command.

Preparing the Spreadsheet

Find the Waterfall Spreadsheet   The next steps we need to take seem absurdly obvious.

We better make sure that we are going to write all this information to the correct spreadsheet! To do this, we will select the Waterfall Spreadsheet by using a Sheets command:

```
Sheets("CFWaterfall").Select
```

This guarantees that we will not overwrite another spreadsheet of the model (including any of the menus)!

Record the Prepayment and Default Speeds of the Cash Flow Set   Now is the time to enter the prepayment and default speeds associated with these cash flows to the header section of the spreadsheet. The prepayment and default speeds are written to two labeled fields on the upper-left-hand section of the spreadsheet. We have created Range names for both the speed and methodology of the default and prepayment assumptions. We will populate the Range "CFDefaultRate" with the default speed and the Range "CFDefaultMethod" with the three letter abbreviation of the default methodology. We will then repeat the processes with the Ranges "CFPrepayRate" and "CFPrepayMethod" to complete this portion of the header of the spreadsheet. How do we know what to print in these cells?

There are two variables in the argument list of the subroutine that we will use as referencing indices to find both the prepayment speeds and their methodologies. They are the variables i_p and i_d, and are passed into the subroutine by the Main Program.

Earlier in the operation of the model, in fact as far back as the time when we were first reading the inputs off the Defaults Menu, we recorded the user's choices of default and prepayment speeds and methods. We generated the various speeds of defaults and prepayments predicated on the Base rate input in the menu and the size of the incremental Step and the Number of Steps. We stored these expanded rates and methods in the arrays named **"g_default_rates"** and **"g_prepay_rates."** All we have to do now is use the values of the variables in the subroutine argument to access the correct rates from this array!

These two variables, i_p and i_d, are used to find the appropriate prepayment and default methodology labels and to place them next to the rate information in the header of the spreadsheet. We will use a Select...Case statement to access the correct methodology.

Clear the Ranges That Will Receive the Cash Flows   Each of the five Ranges that will hold the cash flows for this scenario are now cleared by using the "ClearContents" method against the Range object. This method preserves the formulas (in this case there are none), but also more important, preserves the formatting of the Range.

Write the Cash Flows   We have set the calculation method to Manual. We have selected the correct worksheet. We have labeled the scenario. We have cleared the Ranges into which we are to write the cash flows. The spreadsheet is now in a proper initial condition to receive the cash flow inputs.

We begin by writing the beginning balance of all the eligible collateral into the Range labeled "TotalBeginPrincipal." It is from this cell that all the period remaining principal calculations will be based.

We now use a For...Next loop to load this scenario's cash flows. The loop cycles from 1 to PAY_DATES which is set to 360. Each of the Ranges receives its corresponding strip of cash flows from the global arrays specific to that cash flow.

When the loop finishes, all the cash flows are in the spreadsheet and it is time to issue the Calculate command. The Waterfall Spreadsheet calculates and the results are now available to be read into our result arrays. There they will reside until we output them into the user selected Report Packages.

CAPTURING THE WATERFALL RESULTS

Most structured finance cash flow models are complex. All, even the relatively simple ones, such as the example in this book, can appear complex to the novice. For this reason it is an excellent idea to have a reporting facility in the model that will allow the user to see, very specifically, what is happening.

The Waterfall Report answers this need. This report package is a collection of reproductions of the contents of the complete Waterfall Spreadsheet for each of the unique prepayment and default rate scenarios. The report is written from the contents of the **"g_waterfall_info"** array.

This array is dimensioned in the following manner:

```
Public g_waterfall_info(1 to 100, 1 to PAY_DATES, 1 to PAY_COLS) as Double
```

The first dimension is the maximum number of scenarios (ten Defaults by ten Prepayments). The second dimension is the number of monthly payment periods we designed into the model, 360, which represents the longest original term of the collateral. The third dimension is the number of columns in the Waterfall Spreadsheet, currently 63. We do not print out Columns 64 and 65 in the Waterfall Report

```
Sub Capture_Waterfall_Results(scen)

   'write out the waterfall contents
   For iloop = 1 To PAY_DATES
      For icol = 1 To PAY_COLS
         g_waterfall_info(scen, iloop, icol) = Range("WaterfallCFS").Cells(iloop, icol)
      Next icol
   Next iloop

   'prepayment and default headers
   g_waterfall_misc(scen, 1) = Range("CFDefaultRate")        'prepayment rate
   g_waterfall_misc(scen, 2) = Range("CFPrepayRate")         'default rate
   g_waterfall_method(scen, 1) = Range("CFDefaultMethod")    'prepayment method
   g_waterfall_method(scen, 2) = Range("CFPrepayMethod")     'default method

   'read the components of the Box Score
   Call Get_Waterfall_Box_Score(scen)

End Sub
```

EXHIBIT 15.7   Subroutine that will capture all the Cash Flow Waterfall information from the spreadsheet including the "Box Score" Summary subsection of the worksheet

as 64 is a periods column and 65 contains information available elsewhere on the spreadsheet.

Each time the Waterfall Spreadsheet is calculated, the entire contents of the body of the report are written to this array. The model will also need to store a number of the other Waterfall Spreadsheet inputs that we have transferred from the menus to the spreadsheet. This includes the expenses rates for the various expenses of the deal, and the allocation of principal between the financing unit and the Seller Interest. These are used by the Waterfall Spreadsheet in various calculations. The model will also write the values of the prepayment and default assumptions and the methodology of each to a VBA array named "**g_waterfall_misc**" and "**g_waterfall_method**," respectively. See Exhibit 15.7.

REPORTING THE SUMMARY REPORT OR "BOX SCORE" INFORMATION

You will also note that we are capturing the contents of the summary "Box Score" of the waterfall performance.

The Summary Report box at the leftmost side of the Waterfall Spreadsheet contains the results of the waterfall performance in a condensed format that is accessible at a glance. Each individual item inside the Summary Report box references a cell or Range of the Waterfall Spreadsheet. It pulls all of its information directly from the contents of this worksheet.

It is divided into three sections. The first is a cash flows section that provides a Sources and Uses statement for the structure. This is useful to see if the "cash in = cash out" of the deal is balanced and to give a quick look at all the components of the collateral cash flows and the composition of the expenses and use of funds by the structure.

```
'Waterfall file
Public g_waterfall_file  As String   'waterfall file for scenario outputs
Public g_waterfall_name(1 To MAX_SCEN) As String 'worksheet names in cf output file
Public g_waterfall_info(1 To MAX_SCEN, 1 To PAY_DATES, 1 To PAY_COLS) As Double
Public g_waterfall_misc(1 To MAX_SCEN, 1 To 2) As Double
                                      'prepay and default info for scenario
Public g_waterfall_method(1 To MAX_SCEN, 1 To 2) As String
                                      'prepay and default method
Public g_waterfall_bxscr1(1 To MAX_SCEN, 1 To 14, 1 To 2) As Double
                                      'box score field group 1
Public g_waterfall_bxscr2(1 To MAX_SCEN, 1 To 11, 1 To 2) As Double
                                      'box score field group 2
Public g_waterfall_bxscr3(1 To MAX_SCEN, 1 To 3) As Double
                                      'box score field group 3
```

EXHIBIT 15.8   Declaration in "A_Globals" module to hold the Summary Report information

The second part of the Summary Report contains the performance information for both the Conduit and the Seller Interest. It gives the severity of loss numbers and also the performance statistics of the Conduit financing.

The last part of the Summary Report tells us if any of the three deal triggers have been activated.

In order to be able to write this information into the Waterfall Report Package, we will, along with all the other data, have to move the contents of this part of the Waterfall Spreadsheet in VBA arrays. To accomplish this we will first create three Range names to correspond to each of the major subdivisions of the Summary Report: "WaterfallBox1," "WaterfallBox2," and "WaterfallBox3." Having now defined the segments of the report by these Ranges, we can read their contents into corresponding VBA arrays.

First we will add these array declarations to the others we have already created to capture the contents of the Waterfall Spreadsheet as a whole. See Exhibit 15.8.

Now that we have the arrays in place, we can simply map the contents of the three Ranges, "WaterfallBox1," "WaterfallBox 2," and "WaterfallBox 3," into them. We will do this using the subroutine "Get_Waterfall_Box_Score." This subroutine can be seen in Exhibit 15.9.

We now have all the information we need on hand to write the Waterfall Report Package. Now let us turn to capturing the information we need for the Matrix Report Package!

LOADING THE MATRIX REPORTS INFORMATION

In Exhibit 15.10, the model is capturing all the results information that we will need to populate the Matrix Report Package that we designed back in Chapter 5. Most of the information is a direct item to item read from the Waterfall Spreadsheet. Each time a scenario is produced, this subroutine will transfer the results from the collection of Ranges on the spreadsheets and place them into the arrays.

The model writer has to clearly identify the information and group it by using related naming conventions. These naming conventions should be directly related to the names of the reports or to the uses that the results will be applied to later in the run of the model.

```
Sub Get_Waterfall_Box_Score(scen)

  'cash flow sources and uses block
  For irow = 1 To 14
    For icol = 1 To 2
      g_waterfall_bxscr1(scen, irow, icol) = Range("WaterfallBox1").Cells(irow, icol)
    Next icol
  Next irow

  'position performance statistics block
  For irow = 1 To 11
    For icol = 1 To 2
      If IsNumeric(Range("WaterfallBox2").Cells(irow, icol)) Then
        g_waterfall_bxscr2(scen, irow, icol) = Range("WaterfallBox2").Cells
          (irow,icol)
      End If
    Next icol
  Next irow

  'deal trigger conditions block
  For irow = 1 To 3
    g_waterfall_bxscr3(scen, irow) = Range("WaterfallBox3").Cells(irow)
  Next irow

End Sub
```

EXHIBIT 15.9 Reading the Summary Report contents using the WaterfallBox1, Waterfall-Box2, and WaterfallBox3 Ranges

At the conclusion of these two preceding subroutines, all the results needed to produce the Waterfall Spreadsheet Report Package and the Matrix Report Package has been extracted from the model and stored in VBA arrays ready to be used elsewhere! All that is now left is to write the reports themselves!

PRODUCING THE WATERFALL SPREADSHEET REPORT PACKAGE

We will now create the subroutine to produce the Waterfall Spreadsheet Report Package. This report package is the one that we created back in Chapter 5. The template file consists of a single copy of the Waterfall Spreadsheet and an Assumptions Report Worksheet.

We will need to do the following:

- Locate the template file and open it. After we have it open, rename it to the name entered on the Main Menu.
- Populate the Assumptions Report.
- There is only one Waterfall Spreadsheet template worksheet in the template file. If we need to make additional copies of the worksheet and identify them with their contents, we do so now before anything else is written to the workbook. We know how many individual scenarios there are by the number of prepayment and default rates the model ran. We now create one spreadsheet for each of these scenarios. We will also name each of the worksheets with the prepayment and default speeds used to generate the collateral cash flows for that unique scenario.

```
Sub Capture_Matrix_Report_Results()

    'tenor information for the conduit position
    g_out_avg_life(i_prepay, i_default) = Range("AvgLifeConduit")
    g_out_fin_mat(i_prepay, i_default) = Range("FinalMaturityConduit")
    g_out_mod_durat(i_prepay, i_default) = Range("ConduitModDurat")
    g_out_mac_durat(i_prepay, i_default) = Range("ConduitMacDurat")
    g_out_amt_10yr(i_prepay, i_default) = Range("Conduit10yrBalance")

    'collateral cash flow amounts
    g_out_recoveries(i_prepay, i_default) = Range("sumPrinRecoveries")
    g_out_tot_sch_amort(i_prepay, i_default) = Range("sumPrinRegAmort")
    g_out_tot_prepaid(i_prepay, i_default) = Range("sumPrinPrepayments")
    g_out_tot_coupon(i_prepay, i_default) = Range("sumCoupon")
    g_out_tot_defaults(i_prepay, i_default) = Range("sumPrinDefaults")

    'conduit performance statistics
    g_out_cond_repay(i_prepay, i_default) = Range("sumConduitPrinPaid")
    g_out_cond_debt_service(i_prepay, i_default) = Range("sumConduitDebtService")
    g_out_cond_sol(i_prepay, i_default) = Range("SolConduit")
    If g_out_cond_sol(i_prepay, i_default) > 0.00001 Then
        g_out_cond_cover(i_prepay, i_default) = 0#
        Else
        g_out_cond_cover(i_prepay, i_default) = _
          Range("CFExSprdReleased") / Range("TotalBeginPrincipal")
    End If
    If IsNumeric(Range("CFConduitIRR")) Then
        g_out_cond_irr(i_prepay, i_default) = Range("CFConduitIRR")
        Else
        g_out_cond_irr(i_prepay, i_default) = 999999#
    End If

    'seller interest performance statistics
    If IsNumeric(Range("CFSellerIRR")) Then
        g_out_si_irr(i_prepay, i_default) = Range("CFSellerIRR")
        Else
        g_out_si_irr(i_prepay, i_default) = 999999#
    End If
    g_out_rel_ex_sprd(i_prepay, i_default) = Range("CFExSprdReleased")
    g_out_sel_coverage(i_prepay, i_default) = _
        (Range("CFExSprdReleased") / Range("CFSellerBegBal")) - 1#
    g_out_program_short(i_prepay, i_default) = Range("CFProgFeeShortAmt")
    g_out_servicer_short(i_prepay, i_default) = Range("CFServiceFeeShortAmt")
    g_out_coupon_short(i_prepay, i_default) = Range("CFCouponShortAmt")

End Sub
```

EXHIBIT 15.10   Capture_Matrix_Report_Results subroutine

- We populate each of these worksheets with the contents of the respective VBA arrays we used to capture the results as the model was running.
- When the last worksheet is finished, we Save and Close the worksheet.

We can best facilitate this if we create a subroutine to print out each individual scenario at a time and put it inside of a looping structure that will cycle through the set of scenarios. We can then select the correct set of data from the various arrays we have populated earlier and produce the individual reports one by one.

But first we need to start at the beginning; and the beginning is setting up the template file. Unlike all the other template files, this one needs to be reconfigured before we can use it. We will place the VBA code for this subroutine in the module "WriteSetUpOutputFiles."

Setting Up the Cash Flow Waterfall Workbook

The subroutine "Setup_Cashflow_Waterfall_Workbook" has three major functional sections. The first section finds the correct template file and opens it, immediately making a copy and saving it. As part of the template file set up, it immediately writes the Assumptions Report (better safe then sorry!). See Exhibit 15.11.

```
Sub Setup_Cashflow_Waterfall_Workbook()

Dim waterfall_copy As String

  'Open the template file
  Workbooks.Open Filename:=g_pathway_template & g_template_waterfall
  'Save as the designated report file name
  g_waterfall_file = g_pathway_output & gfn_output_prefix & gfn_waterfall_cfs_file
  ActiveWorkbook.SaveAs Filename:=g_waterfall_file
  Call Write_Assumptions_Page

    'the template file only comes with one blank worksheet, we must add
    'additional waterfall sheets as required; one for each of the prepayment and
     default scenario
    'combinations. Number them sequentially and inset them in the rear of the
      workbook.
    i_name = 1
    p_rate = g_prepay_base_rate
    For ip = 1 To g_prepay_levels
        d_rate = g_default_base_rate
        For id = 1 To g_default_levels
            'name the sheets using the prepayment and default parameters
            g_waterfall_name(i_name) =
               "P-" & (p_rate * 100) & "%" & " D-" & (d_rate * 100) & "%"
                d_rate = d_rate + g_default_increment
            i_name = i_name + 1
        Next id
        p_rate = p_rate + g_prepay_increment
    Next ip

    'Identify the number of reports by the product of the number of
    prepayment and default levels
    num_reports = g_prepay_levels * g_default_levels
    waterfall_copy = g_waterfall_name(1) & " (2)"
    Sheets("CF-1").Name = g_waterfall_name(1)
    For i_rep = 2 To num_reports
        Sheets(g_waterfall_name(1)).Select
        Sheets(g_waterfall_name(1)).Copy After:=Sheets(i_rep - 1)
        Sheets(waterfall_copy).Select
        Sheets(waterfall_copy).Name = g_waterfall_name(i_rep)
    Next i_rep
    Sheets(g_waterfall_name(1)).Move Before:=Sheets(2)  'move to proper place
    ActiveWorkbook.Save

End Sub
```

EXHIBIT 15.11   This expands and modifies the basic waterfall template file, reconfiguring it dynamically for the number of scenario report

Since we designed this template file to accommodate up to one hundred worksheets, we will need to have some way to identify each of them and to ensure that each worksheet contains the correct scenario information. To this end, the subroutine now loops through the number of scenarios and creates a unique name for each spreadsheet using the combination of the prepayment and default rate information.

Finally, the subroutine writes the contents of the waterfall and the Summary Report information to the individual worksheets. After it completes the task, it saves and closes the now complete file. The following sections will go over these processes in more detail.

Open the Template File, Rename, and Write Assumptions   Using the names of the template file and its directory pathway as input by the model user on the Main Menu, we locate and open the Waterfall Spreadsheet template workbook.

Next we create the name and full pathway for the g_waterfall_file variable. It is to the contents of this variable that we perform a SaveAs with the template file on the next line.

Next we find and populate the Assumptions worksheet by using the subroutine "Write_Assumptions_Page." This completes the initial setup of the workbook.

We have only one worksheet available for the Waterfall Spreadsheet results and will probably have to create more. Before that, we will have to create a series of labels to differentiate the results of one scenario from the other. This we will now do. See Exhibit 15.7.

Create the Worksheet Names from the Prepayment/Default Combinations   Here, we want to create an array of unique scenario labels that we can apply to our worksheets to more clearly identify them in the Waterfall Spreadsheet Report Package.

There will be only one worksheet for each of the prepayment and default scenarios. We know how many of them there will be. The number of worksheets will be the number of scenarios as defined by default rate levels multiplied by the number of prepayment rate levels.

We also know how many of each number of default and prepayment scenarios there are because we have stored them in the variables g_default_levels and g_prepay_levels, respectively.

In addition, we have computed each of these prepayment rates and default rates and placed them in the arrays:

```
g_prepay_rate(1 to g_prepay_levels)
```

and

```
g_default_rate(1 to g_default_levels)
```

Thus we have already done most of the work. With this information we will construct a series of names in the form

```
P_rate% D_rate%
```

These we will store until we have created a series of worksheets to apply them to.

We shall create these additional worksheets next.

Create and Rename Additional Worksheets as Needed   How many of these additional copies of the Waterfall Spreadsheet Report do we need?

The answer is one worksheet report for each of the unique scenarios. That is the number equal to the default levels multiplied by the prepayment levels. We assign this value to a variable called num_reports.

Next we will create a name. This name will be the name of each of the copies of the original worksheet that Excel will assign them as they are created. The name of the worksheet in the Waterfall Spreadsheet Report template file is "CF-1."

When Excel creates a copy of this worksheet it will name it "CF-1(2)," if there is not another worksheet in existence with that name already. (We will make sure that *never* happens by renaming these newly created worksheets as soon as they are available!)

We can now loop through the number of reports needed and rename them using the labels we have stored in the **"g_waterfall_name"** array.

The loop will perform the following four operations:

1. Select our original sheet named CF-1
2. Make a copy and place it last in line to the right. We will know where this position is because the loop counter will tell it to do a Copy.After command after the nth worksheet.
3. Select the worksheet named "CF-1(2)." That will always be the newly created worksheet.
4. Rename this worksheet to the next name in **"g_waterfall_name"** array.

These four actions will continually create and rename each worksheet until the loop exhausts itself. The workbook is now ready for the Waterfall Spreadsheet input. The VBA code to write the Waterfall Reports will be placed in the **"WriteWaterfallReports"** module. If you are a bit confused by this, use the VBA Debugger and step through the operation of this part of the subroutine using "F8" the Step command. You will learn how to do this in Chapter 16. Watch the configuration of the workbook change one step at a time and it will become immediately clear what is happening.

Knowing how to write code like this is very important because there are many applications in which the number, sizes, and configurations of the output can be variable across a wide Range of possibilities.

Write the Contents of the Waterfall Spreadsheets

The subroutine "Write_Single_Case_Waterfall" in Exhibit 15.12 is explained step by step in the sections below.

Finding the Correct Worksheet   Earlier, when we prepared the workbook for output, we named each of the worksheets by a unique name. We have all of those names stored in the **"g_waterfall_name"** array. This is a global array so these labels are immediately available to us.

Now all we have to do is run the Sheets(g_waterfall_name(scen)).Select command and we will be immediately directed into the correct spreadsheet one time based on the name in the array!

```
Sub Write_Single_Case_Waterfall(scen)

    Sheets(g_waterfall_name(scen)).Select
    'write the rest of the report
    Call Write_Waterfall_Box_Score(scen)
    Call Write_Waterfall_PrepayDefault_Headers(scen)
    Call Display_Waterfall_ProgressMsg(scen, 1)
    'write out the waterfall contents
    irow = 14
    For iloop = 1 To PAY_DATES
      For icol = 1 To PAY_COLS
          Cells(irow, icol + 10).Value = g_waterfall_info(scen, iloop, icol)
      Next icol
      irow = irow + 1
    Next iloop

    'rewrite the contents of the "Triggers" section
    irow = 14
    For iloop = 1 To PAY_DATES
        For icol = 50 To 53
          If g_waterfall_info(scen, iloop, icol) = 0 Then
              Cells(irow, icol + 10).Value = "TRUE"
          Else
              Cells(irow, icol + 10).Value = "FALSE"
          End If
        Next icol
        irow = irow + 1
      Next iloop
      Call Trim_the_Waterfall_Report

End Sub
```

EXHIBIT 15.12   Populating the Waterfall Spreadsheet worksheets

Printing the Summary Report Information and the Waterfall Spreadsheet Headers

Now we want to write out all the information we read earlier from the Waterfall Spreadsheet.

To do this we can make a copy of the earlier subroutine and simply reverse the assignment statements for each of the blocks of variables.

What was a = b in the "Load_Waterfall_Results" now becomes b = a! The subroutine that performs this task is "Write_Waterfall_Box_Score." You can see this VBA code in Exhibit 15.13.

We next populate the header information for the prepayment and default rates and methodologies. See the subroutine in Exhibit 15.14.

With the Summary Report section and the headers in place, the body of the reports is read into the template file from the array **"g_waterfall_info."** Lastly, we have a bit of housekeeping to do.

In the "Triggers" section of the waterfall, the information will be written to the template file in the form of a numeric "0" for True and "1" for False. We now go through these columns and change the 0s and 1s to the alphabetic "True" and "False."

Trimming the Report   With all the information safely on the sheet, one might think that we are finished. Not at all!

The worksheet has a total of 360 months. None of the loans has a remaining term anywhere near that long! We will therefore have a lot of unused space at the

```
Sub Write_Waterfall_Box_Score(scen)

    'Box Score Section 1 -- Cash Flow Summary
    For irow = 1 To 14
        For icol = 1 To 2
            If irow = 8 Then Exit For
            Cells(irow + 8, icol + 5).Value = g_waterfall_bxscr1(scen, irow, icol)
            If irow = 1 Or irow = 3 Or irow > 5 Then Exit For
        Next icol
    Next irow

    'Box Score Section 2 -- Performance of the Notes and Seller Interest
    For irow = 1 To 11
        For icol = 1 To 2
            If irow = 3 Or irow = 7 Then Exit For
            Cells(irow + 25, icol + 5) = g_waterfall_bxscr2(scen, irow, icol)
            If irow >= 8 Then Exit For
        Next icol
    Next irow

    'Box Score Section 3 -- Triggers
    For irow = 1 To 3
        Cells(irow + 37, 6) = "TRUE"
        If g_waterfall_bxscr3(scen, irow) = 0 Then Cells(irow + 37, 6) = "FALSE"
    Next irow

End Sub
```

EXHIBIT 15.13 Populating the Summary Report section of the Waterfall spreadsheet

bottom of the report. To reduce the file to the minimum, we will trim off these last unneeded months of the waterfall. This is easily done by using a loop counter that counts backwards from the bottom of the report.

When it finds the first cell in the current balance row that has a value greater than $0.01, it stops. From that point to the bottom of the report is deleted and a border line is drawn across the base of the report. *Note*: Here we are making use of the Step option in the For...Next loop to force it to run backward from a higher number to a lower number. This is accomplished by setting the Step value to "−1."

Writing this subroutine is one of the exercises at the end of the period.

PRODUCING THE MATRIX REPORT PACKAGE

Exhibit 15.15 contains the subroutine that initiates and manages the production of the Matrix Summary Report Package.

```
Sub Write_Waterfall_PrepayDefault_Headers(scen As Integer)

    'prepayment and default headers
    Cells(2, 3).Value = g_waterfall_misc(scen, 1)      'default rate
    Cells(3, 3).Value = g_waterfall_misc(scen, 2)      'prepay rate
    Cells(2, 4).Value = g_waterfall_method(scen, 1)    'default method
    Cells(3, 4).Value = g_waterfall_method(scen, 2)    'prepay method

End Sub
```

EXHIBIT 15.14 Populating the prepayment and default header section

```
Sub Write_Matrix_Report_Package()

   'produce the summary matrix reports
   If g_out_matrix Then
         sum_principal = Range("TotalBeginPrincipal")
         Call Setup_Matrix_Workbook
         Call Write_Matrix_Reports(sum_principal)
         ActiveWorkbook.Save
         ActiveWorkbook.Close
   End If

End Sub
```

EXHIBIT 15.15 Main subroutine to produce the Matrix Report Package

Creating the Workbook for the Matrix Reports

Full of confidence with just having polished off the Waterfall Report Package, we can now move on to the Matrix Report Package.

The first step, as always, is to locate the proper template file and rename it to the designated name we entered on the Main Menu. We can accomplish this in two statements. The first using the Workbooks.Open command takes the file name that we construct using the pathway to the template file directory and the name of the template file itself. This is the target file to be opened. Once opened we can save it to a new name, the name we have designated for the output produced by this run of the model. We use the Activeworkbook.SaveAs command to accomplish this. See Exhibit 15.16.

We will add this code to the **"WriteSetUpOutputFiles"** module.

Writing the Matrix Reports

Having opened the template file and renamed it to the designated filename for the Matrix Report Package we are ready to begin writing the reports. We will place all the code that writes the Matrix Reports in its own separate module **"WriteMatrixReports."** See Exhibit 15.17.

There are a total of four Matrix Reports. To make our model more understandable to us and others, we have assigned each of the reports a name in the constants module. See Exhibit 15.18.

The first constant declaration tells the model how many Matrix Reports there currently are. The second assigns a unique numeric code to each of the reports but allows us to use a meaningful label for the report instead of just "6" or "4" or

```
Sub Setup_Matrix_Workbook()

   'Open the template file
   Workbooks.Open Filename:=g_pathway_template & g_template_matrix
   'Save as the designated report file name
   ActiveWorkbook.SaveAs Filename:=g_pathway_output & gfn_output_prefix & _
                    gfn_matrix_file

End Sub
```

EXHIBIT 15.16 Setting Up the Matrix Report workbook

```
Sub Write_Matrix_Reports(sum_principal)

   Call Write_Assumptions_Page

   For i_report = 1 To MATRIX_REPORTS

      If g_matrix_report(i_report) Then
         Select Case i_report
            Case Is = MATRIX_TENOR_REPORT:
                     Call Write_Matrix_Tenor_Report(sum_principal)
            Case Is = MATRIX_CFS_REPORT:
                     Call Write_Matrix_CFs_Report
            Case Is = MATRIX_CONDUIT_REPORT:
                     Call Write_Conduit_Financing_Performance
            Case Is = MATRIX_SELLER_INT_REPORT:
                     Call Write_Matrix_SellerInterest_Report
         End Select
         Call Load_Prepay_Levels       'loads the prepayment rates in the header
         Call Load_Default_Levels      'loads the default rates in the header
         Call Trim_Matrix_Report       'removes unused cells of the matrix
      Else
         Call Delete_UnSelected_Matrix_Report(i_report)
      End If

   Next i_report

End Sub
```

EXHIBIT 15.17   "Write_Matrix_Reports" subroutine

something equally obscure. These constants will allow us to establish loops that will run through the collection of these reports by cycling from 1 to MATRIX_REPORTS, and to select each of the reports by the assigned number of the constant statement.

In fact this is exactly what we are going to do!

We start the process by immediately filling in the Assumptions Page Report so that we can replicate the results if necessary. Then we set up a For...Next loop to cycle through each of the reports of the Martix Report Package.

We will first test to see if the report has been selected for inclusion in the package. If it has been selected, the **"g_matrix_report"** array location corresponding to this report will have been set to "TRUE." This occurred back when the model read our wishes from the Reports Menu.

In that there are three possible choices, we will use a Select Case statement based on the loop value of the For...Next loop. If the report has been selected, the program flow will reach the choice indicated by the value of the "i_report" counter of the loop. A subroutine specifically designed to populate that particular report will be called and the report written into the selected worksheet. The headers and matrix

```
'=============================================================
'Matrix Summary Report Package Constants
'=============================================================
Public Const MATRIX_REPORTS = 4                'total # of reports
Public Const MATRIX_TENOR_REPORT = 1
Public Const MATRIX_CFS_REPORT = 2
Public Const MATRIX_CONDUIT_REPORT = 3
Public Const MATRIX_SELLER_INT_REPORT = 4
```

EXHIBIT 15.18   Declaration of the global constants that support the Matrix Report Package

```
Sub Write_Matrix_Tenor_Report(sum_principal As Double)

    Sheets("Tenor").Select

    icol = 3
    For i_p = 1 To g_prepay_levels
        irow = 14
        For i_d = 1 To g_default_levels
            Cells(irow + 0, icol).Value = g_out_avg_life(i_p, i_d)
            Cells(irow + 1, icol).Value = g_out_fin_mat(i_p, i_d)
            Cells(irow + 2, icol).Value = g_out_mod_durat(i_p, i_d)
            Cells(irow + 3, icol).Value = g_out_mac_durat(i_p, i_d)
            Cells(irow + 4, icol).Value = g_out_amt_10yr(i_p, i_d)
            Cells(irow + 5, icol).Value = g_out_amt_10yr(i_p, i_d) / sum_principal
            irow = irow + 6
        Next i_d
        icol = icol + 1
    Next i_p

End Sub
```

EXHIBIT 15.19 This subroutine writes the contents of six arrays in the Tenor Report template worksheet in the Matrix Report file

prepayment and default values are then added to the report. If the report is not of the maximum size of ten prepayment speeds by ten default speeds, the unused positions are trimmed. See Exhibit 15.19.

The subroutine above is typical of the general form of those that will fill in the report templates of the Matrix Report Package.

This subroutine is used to produce the Matrix Tenor Report.

It populates all six positions of each of the matrix locations. The values by scenario are the average life, final maturity, modified duration, MacCauley duration, the dollar amount of the notes outstanding after ten years, and the percentage of those remaining notes are of the original issuance.

A Matrix Report Is Not Selected

In the case that a report is not selected we will want to delete its template from the Workbook. There's no point in having blank reports in the file and we don't want to give the false impression that the report failed to populate! To delete the unselected reports we merely need to identify them by number, link the number to the appropriate worksheet, and delete the worksheet. See Exhibit 15.20.

```
Sub Delete_UnSelected_Matrix_Report(i_report)

    Select Case i_report
        Case Is = MATRIX_TENOR_REPORT:       Sheets("Tenor").Delete
        Case Is = MATRIX_CFS_REPORT:         Sheets("Cashflows").Delete
        Case Is = MATRIX_CONDUIT_REPORT:     Sheets("SellerInterestPerformance").Delete
        Case Is = MATRIX_SELLER_INT_REPORT:  Sheets("SellerInterestPerformance").Delete
    End Select

End Sub
```

EXHIBIT 15.20 Subroutine that deletes unselected Matrix Summary Reports from the file

Here we can make use of those constants again. We set up a Select...Case statement to identify the report to be deleted and match the numeric value of the constant to the sheet in the workbook. We then simply delete it.

Finishing the Report

The last two things we have to do is to save the report and close the workbook. We accomplish this by the use of our trusty commands,

```
ActiveWorkbook.Save
```

```
ActiveWorkbook.Close
```

and we are done.

DELIVERABLES CHECKLIST

The VBA Knowledge Checklist items for this chapter are:

- Using the "ClearContents" method with the Range object to clear the contents but not the formulas or formatting from the cells of a Range.
- How to rename a worksheet using VBA commands: Sheets("CF-1").Name = new_name.
- How to set the calculation method of the Application object to manual from automatic. This blocks the worksheet caculation sequence until activated by the VBA code directly: Application.Calculation = xlCalculationManual.
- How to copy an existing worksheet and position it after a designated sheet of the workbook.
- How to copy an existing worksheet and position it after a designated sheet of the workbook.
- How to use a Select...Case statement inside of a For...Next loop to test whether a particular individual report has been selected for production by the program.
- How to create a set of public constants that label the reports of a report package so the code that selects them for productionis more transparent: Public Const MATRIX_CF_REPORT =3.
- How to change the color of a cell font based on the value of the output that will go in it. Cells(irow,icol).Font.ColorIndex = 3.
- Use the VBA command to open a workbook: Workbook.Open *filename:* = name_of_file.
- Use the VBA command to save a workbook: Workbook.Save *filename:* = name_of_file.

The Model Production Checklist items for this chapter are:

- Sequentially load the Cash Flow Waterfall spreadsheet with the scenario specific cash flows we have generated, and calculate the worksheet, producing the scenario results.

- A VBA subroutine to find the Cash Flow Waterfall Reports template file, open it, and save it to the designated output file name in the output directory.
- Create the variables and globals needed to hold the contents of each scenario that will be run through the Cash Flow Waterfall spreadsheet.
- Extract the entire contents of the cash flow waterfall on a scenario-by-scenario basis and save the results to a VBA array.
- Write a subroutine to reconfigure the Cash Flow Waterfall Spreadsheet to accommodate as many scenarios as necessary for this run of the model.
- Before writing the reports, populate the Assumption Page of the template file with the criteria of this model run.
- Direct the saved results in the VBA arrays into the Waterfall Report Package on a scenario by scenario basis with one worksheet replicating the contents of each scenario.
- Write a VBA subroutine to trim the Cash Flow Waterfall Report of unused lines.
- Have the report closed and saved automatically upon completion.
- Design a VBA subroutine to find the Matrix Reports template file, open it, and save it to the designated output file name in the output directory.
- Create the variables and globals needed to hold the contents of each scenario that will be run through the Cash Flow Waterfall spreadsheet.
- Extract selected summary results of the cash flow waterfall on a scenario-by-scenario basis and save the results to a VBA arrays that are name coded to each Matrix Report.
- Populate the four Matrix Reports, or be able to delete the unselected reports from the Matrix Report Package.
- Have the facility to trim each of the Matrix Reports of unused row and columns.
- Have the facility to trim each of the Matrix Reports of unused row and columns.

NEXT STEPS

In this chapter, the work of writing the code has come to an end for the moment.

We have built the Menu Support code, Collateral Selection code, the Cash Flow Calculation code, and, finally, the Results Reporting code.

Now it is time to stop building and start testing. Chapter 16, "Debugging the Model," will teach us the use of the VBA Debugger. We will correct any errors we have made while writing the code over the last eight chapters.

When we have a model that runs we will move on to the validation process in Chapter 17.

For now let us concentrate on the debugging process!

ON THE WEB SITE

The material for the Web site for this chapter is the model "MODEL_BASE_Chap15.xls." This model is compiled and will run. It contains the modules that allow it to populate the Excel spreadsheet with the cash flows, trigger the calculation of the worksheet, capture the results of the calculation of the waterfall, produce the Watrefall Report Package and produce the Summary Matrix Report Package.

The model includes the three new modules. There are also additional declarations of the global variables and constants in the **"A_Globals"** and **"A_Constants"** modules. The incremental modules added with this chapter's work are:

"LoadRunCaptureResults"—this module loads the waterfall spreadsheet with the cash flows of the current scenario, triggers it's calculation and captures the results loading them into VBA arrays for use by the subroutines in the modules below.

"WriteWaterfallReports"—this module opens the appropriate template file, renames and saves it, and writes the Waterfall Reports Package.

"WriteMatrixReports"—this module opens the appropriate template file, renames and saves it, and writes the Summary Matrix Report Package.

This chapter effectively ends the first phase of development of the model. We now have a fully functional model that will read a collateral file, error check and read all menu inputs, perform the collateral selection process and report the results, calculate the collateral cash flows, load the waterfall, calculate the results, capture the results, and produce the output report packages we selected!

## CHAPTER 16

Debugging the Model

OVERVIEW

Chapter 15 brought to a close the writing of VBA code (for a while only, until we add enhancements to the model in Chapter 19)!

We now have an Excel/VBA model of moderate size with all the initial development code complete. Just writing the code is only the easier half of the battle. We need to make sure that the VBA compiler can understand the code that we have written, and that it can translate it into a working piece of software.

To do this we will have to make sure we have abided by the rules of the VBA language. The VBA compiler is a sterner task master than any grammar school teacher you ever had. It is sublime in its indifference to your intentions. It can only assess your demonstrated actions when you have written the code it is now asked to peruse. It has a zero tolerance for deviation from the established regulations.

We have one friend to help us through this process. That is the VBA Editor and Debugger. The debugger is invaluable for quickly identifying the source and cause of the errors. It is an essential tool to getting your program in running order.

Even after the program runs, we are still probably not done! Humans, being fallible creatures that we are, often make mistakes. Miscommunications often occur; intentions are often not clearly conveyed. We may intend the model to perform a set of operations and find that the commands that we have written are causing it to do something else. Here again the VBA Debugger can come to our rescue.

The VBA Debugger allows us to examine our code statement by statement while it is running. We can spy on its every action. We can read the values of all of the variables and look into the nooks and crannies of every array if it is necessary! We can stop, restart, and stop the program again and again using a variety of commands and features.

Debugging programs can be a time-consuming and frustrating task. It is a skill that most people will rapidly improve upon with practice. The ironic thing about the use of the VBA Debugger and the debugging process is that the better you get at it, generally, the less you need to use it.

The debugger actually teaches everyone to write better VBA code because it will repeatedly highlight your errors. Being able to clearly see the mistakes you are making is a lot more than half the battle; it is, in my opinion, at least 75% of it. After the third, fourth, or fifth time a person is called to task by the debugger for the same error they get tired of making that mistake in a hurry.

The most important thing is to learn the basic commands selected for this chapter and apply them in a calm and deliberate manner. The more upset you allow yourself to get the longer *any* debugging exercise will take. There will be an advice section at the end of the chapter on what to do if you hit a wall and cannot make any more progress on your own. For now, learn the features and commands and study the examples. These examples will encompass 80 to 90% of the errors that you will make as a beginning modeler. Have patience and a little faith.

DELIVERABLES

VBA Language Knowledge Deliverables

The VBA Editor, VBA Debugger, and VBA language deliverables for this chapter are:

- How to compile a VBA program using the VBA Editor
- Basic instances of each of the four types of common errors
- Commands of the debugger
  - How to enter Break Mode
  - How to set breakpoints in the code
  - How to use the Data Tips function
  - How to use the Step Over and the Step Into commands
  - How to use the Step Out and Run to Cursor commands
  - How to use the Watch feature to check variable values
  - How to use the Immediate Window

Modeling Knowledge Deliverables

The modeling knowledge deliverables for this chapter are:

- The four types of programming errors: syntax, compile, runtime and logical errors
- How to debug a small sample program from scratch

UNDER CONSTRUCTION

Well, if there was ever anyone who deserved a day off we are they! After all the VBA code development of the last four chapters, we can take a break. The task now is to see if what we have written is correct!

The rest of the chapter will teach you how to run the VBA Debugger to check that our development efforts have been on target!

COMPILING THE MODEL

Having finished writing your code, you now wish to run it. To run the code you will first need to enter the VBA Editor by striking the "Alt+F11" keys simultaneously. Once in the VBA Editor you will need to compile the code you have written. See Exhibit 16.1.

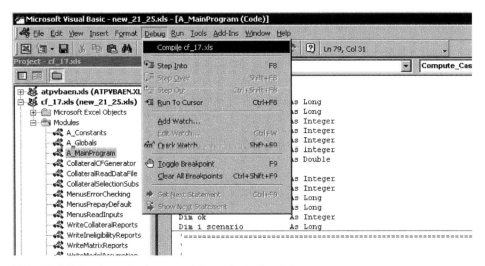

EXHIBIT 16.1   Compile Command from the Debug Menu

This is done in the following manner:

- Pull down the Debug Menu.
- Select the first line labeled "Compile" and the name of the project and select it. The VBA compiler will now attempt to compile the model for you.

If the word "Compile" and the name of the project is faint, then the model does not have any changes to its form that would require it to be recompiled.

At this point the VBA Debugger will begin to identify any errors it has detected in the model. The initial errors that it will address will be the first two types of errors—syntax errors and compile errors—we will talk about in the section immediately following "Types of VBA Errors." Once the program is satisfied that the model is in a sense grammatically correct, we can run the model and see if there are any of the other two types of errors: runtime errors and logical errors.

Before we can start to identify and fix our errors, it would be beneficial to better understand what we are about to encounter.

TYPES OF VBA ERRORS

This chapter will teach you how to identify the various kinds of errors you will encounter in your own and in others' VBA code. It will also familiarize you with the features of the VBA Editor that are particularly helpful in identifying the type of error and its possible resolution.

There are four basic types of errors:

1. Syntax errors—*always* caught at compile time.
2. Compile errors—*always* caught at compile time.

3. Runtime errors—Appear as you run the model and do not allow for its completion.
4. Logical errors—The model compiles, runs, and gives wrong answers. These can sometimes be the subtlest and most frustrating errors to correct. In a word, welcome to hell.

Syntax Errors

These errors are inevitably the results of typing mistakes, such as the misspelling of a VBA keyword, a variable name, a function or subroutine name, and so on. They are usually created at the time that you write your code. They are generally the most numerous of all errors, but they are also the easiest to fix. A quick way to eliminate a large number of syntax errors before you even start is to use the command Option Explicit at the top of each VBA module. Including this command at the top of every VBA module will have the effect of immediately informing you if you have any undeclared variables. Any variables not explicitly declared using "Dim," "Public," or "Constant" will be immediately shown as a syntax error. Using the Option Explicit command, any misspelled variable will not have a corresponding declaration statement attached to it and will be caught as a syntax error at compile time.

Compile Errors

These errors are the results of statements that VBA cannot correctly compile. For example, failure to properly declare variables or Redim variables, errors in assignment code, and missing end of block statements such as a For...Next loop without the Next will trigger a compile error. These errors can be more difficult to resolve than syntax errors for beginners.

Runtime Errors

Runtime errors are the results of expressions or statements that VBA cannot evaluate or execute even though they may be syntactically correct and may compile. These typically include such errors as invalid operations, invalid or mismatched procedure argument lists, or illegal mathematical operations. The classic example is division by zero. If the quantity in the divisor of an expression is unassigned or assumes a value of zero during model execution, a runtime errors will result. Another example of runtime errors are the overflow errors in which a variable declared as a Double is assigned to an Integer declared variable. Another is when a loop control variable is assigning values to an array and overruns the boundaries of the array dimension. We will show examples of these types of errors and the messages they produce later.

Logical Errors

Logical errors are the results of a programmer's errors in reasoning. The model is syntactically correct, the compiler can translate all the statements into compiled code, and the model runs successfully to completion—it just does not produce the desired or expected results. Symptoms include abbreviated runtimes, and incomplete or incorrect task completion. Possible examples in the model would be reports that

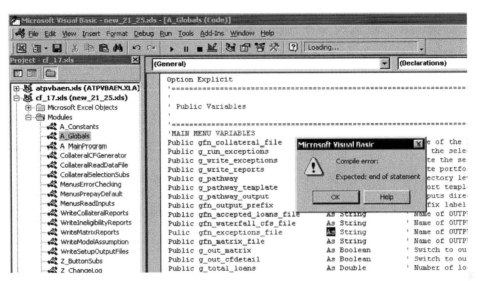

EXHIBIT 16.2   Syntax error created by misspelling the reserved word "Public" in the declaration of the global variable gfn_exceptions_file

have the right data in the wrong columns. These are the most difficult errors to find and correct, and where a solid knowledge of the VBA Debugger comes in most handy.

COMMON SYNTAX ERRORS

The following error in Exhibit 16.2 is an example of some common syntax errors.

Misspelling any VBA Reserved Word
   Misspelled reserved word **"Pulic"** for **"Public."** See Exhibit 16.2.

COMMON COMPILE ERRORS

Misspelling the Name of a Subroutine or Function in a Call Statement
   Subroutine name misspelled in **Call** statement (see Exhibit 16.3).

Redimensioning a Variable Incorrectly
   Original variable type declaration does not match **ReDim** type (see Exhibit 16.4).

Duplicate Declarations of Variables in the same Scope
   Duplicate variable declaration in the same scope (repeats the declaration of **icol**) (see Exhibit 16.5).

Arguments Mismatched between the Sub and the Call
   Call statement and **Sub** declaration have a different number of arguments. This is usually caused by simple carelessness. (See Exhibit 16.6)

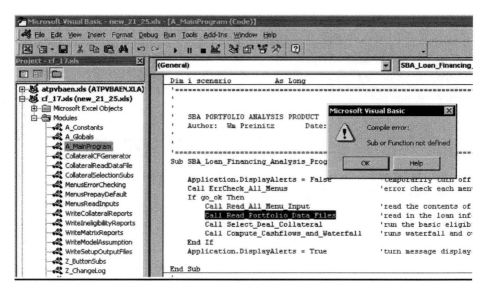

EXHIBIT 16.3 Compile error created by misspelling the name of the subroutine in the Call statement. The program searches to find a Sub by that name and fails

Missing Ending Statements for Decision and Looping Structures

This compile error was triggered because of a missing Next statement in a set of nested For...Next statements. This error will also be prompted by failing to close of Do...Until and Do...While looping statements. (See Exhibit 16.7.)

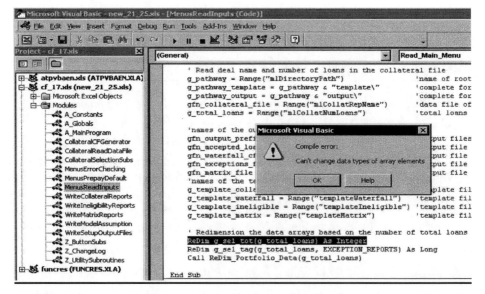

EXHIBIT 16.4 Compile error created by specifying a different data type in the ReDim of a variable than the data type of the original declaration of the variable

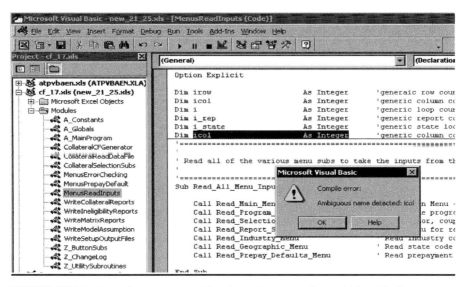

EXHIBIT 16.5 Compile error created by the declaration of a variable with the same name as another variable in the same scope of the declaration of the initial variable

Fortunately, we used labels at the end of each of the For . . . Next loops. These labels, i_period, i_default, and i_prepay, made it immediately apparent that the missing Next statement is attached to the For i_loans . . . Next loop.

HOW TO RUN THE VBA DEBUGGER

The next two types of errors—runtime errors and logical errors—are more difficult to isolate and fix. To be better equipped to address these errors, we need to learn how

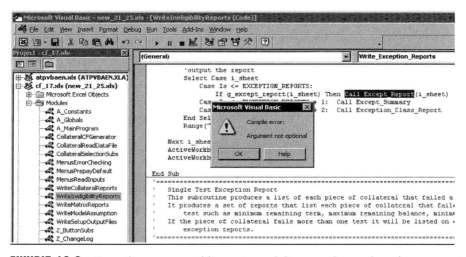

EXHIBIT 16.6 Compile error created by a mismatch between the number of arguments in the Call to the subroutine and the subroutine argument list specified when it was created

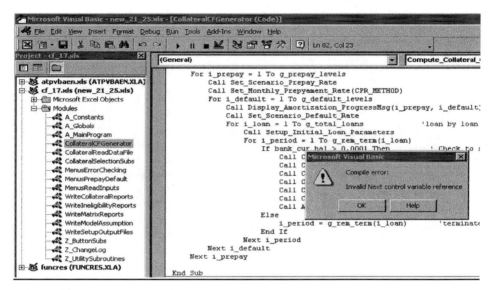

EXHIBIT 16.7   Compile error created by a missing Next statement

to use the debugger. The primary role of the VBA Debugger is to allow us to run the model in a predesignated manner and to be able to stop and start it at various points to examine the current state of variables and watch the flow control structures at work. Fortunately, the VBA Debugger is a powerful one, and a limited number of features will give us all the capacity that we need to find, understand, and fix our errors.

These features fall into two broad categories: the first are flow control features and the second are data examination features.

The features that we will look at are:

- Break Mode
- Setting Breakpoints
- Using Data Tips
- Step Into and Step Over Commands
- Step Out and Run to Cursor Commands
- Using the Watch Feature

Break Mode

The Break Mode is a feature that allows the programmer to single-step through his or her code. Single stepping allows you to view the execution of the model one step at a time. It allows you to see which branches are selected in logical choices and to examine the contents of variables and arrays as the model is executing. It allows you to modify variable values and to edit code that is not currently executing.

Entering Break Mode   There are five ways to enter into Break Mode:

1. If a runtime errors has already been generated, click the Debug button in the Error Dialog Box. You can also enter the Break Mode by entering it from

an Error Dialog Box. Whenever VBA encounters a runtime errors, the model execution is interrupted and an Error Dialog Box is displayed. There are generally four buttons: **Continue, End, Debug, and Help.** If you select the Debug option, it displays the VBA statement causing the runtime errors, opening up to the appropriate project and procedure. All debugging features are activated and the cursor is positioned at the point the error occurred.

2. Hit a previously set breakpoint. If you have already set breakpoints by the use of the "F9" key, the model will stop and enter Break Mode when the first of these are encountered. Remember our use of breakpoints when we were stepping through a recorded macro earlier, in Chapter 7.

3. Hitting a **STOP** command written in the VBA code. The breakpoint set by the "F9" key is in effect only for the current work session. A permanent breakpoint can be established through the entry of a **Stop** statement. The model will enter break mode upon encountering such a statement.

4. Use the **Debug|Step Into** command ("F8"). A procedure can be directly run from its source code by choosing **Debug|Step Into** command. VBA enters into Break Mode and starts at the top of the procedure.

5. Press "Esc" or "Ctrl+Break" simultaneously to interrupt the model while it is running. You can enter Break Mode by interrupting the code execution by pressing the "Esc" key or by pressing the "Ctrl+Break" key combination. VBA will display an Error Dialog Box; select Debug and the procedure currently executing will be displayed.

Leaving Break Mode   To leave Break Mode and continue executing your model at full speed, issue the **Run|Continue** command (F5). The code will continue to run unless it subsequently encounters a breakpoint or a **Stop** statement. Alternatively you can end all execution by issuing the **Run|Reset** command. All execution stops and all variables lose their values.

Setting and Releasing Breakpoints

Setting Breakpoints   Breakpoints are one of the simplest things that you can use in a debug session. A breakpoint is a code roadblock; when the execution of the model reaches the position of a breakpoint set in the code, all code execution stops and the model enters Break Mode.

Breakpoints can only be set on lines of executable code. Breakpoints appear as bright red bans across the Code Window. When the program cursor reaches them, it overlays a portion of the breakpoint line with the cursor line in yellow. See Exhibit 16.8.

You can set a breakpoint in one of two ways:

1. Put the cursor on a line of code and hit the "F9" button.
2. Click the cursor in the left hand margin of the Code Window.

Removing Breakpoints   To remove breakpoints, reverse the process by which you set them. Put the cursor on an executable statement and hit "F9." Click on the red circle in the left-hand margin of the Code Window. To remove all the breakpoints in

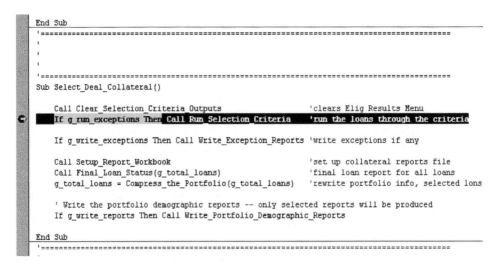

```
End Sub
'==============================================================================
'
'
'
'==============================================================================
Sub Select_Deal_Collateral()

    Call Clear_Selection_Criteria_Outputs              'clears Elig Results Menu
    If g_run_exceptions Then Call Run_Selection_Criteria   'run the loans through the criteria

    If g_write_exceptions Then Call Write_Exception_Reports 'write exceptions if any

    Call Setup_Report_Workbook                         'set up collateral reports file
    Call Final_Loan_Status(g_total_loans)              'final loan report for all loans
    g_total_loans = Compress_the_Portfolio(g_total_loans)  'rewrite portfolio info, selected lons

    ' Write the portfolio demographic reports -- only selected reports will be produced
    If g_write_reports Then Call Write_Portfolio_Demographic_Reports

End Sub
'==============================================================================
```

EXHIBIT 16.8   Breakpoint that had been set is now reached by the program cursor. The program is about to execute the VBA statement upon which the yellow cursor rests

a model: hit the following key combination "Ctl+Shift+F9." Or select off the Debug Menu. See Exhibit 16.9.

Using Data Tips

At times it is only necessary to quickly check the contents or value of an expression, calculation, or variable. The VBA Debugger gives us a fast and easy way to do this. Data Tips is a feature that automatically activates when we place the cursor

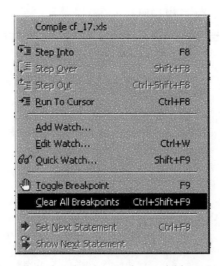

EXHIBIT 16.9   Removing all the breakpoints in the model by using the Debug Option of the VBA Editor

```
' ======================================================================
'
'
'
'
' ======================================================================
Sub Select_Deal_Collateral()

    Call Clear_Selection_Criteria_Outputs              'clears E]
▷   If g_run_exceptions Then Call Run_Selection_Criteria   'run the

    If g_write_exceptions Then Call Write_Exception_Reports 'write exc
        ┌─────────────────────────┐
        │ g_write_exceptions = True │
        └─────────────────────────┘
    Call Setup_Report_Workbook                         'set up co
    Call Final_Loan_Status(g_total_loans)              'final loa
    g_total_loans = Compress_the_Portfolio(g_total_loans)  'rewrite ϝ

    ' Write the portfolio demographic reports -- only selected report:
    If g_write_reports Then Call Write_Portfolio_Demographic_Reports
```

EXHIBIT 16.10 Using the Data Tips feature to check the value of the boolean variable g_write_exceptions, the variable is shown to have a value of True

over any variable. That is the only operation that is required. At the point of the cursor, a small box will appear and the value of the variable will be displayed. See Exhibit 16.10.

Step Into and Step Over Commands

Step Into Command   Once you have entered Break Mode, you can employ the Step Into command to examine the execution of your model on a statement-by-statement basis. You can execute this command by using the "F8" key. Each time you strike it will advance the execution of a single command. The Step Into command will execute each statement sequentially. This allows you to examine the values of the variables and the model settings at each point along the way. It also pauses the model in between steps so that watches or breakpoints can be set on individual variables or breakpoints set further along the execution path.

Sometimes the Step Into command is too much of a good thing.

You may be stepping through your code and encounter a function or subroutine call. You are fairly certain this is not the source of the problem. To avoid entering the procedure with the Step Into command, you can bypass it by using the Step Over command.

Step Over Command   The **Step Over** command will execute the procedure at normal speed and stop upon exit from it. See Exhibit 16.11 as an example.

In Exhibit 16.12 we have just finished executing the "Clear_Selection_Criteria_Outputs" subroutine. We know that the "Run_Selection_Criteria" subroutine is error-free. We do not need to step into this long and involved subroutine, but we would like to proceed without setting any more breakpoints. We can use the Step Over command to execute this subroutine. After it has finished, it will transfer the cursor to the next line where we can continue.

```
Sub Select_Deal_Collateral()

    Call Clear_Selection_Criteria_Outputs                  'clears Elig Results Menu
  ⇨ If g_run_exceptions Then Call Run_Selection_Criteria    'run the loans through the criteria

    If g_write_exceptions Then Call Write_Exception_Reports 'write exceptions if any

    Call Setup_Report_Workbook                             'set up collateral reports file
    Call Final_Loan_Status(g_total_loans)                  'final loan report for all loans
    g_total_loans = Compress_the_Portfolio(g_total_loans)  'rewrite portfolio info, selected lo
```

EXHIBIT 16.11   Getting ready to use the Step Over command on the "Run_Selection_Criteria" subroutine call

In Exhibit 16.13 you can see that the model has just run the subroutine "Run_Selection_Criteria" and the cursor has transferred to the following line without entering the subroutine. This command can save you lots and lots of time if you use it judiciously to bypass parts of your code that you know (or at least strongly suspect) are error free.

Shortcut Keys   Almost all of the VBA Debugger commands have shortcut key combinations so you do not need to spend time pulling down the menus. Shortcuts to **Step Into** and **Step Over** are as follows:

- To execute the Step Into command the shortcut is the "F8" key
- To execute the Step Over command the shortcut is the "Shift+F8" key combination.

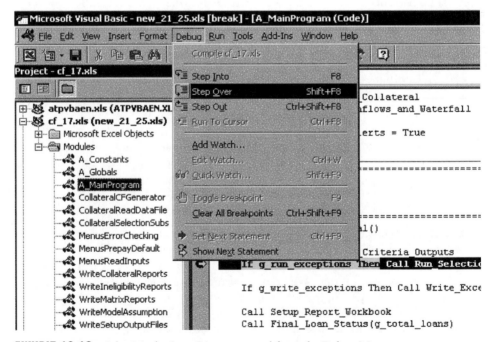

EXHIBIT 16.12   Selecting the Step Over command from the Debug Menu

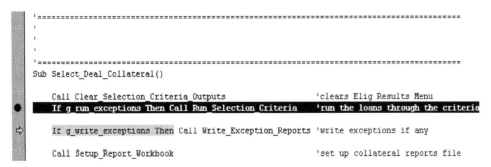

EXHIBIT 16.13 After the Step Over command has executed

Step Out and Run To Cursor Commands

Step Out Command The Step Out command is used to execute the rest of a procedure that you have stepped into and then stop at the first statement outside of the procedure upon completion. To select it, use Debug|Step Out from the menu, or the shortcut key combination "Ctrl+Shift+F8."

This is a great command to use if you had suspicions about part of a subroutine or function, but, having found no errors, need to move on. It stops immediately after it leaves its current subroutine or function and does not advance the code execution any further. Thus you can proceed onward in manageable steps without running every statement in each subroutine that you enter.

Run To Cursor Command This command will allow the model to run at full speed until it hits the current cursor position and then stops. To select it, use Debug|Run to Cursor from the menu, or use the shortcut key "Ctrl+F8."

This command is sort of like setting a temporary breakpoint without all the mess, or the need to remove the breakpoint later. It just runs until it gets to where you are looking at the code and stops!

Watch Feature Sometimes single stepping through your code will not immediately identify the source of the error. When calculation or branching decisions are not being performed properly, the cause may be variables that are improperly set or have been tampered with in other parts of the model. The Watch Window allows you to continually monitor the value of a variable or to pause the execution of the variable when its value changes. In the Code Window, select the text containing the variable, calculation, or expression to monitor. Choose the Debug|Add Watch command and Add Watch dialog box will appear As shown in Exhibits 16.14 and 16.15, respectively.

If you have selected a text piece, it will appear in the **Expression** edit box, this is what will be watched. Specify the **Watch Type** using the radio buttons.

Editing a Watch Expression or Deleting a Watch Expression You can edit any existing **Watch** expression by selecting the **Debug|Edit Watch** command and by then typing into the **Expression** window of the dialog box any changes you want to make. You can also click directly on the variable watch name in the window.

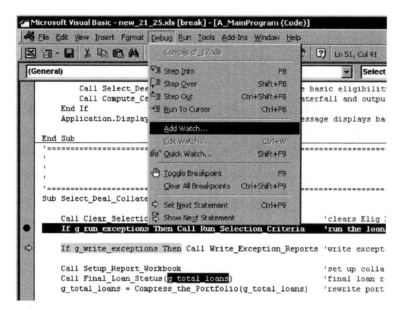

EXHIBIT 16.14   Selecting the Add Watch command from the Debug menu

To delete a **Watch** expression select the **Debug|Edit Watch** command, then click the Delete button to remove the expression from the Watch Window. You can also right click and delete the watch from the menu.

Viewing the Values or Contents of a Watched Variable   Using the right mouse button, click the pop-up menu from the watch line itself. See Exhibit 16.16.

In Exhibit 16.15 and 16.16 we "Watch" the value of the variable g_total_loans, a global variable that holds the count of the number of loans in the portfolio.

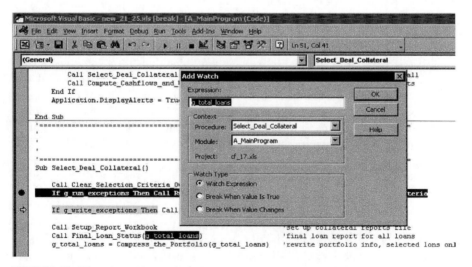

EXHIBIT 16.15   The Add Watch dialog box used to set a Watch condition

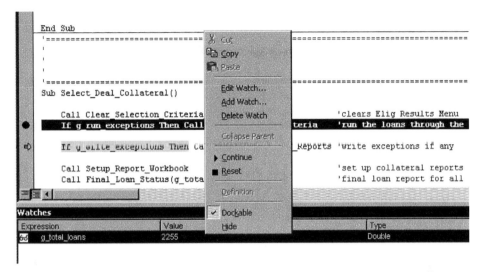

EXHIBIT 16.16   Viewing the value of a watched variable

Using Watch to View Vectors and Arrays   The contents of entire array, or any element of it, can be viewed using the **Watch** command. First select the array name, but not the bracketed indices (otherwise you we see just that value.)

The initial display of an array will appear in the form of the second entry in the Watches window below. There are several things to note:

- A small box has appeared to the left of the array name. It contains a "+" sign. That sign is an indication that this variable has additional information that is not displayed at the moment. See Exhibit 16.17. To display this information simply put the cursor on the box and click. If the array is a vector, a one-dimensional array, a column of entries will appear under the original array name. Each of these entries will display the value of the locations of the array. Each entry will have the index of the array location displayed.

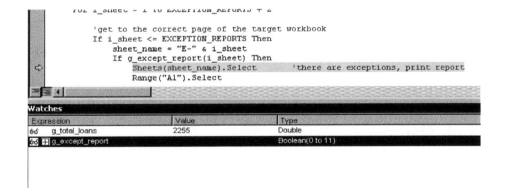

EXHIBIT 16.17   Initial display of an array in the Watches Window

```
'get to the correct page of the target workbook
If i_sheet <= EXCEPTION_REPORTS Then
    sheet_name = "E-" & i_sheet
    If g_except_report(i_sheet) Then
        Sheets(sheet_name).Select        'there are exceptions, print report
        Range("A1").Select
```

Watches		
Expression	Value	Type
g_total_loans	2255	Double
g_except_report		Boolean(0 to 11)
g_except_report(0)	False	Boolean
g_except_report(1)	True	Boolean
g_except_report(2)	True	Boolean
g_except_report(3)	False	Boolean
g_except_report(4)	True	Boolean
g_except_report(5)	True	Boolean
g_except_report(6)	False	Boolean
g_except_report(7)	True	Boolean
g_except_report(8)	True	Boolean
g_except_report(9)	False	Boolean
g_except_report(10)	False	Boolean
g_except_report(11)	True	Boolean

EXHIBIT 16.18   Display of the elements of a one dimensional array

- If the array is a two-dimensional array, a list of the elements of the first dimension will be displayed. Each array element will also have an accompanying small box with a "+" in it. Clicking on the box again will display the second dimension elements of the array and their values. There is an example of this in Exhibit 16.18.
- You can see that the **Watch** window also displays the dimensions of the array in the variable type in the **Type** column.

Note the small box to the left of the array name in the Watches Window. If it contains a "+" it means additional information can be displayed about this variable. In this case, the variable g_exception_report is a Boolean array that tells us which of the Ineligible Collateral Reports are selected for reporting purposes. We will now click on the "+" symbol to display the values of the array in a list. If the array is multidimensional, the next level of the array will also contain "+" in the boxes next to the array name. You can click on these in turn to display the next level of information. See Exhibit 16.18 for an example of this expanded listing format for the "g_exception_report" array showing each value of all the elements of the array.

In Exhibit 16.18, The Watch display for the "g_exception_report" array has now been expanded to display its individual members. It is a Boolean type variable with a dimension of (0 to 11). The 0th, 3rd, 6th, 9th, and 10th elements are "False" all the others are "True."

RUNTIME ERRORS

We have familiarized ourselves with the first two kinds of errors: syntax and compile errors. Next we looked at the core functionality of the VBA Debugger and its commands. We are now ready to move on to runtime errors.

Runtime errors are like the old fashioned jack-in-the-box. You start the program running and all is going along well for a while and then *wham*! You find yourself in

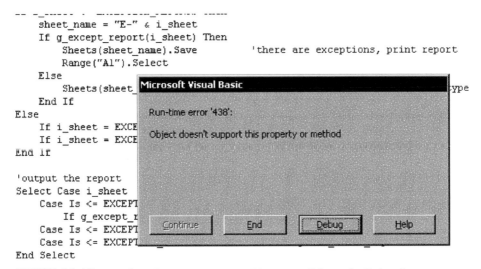

```
     sheet_name = "E-" & i_sheet
     If g_except_report(i_sheet) Then
          Sheets(sheet_name).Save            'there are exceptions, print report
          Range("A1").Select
     Else
          Sheets(sheet_                                                    ype
     End If
Else
     If i_sheet = EXCE
     If i_sheet = EXCE
End If

'output the report
Select Case i_sheet
     Case Is <= EXCEPT
          If g_except_r
     Case Is <= EXCEPT
     Case Is <= EXCEPT
End Select
```

EXHIBIT 16.19   Display of a Runtime errors. You now click on the Debug button to display the screen in Exhibit 16.20

Break Mode in the middle of the VBA Debugger with a message window displayed. An example is shown in Exhibits 16.19 and 16.20.

Exhibits 16.19 and 16.20 show what happens when you encounter a Runtime errors. Wham! Bam! Surprise! What just happened? Click on the "Debug" button to see the VBA statement that caused the problem. This will display the location of the error that caused the problem. In this case, in Exhibits 16.19 and 16.20, we are attempting to apply a Method to an Object that is not supported by the Object. The Method "Save" cannot be applied to the Object "Sheets." You can save an entire Workbook but not an individual worksheet within the Workbook!

Common Runtime Errors   The list below will account for more than 90% of the common runtime errors a beginning modeler will encounter.

```
'Customize the workbook for the exception reports
For i_sheet = 1 To EXCEPTION_REPORTS + 2

    'get to the correct page of the target workbook
    If i_sheet <= EXCEPTION_REPORTS Then
        sheet_name = "E-" & i_sheet
        If g_except_report(i_sheet) Then
            Sheets(sheet_name).Save        'there are exceptions, print report
            Range("A1").Select
        Else
            Sheets(sheet_name).Delete        'there are no exceptions of this type
        End If
    Else
        If i_sheet = EXCEPTION_REPORTS + 1 Then Sheets("E-ALL").Select
        If i_sheet = EXCEPTION_REPORTS + 2 Then Sheets("E-SUM").Select
```

EXHIBIT 16.20   After the Debug button is clicked

Code	Message	Cause
6	Overflow	Value of variable exceeds limits of variable **Type**. Most common cause is a runaway loop counter with a Type of Integer. The number of loop iterations continues until it exceeds the value limit of the Integer.
7	**Out of Memory**	Memory used by model has exceeded machine capacity.
11	**Division by zero**	The denominator of a division calculation equals zero.
13	**Type mismatch**	Model tries to assign the value of one type of variable into another where there is no compatibility such as String to Double.
53	**File not found**	Model tries to open a file that is not at the pathway location it is trying. Usually it is a misspelling or ordering of the pathway components.
70	**Permission denied**	Trying to open a protected file.
76	**Path not found**	See 53 above.
438	**Class doesn't support this property or method.**	You are trying to perform a method against an object that does not exist. See above example with Sheets (Exhibit 16.19).

Code	Solution
6	This is usually the result of an ending condition not being met in the loop. The loop goes on and on and on and the counter goes higher and higher and never stops. This happens more with Do...While and Do...Until loops where there is no fixed end to the loop as in For...Next loops. This can also occur if you try to assign the value of a variable typed as Double into an Integer variable. If the value of the Double is greater than the limits of the Integer you will get an "Overflow" message.
7	Try to **ReDim** or **Erase** large arrays that you are using.
11	This is usually a careless error although sometimes not. Usually the variable in the denominator has not been initialized properly. Other conditions where this occurs are when the model works correctly but there is no check for outlying cases. One such case might occur in this model if a selection criterion were entered that deselected all loans in the portfolio. The portfolio balance would be zero and there would be no cash flows. All calculations that used the portfolio balance as a denominator would generate this error.
13	Model tries to assign the value of one type of variable into another where there is no compatibility such as String to Double.
53	Check for misspelling or ordering of the pathway components. If that doesn't work, see if the pathway and directories actually *do* exist. Adjust accordingly!
70	Change the protection on the file.
76	Check the values of the string variables you are using in the file open statements.
438	Check online help for a listing of compatible objects and methods.

LOGICAL ERRORS

Logical errors are errors where the VBA model does exactly what we have asked it to, with one caveat, it is not doing what we intended it to do.

This is the modern version of "Don't shoot the messenger!"

Logical errors occur when you have given the model instructions to do something, and the results you expected are not what has actually happened. They may be conceptual, or almost annoyingly clerical. Let us look at both types.

An *If ... Then ... Else* Test Fails to Perform as Expected

In the first example we want to highlight in the Seller Interest Summary Matrix Report those cells that have losses to the Seller Interest. To really make them stand out, we are going to change the color combination of the cell from a light yellow background with black font to a red background with a bright yellow font.

To effect this change we add the code in Exhibit 16.21.

We run the model and get the rather confusing pattern we see on the page following the code sample.

Even at first glance we know something is wrong!

If we look at Exhibit 16.22, which displays the first 15 cell values for the prepayment and default combinations, we see a discontinuous pattern. This is unexpected. The prepayment and default methods we are using are linear scaled phenomena and should not produce the kind of spotty results we are seeing. When we examine the individual cells in more detail, we find that there are cells that are displayed with a

```
Sub Write_Conduit_Financing_Performance()

    Sheets("ConduitNotePerformance").Select
    icol = 3
    For i_p = 1 To g_prepay_levels
        irow = 14
        For i_d = 1 To g_default_levels
            Cells(irow + 0, icol).Value = _
                g_out_cond_repay(i_p, i_d) + g_out_cond_debt_service
                (i_p, i_d)
            Cells(irow + 1, icol).Value = g_out_cond_repay(i_p, i_d)
                Cells(irow + 2, icol).Value = g_out_cond_debt_service
                (i_p, i_d)
            Cells(irow + 3, icol).Value = g_out_cond_sol(i_p, i_d)
            Cells(irow + 4, icol).Value = g_out_cond_cover(i_p, i_d)
            If g_out_cond_irr(i_p, i_d) <> 999999# Then
                Cells(irow + 5, icol).Value = g_out_cond_irr(i_p, i_d)
                Else
                Cells(irow + 5, icol).Value = "NA"
            End If
            'highlite if the severity of loss is greater than 0%
            If g_out_cond_sol(i_p, i_d) > 0# Then
                Cells(irow + 3, icol).Font.ColorIndex = 3
                Cells(irow + 3, icol).Font.Bold = True
            End If
            irow = irow + 6
        Next i_d
        icol = icol + 1
    Next i_p

End Sub
```

EXHIBIT 16.21 Code that changes the color pattern of the cells if the loss to the Conduit is greater than 0%

Summary Matrix Report #3
Conduit Note Paydown

Total P&I Payments
Principal Repayments
Debt Service Paid
Severity of Principal Loss
Coverage Ratio
Internal Rate of Return

Default Levels	PSA Prepayment Methodology				
	1	2	3	4	5
	100.00%	150.00%	200.00%	250.00%	300.00%
1	589,246,379	573,228,286	560,822,449	551,139,678	543,479,813
	466,849,358	466,849,358	466,849,358	466,849,358	466,849,358
100.00%	122,397,021	106,378,927	93,973,090	84,290,319	76,630,455
PSA	0.000%	0.000%	0.000%	0.000%	0.000%
	32.85%	29.52%	26.88%	24.73%	22.96%
	3.750%	3.750%	3.750%	3.750%	3.750%
2	586,623,499	571,107,528	559,079,886	549,680,385	542,230,682
	466,849,358	466,849,358	466,849,358	466,849,358	466,849,358
200.00%	119,774,141	104,258,169	92,230,528	82,831,026	75,381,324
PSA	0.000%	0.000%	0.000%	0.000%	0.000%
	31.91%	28.72%	26.18%	24.12%	22.42%
	3.750%	3.750%	3.750%	3.750%	3.750%
3	584,064,376	569,036,126	557,375,596	548,309,189	541,064,067
	466,849,358	466,849,358	466,849,358	466,849,358	466,849,358
300.00%	117,215,018	102,186,768	90,526,238	81,459,831	74,214,709
PSA	0.000%	0.000%	0.000%	0.000%	0.000%
	31.00%	27.93%	25.50%	23.51%	21.87%
	3.750%	3.750%	3.750%	3.750%	3.750%

EXHIBIT 16.22   Code that changes the color pattern of the cells if the loss to the Credit Provider is greater than 0%

red font schema that have a displayed value for the loss number of 0.000%. This labeling should occur only when there is a loss greater than 0.0%. In addition, we know that the loss for these cells cannot possibly be greater than 0.0% because there are positive Coverage Ratios associated with each of the cells!

How can this be?

The answer is that the test for "losses greater than 0%" is not strict enough.

Occasionally when VBA reads values from an Excel cell, it will pick up values that are extremely small numerical values when they should read zero. The best manner to address this phenomenon is to test that and will also encompass vanishingly small, and economically meaningless losses, of say 0.000000000000234%. We need to change the threshold value of the test in the VBA code to something very small and yet larger than the trace values that are appearing. The test is then set to 0.0000000001 and the following results are obtained. The code change is shown in Exhibit 16.23.

The pattern is now correct, only those cells with values of 0.000001% are now displayed.

The corrected report is in Exhibit 16.24.

```
'highlite if the severity of loss is greater than 0%
If g_out_cond_sol(i_p, i_d) > 0.0000000001 Then
    Cells(irow + 3, icol).Font.ColorIndex = 3
    Cells(irow + 3, icol).Font.Bold = True
End If
```

EXHIBIT 16.23   Correct to the test for the Severity of Loss number

Failure of a Flow Control Loop

Another class of logical errors is triggered by incorrectly designated flow control. These errors are those in which all the commands are correct individually, but the sequence of execution is incorrect or incomplete. See Exhibit 16.25.

An obvious error of this type would be to fail to terminate a loop counter correctly, or to hit an Exit...For or an Exit...Sub at the wrong point. Here, without the Exit...For, the irow value will always be 15 and therefore the final maturity value will always be 3.75.

Summary Matrix Report #3
Conduit Note Paydown

Total P&I Payments
Principal Repayments
Debt Service Paid
Severity of Principal Loss
Coverage Ratio
Internal Rate of Return

Default Levels	PSA Prepayment Methodology				
	1	**2**	**3**	**4**	**5**
	100.00%	150.00%	200.00%	250.00%	300.00%
1	589,246,379	573,228,286	560,822,449	551,139,678	543,479,813
	466,849,358	466,849,358	466,849,358	466,849,358	466,849,358
100.00%	122,397,021	106,378,927	93,973,090	84,290,319	76,630,455
PSA	0.000%	0.000%	0.000%	0.000%	0.000%
	32.85%	29.52%	26.88%	24.73%	22.96%
	3.750%	3.750%	3.750%	3.750%	3.750%
2	586,623,499	571,107,528	559,079,886	549,680,385	542,230,682
	466,849,358	466,849,358	466,849,358	466,849,358	466,849,358
200.00%	119,774,141	104,258,169	92,230,528	82,831,026	75,381,324
PSA	0.000%	0.000%	0.000%	0.000%	0.000%
	31.91%	28.72%	26.18%	24.12%	22.42%
	3.750%	3.750%	3.750%	3.750%	3.750%
3	584,064,376	569,036,126	557,375,596	548,309,189	541,064,067
	466,849,358	466,849,358	466,849,358	466,849,358	466,849,358
300.00%	117,215,018	102,186,768	90,526,238	81,459,831	74,214,709
PSA	0.000%	0.000%	0.000%	0.000%	0.000%
	31.00%	27.93%	25.60%	23.51%	21.87%
	3.750%	3.750%	3.750%	3.750%	3.750%
	591,515,560	566,055,163	555,709,021	546,904,128	539,855,028

EXHIBIT 16.24   Corrected report, the bug is dead! We now know a true zero, rather than a false zero, is displayed

```
For i_month = 360 to 1 Step -1
  If Cells(i_month, icol).Value > .00000001 Then
      final_mat_months = i_month
  Endif
Next i_month
final_maturity = final_mat_months/12.0
```

EXHIBIT 16.25   Final maturity bug

In this example a For...Next loop is written to count backwards from the bottom of an Excel spreadsheet column that contains the principal outstanding of the Notes. It is to stop when it finds the first Cell with a value greater than 0.00000001. This Cell will mark the end of the cash flow stream. It will then take the value of the cell with the last cash flow and divide it by 12 to find the actual final maturity.

The problem is that no matter what happens, the final maturity is always 0.0825. The number 0.0825 is the equivalent to 1 month. All final maturities equal 1 month! Why?

As the loop decrements, it will at some point find the first cell location with a value greater than 0.0000001. Let us say that it occurs in i_month = 185. The variable final_mat_months would then have a value of 185. If we were to calculate the value of final_maturity with that value it would be a respectable 15.42 years. However, the loop has not met its stopping criteria so it continues to run and in the next period the value of i_month is reset to 184, because if anything the value of Cells(i_month,icol) must now be greater (it is, after all, the principal balance of the pool 1 month earlier).

This process continues until the counter reaches the value of 1 then the loop stops. At this point, the value of the final_mat_months variable is also 1.

The value of the variable final_maturity is therefore always equal to 1/12 or 0.0825.

The fix is fairly straightforward. If we add an Exit...For statement inside of the If...Then test we will immediate terminate the loop. The value of final_mat_months will be 185 if we assume the values of the previous example. The revised code is in Exhibit 16.26.

A Runaway Train

Another example of a combination of a syntax error and a logical error is shown in Exhibit 16.27. The Main Program starts to run and never, ever, ever stops. You break into the program and use Data Tips to read the value of the variable g_default in subroutine "XYZ." The value is 187,366! Why?

```
For  i_month = 360 to 1 Step -1
  If Cells(i_month, icol).Value > .00000001 Then
      final_mat_months = i_month
      Exit For           'code now breaks out of the loop with correct ending month
Endif
Next i_month
final_maturity = final_mat_months/12.0
```

EXHIBIT 16.26   Final Maturity bug fixed!

```
'=============================================================
Public g_default  As Integer  'number of maximum default cases
'=============================================================
Sub Main_Program
  g_defaults = 0
  Do While g_defaults < 100
    Call XYZ_process
  Loop
End Sub
'=============================================================
Sub XYZ_process
  g_default = g_default + 1
End Sub
'=============================================================
```

EXHIBIT 16.27   This Do While loop will never stop, why?

The variable being tested for the loop terminus is g_defaults, the variable being incremented inside of "XYZ" is g_default, (no "s" on the end). The value of g_defaults will always be zero. It is not being reset.

The fix is to add the Option Explicit statement above the declaration for g_default. It will immediately tell you that the variable g_defaults is undeclared and the problem will be solved!

Parting Admonitions and Advice!

While this chapter seeks to illuminate you as to the most common errors you may encounter, it is certain that you will create things outside the scope of this limited discussion.

With error checking, a good set of rules are the following, to be applied in order, (if feasible):

1. **Stay calm!** Emotion effects perception, anger is the worst! Do not get mad at the compiler, it cannot do anything other than what it is doing—despite all appearances to the contrary the compiler/model/code/product is NOT out to get you personally. The angrier you get, the more you will be unable to focus. Remember most errors are usually simple to see if you take the time to look in a calm collected manner.
2. **Walk away!** (For a while anyway . . . sometimes you will see the problem immediately if you just take a break away from your current framework). This is such a simple tactic and yet many times, people lock horns with a problem and just will not let go. Walk to the bathroom, splash water on your face, then come back and try again. If you cannot do that, then simply push the chair back and stop looking at the screen for at least two minutes. If you get agitated and cannot wait that long, then you really need a *longer* break.
3. **Find help, better yet, step someone else through the problem.** It is *incredible* how quickly this works. Even if the other person does not know VBA and you are explaining just the function of the code, it forces you to verbalize every step. You will find that it's quite edifying to do so. Explaining a process to someone uninvolved makes you rethink it from scratch and frequently, this is just the time you need to unlock the problem.

DELIVERABLES CHECKLIST

The VBA Knowledge Checklist items for this chapter are:

- How to use the Debug=>Compile command in the VBA Editor
- How to run the debugger by entering Break Mode
- The five ways to enter Break Mode: (1) Clicking the "Debug" button on a runtime errors message, (2) hitting a breakpoint, (3) hitting a Stop command, (4) using the Debug|Step Into command, and (5) interrupting the model run using the Esc key or by pressing "Ctl+Break."
- How to leave Break Mode. Hit F5 button of the Run|Continue command on the Debug menu. Alternatively, you can hit Run|Reset to stop the program and initialize everything back to start
- How to set and release Breakpoints
- Use of the Data Tips feature
- Use of the Step Into, Step Over, and Step Out commands,
- Use of the Run To Cursor command
- How to use the Watch feature. How to add or delete a variable from Watch
- How to expand multidimensional arrays in Watch to check all values
- How to identify and fix the eight most common Runtime errors

The Model Knowledge Checklist items for this chapter are:

- Definition of the four types of VBA errors: syntax, compile, runtime, and logical errors
- How to recognize a syntax errors: variable misspelling and so on
- How to recognize a compile time error: Subs of Functions not defined, incorrect variable Type declarations, ReDim errors, duplicate variable declarations, argument list mismatches, errors in looping statements
- How to identify some common causes of failures of If . . . Then . . . Else . . . EndIf statements
- How to debug basic report testing and formatting errors
- The three causes of logical errors: carelessness, fatigue, and time pressure
- Examples of errors when using Do . . . While loops

NEXT STEPS

You should now have a solid understanding of the basic features and operations of the VBA Debugger. This will be especially important in your understanding of Chapter 17, "Validating the Model." We hope that the model code is now error free and we will seek to devise ways of testing this hypothesis.

We will start with a single loan. The first task will be to replicate the 0% prepayment, 0% default cash flows of a nonseasoned loan. We will next introduce seasoning. Finally we will seek to replicate the cash flows of single and multiple loans under several different prepayment and default conditions. As a check to each of these processes, we use Excel to explicitly generate independent cash flows under matching conditions of prepayment and default scenario conditions.

In Chapter 18, "Running the Model," we will run the model. If we have any questions regarding the results we may have to use the debugger again. In Chapter 19, "Building Additional Capabilities," we will expand the features and capacity of the model. Here we will be introducing new code to the process. A number of useful display features will be added as well as an extension of the data file reading capabilities.

It is highly recommended that you complete the debugging exercises at the end of the chapter. Try first to complete the task without reference to the Hints List. If you get stuck, go to the Hints List and try to work through the problem with their help.

Remember, the more you practice, the better and faster you will get.

Stay calm, work diligently, and remember the examples of the chapter.

ON THE WEB SITE

There is no material for this chapter on the Web site.

PART

Six

Testing, Use, and Deployment

## CHAPTER 17

Validating the Model

OVERVIEW

We have now completed the initial stage of model building. Should we immediately run the model for all it's worth as our next stop? Nope. Strange at it may seem, it might be a good idea to test the model before we start putting its output in front of everyone. This way we can save ourselves from some potentially embarrassing moments.

The validation process will be directed against the three main functions of the model, the collateral selection process, the cash flow generation process, and the performance of the waterfall structure. To make sure that these are working properly we will also need to do some testing of the menu support code and the code that reads the collateral data file into the model.

In the first phase, we will check that the selection criteria we have entered into the model are being accepted, transferred into VBA variables, and being applied in the selection process subroutines correctly.

The second phase of the validation effort will involve some straightforward tests of the amortization logic. We can also construct a trace function in VBA to print out the loan-by-loan amortization schedules. The output file for that process can be spot-checked against the Public Securities Administration handbook results.

The last phase of the validation effort will be to examine the function of the Excel cash flow waterfall spreadsheet. This will demonstrate, we hope, that the structure is functioning as expected against a Range of scenarios.

DELIVERABLES

The VBA Language Knowledge Deliverables for this chapter are:

- How to construct a loan-by-loan floating rate loan coupon reset trace function
- How to construct a loan-by-loan cash flow trace module for the model

The Modeling Knowledge Deliverable for this chapter is:

- General common sense ways to validate a structured finance model

UNDER CONSTRUCTION

In this chapter we will add two features to the model to help us trace its calculations and make it easier for us to error check our results both now and with future releases of the model. Both these features may also come in handy when dealing with anyone who will want to examine the model. These may be internal constituencies such as auditors, risk control personnel, credit specialists, or any other business units we may later work with or share the model with. These features may also prove invaluable for outside auditors, investors, rating agency personnel, or regulatory personnel who wish to examine and verify the model in regard to pricing and valuation issues.

A Trace Function for the Floating Rate Loan Coupon Levels

The first of these features will allow us to visually examine the individual coupon pathway of any one of the floating rate notes. Our current portfolio is entirely comprised of these types of loans, and making sure that we have the coupon level reset mechanism functioning correctly is paramount.

To this end we will add a worksheet to the model and create a table for the periodic reset value as well as a graph so that we can visually examine the data. At each of the reset periods we will display the computed coupon level, the index it is based on, the periodic floor and cap constraints, and the lifetime floor and cap constraints.

To accomplish this we will need to add code to a number of modules throughout the model. The modules affected will be:

- **A_Constants.** A constant variable to dimension the trace array.
- **A_Globals.** A set of variables to serve as switches to the trace function and to hold the results that we will capture for later display from the functioning of the coupon reset calculator.
- **CollateralCFGenerator.** The code to capture the coupon levels, index levels, floors and caps information.
- **CollateralReadDataFile.** To redimension the trace array we declared earlier in the A_Globals module.
- **MenusErrorChecking.** To validate the information placed on the "Coup-TraceChart" worksheet before we pass it to the rest of the program.
- **MenusReadInputs.** To read inputs from the "CoupTraceChart" worksheet after we have validated them.
- **Z_ButtonSubs.** We will trigger the worksheet from a button on the sheet itself. We will therefore place the display subroutine in this module. It will be there with others such as those that support Geographic Menu display functionality.
- We will also have to create an action button as we have done previously with the "Run Model" function and the "Run Batch Model" function and link it to the subroutine that will display the information.

A Trace Function for the Monthly Cash Flows

The second of these features is a subroutine we will add to the module that calculates the collateral cash flows, "Collateral CF Generator." This subroutine will allow us to print out each of the collateral cash flow components of the loan on a monthly basis along with the beginning balance for the period. We will call it "Capture Monthly Cash Flow Trace." We will also create a second report-generating subroutine to print a file containing the monthly cash flows of each loan of the portfolio. Consistent with out earlier practices, we will segregate this code in a new module named **"WriteCFTraceReport."**

We will need to add three new input fields to the Main Menu of the model. The first field will be a run option field in the uppermost input block of the model that simply asks the user if they want to turn the cash flow trace function on. The selection of this feature can result in VERY LENGTHLY runtimes, sometimes several hours, in that the model must stop and output the monthly cash flows of each loan to a file after completing its amortization but before beginning the amortization of the next loan. We should therefore make this fact very prominent on the face of the Main Menu. The field should have a distinctly different color from the other run option fields to immediately alert the user of this issue. In addition, a warning message on the menu itself would be a good idea.

The second field will be a file name field for the Cash Flow Trace output file and the third the name of the Cash Flow Trace template file used to produce this report. That takes care of the menu alterations.

In the VBA, we will need to write the subroutines that will gather this information and then produce the appropriate report. The subroutine that will gather the information can be quite simple; we only need to fill one vector with each of the desired cash flow components. We will create the subroutine itself and call it from the appropriate subroutine named "Compute_Colleateal_Cashflows" in the module **"CollateralCFGenerator."** We will need to add code to the model to read this choice from the fields Main Menu and act upon it. That code will go into the **"Menus-ReadInputs"** module in the **"Read_Main_Menu"** subroutine. Next we will need to add appropriate error checking code to the **"MenusErrorChecking"** module to make sure that both the name of the output report file is specified and that the template filename field is filled in if the option to produce the report has been selected.

If we start at the top of the module listing, to implement this feature in VBA we will add code or make changes to the following parts of the model:

- **A_Constants.** We will change the value of the global constant MAIN_MENU _TEMPLATE_FILE_NAME from "6" to "7" to accommodate the additional template filename we have added to the Main Menu.
- **A_Globals.** We will add a block of variables that will all start with the prefix "g_val" to indicate they serve a validation function.
- **MenusErrorCheck.** We will change the values of two constants to reflect the increase by one of the number of report and template files we need to error check. We were also need to modify the subroutine "errMainMenu_ FileCheck-Templates" and the subroutine named "errMainMenu_FilesCheckOutput" to make sure the user has entered a filename in the appropriate fields.
- **MenuReadInputs.** We will modify the subroutine named "ReadMainMenu" to reflect that we have added a new template file name and a new output file name.
- **CollateralCFGenerator.** We will add two calls to the "Compute_Collateral_ Cashflows" subroutine. The first will be to the subroutine that will read the cash flow four cash flow components of the loan on a monthly basis,

"Capture_Monthly_CF_Trace." The second will be the subroutine "Print_Out_Trace_Report" that will produce the report. We will add the first of these subroutines to this module.

■ **WriteCFTraceReport.** This is a new module that we now add to the model. We have already established a practice of segregating the VBA code that writes each of the report packages in a separate module; we will again do so here. We will create "WriteCFTraceReport" and place the main subroutine "Print_Out_Trace_Report" and several other formatting subroutines to support in it.

STEPS IN THE VALIDATION PROCEDURE

Having spent the last three pages outlining the coupon pathway and collateral cash flow components trace functions, we need to pull back and take a minute to organize our thoughts about the validation process. As stated earlier, ***validation is important***!

It is far, far better to catch a small bug or two before you dive into the business of running the model, than to have to redo hours and hours of work. Add to that the discomfort of admitting that it was your mistake that caused all the wasted time and effort and you will see the point I am making.

There are many proverbs that run along the thoughts of "a stitch in time saves nine" or "better safe than sorry." Take a moment now and think seriously about what we are about to do in this chapter. This may be our last time to sit with the model without the pressures of making it produce something for a deal.

We need to assure ourselves that the model is performing as we hoped it would when we designed and built it. As we built the various pieces of the model we did some initial testing to see if the code was working. Now we need to take a systemic approach and test the program from front to back.

This testing approach will perforce follow the developmental stages of the model quite closely. We will start with very basic, almost sophomoric testing, and build gradually upward from there. We will mimic the steps that the model takes in a complete run and test each of the components along the way.

To wit, we will proceed in the testing sequence as follows:

1. Test the error checking subroutines that support the model menus
2. Test the subroutines that read the menu information after it has been error checked
3. Test the subroutines that read the loan-by-loan information from the collateral data file
4. Test the collateral selection process subroutines
5. Test the collateral reporting subroutines
6. Test the collateral cash flow generator

If all these parts of the model function as designed we can be reasonably sure that we have no major errors (we hope)! By performing the testing in an incremental manner, we will be able to build on a slowly accumulating body of validated code before moving on the next step of the process.

I will offer one word of caution for the beginner. Many of these tests will be very simple. There is a great temptation when you have built your first model to begin running it immediately. Why not? We just got done with the hard part, writing the code and debugging it! Now is the time to see the fruits of our labor. While you will never catch all errors no matter how much pre-deployment testing, you need to be as deliberate and careful as possible. Try to catch as many now as you can. As with dental work, the longer the problem exists the worse it gets. Let's try to avoid as many root canals as we can.

VALIDATING THE MENU ERROR CHECKING CODE

All the error checking code of the menus is contained in the VBA module named (appropriately), "**MenusErrorChecking.**" In Chapter 12, "Main Program and Menus," we created the "ErrCheck_All_Menus" subroutine and called seven other subroutines from it.

Test #1. Nonnumeric entries in numeric fields. The first of these subroutines error check the fields of three menus, the Program Costs Menu, the Defaults Menu, and the Program Costs Menu for nonnumeric entries. To test this subroutine, place a nonnumeric entry into every field of these three menus and run the program. The error message will be about a mile long, but it should report each field with the incorrect data on a menu-by-menu basis.

Test#2. Menu entries from the Main Menu. This subroutine tests for three types of errors. These are in order of the test:

- That the fields that contain the main directory path, the name of the collateral data file, and the number of loan records are in that file.
- For the presence of the appropriate template files in the template file directory.
- The upper fields of the menu for report options, that the appropriate filename is already entered in the menu. For example, the option to produce the Summary Matrix report is selected by the user and that the name of the template file and the name of the output have been entered.

To perform the first part of the test, blank out the three fields and run the model. To test the second set of error conditions, simply move the template files from the "template" file directory to any other directory. The program should produce a "file not found" error message for each missing template file. Next put the template files back in place and blank out all the output file names while answering "Y" to all the runtime options that require the production of an output file.

Test #3. The Program Costs Menus error checking test. Blank out all of the fields and run the model. Then put in values that are outside of the acceptable limits for the fields. For the servicing fee, the program expenses, and the spread to the funding index the Range is from 0 to 5%. For the two trigger events the Range is 0 to 10%. For the Advance Rate the number must be greater than 0% and less than 100%

Test #4. The Reports Menu error checking test. The only error condition we need to validate here is that at least one of the component reports of the two report packages must be selected if the option to run the report package is selected from the Main Menu. To test, simply select both of the "Write out Eligible Collateral

Reports" and the "Write out Matrix Summary Reports" option. Deselect all the reports on the menu. Run the model. You should get an error condition for each report package.

Test #5. The Geographic Menu error checking test. The only error in this menu is to deselect all of the states. This condition will then make the entire portfolio ineligible. Go to the "National" button selection line and hit the button marked "Exclude." Then say "Yes" to the Main Menu option "Perform the Collateral Eligibility Test?" An error message should tell you that you need to select at least one state.

Test #6. The Selection Criteria Menu error checking test. There are several error tests in this subroutine. First off, all fields must be positive, next all minimums must be less than or equal to all maximums, next neither the minimum nor the maximum gross coupon can be above 25%, and lastly the maximum LTV allowed for any loan must be less than 100%. Simply set a value to breach these conditions and confirm the appropriate error messages appear.

Test #7. The Defaults Menu error checking test. The error checking subroutine for this menu tests that all entries must be greater than zero. It next tests that the number of prepayment or default scenarios cannot exceed ten, the limit of the Matrix Summary Report template. It then tests that the recovery period cannot exceed 60 months. The Market Value Decline cannot exceed 100%. The last test is that all the annual distributions of defaults under the User Default option cannot exceed 100%, (the total amount of the indicated speed). These are easy tests to fail and the error messages should appear after you have done so.

VALIDATING THE MENU INPUTS

Before we run off in high spirits to test the collateral selection process, the cash flow calculations, and the waterfall structure, we should first verify that the menu inputs are correctly being transferred to the VBA variables. We can easily accomplish this using the VBA Debugger and positioning a break point at the end of the subroutines that read the menus. Use the Add Watch command on arrays and large collections of data and save the simple solution of positioning the cursor over each of the individual variables using the Data Tips feature.

Go to the module "MenusReadInputs" and place a breakpoint at the "End Sub" command of each of the menu reading subroutines of the module.

Test #1. The "Read_Main_Menu" subroutine. Everything in this subroutine can be confirmed by the use of Data Tips. Simply start at the top of the subroutine and one-by-one run the cursor over each of the assignment variables to confirm that they are correctly mapped to the menu fields.

Test #2. The "Read_The_Program_Costs_Menu" subroutine. Use the Data Tips feature on each variable.

Test #3. The "Read_Selection_Criteria_Menu" subroutine. Use Data tips to confirm all but the two arrays of the index selection fields. Use the Add Watch feature for both the "g_crit_acc_index" and "g_crit_min_spread" arrays.

Test #4. The "Read_Report_Selection_Menu" subroutine. Use the Add Watch feature to match the menu selections against the contents of the "g_reports" and "g_matrix_reports" arrays.

Test #5. The "Read_Geographic_Selection_Menu" subroutine. Use the Add Watch command to match the contents of the four arrays initialized by the subroutine "g_state_select," "g_state_postal," "g_state_name," and "g_state_id_number."

Test #6. The "Read_PrepayDefaults_Menu" subroutine. This menu has by far the most data on it. Be particularly careful checking the day count arrays, **"g_day_count"** array, and the rate array, **"g_index_level."** There is also the conduit funding level array, **"g_fund_conduit"** and the **"g_ann_def_dist"** array which contains the annual default distribution pattern of the User prepayment method. All the other entries can be checked with Data Tips.

VALIDATING THE CODE FOR READING THE PORTFOLIO DATA FILE

It is vitally important that the information from the collateral data file is being correctly read into the model. Without the collateral there simply is no deal. The two subroutines that we will be most concerned with are the "Read_Portfolio_Data_File" and the "Read_Portfolio_Data" subroutine, both of which are in the **"Collateral-ReadDataFile"** module.

Test #1. Record count check. Make sure the record count VBA code is performing correctly. There are two modes of input from the Main Menu. If the user enters "0," the model will count the number of records and stop at the first blank line in the data file. If the user enters a number, the model will read that many records and stop. Put a breakpoint at the end of the If...Then...Else statement in the "Read_Collateral_Data_File" subroutine. Then read the value of the row_stop variable. Subtract the 2 (the number of header rows in the data file) from the row_stop and you should have the number of records in the file. Next introduce a blank line after the tenth record of the file. Restart the process. The value of the row row_stop variable should be 12.

Test #2. Make sure the contents of the file are being correctly assigned to the global variable arrays correctly. We need to determine that the collateral information is being placed in the correct global variable arrays. All of these activities are performed in the "Read_Collateral_Data" subroutine. Place a breakpoint at the top of the loop and then step through the first record of the file. This process will go a lot faster if you print out the first few records and can directly compare them to the contents of the file.

VALIDATING THE COLLATERAL SELECTION CODE

The performance of the waterfall structure is dependent on the cash flow vectors that are written into it on a scenario-by-scenario basis. Those cash flows are directly derived from the loans that have passed the collateral selection process. If the collateral selection process is unreliable, then we can have no confidence in the rest of the modeling process.

Fortunately, the collateral selection process is one of the more straightforward portions of the model to validate. We are particularly fortunate in this deal because we have only a small loan portfolio. We will use the collateral data file named

Collateral Selection Criteria Menu

Minimum	Maximum	
0	360	Original Term (Months)
0	360	Remaining Term (Months)
$0	$5,000,000	Original Balance
$0	$999,999	Remaining Balance
0.000%	25.000%	Gross Coupon
	100.000%	Maximum Total Project LTV%
	$100,000	Difference Stated-Calculated Pmt

Run the Model

Indices & Minimum Spreads

Index Code	Min Spread	
PRIME	0.000%	Index #1 and Minimum Spread
		Index #2 and Minimum Spread
		Index #3 and Minimum Spread
		Index #4 and Minimum Spread
		Index #5 and Minimum Spread
		Index #6 and Minimum Spread

EXHIBIT 17.1   Collateral Selection code to deselect only loans with current balances of $1,000,000 or greater; all other selection criteria set "wide" to eliminate any other selection from taking place

"portfolio_orig.xls" for the tests. To validate the collateral selection subroutines we will perform the following tests:

Test #1. No selection process. Run the model with the selection process turned off and produce the eligible collateral report package. The resultant eligible loans should be identical to the base collateral file. Simple but effective.

Test #2. Portfolio totals are correct. Open the data file. Place an Excel SUM function in the first cell of each of the following columns; "B" original loan balance and "C" current loan balance. Make a copy of the file. Using the Excel "Sort" command, sort the file by current balance in descending order, which will put the largest loans at the top of the file. Select this portion of the portfolio and print the records then delete all loan records with balances above $1,000,000. On the Selection Criteria Menu set the selection criteria of "Maximum Loan Balance" to $999,999. Put the rest of the selection criteria values to levels that will not deselect any other loans. See Exhibit 17.1. Run the model with the selection process and the print ineligibility reports turned on. The portfolio total of this run should match the portfolio total of the edited collateral file. In addition, the contents of the Ineligible Collateral report #4, selection for minimum/maximum current loan value, will be the list of loans that you deleted.

Test #3. Test the selection process by each of the ineligibility tests. We will now construct a series of tests that will focus on the ineligibility criteria one-by-one. We will walk through the process for the first of these tests as a general guide and establish the procedures that can be used for all of the following. When we ran Test #1 above, we produced a set of Eligible Collateral Reports for the entire portfolio. The portfolio demographic report Elig-2 Current Balances Distribution by Remaining Term lists all the loans of the portfolio by remaining term in 6-month intervals. There are no loans with less than 12 months remaining terms, and only one loan with a remaining term between 13 and 24 months. This loan has a remaining balance of $17,502. If

Collateral Selection Criteria Menu

Minimum	Maximum	
0	360	Original Term (Months)
25	360	Remaining Term (Months)
$0	$5,000,000	Original Balance
$0	$5,000,000	Remaining Balance
0.000%	25.000%	Gross Coupon
	100.000%	Maximum Total Project LTV%
	$100,000	Difference Stated-Calculated Pmt

Run the Model

Indices & Minimum Spreads		
Index Code	Min Spread	
PRIME	0.000%	Index #1 and Minimum Spread
		Index #2 and Minimum Spread
		Index #3 and Minimum Spread
		Index #4 and Minimum Spread
		Index #5 and Minimum Spread
		Index #6 and Minimum Spread

EXHIBIT 17.2 Collateral Selection code to deselect the only loan in the portfolio with a remaining term less that 25 months

we subsequently configure the selection criteria test for a minimum remaining term of 25 and a maximum remaining term of 360, we will eliminate only this single loan. See Exhibit 17.2. If the selection process works correctly we will see a single loan of this amount appear in the Ineligible Collateral Report Inelig1 Min/Max Remaining Term.

Similarly there are 336 loans with remaining terms of between 109 and 120 months with a collective current balance of $25,966,112. If we set the minimum remaining term test to 108 and the maximum remaining term test to 120, then we should select these and only these loans.

We can apply this process to each of the other tests for balances and terms, gross coupons, the Loan To Value ratio, and the payment difference amount. For example, there is only one loan with a spread to PRIME of 1.50%, one with a spread of 1.75%, and two with a spread of 2.00%. If we set the minimum spread to 2.01% we should net four ineligible loans under that test.

Each time you repeat the process, make sure that you return the settings to those shown in Exhibit 17.1 so that you do not accidentally deselect any other loans that the owner targeted in the test.

Test #4. The Geographic Menu Selection test. The process is even more easily accomplished when there is only a single selection criteria test such as state geographic code. To make sure that no other loans are eliminated under other selection criteria, reset the Selection Criteria Menu to the settings shown in Exhibit 17.1. The next step is to simply omit any state from the eligible list and compare the number of loans and their characteristics against that line on the Elig-11 Current Balances by State or Territory report. Exclusion of loans from my home state, Connecticut, for example, should yield 99 ineligible loans for a whopping current balance of $6,585,079 that constitutes 3.255% of the portfolio current balances. The total of the Inelig8 Ineligible by State or Territory Code report should equal the single line on the demographic report. This approach can also be applied against combination of states.

Test #5. **Joint selection conditions across two or more criteria.** How do we know that the selection tests will work for joint conditions? Using the preceding test as an example, we can construct a fairly simple joint test. There are 22 loans in the portfolio that have individual current balances greater than $1 million. These loans represent a sum total of $27,079,714 of the current balance of the portfolio. These 22 loans were originated in only 12 of the 54 total states and territories. Of these 22 loans, only one loan was originated in West Virginia and three other loans originated in Arizona. The four loans from these two states total $4,953,438 of the current balance. A listing of these loans is shown in Exhibit 17.3.

We should see these numbers reflected in the two Selection Summary Reports. Keep in mind that the program will also deselect all other loans in Arizona and West Virginia in the selection process. There are a total of 96 loans that have balances less

EXHIBIT 17.3 There are 22 loans with current balances over $1 million and 4 of them are from either Arizona or West Virginia

	Loan ID	Current Loan Balance	State	Criteria		Results	
				Test 1 Cur Balance $ 1,000,000	Test 2 State WV & AZ	1 Only	1 & 2
1	1774	1,640,244	WV	1	1		1,640,244
2	1424	1,555,637	NY	1	0	1,555,637	
3	155	1,401,406	AL	1	0	1,401,406	
4	630	1,389,417	TX	1	0	1,389,417	
5	439	1,354,577	MS	1	0	1,354,577	
6	554	1,299,936	TN	1	0	1,299,936	
7	1247	1,278,253	FL	1	0	1,278,253	
8	593	1,263,027	CA	1	0	1,263,027	
9	545	1,239,752	NJ	1	0	1,239,752	
10	622	1,227,851	MS	1	0	1,227,851	
11	2239	1,227,729	AZ	1	1		1,227,729
12	750	1,225,381	FL	1	0	1,225,381	
13	333	1,185,582	FL	1	0	1,185,582	
14	814	1,169,808	NY	1	0	1,169,808	
15	625	1,168,898	TX	1	0	1,168,898	
16	1670	1,117,641	CO	1	0	1,117,641	
17	595	1,088,937	TX	1	0	1,088,937	
18	1837	1,085,777	PA	1	0	1,085,777	
19	1025	1,079,166	AZ	1	1		1,079,166
20	810	1,038,384	TX	1	0	1,038,384	
21	2242	1,036,012	NJ	1	0	1,036,012	
22	739	1,006,299	AZ	1	1		1,006,299
		27,079,714		22	4	22,126,276	4,953,438
						18	4

Table title: **Test of Joint Selection Criteria**

Loan Listing Exception Report
Individual Loan Ineligibility Conditions

Ineligibility Condition Reference	
1 = Min/Max Remaining Term	7 = Excluded State or Geographic Region
2 = Min/Max Original Term	8 = Inconsistent Original vs. Remaining Term
3 = Min Max Original Balance	9 = Inconsistent Original vs. Remaining Balance
4 = Min/Max Current Balance	10 = Calculated vs. Stated Payment Differences
5 = Exceeds Maximum LTV	11 = Unacceptable Gross Coupon
6 = Unacceptable Floater Indice/Spread	

Total Loans Rejected	Loan Number	1	2	3	4	5	6	7	8	9	10	11	Loan Yield	Current Balance
118		0	0	0	22	0	0	4	0	0	0	0	8.241%	27,079,714
6	155				1								8.250%	1,401,406
20	333				1								8.250%	1,185,582
23	439				1								8.000%	1,354,577
30	545				1								7.750%	1,239,752
31	554				1								8.250%	1,299,936
33	593				1								7.750%	1,263,027
34	595				1								7.750%	1,088,937
36	622				1								8.250%	1,227,851
37	625				1								7.750%	1,168,898
38	630				1								7.750%	1,389,417
44	739				1			1					9.000%	1,006,299
48	750				1								8.750%	1,225,381
51	810				1								7.250%	1,038,384
52	814				1			1					8.750%	1,169,808
59	1025				1								8.500%	1,079,166
68	1247				1								8.750%	1,278,253
81	1424				1								8.000%	1,555,637
92	1670				1			1					9.000%	1,117,641
99	1774				1								8.000%	1,640,244
103	1837				1			1					8.750%	1,085,777
117	2239				1								8.250%	1,227,729
118	2242				1								9.000%	1,036,012

EXHIBIT 17.4   Loans with balances greater than $1 million in the states of Arizona and West Virginia; for the sake of brevity all loans deselected for geographic location alone have been dropped from the report (a total of 96 loans)

than $1 million in Arizona and West Virginia. If we run the selection process we will see the following Loan Listing Exception Report produced, see Exhibit 17.4.

The second report also confirms that the program is working correctly in regards to combination criteria selection. See Exhibit 17.5.

VALIDATING THE ELIGIBLE COLLATERAL REPORTING CODE

The next step in the validation process is to test the performance of the subroutines that construct the stratification reports of the Eligible Collateral Report Package. These reports are very easy to test and a single simple technique can be applied across all of the various tests.

Test #1. Validate a stratification report. Make a copy of the **"portfolio_orig.xls"** data file. Using the Excel Sort option, select one of the parameters that is the criteria

Summary Exception Report
Contracts Grouped By Unique Ineligibility Combinations

Ineligibility Condition Reference	
1 = Min/Max Remaining Term	7 = Excluded State or Geographic Region
2 = Min/Max Original Term	8 = Inconsistent Original vs. Remaining Term
3 = Min Max Original Balance	9 = Inconsistent Original vs. Remaining Balance
4 = Min/Max Current Balance	10 = Calculated vs. Stated Payment Differences
5 = Exceeds Maximum LTV	11 = Unacceptable Gross Coupon
6 = Unacceptable Floater Indice/Spread	

Unique Ineligibility Code	Ineligibility Condition											Number of Loans	Total Current Balance	Total Equity Position
	1	2	3	4	5	6	7	8	9	10	11			
	0	0	0	2	0	0	2	0	0	0	0	118	46,481,595	1,592,157
8				1								18	22,126,276	693,988
64							1					96	19,401,881	345,898
72				1			1					4	4,953,438	552,271

EXHIBIT 17.5 A total of 22 loans have failed criteria Test #4, balances over $1 million; of these a total of four have failed Test #4 and Test #7 jointly. The balances match the schedule in Exhibit 17.3! The program works!

variable for one of the stratification reports. Let's pick Gross Coupon in column "C" of the spreadsheet. Sort the file by column "C" in ascending order. After the file is sorted break the file at one of the stratification points with three blank lines. Use the "Sum" function to sum the original and current loan balances. In the first blank line under the column "C" use the "SumProduct" function to take the sum product of the current loan balance column and the coupon column. Divide the result by the sum of the current loan balance column for this interval. It should match the equivalent bracket in the report Eligible Collateral Report #4, Current Balances Distribution by Current Coupon. See Exhibits 17.6 and 17.7.

VALIDATING THE FLOATING RATE LOAN RESET PERIOD LEVELS

Balance, term, and coupon information are the three building blocks that form the basis for computing the amortization pattern of any loan. Starting with these three items, we can construct the basic amortization pattern for any loan or note. After we are confident that this pattern is sound we can then layer in the aspects of prepayment and default effects.

Since none of our loans allow for negative amortization, our balance calculations are fairly straightforward. None of the loans have extendable terms so the term information is also quite simple. This is not the case with the issue of monthly coupon level. The coupons of these loans are determined, as we have seen earlier, by the interaction of several factors working simultaneously at any of the scheduled reset periods. These are:

- The current level of the reference index
- The spread of the loan, established at its inception and constant throughout the life of the loan

EXHIBIT 17.6   Manually computed stratification interval for loans with a coupon of 7.26 to 7.50%

CONTENTS OF COLLATERAL DATA FILE FOR COUPON INTERVAL 7.26% TO 7.50%

	Loan #	Orig Bal	Cur Bal	Coupon	OrigTerm	RemTerm	Season	Appraisal	Cur Equity
1	417	1,035,000	988,222	7.500%	300	295	5	1,350,000	391,778
2	404	890,100	774,003	7.500%	299	285	14	1,230,000	515,997
3	1641	555,900	535,867	7.500%	289	285	4	1,090,000	554,133
4	518	524,800	481,530	7.500%	287	278	9	820,000	338,470
5	490	540,000	442,781	7.500%	298	279	19	750,000	307,219
6	926	468,000	393,122	7.500%	300	283	17	750,000	386,878
7	488	436,600	388,117	7.500%	300	288	12	530,000	201,883
8	841	435,200	382,668	7.500%	240	227	13	680,000	297,332
9	451	351,000	347,869	7.500%	300	299	1	650,000	302,131
10	420	283,500	257,441	7.500%	240	230	10	450,000	192,559
11	2051	331,500	215,374	7.500%	300	265	35	510,000	294,626
12	297	214,200	204,519	7.500%	243	238	5	420,000	215,481
13	2237	256,500	183,571	7.500%	228	199	29	450,000	266,429
14	1560	180,000	170,205	7.500%	294	288	6	330,000	129,795
15	482	199,800	159,772	7.500%	300	279	21	270,000	110,228
16	633	177,500	156,074	7.500%	251	238	13	250,000	93,926
Totals/SumProd.		**6,879,600**	**6,081,136**	456,085	1,738,576,597	1,668,382,260	70,194,337	**10,630,000**	**4,598,864**
Averages/$ Weighted Averages		**380,071**		7.500%	285.90	274.35	11.54	56.239%	43.061%

Portfolio Total $ 461,898,460
% Current Bal   1.317%

429

EXHIBIT 17.7 The stratification report, if we compare the numbers in the sixth line of the report for the interval 7.25 to 7.50% we see that they match!

Eligible Collateral Report #4
Current Balances Distribution by Current Coupon

	4	5	6	7	8	9	10	11	12	13	15	17	18
Current Coupon Range	Number of Loans	Current Loan Balance	Current Loan LTV	% Current Balances	Cum % Current Balances	Average Loan Balance	WtAvg Current Yield	WtAvg Original Term	WtAvg Remain Term	WtAvg Current Seasoning	Equity Balance	Equity % Appraisal	Total Appraisal
	2,255	**461,898,460**									**365,601,540**		**827,500,000**
6.50% to 6.75%	1	429,347	44.263%	0.093%	0.093%	429,347	6.750%	279.00	243.00	36.00	540,653	55.737%	970,000
6.75% to 7.00%	1	539,480	62.009%	0.117%	0.210%	539,480	7.000%	300.00	295.00	5.00	330,520	37.991%	870,000
7.00% to 7.25%	2	1,078,705	63.082%	0.234%	0.443%	539,352	7.250%	258.62	252.20	6.42	631,295	36.918%	1,710,000
7.25% to 7.50%	16	6,081,136	56.939%	1.317%	1.760%	380,071	7.500%	285.90	274.35	11.54	4,598,864	43.061%	10,680,000
7.50% to 7.75%	80	37,157,383	60.458%	8.044%	9.804%	464,467	7.750%	272.80	263.13	9.67	24,302,617	39.542%	61,460,000
7.75% to 8.00%	116	42,955,794	58.844%	9.300%	19.104%	370,309	8.000%	246.42	234.03	12.39	30,044,206	41.156%	73,000,000
8.00% to 8.25%	376	107,639,566	57.212%	23.304%	42.408%	286,275	8.250%	220.41	206.90	13.51	80,500,434	42.788%	188,140,000
8.25% to 8.50%	218	58,679,918	55.758%	12.704%	55.112%	269,174	8.500%	197.23	181.60	15.62	46,560,082	44.242%	105,240,000
8.50% to 8.75%	271	62,674,430	54.666%	13.569%	68.681%	231,271	8.749%	191.27	174.11	17.16	51,975,570	45.334%	114,650,000
8.75% to 9.00%	1095	141,665,961	53.406%	30.670%	99.351%	129,375	9.000%	160.47	142.22	18.25	123,594,039	46.594%	265,260,000
9.00% to 9.25%	2	1,070,697	56.352%	0.232%	99.583%	535,349	9.250%	287.91	260.56	27.35	829,303	43.648%	1,900,000
9.75% to 10.00%	68	1,801,603	53.302%	0.390%	99.973%	26,494	10.000%	88.34	66.62	21.72	1,578,397	46.698%	3,380,000
10.75% to 11.00%	9	124,441	51.851%	0.027%	100.000%	13,827	11.000%	83.88	62.61	21.27	115,559	48.149%	240,000

- The current coupon level
- The periodic floor and cap spread from the current coupon level
- The lifetime floor and cap set the limits to the movement of the coupon rate

What we would like to arrive at is a method to quickly and easily spot-check the coupon level reset pattern for any loan in the portfolio. The most effective way to accomplish this is to provide ourselves with both a graphic and tabular display of the information. The graphic display should clearly display the path of the current coupon as being consistent with the constraints of the various floors and caps. The tabular information will provide a period-by-period detail of each of the components contributing to the reset calculation. We can then switch back and forth between the less-detailed versus more-detailed presentation.

So to start the ball rolling let's go back to the design principles we learned earlier "Last Things First, First Things Last," and begin by designing the report.

We will want the graph to be fairly large so we can see as much of the detail as possible at a glance without having to immediately refer to the table. With this in mind we can position the chart across the entire width of the screen by placing the tabular information *below* it, instead of out to one side or the other as we might usually do. This will give us plenty of room to work with and still leave the table and all its details readily accessible.

The remaining items on the worksheet are almost trivial when compared to the other menus and reports we have already built. We will need two input fields only:

1. A switch to indicate to the program that we want to capture the trace information
2. A field to take the identification number of the loan we wish to see displayed in the chart and table

That's about it for the information. Now we need to think about display. What we are trying to verify is that the pattern of the coupon reset levels of the loan are consistent with the boundaries of the four constraints of the two pairs of floors and caps. We are lucky that the caps and floors relate only to their gross coupons and are not percentages of existing payments of other more annoying calculations.

We therefore are really dealing with two pairs of matched constraints, a pair of high-lows, in effect. We will visually link these pairs by using the same color for both the periodic floor and cap, and a second color to represent the lifetime floor and cap. This will create a visual image of a set of corridors, bounded by the same color lines. We will make these lines more subdued than the coupon level line that will be the focus of out attention. If we make the floor and cap lines blue or green and select red for the coupon level we should have no difficulty at all in quickly seeing a violation of the rules.

As a final refinement to the graph design we will give the coupon line a bit of texture. Remember it is possible that at some time the coupon level may lie directly above one of the floor or cap lines and we need to be aware of this situation. We will position this report on the worksheet we will add to the model named "CoupTraceChart." Combining all of the above, we end up with the report in Exhibit 17.8.

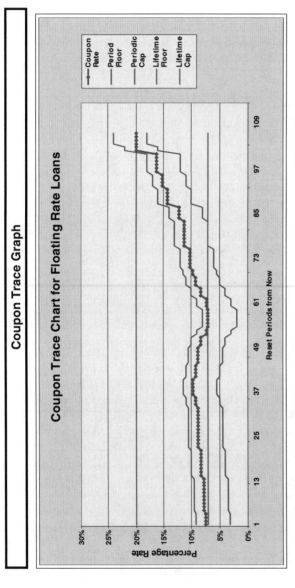

Coupon Trace Graph

Coupon Trace Chart for Floating Rate Loans

Plot Coupon Pathway

| Coupon Trace Switch | Y |
| Loan Number | 5 |

Period	Coupon Level	Index Level	Periodic Floor	Period Cap	Lifetime Floor	Lifetime Cap
1	7.50%	5.25%	3.25%	9.25%	7.00%	20.00%
2	7.50%	5.25%	3.25%	9.25%	7.00%	20.00%
3	7.50%	5.25%	3.25%	9.25%	7.00%	20.00%
4	7.50%	5.25%	3.25%	9.25%	7.00%	20.00%
5	7.75%	5.50%	3.50%	9.50%	7.00%	20.00%
6	7.75%	5.50%	3.50%	9.50%	7.00%	20.00%
7	7.75%	5.50%	3.50%	9.50%	7.00%	20.00%
8	7.75%	5.50%	3.50%	9.50%	7.00%	20.00%
9	7.75%	5.50%	3.50%	9.50%	7.00%	20.00%
10	7.75%	5.50%	3.50%	9.50%	7.00%	20.00%
11	7.75%	5.50%	3.50%	9.50%	7.00%	20.00%
12	7.75%	5.50%	3.50%	9.50%	7.00%	20.00%
13	7.75%	5.50%	3.50%	9.50%	7.00%	20.00%
14	7.75%	5.50%	3.50%	9.50%	7.00%	20.00%
15	8.25%	6.00%	4.00%	10.00%	7.00%	20.00%
16	8.25%	6.00%	4.00%	10.00%	7.00%	20.00%
17	8.25%	6.00%	4.00%	10.00%	7.00%	20.00%

EXHIBIT 17.8   The overall design of the Coupon Trace Report

The graph dominates the display, giving immediate information as to the compliance of the coupon reset levels to the constraints of the floor and caps. The table provides detail. There is a button linked to the display subroutine that will also call an error message if necessary.

There are only two input fields both on the lower right of the screen: the first to turn the trace function on, the second to validate the loan number. One only needs to place a "Y" in the "Coupon Trace Switch" before the model is run to capture the information for display later. After the model has run the user enters the name of the loan whose coupon reset pattern they want to verify.

In the model on the Web site, the lines for the periodic floor and cap are deep blue, the lines for the lifetime floor and cap are green, and the coupon reset pathway is red with an embedded diamond symbol to help it stand out when it overlays the others.

Now let us look at the changes to the screen and to the VBA code we will add to the model to implement this feature.

If we start with our screen report and work backward we can see that this entire feature hinges on the contents of the table that holds the coupon, index, and floor and cap information. We will also need to tell the program that we want to collect the data in the first place (the switch field), and later, after the program run, what loan we wish to display.

We start by declaring three Range names for the report screen:

1. "Coupon Trace Switch" will cover the cells (L40:M40) and accept "Y" or "N" to turn the option to capture the interest rate pathway information on or off, respectively.
2. "CouponTraceLoan" will cover the cells (L41:M41) and accept any number. This entry will be tested later to determine if it is numeric and if it is less than the maximum number of accepted loans in the portfolio. Obviously if there are six loans in the portfolio we cannot display the tenth loan!
3. "CouponTraceSch" will comprise the table. The table covers the region of cells (C35:H154). This is the table that we will populate from the model and that the graph at the top of the screen will reference.

Note that since this is *not* an input menu per se, we will not prefix the Ranges on it with the "m#" designation that we have used earlier. We did, however, start all the Range names with the "CouponTrace" prefix to make them an easily recognized group.

With these Ranges in place, we can now proceed to add the VBA code. We will organize this code addition along the lines of the modules mentioned earlier and in the order you should be thinking about the problem. Broadly speaking, we need to set up an array to hold the data we will put in the table and a pair of variables for the switch and the selected loan number. If we need to declare any constants to support the array, we should do that next. Next we will be preparing the array to receive that data, then loading the array. That should get the data portion of the project complete. Then we will deal with the display of the data now in hand. To do this we will create the display subroutine and in the process read the information from the screen, error check it, and use it to populate the screen table, triggering the population of the graph. The process of writing this VBA will involve eight steps.

```
'LOAN COUPON LEVEL TRACE REPORT
Public g_val_coup_trace()    As Double    'coupon pathway trace information
Public g_val_coup_trace_switch    As Boolean    'turn trace on or off
```

EXHIBIT 17.9   The declaration of the global variables for the table and the switch (the loan selected variable will be declared later)

Step #1. "A_Globals." Add a declaration of the array that will hold the data for the large table and variables for the two input fields of the screen. We will prefix these variables and all others that we create for this feature with "val_coup" to stand for "validation process, coupon." See Exhibit 17.9.

Step #2. "A_Constants." Add a constant variable for the number of columns of the table and one for the number of rows. This will make it much easier to change the model if we need to expand this feature at a later date. The contents of the rows are displayed in order as a form of online documentation. Why do we declare this array for only four items when the table on the "CoupTraceChart" worksheet has six items? The first four items can, and frequently do, change value at a reset period. The last two items of the chart are constant throughout the life of the loan; they are the lifetime floor and cap. In that they do not change and are not calculated, we can populate the table directly by using the values of the two global variables g_loan_life_cap and g_loan_life_floor that we will read from the collateral data file. See Exhibit 17.10.

Step #3. At a point in the program when the collateral selection process is complete, redimension the array to the number of active loans in the portfolio. The "Read_Portfolio_Data_File" subroutine is just the place! It is the earliest point at which we know the number of loans in the portfolio. This redimension is triggered only if the value of the Boolean variable g_val_coup_trace_switch is "TRUE," meaning that we wish to collect this information as the model is running for display later. See Exhibit 17.11.

Step #4. Having declared and dimensioned the array, we move to the next step. We now need to read the coupon reset period information into the array. Keep in mind that the coupon reset occurs quarterly for the loans of the portfolio and we need to keep the information for those dates only as it remains constant for the periods between the dates. The subroutine "Calculate_Loan_Floater_Coupon_Levels" is the place where this activity occurs. The subroutine is in the "CollateralCFGenerator" subroutine. The main loop in this subroutine runs through each month of the

```
'================================================================
'Coupon Trace Constants -- Floating Rate Loans Only
' 1 = computed coupon level
' 2 = index level
' 3 = periodic floor
' 4 = periodic cap
'================================================================
Public Const COUP_TRACE_ITEMS = 4      'data we need to store by reset period
Public Const COUP_TRACE_ROWS = 120     'quarterly for 30 years
```

EXHIBIT 17.10   The declaration of the constant variables to dimension the array that will hold the data for the table

```
Sub Read_Portfolio_Data_File()

  Workbooks.Open Filename:=g_pathway & "data\" & gfn_collateral_file
  j = 1
  current_row = FIRST_DATA_ROW
  Sheets("LoanInformation").Select
  Range("A1").Select
  'if the number of loans in the portfolio is entered as 0 count the file
  'if a number greater than zero is entered read that number of records
  [Code omitted - Loop that counts the # of loans in the portfolio]
  'redimension the data arrays based on the number of total loans in the portfolio
  ReDim g_col_tot(1 To g_total_loans) As Double
  ReDim g_sel_tag(1 To g_total_loans, 1 To INELIG_SINGLE_REPS) As Boolean
  Call ReDim_Portfolio_Data_Arrays(g_total_loans)
  'redimension the coupon trace array if it is selected
  If g_val_coup_trace_switch Then
     ReDim g_val_coup_trace(1 To g_total_loans, 1 To COUP_TRACE_ROWS, _
                            1 to COUP_TRACE_ITEMS) As Double
  End If
  'read the loans data file based on the program count or the input count
  j = Read_Portfolio_Data(FIRST_DATA_ROW, row_stop, j)
  'Total lines read minus one = number of collateral pieces
  ActiveWorkbook.Close

End Sub
```

EXHIBIT 17.11   Redimensioning of the "g_val_coup_trace" array

remaining life of the loan. If the current period is a periodic reset event, it calculates the new coupon. We will simply load the results of those calculations into our new array. Remember we are not capturing each monthly coupon level that the subroutine calculates; only those on the reset dates. For this reason we need to create a variable to keep track of the reset periods aside from the monthly periods that are the main focus of the activities of this subroutine. This variable we will name itrace to distinguish it from the regular monthly loop counter im (which stands for a monthly frequency). See Exhibit 17.12.

Step #5. We now have the array completely populated! All we need to do is print out the contents into the table on the screen. We now write the subroutine to do this. We will trigger this subroutine from a button. The subroutine itself is a standalone. It is not part of the flow of the Main Program. No other subroutine in the Main Program sequence will call it. It is different, but we do have precedence for these types of subroutines. They are found associated with the Geographic Selection Menu and the Defaults Menu. On the Geographic Menu, subroutines of this type populate or clear various combinations of states by their regional location. On the Default Menu, the button clears the distribution default timing for the User default annual table. All of these subs reside in the module "**Z_ButtonSubs**" and that is where we will place this one.

The subroutine "Populate_Coupon_Trace_Graph" will do just that. See Exhibit 17.13.

Step #6. As the subroutine "Populate_Coupon_Trace_Graph" starts to work, one of its first tasks is to error check the inputs from the report screen. "Error_Check_Coupon_Trace_Graph" will check four conditions. The first, if the model has been run and the coupon reset information is available; second, if the loan number is a numeric; third, if the loan number is within the Range of loan numbers of the

```
Sub Calculate_Loan_Floater_Coupon_Levels(iloan As Long)

Dim beg_rate    As Double     'rate at beginning of the period
Dim now_rate    As Double     'rate at reset event
Dim im          As Integer    'monthly loop counter
Dim ifloat      As Integer    'type of floater
Dim itrace      As Long       'period of the trace information

  itrace = 0 'start at zero
  ifloat = g_loan_floater_code(iloan)
  'set the initial rate to the current index rate and the spread of the loan
  beg_rate = g_index_levels(1, ifloat) + g_loan_spread(iloan)
  g_loan_coupon(iloan, 1) = beg_rate

For im = 2 To g_loan_rem_term(iloan)
   If (g_loan_season(iloan) + im - 1) Mod g_loan_reset_rate(iloan) = 0 Then
       itrace = itrace + 1
       'its a reset month
       now_rate = g_index_levels(im, ifloat) + g_loan_spread(iloan)
       'two checks for limits on periodic resets
       If now_rate >= beg_rate + g_loan_reset_cap(iloan) Then
           now_rate = beg_rate + g_loan_reset_cap(iloan)
       End If
       If now_rate <= beg_rate - g_loan_reset_floor(iloan) Then
           now_rate = beg_rate - g_loan_reset_floor(iloan)
       End If
       'check results against the lifetime cap and floor for the loan
       If now_rate>=g_loan_life_cap(iloan) Then now_rate = g_loan_life_cap(iloan)
       If now_rate <= g_loan_life_floor(iloan) Then now_rate = g_loan_life_floor(iloan)
       'if we are doing a coupon rate trace catch that information now
       '1 = computed coupon level, 2 = current index level, 3 = period floor,
       '4 = periodic cap, the life time floor and caps are constant
       If g_val_coup_trace_switch Then
          g_val_coup_trace(iloan, itrace, 1) = beg_rate
          g_val_coup_trace(iloan, itrace, 2) = g_index_levels(itrace, ifloat)
          g_val_coup_trace(iloan, itrace, 3) = beg_rate - g_loan_reset_cap(iloan)
          g_val_coup_trace(iloan, itrace, 4) = beg_rate + g_loan_reset_cap(iloan)
       End If
       'reset the beginning rate to this rate
       g_loan_coupon(iloan, im) = now_rate
       beg_rate = now_rate
    Else
      g_loan_coupon(iloan, im) = beg_rate
    End If
  Next im

End Sub
```

EXHIBIT 17.12   Reading the coupon reset event values into the "g_val_coup_trace" array

portfolio; and last, if a "Y" or a "N" has been entered in the coupon trace switch field.

This subroutine follows the error checking code format that we had developed earlier and so its organization and function look familiar. See Exhibit 17.14.

Step #7. Our next task is to record the value input into the trace switch field. We will place this code in the **"ReadMenusInputs"** module. See Exhibit 17.15.

Step #8. Our last task is to create the button to trigger the display function. We will give the button the title "Plot Coupon Pathway" and link it to the "Populate_Coupon_Trace_Graph" subroutine. When the button is pressed, the subroutine

```
'==============================================================================
' Populate the Loan Coupon Trace Graph
'==============================================================================
Sub Populate_Coupon_Trace_Graph()

Dim t_loan  As Long     '# of the loan selected for trace

  'error check the input number and the trace switch field value
  Call Error_Check_Coupon_Trace_Graph

  'if you get to here the input has passed and we can proceed
  t_loan = Trim(Range("CouponTraceLoan"))
  'clear the current contents of the range if any
  Range("CouponTraceSch").ClearContents
  Calculate     'this will clear the graph area

  'load the new contents in based on the loan #
  For i = 1 To PAY_DATES
    If g_val_coup_trace(t_loan, i, 4) > 0# Then
        Range("CouponTraceSch").Cells(i, 1) = _
                       g_val_coup_trace(t_loan, i, 1) 'coupon rate
        Range("CouponTraceSch").Cells(i, 2) = _
                       g_val_coup_trace(t_loan, i, 2) 'index
        Range("CouponTraceSch").Cells(i, 3) = _
                       g_val_coup_trace(t_loan, i, 3) 'period floor
        Range("CouponTraceSch").Cells(i, 4) = _
                       g_val_coup_trace(t_loan, i, 4) 'period cap
        Range("CouponTraceSch").Cells(i, 5) = _
                       g_loan_life_floor(t_loan) 'life floor
        Range("CouponTraceSch").Cells(i, 6) = _
                       g_loan_life_cap(t_loan) 'life cap
    Else
        Calculate    'refresh the graph
        Exit For     'loaded all data, we are done
    End If
  Next i

End Sub
```

EXHIBIT 17.13   Error checking and reading the data into the table

acts as a mini Main Program and activates, running to conclusion. This button will
be directly linked to the Main Program subroutine and, when pressed, will start the
model running. Providing additional copies of the button on the other menus allows
the user to start the model from any location.

Buttons are objects and can be installed by using the View|Toolbars|Forms
command. Once you reach the Forms Menu, select the button option. See Exhibits
17.16 and 17.17.

Draw the general shape of the button, and then use the Format command to
insert text so that the user knows what it is for. Make the button large enough so
that it is clearly visible on the screen. Next, format the button font to be a very
bright color; red or yellow work best against the standard gray button background.
See Exhibits 17.17 and 17.18.

The next step is to right click on the button and select the "Assign Macro"
option. The dialog box will appear. Simply scroll down to the macro you wish to
assign and click on it. Activating the button will immediately start running the VBA
code in the associated subroutine. See Exhibit 17.19.

```
Sub Error_Check_Coupon_Trace_Graph()

Dim error_type(1 To 4)  As Boolean  'there are 3 types of errors
Dim t_loan              As Long     '# of the trace loan input
Dim switch_test(1 To 2) As Boolean  'test to see if switch = "Y" or "N"
Dim i_err               As Integer  'loop counter

  'Error check the input number and the switch option
  error_type(1) = False   'g_total_loans is 0, program not run yet
  error_type(2) = False   'loan # OK but too large for portfolio
  error_type(3) = False   'loan # entered not numeric
  error_type(4) = False   'trace switch is either "Y" or "N"

  'test to see if the program has been run prior to the request for  the loan
  'coupon reset information, if it has not the global variable g_total_loans
  'will be zero
  If g_total_loans = 0 Then
     error_type(1) = True
     msgInfo(1) = " You need to run the model first to make" & Chr(13) _
         &" this information available!" & Chr(13)
  End If
  'Test for a non-numeric first if it passes that test, test if the input loan
  '  number is greater than the largest loan number in the portfolio
  If error_type(1) = False Then
     If IsNumeric(Trim(Range("CouponTraceLoan"))) Then
        t_loan = Range("CouponTraceLoan")
        If t_loan > g_total_loans Then
           'loan # greater than portfolio limit
           error_type(2) = True
           msgInfo(2) = " Loan Number greater than portfolio size " & _
              Chr(13) & g_total_loans
        End If
     Else
       'non numeric loan number requested
       error_type(3) = True
       msgInfo(3) = " Invalid non-Numeric Loan Number" & Chr(13)
     End If
  End If
  'Test for a "Y" or "N" in the coupon trace switch field
  switch_test(1) = (UCase(Trim(Range("CouponTraceSwitch"))) = "Y")
  switch_test(2) = (UCase(Trim(Range("CouponTraceSwitch"))) = "N")
  If switch_test(1) = False And switch_test(2) = False Then
     'neither "Y" or "N" entered
     error_type(4) = True
     msgInfo(4) = " Please enter either Y or N in the " & Chr(13) _
                       & "  coupon trace switch field" & Chr(13)
  End If

  'Construct and print out the message
  If error_type(1) Or error_type(2) Then
     Sheets("CoupTraceChart").Select
     msgTotal = "Floater Loan Coupon Trace Chart" & Chr(13)
     For i_err = 1 To 4
       If error_type(i_err) Then msgTotal = msgTotal & msgInfo(i_err)
     Next i_err
     msgPrompt = msgTotal
     msgResult = MsgBox(msgPrompt, cMsgButtonCode1, msgTitle)
     End
  End If

End Sub
```

EXHIBIT 17.14   Error checking the switch field and the loan number field

```
'=========================================================================
' Reads the coupon trace switch
'=========================================================================
Sub Read_Coupon_Trace_Screen()

  g_val_coup_trace_switch = False
  g_val_coup_trace_switch = (UCase(Trim(Range("CouponTraceSwitch")))) = "Y"

End Sub
```

EXHIBIT 17.15 Reading in the trace switch field

VALIDATING THE CASH FLOW CALCULATION CODE

Having some assurance that the inputs from both the menus and the collateral file are being read correctly, the collateral selection process is sound, and the monthly coupon levels for the portfolio are being correctly set, we can now turn our attention to the validation of the cash flow calculations.

To review: the cash flow calculation subroutines produce six vectors of cash flows for the portfolio as a whole. These are as follows: beginning period balance, defaulted principal, scheduled amortization of principal, coupon payments, prepayments of principal, and recoveries of defaulted principal. These vectors are aggregated from

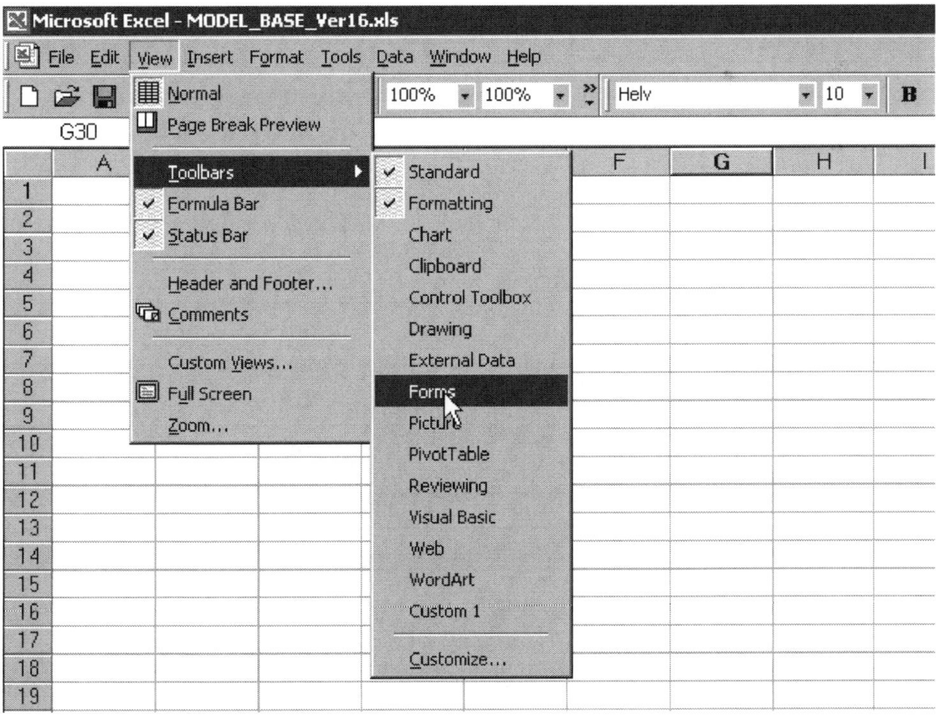

EXHIBIT 17.16 Getting to the Forms Menu to draw a button

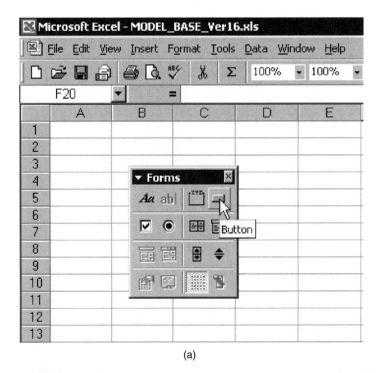

(a)

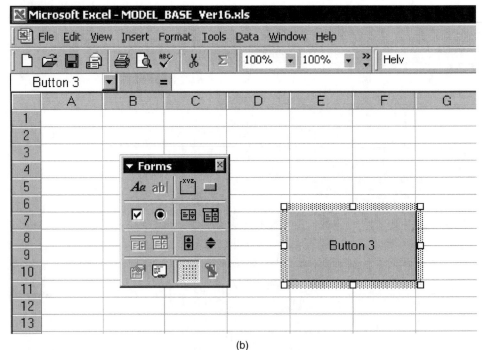

(b)

EXHIBIT 17.17 (a) Click on the Button icon and (b) a cursor appears and draws the button

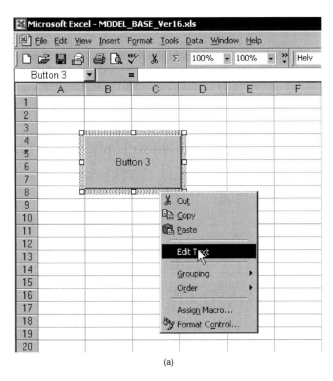

(a)

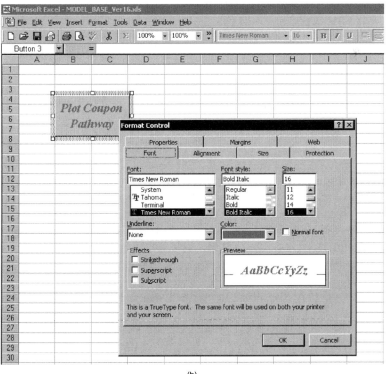

(b)

EXHIBIT 17.18   (a) Click on the Edit Text option and (b) edit the button text

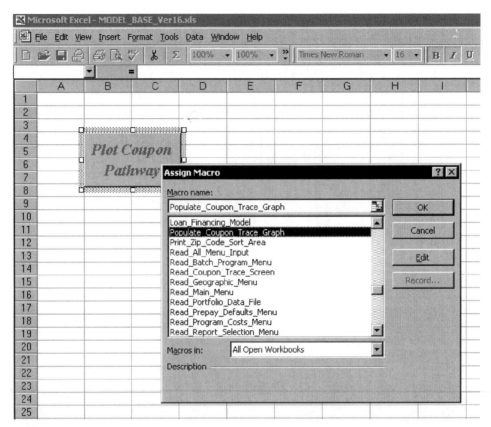

EXHIBIT 17.19   Assign the "Populate_Coupon_Trace_Graph" subroutine to the button

successive single loan amortization exercises and collectively summed before being written into the portfolio.

How can we look at them in the waterfall and tell if they are correct?

We cannot. There are too many loans with all kinds of different terms, coupons, and balances. So what do we do? There are basically two very different approaches that we can take. One is an essentially external approach to simplifying the process and the second is an internal approach that requires a bit of coding to accomplish. Both are useful in their own ways. We will start with the no-additional-code approach first.

Cash Flow Validation Using the Waterfall Spreadsheet

We clearly cannot verify the collective cash flows of a loan portfolio, but that should not stop us from trying to validate single loans or small groups of loans. We can specify any kind of loan we want, whether it is in the proposed portfolio or not by entering its characteristics into the collateral file as a single record. We can then run this record through the model. It is essentially a one-loan portfolio.

Test #1. Amortization of a fixed rate loan. Create a single fixed rate loan of a given term and coupon. This loan can look just like a residential first mortgage. It has a coupon of 7%, original and remaining terms of 360 months, and a balance of $100 million. While $100 million is a fairly large balance, it will display a large number of digits in the amortization process when displayed in the Excel Waterfall worksheet. Waive the collateral selection process eligibility tests. Specify a Range of prepayment and default terms of ten steps each for levels of 10% increments. This will produce a file of 100 waterfalls with some interesting characteristics. Start with the CPR, and then the PSA methodology. Put the market value decline factor at 0%. This will result in all defaulted principal being recovered with a lag.

Test #2. Fixed rate loan 0% Prepayments, 0% Defaults. This should look exactly like a standard amortization table from the PSA Securitization Handbook or other available sources. The monthly coupon payment can be calculated by hand and confirmed. The sum of the principal and coupon expense will be constant over the life of the loan because there is no payment attrition caused by either prepayment or defaults.

Test #3. Fixed rate loan 0% Prepayments, N% Defaults compared to N% Prepayments, 0% Defaults. If we use the CPR calculation methodology, we will pair up what are essentially mirror images of the amortization process. We will take the pair of scenarios 0%Prepay/10%Defaults and 10%Prepay/0%Defaults where the prepayment and default methodologies are both CPR. The amount of monthly defaults of principal and the monthly amounts of prepaid principal amounts will be identical in both cases. The amortization of principal will also be identical. The coupon and the payment levels on a period-by-period basis will also be the same. The aggregate cash flows will be very different because all the prepayments will result in principal being available to the deal while the defaulted principal will only result in principal available after the recovery period delay. While not conclusive, the evidence would suggest that if the balances are the same, either the calculations are correct, or if there is an error that it is systemic. Fortunately you can also compare a number of these cash flow scenarios with those that are available online to verify the contents

Test #4. Fixed rate loan N% Prepayments, N% Defaults. These scenarios will exhibit payment attrition and balance attrition that is in a systematic and recognizable pattern. As the combined rates increase, no scenario with a lesser Prepay+Default Rate sum should have a shorter average life, final maturity, or duration than a combination with a high sum. If you graph the principal outstanding curves of successive prepayment rates holding the default rate steady, you should see a consistent set of parallel amortization curves.

Test #5. Adding the Market Value Decline Factor. Now set the market value decline (MVD) factor to 100% and run the model. There will be no recovery of principal. Reset the MVD factor to be 50%. Now vary the starting appraisal values of the property. There is only one loan. It should be possible to calculate the monthly value of the recovered principal manually. Review the material in Chapter 14, "Calculating the Cash Flows," on the calculation of recoveries.

Floating Rate Loans

Things get somewhat more complicated for floating rate loans. If we stay calm and take things in a logical manner, you will see that it is not terribly more complicated, we just need to track a few other items. The first thing we can do is to print out to the Waterfall Spreadsheet, the monthly coupon rate of the note, and the monthly level of the index for that month. We can put this in a pair of the rightmost columns of the spreadsheet. The variables that we will print out are the g_loan_coupon, g_loan_spread, and g_index_level. Once we have these we can quickly compare the behavior of the floating rate coupon.

Test #6. Mimic the behavior of a fixed rate note. Put the index level for the floating rate note constant over its life. It now has become a fixed rate note. Run Test #1 under the fixed rate note test above. The results should be identical if the coupon rates are identical.

Test #7. Step the index by a fixed amount (0.5%) at one-year intervals. Run the program for the 100 scenarios using a pair of counter-balancing prepayment and default rates as we did above for the fixed rate loans. This will give you the same mirror imaging for the defaults and prepayment amounts now working with a floating rate note.

Test #8. Run a single scenario 0% Prepayments, 0% Defaults with a steady constant decline of 1.00% in the index. This will test the floor interest rate setting feature. This will give a clear amortization pattern with the only difference being a decrease in the amount of coupon paid over the life of the loan and a shortening of the loan average life due to more rapid principal amortization.

Test #9. Test #8 above with steady, one-year, increases of 1.00% per year in the index. This will test the interest rate cap setting logic in the program. This will give a clear amortization pattern with the only difference being an increase in the amount of coupon paid over the life of the loan and a lengthening of the loan average life due to more gradual principal amortization.

Cash Flow Validation Using a Purpose to Build VBA Subroutine

While the above methods will be very helpful in determining if we are on the right track, it does nothing at all to help verify the cash flows of the actual proposed portfolio on a loan-by-loan basis. For this we are going to need a bit of template file magic.

What we want to end up with are the monthly cash flows for each loan in the portfolio. We have to give this some thought. There are 2,000+ loans if all are deemed eligible for inclusion in the securitization. Approximately 40% of the portfolio has remaining terms greater than 120 months. The most useful display would be the beginning period balance, defaults, coupon income, scheduled amortization, prepayments and the ending balance. Displaying the coupon would also be very helpful in that we could immediately check its level at any point in time and confirm that neither the caps nor floors had been violated.

Excel spreadsheets are very long, 65,536 rows but only 256 columns wide. This would argue for writing the information in columns. If we look at the Eligible Collateral report Elig-2 Current Balances by Remaining Term, we can estimate how many cells of cash flows will be generated. The sum product of the number of loans by the maximum of the remaining term is 345,636, using the minimum it is 320,831! If we assume the worst-case scenario is 0% Prepayments and 0% Defaults, all loans will run to term. Printing the loan cash flows in a continuous column, one after the other, and stop printing when we hit the 65,000[th] row, we would need six columns of information each being eight cells wide. We would only use 48 of the available 256 columns!

To do this, an Excel file template has to be created and populated with formulas that will calculate when the information is written to the appropriate cells. Each column will have the following formulas or results:

- Column #1 – Nth Monthly period
- Column #2 – Beginning period principal balance for the period
- Column #3 – Defaulted principal for the period
- Column #4 – Coupon payments for the period
- Column #5 – Scheduled principal amortization for the period
- Column #6 – Prepayments of principal for the period
- Column #7 – Ending period principal balance
- Column #8 – Coupon rate of the loan for the period

> Column#7 would have as its formula (Column#2 − (Column#3 + Column#5 + Column#6)).

Field #1 would be equal to Field #7 (from the previous period).

At the beginning of each of the loan records the model will print the column headers. These would overwrite the formulas in the cells. The loan ID number would be placed in Column #1. The cash flow components would then be written in Columns 3, 4, 5, and 6. In period one of the loan the beginning principal balance would be written into Column 1, overwriting the formula in that cell. After every loan in the portfolio is completely written, the entire file would then be calculated. We would then have a period-by-period cash flow components schedule for the entire portfolio. We could confirm not only the per-period calculations but the entire amortization sequence of the entire loan.

Some Essential Preparatory Work   The one drawback to this approach is that we have to write some more VBA code and that the process, when run for the entire portfolio, takes a significant period of time.

To capture the information we need, we will have to declare some global variables, one for each of the cash flow components we are interested in. See Exhibit 17.20.

We will also need to change or declare some additional variables to handle the output filename, the template filename, the option choice to produce the report, and two constants to help with the error checking subroutines.

```
'CASH FLOW TRACE REPORT VARIABLES
Public g_val_defaults(1 To PAY_DATES)     As Double   'monthly defaults per loan
Public g_val_coup_income(1 To PAY_DATES)  As Double   'monthly coupon per loan
Public g_val_prin_ret(1 To PAY_DATES)     As Double   'monthly princpal per loan
Public g_val_prepays(1 To PAY_DATES)      As Double   'monthly prepays per loan
```

EXHIBIT 17.20   The global variables for the cash flow components

We will make the following declaration of a global variable to record the election of producing the report:

```
Public g_out_cftrace          As Boolean      'Switch to output CF Trace report
```

We will declare a global variable to record the name of the template file we have created for the Cash Flow Trace Report:

```
Public g_template_cf_trace_file As String 'template file name for cf trace report file
```

We will declare a global variable to record the name of the output file we will create using the template file above:

```
Public gfn_cf_trace_file    As String      'Name of OUTPUT cash flows trace file
```

These variables will be added to the **"A_Globals"** module.

We also need to add and change the value of a public constant to reflect the fact that we have an additional template filename and an additional output filename to error check on the Main Menu. In the module **"A_Constants"** we will change the value of the following constant from "6" to "7":

```
Public Const MAIN_MENU_TEMPLATE_FILE_NAMES = 7 '# of the names of template files
```

In the module **"MenusErrorCheck"** we will also change the values of the following constants from "6" to "7" so that the loops they control will now include error checking for the new filename and template filename.

```
'Number of output file sets we need to check to prevent overwrtting of existing files
Const OUTPUT_FILE_TESTS = 7   '# types of election tests (file name entered?)
Const OUTPUT_FILE_EXISTS = 7  '# tests for overwritting existing output files
```

Lastly, in the module **"CollateralCFGenerator"** we will add two calls to the subroutine "Compute_Collateral_Cashflows." The first one will be to a subroutine that will collect the monthly cash flow information for each piece of collateral and the second is the one that will print the results. The added calls are highlighted in Exhibit 17.21

Capturing the Monthly Cash Flows   The following subroutine will begin the process of building the trace file by capturing the amount of each of the cash flow components on a monthly basis. See Exhibit 17.22. Once we have these cash flows in hand we can move to printing them out, which we will do in the subroutine listed in the next section.

Writing the Cash Flow Trace File   This subroutine will have to perform the following steps:

```
Sub Compute_Collateral_Cashflows()

  If g_out_matrix Or g_out_waterfall Or g_out_scen_file Then

    Call Clear_Cashflow_Arrays          'zero out the payment components
    Call Redim_All_CashFlowComponent_Vectors 'redims the cash flow vectors
    Sheets("Main Menu").Select          'display the progress counter on Main Menu
    m_complete = 0
    Call Set_Scenario_Prepay_Rate       'expand the Base Rate scenarios
    Call Set_Scenario_Default_Rate      'expand the Base Rate scenarios
    Call Set_Monthly_Prepay_Factors     'calc monthly prepayments factors
                                               for each loan
    Call Set_Monthly_Default_Factors   'calc monthly prepayments factors
                                              for each loan
    Call Calc_Coupon_Factors            'set coupon and payment resets by loan
    Call Calc_SchAmortization_Factors 'set principal amortization by period

    For iprepay = 1 To g_prepay_levels            'loop through the Base Rates
       For idefault = 1 To g_default_levels        'loop through the Base Rates
          For iloan = 1 To g_total_loans           'loop loan-by-loan
             Call Setup_Initial_Loan_Parameters
             For iperiod = 1 To g_loan_rem_term(iloan)
                Call Calculate_Default_Effects(iloan)
                Call Calculate_Coupon_Payments
                Call Calculate_Scheduled_Amortization
                Call Calculate_Prepayments_of_Principal
                Call Calculate_Recoveries
                Call Accumulate_CF_Components
                If g_out_cftrace Then Call Capture_Monthly_CF_Trace(iperiod)
             Next iperiod
             If g_out_cftrace Then Call Print_Out_Trace_Report(iprepay, idefault)
          Next iloan
          Call Display_Amortization_ProgressMsg(iprepay, idefault)
       Next idefault
    Next iprepay

  End If

End Sub
```

EXHIBIT 17.21 The two subroutine call added to the "Compute_Collateral_Cashflows" subroutine

1. If this is the first loan of the portfolio, open the template file and rename it, saving it to the new name. The name is constructed using the prepayment and default rate assumptions associated with these cash flows.
2. Write the standard Assumptions Page Report into the template file so that we know all the selection criteria used.

```
Sub Capture_Monthly_CF_Trace(iperiod As Long)

  g_val_defaults(iperiod) = m_loan_defaults
  g_val_coup_income(iperiod) = m_loan_coup_income
  g_val_prin_ret(iperiod) = m_loan_prin_ret
  g_val_prepays(iperiod) = m_loan_prepays

End Sub
```

EXHIBIT 17.22 The two subroutine call added to the "Compute_Collateral_Cashflows" subroutine

3. Write out the loan-by-loan Final Loan Status Report so that we have a listing of every single loan in the cash flow file.
4. Write the individual loan block. First the headers and then the period-by-period cash flows.
5. Test to see if this loan is the last loan in the portfolio. If it is, erase the rest of the unused formulas in the workbook, calculate the formulas, and then copy the contents as values that wipe out the formulas, and close the worksheet. If it is not the last loan, then continue.
6. If the last print line is greater than 20,000, clear the rest of the column and start a new column. If it is not, go to the next loan and write it into this column.

Exhibit 17.23 displays the VBA code that will do this for us. As noted in the "Under Construction" section earlier in the chapter, this subroutine and three other

```
Sub Print_Out_Trace_Report(fin_type)

Dim i               As Long      'generic loop counter
Dim trace_file      As String    'full pathway of trace file
Dim trace_name      As String    'full file name
Dim trace_prepay    As String    'prepayment portion of file name
Dim trace_default   As String    'default portion of file
Dim v_cur_balance   As Double    'running cur balance number

  'Open the template file and populate it with the list of
  'eligible collateral, the data file, and the assumptions
  If iloan = 1 Then
       'this is the first report, open the file
       Workbooks.Open Filename:=g_pathway_template & "cf_trace_template.xls"
       trace_prepay = "P" & g_prepay_rate(iprepay) * 100 & "%_"
       trace_default = "D" & g_default_rate(idefault) * 100 & "%.xls"
       trace_name = "CFTrace_" & trace_prepay & trace_default
       trace_file = g_pathway_output & gfn_output_prefix & trace_name
       ActiveWorkbook.SaveAs Filename:=trace_file
       icol = 1
       row_num = 1
       cf_trace_col_num = 1
       Call Write_Assumptions_Page
       Call Final_Loan_Status(False)
       Sheets("MonthlyCF").Select
       ActiveWorkbook.Save
  End If

  'print out the monthy cash flows
v_cur_balance = g_loan_cur_bal(iloan)
Call Write_Loan_Trace_Headers
For i = 1 To g_loan_rem_term(iloan)
  If v_cur_balance > 0.01 Then
        Cells(row_num, icol).Value = i
        'set the beginning balance of the loan
        Cells(row_num, icol + 1).Value = g_loan_cur_bal(iloan)
        Cells(row_num, icol + 2).Value = v_defaults(i)
        Cells(row_num, icol + 3).Value = v_coup_income(i)
        Cells(row_num, icol + 4).Value = v_prin_ret(i)
        Cells(row_num, icol + 5).Value = v_prepays(i)
        'icol+6 is a calculation column for ending balance
        Cells(row_num, icol + 7).Value = g_loan_coupon(iloan, i)
        v_cur_balance = v_cur_balance - v_defaults(i) -
          v_prin_ret(i) - v_prepays(i)
```

EXHIBIT 17.23 Code from the "Cash Flow Trace" function

```
                    row_num = row_num + 1
        End If
    Next i
    'clear the accumulators
    Erase v_defaults
    Erase v_coup_income
    Erase v_prin_ret
    Erase v_prepays
    'put out a progress message
    Application.StatusBar = "Finished cashflows for loan = " & iloan & _
        " column=" & cf_trace_col_num & "  row_num=" & row_num

'Test to see if we are finished with the portfolio clear the unused columns and save
  If iloan = g_total_loans Then
        Call Clear_Unused_Column_Space   'current column only
        If cf_trace_col_num < 20 Then
           'clear all the additonal columns
           For i = cf_trace_col_num + 1 To 20
             row_num = 1
             cf_trace_col_num = cf_trace_col_num + 1
             Call Clear_Unused_Column_Space
           Next i
        End If
        Calculate
        Call Copy_Worksheet_as_Values_and_Save
  End If

'We are going to write in the first 20,000 rows of each column otherwise we will
spend 'half our lives scrolling down, test to see if we are at the end of a column.
If we are clear the 'remainder of the column.
  If row_num > 20000 Then
        Call Clear_Unused_Column_Space
        'need to start a new column
        cf_trace_col_num = cf_trace_col_num + 1
        'there are only twenty columns available
        If cf_trace_col_num <= 20 Then
            icol = 1 + ((cf_trace_col_num - 1) * 8)
             row_num = 1
            Calculate
            ActiveWorkbook.Save
        Else
           'no more columns left to write to!
           Call Copy_Worksheet_as_Values_and_Save
        End If
  End If
End If

End Sub
```

EXHIBIT 17.23   (*Continued*)

formatting subroutines that support it will be placed in a newly created module named "WriteCFTraceReport."

This will produce the following report block for each loan as shown in Exhibit 17.24.

VALIDATING THE CASH FLOW WATERFALL SPREADSHEET

We can have a high degree of confidence that the calculation of the collateral cash flows is correct. These cash flows are now fed into the waterfall spreadsheet.

EXHIBIT 17.24 This is a sample of a section of the Cash Flow Trace Report for a single loan

1	Beg Bal	Defaults	Coup Inc	Sch Amort	Prepay	End Bal	Coup Level
1	459,000.00	7,299.56	3,764.17	272.18	3,946.21	447,482.05	10.000%
2	447,482.05	7,116.39	3,669.71	267.72	3,847.17	436,250.78	10.000%
3	436,250.78	6,937.77	3,577.61	263.33	3,750.59	425,299.09	10.000%
4	425,299.09	6,763.61	3,574.99	265.50	3,656.35	414,613.63	10.250%
[20 periods omitted]							
24	255,230.93	4,058.98	2,354.74	211.57	2,193.80	248,766.58	11.250%
[86 periods omitted]							
120	20,252.59	322.08	166.09	44.64	173.83	19,712.03	10.0000%
[100 periods omitted]							
220	1,105.32	17.58	9.06	8.56	9.43	1,069.75	10.0000%
[80 periods omitted]							
300	16.67	0.27	0.14	2.29	0.12	13.99	10.0000%
301	13.99	0.22	0.11	2.25	0.10	11.42	10.0000%
302	11.42	0.18	0.09	2.21	0.08	8.95	10.0000%
303	8.95	0.14	0.07	2.17	0.06	6.58	10.0000%
304	6.58	0.10	0.05	2.14	0.04	4.29	10.0000%
305	4.29	0.07	0.04	2.10	0.02	2.10	10.0000%
306	2.10	0.03	0.02	2.07	0.00	0.00	10.0000%

EXHIBIT 17.25   Sources and Uses of the cash flow waterfall spreadsheet

Summary Report		
Collateral Cash Flows		
Scheduled Amortization	87,626,033	21.45%
Prepayments to Principal	148,067,224	36.24%
Total Principal Retired	235,693,258	
Defaulted Principal	172,877,718	42.31%
Recoveries of Principal (& rate)	150,537,927	87.08%
Coupon Income	127,388,641	
Total Cash Sources	**513,619,826**	
Debt Cash Flows		
Program Fees	2,871,882	
Servicing Fee	10,749,195	
Conduit Debt Service	108,309,085	
Conduit Principal Payments	388,142,427	
Released to Seller	3,547,237	
Total Cash Uses	**513,619,826**	

Balancing Sources and Uses

The first thing we should check is that the total sources of cash flows for each period is equal to the total uses.

The Waterfall has a "Box Score" area, as shown in Exhibits 17.25 and 17.26 that will tell us just that.

EXHIBIT 17.26   Summary performance statistics for both the Conduit and the Seller Interest

Performance	Conduit	Seller Interest
Structuring		
Beginning Balance	388,142,427	20,428,549
Ownership Interest	95.00%	5.00%
Performance		
Principal Outstanding	$0.00	0.00%
Severity of Loss	0.000%	0.00%
IRR	7.478%	−15.257%
Tenor		
Average Life (yrs)	3.700	
Final Maturity (yrs)	10.917	
Modified Duration	3.052	
Macauley Duration	2.880	
Checks		
Program Fee Shortfall	FALSE	
Servicing Fee Shortfall	FALSE	
Interest Shortfall	TRUE	

In addition, we have another section of the Box Score that contains the summary performance statistics for the Conduit Financing and the Seller Interest.

These two sections can be used to independently verify the performance of the structure. We can see the period-by-period cash flows in the spreadsheet. Using these we can independently confirm the average lives, final maturities, and durations by running them through other software or calculators.

Performance Triggers

There are three performance triggers in the deal that will immediately force all payments to go to the Conduit Financing until it is paid out. These are:

1. Breach of the three-month rolling default threshold of 10% of the original balance of the collateral
2. Clean up call when the balance of the Conduit financing is less than 10% of its original amount
3. Qualitative breach such as a servicer default or a performance failure

These trigger events should be clearly identifiable in the model. For the qualitative breach, apply the trigger at various points in the waterfall and observe the results of the accelerated principal payments to the Conduit financing position.

Delinquency Reserve Fund Performance

Verifying that the Delinquency Reserve Fund is performing as expected is greatly facilitated by a special section of the spreadsheet solely dedicated to detailing its activities.

In Columns 44 to 49 of the cash flow waterfall, we have a column-by-column description of the monthly transactions of the account. The section details balances, funding, and draw activities. We can specifically trace under which conditions the account can fund, using Excess Servicing from the deal. The current cap for the account is also displayed so that we know what the funding limitations are.

FUTURE BACK TESTING ACTIVITY

There is one further validation task that we have to start thinking about. This is the subject of back testing. Back testing occurs just before the time a new version of the model is released to the users. It falls under the "better to be safe than to be sorry" rule.

The process of back testing begins with the specification of a number of model functions that are critical and core to the model. Obviously any impairment of these functions is undesirable. But how will we know if anything in the existing model has been impacted in the course of the changes we made to the newer version? We can design a suite of runs and a list of functions that we will check across the version change. If it worked before it should continue to work in the new version as long as the change to the new version was not specifically designed to change something in the test numbers.

So, for each model, we run a specific series of analysis and then compare the results. They should be identical. This will be added in because we had the foresight to include an Assumptions Report in every file we produced. The formats of the report packages will probably not change from one release of the model to another, allowing us to write a VBA/Excel program to sequentially compare each pair of files, existing version to new version results.

In that this discussion is more properly presented later, in Chapter 21, "Managing the Growth of the Model," we have only outlined it here. In Chapter 21 we will design the test cases and show you how to write the file-parsing program that will alleviate the necessity of comparing the files manually.

VALIDATION ACTIVITIES BY THIRD PARTIES

Depending on the issuance conventions for the asset class that you are modeling, you may well find yourself having to verify the model with a third party, most likely an audit firm. In the case of public issuance where the deal is syndicated, the members of the syndicate will all run their own models and confirm the results among themselves before approaching an audit firm.

These audit requirements will specify a list of all items to be verified. There will also be criteria as to the degree of accuracy needed for the confirmation to be affirmed. You should conduct your validation activities with a special emphasis on these items. Doing so will save you a lot of time and embarrassment as the time to close the transaction approaches.

DELIVERABLES CHECKLIST

The VBA Knowledge Checklist item for this chapter is:

- How to write a period-by-period cash flow component Trace Program

The Model Knowledge Checklist for this chapter is:

- Testing techniques for verifying loan portfolio cash flows

NEXT STEPS

Having validated the model we are *now* ready to use it. In Chapter 18, "Running the Model," we will lay out the typical series of runs that are used to move the deal from a proposal to a finished financing.

ON THE WEB SITE

On the Web site you will find **"MODEL_BASE_17.xls"** that contains the incremental code for the cash flow trace functionality.

You will also find the template file for the Cash Flow Trace report and a finished report (which is very *large*!).

CHAPTER **18**

Running the Model

OVERVIEW

We are now ready to run the model. In this chapter we will step through the process of modeling a simplified Conduit Financing deal. We will identify the collateral offered by the Seller. We will then sort through the pool and select a subset of loans that are individually and collectively eligible for inclusion in the deal. Once we have the collateral in hand, we can run the Expected Case cash flows. These represent our best estimates of the anticipated performance of the deal over its lifetime, the base case. From this Expected Case we will identify certain critical inputs and the Range of values these inputs have historically assumed. In a series of model runs, we will run the model across these values and measure the deal's sensitivity to a Range of variances in their values. To complete our internal credit analysis, we will apply our institutional stress tests.

Lastly, we will subject the deal to specific conditions as set forth by the rating agencies. These assumptions will be considerably more severe than the Expected Case assumptions. The performance of the structure against these Rating Agency Stress Case criteria will be the basis for the credit rating of the deal.

If this sounds like it entails a lot of work, you are right, it does!

There are certain things that we can do to make things easier on ourselves. Most of the sensitivity and stress runs require that we produce sets of reports. These sets of reports will keep some inputs constant while varying one, two, or three parameters at a time. We may be able to modify the model so that it is capable of running multiple scenario sets instead of having to enter each scenario by hand. This is a model evolution that was alluded to in Chapter 1. By being able to specify many related scenarios at a single time we will greatly reduce the amount of repetitive data entry to the menus that we would otherwise have to do. This functionality will also tend to significantly lower data entry errors due to fatigue and carelessness. If we have a menu to specify multiple scenarios we will quickly see the underlying input patterns and spot errors and omissions before we waste time running the model from the wrong input set. It will also avoid the requirement to constantly monitor the progress of the model. We should be able to start the model on a set of runs and let the machine finish on its own while we are doing something else (like eating lunch).

The Sensitivity and Stress runs will produce a large number of related output files. The vast majority of these files will be Summary Matrix files. By the time we are running Sensitivity and Stress runs we will be tightly focused on only a few of the output results. The most critical results at this point in the process will be the Severity of Loss to and the Coverage Ratio of the Conduit Financing.

Upon completion of these runs we will be faced with another problem. It is called the "too much of a good thing" problem. If we are trying to quickly compare the variation of a single parameter across ten different scenarios we will have no effective or efficient way to do it! We could print out all ten Summary Matrix Reports and line them up side up side, but there is a much better solution.

We can build another VBA program to help us organize and present the model outputs in a more intelligible form. We will build a "post-processing" program. A "post-processing" program goes to work after the model has finished all its runs. It is a separate VBA/Excel program that will allow us to open sets of Matrix Summary Reports and extract from them targeted individual outputs. One of these outputs, Severity of Loss to the Conduit Financing, will be critical in the later portion of the structuring process. The program, which we will call simply Extractor.xls, will greatly speed up and simplify the process of isolating critical information from many different output files.

DELIVERABLES

VBA Language Knowledge Deliverables
- How to build an ability to run the model in a "Batch Mode" to produce multiple scenarios in a single model run
- How to design a post-processing program to help us organize the output of the model more effectively and efficiently

Modeling Knowledge Deliverable
- How to perform the tasks needed to structure a deal

UNDER CONSTRUCTION

While the main focus of this chapter will be the use of the model to structure a deal, we will conduct two distinct development activities.

The first will be to build a "batch" processing capability into the model. The capability will allow us to specify the most frequently used parameters of the model, market value decline, recovery lag period, and Conduit pricing spread for up to 50 different individual scenarios at one time. We can then run these scenarios without the necessity of manually loading each scenario's inputs before we run it. This facility will also allow us to establish files of the conditions of stress tests, investor requests, and the like, for use in structuring other deals.

The second will be the development of a program that will sit outside the model, the "Matrix_Extractor.xls" program. This program will allow us to aggregate the results of several Summary Matrix Report packages into a single file. This will allow use to compare, review and interpret the results of the various model runs more easily.

To implement the "batch" feature in the model we will develop a short but highly efficient set of subroutines that will allow us to make multiple runs of the model without manual intervention. To do this we will essentially have to persuade the existing model into thinking that *we* are making the inputs and triggering the calculation sequences. To this end we need to make several changes and additions to the model.

The first thing on our list of "Things To Do" to build a multiple scenario model is to contract a menu that will contain the set of inputs that we want to mimic as user inputs.

We next need to create VBA code to read the menu, transfer its contents to the model, and trigger the calculation of the model. The code that we will develop will be specifically related to this purpose and this purpose only. We should therefore create a separate module for this code and name it "A_BatchFileProgram."

Into this module we will place four relatively short subroutines. The first subroutine will count the number of scenarios that have been entered. The second subroutine will error check the contents of the Batch File Menu. The third will read the contents of the menu into arrays in the model. The last subroutine will write the contents to the model and trigger its calculations.

All variables we will need for these subroutines will be modular level variables so that we will not need to alter the **"A_Constants"** or the **"A_Globals"** modules.

The second project will be the development of the standalone program "Matrix_Extractor.xls." In this program we create a single menu and a series of five VBA modules. The modules will mirror the module structure of our original model. There will be modules to hold the public constants and global variables, the main program, to read the menu, to read the data files, and to write the report.

INSTALLING A "RUN BUTTON"

Before we start making repeated runs of the model, it would be convenient not to have to enter the VBA Editor, go to the Main Program, and hit the "F5" button. Instead, we are going to create a "Run Model" button on each of the menus. This button will be directly linked to the Main Program subroutine and when pressed, it will start the model running. Providing additional copies of the button on the other menus allows the user to start the model from any location.

Linking the Button to the Main Model

Buttons are objects and can be installed by using the View|Toolbars|Forms command, then selecting the button option. Draw the general shape of the button, and then use the Format command to insert text so that the user knows what it is for. Make the button large enough so that it is clearly visible on the screen. Next, format the button font to be a very bright color; red or yellow work best against the standard gray button background.

Assigning, Labeling, and Formatting the Button

The next step is to right click on the button and select the "Assign Macro" option. The dialog box will appear. Simply scroll down to the macro you wish to assign and click on it. Activating the button will immediately start running the VBA code in the associated subroutine.

Right click the button again and select the Font option to format the button label.

STEPS OF THE STRUCTURING PROCESS

The following are steps that we will follow to structure a basic deal:

1. **Determine the composition of the proposed collateral portfolio.** Run the proposed collateral file through the model with the Collateral Selection and all the Cash Flow report-generating options turned off. Enter a "YES" to the "Write Out Eligible Collateral Reports?" option. This will produce a set of collateral stratification reports based on the entire contents of the proposed portfolio. We will use these reports to determine the basic structure of the collateral. These reports will also identify any concentration issues in the portfolio related to geographic location or large balances.

2. **Perform the initial selection activity.** Now we will enter the selection criteria that we will apply on the loan-by-loan level. These parameters will be entered in the Collateral Criteria Menu. Answer "Y" to the first three options on the Main Menu. These will perform the selection process, print the ineligible loans, and print the new Eligible Collateral Stratification Reports.

3. **Examine the initially selected portfolio for concentration issues.** Concentration issues relate to the clustering of loans with similar characteristics. These may be coupon rate, balance, geographic, tenor, fixed/floating features, or any other aggregation of common characteristics that can make the portfolio vulnerable. The key concentration issues we will have to concern ourselves with in this portfolio are current balance concentrations in large loans and geographic concentration. Geographic concentration is of particular interest due to the fact that both physical and economic disasters can affect clustered loans strongly. We have two ways of dealing with concentration issues. The first is to disqualify loans with the concentrated characteristic. The second is to add additional collateral to the portfolio to limit the concentration by increasing the overall pool size.

4. **Correction of any concentration issues.** If there are concentration issues, we may move to solve them by one of the two methods. We may add eligible collateral, if it is available, or we may disqualify collateral that is eligible on an individual basis but not on a collective basis.

5. **Run the Expected Case cash flow analysis.** After having addressed the concentration issues in step four, we are now able to begin to run the model and determine the Conduit advance rate to the Seller. The Expected Case is just that, what we realistically expect to happen over the life of the deal. We will run the cash flows based on a Range of prepayment and default assumptions that encompass the observed empirical rates for collateral portfolios of this type. We will look at the performance of the Conduit financing to determine the expected repayment patterns. We will also look at the ability of the proposed Seller Interest to absorb defaults and payment dilution of the collateral.

6. **Performing Sensitivity Analysis of the Expected Case.** Due to the limited space in the book, we will conduct sensitivity analysis on three factors as they relate to the Expected Case. The three most sensitive factors are the percentage of the Market Value Decline (MVD) parameter, the length of the Recovery Lag Period (RLP), and the Conduit Financing Spread. The first will tell us what our expected recoveries are relative to the Owners Equity in each of the loans. The second will tell us how long we have to wait for the recovered principal to be realized in the

cash flows. The third, the Conduit Financing Spread, will determine the magnitude of the coupon income between the collateral coupon payments and the gross Conduit financing interest expense. We will run an increasing percentage of MVD, longer and longer RLP, and higher financing spreads. Once we have completed these runs, we will progress to the rating agency stress tests.

7. **Performing the rating agency stress tests.** The assumptions of these tests are specified by the rating agencies. They involve setting a specific percentage of the original principal to default over a compressed timeframe at the beginning of the deal. As such we will select the "User Defined" default methodology that targets a specific percentage of the principal and then spreads it across the annual schedule table according to the pattern indicated. Both the MVD and the RLP will be more severe to simulate a widespread and severe downturn in the economic environment. We will then see where the Seller Interest fails to protect the Conduit Financing and what losses the Conduit Financing sustains.

8. **Adjustments to the Seller Interest based on the stress test outcomes.** Finally we may need to adjust the Seller Interest and rerun the rating agency stress tests to meet the requirements of the desired rating. When this step is complete we will have completed our initial sizing of the deal. In the real world we may do this numerous times, but these steps are fully representative of the process as a whole.

ORGANIZING THE OUTPUT

We are about to go through a structuring run step by step. Along the way we will generate over 100 output files. To avoid confusion, misplaced or overwritten output files, it is a good idea to organize the output directory to accommodate this future activity.

Creating Subdirectories to Store the Output

To be sure that we preserve the output of the various model runs specified above, we will create a series of subdirectories under the output directory. These subdirectories will be organized along the steps of the structuring process. When a step in the process requires segregation of a series of results, sensitivity runs, or stress tests, we will create further subdirectories. These will hold a collection of files related to the subprocesses or case specific conditions under the main activity.

The names of the first level subdirectories are shown in Exhibit 18.1.

This directory structure will give us an organized way to store the various sets of outputs we will generate.

In practice, it is best to route all the results files to the output directory first and then move them to the subdirectories after the run is complete. This will allow you to look at each set of results before you store them for more or less permanent keeping in the subdirectories. (It also makes for considerably shorter pathway names in the menu fields.)

Now that we have the structure established to receive the files, let us start generating them!

```
\output
    \run01_base_portfolio   'Step#1 description of collateral portfolio no selection
    \run02_first_selection  'Step#2 initial collateral selection process results
    \run03_comb_selection   'Step#3 and #4 subsequent selection processes
    \run04_expect_case      'Step#5 expected economic case cash flows
    \run04_sen              'Step#6 sensitivities of the expected economic case
        \01_lag_only        '       sensitivity to recovery lag period only
        \02_mvd_only        '       sensitivity to market value decline only
        \03_spread_only     '       sensitivity to Cond Fin spread changes only
        \04_lag_mvd         '       sensitivity to RPL and MVD changes
        \05_spread_mvd      '       sensitivity to Spread and MVD changes
        \06_lag_spread      '       sensitivity to RPL and Spread
        \07_all_3           '       sensitivity to RPL, 2-3% Spread and MVD
        \08_all_3_CFS400    '       sensitivity to RPL, 4% Spread, and MVD
        \09_first10yrs      'Stress test of Expected Case all losses in 1st 10 years
    \run05_rating_agency    'Step#7 rating agency stress tests
        \01_first5yrs       '       default timing 5%-30%-30%-30%-5%
    \run06_final_sizing     'Step#8 files for the final sizing of the deal
        \825_advance        '       structure performance 82.5% advance rate
        \90_advance         '       structure performance 90% advance rate
        \95_advance         '       structure performance 95% advance rate
        \final_sizings      '       final sizings for BBB, A, AA, AAA
```

EXHIBIT 18.1   Output directory structure we will create to hold the results of the structuring runs

STEP 1: DETERMINE COMPOSITION OF PROPOSED COLLATERAL PORTFOLIO

As indicated above in the outline of the steps, the first thing we need to determine is what kind of a hand we have been dealt by the Seller. To get an overall view of the collateral portfolio without applying any of the selection criteria, we will set the model up with these options:

- "Write Out Eligible Collateral Reports" option turned on and all the other options turned off. This will treat all loans as eligible and produce the collateral stratification reports for the entire portfolio.
- The data file is "collateral_orig.xls" and can be found in the "\data" directory. We enter this name in the input field "Collateral Data File Name."
- Enter "NoSelect_" in the "Report Group Prefix" field to tag the eligible reports file with this name.

When you are finished the Main Menu should look like Exhibit 18.2. We will not have to make any other inputs to the model. Again we are not performing a selection activity against the collateral merely getting all of it to print out so we can look at it.

We run the model and the results are as follows:

Total loans:	2,255	Total Current Balance:	$461,898,460
Wght Avg Orig Term:	202.47 months	Total Equity Balance:	$365,601,540
Wght Avg Rem Term:	187.11 months		
Wght Avg Coupon:	8.511%		

This looks like a fairly robust portfolio. It is somewhat seasoned but not overly so. The collateral pool has a wide spread to the index rate upon which it floats, Prime. The loans also tend to have large equity balances as it relates to the current balances

Loan Securitization Model Main Menu

Program Execution Options	(Y=YES; N=NO)
N	Perform the Collateral Eligibility Test?
N	Write out Ineligible Collateral Reports?
Y	Write out Eligible Collateral Reports?
N	Write out Eligible Collateral Loan File?
N	Write out Cash Flow Waterfall Reports?
N	Write out Matrix Summary Reports?
N	Write out Cash Flow Trace files? (*Caution: can generate VERY LENGTHY run times!*)

Run the Model

Input File Information

C:\VBA_Class\VBA_Book\

portfolio_orig.xls	Collateral Data File Name
0	# of Loans *Enter "0" to read all available, otherwise enter the number of loans that you want to have read from the top of the file.*

	Report Group Prefix (attached to alll output files)		Template File Names
NoSelect			
Ineligibles.xls	Ineligible Collateral Reports File Name	<=======	inelig_template.xls
Collateral.xls	Eligible Collateral Reports File Name	<=======	collat_template.xls
Waterfall.xls	Cash Flow Waterfalls Report File Name	<=======	waterfall_template.xls
Matrix.xls	Summary Matrix Reports Files	<=======	matrix_template.xls
	Eligible Collateral File	<=======	datafile_template.xls
Scenario.xls	Scenario Summary Reports File	<=======	scenario_template.xls

EXHIBIT 18.2   Main Menu inputs to produce the set or collateral demographic reports

and project appraisal estimates. We will now go through the collateral reports one by one and look at the characteristics of the portfolio.

- **Elig-1, Current Balances by Original Terms.** This report shows us that the Seller was originating loans clustered around four original terms of 10, 15, 20, and 25 years.
- **Elig-2, Current Balances by Remaining Term.** Approximately 40% of the portfolio has a remaining term of under 10 years, 63% under 20 years, and 99% under 25 years or less. The longest remaining term is 26 years. Except for concentrations at 10 years and 29 years, the distribution of remaining term at 12-month intervals is relatively smooth.
- **Elig-3, Current Balances Distribution by Seasoning.** The portfolio is new. Most of it, 87%, is less than 30 months old. This could be a problem in regards to servicing history and performance history. There is not a long-term history available unless the Seller has historical data on other similar and more seasoned portfolios. We could then make use of that experience as a proxy for this portfolio all other things being equal (underwriting, due diligence, etc.).
- **Elig-4, Current Balances Distributed by Current Coupon.** The overwhelming amount of current balances is concentrated in the Range of 7.50 to 9.00% coupon. Within that overall Range there are substantial balances in every single 0.25% interval. This would tend to make the portfolio less vulnerable to prepayment effects.
- **Elig-5, Current Distributed by Spread.** In that all loans are indexed off of the Prime Rate, the spread distribution mirrors the coupon distribution. The spreads are robust with the bulk of the loans in the stratification for spread level between the 2.75 to 3.75% Range.
- **Elig-6, Current Balances by Percentage of Owners Equity.** The key item in this report is to note that 21% of the loans in the portfolio have an Owner's Equity

position that is greater than 50%. The 50% number is significant in that it is the standard base MVD number for this asset class. This is to say that 21% of the loans will experience 100% recovery of the principal if they default. In addition 74% of the loan balances are in loans with a 30% or greater equity position which will also serve to limit net losses.

- **Elig-7, Current Balances by Loan-to-Value Ratio.** This is the mirror image report of the one above. This ratio is computed by dividing the current balance of the loan by the appraisal value of the project. The loan-to-value (LTV) is the inverse of the Owners Equity percentage. A loan with a 40% LTV will have a 60% Owners Equity position.

- **Elig-8, Current Balances by Current Balance Distribution.** The portfolio is made up of smaller balance loans. Over 30% of the current balances are in loans under $200,000. Over 77% of the balances are in loans under $600,000. Only 5% of the loan balances are in loans of over $1 million. This is, however, a problem: currently there is a rating agency limitation of 2% on loans over $1 million in portfolios under $500 million. We may have our first small concentration issue.

- **Elig-9, Current Balances by Original Balance Distribution.** This report gives us information on the distribution of the number of loans and their remaining balances by the original balance of the loan. It indirectly tells us how "chunky" the loans are from a payment standpoint. It is also indicative of how much exposure we have to large balance loan concentrations. As noted in the comments in Elig-8, this is something we need to keep an eye on.

- **Elig-10, Current Balances Distribution by State or Territory.** This report shows that five states account for 35% of the current balances. In addition, two states, California and New Jersey, each account for over 8% of the current balances. We have a 7.5% cap for the portfolio as a whole for current balances from any one state. This state level concentration might possibly be a second concentration issue.

- **Elig-11, Current Balances in Top 50 ZIP Codes.** The top five ZIP codes account for 2.4% of the current balance of the portfolio. None of the top three ZIP codes, Alabama 35209, Nevada 89118, and Texas 76028, have over 0.70% of the total portfolio balances that is the concentration limit for a single ZIP code. In addition, the top five ZIP codes cannot collectively have more than 3% of the total principal, so, as noted above, we are well under that concentration limit also.

The initial review of the portfolio is now complete. We have identified a number of strengths in the portfolio and a number of weaknesses. The weaknesses are a lack of seasoning, large loan balance concentration, and both state and ZIP code level geographic concentration. The strengths are wide collateral coupon spreads in regards to the financing costs and very strong equity positions. These two factors in combination will be significant risk mitigants.

STEP 2: INITIAL COLLATERAL SELECTION

We will now apply a set of selection criteria against the portfolio. The first thing to do is set the initial three choices in the model options block to "Y." All other model option settings will be turned to "N." The effect of this will be to run the collateral

Loan Securitization Model Main Menu

Program Execution Options	(Y=YES; N=NO)	
Y	Perform the Collateral Eligibility Test?	
Y	Write out Ineligible Collateral Reports?	**Run the**
Y	Write out Eligible Collateral Reports?	**Model**
N	Write out Eligible Collateral Loan File?	
N	Write out Cash Flow Waterfall Reports?	
N	Write out Matrix Summary Reports?	
N	Write out Cash Flow Trace Files? (*Caution: can generate VERY LENGTHY run times!*)	

Input File Information

C:\VBA_Class\AnalystProgram	
portfolio_orig.xls	Collateral Data File Name
0	# of Loans *Enter "0" to read all available, otherwise enter the number of loans that you want to have read from the top of the file.*

Output File Information

		Template File Names
Select_01_	Report Group Prefix (attached to alll output files)	
Ineligibles.xls	Ineligible Collateral Reports File Name <=======	inelig_template.xls
Collateral.xls	Eligible Collateral Reports File Name <=======	collat_template.xls
Waterfall.xls	Cash Flow Waterfalls Report File Name <=======	waterfall_template.xls
Matrix.xls	Summary Matrix Reports Files <=======	matrix_template.xls
	Eligible Collateral File <=======	datafile_template.xls

EXHIBIT 18.3   Main Menu settings for the run

file through the selection process but not produce any cash flows. We do not want to run cash flows just yet because we do not know how many of the loans of the portfolio will survive the portfolio selection process. In addition, we will not select to produce a new collateral data file because we do not know if or when the selection process will be over. We will call the output file prefix of the Eligible and Ineligible Collateral Report Package as "Select01_."

We will not change the name of the collateral data file, as we want to use the same data set as before. We keep the number of loans at "0," the option to read every loan in the entire file. The names of the template files and the names of the output files will not change either.

See Exhibit 18.3 to view the Main Menu configuration for this run.

We now enter the selection criteria. See Exhibit 18.4.

We are making these selections for the following reasons. Minimum remaining and original term is set to 12. It may take four to six months to put the deal together. The information about the loans is current as of now. If, however, we closed the deal four to eight months from now, they will have four to eight months less cash flows. We therefore need to be sure that the loans will not have paid out prior to closing the deal.

We will set the remaining and original minimum principal balances to $25,000 to eliminate the very small loans of the portfolio that would not be economically feasible to service. We will set the minimum spread for any loan to 2.25%. After the selection is complete, we will review the two geographic concentration issues to see if they have improved.

We hit the "Run the Model" button and the Ineligible Loan Report in Exhibit 18.5 is produced.

A total of 56 loans are ineligible for a total current balance of $3.024MM. These results can be seen in Exhibit 18.5.

Collateral Selection Criteria Menu

Minimum	Maximum	
12	360	Original Term (Months)
12	360	Remaining Term (Months)
$25,000	$2,000,000	Original Balance
$25,000	$2,000,000	Remaining Balance
7.000%	11.000%	Gross Coupon
	80.000%	Maximum Total Project LTV%
	$5	Difference Stated-Calculated Pmt

Run the Model

Indices & Minimum Spreads		
Index Code	Min Spread	
PRIME	2.250%	Index #1 and Minimum Spread
		Index #2 and Minimum Spread
		Index #3 and Minimum Spread
		Index #4 and Minimum Spread
		Index #5 and Minimum Spread
		Index #6 and Minimum Spread

EXHIBIT 18.4 Collateral Selection Criteria menu settings

Summary Exception Report
Contracts Grouped By Unique Ineligibility Combinations

Ineligibility Condition Reference	
1 = Min/Max Remaining Term	7 = Excluded State or Geographic Region
2 = Min/Max Original Term	8 = Inconsistent Original vs. Remaining Term
3 = Min Max Original Balance	9 = Inconsistent Original vs. Remaining Balance
4 = Min/Max Current Balance	10 = Calculated vs. Stated Payment Differences
5 = Exceeds Maximum LTV	11 = Unacceptable Gross Coupon
6 = Unacceptable Floater Indice/Spread	

Unique Ineligibility Code	Ineligibility Condition											Number of Loans	Total Current Balance	Total Equity Position
	1	2	3	4	5	6	7	8	9	10	11			
	0	0	1	2	0	2	0	0	0	0	1	56	3,024,285	646,065
8								1				28	620,496	25,150
12		1	1									24	356,258	10,582
32				1								3	1,618,184	69,679
1056				1							1	1	429,347	540,653

EXHIBIT 18.5 Summary Exception Report in the file "Select01_Ineligibles.xls"

STEP 3: ADDRESSING PORTFOLIO CONCENTRATION ISSUES

Besides producing the Ineligible Collateral File Reports, the model will also provide use with the same collateral demographic reports shown before. If we look at the report Elig-8, we still have the concentration issue concerning large balance loans. A total of 4.5% of the portfolio comprises of loans with over $1 million current balances. In addition, we still have problems with the state level geographic concentrations. The loans are concentrated in the states of California and New Jersey with over 7.5% of the portfolio balances. We may be able to kill two birds with one stone.

Loan Securitization Model Main Menu

Program Execution Options   (Y=YES; N=NO)

Y	Perform the Collateral Eligibility Test?
Y	Write out Ineligible Collateral Reports?
Y	Write out Eligible Collateral Reports?
N	Write out Eligible Collateral Loan File?
N	Write out Cash Flow Waterfall Reports?
N	Write out Matrix Summary Reports?
N	Write out Cash Flow Trace Files? *(Caution: can generate VERY LENGTHY runtimes!)*

Run the Model

Input File Information

C:\VBA_Class\AnalystProgram

portfolio_orig.xls	Collateral Data File Name
0	# of Loans *Enter "0" to read all available, otherwise enter the number of loans that you want to have read from the top of the file.*

Output File Information

Select_02_	Report Group Prefix (attached to all output files)	Template File Names
Ineligibles.xls	Ineligible Collateral Reports File Name <======	inelig_template.xls
Collateral.xls	Eligible Collateral Reports File Name <======	collat_template.xls
Waterfall.xls	Cash Flow Waterfalls Report File Name <======	waterfall_template.xls
Matrix.xls	Summary Matrix Reports Files <======	matrix_template.xls
	Eligible Collateral File <======	datafile_template.xls

EXHIBIT 18.6   Main Menu settings for the second selection

It may be that the loans in California and New Jersey are big balance loans and that is the cause of the concentration of balances in those two states. We will set the maximum current balance criteria to $1.1 million. This will immediately address the large loan balance concentration. It may also eliminate balances in California and New Jersey to the point where their loans are less than 7.5% of the total portfolio.

We will call this run "Select02_." The Main Menu configuration is shown in Exhibit 18.6. The entries for the Collateral Selection Menu is shown in Exhibit 18.7.

Rerunning the revised selection criteria gives the following results, as seen in Exhibit 18.8.

A total of 72 loans with a combined balance of $23.77 million in loans are now ineligible. The current balance of the eligible loans in the portfolio is now $438,129,036.

We have fixed the large loan balance concentration issue. A total of only 1.2% of the portfolio consists of loans larger than $1 million. The geographic concentration at the state level remains an open question. The top state, California, contains 8.22% of the current balances and the number two state, New Jersey has 8.18%. This is above the acceptable current rating agency concentration limit of 7.5%. One approach aimed at lowering these concentrations would be to remove loans from California and New Jersey from the portfolio.

Unfortunately, this is not possible. The Seller needs to realize at least $450 million from the deal. Removing more loans will make that impossible. We are already down to $438 million. In addition, keep in mind that we will not be able to finance 100% of the collateral of the portfolio. If we end up financing at a 95% advance rate, we will reduce the amount the Seller receives roughly $416 million,

Collateral Selection Criteria Menu

Minimum	Maximum	
12	360	Original Term (Months)
12	360	Remaining Term (Months)
$25,000	$2,000,000	Original Balance
$25,000	$1,000,000	Remaining Balance
7.000%	11.000%	Gross Coupon
	80.000%	Maximum Total Project LTV%
	$5	Difference Stated-Calculated Pmt

Run the Model

Indices & Minimum Spreads

Index Code	Min Spread	
PRIME	2.250%	Index #1 and Minimum Spread
		Index #2 and Minimum Spread
		Index #3 and Minimum Spread
		Index #4 and Minimum Spread
		Index #5 and Minimum Spread
		Index #6 and Minimum Spread

EXHIBIT 18.7 Inputs to the Collateral Selection Criteria Menu for the second selection process

which is 95% of the current eligible collateral balance of $438 million. The $416 million would then be $34 million less than the stated minimum amount needed of $450 million. There is, however, another solution.

We can lower the concentrations by adding collateral. The Seller has a recently acquired a portfolio of similar loans. It consists of 112 loans with a combined current balance of $75,953,811. We will add these loans to the initial portfolio of loans and reapply the selection criteria to the now combined portfolio. The information on these loans is contained in the data file **"portfolio_add.xls."** We can combine

Summary Exception Report
Contracts Grouped By Unique Ineligibility Combinations

Ineligibility Condition Reference

1 = Min/Max Remaining Term	7 = Excluded State or Geographic Region
2 = Min/Max Original Term	8 = Inconsistent Original vs. Remaining Term
3 = Min Max Original Balance	9 = Inconsistent Original vs. Remaining Balance
4 = Min/Max Current Balance	10 = Calculated vs. Stated Payment Differences
5 = Exceeds Maximum LTV	11 = Unacceptable Gross Coupon
6 = Unacceptable Floater Indice/Spread	

Unique Ineligibility Code	1	2	3	4	5	6	7	8	9	10	11	Number of Loans	Total Current Balance	Total Equity Position
	0	0	1	2	0	2	0	0	0	0	1	72	23,769,424	1,173,186
8				1								44	21,365,635	552,271
12			1	1								24	356,258	10,582
32						1						3	1,618,184	69,679
1056						1					1	1	429,347	540,653

EXHIBIT 18.8 Summary Exception Report

these loans with the original portfolio and call the new collateral portfolio "**port-folio_comb.xls.**" We will run the selection criteria against this portfolio that now consists of 2,367 loans for a total of $537,852,271 current balance.

STEP 4: CORRECTING CONCENTRATION ISSUES

We first combine the collateral files. We are fortunate that this portfolio was recently incorporated into the client's servicing and accounting system, or we could have had a real problem tying to reconcile the two portfolios.

We will keep all the settings the same from the previous "Select02_" run. We just want to apply the same criteria to the larger combined portfolio. We set the "Report Group Prefix" name to "Select03_." We will make two other changes however. In the model options section we will set the fourth option, "Write Out Eligible Collateral Loan File?" to "Y." This will create a file with the prefix of "Select03_" and the filename entered in the sixth field of the filename section. Into the sixth field, named "Eligible Collateral File," we will enter the name "CollateralData." When the model has completed the selection process it will produce a file identical in format to "**portfolio_comb.xls**" the collateral files we have been using with the name "**Select03_CollateralData.**" If the selection process is successful in eliminating the state level geographic concentration issues, we can use this file as our working portfolio file for the deal. Still leaving the cash flow reports turned off, we run the model. The settings of the Main Menu for this run are shown in Exhibit 18.9.

Loan Securitization Model Main Menu

Program Execution Options (Y=YES; N=NO)

Y	Perform the Collateral Eligibility Test?
Y	Write out Ineligible Collateral Reports?
Y	Write out Eligible Collateral Reports?
N	Write out Eligible Collateral Loan File?
N	Write out Cash Flow Waterfall Reports?
N	Write out Matrix Summary Reports?
N	Write out Cash Flow Trace Files? *(Caution: can generate VERY LENGTHY runtimes!)*

Run the Model

Input File Information

C:\VBA_Class\AnalystProgram	
portfolio_comb.xls	Collateral Data File Name
0	# of Loans *Enter "0" to read all available, otherwise enter the number of loans that you want to have read from the top of the file.*

Output File Information

		Template File Names
Select03_	Report Group Prefix (attached to all output files)	
Ineligibles.xls	Ineligible Collateral Reports File Name <======	inelig_template.xls
Collateral.xls	Eligible Collateral Reports File Name <======	collat template.xls
Waterfall.xls	Cash Flow Waterfalls Report File Name <======	waterfall template.xls
Matrix.xls	Summary Matrix Reports Files <======	matrix template.xls
CollateralData.xls	Eligible Collateral File <======	datafile template.xls

EXHIBIT 18.9 Main Menu settings for the collateral selection run against the combined portfolio

Summary Exception Report
Contracts Grouped By Unique Ineligibility Combinations

Ineligibility Condition Reference	
1 = Min/Max Remaining Term	7 = Excluded State or Geographic Region
2 = Min/Max Original Term	8 = Inconsistent Original vs. Remaining Term
3 = Min Max Original Balance	9 = Inconsistent Original vs. Remaining Balance
4 = Min/Max Current Balance	10 = Calculated vs. Stated Payment Differences
5 = Exceeds Maximum LTV	11 = Unacceptable Gross Coupon
6 = Unacceptable Floater Indice/Spread	

Unique Ineligibility Code	Ineligibility Condition											Number of Loans	Total Current Balance	Total Equity Position
	1	2	3	4	5	6	7	8	9	10	11			
	0	0	1	2	0	2	0	0	0	0	1	88	46,431,894	2,696,065
8				1								58	41,544,894	575,123
12			1	1								25	2,111,171	1,134,087
32						1						4	2,346,482	446,202
1056						1					1	1	429,347	540,653

EXHIBIT 18.10   Summary Exception Report for the "Select03_Ineligibles.xls" file

Applying the same set of selection criteria we entered for the previous "Select02_" model run, we arrive at the results as seen in Exhibit 18.10.

We now have 88 loans ineligible for a combined balance of $46.4 million.

The remaining eligible loan portfolio consists of 2,279 loans for a current balance of $491,420,377. This will easily meet the targeted finance amount of $450 even with a 5 to 7% advance rate. Have we solved the concentration issues?

Yes. The large loan concentration is six loans of 1.29% of the portfolio. The highest state level concentration is 7.33% in California, followed by New Jersey at 7.29%. The combined five states are a total of 32.24% of the portfolio. This is down from 34.8% in the initial run.

We would appear to have a workable first cut portfolio!

We will save the resultant portfolio in the file **"Select03_CollateralData.xls"** and use this file for the remainder of the analysis.

STEP 5: RUNNING THE EXPECTED CASE CASH FLOWS

Now that we have a preliminary portfolio we can start to run the cash flows. The first cash flow runs we will perform will be those centered on what is called the Expected Case.

The Expected Case (EC) is, in our best opinion, the payment behavior we expect to see from the collateral. We start by looking at historical loss curves for this pool and others like it. We also take into consideration the underwriting practices and due diligence practiced by the Seller in their lending practices. The demographics of the collateral, especially concentrations, as noted above are also important in future loss estimations. Lastly, we need to factor in the general economic outlook, especially for the next several years.

This portfolio has two important characteristics that will serve to mitigate large losses. The first is that a substantial number of loans have very low LTV ratios. Thus many of the loans will recover all or most of their defaulted principal even with a 50% market value decline at the end of the recovery period. In these cases, the deal will only suffer the loss of the defaulted principal for the lag period. The deal will, of course, lose the coupon income from these loans permanently from the point of their default. The recovery of a significant percentage of the defaulted principal is a very important factor in the successful repayment of the Conduit Financing. The second factor is the high spread the loans have to their benchmark index, about 3.255%. This is a tremendous amount of excess spread. Not only is this a wide spread, but the base rate of the Prime Rate is considerably higher that that of LIBOR, the rate that the financing costs are based. This difference between the financing costs and the Prime Rate plus spread in the coupon of the collateral is immediately available to the Conduit Financing and will help fund the Delinquent Account Reserve and to defease losses.

Entries to the Main Menu

Starting at the top of the Main Menu and working down, we will make the following entries. The first three menu run options will be set to "N." We do not need to perform any further collateral testing or reporting because we produced a collateral loan file of the eligible collateral **"Select03_CollateralData.xls"** on the last run. We will enter "Y" into the next three fields. This will produce a loan file that we can store with the cash flow reports (in case we need to replicate them), and the Waterfall Report Package and the Matrix Package. We will enter "N" in the last two options, the Single Case Summary Option and the Trace Cash Flows.

Next we will enter the name of the collateral loan data file we created in the field "Collateral Data File Name." This is the file **"Select03_CollateralData.xls."** We will set the Output File Prefix for this run to "BaseEC_," our Base Expected Case.

The entries for this run in the Main Menu are shown in Exhibit 18.11.

Entries to the Default/Prepayment Menu

The Expected Case analysis will be a broad-brush look at the Range of possible prepayment and default speeds the portfolio may experience. We will set the default Range to be from 100% to 500% PSA by 50% PSA increments, nine cases. The prepayments will be set from 100% to 300% PSA by 25% PSA increments, which results in nine cases. This will produce a total of 81 scenarios. Current performance of the collateral portfolio indicates that a base line prepayment speed of about 200 to 250% PSA is the most probable future behavior. Default rates have had Ranges of 300 to 400% PSA for similar portfolios with national level distributions of loans.

The MVD factor will be set to 50%, and the RLP to 12 months. The Advance Rate on the portfolio will be set at 95%.

Lastly, we will set the Prime Rate, in Column S, to 5.25% for all 360 months and the LIBOR Rate in Column T to 2.75% for all months. The entries for the default and prepayment criteria are shown in Exhibit 18.12.

Loan Securitization Model Main Menu

Program Execution Options	(Y=YES; N=NO)
N	Perform the Collateral Eligibility Test?
N	Write out Ineligible Collateral Reports?
N	Write out Eligible Collateral Reports?
N	Write out Eligible Collateral Loan File?
Y	Write out Cash Flow Waterfall Reports?
Y	Write out Matrix Summary Reports ?
N	Write out Cash Flow Trace Files? *(Caution: can generate VERY LENGTHY runtimes!)*

Run the Model

Input File Information

C:\VBA_Class\AnalystProgram	
Select03_CollateralData.xls	Collateral Data File Name
0	# of Loans *Enter "0" to read all available, otherwise enter the number of loans that you want to have read from the top of the file.*

Output File Information

	Report Group Prefix (attached to all output files)	Template File Names
BaseEC_		
Ineligibles.xls	Ineligible Collateral Reports File Name <======	inelig_template.xls
Collateral.xls	Eligible Collateral Reports File Name <======	collat_template.xls
Waterfall.xls	Cash Flow Waterfalls Report File Name <======	waterfall_template.xls
Matrix.xls	Summary Matrix Reports Files <======	matrix_template.xls
	Eligible Collateral File <======	datafile_template.xls

EXHIBIT 18.11 Main Menu entries for running the Expected Case

Default Rates

		Default Methodology Codes
Default Rate	100.00%	1=CPR, 2=PSA
Default Rate Step	50.00%	3=User Defined
# Default Steps	9	
Methodology	2	

Prepayment Rates

		Prepay Method Codes
Prepay Base Rate	100.00%	
Prepay Rate Step	25.00%	1=CPR, 2=PSA,
# Prepay Steps	9	
Methodology	2	

Distribution of Portfolio Lifetime Annual Defaults

Year 1		Year 11		Year 21	
Year 2		Year 12		Year 22	
Year 3		Year 13		Year 23	
Year 4		Year 14		Year 24	
Year 5		Year 15		Year 25	
Year 6		Year 16		Year 26	
Year 7		Year 17		Year 27	
Year 8		Year 18		Year 28	
Year 9		Year 19		Year 29	
Year 10		Year 20		Year 30	
			Percentage Sum for all Years=>	0.00%	

Run the Model

Mkt Value Decline	50.00%
Recovery Lag	12 Months

Clear All

EXHIBIT 18.12 Entries to the Default and Prepayment Menu for running the Expected Case

Entries to the Program Costs Menu

We will set the following entries into the Program Costs Menu:

Servicer Fees	0.75%
Program Fees	0.20%
Clean Up Call Level	10.00%
Rolling Three-Month Default Rate	5.00%
Conduit Advance Rate	95.00%
Conduit Financing Spread	1.00%

Running the Program

We now run the program.

The results are very encouraging! If we look at the "ConduitNotePerfromance" worksheet in the **"BaseEC_Matrix.xls"** file, we see that we have *no* cases where the Conduit Financing suffers a loss. The coverage ratio of the Conduit Financing Ranges from a high of 22.08% to a low of 14.30%. The yield for the Conduit Financing is 3.75%, the 2.75% LIBOR rate plus the 1.00% Conduit Financing Spread (CFS).

The tenor Ranges on the Conduit Financing was as follows:

Average Life	4.10 years to 6.99 years
Final Maturity	13.92 years to 20.83 years
Modified Duration	3.54 years to 5.59 years
Macauley Duration	3.58 years to 5.80 years

The excess servicing income released to the Seller Ranged from $102.4 million to $161.4 million.

The Expected Case is therefore quite satisfactory. The amount of excess servicing income is extremely robust. This is because in the Expected Case the CFS is 1.00%, which combined with a uniform assumption of LIBOR at 2.75% gives us an all in funding costs across the life of the deal of 3.75%. The returns from the loans of the portfolio are substantially higher. To start out with the base assumption for the level of Prime is 5.25%, a full 2.5% greater than LIBOR. On top of this, the average spread on the portfolio is, on a dollar-weighted balance, an additional 3.25%! That means that at the inception of the deal the coupon income to the deal produced by the collateral will be $(5.25\% + 3.25\%) = 8.50$ as compared to the coupon expense of the financing of $(2.75\% + 1.00\%) = 3.75\%$, or $(8.50\% - 3.75\%) = 4.75\%$ of excess spread available from the portfolio to absorb losses and expenses. That is a lot of excess spread! Remember that this is on an original loan balance of nearly $500 million!

This is *not,* however, the entire story.

We now need to perform sensitivity analysis on the Expected Case to see how changes to the key assumptions will affect the deal performance.

One other thing that is very noticeable in the Expected Case is that the percentage of recovered principal across most of the scenarios is approximately 85%. That is to say that the collateral pool only experiences a 15% net loss on defaulted principal. For every $1 that defaults approximately $0.85 is realized at the end of the recovery period.

One obvious set of sensitivities to explore is the effect of changes in the MVD rate. What would be the effect of MVDs in excess of 50%? Are MVDs greater than 50% likely? While not *likely* they are *possible* in certain economic conditions. If lenders reclaim large numbers of properties during a period of economic recession these declines could occur. In addition, it is important to find out the conditions under which the Conduit Financing will suffer losses. We have not found that set of conditions in the Expected Case. It is also quite reasonable to assume that the RLPs will significantly lengthen if there is a glut of repossessed properties available for sale. We should explore a series of lengthening recovery period times moving out from 12 to 36 months.

The results of the future sensitivity analysis aside we are off to a strong start with the Expected Case results. Let us see how the deal holds up under additional stress tests and see if we can determine under what conditions we start to see losses to the Conduit Financing.

STEP 6: EXPECTED CASE SENSITIVITY ANALYSIS

Key Parameters

Having completed the Expected Case, we now move on to determining the effects that changing some of the assumptions will have on the behavior of the deal. There are four major input assumptions that have the capacity to significantly alter the timing and magnitude of the cash flows. These are:

1. Timing and magnitude of default activity
2. Severity of Market Value Decline assumptions
3. Variations in the length of the Recovery Lag Period
4. Changes in the relationship between LIBOR and Prime

Changes in each of these assumptions can act to deprive the deal for cash in different ways. Obviously the greater and sooner the default activity occurs, the less cash the deal will receive in principal and interest payments from the collateral over the remainder of its life. Higher than expected MVD rates will limit the amount of recovered principal despite the very strong equity positions in the collateral portfolio. As RLPs are extended, from 12 months out to 36 months, the receipt of that portion of the principal that is recovered is greatly delayed. This delay causes a slowdown in the retirement of the Conduit Financing position, generating greater amounts of debt service than in the Expected Case. Lastly, if the difference between the current coupon levels of the Prime Rate and LIBOR becomes smaller, this will immediately decrease the excess cash flows generated when compared to the current relationship between the two rate levels.

Finding the "Breaking Point" of the Deal

During this process we will look at increasing MVDs, up to 70%. RLPs will be extended from 12 to 36 months. Are these assumptions rational, or do they need to be? The answer is "Yes" and "Yes." One of the objectives of the exercise that we are about to undertake is to find the "breaking point" of the deal. The point at which the first losses occur to the Conduit Financing is a very important piece of information to know! The conditions in which substantial losses occur are even more important. If it happens that these conditions are not only possible but also are indeed probable, we will have to make major changes to the deal. One of these changes could be substantially lowering the Advance Rate to the Seller. The Seller would lose the availability of $4.91 million for each 1% decrease in the Advance Rate. If we had to lower the Advance Rate to 90% from 95%, it would result in an availability loss of approximately $25 million.

Equally we need to be able to specifically describe to ourselves the risks that the Conduit is exposing itself to. MVDs in excess of 50% can easily occur. If the property was initially abandoned and it needs to be brought up to a condition to which it can be sold, costs can be easily up to 10–15% of the project. "Fire Sale" pricing can also substantially lower recovery values.

For these reasons, we will now run the following scenarios. We will vary the MVDs from 50% to 70% by 5% intervals in conjunction with RLPs from 12 to 36 months at 6-month intervals.

To speed this process, we will also reduce the number of individual scenarios per run. We will now run 25 scenarios per run, assuming five prepayment speeds, and five default speeds. We can reduce the number of scenarios because we are most interested in producing an overview. Once we have the lay of the land "from 50,000 feet," we can return to specific cases at our leisure.

Sticking with the plan above, we will run 25 model runs, each of which will produce 25 scenarios. This will be a lot of information to deal with and we will need to be careful when generating all these files. To clearly differentiate which information is in which file, we will set up the following file naming convention.

Each time we run the model we will enter a new name into the Report Group Prefix field on the Main Menu. The convention will be as follows: "ECS_" for Expected Case Sensitivity, "MVDnn_" where nn for 55% is 55, and "Lnn_" for the lag period, and "Snnn_" is the spread over LIBOR of the Conduit financing assumption. Thus the Report Group Prefix for a set of runs that had a 60% MVD and a 24 month Recovery Lag period and a spread of 1.00% to LIBOR would be "ECS_MVD60_L24_S100."

We will set the Main Menu to the following condition and begin our runs. Remember to go to the Defaults Menu to update the MVD and RLP as necessary before each of the runs.

Organizing the Sensitivity Tests

Until you gain more experience in organizing a set of stress tests it is best to start with simple one parameter sensitivity runs and work upward from there. Once these have been prepared, two parameters can be combined and then three or more for the final runs.

The Expected Case has the following key assumptions:

- PSA Prepayment Methodology, speeds of 100 to 300% by 50% intervals
- PSA Default Methodology, speeds of 100 to 500% by 100% intervals
- Recovery Lag Period of 12 months
- Conduit Spread of 1.00%
- Market Value Decline percentage of 50%

Single Parameter Sensitivity Tests   Our first sensitivity runs will be to vary a single parameter across a Range of values keeping all other Expected Case assumptions constant.

> **Sensitivity Runs #1: Recovery Lag Period** only. Vary the RLP assuming values from 18 to 36 months by 6-month increments (four model runs).

> **Sensitivity Runs #2: Market Value Decline only.** Vary the MVD percentage from 30% to 70 % by 5% increments (nine model runs).

> **Sensitivity Runs #3: Financing Spread only.** Vary the Conduit Financing Spread from 1.00% to 4.00% by 0.50% increments (seven model runs).

Two Parameter Sensitivity Tests   Our next set of sensitivity runs will combine pairs of these factors:

> **Sensitivity Runs #4: RLP and MVD.** Vary the RLP through values from 18 to 36 months by 6-month increments, vary the MVDs from 60% to 70% by 10% (eight model runs).

> **Sensitivity Runs #5: MVD and Spread.** Vary the MVD percentage from 50 to 70 % by 10% increments, vary the Spread from 2.00 to 4.00% by 1.00% (nine model runs).

> **Sensitivity Runs #6: Spread and RLP.** Vary the CFS from 2.00 to 4.00% by 1.00% increments, vary the RLP from 12 to 36 months by 6-month increments (15 model runs).

Three Parameters Sensitivity Tests   Lastly, we will combine changes to all three parameters:

> **Sensitivity Runs #7: MVD and RLP and Spread.** Vary the RLP from 12 to 36 months by 6-month intervals, vary the MVD from 50 to 70% by 10%, and the financing spread from 2.00 to 3.00% by 1.00% increments (30 model runs).

TIME OUT! BUILDING A BATCH PROCESSING CAPABILITY

Did you just see what I saw?

If we look again at the list of sensitivity runs above, we can see that we will really be running this model very hard for some period of time. By the looks of it we have:

$$4 + 9 + 7 + 8 + 9 + 15 + 30 = 82 \text{ model runs ahead of us!}$$

(No wonder we get paid the big bucks!) Seriously though, what a nightmare! No one wants to sit in front of a computer and enter one scenario after another 82 times! I have done it and it is not fun in any definition of the word! Not only is it tedious, but it is an input method fraught with the possibility of error. There **must** be a better way.

There *is*!

As intimated in the "Overview" section of this chapter, we can program a way to have the model run sets of scenarios instead of running them one at a time. What we need to do is to convince the model that *we are* there all the time. If the model cannot tell the difference between us entering the scenario inputs one after another and another program doing it, we are set!

What we are now going to do is build a subroutine that will supersede the Main Program of the model. This subroutine will call the Main Program and treat it as a subordinate subroutine. In essence, we will be treating the entire model as a single subroutine call! We will create a new VBA module and name it "**A_BatchFileProgram.**" We will put all of the code we develop for this feature into that module.

The steps of this program will be:

1. Read the Batch Program menu with a list of single scenario conditions, placing the information in VBA arrays.
2. Using a looping structure, load the first set of specifications into the appropriate menu input fields of the model.
3. Call the Loan_Financing_Model main model as a subroutine after the inputs are complete. The model runs to completion producing whatever output is specified. As the model finishes running, it returns control to the Batch subroutine which called it.
4. Go back to Step #2 and complete as many loops as there are separate scenarios listed on the Batch Program Menu.

To understand this process better let's look at the Batch Program Menu in Exhibit 18.13.

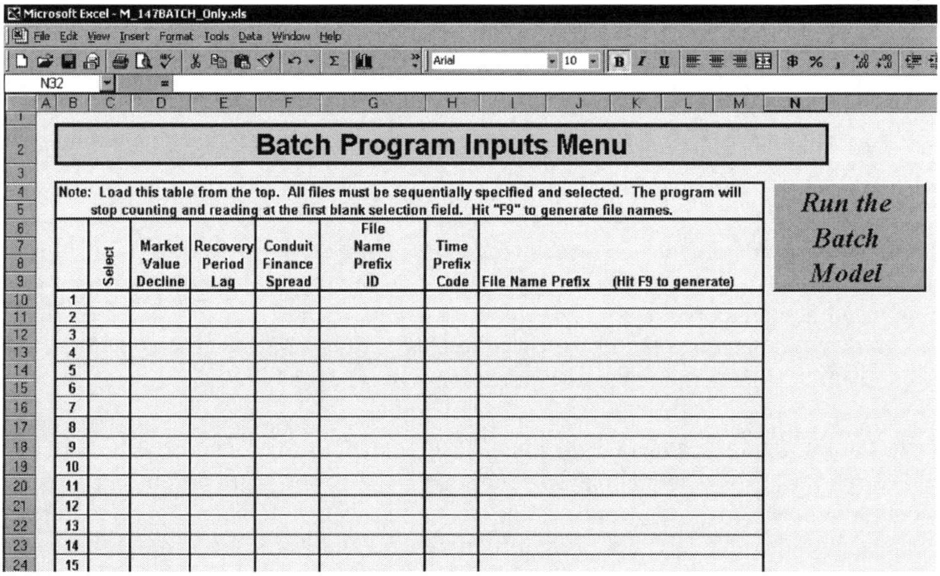

EXHIBIT 18.13 Menu of the Batch Program

Each row of the menu is a separate scenario. We will enter the key sensitivity variables in the row to generate a single model run under those conditions. The layout of this menu is as follows:

1. **Column C: Select Column.** This column indicates to the model which of the listed scenarios are to be run in this Batch Run of the model. The scenarios must be selected without a break in the sequence. If you want to run eight scenarios, enter them in the first eight rows of the menu and place an "X" in each row.
2. **Column D: Market Value Decline.** Enter the value for the MVD in this column. If you want a 50% MVD for the scenario, enter "50" and the field will display 50%.
3. **Column E: Recovery Lag Period.** Enter the number of months in the RLP for this scenario.
4. **Column F: Conduit Financing Spread.** Enter the CFS for the scenario. For 1.00% enter "1"; the menu will do the conversion for you as the column is set to a percentage format.
5. **Column G: File Name Prefix.** Enter a prefix that will identify any related files of this batch run to yourself and others.
6. **Column H: Time Prefix Code:** Enter a code to distinguish a time pattern, essentially a vector. This is mostly used with the USER default methodology to distinguish between default time periods. For example, T1 might mean a five-year distribution of defaulted principal as follows: 5%, 30%, 30%, 30%, 5%. Alternatively, T2 might mean a pattern of 40%, 30%, 20%, 10% over four years.
7. **Column I: File Name Prefix.** This is the filename prefix that is generated by Excel when the user hits the "F9" key. It creates the filename from the preceding five columns of inputs. For an MVD of 70%, an RLP of 12, a CFS of 1%, a file prefix of SEN, and a time prefix of T2, the output files for the model run would have the prefix of:

```
SEN_MVD70_L12_S100_T2
```

If a Summary Matrix Report was generated during the run, its name would be:

```
SEN_MVD70_L12_S100_T2_Matrix.xls
```

If we wanted to generate the file names for the Sensitivity Run #2 above, the menu would look like this after all inputs and striking the F9 button to generate the completed filename prefixes.

In that the default method for these runs is "PSA" and not "User" there is no need to enter a time tag for the filenames. See Exhibit 18.14.

Code for the Batch Scenario Program   The Batch Scenario Program is comprised of less than 50 VBA statements, yet it will save us hours of aggravation and clerical work! It will also give you a comfortable feeling knowing that when you go to lunch, 40 runs of the model will be waiting for you when you return. We will put this code in a separate Module named "**A_BatchFileProgram**" that we will add to the model just to hold this code.

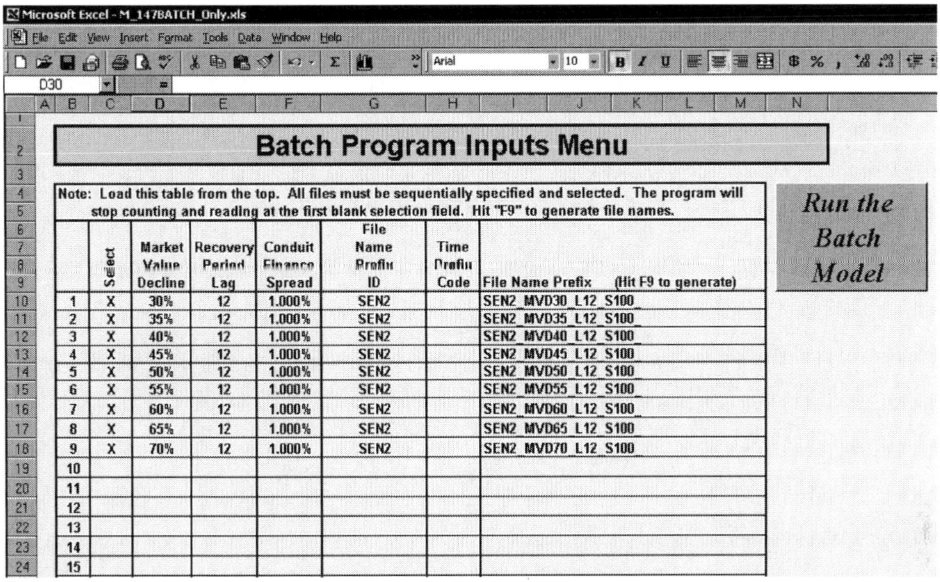

Batch Program Inputs Menu

Note: Load this table from the top. All files must be sequentially specified and selected. The program will stop counting and reading at the first blank selection field. Hit "F9" to generate file names.

	Select	Market Value Decline	Recovery Period Lag	Conduit Finance Spread	File Name Prefix ID	Time Prefix Code	File Name Prefix (Hit F9 to generate)
1	X	30%	12	1.000%	SEN2		SEN2_MVD30_L12_S100_
2	X	35%	12	1.000%	SEN2		SEN2_MVD35_L12_S100_
3	X	40%	12	1.000%	SEN2		SEN2_MVD40_L12_S100_
4	X	45%	12	1.000%	SEN2		SEN2_MVD45_L12_S100_
5	X	50%	12	1.000%	SEN2		SEN2_MVD50_L12_S100_
6	X	55%	12	1.000%	SEN2		SEN2_MVD55_L12_S100_
7	X	60%	12	1.000%	SEN2		SEN2_MVD60_L12_S100_
8	X	65%	12	1.000%	SEN2		SEN2_MVD65_L12_S100_
9	X	70%	12	1.000%	SEN2		SEN2_MVD70_L12_S100_
10							
11							
12							
13							
14							
15							

EXHIBIT 18.14 Menu of the Batch Program with fields input and the file prefixes completed for Sensitivity Run #2

The first subroutine, "Count_Number_Of_Scenarios," runs down Column C and counts the number of selected scenarios.

The second subroutine "Read_Batch_Program_Menu" reads the inputs of up to 50 different scenarios from the "m10" Range names that we designated on the menu.

The last subroutine uses a For...Next loop to sequentially populate the fields on three menus of the model. These are the Defaults Menu, the Program Costs Menu, and the Main Menu. It then triggers the model run by calling the Loan_Financing_Model as a subroutine. The model runs and produces its designated output as if it were a standalone program. See Exhibit 18.15.

With the Batch Scenario Program at our disposal, we can now face the 82 sensitivity runs with significantly less trepidation. In fact we can produce all 20 of the first three sets of sensitivity runs at one time by entering the following information on the Batch Menu, as seen in Exhibit 18.16.

The last step in installing the Batch Scenario Program code will be to create and install a Run button for this code. We go through the same steps as we did when we created the Run button for the single scenario model. The difference is solely in the label of the button and the subroutine that it is assigned to.

SENSITIVITY ANALYSIS RESULTS

Results of the Single Parameter Sensitivity Runs

The results of the three Expected Case sensitivity model runs are summarized in Exhibit 18.17.

```
Option Explicit
Const NUM_OF_BATCH_FILES = 50              'max number of files
Dim i_file                As Integer       'scenario loop counter
Dim num_file              As Integer       'number of files requested
Dim batch_mvd_factor()    As Double        'market value decline vector
Dim batch_lag_period()    As Integer       'recovery lag period in months
Dim batch_conduit_sprd()  As Double        'conduit financing spread
Dim batch_file_name()     As String        'name of the inidividual file
'===============================================================================
'    BATCH SCENARIO PROGRAM
'    Author:  Wm Preinitz       Date:     20-DECEMBER-2008
'===============================================================================
Sub Run_Batch_Program()
    Sheets("Batch Run Menu").Select
    Call Count_Number_Of_Scenarios
    Call Read_Batch_Program_Menu
    Call Load_and_Run_Loan_Financing_Model
End Sub
'===============================================================================
' Read the number of selected scenarios in the menu
'===============================================================================
Sub Count_Number_Of_Scenarios()
    'count the number of designated scenarios
    For i_file = 1 To NUM_OF_BATCH_FILES
            If Range("m10SelectScenario").Cells(i_file) <> "" And _
              Range("m10MktValueDecline").Cells(i_file) <> "" Then
                  num_file = i_file
            Else
                    Exit For
            End If
    Next i_file
End Sub
'===================================================------■■■■■----------------
' Read the menu entries for the selected scenarios
'===============================================================================
Sub Read_Batch_Program_Menu()
    'read the contents of the ranges
    ReDim batch_mvd_factor(1 To num_file) As Double    'market value decline vector
    ReDim batch_lag_period(1 To num_file) As Integer   'recovery lag period in months
    ReDim batch_conduit_sprd(1 To num_file) As Double  'conduit financing spread
    ReDim batch_file_name(1 To num_file) As String     'name of the inidividual file
    For i_file = 1 To num_file
        batch_mvd_factor(i_file) = Range("m10MktValueDecline").Cells(i_file).Value
        batch_lag_period(i_file) = Range("m10RecPeriodLag").Cells(i_file).Value
        batch_conduit_sprd(i_file) = Range("m10ConduitSpread").Cells(i_file).Value
        batch_file_name(i_file) = Range("m10FilePrefixName").Cells(i_file).Value
    Next i_file
End Sub
'===============================================================================
' Read the menu entries for the selected scenarios
'===============================================================================
Sub Load_and_Run_Loan_Financing_Model()
    For i_file = 1 To num_file
        Sheets("Defaults Menu").Select
        Cells(23, 4).Value = batch_mvd_factor(i_file)
        Cells(24, 4).Value = batch_lag_period(i_file)
        Sheets("Program Costs Menu").Select
        Cells(16, 3).Value = batch_conduit_sprd(i_file)
        Sheets("Defaults Menu").Calculate
        Sheets("Main Menu").Select
        Cells(19, 3).Value = batch_file_name(i_file)
        Call Loan_Financing_Model
    Next i_file
End Sub
```

EXHIBIT 18.15 VBA code of the Batch Scenario Program

Microsoft Excel - M_147BATCH_Only.xls

File Edit View Insert Format Tools Data Window Help

N32

Batch Program Inputs Menu

Note: Load this table from the top. All files must be sequentially specified and selected. The program will stop counting and reading at the first blank selection field. Hit "F9" to generate file names.

Run the Batch Model

	Select	Market Value Decline	Recovery Period Lag	Conduit Finance Spread	File Name Prefix ID	Time Prefix Code	File Name Prefix (Hit F9 to generate)
1	X	50%	12	1.000%	SEN1		SEN1_MVD50_L12_S100
2	X	50%	12	1.000%	SEN1		SEN1_MVD50_L12_S100
3	X	50%	12	1.000%	SEN1		SEN1_MVD50_L12_S100
4	X	50%	12	1.000%	SEN1		SEN1_MVD50_L12_S100
5	X	30%	12	1.000%	SEN2		SEN2_MVD30_L12_S100
6	X	35%	12	1.000%	SEN2		SEN2_MVD35_L12_S100
7	X	40%	12	1.000%	SEN2		SEN2_MVD40_L12_S100
8	X	45%	12	1.000%	SEN2		SEN2_MVD45_L12_S100
9	X	50%	12	1.000%	SEN2		SEN2_MVD50_L12_S100
10	X	55%	12	1.000%	SEN2		SEN2_MVD55_L12_S100
11	X	60%	12	1.000%	SEN2		SEN2_MVD60_L12_S100
12	X	65%	12	1.000%	SEN2		SEN2_MVD65_L12_S100
13	X	70%	12	1.000%	SEN2		SEN2_MVD70_L12_S100
14	X	50%	12	1.000%	SEN3		SEN3_MVD50_L12_S100
15	X	50%	12	1.500%	SEN3		SEN3_MVD50_L12_S150
16	X	50%	12	2.000%	SEN3		SEN3_MVD50_L12_S200
17	X	50%	12	2.500%	SEN3		SEN3_MVD50_L12_S250
18	X	50%	12	3.000%	SEN3		SEN3_MVD50_L12_S300
19	X	50%	12	3.500%	SEN3		SEN3_MVD50_L12_S350
20	X	50%	12	4.000%	SEN3		SEN3_MVD50_L12_S400

EXHIBIT 18.16 Batch Program Inputs Menu completed for the first three sets of Sensitivity Runs

The results for the first three sensitivity runs are very impressive. Varying any of these parameters across the Range of values of the tests does not result in any meaningful degradation to the ability of the collateral to repay the Conduit Financing.

There are *no* losses *at all* to the Conduit Financing across all conditions of Tests 1, 2, and 3. Losses do not even occur in these sensitivity runs even if they were the equivalent of a 4.00% Conduit Financing Spread, (CFS).

Let us take a minute to clarify one point. The CFS is a cost of the deal and is set once at the inception of the deal and never changed. Why then are we varying it across these runs within the sensitivity set? There is a phenomenon known as "spread compression." Spread compression occurs when two normally related indices, which customarily move in a parallel manner for a time, do not. What this is to say is that in general, over long periods of time when the LIBOR Rate rises the Prime Rate will also increase. What happens, however, if this relationship is temporarily not operant? In this case LIBOR may rise and Prime may fall. If LIBOR, the funding cost rate increases and the Prime rate upon which the coupon payments of the collateral are based falls, we will have less cash, and, dependent on the magnitude of the move, much less cash, coming into the deal than we originally anticipated.

The effect of a movement in LIBOR as the funding benchmark versus Prime as the collateral benchmark would be most pronounced if it occurred immediately on the issuance of the deal and then stayed in that configuration for the remainder

EXHIBIT 18.17   Initial Sensitivity of Recovery Lag Period, Market Value Decline, and Conduit Financing Spread

	Run #1 Recovery Lag Period Only	Run #2 Market Value Decline Only	Run #3 Spread Financing Only
CONDUIT PERFORMANCE			
Loss Cases to the Conduit Financing?	NO	NO	NO
Number of Loss Cases	0	0	0
Maximum Loss	0%	0%	0%
Minimum Loss	0%	0%	0%
Cases of Full IRR	All	All	All
Maximum Coverage Ratio	32.8%	33.8%	32.8%
Minimum Coverage Ratio	20.8%	17.8%	8.9%
SELLER INTEREST PERFORMANCE			
Maximum Internal Rate of Return	60.19%	60.14%	60.19%
Minimum Internal Rate of Return	36.44%	39.55%	9.94%
Maximum Excess Servicing Released	$161.5 MM	$163.2 MM	$161.4 MM
Minimum Excess Servicing Released	$102.4 MM	$87.4 MM	$43.7 MM
Maximum Coverage Ratio	557.0%	564.2%	557.0%
Minimum Coverage Ratio	316.7%	255.8%	77.8%
STRUCTURE PERFORMANCE			
Program Fees Payment Shortfall?	NO	NO	NO
Servicing Fees Payment Shortfall?	NO	NO	NO
Conduit Interest Payment Shortfall?	NO	NO	NO

of the life of the deal. You and everyone else thought LIBOR was going to stay at roughly around its current level, and suddenly it has increased 1%, 2%, 3%, or even 4%! We have two ways that we can simulate that set of circumstances in the model. Firstly, we can change all the entries in the LIBOR column each time we run the model. The second way is to simply increase the level of the CFS. Both will have *exactly* the same effect. In the real world, as noted, the CFS will *never* change. In the model there is no difference in the cash flow calculations if the LIBOR Rate is constant for the scenario and the CFS increase from 1% to 3% or if the CFS stays constant at 1% and the LIBOR level changes immediately to a rate 2% higher and stays for all remaining time periods of the model.

It is *very important* to note that the effects on the deal structure of the funding costs based on *LIBOR increasing* 2% will *not* be the same as the *LIBOR increasing* 1% *and the Prime decreasing* 1%! Why?

If we had $100 of collateral and the deal had a 95% Advance Rate, (as currently modeled), we would have lent $95 of Conduit principal against the $100 of loan collateral.

Case #1—If the LIBOR Rate increased 2%, the financing costs for the Conduit principal would increase by $95 times 2%.

Case #2—If the LIBOR Rate increased 1%, the financing costs of the Conduit principal would increase by $95 times 1%. The loss of coupon income from the collateral pool with a 1% decline in the Prime Rate would be $100 times 1%.

We can see at a glance that:

$$(\$95 * 2\%) \text{ does not equal } ((\$95 * 1\%) + (\$100 * 1\%))!$$

Later we may wish to model movements in which LIBOR increases at the same time as the Prime Rate decreases by changing elements in both of the rate schedules over the life of the deal. You may also want to look at the effects of a series of compression and/or widening episodes between LIBOR and Prime at various points in time over the life of the deal. The model as currently designed will accommodate that line of inquiry.

For the moment, in the following sensitivity run we will move only one of the index rates, LIBOR. We will simulate an instantaneous increase in the funding rate in the first month of the deal that continues unchanged throughout the remainder of the life of the deal by changing the CFS level.

We can now return to the results of our runs. It can also be seen that across the Range of values used in the sensitivity analysis, the structure is immune to single parameter variance. This does assume that the timing of the defaults are as predicted. This timing is very benign in that the events of defaulted principal are spread across the life of the deal where it is more easily and gradually defused by excess spread. Another advantage to gradually distributed default activity is that the surviving collateral continues to amortize and produce coupon income over the life of the deal. Also, as long regular monthly loan payments are made the current balance of the loan, declines and increases in the equity ratios of the surviving loans will continue to improve. The higher the equity ratios the more limited the ability of high MVDs to trigger losses.

Results of the Two Parameter Sensitivity Runs

The results of two variable sensitivity runs are summarized in Exhibit 18.18.

Here again the structure performs extremely well despite adverse values to the various pairs of parameters.

In Run #4 there are *no* losses to the Conduit Financing. The minimum amounts of excess servicing released to the Seller Interest, and the minimum Seller Interest coverage ratios are robust. There are no payment shortfalls for any of the expenses.

In Run #5 there are no losses to the Conduit Financing despite cases that include a 4.00% change in the CFS. In the worst case of this run the Seller Interest retains a 16% Coverage Ratio!

In Run #6 there are *no* losses to the Conduit Financing. It should be noted that these scenarios do not include any 4.00% CFS sensitivities. The Range of CFS variance is confined to 2.00 to 3.00%.

This clearly indicates that given the Range of PSA prepayment and default speeds and tests with the variations in pairs of the three key parameters, the deal is sound.

It is, however, much clearer here than in Cases 1, 2, and 3 that the robustness of the deal rests on two major supports. There is a wide spread between the Conduit

EXHIBIT 18.18   Sensitivity results for two variable pairings of Recovery Lag Period, Market Value Decline, and Conduit Financing Spread

	Run #4 MVD 60–70% and RPL 12–36	Run #5 MVD 50–70% and CFS 1% to 4%	Run #6 Spread 2% to 3% and RPL 12–36
CONDUIT PERFORMANCE			
Loss Cases to the Conduit Financing?	NO	NO	NO
Number of Loss Cases	0	0	0
Maximum Loss	0%	0%	0%
Minimum Loss	0%	0%	0%
Cases of Full IRR	All	All	All
Maximum Coverage Ratio	32.4%	32.9%	25.6%
Minimum Coverage Ratio	17.9%	5.8%	9.9%
SELLER INTEREST PERFORMANCE			
Maximum Internal Rate of Return	59.50%	60.12%	44.36%
Minimum Internal Rate of Return	32.80%	1.88%	7.40%
Maximum Excess Servicing Released	$159.6 MM	$161.4 MM	$125.7 MM
Minimum Excess Servicing Released	$87.7 MM	$28.6 MM	$49.1 MM
Maximum Coverage Ratio	549.4%	557.0%	411.6%
Minimum Coverage Ratio	255.8%	16.5%	99.7%
STRUCTURE PERFORMANCE			
Program Fees Payment Shortfall?	NO	NO	NO
Servicing Fees Payment Shortfall?	NO	NO	NO
Conduit Interest Payment Shortfall?	NO	NO	NO

Financing rate of 3.75% and the 8.50% average yield of the coupons of the loan portfolio. In addition, the large equity positions of the loans will serve to mitigate losses even under higher MVDs. The equity positions of the loans are very strong and will not produce losses even when the MVDs are as high as 70% (indicative of a strong recession or a depression). In addition, in these cases, the defaults are spread across the life of the deal where their effects can be absorbed and offset by the excess spread and high loss recovery rates.

Results of the Three Parameter Sensitivity Run

The results contained in Exhibit 18.19 are of a three variable sensitivity run, broken into three subsets by different MVD rates.

Case #7 is really composed of three distinct subcases: #7a, #7b, and #7c, identified by increasing MVD percentages. None of these cases show losses. The maximum increase in the CFS used in these cases was 3.00%. There are *no* losses to the Conduit Financing in any of these cases. The minimum Conduit Financing Coverage Ratio declines somewhat, but never gets close to zero.

EXHIBIT 18.19   Sensitivity results for three variable variance of Recovery Lag Period, Market Value Decline, and Conduit Financing Spread, broken out across 50%–60%–70% MVD

	Run #7a MVD 50%, RPL 12–36, CFS 2%–3%	Run #7b MVD 60%, RPL 12–36, CFS 2%–3%	Run #7c MVD 70%, RPL 12–36, CFS 2%–3%
CONDUIT PERFORMANCE			
Loss Cases to the Conduit Financing?	NO	NO	NO
Number of Loss Cases	0	0	0
Maximum Loss	0%	0%	0%
Minimum Loss	0%	0%	0%
Cases of Full IRR	All	All	All
Maximum Coverage Ratio	26.2%	25.8%	25.3%
Minimum Coverage Ratio	12.9%	11.6%	9.9%
SELLER INTEREST PERFORMANCE			
Maximum Internal Rate of Return	45.29%	44.57%	43.72%
Minimum Internal Rate of Return	15.47%	13.10%	10.12%
Maximum Excess Servicing Released	$128.5 MM	$126.7 MM	$124.5 MM
Minimum Excess Servicing Released	$63.5 MM	$56.4 MM	$48.1 MM
Maximum Coverage Ratio	423.1%	415.5%	406.8%
Minimum Coverage Ratio	158.3%	129.7%	97.25%
STRUCTURE PERFORMANCE			
Program Fees Payment Shortfall?	NO	NO	NO
Servicing Fees Payment Shortfall?	NO	NO	NO
Conduit Interest Payment Shortfall?	NO	NO	NO

Case #7c is the most stressful of the cases, but even here the Coverage ratios for both the Conduit Financing and the Seller Interest remain positive.

Breaking Point: Sensitivity to a 5% CFS

At the beginning of this section we said that the goal of the sensitivity analysis was to identify conditions that would break the Conduit Financing causing systemic losses.

We failed to find this breaking point through any of the single parameter sensitivities; Cases 1, 2, or 3; or the multiple parameter sensitivities of Cases 4, 5, 6, and 7 when they were applied to the Expected Case. We have therefore failed to identify a breaking point for the structure based on manipulations of the three parameters so far.

We will now run the three subcases of Case 7 with a 5.00% CFS. We will call these cases Run #8. The results are shown in Exhibit 18.20.

This is clearly the breaking point of the structure, given no changes to the prepayment and default assumptions. Here there is so little spread to support the losses that the cushion of the Seller Interest is quickly exhausted. In Cases 8b and 8c

EXHIBIT 18.20 Finding the conditions that result in systemic losses

	Run #8a MVD 50%, RPL 12–36, CFS 5.00%	Run #8b MVD 60%, RPL 12–36, CFS 5.00%	Run #8c MVD 70%, RPL 12–36, CFS 5.00%
CONDUIT PERFORMANCE			
Loss Cases to the Conduit Financing?	NO	YES	YES
Number of Loss Cases	0	2 of 125	28 of 125
Maximum Loss	0%	2.45%	10.68%
Minimum Loss	0%	0.93%	0%
Cases of Full IRR	All	123 of 125	97 of 125
Maximum Coverage Ratio	5.9%	5.6%	5.28%
Minimum Coverage Ratio	2.4%	0%	0%
SELLER INTEREST PERFORMANCE			
Maximum Internal Rate of Return	2.41%	−1.60%	0.70%
Minimum Internal Rate of Return	−4.20%	−8.9%	−10.03%
Maximum Excess Servicing Released	$29.0 MM	$27.6 MM	$25.9 MM
Minimum Excess Servicing Released	$12.0 MM	$0	$0
Maximum Coverage Ratio	18.29%	−39.43%	6.21%
Minimum Coverage Ratio	−51.31%	−100.00%	−100.00%
STRUCTURE PERFORMANCE			
Program Fees Payment Shortfall?	NO	YES	YES
Servicing Fees Payment Shortfall?	NO	NO	NO
Conduit Interest Payment Shortfall?	NO	NO	NO

the Conduit financing begins to capitalize small amounts of interest when the excess spread from the collateral proves insufficient to pay current interest.

Based on these sensitivity cases it would appear that we have little to fear.

The scenarios of Case 8 are very unlikely to occur.

Are we finished? One unanswered question remains. All of these previous sensitivity scenarios are based on the assumptions that the defaults will be distributed evenly over the life of the deal. This is consistent with the PSA methodology. In addition, the PSA methodology looks at defaults as a current percentage of *remaining principal balance outstanding*. Thus, as the portfolio amortizes and prepayments retire other principal amounts, the defaults decrease in magnitude as time goes on. What would happen if the default methodology calculated losses as a fixed percentage based on outstanding principal balance at the inception of the deal, and, in addition, moved the occurrence of the defaults to earlier in the life of the deal?

This change would have three immediate effects. The first would be a significant increase in the total amount of defaulted principal combined with an "early arrival" of the defaults in the deal. The second would be an immediate decline in the total amount of excess spread available to the deal due to the loss of coupon payments from these defaulted loan balances. The third effect triggered by the first two would be a rapid depletion of the Seller Interest. The loss of the Seller Interest would then result in the application of all losses directly against the Conduit Financing.

Stress Case of an Accelerated Default Pattern

We will now create our first Stress Case. A Stress Case differs from an Expected Case sensitivity in that some of the values of the inputs will lie outside of the Ranges used for sensitivity analysis (that is why it is called a *Stress Case!*).

Stress tests are designed to reflect nightmare scenarios. They are the outliers that may appear without regard to the existing set of empirical observations. These are not second or even third standard deviation events, but may instead represent conditions that, though possible, may seem remote.

Stress tests are not necessarily designed to be structuring criteria, but they can be. Many of the higher investment grade ratings such as A+, AA, and AAA, may require that the structure withstand 300 to 500% of base case empirical levels of defaults or prepayments. Alternatively, they may require a combination of overemphasized inputs such as 300% of one parameter and 400% of another.

In this case we have been asked to construct a stress test in which all the losses are calculated on the current balances of the collateral portfolio at the time of securitization. This is in direct contrast to a method that uses the ongoing current balance as the basis of the default calculation as is the case with the PSA methodology. The absolute dollar amount of the losses will be significantly higher, approaching worst-case historical levels for this type of collateral. As noted before, the total amounts of principal defaulted using a current balance default calculation methodology is strongly influenced by the amount of principal outstanding over the life. If large amounts of principal are retired through scheduled amortization or prepayment activity, the gross defaults will decline, in some cases precipitously. Exhibit 18.21 illustrates the amount of principal defaulted as a product of the PSA prepayment/default combinations we used in the Expected Case sensitivity runs.

Reductions of Defaults as a Percentage of Original Balance Due to Prepayment Effects
As this clearly shows 100%, 200%, 300%, 400%, or 500% PSA defaults is not a constant amount but is *critically* dependent on the accompanying prepayment speed specified. Moving away from the PSA methodology to the User methodology

EXHIBIT 18.21 Reductions in dollar default levels due to influence of high prepayment rates

PREPAYMENT SPEEDS	100 PSA	150 PSA	200 PSA	250 PSA	300 PSA
DEFAULT SPEED					
100 PSA	2.47%	2.31%	2.17%	2.05%	1.93%
200 PSA	4.87%	4.57%	4.30%	4.05%	3.82%
300 PSA	7.22%	6.77%	6.36%	6.00%	5.67%
400 PSA	9.51%	8.92%	8.40%	7.92%	7.48%
500 PSA	11.73%	11.02%	10.37%	9.78%	9.25%

changes the basis of the default percentage to one based on original balance. Thus if a 10% Default Rate is specified, it is calculated from the original principal balance, in this case at $491.4 million, the total defaults will be $49.14 million or exactly 10%, regardless of the prepayment activity. The stress tests that follow and the rating agency stress tests will both use this approach.

The USER methodology also requires that the distribution of the defaulted principal be specified on an annual basis. This annual proportioning can occur in any pattern as long as the total of the User annual allocations over the life of the deal total 100%. In the following stress test of the Expected Case, we will specify that the defaults be distributed equally across the first ten years of the deal, 10% per year. If the overall Default Rate is set to 20% a total of $98.28 million of defaults will occur at a rate of $9.828 million per year.

We will generate the Matrix Reports for the combination of each of the following conditions:

Market Value Declines	50%, 60%, 70%
Conduit Funding Spreads	2%, 3% 4%, 5%
Recovery Lag Periods	12, 24, 36 months

This sensitivity analysis will produce 36 files containing 25 scenarios each.

Defaults Range from 5 to 25% of the original principal balance of the portfolio by 5% intervals. Prepayments will remain under the PSA methodology and will be consistent with those used in the sensitivity analysis. They are 100% PSA to 300% PSA by 50% intervals. Exhibit 18.22 shows the entries to the Defaults and Prepayments Menu to specify this User default methodology.

Default Rates

Default Rate	5.00%	Default Methodology Codes
Default Rate Step	5.00%	1=CPR, 2=PSA
# Default Steps	5	3=User Defined
Methodology	3	

Prepayment Rates

Prepay Base Rate	100.00%	Prepay Method
Prepay Rate Step	50.00%	Codes
# Prepay Steps	5	1=CPR, 2=PSA,
Methodology	2	

Distribution of Portfolio Lifetime Annual Defaults

Year 1	10.00%	Year 11		Year 21	
Year 2	10.00%	Year 12		Year 22	
Year 3	10.00%	Year 13		Year 23	
Year 4	10.00%	Year 14		Year 24	
Year 5	10.00%	Year 15		Year 25	
Year 6	10.00%	Year 16		Year 26	
Year 7	10.00%	Year 17		Year 27	
Year 8	10.00%	Year 18		Year 28	
Year 9	10.00%	Year 19		Year 29	
Year 10	10.00%	Year 20		Year 30	
Percentage Sum for all Years=>				100.00%	

Run the Model

Mkt Value Decline	50.00%	
Recovery Lag	12	Months

Clear All

EXHIBIT 18.22   Entries to the Default/Prepayment Menu for the User methodology accelerated default pattern

HELP! A POST-PROCESSING PROGRAM

If we want to compare the performance of a single output result such as the Conduit Financing Severity of Loss numbers for each of the above 36 stress cases, we will need to page through 36 separate Summary Matrix Reports!

Post-processing programs stand outside of the model and are used to extract information from sets of related output reports. For example, you may want to examine the value of a single parameter contained in ten different output reports. You will find it much easier to spend some time writing a program to extract that information automatically from a series of report files rather than paging endlessly through a set of printed reports. If we put the extracted information into an Excel workbook, it can then be perused, displayed, or graphed by you at your leisure! Always try to avoid digging the hole with the coffee scoop!

When we look at a collection of stress cases, it would be very helpful to be able to have all the values for a single parameter grouped on a single page.

It will be much easier for us to have the results data grouped by individual parameters across cases in a one-page report. If all the Summary Matrix Reports have the same default and prepayment matrix speeds, we can group any of the output data along this framework.

This will allow us to view the continuum of changes in values across closely related cases.

The name of this program is **EXTRACTOR.xls**. A discussion of how to use it and its limitations can be found at the end of this chapter

An example of the reports produced by the program is shown in Exhibit 18.23.

Results of the Stress Test: All Defaults Distributed in First Ten Years

Exhibit 18.24 displays the results of the first User specified stress tests.

Default Levels	Type	MVD	RPL	Spread	Prepayment L PSA Prepayment Methodology					
					1	2	3	4	5	
					100.00%	150.00%	200.00%	250.00%		
1	ECSLagSprd	50.00%	12	200	22.49%	22.37%	22.24%	22.09%	21.95%	C:\VBA_Class\Anal
100.00%	ECSLagSprd	50.00%	18	200	21.97%	21.85%	21.71%	21.56%	21.41%	C:\VBA_Class\Anal
PSA	ECSLagSprd	50.00%	24	200	21.52%	21.39%	21.25%	21.09%	20.94%	C:\VBA_Class\Anal
	ECSLagSprd	50.00%	30	200	21.13%	21.00%	20.84%	20.68%	20.52%	C:\VBA_Class\Anal
	ECSLagSprd	50.00%	36	200	20.79%	20.65%	20.49%	20.31%	20.14%	C:\VBA_Class\Anal
	ECSLagSprd	50.00%	12	300	8.00%	7.88%	7.78%	7.69%	7.61%	C:\VBA_Class\Anal
	ECSLagSprd	50.00%	18	300	7.83%	7.71%	7.60%	7.51%	7.43%	C:\VBA_Class\Anal
	ECSLagSprd	50.00%	24	300	7.66%	7.54%	7.43%	7.33%	7.25%	C:\VBA_Class\Anal
	ECSLagSprd	50.00%	30	300	7.50%	7.38%	7.26%	7.17%	7.08%	C:\VBA_Class\Anal
	ECSLagSprd	50.00%	36	300	7.35%	7.23%	7.11%	7.01%	6.93%	C:\VBA_Class\Anal
2	ECSLagSprd	50.00%	12	200	20.44%	20.29%	20.13%	19.96%	19.82%	C:\VBA_Class\Anal
200.00%	ECSLagSprd	50.00%	18	200	19.55%	19.39%	19.21%	19.03%	18.88%	C:\VBA_Class\Anal
PSA	ECSLagSprd	50.00%	24	200	18.80%	18.62%	18.44%	18.24%	18.06%	C:\VBA_Class\Anal
	ECSLagSprd	50.00%	30	200	18.15%	17.96%	17.76%	17.55%	17.37%	C:\VBA_Class\Anal
	ECSLagSprd	50.00%	36	200	17.58%	17.38%	17.17%	16.94%	16.75%	C:\VBA_Class\Anal
	ECSLagSprd	50.00%	12	300	6.83%	6.69%	6.58%	6.48%	6.40%	C:\VBA_Class\Anal
	ECSLagSprd	50.00%	18	300	6.60%	6.45%	6.33%	6.23%	6.14%	C:\VBA_Class\Anal
	ECSLagSprd	50.00%	24	300	6.38%	6.23%	6.10%	5.99%	5.90%	C:\VBA_Class\Anal
	ECSLagSprd	50.00%	30	300	6.18%	6.01%	5.87%	5.76%	5.67%	C:\VBA_Class\Anal
	ECSLagSprd	50.00%	36	300	5.99%	5.81%	5.67%	5.55%	5.46%	C:\VBA_Class\Anal

Summary Matrix Report - Seller Interest Performance
Seller Interest IRR

EXHIBIT 18.23   Summary Matrix Extraction Report

EXHIBIT 18.24   Initial Sensitivity results of the first USER defined stress tests

	Run #9a MVD 50-70%, RPL 12,24,36, CFS 2.00%	Run #9b MVD 50-70%, RPL 12,24,36, CFS 3.00%	Run #9c MVD 50-70%, RPL 12,24,36, CFS 4.00%	Run #9d MVD 50-70%, RPL 12,24,36, CFS 5.00%
CONDUIT PERFORMANCE				
Loss Cases?	NO	YES	YES	YES
# of Loss Cases	0	2 of 225	19 of 225	94 of 225
Max Loss	0%	1.41%	7.88%	26.75%
Min Loss	0%	0.27%	0.13%	0.53%
# of Full IRR	All	223 of 225	206 of 225	131 of 225
Max Coverage Ratio	21.6%	18.94%	12.26%	6.08%
Min Coverage Ratio	6.1%	0%	0%	0%
SELLER INTEREST PERFORMANCE				
Maximum IRR	36.22%	29.6%	15.01%	1.00%
Minimum IRR	−2.71%	−20.1%	NA	NA
Max Excess Servicing	$105.8 MM	$93.9 MM	$60.2 MM	$27.2 MM
Min Excess Servicing	$18.4 MM	$10.9 MM	$0	$0
Max Coverage Ratio	330.82%	278.7%	145.2%	10.56%
Min Coverage Ratio	−25.75%	−53.6%	−100.0%	−100.0%
STRUCTURE PERFORMANCE				
Program Fees Shortfall?	NO	NO	NO	NO
Servicing Fees Shortfall?	NO	NO	NO	NO
Conduit Interest Shortfall?	YES	YES	YES	YES

Default Rates 5% to 25% User, Distributed First 10 Years, Prepayments 100% to 300% PSA   Moving the defaults to the first ten years of the deal changes the picture immediately.

The number of loss cases increases sharply for each lost 1% increase in CFS. With less time for the collateral to amortize before defaults occur, the severity of loss figures also increase sharply. The movement of the defaults to the early (one to ten years) of the deal is the sensitivity that "breaks the deal." This phenomenon anticipates the next set of analysis that we will perform the stress tests for the rating agencies.

STEP 7: RATING AGENCY STRESS TESTS

Having finished all the internally required runs, we are about to embark upon our first exercise in running numbers for external parties, the rating agencies. Our deal is a Conduit deal and as such will not be sold as an individual deal to investors. Instead, commercial paper, backed by the cash flows of this deal and hundreds of others, will be purchased based on the overall rating of the Conduit. This does not mean that we are immune to the ratings process.

Inputs for the Rating Agency Stress Test

We need to represent to the ratings agencies that this deal is structured to acceptable criteria for inclusion in the Conduit vehicle. The Conduit will have specific buckets within it for deals with the various investment grade ratings. We may be limited to specific ratings if we wish to place this deal in the existing Conduit.

For the moment we will assume that we are free to meet any of the criteria for the A, AA, or AAA ratings.

The stress tests that we will be asked to produce are:

Prepayment Range	100% to 300% PSA by 50% increment
Defaults Range	5% to 25% USER by 5% increments
Default Distribution	5%, 30%, 30%, 30%, 5% (1st 5 years only)
Conduit Funding Spread	2.00%, 3.00%, 4.00%
Market Value Decline %	50%, 60%, 70%
Recovery Lag Period	12, 24, 36

These tests also employ a "User" defined method that requires that the user specify an absolute percentage of the beginning current balance of the collateral as the total lifetime defaults. To briefly recap this method, if the aggregate portfolio current balance at the inception of the deal was $400 million and the User default percentage was set to 15%, a total of $60 million of principal would be defaulted over the time period specified. The period over which the defaults are applied are entered in the table entitled "Distribution of Portfolio Lifetime Annual Defaults." Again remember, the annual percentages of this table *must* total 100% as they are used to distribute the $60 million of defaulted principal (in our above example) over the specified years of the deal. The entries required to specify the default pattern of the rating agency stress cases are shown in Exhibit 18.25.

The initial results of this test are found in Exhibit 18.26.

Default Rates		
Default Rate	5.00%	**Default Methodology Codes**
Default Rate Step	5.00%	1=CPR, 2=PSA
# Default Steps	5	3=User Defined
Methodology	3	

Prepayment Rates		
Prepay Base Rate	100.00%	**Prepay Method**
Prepay Rate Step	50.00%	**Codes**
# Prepay Steps	5	1=CPR, 2=PSA,
Methodology	2	

Distribution of Portfolio Lifetime Annual Defaults

Year	%	Year	%	Year	%
Year 1	5.00%	Year 11		Year 21	
Year 2	30.00%	Year 12		Year 22	
Year 3	30.00%	Year 13		Year 23	
Year 4	30.00%	Year 14		Year 24	
Year 5	5.00%	Year 15		Year 25	
Year 6		Year 16		Year 26	
Year 7		Year 17		Year 27	
Year 8		Year 18		Year 28	
Year 9		Year 19		Year 29	
Year 10		Year 20		Year 30	

Percentage Sum for all Years=> 0.00%

Mkt Value Decline	50.00%
Recovery Lag	12 Months

Run the Model

Clear All

EXHIBIT 18.25 Default/Prepayments menu settings for the rating agency stress tests

EXHIBIT 18.26   Initial rating agency stress test results

	Run #10a MVD 50–70%, RPL 12,24,36, CFS 2.00%	Run #10b MVD 50–70%, RPL 12,24,36, CFS 3.00%	Run #10c MVD 50–70%, RPL 12,24,36, CFS 4.00%
CONDUIT PERFORMANCE			
Loss Cases?	YES	YES	YES
# of Loss Cases	54 of 225	86 of 225	134 of 225
Max Loss	26.34%	36.62%	45.54%
Min Loss	0.81%	0.89%	1.30%

Default Rates 5% to 25% User, Distributed 5%-30%-30%-30%-5% for First Five Years, Prepayments 100% to 300% PSA   We can readily see from the results that changing the distribution of the defaulted principal from a ten-year to a five-year period has a significant impact on the ability of the structure to withstand losses to the Conduit Financing.

The concentration of these losses in the first five years of the deal and a 4.00% CFS will produce losses in almost every scenario. We should, however, remember that stress runs are meant to be exactly that *stressful*! They are designed to produce widespread pressure on the elements of the deal structure.

While these results may appear shocking at first, you will soon discover that they should be judged in the context of the credit rating that we want to receive from the agencies. In the next section we will look at a set of hypothetical rating criteria. We will see how the results fit into this framework of tests and what ratings we think can be achieved by the structure.

STEP 8: ADJUSTING THE SELLER INTEREST

Rating Levels Criteria

The rating criteria outlined below are hypothetical standards for this deal. They represent broad constructs of the tiered approach used by rating agencies to rate structured deals. These are analytical guidelines only and do not relate to the legal framework of the deal or any due diligence issues connected with the collateral. It is assumed that all other nonanalytical criteria for the rating level have been met and that the remaining issues relate to the results of the model. It also assumes that the calculation methodologies of the model conform to the rating criteria requirements and that both sides agree that these are appropriate for the structure. Remember, in the real world there will be multiple and sometimes interlocking criteria to be meet. This simplified example can serve as an introduction to the real criteria that will be much more complex for a real deal!

BBB Rating Level

No Losses; 15% User Defaults; MVD=50%; Recovery Lag=18; CFS=3.00%;

A Ratings Level

No Losses; 20% User Defaults; MVD=60%; Recovery Lag=18; CFS=3.00%;

AA Ratings Level

No Losses; 30% User Defaults; MVD=60%; Recovery Lag=24; CFS=4.00%;

AAA Ratings Level

No Losses; 40% User Defaults; MVD=70%; Recovery Lag=30; CFS=5.00%;

Current Performance as Structured

If the Seller Interest Advance Rate is maintained at 95%, we have the following results:

- The size of the deal will be $ 466.85 million, which meets the financing target for the Seller, $450 million with $16 million extra.
- The deal meets all the criteria for a BBB rating without modification.
- The deal also just squeaks by the A level criteria.

Let us look at the case of the A rating. In that the initial CFS was set to 1.00% over LIBOR for an "A" rated deal, we will not have to do further runs of the structure. It is currently priced appropriately for an "A" transaction.

This is *not* the case for the BBB rating however. The initial pricing of the Conduit Financing Spread was set to 1.00%. If we do the deal at a BBB level, we will probably have to raise the financing spread to 1.50%. This means that all the stress financing rates that had been set at 2%, 3%, and 4% would now rise to 2.5%, 3.5%, and 4.5%. This might well lower the issuance amount. Or it might not. There might be enough room for the increased financing rates to be absorbed by the deal without changing its performance against the BBB rating criteria stated above.

One thing is clear, however.

We will have to reduce the Seller Interest advance rate to meet the AA structure criteria, and major reductions in the advance rate will be required to meet the AAA rating.

AA Rating: Changing the Seller Interest Advance Rate from 95% to 90%

By reducing the Seller Interest Advance Rate to 90% we will meet all the AA criteria. This puts the deal size at $442.3 million, slightly below the $450 million target for the deal.

We may be able to raise the advance rate because we will reduce the Conduit Financing from 1.00% to 0.85% if the deal is an AA. It is unlikely that the Seller will want to go through this exercise. The Seller has strongly insisted on a $450 million target as the absolute irreducible minimum needed from the deal. With an A rating discussed above, they meet that goal with a $16 million cushion.

AAA Rating: Changing the Seller Interest Advance Rate from 95% to 82.5%

By reducing the Seller Interest Advance Rate to 82.5% we will meet all the AAA criteria. This puts the deal size at $405.4 million, significantly below the $450 million target for the deal.

This is the least attractive of the options. Again we would rerun this structure with a lower financing spread, possibly as low as 0.50%. This would raise the advance rate due to lower coupon expense. We will address the issue of resizing for this level and the AA level in Chapter 19.

SIZING RESULTS TABLE

Exhibit 18.27 displays the sizing results table for the performance of the deal at the BBB, A, AA, and AAA levels. The results are based on the maximum Advance

EXHIBIT 18.27   Performance of the structure at the various target ratings levels

| | Perfromance Statistics by Ratings Levels | | | |
	BBB	A	AA	AAA
ADVANCE RATE	95%	95%	90%	82.5%
FINANCING AMOUNT	$466.9 MM	$466.9 MM	$442.28 MM	$405.4 MM
SELLER INTEREST	$24.6 MM	$24.6 MM	$49.14 MM	$86.0 MM
CONDUIT SPREAD	2.00%	1.00%	0.65%	0.35%
Meets Seller Require?	YES	YES	NO	NO
Meets Conduit Require?	YES	YES	YES	YES
TENOR PERFORMANCE (yrs)				
Average Life	5.85	5.84	5.80	5.74
Final Maturity	19.25	18.91	17.91	16.75
Macauley Duration	4.78	4.97	5.02	5.05
Modified Duration	4.57	4.80	4.81	4.89
COLLATERAL CASH FLOWS				
Scheduled Amortization	$237.3 MM	$237.3 MM	$237.3 MM	$237.3 MM
Prepayments	$220.4 MM	$220.4 MM	$220.4 MM	$220.4 MM
Total Principal Retired	$457.7 MM	$457.7 MM	$457.7 MM	$457.7 MM
Defaults	$33.7 MM	$33.7 MM	$33.7 MM	$33.7 MM
Default Recoveries	$28.8 MM	$28.8 MM	$28.8 MM	$28.8 MM
Total Coupon	$247.2 MM	$247.2 MM	$247.2 MM	$247.2 MM
CONDUIT NOTE PAYDOWN				
Total Principal & Interest	$596.6 MM	$567.29 MM	$529.4 MM	$477.5 MM
Principal Repayments	$466.9 MM	$466.9 MM	$442.28 MM	$405.4 MM
Interest Payments	$129.7 MM	$102.2 MM	$87.2 MM	$72.1 MM
Severity of Loss	0%	0%	0%	0%
Coverage Ratio	22.32%	27.93%	36.06%	36.91%
Internal Rate of Return	4.75%	3.750%	3.40%	3.10%
SELLER INTEREST PERFORMANCE				
Internal Rate of Return	39.29%	53.07%	34.79%	23.98%
Release of Ex Servicing	$109.7 MM	$137.3 MM	$177.2 MM	$229.6 MM
Coverage	346%	459%	260%	167%

Rates that meet the rating agency requirements for each of the credit levels. The assumptions are the Economic Case midrange assumptions:

Prepayment Speed	150% PSA
Defaults Rate	300% PSA
Conduit Funding Spread	1.00%
Market Value Decline %	50%
Recovery Lag Period	12

WE ARE DONE!

We should be ***pretty darn pleased*** with ourselves!

All in all it looks like we have achieved our objective. We have a credit level and structure that we feel are appropriate for inclusion in the Conduit and the Seller has a deal that meets the $450 million financing proceeds requirements!

DELIVERABLES CHECKLIST

The Modeling Deliverables for this chapter are:

- Learning the steps necessary to perform a basic structuring exercise
- Understanding the use of the model to provide the necessary information at each stage of the structuring process.

NEXT STEPS

We have now completed a basic structuring exercise.

Our next goal is to take the lessons we have learned and improve the model so that structuring exercise will be easier the next time. Having survived the ordeal of the sensitivity runs and the rating agency stress runs, one immediate improvement springs to mind.

Most of the effort in this chapter has been concentrated on sizing the deal and testing the deal against various internal and external criteria. We may, in the near future, have to take the results and present them in detail to our own internal risk personnel or rating agency personnel.

The Cash Flow Waterfall Reports provide us with a complete period-by-period analysis of a given scenario. The Matrix Summary and the Extractor reports provide us with high-level summaries with multiple scenario information. We are, however, lacking a report to address the midrange of information. We need a report more general than the Waterfall and more specific than the Matrix Summary Report.

This would be a report that would fit on a single page and ideally contain the following:

1. The assumptions of the scenario,
2. The "Box Score" section we developed for the Waterfall report,
3. An abbreviated, perhaps annual, cash flow table of the key Sources, and Uses of the deal,
4. A graphic representation of 3 above.

This is one of the "added features" that we will create to improve the model. Now that we are getting to feel more comfortable using VBA, we should find that writing these improvements is a somewhat less daunting task than we did ten chapters ago!

Before you leave this chapter, make sure that you spend time studying the Extractor.xls program. It and other programs that you will create will save you hundreds of hours of boring, tedious, and excruciatingly annoying work!

Or, if you like that kind of activity just skip it!

Or not.

ON THE WEB SITE

On the Web site you will find three new things.

The first is a copy of **"MODEL_BASE_18.xls"** that contains the additional VBA module named **"A_BatchFileProgram,"** which allows you to run multiple scenarios from a new menu input schema.

The second are the sets of files produced in the issuance and rating process of the deals. These are organized in the following manner, in the order that they were created for the structuring process

Step #1 — Directory **"run01_base_noselect."** This directory contains a single file which is the Collateral Stratification Report of the loans in the file **"portfolio_orig.xls."** This is a pure stratification report without any selection criteria applied against the loans.

Step #2 — Directory **"run02_base_select."** This directory contains the results of the two initial selection processes.

Step #3 — Directory **"run03_comb_select."** This directory contains two files, an eligible collateral stratification file and an ineligibles file. These files are the results of adding more collateral to the deal to address concentration issues.

Step #4a —Directory **"run04_break_deal."** This directory contains 25 files that look at breaking the deal, causing losses to the Conduit financing position, by varying the MVD between 50% and 70% and the RPL from 12 months to 36 months.

Step #4b — Directory **"run04_expected_case."** This directory contains a set of four files, the Collateral Stratification Reports, the Ineligible Collateral Report, the Matrix Summary Reports, and the Waterfall Reports.

Step#4c — Directory **"run04_sensitivity."** This directory contains nine subdirectories each of which contains a series of files measuring the deals sensitivities to MVD, RPL, and Conduit pricing spread. The first three directories are test results of sensitivity of changes to one input. The second three directories measure sensitivity to combinations of two variables. The seventh and eighth directories contain files for sensitivities to all three factors simultaneously. The ninth directory contains sensitivities to the deal when all defaults are clustered in the first ten years.

Step #5 — Directory **"run05_rating_stress."** This is the directory that holds four sets of rating agency stresses.

Step #6 — Directory **"run06_resize."** There are three subdirectories for the various advance rates and one, named "Results," that contains the final sizing runs of the deal.

The third is the program **"Matrix_Extractor.xls"** which is used to compare the results of various Summary Matrix Report Packages in a single file.

EXTRACTOR.XLS PROGRAM

In the later part of the structuring process, after the collateral selection and the Expected Case has been run, we needed to look at large numbers of related model outputs. The Matrix Summary Reports were the source of almost all of this information. Unfortunately, these reports represent the results of a single model run. We have no good way to easily compare results across sets of several Summary Matrix Reports. For example, what if we wanted to look at the Severity of Loss to the Conduit Position, or the Internal Rate of Return to the Seller Position across ten model runs? We would have to layout the ten pages containing that information from the ten separate Summary Matrix Reports.

We will put the Extractor.xls program in the "\model" directory.

Overview of the Role and Function of the Extractor Program

The Extractor Program is meant to be a solution to this problem. The Extractor Program is not a model. It is merely a program to help us more effectively use the information generated by the model itself. It is called a post processor program because it comes into play *after* the model has run and created its output reports. It allows us to extract and concentrate information that is otherwise diffused across many separate reports making it cumbersome or impossible to analyze in its current form.

Like the Loan Financing Model, the Extractor has a menu that serves as the driver of the program. On this menu we will specify which Matrix Summary Reports we want the program to open and which individual data items we will want it to retrieve for us. This information will then be stored in arrays and output to a template file. It is general in design and is very similar to the model and you should feel immediately at home with its organization.

The Extractor Program performs the following operations:

- Reads the contents of the Main Menu
- Uses those inputs to build a series of target file names from which it will retrieve the data
- Uses those inputs to build file pathways to the output files in the "\output" directory
- Opens the files, finds the correct worksheet, and extracts the information from the location specified
- Stores the information in VBA arrays
- Closes the output file workbook and opens the next repeating the process for each of the specified files
- When retrieval is complete, opens a template file, renaming it to a filename input on the Main Menu
- Populates the renamed template file, saves it, and closes it

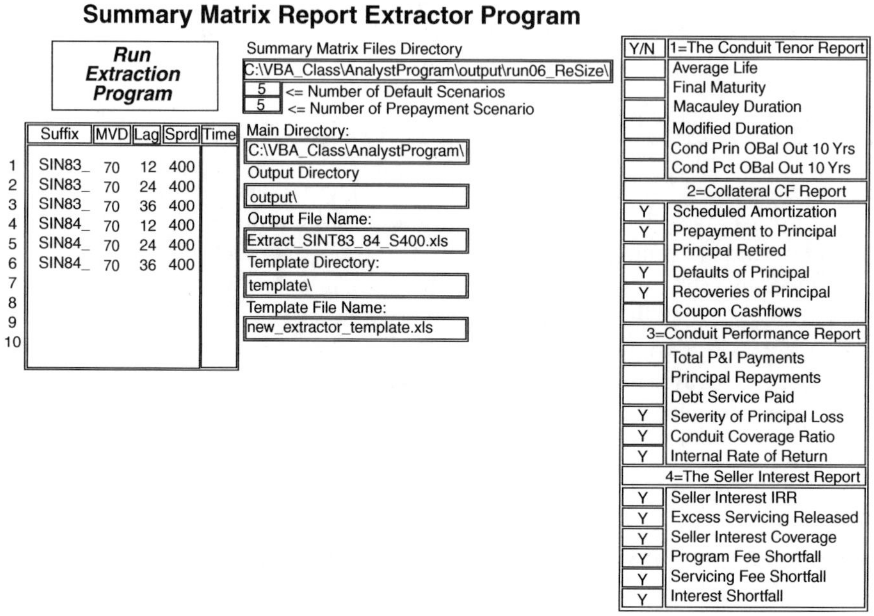

Summary Matrix Report Extractor Program

EXHIBIT 18.28   Main Menu of the Extractor Program

Well, that process certainly sounds familiar! It is virtually the step-by-step macro overview of the functionality of the model. The Extractor Program will save you immense amounts of time and trouble when you have generated large numbers of identically formatted output and need to make sense of it in a hurry!

I have also personally thought that these programs are not only useful but also fun to watch. Depending on the number of files involved and the number of data items, the screen can get quite busy when the Extractor Program is running. I often feel that it is like having a high speed, cheerful, indefatigable, file clerk furiously running here and there (a maniacal gleam in their eye), relentlessly snatching the data from wherever it is hiding.

A picture of the Main Menu and the description of its fields are shown in Exhibit 18.28.

Extractor Program Main Menu

The fields of the menu, shown in Exhibit 18.28, and their uses are as follows:

The File Name Specification Box: Enter the file prefix of the target Summary Report target files, the MVD value, the RPL value, and the CFS assumption for the run. If the file name has a Time Pattern designator, enter it also. The Extractor uses this information to construct the file name that it will open to retrieve the data. Files are opened and their data displayed in the order that they are in the list. The filename construct from the following inputs:

TEST01_   70   12   400   3

would be translated into a file name of:

```
"TEST01_MVD70_L12_S400_T3.xls"
```

This filename follows the conventions of the chapter and is in the general style format of the Summary Report files.

Summary Report Files Directory: Where the Summary Matrix Reports are to be found.

Number of Default Scenarios and Number of Prepayment Scenarios: Number of default and prepayment scenarios to be retrieved. Note: this retrieval process will ALWAYS start with the northwest corner of the report so you can draw out smaller sections of the Summary Matrix Report fields. If the Summary Report is five rows of default speeds and six columns of prepayment speeds, you could elect to retrieve only the first row and first three columns by specifying 1, 3 in the boxes. You would, however, get only the first row and first three columns.

Main Directory: Main directory of the project.

Output Directory: Output directory into which the finished extraction report is written.

Output File Name: Your name for the extraction report.

Template Directory: Subdirectory where the template file for the extraction report is stored.

Template File Name: Name of the template to be used to write the extracted results.

Parameter Check List: This is the listing, by worksheet, of all the parameters in the Summary Matrix Report target files, by worksheet. Enter a "Y" to retrieve the data item.

Program Operation

Place all entries in the Main Menu.

Hit the "Run Extractor Program" button. Based on the number of files selected and the number of data items specified, the screen will start flashing as each file is open and read.

Results

The program will produce a file with a single page for each of the data items selected. The pages will be in the order of the items on the Main Menu list. Each file will be grouped by default/prepayment combination in sets of up to ten files which is the limit of the template format.

An example of the report is shown in Exhibit 18.29.

Summary Matrix Report - Seller Interest Performance
Seller Interest IRR

Default Levels	Type	MVD	RPL	Spread	Prepayment L(PSA Prepayment Methodology)					
					1	2	3	4	5	
					100.00%	150.00%	200.00%	250.00%		
1	ECSLagSprd	50.00%	12	200	22.49%	22.37%	22.24%	22.09%	21.95%	C:\VBA_Class\Anal
100.00%	ECSLagSprd	50.00%	18	200	21.97%	21.85%	21.71%	21.56%	21.41%	C:\VBA_Class\Anal
PSA	ECSLagSprd	50.00%	24	200	21.52%	21.39%	21.25%	21.09%	20.94%	C:\VBA_Class\Anal
	ECSLagSprd	50.00%	30	200	21.13%	21.00%	20.84%	20.68%	20.52%	C:\VBA_Class\Anal
	ECSLagSprd	50.00%	36	200	20.79%	20.65%	20.49%	20.31%	20.14%	C:\VBA_Class\Anal
	ECSLagSprd	50.00%	12	300	8.00%	7.88%	7.78%	7.69%	7.61%	C:\VBA_Class\Anal
	ECSLagSprd	50.00%	18	300	7.83%	7.71%	7.60%	7.51%	7.43%	C:\VBA_Class\Anal
	ECSLagSprd	50.00%	24	300	7.66%	7.54%	7.43%	7.33%	7.25%	C:\VBA_Class\Anal
	ECSLagSprd	50.00%	30	300	7.50%	7.38%	7.26%	7.17%	7.08%	C:\VBA_Class\Anal
	ECSLagSprd	50.00%	36	300	7.35%	7.23%	7.11%	7.01%	6.93%	C:\VBA_Class\Anal
2	ECSLagSprd	50.00%	12	200	20.44%	20.29%	20.13%	19.96%	19.82%	C:\VBA_Class\Anal
200.00%	ECSLagSprd	50.00%	18	200	19.55%	19.39%	19.21%	19.03%	18.88%	C:\VBA_Class\Anal
PSA	ECSLagSprd	50.00%	24	200	18.80%	18.62%	18.44%	18.24%	18.08%	C:\VBA_Class\Anal
	ECSLagSprd	50.00%	30	200	18.15%	17.96%	17.76%	17.55%	17.37%	C:\VBA_Class\Anal
	ECSLagSprd	50.00%	36	200	17.58%	17.38%	17.17%	16.94%	16.75%	C:\VBA_Class\Anal
	ECSLagSprd	50.00%	12	300	6.83%	6.69%	6.58%	6.48%	6.40%	C:\VBA_Class\Anal
	ECSLagSprd	50.00%	18	300	6.60%	6.45%	6.33%	6.23%	6.14%	C:\VBA_Class\Anal
	ECSLagSprd	50.00%	24	300	6.38%	6.23%	6.10%	5.99%	5.90%	C:\VBA_Class\Anal
	ECSLagSprd	50.00%	30	300	6.18%	6.01%	5.87%	5.76%	5.67%	C:\VBA_Class\Anal
	ECSLagSprd	50.00%	36	300	5.99%	5.81%	5.67%	5.55%	5.46%	C:\VBA_Class\Anal

EXHIBIT 18.29 Finished Extraction Report. This report shows the IRR for the Seller Interest across nine different sets of Summary Matrix Reports.

The report fields are as follows, columns across the top of the report.

- Default Speed
- File Prefix Label to identify the run
- Market Value Decline of the run
- Recovery Lag Period of the run
- Conduit Financing Spread of the run
- Up to 10 columns of data, by prepayment speed
- The name of the target Summary Matrix file from which the data was extracted

Batch Program Inputs Menu

Note: Load this table from the top. All files must be sequentially specified and selected. The program will stop counting and reading at the first blank selection field. Hit "F9" to generate file names.

Run the Batch Model

	Select	Market Value Decline	Recovery Period Lag	Conduit Finance Spread	File Name Prefix ID	Time Prefix Code	File Name Prefix (Hit F9 to generate)
1	x	60%	12	1.000%	ECSMvdLag		ECSMvdLag_MVD60_L12_S100_
2	x	60%	18	1.000%	ECSMvdLag		ECSMvdLag_MVD60_L18_S100_
3	x	60%	24	1.000%	ECSMvdLag		ECSMvdLag_MVD60_L24_S100_
4	x	60%	30	1.000%	ECSMvdLag		ECSMvdLag_MVD60_L30_S100_
5	x	60%	36	1.000%	ECSMvdLag		ECSMvdLag_MVD60_L36_S100_
6	x	70%	12	1.000%	ECSMvdLag		ECSMvdLag_MVD70_L12_S100_
7	x	70%	18	1.000%	ECSMvdLag		ECSMvdLag_MVD70_L18_S100_
8	x	70%	24	1.000%	ECSMvdLag		ECSMvdLag_MVD70_L24_S100_
9	x	70%	30	1.000%	ECSMvdLag		ECSMvdLag_MVD70_L30_S100_
10	x	70%	36	1.000%	ECSMvdLag		ECSMvdLag_MVD70_L36_S100_

EXHIBIT 18.30 Batch Menu setup for Run #4

Batch Program Inputs Menu

Note: Load this table from the top. All files must be sequentially specified and selected. The program will stop counting and reading at the first blank selection field. Hit "F9" to generate file names.

Run the Batch Model

	Select	Market Value Decline	Recovery Period Lag	Conduit Finance Spread	File Name Prefix ID	Time Prefix Code	File Name Prefix (Hit F9 to generate)
1	x	50%	12	1.000%	ECSMvdSprd		ECSMvdSprd_MVD50_L12_S100_
2	x	50%	12	2.000%	ECSMvdSprd		ECSMvdSprd_MVD50_L12_S200_
3	x	50%	12	3.000%	ECSMvdSprd		ECSMvdSprd_MVD50_L12_S300_
4	x	50%	12	4.000%	ECSMvdSprd		ECSMvdSprd_MVD50_L12_S400_
5	x	60%	12	1.000%	ECSMvdSprd		ECSMvdSprd_MVD60_L12_S100_
6	x	60%	12	2.000%	ECSMvdSprd		ECSMvdSprd_MVD60_L12_S200_
7	x	60%	12	3.000%	ECSMvdSprd		ECSMvdSprd_MVD60_L12_S300_
8	x	60%	12	4.000%	ECSMvdSprd		ECSMvdSprd_MVD60_L12_S400_
9	x	70%	12	1.000%	ECSMvdSprd		ECSMvdSprd_MVD70_L12_S100_
10	x	70%	12	2.000%	ECSMvdSprd		ECSMvdSprd_MVD70_L12_S200_
11	x	70%	12	3.000%	ECSMvdSprd		ECSMvdSprd_MVD70_L12_S300_
12	x	70%	12	4.000%	ECSMvdSprd		ECSMvdSprd_MVD70_L12_S400_

EXHIBIT 18.31   Batch Menu setup for Run #5

I hope you have as much fun running this against your result sets as I had writing and running it myself!

BATCH PROGRAM INPUTS MENU ENTRIES

In case you wish to replicate all the runs of the model, here are the entries to the Batch Program Input Menu for the sensitivity and the sizing runs in this chapter.

Batch Program Inputs Menu

Note: Load this table from the top. All files must be sequentially specified and selected. The program will stop counting and reading at the first blank selection field. Hit "F9" to generate file names.

Run the Batch Model

	Select	Market Value Decline	Recovery Period Lag	Conduit Finance Spread	File Name Prefix ID	Time Prefix Code	File Name Prefix (Hit F9 to generate)
1	x	50%	12	2.000%	ECSLagSprd		ECSLagSprd_MVD50_L12_S200_
2	x	50%	18	2.000%	ECSLagSprd		ECSLagSprd_MVD50_L18_S200_
3	x	50%	24	2.000%	ECSLagSprd		ECSLagSprd_MVD50_L24_S200_
4	x	50%	30	2.000%	ECSLagSprd		ECSLagSprd_MVD50_L30_S200_
5	x	50%	36	2.000%	ECSLagSprd		ECSLagSprd_MVD50_L36_S200_
6	x	50%	12	3.000%	ECSLagSprd		ECSLagSprd_MVD50_L12_S300_
7	x	50%	18	3.000%	ECSLagSprd		ECSLagSprd_MVD50_L18_S300_
8	x	50%	24	3.000%	ECSLagSprd		ECSLagSprd_MVD50_L24_S300_
9	x	50%	30	3.000%	ECSLagSprd		ECSLagSprd_MVD50_L30_S300_
10	x	50%	36	3.000%	ECSLagSprd		ECSLagSprd_MVD50_L36_S300_

EXHIBIT 18.32   Batch Menu setup for Run #6

| | | **Batch Program Inputs Menu** | | | | |

Note: Load this table from the top. All files must be sequentially specified and selected. The program will stop counting and reading at the first blank selection field. Hit "F9" to generate file names.

Run the Batch Model

	Select	Market Value Decline	Recovery Period Lag	Conduit Finance Spread	File Name Prefix ID	Time Prefix Code	File Name Prefix (Hit F9 to generate)
1	x	50%	12	2.000%	ECSAII		ECSAII_MVD50_L12_S200_
2	x	50%	18	2.000%	ECSAII		ECSAII_MVD50_L18_S200_
3	x	50%	24	2.000%	ECSAII		ECSAII_MVD50_L24_S200_
4	x	50%	30	2.000%	ECSAII		ECSAII_MVD50_L30_S200_
5	x	50%	36	2.000%	ECSAII		ECSAII_MVD50_L36_S200_
6	x	50%	12	3.000%	ECSAII		ECSAII_MVD50_L12_S300_
7	x	50%	18	3.000%	ECSAII		ECSAII_MVD50_L18_S300_
8	x	50%	24	3.000%	ECSAII		ECSAII_MVD50_L24_S300_
9	x	50%	30	3.000%	ECSAII		ECSAII_MVD50_L30_S300_
10	x	50%	36	3.000%	ECSAII		ECSAII_MVD50_L36_S300_
11	x	60%	12	2.000%	ECSAII		ECSAII_MVD60_L12_S200_
12	x	60%	18	2.000%	ECSAII		ECSAII_MVD60_L18_S200_
13	x	60%	24	2.000%	ECSAII		ECSAII_MVD60_L24_S200_
14	x	60%	30	2.000%	ECSAII		ECSAII_MVD60_L30_S200_
15	x	60%	36	2.000%	ECSAII		ECSAII_MVD60_L36_S200_
16	x	60%	12	3.000%	ECSAII		ECSAII_MVD60_L12_S300_
17	x	60%	18	3.000%	ECSAII		ECSAII_MVD60_L18_S300_
18	x	60%	24	3.000%	ECSAII		ECSAII_MVD60_L24_S300_
19	x	60%	30	3.000%	ECSAII		ECSAII_MVD60_L30_S300_
20	x	60%	36	3.000%	ECSAII		ECSAII_MVD60_L36_S300_
21	x	70%	12	2.000%	ECSAII		ECSAII_MVD70_L12_S200_
22	x	70%	18	2.000%	ECSAII		ECSAII_MVD70_L18_S200_
23	x	70%	24	2.000%	ECSAII		ECSAII_MVD70_L24_S200_
24	x	70%	30	2.000%	ECSAII		ECSAII_MVD70_L30_S200_
25	x	70%	36	2.000%	ECSAII		ECSAII_MVD70_L36_S200_
26	x	70%	12	3.000%	ECSAII		ECSAII_MVD70_L12_S300_
27	x	70%	18	3.000%	ECSAII		ECSAII_MVD70_L18_S300_
28	x	70%	24	3.000%	ECSAII		ECSAII_ MVD70_L24_S300_
29	x	70%	30	3.000%	ECSAII		ECSAII_MVD70_L30_S300_
30	x	70%	36	3.000%	ECSAII		ECSAII_MVD70_L36_S300_

EXHIBIT 18.33   Batch Menu setup for Run #7. The entries for Run #7a are lines 1 to 10, for Run #7b lines 11 to 20, and Run #7c lines 21 to 30.

Sensitivity Runs

For the Two Parameter runs, Run #4, Run #5, and Run #6, see Exhibits 18.30, 18.31, and 18.32 respectively.

For the Three Parameter runs, Run #7a, #7b, and #7c, see Exhibit 18.33.

For the Breaking Point runs, Runs #8a, #8b, and #8c, see Exhibit 18.34.

Sizing Runs

For the Internal Stress Tests Run, #9a and #9b, see Exhibit 18.35.

To produce the inputs for Run #9c, change the names in lines 1 to 9 to "ES-CAll_9c" and the CFS to 4%. To produce the inputs for Run #9d, change the names in lines 10 to 18 to "ESCAll_9d" and the CFS to 5%.

Batch Program Inputs Menu

Note: Load this table from the top. All files must be sequentially specified and selected. The program will stop counting and reading at the first blank selection field. Hit "F9" to generate file names.

Run the Batch Model

	Select	Market Value Decline	Recovery Period Lag	Conduit Finance Spread	File Name Prefix ID	Time Prefix Code	File Name Prefix (Hit F9 to generate)
1	x	50%	12	5.000%	ECS_08a		ECS_08a_MVD50_L12_S500_
2	x	50%	18	5.000%	ECS_08a		ECS_08a_MVD50_L18_S500_
3	x	50%	24	5.000%	ECS_08a		ECS_08a_MVD50_L24_S500_
4	x	50%	30	5.000%	ECS_08a		ECS_08a_MVD50_L30_S500_
5	x	50%	36	5.000%	ECS_08a		ECS_08a_MVD50_L36_S500_
6	x	60%	12	5.000%	ECS_08b		ECS_08b_MVD60_L12_S500_
7	x	60%	18	5.000%	ECS_08b		ECS_08b_MVD60_L18_S500_
8	x	60%	24	5.000%	ECS_08b		ECS_08b_MVD60_L24_S500_
9	x	60%	30	5.000%	ECS_08b		ECS_08b_MVD60_L30_S500_
10	x	60%	36	5.000%	ECS_08b		ECS_08b_MVD60_L36_S500_
11	x	70%	12	5.000%	ECS_08c		ECS_08c_MVD70_L12_S500_
12	x	70%	18	5.000%	ECS_08c		ECS_08c_MVD70_L18_S500_
13	x	70%	24	5.000%	ECS_08c		ECS_08c_MVD70_L24_S500_
14	x	70%	30	5.000%	ECS_08c		ECS_08c_MVD70_L30_S500_
15	x	70%	36	5.000%	ECS_08c		ECS_08c_MVD70_L36_S500_

EXHIBIT 18.34 Batch Menu setup for Run #8. The entries for Run #8a are in line 1 to 5, for Run #8b are in lines 6 to 10, and the entries for Run #8c are in lines 11 to 15.

Batch Program Inputs Menu

Note: Load this table from the top. All files must be sequentially specified and selected. The program will stop counting and reading at the first blank selection field. Hit "F9" to generate file names.

Run the Batch Model

	Select	Market Value Decline	Recovery Period Lag	Conduit Finance Spread	File Name Prefix ID	Time Prefix Code	File Name Prefix (Hit F9 to generate)
1	x	50%	12	2.000%	ECSAII_09a		ECSAII_09a_MVD50_L12_S200_
2	x	50%	24	2.000%	ECSAII_09a		ECSAII_09a_MVD50_L24_S200_
3	x	50%	36	2.000%	ECSAII_09a		ECSAII_09a_MVD50_L36_S200_
4	x	60%	12	2.000%	ECSAII_09a		ECSAII_09a_MVD60_L12_S200_
5	x	60%	24	2.000%	ECSAII_09a		ECSAII_09a_MVD60_L24_S200_
6	x	60%	36	2.000%	ECSAII_09a		ECSAII_09a_MVD60_L36_S200_
7	x	70%	12	2.000%	ECSAII_09a		ECSAII_09a_MVD70_L12_S200_
8	x	70%	24	2.000%	ECSAII_09a		ECSAII_09a_MVD70_L24_S200_
9	x	70%	36	2.000%	ECSAII_09a		ECSAII_09a_MVD70_L36_S200_
10	x	50%	12	3.000%	ECSAII_09b		ECSAII_09b_MVD50_L12_S300_
11	x	50%	24	3.000%	ECSAII_09b		ECSAII_09b_MVD50_L24_S300_
12	x	50%	36	3.000%	ECSAII_09b		ECSAII_09b_MVD50_L36_S300_
13	x	60%	12	3.000%	ECSAII_09b		ECSAII_09b_MVD60_L12_S300_
14	x	60%	24	3.000%	ECSAII_09b		ECSAII_09b_MVD60_L24_S300_
15	x	60%	36	3.000%	ECSAII_09b		ECSAII_09b_MVD60_L36_S300_
16	x	70%	12	3.000%	ECSAII_09b		ECSAII_09b_MVD70_L12_S300_
17	x	70%	24	3.000%	ECSAII_09b		ECSAII_09b_MVD70_L24_S300_
18	x	70%	36	3.000%	ECSAII_09b		ECSAII_09b_MVD70_L36_S300_

EXHIBIT 18.35 Batch Menu setup for the first two cases #9a and #9b of Run #9. The entries for Run #9a are in lines 1 to 9 and the entries for Run #9b are in lines 10 to 18.

	Batch Program Inputs Menu					

Note: Load this table from the top. All files must be sequentially specified and selected. The program will stop counting and reading at the first blank selection field. Hit "F9" to generate file names.

Run the Batch Model

	Select	Market Value Decline	Recovery Period Lag	Conduit Finance Spread	File Name Prefix ID	Time Prefix Code	File Name Prefix (Hit F9 to generate)
1	x	50%	12	2.000%	RAS_10a		RAS_10a_MVD50_L12_S200_
2	x	50%	24	2.000%	RAS_10a		RAS_10a_MVD50_L24_S200_
3	x	50%	36	2.000%	RAS_10a		RAS_10a_MVD50_L36_S200_
4	x	60%	12	2.000%	RAS_10a		RAS_10a_MVD60_L12_S200_
5	x	60%	24	2.000%	RAS_10a		RAS_10a_MVD60_L24_S200_
6	x	60%	36	2.000%	RAS_10a		RAS_10a_MVD60_L36_S200_
7	x	70%	12	2.000%	RAS_10a		RAS_10a_MVD70_L12_S200_
8	x	70%	24	2.000%	RAS_10a		RAS_10a_MVD70_L24_S200_
9	x	70%	36	2.000%	RAS_10a		RAS_10a_MVD70_L36_S200_
10	x	50%	12	3.000%	RAS_10b		RAS_10b_MVD50_L12_S300_
11	x	50%	24	3.000%	RAS_10b		RAS_10b_MVD50_L24_S300_
12	x	50%	36	3.000%	RAS_10b		RAS_10b_MVD50_L36_S300_
13	x	60%	12	3.000%	RAS_10b		RAS_10b_MVD60_L12_S300_
14	x	60%	24	3.000%	RAS_10b		RAS_10b_MVD60_L24_S300_
15	x	60%	36	3.000%	RAS_10b		RAS_10b_MVD60_L36_S300_
16	x	70%	12	3.000%	RAS_10b		RAS_10b_MVD70_L12_S300_
17	x	70%	24	3.000%	RAS_10b		RAS_10b_MVD70_L24_S300_
18	x	70%	36	3.000%	RAS_10b		RAS_10b_MVD70_L36_S300_

EXHIBIT 18.36 Batch Menu entries for Rating Agency Stress Run #10a and Run #10b

Rating Agency Stress Runs

For the Rating Agency Stress Tests Run #10a, see Exhibit 18.36.

The inputs for the last run of the #10 set, #10c, would involve changing the file prefix name to "RAS_10c" and the CFS to 4%.

## CHAPTER 19

Building Additional Capabilities

OVERVIEW

No matter how well designed an initial development application is, it will soon experience growing pains. Many well-designed applications will generate the need for improvements simply because they are *so* useful. Nobody cares to improve models that are not used or not needed.

This chapter will look at how to make improvements to our model and why it would be reasonable to do so. These additional features will either improve the analytical abilities of the model or its execution efficiency or both.

We will use the methodologies that we have already mastered to implement these changes.

These additional capabilities will be in the following areas:

- Adding buttons to directly open the most recently run set of output files. With these buttons installed we can directly view the contents of the last set of files produced by the model. We will not have to leave the model or change screens to immediately view the results.
- Design and program a new report, the Single Scenario Report. This report will display the results of a pair of prepayment and default assumptions for a single case. This report will fall into the mid-ground of detail between the Waterfall Report and the Summary Matrix Report. It will be an ideal report to include in client presentations.
- The ability to model a single case or a batch run of different interest rate scenarios for either the LIBOR (London Interbank Offering Rate) Rate, the Prime Rate, and the Conduit Financing Spread (CFS), or any combination of these three. We will split the dates and rate information from the Default Menu and place these schedules in a new menu—Rates Dates Menu. This will allow us to specify the rate level of any of these assumptions individually for every month of the deal.
- Add more information about the collateral pool, the day count factors, and interest rate pathways to the Assumptions Report that accompanies all the files.

UNDER CONSTRUCTION

In this chapter we are going to implement the changes that have been suggested by those, including us, who are using the model.

As listed in the "Deliverables" section, these changes will be focused on three major improvements.

For the first modification to the model, building the button code to open an output file we will work entirely from within the program, we will work exclusively in the **"Z_ButtonSubs"** module.

For the second modification of the program we will need to do several different things. The first thing is create the template file for the new report. This is named **"template_scenario.xls"** and is on the Web site. Next we will need to add an entirely new module to the model named **"WriteScenarioReports."** Into this module we will place all the code needed to produce the report. Fortunately for us all the data that will populate this report already exists. We simply need to aggregate it and then print it out. To this end we will declare a number of variables and place them under the heading "Single Scenario Reports" at the bottom of the module. There is little or no computational burden to producing the report aside from aggregating monthly cash flows into annual ones so we can put all the rest of the report writing code in the separate module we created earlier.

Our last project is to allow the Batch File capability a greater Range of action by allowing several more variables to be specified on the Batch File Menu fields. We will need to modify the Batch File Menu and to expand the error checking to include these new variables, as appropriate. Next we will need to transfer the information from the menu to the model and apply it in running the model one step at a time.

The lion's share of this development will be solely within the confines of the **"A_BatchFileProgram"** module.

We will, however, change the menu layout of the Program Costs Menu. We will need to modify the menu reading and menu error checking subroutines in the **"MenusErrorChecking"** and the **"MenusReadInputs"** modules.

In addition, we will create a new menu named "Rate and Dates" and transfer the various interest rates and day count information to it from its original location on the right of the Defaults Menu.

Lastly, we will need to modify the VBA code inside of the **"WriteAssumptionsReport"** module to reflect the differences in the form of the inputs attendant upon the above changes to the model.

DELIVERABLES

The VBA Language Knowledge Deliverables for this chapter are:

- How to use buttons on a menu to open output report files
- How to add a report to the existing model
- How to add a new sensitivity feature to the model, both in the single case and the batch run mode of operation

PEEK-A-BOO! IMMEDIATE ACCESS TO MODEL RESULTS

Adding Action Buttons to the Main Menu

It would be a convenient and civilized touch to be able to view the latest run output files with just the click of a button. We can do this quite easily. As we create the

Loan Securitization Model Main Menu

Program Execution Options	(Y=YES; N=NO)			
N	Perform the Collateral Eligibility Test?		**Run the Model**	**Run the Batch Model**
N	Write out Ineligible Collateral Reports?			
N	Write out Eligible Collateral Reports?			
N	Write out Eligible Collateral Loan File?			
N	Write out Cash Flow Waterfall Reports?			
Y	Write out Matrix Summary Reports?			
N	Write out Cash Flow Trace Files? *(Caution: can generate VERY LENGTHY runtimes!)*			

Input File Information

C:\VBA_Class\AnalystProgram

Data3.xls	Collateral Data File Name	
0	# of Loans	*Enter "0" to read all available, otherwise enter the number of loans that you want to have read from the top of the file.*

	A_AR95_EC	Report Group Prefix (attached to all output files)	Template File Names
View	Ineligibles.xls	Ineligible Collateral Reports File Name <======	ac_inelig_template.xls
View	Collateral.xls	Eligible Collateral Reports File Name <======	ac_collat_template.xls
View	Waterfall.xls	Cash Flow Waterfalls Report File Name <======	ac_waterfall_template.xls
View	Matrix.xls	Summary Matrix Reports Files <======	ac_matrix_template.xls
View	Eligibles.xls	Eligible Collateral File <======	ac_datafile_template.xls
View	Scenario.xls	Scenario Summary Reports File <======	ac_scenario_template.xls
	CFTrace.xls	Cash Flow Trace Report File <======	cf_trace_template.xls

EXHIBIT 19.1 Menu with file "View" buttons added

output files, we build pathways to them. These pathways are assembled in the setup file subroutines we use to copy the template files and rename them to the output files we will use later.

Once the model has run the file pathways to all, output files are immediately available. We need only find the output pathway: write an Open.Filename command code and link it to some buttons. We will start on the Main Menu and create, position, and label a single button, marked "View," next to each of the names of the output files.

It should look like Exhibit 19.1 when it is completed.

Adding VBA Button Support Code

This functionality will require some VBA to link the buttons with the program and get them pointed in the right direction to open the files. Fortunately, a million years ago, in Chapter 6, "Laying the Model Groundwork," we created a module to house buttons related VBA code.

This is the module where the button support code will reside, "**Z_ButtonSubs.**" See Exhibit 19.2.

Each button will need its own subroutine.

The subroutines will be very brief. They will each have a single executable VBA statement that will simply open the appropriate file using the Workbooks.Open Filename command. All the files are in the output directory and so have the same pathway. Each will share an output file prefix if one was entered when the model was run. The specific filenames for each of the output files are stored in global variables and are readily available.

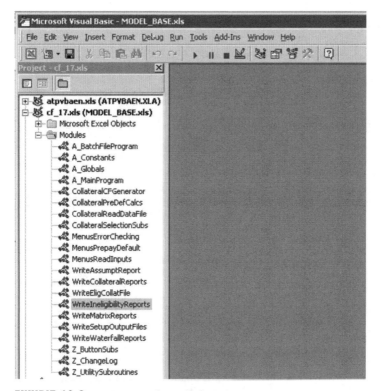

EXHIBIT 19.2   Z_ButtonSubs module

The VBA code for the four subroutines is shown in Exhibit 19.3.

The last thing we have to do is link these five subroutines with the corresponding buttons on the Main Menu. We can do this by placing the cursor on the button and striking the right mouse button. The menu will appear and the "Assign Macro" choice is selected.

Then simply choose the name of the VBA subroutine from the list of available subroutines.

The feature is now complete!

After the model run has completed, select the "View" button next to the report and you will be placed directly into the file.

That was easy! The next improvement is somewhat more involved.

SINGLE SCENARIO REPORT FILE

As we have run the model over the last week, we have noticed that we have a hole in our spectrum of reports. The Cash Flow Waterfall Reports provide us with a very detailed picture of what is going on anywhere in the deal on a monthly basis. The Summary Matrix Report Package will tell us what is transpiring across multiple scenarios of the same model run. At the highest level of reporting, the Extractor.xls program can produce a report that spans many different sets of model runs in a single report.

```
'=======================================================================================
' Open Output reports
'=======================================================================================
Sub Button_View_Collateral_Reports_File()
  Workbooks.Open Filename:= _
           g_pathway_output & gfn_output_prefix & gfn_accepted_loans_file
End Sub
'=======================================================================================
Sub Button_View_Ineligible_Loans_File()
  Workbooks.Open Filename:=g_pathway_output & gfn_output_prefix & gfn_exceptions_file
End Sub
'=======================================================================================
Sub Button_View_Cash_Flow_Waterfall_File()
  Workbooks.Open Filename:=g_pathway_output & gfn_output_prefix & gfn_waterfall_cfs_file
End Sub
'=======================================================================================
Sub Button_View_Matrix_File()
  Workbooks.Open Filename:=g_pathway_output & gfn_output_prefix & gfn_matrix_file
End Sub
'=======================================================================================
Sub Button_View_Collateral_File()
  Workbooks.Open Filename:=g_pathway_output & gfn_output_prefix & gfn_elig_collat_file
End Sub
```

EXHIBIT 19.3 VBA code for the "View" files buttons

But what if we want a comprehensive view of the performance of a single scenario? Ideally this report should be no longer than a single page. It should be a report that we can easily print out and pass around to all interested parties. A single-page report is the perfect size for inclusion directly in sales and marketing presentations to investors, rating agencies, credit wrap providers, and our own internal review personnel.

The wonderful thing about this report is that the information is already available. We will have to generate absolutely no additional information to produce it! We may have to repackage some of the information that we have, but again, this report will not require the additional generation of a single piece of data.

We should also be able to isolate the code for this report the way that we have for the other reporting functions. We will create a VBA module named **"OutputScenarioReports"** and place the vast majority of the code in it.

Design of the Single Scenario Report

The report will consist of four sections:

1. The Assumptions Section
2. The "Box Score" Section
3. The Annual Cash Flow Table Section
4. The Graphics Section that will contain two graphs: the Collateral Cash Flows Graph and the Conduit Cash Flows Graph

If some of these sections look familiar, it is because they are. The Assumptions Section will merely be the Assumptions Worksheet information reconfigured to fit on a single page, without the geographic selection options. The "Box Score" section will be identical to that displayed in the *Cash Flow Waterfall Report*.

The Annual Cash Flows Section will be a condensation of the contents of the Waterfall also. It is impossible to visually display hundreds of months of cash flow periods on a single-page report. We will therefore aggregate the monthly cash flows into annual totals. Along with these, we will also publish the beginning of the year balances of the collateral principal and the Conduit financing outstanding. The key expenses of the deal, the Program Fee, the Servicing Fees, and the Conduit Interest Expense will also be displayed.

Lastly we will graph the key collateral and Conduit cash flow components on two separate graphs at the bottom of the report.

Steps to Take in the Process of Developing the Report

We will need to complete the following tasks to bring the Single Scenario Report file into being:

- Design a template file for the report.
- Declare variables in the "A_Globals" module to hold the Single Scenario Report information.
- Add a field to the Main Menu allowing us to select this report set for production, designate the name of the template file, and of the finished file suffix.
- Write a VBA subroutine to reconfigure the basic template field to accommodate the number of prepayment and default combination scenarios we will be producing.
- Add a VBA module to the model named "WriteScenarioReport" to hold the code for this application.
- Write a VBA subroutine to capture the data from the Waterfall Spreadsheet after the model has been run.
- Write a VBA subroutine to produce the reformatted Assumptions Section.
- Write a VBA subroutine to produce the "Box Score" Section of the report.
- Write a VBA subroutine to produce the Annual Cash Flow Section of the report.

Template File

The template file will consist of an Assumptions Worksheet and a single worksheet configured to the layout of the Single Scenario Report. As we did in the case of the Waterfall Report file, we will copy instances of this single worksheet as many times as we need to accommodate the number of prepayment and default scenarios of the model run. For this we can use the VBA code that we developed for the Waterfall Reports to set up the Single Scenario file.

The report worksheet is shown in Exhibit 19.4.

Writing the Code

Create a New Module to Hold the Code   As we have done earlier in the book, we will start by creating a home for whatever code we will need to produce this report by creating a new VBA Module, "WriteScenarioReport." If you need to refresh yourself on how to create and name a new module, just refer back to Chapter 6, "Laying the Model Groundwork."

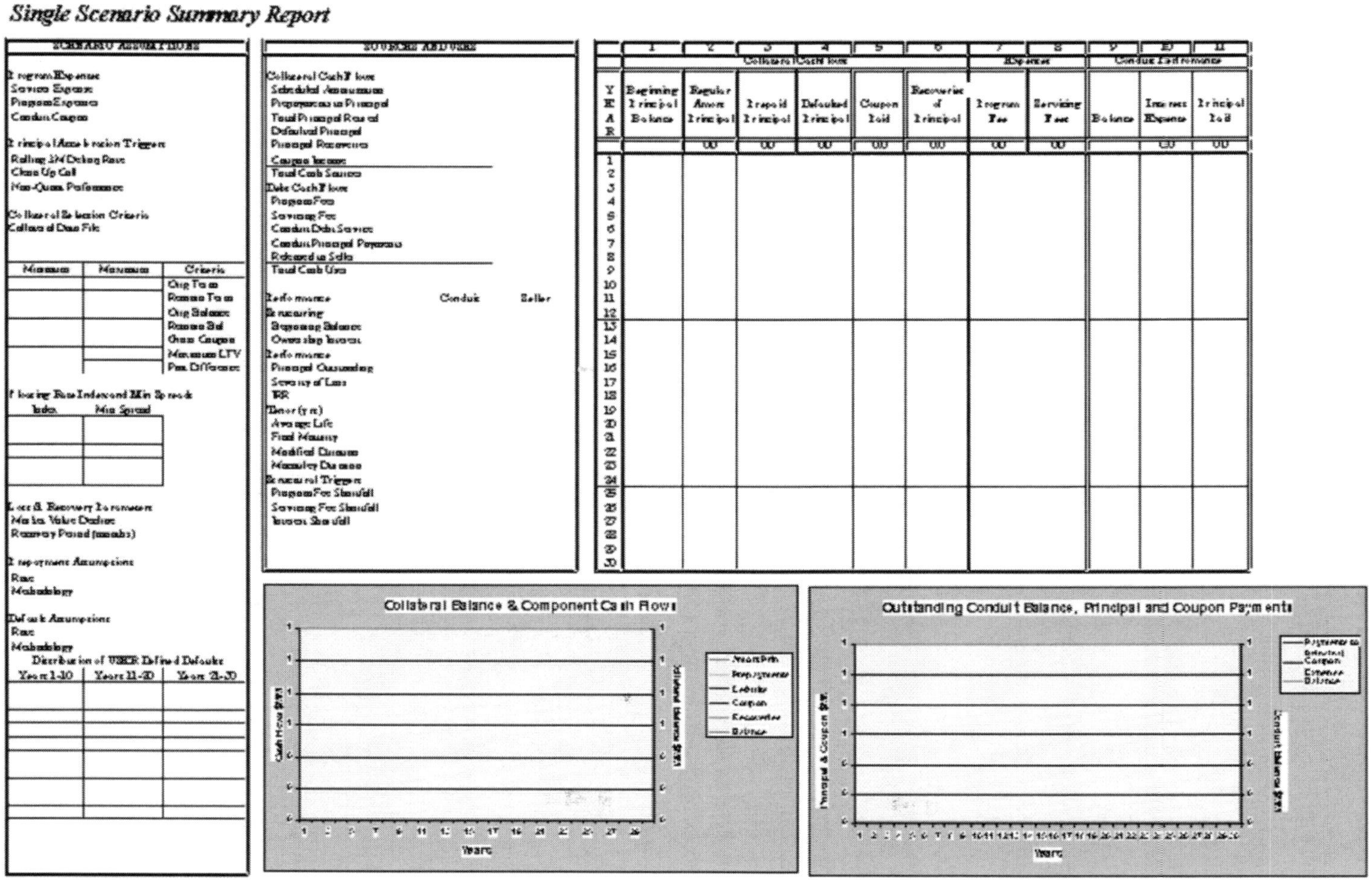

EXHIBIT 19.4 Single Scenario Template File worksheet

```
Public gfn_scenario_file      As String   'Name of  single scenario report file
Public g_out_scen_file        As Boolean  'Switch to output the single scenario file
Public g_template_scenario    As String   'Template file name for single scenarios file
```

EXHIBIT 19.5   Declaration Main Menu support variables for template and output file names

```
' Single Scenario file
Public g_scenario_file                     As String   'waterfall file for scenario outputs
Public g_scen_name(1 To MAX_SCEN)          As String   'worksheet names in cf output file
Public g_scen_info(1 To MAX_SCEN, 1 To MAX_YEARS, 1 To SCEN_ITEMS) As Double
Public g_scen_misc(1 To MAX_SCEN, 1 To 2)  As Double 'prepay/default info
Public g_scen_method(1 To MAX_SCEN, 1 To 2) As String 'prepay and default method
Public g_scen_bxscr1(1 To MAX_SCEN, 1 To 14, 1 To 2) As Double 'box score field group 1
Public g_scen_bxscr2(1 To MAX_SCEN, 1 To 11, 1 To 2) As Double 'box score field group 2
Public g_scen_bxscr3(1 To MAX_SCEN, 1 To 3)          As Double 'box score field group 3
```

EXHIBIT 19.6   Declaration of the variables to hold the information for the Single Scenario Report Files

Declaring the File and Template Name Variables   These variables will be declared in the "A_Globals" module. See Exhibits 19.5 and 19.6.

Modifying the Main Menu   Before we do anything else, we need to modify the Main Menu to allow for the following items, as shown in Exhibit 19.7.

- A field to allow for the selection of the Single Scenario reporting option
- A field with the name of the template file

Loan Securitization Model Main Menu

Program Execution Options	(Y=YES; N=NO)	
N	Perform the Collateral Eligibility Test?	
N	Write out Ineligible Collateral Reports?	**Run the Model** **Run the Batch Model**
N	Write out Eligible Collateral Reports?	
N	Write out Eligible Collateral Loan File?	
N	Write out Cash Flow Waterfall Reports?	
Y	Write out Matrix Summary Reports?	
N	Write out Single Scenario Reports?	
N	Write out Cash Flow Trace Files? *(Caution: can generate VERY LENGTHY runtimes!)*	

Input File Information

C:\VBA_Class\AnalystProgram	
Data3.xls	Collateral Data File Name
0	# of Loans *Enter "0" to read all available, otherwise enter the number of loans that you want to have read from the top of the file.*

				Template File Names
	A_AR95_EC	Report Group Prefix (attached to all output files)		
View	Ineligibles.xls	Ineligible Collateral Reports File Name	<======	ac_inelig_template.xls
View	Collateral.xls	Eligible Collateral Reports File Name	<======	ac_collat_template.xls
View	Waterfall.xls	Cash Flow Waterfalls Report File Name	<======	ac_waterfall_template.xls
View	Matrix.xls	Summary Matrix Reports Files	<======	ac_matrix_template.xls
View	Eligibles.xls	Eligible Collateral File	<======	ac_datafile_template.xls
View	Scenario.xls	Scenario Summary Reports File	<======	ac_scnario_emplate.xls
	CFTrace.xls	Cash Flow Trace Report File	<======	cf_trace_template.xls

EXHIBIT 19.7   Revised Main Menu

```
Sub Read_Main_Menu()
  Sheets("Main Menu").Select
  Range("A1").Select
  ' Read the program runtime options selections
  [7 lines of code not shown]
  g_out_scen_file = UCase(Range("m1WriteScenSummary")) = "Y"
  'Read deal name and number of loans in the collateral file
  [4 lines of code not shown]
  'Names of the output report files
  [7 lines of code not shown]
  gfn_scenario_file = Range("m1ScenarioName") 'output file for single scenario report
  'names of the template files
  [6 lines of code not shown]
  g_template_scenario = Range("templateScenario")'template of the single scenario file
End Sub
```

EXHIBIT 19.8   Additional code to the "Read_Main_Menu" subroutine

- A field with the name of the file extension to use when the file is written to the "\output" directory

We will now need to write code to extract this information from the Main Menu. Moving to the "Read_Main_Menu" subroutine in the **"ReadMenus"** module, we will add the lines shown in Exhibit 19.8.

Reconfiguring the Template Report   The next thing on our "To Do" list is to write the code to prepare the Single Scenario Template Report file to receive the proper number of scenarios from the model run. This subroutine is very similar in function to the one that sets up the Cash Flow Waterfall Report file. This subroutine will be added to the **"WriteSetupOutputFiles"** module. The VBA code is shown in Exhibit 19.9.

Capturing the Data from the Waterfall Spreadsheet   Now that we have variables declared, a template file designed, and a subroutine to modify the template file into as many reports as we need, we can begin to write the code to capture the information we need.

Both of the subroutines below will be added to the **"A_MainProgram"** module.

We need to inform the Main Program that we are going to capture information from the Cash Flow Waterfall worksheet and we do it as shown in Exhibit 19.10, 19.11, and 19.12.

The subroutine in Exhibit 19.12 captures all the information we need from the Waterfall worksheet. Its main looping structure counts the months and sums the information by annual periods. When the period is the first month of the year it captures the balance information. At the end of the year it clears the summation variables. We will place this code in the **"WriteScenarioReports"** module.

Master Subroutine to Write the Single Scenario Report File—Putting All the Pieces Together   This will be our high-level subroutine to control the process of writing the Single Scenario Report file. It begins with a call to the set up subroutine we created above. Having already captured all the data from the Waterfall worksheet, we can begin to populate the reports that the loop will create (see Exhibit 19.13).

```
'========================================================================
' Sets up the single scenario report file
'========================================================================
Sub Setup_Single_Scenario_Workbook()

Dim scen_copy As String

    'Open the template file
    Workbooks.Open Filename:=g_pathway_template & g_template_scenario
    'Save as the designated report file name
    g_scenario_file = g_pathway_output & gfn_output_prefix & gfn_scenario_file
    ActiveWorkbook.SaveAs Filename:=g_scenario_file

    'The template file only comes with one blank worksheet, we must add additional
    sheets ' as required; one for each of the prepayment and default scenario
    combinations. ' Number them sequentially and inset them in the rear of the
    workbook.
    i_name = 1
    p_rate = g_prepay_base_rate
    For ip = 1 To g_prepay_levels
        d_rate = g_default_base_rate
        For id = 1 To g_default_levels
            ' name the sheets using the prepayment and default parameters
            g_scen_name(i_name) = "P-" & (p_rate * 100) & "%" & _
                                " D-" & (d_rate * 100) & "%"
            d_rate = d_rate + g_default_increment
            i_name = i_name + 1
        Next id
        p_rate = p_rate + g_prepay_increment
    Next ip
    'Identify the number of reports by the product of the number of prepay and default
    levels num_reports = g_prepay_levels * g_default_levels
    scen_copy = g_scen_name(1) & " (2)"
    Sheets("SS-1").Name = g_scen_name(1)
    For i_rep = 2 To num_reports
        Sheets(g_scen_name(1)).Select
        Sheets(g_scen_name(1)).Copy After:=Sheets(i_rep - 1)
        Sheets(scen_copy).Select
        Sheets(scen_copy).Name = g_scen_name(i_rep)
    Next i_rep
    Sheets(g_scen_name(1)).Move Before:=Sheets(2)   'move to proper place
    ActiveWorkbook.Save

End Sub
```

EXHIBIT 19.9   Subroutine "Setup_Single_Scenario_Workbook"

Writing the Report   This is now all we need to control the report writing process. A series of subroutine calls will populate the various sections of the report.
We have already summed all the monthly information on the cash flows and selected the beginning year balances and placed them in the appropriate location
in the "g_scen_info" array. All we need now is to just fill in the blanks of the
template file.

   You can examine the code that writes the prepayment headers, the "Box
Score" section, and the Assumptions Section on your own. It is virtually identical to that of the Waterfall report. All of these report writing subroutines
are found in the **"WriteScenarioReports"** module. The code for the subroutine
"Write_Single_Case_Scenario_File" is shown in Exhibit 19.14.

```
Sub Loan_Financing_Model()
    Application_DisplayAlerts = False    'temporarily turn off the warning messages
    Call Display_PrepayDefault_ProgressMsg(99) 'display program progress msg (null)
    Call ErrCheck_All_Menus              'error check all menu entries
    Call Read_All_Menu_Input             'transfer the menu entries to variables
    Call Read_Portfolio_Data_File        'read in the loan information to variables
    Call Select_Deal_Collateral          'select collateral, print eligibility reports
    g_main_filename = ActiveWorkbook.Name
    'run the cash flow waterfall model
    Call Compute_Collateral_Cashflows    'generate the cash flows
    Call Load_and_Run_the_Waterfall      'loads scenario cfs and runs the waterfall
    'Apply the cash flows to the waterfall, scenario by scenario and capture results
    Call Compute_Collateral_Cashflows    'generating the cash flows
    Call Load_and_Run_the_Waterfall      'loads scenario cfs and runs the waterfall
    Call Write_Waterfall_Report_Package  'package of waterfall reports in detail
    Call Write_Matrix_Report_Package     'pacakge of 4 matrix reports
    Call Write_Scenario_Report_Package   'package of single scenario reports
End Sub
```

EXHIBIT 19.10　　Additional code to the Main Model

```
Sub Load_and_Run_the_Waterfall()

  i_scenario = 0
  For i_prepay = 1 To g_prepay_levels
      For i_default = 1 To g_default_levels
          i_scenario = i_scenario + 1
          Call Load_Collateral_Cashflows(i_prepay, i_default)
          Call Load_Funding_Rate_Levels
          Calculate
          If g_out_cfdetail Then Call Capture_Waterfall_Results(i_scenario)
          If g_out_scen_file Then Call Capture_Scenario_Results(i_scenario)
          If g_out_matrix Then Call Capture_Matrix_Report_Results
          Call Display_Waterfall_ProgressMsg(i_scenario, 2)
      Next i_default
  Next i_prepay

End Sub
```

EXHIBIT 19.11　　Code added to the "Load_and_Run_the_Waterfall" subroutine. This will call a data capture subroutine below to get the information we need for the Single Scenario Report file.

The Finished Product　　I hope that this exercise has demonstrated to you the flexibility of VBA to create new reports quickly and easily. Remember that this flexibility comes at a price of having spent the time and effort to initially organize and structure the original model. Because of that earlier effort, we were able to reuse some existing code and build off of existing template sections to create something that fits a real informational need. It is useful not only for ourselves but to many other constituencies of the process. Due to the large size of this report, a schematic is shown in Exhibit 19.15.

ABILITY TO RUN INTEREST RATE SENSITIVITIES

In Chapter 18 we ran the model many times to produce sets of sensitivity results from the Expected Case and for the rating agency stress runs. In these runs we

```
Sub Capture_Scenario_Results(scen)

Dim ip          As Integer   'period counter
Dim ibeg        As Integer   'beginning period
Dim iend        As Integer   'ending period
Dim scen_sum(1 To SCEN_ITEMS)    As Double      'annual sum or end balance
Dim isum        As Double    'item counter

      'write out the waterfall contents
      ibeg = 1
      iend = 12
      For iloop = 1 To MAX_YEARS
            'get the year end balances or sum the yearly cash flows
            For ip = ibeg To iend
                  'collateral balance
                  If ip = iend Then scen_sum(1) = Range("WaterfallCFS").Cells(ip, 1)
                  'sum the cash flows, scheduled amortization of principal,
                  ' prepayments, defaults, coupon, recoveries
                  scen_sum(2) = scen_sum(2) + Range("WaterfallCFS").Cells(ip, 3)
                  scen_sum(3) = scen_sum(3) + Range("WaterfallCFS").Cells(ip, 4)
                  scen_sum(4) = scen_sum(4) + Range("WaterfallCFS").Cells(ip, 5)
                  scen_sum(5) = scen_sum(5) + Range("WaterfallCFS").Cells(ip, 8)
                  scen_sum(6) = scen_sum(6) + Range("WaterfallCFS").Cells(ip, 9)
                  'program, servicing, and conduit coupon expenses
                  scen_sum(7) = scen_sum(7) + Range("WaterfallCFS").Cells(ip, 14)
                  scen_sum(8) = scen_sum(8) + Range("WaterfallCFS").Cells(ip, 18)
                  'conduit balance outstanding and conduit principal paid
                  If ip = iend Then scen_sum(9) = Range("WaterfallCFS").Cells(ip, 37)
                  scen_sum(10) = scen_sum(10) + Range("WaterfallCFS").Cells(ip, 23)
                  scen_sum(11) = scen_sum(11) + Range("WaterfallCFS").Cells(ip, 30)
            Next ip
            ibeg = ibeg + 12
            iend = iend + 12
            For isum = 1 To SCEN_ITEMS
              g_scen_info(scen, iloop, isum) = scen_sum(isum)
              scen_sum(isum) = 0#
            Next isum
      Next iloop
      'prepayment and default headers
      g_scen_misc(scen, 1) = Range("CFDefaultRate")         'prepayment rate
      g_scen_misc(scen, 2) = Range("CFPrepayRate")          'default rate
      g_scen_method(scen, 1) = Range("CFDefaultMethod")     'prepayment method
      g_scen_method(scen, 2) = Range("CFPrepayMethod")      'default method
      'get the components of the Box Score
      Call Get_Scenario_Box_Score(scen)

End Sub
```

EXHIBIT 19.12   "Capture_Scenario_Results" subroutine

concentrated on varying the Market Value Decline (MVD) Factor, the Recovery Lag Period (RLP), and the Conduit Financing Spread (CFS).

The sensitivity analysis was limited in these cases to a single set of interest rate assumptions that maintained both LIBOR and Prime at constant levels throughout the life of the deal. This was clearly a simplifying device based on space consideration for the chapter and the book. In the real world, however, we will be asked to examine the effects of rate pathways for either or both of the indices. The scenarios of most interest will be when the Conduit funding rate closes with the gross coupon levels of the collateral. If the margin between the coupon expense of the debt in the Conduit

```
Sub Write_Scenario_Report_Package()

   'produce the single scenario reports
   If g_out_scen_file Then
          Call Setup_Single_Scenario_Workbook
          For i_scenario = 1 To (g_prepay_levels * g_default_levels)
               Call Write_Single_Case_Scenario_File(i_scenario)
          Next i_scenario
          Calculate
          ActiveWorkbook.Save
          ActiveWorkbook.Close
   End If

End Sub
```

EXHIBIT 19.13   Write_Scenario_Report_Package subroutine

```
Sub Write_Single_Case_Scenario_File(scen)

   Sheets(g_scen_name(scen)).Select

   'write the rest of the report
   Call Write_Scenario_Box_Score(scen)
   Call Write_Scenario_PrepayDefault_Headers(scen)
   Call Write_Scenario_Assumptions_Section
   'write out the waterfall contents
   irow = 11
   For iloop = 1 To MAX_YEARS
      For icol = 1 To SCEN_ITEMS
         'scales the contents of the Waterfall to $ millions
         Cells(irow, icol + 12).Value = g_scen_info(scen, iloop, icol) / 1000000#
      Next icol
      irow = irow + 1
   Next iloop

End Sub
```

EXHIBIT 19.14   "Write_Single_Case Scenario_File" subroutine—the high-level write subroutine that will call other subroutines to fill in each portion of the report

and the coupon income from the collateral of the portfolio becomes less than at the inception of the deal, the excess cash generated by the collateral will be significantly less.

While this may sound like a complicated feature to implement, I think you will be surprised at how easily we can make it happen. (Especially since we are ready and eager to employ some of our newly acquired VBA/Excel modeling skills!)

Doing Some Menu Work: Splitting the Date and Rate Information from the Defaults Menu

To create this new feature in the model, we will be adding two tables of five pathways with 360 months in each for the LIBOR and Prime Rate assumptions. In addition, we will add a small table for five alternative Conduit Financing Spreads.

This means we will add 11 columns to a menu somewhere! There will be five columns for the LIBOR assumptions, five for the Prime Rate assumptions, and one column for the spread assumptions.

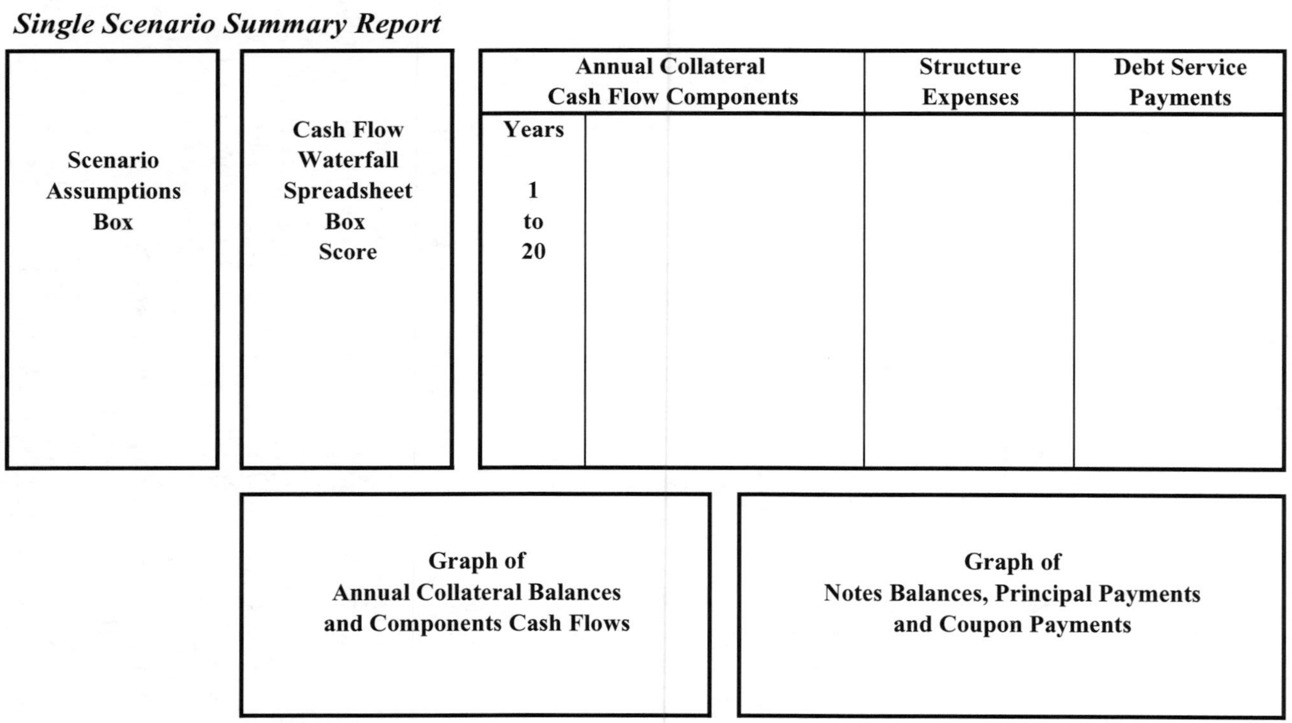

Single Scenario Summary Report

	Annual Collateral Cash Flow Components		Structure Expenses	Debt Service Payments
Years				
1				
to				
20				

Scenario Assumptions Box

Cash Flow Waterfall Spreadsheet Box Score

Graph of Annual Collateral Balances and Components Cash Flows

Graph of Notes Balances, Principal Payments and Coupon Payments

EXHIBIT 19.15 Completed Single Scenario Report

The rates and time period decimal factors are directly related, but as a group they are less related to the defaults and prepayment assumptions than they are to each other. This relationship and the fact that we are talking about a large additional set of menu inputs would strongly argue for splitting the date and rate information off of the Defaults Menu. We also have to give some thought to the future. The loans in the current collateral portfolio all float off of Prime, but we may end up, in future deals, with others that do not. By splitting the menus now we also allow ourselves some growth room for future expansion.

To meet all these requirements, we will therefore establish a new menu named the "Rate Date Menu." We will move all the existing rate and date information from the Defaults Menu to this new menu. On the new menu we will add the ability to specify five pathways for the LIBOR and Prime assumptions and up to five assumptions for the spread assumptions.

This menu will be laid out with five tables. Moving across the Excel spreadsheet from right to left, we will create the following tables:

- The Selected Rate Table—This table in columns B to F will contain the rate schedules that we have selected from the other three tables. This table will consist of four columns which contain in order: in column C, the 360 months of Prime Rate coupon levels; in column D, the selected assumptions of the LIBOR rate; in column E, the selected assumption of the Conduit Financing Spread; and in column F, the Conduit Financing Rates, which is the sum of columns D and F. The columns C, D, and E, which contain the Prime Rate, LIBOR Rate, and Conduit Funding Spread will be collectively grouped in a single Range named "m11IndexLevels." The Conduit Funding Rate in column F will be given the Range name "m11FundConduit."
- The five-column table of alternative LIBOR Rates, in columns H to L. This table will be given the Range name of "m11AltLiborPaths."
- The one column table of alternative Conduit Financing Spreads in column N. This table will be given the Range name of "m11AltConduitSpreads."
- The five column table of alternative Prime Rates, in columns P to T. This table will be given the Range name of "m11AltPrimePaths."
- The four-column table of day count factors in columns V to Y. This table will be given the Range name of "m11DayCntFactors."

When we are done, the menu should look like Exhibit 19.16.

Reading the Pathway Information Into the Model

Once we have the information about the pathways entered into the Rates Dates Menu, how do we make it accessible to the model? The first thing we have to do is give the user (which may well be us) a way to specify which set of LIBOR, Prime, or Spread assumptions are to be used in the current model run. The way we will do this is to add some entry fields to the Program Costs Menu.

The Program Costs Menu is the current home to the field that allowed us to specify the CFS. We now no longer need this field because any information about the CFS is going to be contained in one of the five alternatives on the Rates Dates Menu. Ah yes! But which alternative is it?

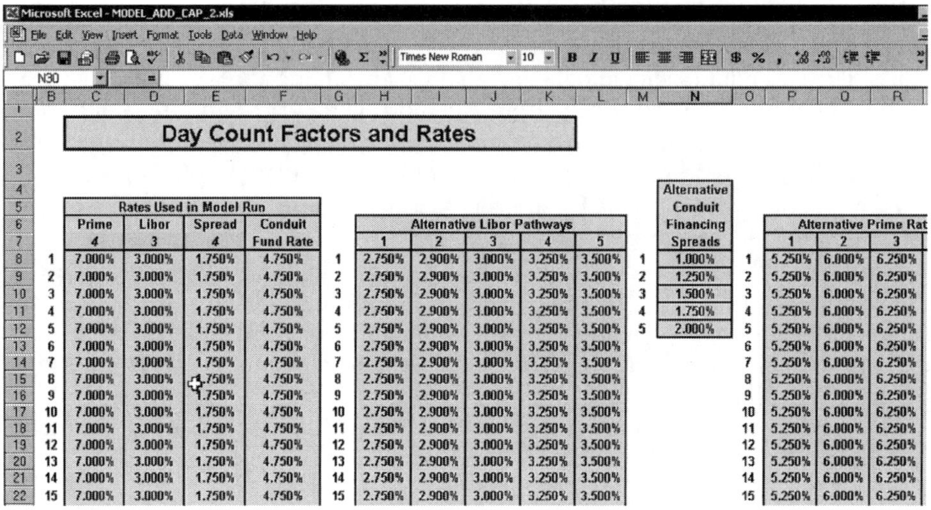

Day Count Factors and Rates

	Rates Used in Model Run			
	Prime 4	Libor 3	Spread 4	Conduit Fund Rate
1	7.000%	3.000%	1.750%	4.750%
2	7.000%	3.000%	1.750%	4.750%
3	7.000%	3.000%	1.750%	4.750%
4	7.000%	3.000%	1.750%	4.750%
5	7.000%	3.000%	1.750%	4.750%
6	7.000%	3.000%	1.750%	4.750%
7	7.000%	3.000%	1.750%	4.750%
8	7.000%	3.000%	1.750%	4.750%
9	7.000%	3.000%	1.750%	4.750%
10	7.000%	3.000%	1.750%	4.750%
11	7.000%	3.000%	1.750%	4.750%
12	7.000%	3.000%	1.750%	4.750%
13	7.000%	3.000%	1.750%	4.750%
14	7.000%	3.000%	1.750%	4.750%
15	7.000%	3.000%	1.750%	4.750%

	Alternative Libor Pathways				
	1	2	3	4	5
1	2.750%	2.900%	3.000%	3.250%	3.500%
2	2.750%	2.900%	3.000%	3.250%	3.500%
3	2.750%	2.900%	3.000%	3.250%	3.500%
4	2.750%	2.900%	3.000%	3.250%	3.500%
5	2.750%	2.900%	3.000%	3.250%	3.500%
6	2.750%	2.900%	3.000%	3.250%	3.500%
7	2.750%	2.900%	3.000%	3.250%	3.500%
8	2.750%	2.900%	3.000%	3.250%	3.500%
9	2.750%	2.900%	3.000%	3.250%	3.500%
10	2.750%	2.900%	3.000%	3.250%	3.500%
11	2.750%	2.900%	3.000%	3.250%	3.500%
12	2.750%	2.900%	3.000%	3.250%	3.500%
13	2.750%	2.900%	3.000%	3.250%	3.500%
14	2.750%	2.900%	3.000%	3.250%	3.500%
15	2.750%	2.900%	3.000%	3.250%	3.500%

	Alternative Conduit Financing Spreads
1	1.000%
2	1.250%
3	1.500%
4	1.750%
5	2.000%

	Alternative Prime Rat		
	1	2	3
1	5.250%	6.000%	6.250%
2	5.250%	6.000%	6.250%
3	5.250%	6.000%	6.250%
4	5.250%	6.000%	6.250%
5	5.250%	6.000%	6.250%
6	5.250%	6.000%	6.250%
7	5.250%	6.000%	6.250%
8	5.250%	6.000%	6.250%
9	5.250%	6.000%	6.250%
10	5.250%	6.000%	6.250%
11	5.250%	6.000%	6.250%
12	5.250%	6.000%	6.250%
13	5.250%	6.000%	6.250%
14	5.250%	6.000%	6.250%
15	5.250%	6.000%	6.250%

EXHIBIT 19.16 Rates Dates Menu

We do not know and have no way of knowing unless we allow the user to make the choice and that choice can be transferred to the model. We will therefore add three new fields to the Program Costs Menu and drop the previous field of the Conduit Spread. The three new fields will ask the user which of the LIBOR, Prime, and Spread pathways they want to use in the analysis.

We will then enter a formula to access the values of these fields on the top of the three columns where the selected pathway is displayed. Each of these formulas will be over their respective columns and will read the choice entered for the pathway election from the Program Costs Menu field. Each of the columns will then use this pathway designation to access the appropriate column of the five alternative pathways per rate.

You may have noticed that so far, we have not used a single line of VBA to implement this feature into the model. Nor do we need to. The model is already set up to read the necessary information from the Range that contains the values of the Prime Rate schedule. Whatever values are therefore present in that column are those used to amortize the collateral. The same is the case for reading into the model the current CFR to determine the debt service costs of the Conduit Financing.

Once we create the fields on the Program Menu and link them to the Excel formulas in the Rates Dates Menu, we are done for the moment. We will assign these fields the Range names "m2SpreadChoice," "m2LiborPathway,"and "m2PrimePathway" respectively, from top to bottom. We need to assign these input fields Range names so we can error check them later. The user makes his other election in the three new fields of the Program Costs Menu and the respective pathways from each of the tables are displayed in columns C, D, or E, respectively! See Exhibits 19.17 and 19.18.

Let us look at Exhibit 19.18 for a moment. In this case the cells C6, D6, and E6 contain the numbers 4, 3, and 4, respectively. These match the numbers shown

Program Costs Menu

Program Expenses

0.75%	Servicer Fee (off of Asset Balance)
0.20%	Program Fees (off of Note Balance)

Principal Reallocation Triggers

10.00%	Clean Up Call Level
5.00%	Rolling 3 Month Default Rate

Advance Rate

95.00%	Conduit Percentage

4	Conduit Spread Choice
3	Libor Pathway
4	Prime Rate Pathway

Run the Model

EXHIBIT 19.17 Program Costs Menu

on the three fields of the Program Costs Menu. The formulas in these cells reference the selections that we have entered on the Program Costs Menu to designate the pathway information we will use on the next run of the model. The Excel formula for cell C6 is as follows:

```
"=m2LiborPathway"
```

which is the Range name of the LIBOR Pathway field.

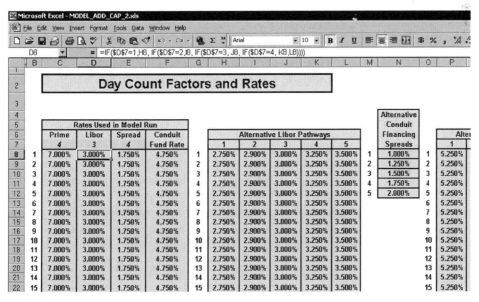

EXHIBIT 19.18 Rate Date Menu with the fourth Prime pathway, the Third LIBOR pathway, and the Fourth Conduit Spread selected

```
Sub Read_All_Menu_Input()

    Call Read_Main_Menu                 'Read Main Menu -- set program run options
    Call Read_Program_Costs_Menu        'Reads the program costs inputs
    Call Read_Selection_Criteria_Menu   'Read tenor, coupon & balance selection criteria
    Call Read_Report_Selection_Menu     'Read menu for report selections
    Call Read_Geographic_Menu           'Read state code geographic selection criteria
    Call Read_Prepay_Defaults_Menu      'Read prepayment and default schedule to apply
    Call Read_Rates_and_Dates_Menu      'Read the rates and dates menu

End Sub
```

EXHIBIT 19.19 Adding the call to read the contents of the Rates Dates Menu

The Excel spreadsheet will now use the entry in this field in the formula shown in the formula window above to populate cell C7.

```
"=IF($D$6=1,H7, IF($D$6=2,I7, IF($D$6=3, J7, IF($D$6=4, K7,L7))))"
```

This formula will select the corresponding rate entry from the LIBOR Rate table based on a value between one and five. We will need to make sure to build an error check for these values in the "errProgramCostsMenu" subroutine to make sure the entries are within the limits of acceptable values. Once the Rates Dates Menu has read the information from the Program Costs Menu, it can fill up the columns C, D, and E with the specified pathway from the three tables.

What else do we need to do? Just getting the rate and spread information into the correct columns of the Rates Dates Menu is not enough! We need to make the contents of these columns available to the VBA variables used by the model. To accomplish this we will add VBA code to the module **"MenuReadInputs."** The highest-level subroutine in that module is "Read_All_Menu_Input." To this subroutine we will add a call to a new subroutine we will now create. The new subroutine will be named "Read_Rates_and_Dates_Menu." When we are done, the "Read_All_Menu_Input" subroutine will look like Exhibit 19.19. The new subroutine that it will call is shown in Exhibit 19.20.

Error Checking the Program Costs Menus

"Here he goes again!" you say, "Just when I thought that we had avoided this subject!" Yes, you can now add "error checking" to the short list of *death* and *taxes* that cannot be avoided in your life. If, however, you want to skip this, go right ahead. You are only hurting yourself.

We need to add some additional code to the "errProgramCostsMenu" subroutine to check that the values of these three fields is between one and five. The code is fairly obvious, so I will not spend too much time on it. The code additions can be seen in Exhibit 19.21. The incremental code is in bold type.

Error Checking the Rates Dates Menu

We now need to write some error checking code for the contents of the three tables, the LIBOR Rates Table, the Prime Rates Table, and the Conduit Spreads Table on

```
Sub Read_Rates_and_Dates_Menu()

    Sheets("Rates Dates Menu").Select
    Range("A1").Select
    Calculate

    'read the day count factors for 30/360, Act/360, Act/Act
    For irow = 1 To PAY_DATES
        For icol = 1 To 3
            g_day_factors(irow, icol) = Range("m11DayCntFactors").Cells(irow, icol)
        Next icol
    Next irow

    'index interest level;  Prime, LIBOR, 10 yr TSY
    For irow = 1 To PAY_DATES
        For icol = 1 To 3
            g_index_levels(irow, icol) = Range("m11IndexLevels").Cells(irow, icol)
        Next icol
    Next irow

    'funding rates for the conduit
    For irow = 1 To PAY_DATES
        g_fund_conduit(irow) = Range("m11FundConduit").Cells(irow)
    Next irow

End Sub
```

EXHIBIT 19.20   Subroutine that reads the contents of the Rates Dates Menu and puts the selected pathways into the appropriate VBA variables

the Rates Dates Menu. After all, what good does it do to correctly select one of the five pathways in these tables only to find that it is full of junk information? This test will not be an exhaustive test. We will not test for negative values or for values failing outside of a Range. Once we have built this test, however, we could easily add those features to the model by creating a separate subroutine to perform the tests. Now we will content ourselves with an error check for numeric data only. These are large tables. There are two of them and each has 360 rows and five columns. It would be helpful to be able to assure the user that all the information is numeric in nature. In that the tables are so large, it would also be informative to tell the user which column in which of the tables has the defective data. We will start with the additional code needed in the subroutine "errAllMenus_for_IsNumerics." See Exhibit 19.22.

We will now look at the code for the "IsNumerics_RatesDatesInfo" subroutine. This subroutine is composed of five major sections. The functional requirements for each, in order, are:

1. Declare the working variables needed to perform the tests.
2. Declare the error message components.
3. Test the LIBOR rate and Prime rate table values and record the presence of errors, if they are found.
4. Test the Conduit Financing Spread alternatives table and record the presence of errors, if they are found.
5. Assemble the error message components.

```
Sub errProgramCostsMenu()

    'menu location masthead statement for top of error message
    msgTotal = "Program Cost Menu   => " & Chr(13)
    'group error conditions
    (4 lines of code omitted)
    msgInfo(5) = " Pathway Choice must be between 1 and 5" & Chr(13)
    'individual field error conditions
    (5 lines of code omitted)
    msgComp(6) = " Conduit Spread Pathway Choice" & Chr(13)
    msgComp(7) = " LIBOR Rate Pathway Choice" & Chr(13)
    msgComp(8) = " Prime Rate Pathway Choice" & Chr(13)

    'test the values of each of the fields of the menu
    For itest = 1 To 8
      err_result(itest) = False
      Select Case itest
          (5 lines of code omitted)
          Case Is = 6: x = Range("m2SpreadPathway")
          Case Is = 7: x = Range("m2LiborPathway")
          Case Is = 8: x = Range("m2PrimePathway")
      End Select
      (9 lines of code omitted)
      If itest >= 6 And itest <= 8 Then
          If x >= 0 Or x <= 6 Then err_result(itest) = True
      End If
    Next itest

    (23 lines of code omitted)
    'test for rate pathways
    For itest = 6 To 8
      If err_result(itest) = True Then  'got one!
          msgInfo(5) = msgInfo(5) & msgComp(itest) 'add pathway error
          errcase(5) = errcase(5) + 1   'tell calling sub to print out
      End If
    Next itest

    'Print the combination of errors
    If (errcase(1) + errcase(2) + errcase(3) + errcase(4) + errcase(5)) > 0 Then
          (5 lines of code omitted)
          If errcase(5) > 0 Then msgTotal = msgTotal & msgInfo(5)
          (3 lines of code omitted)
    End If

End Sub
```

EXHIBIT 19.21   Additional code in "errProgramCostsMenu" to error check the three pathway election fields

This is a large subroutine and before we begin to step through it we should review just what we are trying to accomplish. The objective of this piece of code is to hunt through all three of the tables, the LIBOR Table, the Prime Table, and the Conduit Spread Table, and determine if all of the inputs are numeric.

Declarations of the Variables   Since there are three columns each having five columns, we will be searching and holding results with those numbers in mind. The numbers, currently three and five, will be used in a number of places, and if we need to change them in the future it might be easier to change them now. We will therefore declare them as constant variables. Next we will declare three scalar

```
Sub errAllMenus_for_IsNumerics()

    For itable = 1 To 4
        Select Case itable
            Case Is = 1: Call IsNumeric_ProgramCostsInfo
            (2 lines of code omitted)
            Case Is = 4: Call IsNumeric_RatesDatesInfo
        End Select
    Next itable

    'If there are errors to print -- print them!
    err_total = errcase(1) + errcase(2) + errcase(3) + errcase(4)
    If err_total > 0 Then
        'Error box title -- displayed above any errors
        msgTotal = "Non-numeric Inputs for the following Tables" & Chr(13) & Chr(13)
        'Print the combination of errors based on the error code value
        (3 lines of code omitted)
        If errcase(4) > 0 Then msgTotal = msgTotal & msgInfo(4)
        msgPrompt = msgTotal
        msgResult = MsgBox(msgPrompt, cMsgButtonCode1, msgTitle)
        go_ok = False
    End If

End Sub
```

EXHIBIT 19.22   Additional code in "errAllMenus_for_IsNumerics" subroutine

variables to hold the current value from each of the tables we are currently reading from. The next variable, column_err, will hold the total number of errors from each of the columns of all of the tables. Thus if the first column of the first table has three errors detected, the value of column_err(1,1) will be equal to 3. The variable table_total will hold the number of errors found in each table as a whole. These two variables will allow us to first test if the table as a whole has any errors, and then if it does, which columns have errors. See Exhibit 19.23.

Declarations of the Message Components (msgInfo(4) and msgComp array)   The next six lines of the subroutine declare the values of the components of the error message that we want to build. As with the other message components in existing subroutines, we will start with a base message fragment and continually concatenate other string messages onto the seed message to build the entire complex message. The variable msgInfo(4) is the base component of the error message. If the value of variable errcase(4) is set to 1 and an error has occurred, we will start building

```
Sub IsNumeric_RatesDatesInfo()

Const NUM_TABLES = 3                           'number of rates tables
Const NUM_COLS = 5                             'number of columns per table
Dim libor_value  As String                     'test value for the libor rate
Dim condt_value  As String                     'test value for the conduit spread
Dim prime_value  As String                     'test value for the prime rate
Dim column_err(1 To NUM_COLS, 1 To NUM_TABLES) As Double
                                               'number of errors in column
Dim table_total(1 To NUM_TABLES) As Double     'number of errors in table
Dim rtable        As Integer                   'counter for looping through tables
```

EXHIBIT 19.23   Variable declaration code in "IsNumeric_RateDatesInfo" subroutine

```
msgInfo(4) = "Rates & Dates Menu   => non-numeric entry in table" & Chr(13)
 msgComp(1) = "   LIBOR Rate Table in Pathway "
 msgComp(2) = "   Prime Spread Table in Pathway "
 msgComp(3) = "   Conduit Spread Table in Entry "
 msgComp(4) = Chr(13)
 errcase(4) = 0      'tells the calling subroutine we have error if = 1
```

EXHIBIT 19.24 Message components declaration code in "IsNumeric_RateDatesInfo" subroutine

the complex error message. If errcase(4) is 1, it will alert the subroutine "errAll-Menus_for_IsNumerics" that something is wrong on the RatesDatesMenu and to subsequently print out the contents of msgInfo(4) message. What we want to end up with is an error message that looks like this, if, for example, there was an error in columns 1 and 3 of the LIBOR Rate table.

Rates & Dates Menu $\Rightarrow$ non $-$ numeric entry in table
LIBOR Rate Table in Pathway 1, 3,

To accomplish this we will use the code in Exhibit 19.24.

Initialization of the Testing Variables Here we take a few lines to initialize the values of the testing variables. We will set the number of errors in each of the tables to zero and the number of error in each of the columns to zero. See Exhibit 19.25.

Test the Values, Record the Errors This code will go down the first column of both the LIBOR and Prime Rate table simultaneously, then the second column, the third, and so on until the entire contents of all the columns are examined. There are three nested For...Next loops. The outermost cycles through the column number one to five. The next innermost cycles through the 360 dates of the table. Immediately inside of this loop is the code to read a single cell value from the selected column and row of each of the three tables. The contents of the Range location are stored in the working variables "libor_value," "condt_value," or "prime_value," depending on the table from which they were read.

Next the first two elements of the **"err_result"** array are initialized to "FALSE." We can put these related statements on a single line by ending each with the ":" sign. The compiler then treats them are if they were on separate lines.

The contents of the three working variables are then tested to see if they are numeric in nature. If they are not, the value of IsNumeric(libor_rate) would be "FALSE." The right side of the equal sign will then compare the term as if it reads

```
For itest = 1 To NUM_TABLES+1
    table_total(itest) = 0
    For icase = 1 To 5
        column_err(icase, itest) = 0#
    Next icase
Next itest
```

EXHIBIT 19.25 Initialization of the testing variables in "IsNumeric_RateDatesInfo" subroutine

```
'check each of the fields for non numerics
For icase = 1 To NUM_COLS
 For imonth = 1 To PAY_DATES
     libor_value = Range("m11AltLiborPaths").Cells(imonth, icase)
     prime_value = Range("m11AltPrimePaths").Cells(imonth, icase)
     'if the cell is not blank then test the value for numeric
     err_result(1) = False:  err_result(2)=False:
     If libor_value <> "" Then err_result(1) = (IsNumeric(libor_value) = False)
     If prime_value <> "" Then err_result(3) = (IsNumeric(prime_value) = False)
     'if we find an error, increment the counter and table of the error
     For itable = 1 To NUM_TABLES
         If err_result(itable) Then
             column_err(icase, itable) = column_err(icase, itable) + 1
             table_total(itable) = table_total(itable) + column_err(icase, itable)
             errcase(4) = 1              'error of this type detected
         End If
     Next itable
 Next imonth
Next icase
```

EXHIBIT 19.26   Testing the contents of the tables in "IsNumeric_RateDatesInfo" subroutine

(FALSE=FALSE), which as we all know is TRUE! The value of "err_result(n)" is then set to "TRUE" and we know we have a non-numeric entry at that location.

   The For...Next loop that follows reads each of the three err_result values and increments both the appropriate column_err and table_total variable values to record the error. We will use the contents of both of the variables to construct the complex error message in the next section of the subroutine. The "table_total" will be tested to determine which table has errors and the "column_err" array to print the column numbers in the error message. See Exhibit 19.26 for the VBA code that performs these tasks.

Assemble the Error Message Components   Now all we need to do is test the five entries in the Conduit Spread Table and we are done. The code will be considerably shorter and less complex because it is a single column table. See Exhibit 19.27.

Assemble the error message components   The VBA code in Exhibit 19.28 uses two nested For...Next loops to assemble the complete error message. The outer of the two loops triggers the printing of the Table component of the message. If

```
'Conduit Spread Table
For icase = 1 To 5
    condt_value = Range("m11AltConduitSpreads").Cells(icase)
    'if the cell is not blank then test the value for numeric
    err_result(3) = False:
    If condt_value <> "" Then err_result(3) = (IsNumeric(condt_value) = False)
    'if we find an error, increment the counter and table of the error
    If err_result(3) Then
        column_err(icase, 3) = column_err(icase, 3) + 1
        table_total(3) = table_total(3) + 1
        errcase(4) = 1                  'error of this type detected
    End If
Next icase
```

EXHIBIT 19.27   Error testing code for non-numeric entries in the Conduit Spread Table

```
For itest = 1 To NUM_TABLES+1                    '1=Libor, 2=Prime, 3=Conduit Spread
    If table_total(itest) > 0 Then               'got one!
        msgInfo(4) = msgInfo(4) & msgComp(itest)    'add table location
        For icase = 1 To 5
          If column_err(icase, itest) > 0 Then   'add the pathway(s) numbers
                msgInfo(4) = msgInfo(4) & " " & icase & ","
          End If
        Next icase
        msgInfo(4) = msgInfo(4) & msgComp(4)          'close with a line return
    End If
  Next itest

End Sub
```

EXHIBIT 19.28   Assemble the error message in "IsNumeric_RateDatesInfo" subroutine

there are errors found in the Table, a subsequent inner For... Next loop triggers the printing of any individual columns in which the errors were detected for this table.

When completed, the subroutine should produce a message box that looks like the one in Exhibit 19.29.

We can now load the pathways of the tables with whatever Interest Rate patterns we like and run them by simply entering three numbers in the Program Costs Menu. Are we done? No! Like those late night television commercial announcements about the Ginsu Knife, we have more, much more! Let us implement this feature in the code of the Batch Processor.

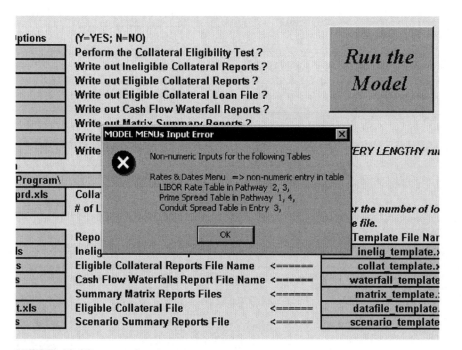

EXHIBIT 19.29   Completed error message

Building This Capability into the Batch Processing Module

Adding the LIBOR, Prime, and Conduit choices using the framework that we have already developed for the batch processing function should be a fairly straightforward task!

As we did before, all we need to do in the batch processing function is to fool the model into thinking that a human user is making all the Assumptions entries. We can do this by building additional code into the existing batch processing subroutines to drop our choices into the Program Costs Menu. The model will then be updated, especially if we issue a Calculate command immediately upon entry, and the proper schedules will be read into the pathway displays on the Rates Dates Menu.

To this end we will first reconfigure the Batch Run Menu to include three new columns of assumptions related to which pathway is to be used with the model run specified. The model will read these selections and then place them in Program Cost Menu just as if we had done it ourselves. "Drats! Fooled again!" says the model! The revised Batch Run Menu will look like Exhibit 19.30.

Are we done? No. We must now use our standard bag of menu tricks to move the information from the menu into the VBA and over to where we can use it.

The first step will be applying a Range name to each of the newly added columns in the menu. These Range names will be congruent with the naming convention of this menu having the "m10" suffix. Their names will be, respectively, "m10LiborPathway," m10PrimePathway," and "m10SpreadPathway." We can now use our standard reading VBA statements to transfer the information to VBA variables and then back to the Program Cost Menu at the appropriate time.

We will next need to declare variables to hold the rate pathway choice information. In that all the code for the "Batch Run" function is contained in the "**A_BatchFileProgram**" module, we will add these to the list at the top, making them Module scope variables. These declarations can be seen in Exhibit 19.31.

Batch Output File Menu

	Select	Market Value Decline	Recovery Period Lag	Conduit Finance Spread	File Name Prefix ID	Time Prefix Code	Conduit Spread Choice	Libor Rates Path	Prime Rates Path	File Name Prefix
1	X	50%	12	2.000%	BBB_Test1		1	3	2	BBB_Test1_MVD50_L12_S200_
2	X	50%	24	2.000%	BBB_Test1		5	5	5	BBB_Test1_MVD50_L24_S200_
3	X	50%	36	2.000%	BBB_Test1		4	3	1	BBB_Test1_MVD50_L36_S200_
4										
5										
6										
7										
8										
9										
10										
11										
12										
13										
14										
15										
16										

EXHIBIT 19.30　New and improved Batch Run Menu

```
Dim batch_spread_path()        As Integer    'conduit spread choice
Dim batch_libor_path()         As Integer    'libor spread pathway
Dim batch_prime_path()         As Integer    'prime rate pathway
```

EXHIBIT 19.31   Declaration of the variables to hold the rate information pathway choices

With the pathway choices ensconced in VBA arrays, we can now move them and put them to work. We now add the code (in bold), to read the information from the Ranges into the variables after first ReDimming them to the number of active batch runs selected. See Exhibit 19.32.

The last step is to transfer the choices to the Program Menu file and let the model work its magic after that. See Exhibit 19.33.

We have now completed installing this additional feature to the model!

```
Sub Read_Batch_Program_Menu()

  'read the contents of the ranges
  ReDim batch_mvd_factor(1 To num_file) As Double      'market value decline vector
  ReDim batch_lag_period(1 To num_file) As Integer     'recovery lag period in months
  ReDim batch_conduit_sprd(1 To num_file) As Double    'conduit financing spread
  ReDim batch_file_name(1 To num_file) As String       'name of the individual file
  ReDim batch_spread_path(1 To num_file) As Integer    'conduit spread pathway
  ReDim batch_libor_path(1 To num_file) As Integer     'libor spread pathway
  ReDim batch_prime_path(1 To num_file) As Integer     'prime rate pathway

    For i_file = 1 To num_file
        batch_mvd_factor(i_file) = Range("m10MktValueDecline").Cells(i_file).Value
        batch_lag_period(i_file) = Range("m10RecPeriodLag").Cells(i_file).Value
        batch_conduit_sprd(i_file) = Range("m10ConduitSpread").Cells(i_file).Value
        batch_file_name(i_file) = Range("m10FilePrefixName").Cells(i_file).Value
        batch_spread_path(i_file) = Range("m10SpreadPathway").Cells(i_file).Value
        batch_libor_path(i_file) = Range("m10LiborPathway").Cells(i_file).Value
        batch_prime_path(i_file) = Range("m10PrimePathway").Cells(i_file).Value
    Next i_file

End Sub
```

EXHIBIT 19.32   Reading the new information from the menu

```
Sub Load_and_Run_Loan_Financing_Model()

  For i_file = 1 To num_file
      Sheets("Defaults Menu").Select
      Cells(23, 4).Value = batch_mvd_factor(i_file)
      Cells(24, 4).Value = batch_lag_period(i_file)
      Sheets("Program Costs Menu").Select
      Cells(16, 3).Value = batch_spread_path(i_file)
      Cells(17, 3).Value = batch_libor_path(i_file)
      Cells(18, 3).Value = batch_prime_path(i_file)
      Sheets("Defaults Menu").Calculate
      Sheets("Main Menu").Select
      Cells(19, 3).Value = batch_file_name(i_file)
      Call Loan_Financing_Model
  Next i_file

End Sub
```

EXHIBIT 19.33   Loading the pathway choices into the Program Cost Menu

ADDING INFORMATION TO THE ASSUMPTIONS PAGE

As pointed out earlier, the role of the Assumptions Page in each of the output report files is to recapitulate the conditions under which the model was run that produced the report results. To this end we need to add some incremental information that we will find invaluable if we have to recreate the model run at some later (sometimes much later) date. To this end we are going to add the contents of the "Eligibility Results" menu, the schedule of Index Rates, and the Day Count Factor Table to the Assumptions Report.

Adding the Eligibility Results Menu Information

The Eligibility Results Menu is populated by the subroutine "Update_Selection_Criteria_Outputs." This subroutine examines each of the loans of the portfolio and then separates them based on whether they are eligible or ineligible. It counts the number of ineligibles and sums their balances. For the eligible loans, it counts the eligible loans, sums their balances, calculates the percentage of eligible balances of the total, and computes several portfolio measures such as weighted average coupon (WAC), weighted average remaining term (WART), and weighted average seasoning.

Unfortunately, nearly all of these calculations are conducted using local variables. The results are therefore inaccessible to other portions of the program. We will therefore convert the variables we need to be global variables and move their declarations to the "A_Globals" module. Once we have completed this task, we can then reconfigure the Assumptions Page in one (and only one) of the report files. We will then add the VBA code we need to the "Write_Assumptions_Page" subroutine. That will complete the process.

Creating the Global Variables   The variables we need to move to the "A_Globals" module are currently module-level variables in the "CollateralSelectionSubs" module. We will cut these out of the top of the module and paste them in the "A_Globals" module at the bottom. We will change the declaration from Dim to Public and put the "g_" prefix on each of them to identify their change in status. The renamed and redeclared variable block can be seen in Exhibit 19.34.

```
' Assumption Report Variables
Public g_sum_wac_1          As Double   'final eligible wac
Public g_sum_rem_1          As Double   'final eligible wgh rem term
Public g_sum_sea_1          As Double   'final eligible wgh seasoning
Public g_acc_cur_bal        As Double   'eligibal balances
Public g_rej_cur_bal        As Double   'ineligible balances
Public g_grand_total        As Double   'total portfolio balances
Public g_pct_accepted       As Double   '% balances eligible
Public g_pct_rejected       As Double   '% balances ineligible
Public g_number_accepted    As Double   'loan count eligible
Public g_number_rejected    As Double   'loan count ineligible
Public g_inelig_loan(1 To INELIGIBLE_REPORTS) As Long     'by type ineligible loans
Public g_inelig_bals(1 To INELIGIBLE_REPORTS) As Double   'by type ineligible balances
```

EXHIBIT 19.34   New global variables

With our new variables declared, we now need to change the names of these variables to reflect the "g_" prefix in the code of the "Update_Selection_Criteria_Outputs" subroutine where the results that we wish to capture for the Assumptions Page are computed.

We will also need to change the names in the "Update_Totals_Columns" and the "Update_Detail_Columns" subroutines in the same module. The changes to these subroutines are necessary because although they write to the Eligibility Results Menu, only the redeclaration of the variables in Exhibit 19.34 will make these subroutines inoperative. The revised VBA code for these subroutines is presented in Exhibits 19.35, 19.36, and 19.37. Variable name changes are highlighted in bold. The subroutine "Clear_Eligibility_Accumulators" will also need to reflect these revised names.

```
Sub Update_Selection_Criteria_Outputs()

  ' Display the results to the selection screen
  Sheets("Eligibility Results").Select
  Range("A1").Select

  For iloan = 1 To g_total_loans

      g_grand_total = g_grand_total + g_loan_cur_bal(iloan)
      If g_loan_ok(iloan) Then
          g_acc_cur_bal = g_acc_cur_bal + g_loan_cur_bal(iloan)
          sum_wac = sum_wac + (g_loan_coup(iloan) * g_loan_cur_bal(iloan))
          sum_rem = sum_rem + (g_loan_rem_term(iloan) * g_loan_cur_bal(iloan))
          sum_sea = sum_sea + (g_loan_season(iloan) * g_loan_cur_bal(iloan))
          g_number_accepted = g_number_accepted + 1
      Else
          g_rej_cur_bal = g_rej_cur_bal + g_loan_cur_bal(iloan)
          g_number_rejected = g_number_rejected + 1
          For icondition = 1 To INELIGIBLE_REPORTS
              If g_sel_tag(iloan, icondition) Then
                  g_inelig_loan(icondition) = g_inelig_loan(icondition) + 1
                  g_inelig_bals(icondition) = g_inelig_bals(icondition) + g_loan_cur_bal
                      (iloan)
              End If
          Next icondition
      End If

      'calculate the total column display values
      g_pct_accepted = g_acc_cur_bal / g_grand_total
      g_pct_rejected = g_rej_cur_bal / g_grand_total
      If g_acc_cur_bal > 0# Then
          g_sum_wac_1 = sum_wac / g_acc_cur_bal
          g_sum_rem_1 = sum_rem / g_acc_cur_bal
          g_sum_sea_1 = sum_sea / g_acc_cur_bal
          Else
          sum_wac = 0#
          sum_rem = 0#
          sum_sea = 0#
      End If
      (5 lines of code omitted)
  Next iloan
  (2 lines of code omitted)

End Sub
```

EXHIBIT 19.35   Changing the local variables to global variables so we can use their values in the revised Assumptions Report

```
Sub Update_Totals_Columns()

    Range("m3TotalNumLoans") = iloan
    Range("m3TotalCurBals") = g_grand_total
    Range("m3NumLoansRejected") = g_number_rejected
    Range("m3CurBalRejected") = g_rej_cur_bal
    Range("m3CurBalRejPct") = g_pct_rejected
    Range("m3NumLoansOK") = g_number_accepted
    Range("m3CurBalOK") = g_acc_cur_bal
    Range("m3CurBalOKPct") = g_pct_accepted
    Range("m3LoansOKWAC") = g_sum_wac_1
    Range("m3LoansOKWART") = g_sum_rem_1
    Range("m3LoansOKWASeason") = g_sum_sea_1

End Sub
```

EXHIBIT 19.36   Subroutine that writes the selection results to the Assumptions Report

```
Sub Update_Detail_Columns()

  For icondition = 1 To INELIGIBLE_REPORTS
    If g_inelig_bals(icondition) > 0# Then
        Range("m3IneligibleBals").Cells(icondition) = g_inelig_bals(icondition)
    End If
    If g_inelig_loan(icondition) > 0# Then
        Range("m3IneligibleLoans").Cells(icondition) = g_inelig_loan(icondition)
    End If
  Next icondition

End Sub
```

EXHIBIT 19.37   Subroutine that writes the results of the Collateral Selection process to the Assumptions Report

Reconfiguring the Assumptions Page   Now that we have the data in hand we need a place to put it. We will now modify the lower left-hand corner of the current Assumption Page by adding an information block very similar to that of the Eligibility Results Menu. This block will start in Column B, Row 32, and extend to Column H, Row 46. See Exhibit 19.38.

31					
32	**Collateral Characteristics**				
33	**Portfolio Totals**				
34		Number of Loans			
35		Current Balances	**Ineligible Collateral Detail**		
36	**Ineligible Collateral**				Min/Max Remaining Term
37		Number of Loans			Min/Max Original Term
38		Current Balances			Min/Max Original Balance
39		% Balances			Min/Max Remaining Balance
40	**Eligible Collateral Summary**				Exceeded Max LTV
41		Number of Loans			Min Floater Spread
42		Current Balances			Excluded Geographic Region
43		% Balances			Inconsistent Orig vs. Rem Term
44		Wght Avg Coupon			Inconsistent Orig vs. Rem Bal
45		Wght Avg Rem Term			Exceeded Calc vs. Stated Pmt
46		Wght Avg Seasoning			Unacceptable Gross Coupon
47					

EXHIBIT 19.38   Collateral Characteristics section of the Assumptions Page

```
'SECTION IV - Collateral Selection Results
'summary statistics
Cells(34, 2).Value = g_total_loans
Cells(35, 2).Value = g_grand_total
Cells(37, 2).Value = g_number_rejected
Cells(38, 2).Value = g_rej_cur_bal
Cells(39, 2).Value = g_pct_rejected
Cells(41, 2).Value = g_number_accepted
Cells(42, 2).Value = g_acc_cur_bal
Cells(43, 2).Value = g_pct_accepted
Cells(44, 2).Value = g_sum_wac_1
Cells(45, 2).Value = g_sum_rem_1
Cells(46, 2).Value = g_sum_sea_1
'ineligibles by rejection condition
For irow = 1 To INELIGIBLE_REPORTS
    Cells(irow + 35, 6) = ""
    Cells(irow + 35, 7) = ""
    If g_inelig_bals(irow) > 0# Then
        Cells(irow + 35, 7) = g_inelig_bals(irow)
    End If
    If g_inelig_loan(irow) > 0# Then
        Cells(irow + 35, 6) = g_inelig_loan(irow)
    End If
Next irow
```

EXHIBIT 19.39   Additional code in the "Write_Assumptions_Page" subroutine

Adding the Code to Write the Eligiblity Results   We now have the data and the place to put it. We need only modify the subroutine that writes the Assumptions Page and we are finished. We will of course add the code to existing subroutine "Write_Assumption_Report." Only the incremental code is displayed in Exhibit 19.39. Remember we cannot use Range names here because this is not a single spreadsheet; it is copied across no less than six different template files.

The upper half of these lines will populate the left column of output. The two loops at the bottom populate the two columns of information to the right of the section. When complete, we will have a section like that in Exhibit 19.40.

Let us move on to the next section of Rates and Dates.

	Collateral Characteristics				
31					
32	**Collateral Characteristics**				
33	**Portfolio Totals**				
34	2,279	Number of Loans			
35	$537,852,271	Current Balances	**Ineligible Collateral Detail**		
36	**Ineligible Collateral**				Min/Max Remaining Term
37	88	Number of Loans			Min/Max Original Term
38	$46,431,894	Current Balances	25	$2,111,171	Min/Max Original Balance
39	8.633%	% Balances	83	$43,656,065	Min/Max Remaining Balance
40	**Eligible Collateral Summary**				Exceeded Max LTV
41	2,279	Number of Loans	5	$2,775,829	Min Floater Spread
42	$491,420,377	Current Balances			Excluded Geographic Region
43	91.367%	% Balances			Inconsistent Orig vs. Rem Term
44	8.505%	Wght Avg Coupon			Inconsistent Orig vs. Rem Bal
45	191.62	Wght Avg Rem Term			Exceeded Calc vs. Stated Pmt
46	15.19	Wght Avg Seasoning	1	$429,347	Unacceptable Gross Coupon
47					

EXHIBIT 19.40   Populated Collateral Characteristics Section

Adding the Rates and Dates

The last portion of the expanded Assumptions Report will be the addition of the Rates and Dates information. This portion consists of two tables. The first one contains the Rates information: the Prime and LIBOR Rate levels and the Conduit Funding Costs. The other, the final table of information we should add to the report, is the Date Sequence of the model and the various decimal day count factors for each month.

There is one other detail that we will need to clarify. That is the monthly schedule of the deal. We will capture this information by declaring a global variable call g_months and dimension it to the number of PAY_DATES of the model. See Exhibit 19.41.

Once we have declared this variable we can add a line of code to the subroutine that captures the data from the Rates and Dates Menu. See Exhibit 19.42.

With all the variables now in place we simply write a loop to print out both of the tables. See Exhibit 19.43.

The new section of the Assumptions Report should look like Exhibit 19.44.

```
Public g_months(1 To PAY_DATES)      As Date      'beginning month dates
```

EXHIBIT 19.41   Declaration of the g_months variable in the "A_Globals" module

```
Sub Read_Rates_and_Dates_Menu()

    (3 lines of code omitted)
    'read the day count factors for 30/360, Act/360, Act/Act
    For irow = 1 To PAY_DATES
        For icol = 1 To 3
            g_day_factors(irow, icol) = Range("m11DayCntFactors").Cells(irow, icol)
        Next icol
        g_months(irow) = Range("m11Months").Cells(irow)
    Next irow
    (10 lines of code omitted)

End Sub
```

EXHIBIT 19.42   Insert a line to populate the g_months variable from the Rates and Dates Menu.

```
            'SECTION V - Rates and Dates Schedule
            For irow = 1 To PAY_DATES
              Cells(irow + 5, 20).Value = g_index_levels(irow, 1)
              Cells(irow + 5, 21).Value = g_index_levels(irow, 2)
              Cells(irow + 5, 22).Value = g_fund_conduit(irow)
              Cells(irow + 5, 24).Value = g_months(irow)
              Cells(irow + 5, 25).Value = g_day_factors(irow, 1)
              Cells(irow + 5, 26).Value = g_day_factors(irow, 2)
              Cells(irow + 5, 27).Value = g_day_factors(irow, 3)
            Next irow
```

EXHIBIT 19.43   Subroutine that populates the rates and dates information on the Assumptions Report

Microsoft Excel - test_ac2_Scenario.xls

File Edit View Insert Format Tools Data Window Help

Geographic Selection				Rates Used in Model Run					Day Count			
				Prime	Libor	Conduit				Factors		
TRUE	AK	Alaska		Pathway	Pathway	Fund Rate		Month	30/360	Act/360	Act/Act
TRUE	AL	Alabama	1	5.250%	2.750%	3.750%	1	1-Jan-08	0.08333	0.08611	0.08493
TRUE	AR	Arkansas	2	5.250%	2.750%	3.750%	2	1-Feb-08	0.08333	0.08056	0.07945
TRUE	AZ	Arizona	3	5.250%	2.750%	3.750%	3	1-Mar-08	0.08333	0.08611	0.08493
TRUE	CA	California	4	5.250%	2.750%	3.750%	4	1-Apr-08	0.08333	0.08333	0.08219
TRUE	CO	Colorado	5	5.250%	2.750%	3.750%	5	1-May-08	0.08333	0.08611	0.08493
TRUE	CT	Connecticut	6	5.250%	2.750%	3.750%	6	1-Jun-08	0.08333	0.08333	0.08219
TRUE	DE	Delaware	7	5.250%	2.750%	3.750%	7	1-Jul-08	0.08333	0.08611	0.08493
TRUE	FL	Florida	8	5.250%	2.750%	3.750%	8	1-Aug-08	0.08333	0.08611	0.08493
TRUE	GA	Georgia	9	5.250%	2.750%	3.750%	9	1-Sep-08	0.08333	0.08333	0.08219
TRUE	HI	Hawaii	10	5.250%	2.750%	3.750%	10	1-Oct-08	0.08333	0.08611	0.08493
TRUE	IA	Iowa	11	5.250%	2.750%	3.750%	11	1-Nov-08	0.08333	0.08333	0.08219
TRUE	ID	Idaho	12	5.250%	2.750%	3.750%	12	1-Dec-08	0.08333	0.08611	0.08493
TRUE	IL	Illinois	13	5.250%	2.750%	3.750%	13	1-Jan-09	0.08333	0.08611	0.08493
TRUE	IN	Indiana	14	5.250%	2.750%	3.750%	14	1-Feb-09	0.08333	0.07778	0.07671
TRUE	KS	Kansas									

EXHIBIT 19.44   Populated Rates and Dates section of the Assumptions Report

NEXT STEPS

We have now finished the last coding chapter of the book. How do you feel? Exhausted? Exhilarated? Euphoric? Some of these feelings or all of them? Well relax!

The next two chapters are about the afterlife of the model but they are critical nevertheless. Chapter 20, "Documentation of the Model," deals, obviously, with the subject of documentation. Documentation is at times boring but can save your life if you have to be away from the model for an extended period of time. *It is also helpful if you need to turn the model over to a successor so that you can be promoted!*

Chapter 21, "Managing the Growth of the Model," deals with future model growth. No one can say what the lifetime of a model is, how long it will be used, or over how many deals. If the model is heavily used it will grow over time and you have to be prepared for that. Chapter 21 will outline the general things you can expect to happen over time.

But for now congratulations! You have written and improved your first real model!

ON THE WEB SITE

The model "MODEL_ADD_CAP_01.xls" and its attendant report file templates. The templates reflect the updated and expanded Assumptions Pages. They are as follows:

The file "ac_cf_trace_template.xls," the revised cash flow trace template file.

The file "ac_collat_template.xls," the revised Eligible Collateral Stratification Reports template.

The file "ac_inelig_template.xls," the revised Ineligible Collateral template file.

The file **"ac_datafile_template.xls,"** the revised template for writing a collateral data file.

The file **"ac_matrix_template.xls,"** the revised Matrix Summary Report Package template file.

The file **"ac_scenario_template.xls,"** the revised Single Scenario Report Package template file.

The file **"ac_waterfall_template.xls,"** the revised Waterfall Cash Flow Report Package template file.

There is also a complete set of output reports and the collateral file **"Data3.xls"** that was the collateral file for the model run.

After the Model Is Written

Documentation of the Model

OVERVIEW

This chapter will deal with documentation. The usual reaction to hearing the term "documentation" is a feeling of vague nausea, slight dizziness, and an overpowering urge to flee from the room. Is this an appropriate response? It possibly is.

If you have left the task of documentation as the last thing to do, you may be justified in evidencing this typical Pavlovian response to the task! The process does not have to be traumatic at all. There are lots of simple things that you can do to document your program while you are writing it. This is the best approach to the problem. By spreading the documentation effort into hundreds, (or even thousands), of tiny nano-episodes, you will finish the model with the task mostly complete!

Then when the subject comes up you can say one of two things: "Yes, all the online documentation is complete, what else did you have in mind?" or the duplicitous, "Oh yes, I can start tomorrow and work on it from home for a few days!" If you adhere to the following practices as you build the code, you will at this point look like either the most forward thinking person your manager has ever seen, or you will have just gotten yourself two extra vacation days.

Online documentation has one important and immediate beneficiary, *you*. If you are separated from the model for any period of time it will be necessary to reacquaint yourself with it before you begin using it again. This task is made hundreds of times easier if you have left yourself helpful hints across the model. In addition, if you are recognized for your great work on this model and are promoted, another person will have to pick up the model. It will be of credit to you, and you will save yourself a lot of time and effort, if you have left an in-model road map for the person to follow. There is nothing worse than having to be called off of a current project to sit for several days with someone else teaching them your model. You will undoubtedly have to make up the time on the other project and that just means longer days for *you*.

Offline documentation is different. Nearly all of the online documentation can be accomplished while you are building the model; the same cannot be said for offline documentation. Some types of offline are developed for the people running the model but it is primarily for the benefit of external constituencies. These other groups are external to the model group and can consist of such entities as your auditors (both internal and external), model validation groups, training groups, internal risk assessment personnel, rating agency personal, credit wrap providers, and in rare instances, investors. The offline documentation will consist of documents and files completely segregated from the model itself, deliberately so, in most cases.

This documentation will take the form of Standard Operating Procedures (SOPs), training program documents, validation runs, benchmark runs, and descriptions of the key assumptions and algorithms of the model.

Having said all of this, let us see how we can keep everyone happy.

DELIVERABLES

The following are the list of deliverables for this chapter:

- How to write various complimentary forms of online documentation into the model as you build it
- A description of the contents of a Runtime Standard Operating Procedure, the most common form of offline documentation
- A brief outline of the suggested contents of a User Manual

UNDER CONSTRUCTION

We will not add any VBA code to the model in this chapter.

ONLINE DOCUMENTATION

We will start with online documentation. I think you will be surprised how much online documentation you already have in the model. Online documentation is ***anything*** in the form of comments and explanatory text that is in the Excel spreadsheets and VBA modules and that are not executable code. I have suggested nine broad categories of online documentation.

Menu Documentation Comments

It is always a good idea to clearly label every input position on every menu. For complicated menus, you may wish to add a block of explanation, especially if the information must be consistent with the data on other menus.

If a specific field is particularly important or needs to be supported with an explanatory or cautionary comment the Excel **Insert => Comments** feature is perfect for the job.

Variable Name Conventions

We have already discussed variable naming conventions. The most important of these is to clearly differentiate between global, module, and local variables. Global variables should always be prefixed with a "g_." Module variables should always be prefixed by "m_." The exception to this rule is when the module is small and it is immediately obvious that the variable is modular in scope.

You will have variables that are related in function, such as all the variables that are used to populate a single report or set of reports. An example in the module

```
Public g_crit_min_orig_term       As Double       'Min original term in months
Public g_crit_max_orig_term       As Double       'Max original term in months
Public g_crit_min_rem_term        As Double       'Min remaining term in months
Public g_crit_max_rem_term        As Double       'Max remaining term in months
Public g_crit_min_orig_bal        As Double       'Min original balance
Public g_crit_max_orig_bal        As Double       'Max original balance
```

EXHIBIT 20.1   Inline comments following a series of global variable declarations

is the variables for the Summary Matrix Reports. Each of these is global in scope and therefore has the "g_" prefix. In addition to that, each has an "m#" prefix immediately after the "g." Thus we know that all the variables populating the Fifth Summary Matrix Report are prefixed "gm5_."

This naming convention should also be applied to variables that are used for a related functional purpose. An example is the set of variables that are used as the collateral selection criteria values. All of these variables have their values populated by the fields on the Collateral Criteria Menu. Each of them begins with the "g_crit_" prefix. See Exhibit 20.1.

Although many people overlook variable names as a form of online documentation, they are very shortsighted to do so. A set of consistent, clear, and recognizable variable names will go far in helping you and others work with your program.

Developing Module Name Conventions

Module names can also immediate contribute to documenting the structure and contents of the model. Module names should start with the major functional role of the module. What is the key role of the module in the model?

You can develop your own naming conventions. The ones used in the model will tell anyone what is the immediate primary function of the VBA code contained within.

"Menu" prefixes for all menu input activity. "Write" prefix for all output. "Collateral" for all subroutines doing selection and amortization. "A_" for the global variable declarations, the constant variable declaration, and the Main Program code to get them to the top of the list. "Z_" for all utility and basic support code. The primary purpose of these naming conventions is to bring a structure and clarity to the module organization. You want to help a new or returning user to find their way with the minimum of confusion and delay.

In Line Comments for Global and Constant Variables

In line explanatory comments for all global and constant variables is an absolutely nonnegotiable part of online documentation. Every single global variable and constant *must* have an inline comment. End of story!

Perform this function every time you create a variable. If you get used to doing it automatically it will become painless and routine. This practice also has the advantage of always keeping the program up to date.

This is the ***most important single thing you can do*** to help a new developer or user of your model. It is also the most important thing you can do to help yourself! If you think that you will remember every variable when you are called back to the

```
'=============================================================================
' Compress_the_Portfolio
' All of the remaining reports deal with collateral that has passed all the selection
' criteria for securitization. To save time, especially when dealing with very large
' portfolios we will now compress the arrays holding the collateral information.
' Only the approved loan records will be rewritten into the new arrays. The size of
' those arrays will be reduced by the rejected loans.
'=============================================================================
```

EXHIBIT 20.2   Subroutine masthead comment sections for Compress_the_Portfolio

model after a six-month hiatus, you are kidding yourself. The worst thing in the world is to be called back into a time pressure situation and have to pick up a model lacking such comments.

Group the variables by function make the names consistent and then comment, comment, comment. I cannot emphasize this enough!

How many global variables need to be commented? All of them.

Subroutine Masthead Comment Section

Create a box made out of comment lines, like those in Exhibits 20.2 and 20.3, at the top of every subroutine. This serves two purposes. One it provides an immediate visual break between that subroutine, its predecessor, and its successor, in the module. Second it gives you a place for additional general comments. Typical masthead comment blocks are shown in Exhibits 20.2 and 20.3.

This is also useful if you need to explain a particular calculation or activity.

Module Masthead Comment Section

My comment about the value of the masthead comment block goes double for subroutine masthead comments if you have a module that has a collection of code that would be difficult to understand without some guidance.

```
'=============================================================================
' Calculate_Recoveries
' If the severity of loss of the scenario is less than the current cltv of the
'  loan to the project there are 100% recoveries. Remember the severity of loss is
'  on the entire project and will hit the equity first, and the conduit position
'  last.
' If there is a 50% MarketValueDecline (SOL) against a 45% LTV then the first
'  expression will be true (1-.50)=.50 .50>=.45 you will recover everything!
' If there is a 75% SOL against a 50% LTV then the second expression will be true:
'      recovery_factor = (.75-.50)/.50 = .50
'      recoveries     = total balance defaulted * (1.00-.50) or 50% of the position
' this is easy to check in that a $1,000,000 project with a 50% LTV suffering
! a 75% SOL will wipe out the $500,000 above the loan, and $250,000 of the loan
! position leaving the recovery of
!    $500,000 (loan)- $250,000 loan loss = $250,000 loan recovery
'    $250,000 is 50% of the loans position of $250,000
' Remember you can only recover the amount of the default, not more than the amount
! you have outstanding.
'=============================================================================
```

EXHIBIT 20.3   Subroutine masthead comment sections for Calculate_Recoveries

```
'======================================================================
'The code of this module is completely independent from the rest of the
'model. Its sole purpose is to populate and correctly display single
'results information in the "Cash Flow Results" output screen.
'The module consists of the following:
' 1) A large block of Constants that link the buttons to specific outputs.
' 2) Load_Screen_Matrix_Output subroutine which is the master of the module.
' 3) The Clear_MatrixScreen_Output_Area subroutine clears the display area.
' 4) The Set_MatrixScreen_Header_Rates subroutine populates the prepayment.
'    and default rates on the periphery of the display area.
' 5) The Set_MatrixScreen_Field_Formating subroutine sets the form of the
'    data display to dollars, time, or percentages.
' 6) The Set_MatrixScreen_Title displays the name of the datum.
' 7) The Fill_MatrixScreen_Data subroutine fills the display.
' 8) The Fill_MatrixScreen_DefaultColors subroutine changes the font and
'    background colors of the cells that display losses.
' 9) The Update_Graphic_Display subroutine updates the format of the graph to
'    right of the display matrix.
'======================================================================
```

EXHIBIT 20.4 Module masthead comment for the **"WriteMatrixScreen"** module

The masthead module comment for the **"WriteMatrixScreen"** module can be seen in Exhibit 20.4.

Development History Module

The last item on the online documentation agenda is the **"History"** Module. This is a separate VBA module in which you should laundry-list major episodic additions to the model. A perfect example of this is the additional capabilities we added to the model in Chapter 19. There should be a comment section for each with the name of the developer, their phone number, and e-mail address. Also include the then current version number of the model as it may change over time as successive changes accumulate in the model. A brief description of what changes were made and which subroutines and modules were affected should also be included. This is especially important if the changes were scattered across several subroutines and modules. Exhibit 20.5 shows the log entry in **Z_ChangeLog** for the modifications of Chapter 19.

You will notice that the Version Number of the model, "Version 100_30" has not changed even though we have added three additional features to the model. It will be up to you to determine how much cumulative change constitutes enough change to increment the Version Number. There is no relationship between the number of lines of VBA code added to the model and when the next Version Number is announced. It is more dependent upon the functional or computational significance of the change than it is the amount of the code needed to affect it.

A significant bug fix would immediately trigger a Version Number change, while a change to the format of a report might not.

If you keep this up to date it will be of tremendous help. It only takes three to four minutes to write these comment blocks, especially if you do it immediately after you have written and tested the code. After a year you can begin to discard some of the earlier entries or simply create another module, (this saves scrolling down).

```
'========================================================================================
' 2/7/2008  William Preinitz [telephone number] [email address]
' Version 100_30
' Added the ability to view the output files from buttons on the Main Menu.
'  Buttons code is contained in A_ButtonSubs, one subroutine for each button
'  Button_View_Collateral_Reports_File, Button_View_Ineligible_Loans_File,
'    Button_View_Cash_Flow_Waterfall_File, Button_View_Matrix_File
'----------------------------------------------------------------------------------------
' 2/11/2008  William Preinitz [telephone number] [email address]
' Version 100_30
' Added the Single Result Matrix Screen
'  Matrix screen displays a single result across all the prepay/default matrix
'  All the code to accommodate this feature is completely contained in
'  "WriteMatrixScreen" module and does not interact with the rest of the program.
'  This feature can only be run after the model has run and will display only
'  the contents of the last model run.
'----------------------------------------------------------------------------------------
' 2/20/2008  William Preinitz [telephone number] [email address]
' Version 100_30
' Added the ability to read up to 5 collateral files.
'  Added 5 additonal fields to the Main Menu. Added range name "m1CollatFile01 to 05"
'  Added constant MAC_COLAT_FILES to A_Globals, changed declaration
'  of "gfn_collat_files" variable. Added code to read file names in Read_Main_Menu
'  sub. Major rewrite of the subs Read_Portfolio_Data_File and Read_Portfolio_Data in
'  the module CollateralReadDataFile.
'========================================================================================
```

EXHIBIT 20.5   Change entries for the additional capabilities added to the model in Chapter 19

Rating Agency Criteria

You may wish to include a comment section at the location of your choice that outlines particularly important structuring or rating agency criteria. This is useful because it is right there in the model for the benefit of you and the new users. Some of these criteria are already explicitly in the model. The timing of the default rates in the rating agency shock criteria for example. There may be restrictions as to various concentration measurements at the portfolio level that you may want to currently annotate on the Selection Criteria Menu. A case in point is that no state may have more than 7% of the portfolio balance and that the top three states may have no more that 12%. No ZIP code may have more than 0.75% of the current balances (or the payment stream). Certain industry groups will always be ineligible collateral and others may be subject to specific restrictions. For example, restaurants and other eating places may constitute no more than 10%, while gas stations are always ineligible for inclusion.

Another useful list is the criteria for particular stress tests that the agencies will ask for. Usually, these comments are quite brief but can be helpful if, for example, it is a list of ten stress tests and their input criteria. You have the specifications immediately available and immediately associated with the model that will produce them.

Standard Analysis Benchmark Packages

The development of a set of files in the output directory, under a subdirectory named "benchmarks" is a quick and easy way to provide a guide as to the form of a typical model run. These runs can be created with current values and then transferred to the subdirectory as an archival reference. With this in hand it is then easy to reactivate the model after a period of time has elapsed and to have a degree of confidence that it is working correctly.

EXTERNAL DOCUMENTATION

Runtime Standard Operating Procedures

A Runtime Standard Operating Procedure (RTSOP) is a document that provides a detailed guide to all steps in the process of running the model from the collection of information about the proposed collateral to the final modeling runs delivered to the rating agencies, credit wrap providers, or the investors.

While not as extensive as its larger and greatly-to-be-feared nemesis, the User Manual, the RTSOP is a nontrivial document. If the model is being used on a regular basis and is important to the business function, you will almost certainly need to develop one of these.

The RTSOP explicitly states in excruciating detail each step that is taken from first to last in using the model to support the structuring effort. It should be designed so that an intelligent person who is unfamiliar with the model, but familiar with the business can use the model effectively.

It should consist of, at a minimum, the following information:

- A description of the business purpose of the model
- A set of deal criteria from the appropriate rating agencies, your own internal credit, and any other constituencies whose requirements will affect the character of the deal
- A detailed description of the sources, size, complexity, form, and reasonable value Ranges of model inputs, how they are entered into the model, and how the model will make use of them
- A listing of all key formula (not bond math per se), but algorithms or any proprietary assessment methodologies used in the model
- A step-by-step guide to mechanically running the model
- A sample of expected output and how it is used
- A base test case to compare the initial runs of the model to a proven standard result
- A list of how the results are used and who uses them
- A list of personnel who are practiced users of the model and who could reasonably be called on to help

Audit Criteria

Depending on the uses of the model, there may come a time when you will have to have it put through a model validation process. This process may Range in scope from merely providing a series of scenario runs to a full blown reverse-engineer-from-scratch effort. If the model is used to evaluate the risk of a retained portion of the deal held by the bank, the review process would be extensive. If that is the case, it is imperative that you retain every single scrap of material that is produced during the process.

Make every effort to have this material available so that if significant changes are made to the model you will be able to verify that the base results have not changed.

USER TRAINING DOCUMENTATION

User Manual

Developing a User Manual (UM) is a big step. It is a lot of work and generally something that should not be undertaken lightly. If you have to write a UM, your first step is to go and get help. Provide whoever is helping you with outline, raw material such as screen shots, and commentary, and then step out of the way and try to act only as an editor.

At a bare minimum the UM will contain most, if not all, of the contents of the Runtime SOP material. It will also have to cover a training approach and a series of tests or measurements of the student's progress in understanding the material.

It should also cover the most common errors that can be made. This relates both to data, input sequences, and model use.

You should also include a case study or two. This is especially true if you have two deals that are different enough to be instructive. Build the case studies with an idea of covering the following items:

- The business situation, client goals, and your firms' internal requirements to do the deal.
- How to get and qualify the data.
- Those factors that affect the way the deal is structured such as regulatory constraints, accounting policies, risk management restrictions, and third-party criteria (rating agencies and their ilk).
- The steps for running the model.
- The production of general and specialty runs.
- How to validate the model output to be sure it is mathematically and financially correct. Even more important is to be sure the runs are appropriate to the questions being asked.
- How to use the material for presentations to clients and others.
- How to preserve the material after the deal is issued, either for research or for monitoring processes.

DELIVERABLES CHECKLIST

The VBA Knowledge Checklist items for this chapter are:

- Develop and adhere to naming conventions for global variables.
- Name your VBA modules according to function and group them as they relate to larger functionality.

- *Always* comment global and constant variable declarations.
- Use subroutine and module level masthead comments for difficult or involved processes
- Add comments liberally through the executable code to guide yourself and other users.
- Develop a **"Z_ChangeLog"** module and enter the episodes of major model changes in it.

NEXT STEPS

We now need to plan for the further growth of the model.

This may involve as much or more work than we have done already although it will probably be spread out across a longer period of time.

Chapter 21, "Managing the Growth of the Model," will look at some of the issues we may face in the future.

ON THE WEB SITE

There is no Web site material for this chapter.

Managing the Growth of the Model

OVERVIEW

In Chapter 20, we examined how to effectively and efficiently document the model. The documentation effort was, in a way, an effort in self-protection at the code level. We will now move one level up and look at what we need to preserve and grow the model over time. Models, like people, grow. They experience a growth pattern passing through the stages of infancy, youth, young adult, maturity, and in many cases death.

Infancy is the early design phase, the specification of the output reporting, the menu structure and the description and construction of the basic module structure of the VBA code. In youth we write the first code, test, and validate the basic model, and do the first deal. We looked at the first stages of growth into young adulthood in Chapter 19, "Building Additional Capabilities." Here, the model begins to grow inwardly, the basic framework and form is intact, but the complexity and Range of operations increases. The modeling framework becomes "richer," able to accomplish more varied operations and perhaps become subtler in its analytical capacity.

This chapter will look at those aspects of modeling that you may have to grapple with as the model enters its maturity.

The four issues we will cover here are:

1. The evolutionary steps concerned with maintaining control of the model no matter what form it eventually migrates to. This will concern the subjects of version release and the protected segregation of the code.
2. Making the model promotion and ongoing validation processes more robust.
3. The potential software evolutions the model may experience.
4. The structural evolution of the model and possible bifurcation of its functionality.

DELIVERABLES

The VBA Language Knowledge Deliverables for this chapter are:

■ How to establish a procedure to update development and production versions of the model, along with their attendant data files and template reports.

- How to design and automate a procedure for back testing new versions of the model prior to release. Back testing is designed to verify that the newest set of modifications to the model have not changed any of the existing functionality of the earlier versions.
- How to split the "Collateral Selection" function from the model.
- How to split the "Cash Flow modeling" function from the model.

The Modeling Knowledge Deliverables for this chapter are:

- What a model "Gold Copy" is and why is it vitally important to have one
- What the model promotion sequence is, from moving a new version of the model from the development environment into production
- How models evolve structurally over time
- How the software composition of a model may change as it evolves from a VBA/Excel construct
- How to establish a base set of model back testing scenarios
- A suggested version number release convention
- Setting up online and offline version release documentation procedures

UNDER CONSTRUCTION

In this chapter we will build a program that will not be part of the model itself. Earlier we build the "Extractor.xls" program to help use pull information from a set of files and display the same datum in a comparative report.

As we continue to develop the model we will need to test each successive version against the existing version to make sure that we have not introduced any errors into our new model before we deploy it. To this end we will build a program named "Auto_Validate.xls" that will help us compare the contents of a pair of Cash Flow Waterfall Reports. If we generate two sets of these reports, one from each model version, using the same set of inputs, the files should be identical.

This standalone program will allow us to compare these file sets automatically and as part of a systemic promotion effort to assure us control over our code.

MAINTAINING THE MODEL ENVIRONMENT

Most of the modeling activity in the book has assumed that you will be working with a structuring team, but that when it comes to "putting the munitions on the target" VBA and Excel-wise, you are on your own. This is, in a way, a fool's paradise. It is an almost completely free state of nature. You can do what you want, when you want, without anyone looking over your shoulder.

Enjoy it while it lasts.

If you do not intend to do anything else with your life except run numbers with this model, you may be okay. If, however, you want to use this experience as a springboard to greater responsibility, recognition, and reward, things will have to change. By the way, the key word in that last sentence in case you missed it was *reward*. At some point, and it may come much sooner than you think, you will become a hot property. You will become someone whose experience and skill (not to mention charisma), will be in demand.

You may no longer be the sole modeling person working on the project.

It now becomes desirable to leverage up the value of your original work. This is especially true if you are trying to run several or many deals simultaneously. You will need to train others to run the model. Clearly, they cannot be running the same copy of the model you are currently working on. Neither can you simply "give" them an unmodified copy of the model and let them loose.

It is this brave new world that we will now address.

Do not worry; this is primarily an exercise in basic common sense. If you use a little forethought and judgment, everything should be fine.

Access to the Model

Once there are two or more people using the same model, you must immediately develop a production and development environment. This is only common sense. You may still be the only developer but the model is now sufficiently robust for others to use. You will now need to make sure that people who are only users of the model do not stray over into the development space.

The worst possible scenario is that they decide that they understand the model enough to "improve" it without either your knowledge or approval.

How is this to be prevented? The simplest way is to move the development model and its attendant files to a shared drive that the users do not have access to. Failing that, you can protect the development model itself with a password and move it to another directory. Depending on the environment of the firm, you may be able to hide the development environment altogether so the user group cannot even see it.

Users are then allowed access to and perhaps even the ability to copy read-only versions of the model.

Segregation of the Development Code

However it is accomplished, the development code must be segregated from the user code.

It also needs to be segregated from the most dangerous person of all—you.

While this sounds strange, we should remember the adage, "Pride goeth before the fall!" You need to isolate and preserve the first stable version of the model. This version will certainly be the one that you first release to a user, but it may be a much earlier version of the model.

Every change you make to the model, no matter how well you think you know the code and no matter how small the change, introduces the possibility of error. You should not expose yourself to this risk on an ongoing basis when you do not need to. Once the first stable version of the model has been tested, you need to do the following:

- Establish a "Gold Copy" that is protected from everyone, even you.
- Start a version numbering system to identify successive copies of the code. This version numbering system will be discussed below, but you need to start with "Model 0" or whatever you want to call it.

- Establish a set of back testing criteria. Back tests produce much if not all of the previous output of the model from a designated set of inputs. An example would be different combinations of prepayment and default rates with a designated collateral file. The collateral is run through the selection process and the cash flows are calculated. The results are output to a standard file. These results can then be compared against the outputs of successive release versions of the model. This will make sure that none of the core functionality of the model has changed.
- Establish how much change constitutes the need to generate a new development and user model. Remember that as the versions of the model change, so will the development base model, the model that the users see, and the Gold Copy. You may not want to change the versions for very minor changes, but you should have a clear criterion of when a model promotion should occur.
- Have a very specific Standard Operating Procedure (SOP) on what actions need to be taken during a model version promotion. Who is the maker, checker, and approver? Who talks to the keeper of the Gold Copy? What back tests need to be confirmed? Does the back testing need to be expanded to encompass the new features or functions?

Establishment of Model Version Numbering System

How do we establish a version numbering system for your code? The answer, "Any way you want!" As long as it is clear, concise, intelligible, and ruthlessly enforced.

My favorite is the following:

```
MODEL_NAME_001_01.xls
```

Which is to say:

```
MODEL_NAME_(major version)_(minor_version).xls
```

This system would take the name "**LOAN_FIN_001_00.xls**" for the current model. For each minor change, the second number would increment by 1. For each major change, the first number would increment by one and the second number would be set to zero. If the second number, the number of small changes ever reaches 10, the successive changes would be considered the equivalent of a major change. The first number would increment and the second number would reset to 0.

You can establish a list of what a major change is versus a minor one, but here are some suggestions:

Major Change	Minor Change
Changes to the Cash Flow Waterfall spreadsheet	Reformat a report header/footer
Add a new prepayment/default methodology	Add comments to the code
Correct a calculation error	
Add/Delete a new report	

The absolutely critical thing is that you keep the version codes in sync with both the online and offline documentation, and that the causes for the changes are clearly recorded in an accessible area.

The last thing that is needed to complete the process is to include the version number of the model in every report or back testing output file that the model produces. This makes it extremely easy to identify where the results came from, and in many cases whom they came from. You can do this very easily by placing a footer section in each of the report packages.

Establishment of a "Gold Copy"

A true gold copy is a copy of the software that is not available to anyone, even the developers. It customarily resides on a shared drive that is not accessible to *anyone* in the business unit. The purpose of the Gold Copy is to keep a working version of the model safe, no matter what changes are made in the development environment. After a period of extensive testing, a new version of the model can be designated the Gold Copies and the current Gold Copy will be archived and replaced. The prior Gold Copy is never deleted and is preserved, along with all other files, data, template, or others needed to run it.

Online Developer Documentation Log

The online development log should be in the form discussed earlier in Chapter 20, "Documentation of the Model."

Keep it basic; make sure you identify the code and the person making the changes. If it is a big change reference the off line documentation and the validation files and processes.

Off-Line Developer Documentation Log

This is best embodied in the form of a three-ring binder with a set of standardized pages. Each page documents a promotion event. At a minimum the form must contain the following:

- The new version number of the model.
- The date of the change.
- The nature of the change, if it is minor or major, and what functionality of the model the change affects.
- The maker of the change, the checker, and the approver. All should be different people if possible.
- If the change is extensive, a list of all portions of the code modified or added. This should include the VBA module and the names of the subroutines. This is especially true of code that is removed from the model.
- A notation as to what the validation tests were and where the results are stored.
- A notation of any files external to the model that have been created, changed, or eliminated to facilitate the change.

Making Internal Auditors Happy

It is not a universal requirement that every model in the firm undergo an audit process. Many models are not directly audited. Three of the main criteria for whether a model needs to be audited or not are the following:

- Do the results of the model serve as a mark-to-market valuation of securities held by the firm?
- Is the model used for pricing of publicly traded securities in the open market?
- Is the model used for the pricing of complex or illiquid securities or positions, and therefore has no readily available industry comparable valuations?

If any of the above is true, or if your firm requires the model to be audited for any other reason, you can use another approach. The best way to kill two birds with one stone is to build your control environment around to the firm's audit standards. These standards will often layout the exact environment, forms, and software management practices required. It will also free you of the burden of choice. The firm may, for example, have a preferred third-party vendor of software environment management tools.

If you work within this framework, you will build what is the firm-recommended environment and control procedures and satisfy your own needs at the department level simultaneously.

STREAMLINING THE VALIDATION AND PROMOTION PROCESS

Establishing a Test Suite of Runs Using Standardized Reports

As the models advance from one major version to the next, we will have to satisfy ourselves of two things. The first is that the newly implemented changes are working correctly. The second is that these changes have not triggered any other errors or unanticipated changes in the remaining portion of the model.

The way that we can most efficiently test that no unforeseen changes have occurred is to design a series of model runs that will be produced after each new version of the model is promoted. These report packages will then be compared with the report set from the most immediately prior model version. If there are any changes that cannot be explained as a direct influence of the new changes, we will need to investigate the source of the discrepancies.

Base Case Cash Flow Back Testing

The first place to start in the establishment of a back testing system is to run a series of reports from the first version of the model. This set of output results will contain the collateral data file used in the model, the set of collateral selection reports, a Cash Flow Waterfall Report, and the Summary Matrix Report Package.

The initial runs should be performed with what is a representative set of values used in the current modeling process. If the market convention for prepayment and default is expressed in terms of CPR rates, that is the methodology that should be applied. The same applies to current collateral selection criteria, coupon rates, reserve fund levels, market value decline estimates, recovery delays, and so on.

The base set of back testing runs would contain a Range of prepayment and default scenarios as follows (all scenario speeds in CPR):

- Prepayment Rates 0% to 20% by 2% intervals, Default Rates 0 to 20% by 2% intervals
- Prepayment Rates 20% to 100% by 10% intervals, Default Rates 20 to 100% by 10% intervals
- Prepayment Rates 0% to 5% by 0.5% intervals, Default Rates 0% to 5% by 0.5% intervals

This back testing schedule consists of two sets of 100 scenarios each (which is a lot of scenarios to check). The next scenario would be the rating agency stress tests applying the following default and prepayment rates:

1. Prepayment Rates 0% to 20% by 2% intervals, Default Rates 0% to 100% by 10% intervals
2. Prepayment Rates 20% to 100% by 10% intervals, Default Rates 0% to 100% by 10% intervals

These two report sets add another 200 scenarios to the back testing package. The last set would be to run the following three sets of reports:

1. Prepayment Rates 0% to 20% by 5% intervals, Default Rates 0% to 20% by 5% intervals. Change recovery period from 12? to 18 months.
2. Prepayment Rates 0% to 20% by 5% intervals, Default Rates 0% to 20% by 5% intervals. Change market value decline % from 50% to 80% months.
3. Prepayment Rates 0% to 20% by 5% intervals, Default Rates 0% to 20% by 5% intervals. Change recovery period from 12 to 18 months and change market value decline % from 50% to 80% months.

Each of these model runs will add an incremental 25 scenarios. That brings the total to 575 cash flow scenarios to confirm. At this point we have to ask ourselves two additional questions:

1. Who is going to check all these numbers?
2. Is this direct evidence that the author has finally "jumped the tracks," (to put it politely)?

The answers are (unexpectedly), "no one" and "No." I don't care how persnickety you are, no one can check that much data and be assured that they have done it correctly; no one.

Then again, no one has to.

As long as we keep the formats of the reports in the output packages constant, we do not need to do anything except run a validation checking program.

Automation of the Validation Process

We can write a program to assist us in the validation program. We need to compare two sets of output reports. The fact will be made easier in that we will use standard names for each of these report packages. These are eight report packages from the new version that have to be compared to eight report packages from the existing version of the model.

Each report has the same physical configuration of rows and columns. Each report will have a corresponding name based on the scenario set and the file prefix. The following file naming convention is adopted. For example, we are comparing the previous version release, which was "**LOAN_FIN_109_00.xls**" to the new version release "**LOAN_FIN_110_00.xls.**"

Each of the eight files would be named:

```
VERSION109_(file type)_(IdNumber).xls
```

Thus the files for this version for the first prepayment and default matrix are:

```
VERSION109_Inelig_1.xls      Ineligible Collateral reports
VERSION109_Strat_1.xls       Collateral Stratification reports
VERSION109_CFW_1.xls         Cash Flow Waterfall reports
VERSION109_SM_1.xls          Summary Matrix reports
VERSION109_Single_1.xls      Single Page Scenario reports
```

The remaining seven Cash Flow Waterfall files would be "**VERSION109_CFW_2.xls**" through filename "**VERSION109_CFW_8.xls.**"

The program would perform the following steps:

1. Read a menu with the directory information where each of the back test file sets are located.
2. Loop through each of the five types of files in the outermost For ... Next loop.
3. Dependent upon the type of file that is currently being scanned, begin loading the contents of each report for the old version into an array. For the Cash Flow Waterfall the array would be identical to the one used in the model:

```
Public g_waterfall_old(1 To 100, 1 To PAY_DATES, 1 To PAY_COLS) As Double
```

4. The program would then open the "**VERSION110_CFW_1.xls**" file and read in the contents into another similar array "**Public g_waterfall_old**" of identical dimensions.
5. The program then calls a report specific comparison function that simply overlays each of the reports and takes the differences of the two arrays. If any of the differences are above a critical amount, say $1, the difference is printed out into a report named after the two versions: "**DIFF_109_110_CFW_1.xls.**"
6. If there are no differences, a report is prepared in the "**DIFF_109_100_CFW.xls**" stating that, so we have direct confirmation.

A copy of this program can be found on the Web site for this book. It is called "**Auto_Validate_100.xls.**"

Automation of the Model Promotion Process

Now that we have automated the model validation process for two consecutive model versions, we can take another step forward in automation.

We now know how to perform the following tasks on files: open, close, save, and save as. With these four commands, we can build a small VBA program that will move files from one directory to another, copy files, or save them to a specified name. To promote a major version change, the procedures would follow this broad pattern:

- Rename the current user file to the next Gold Copy standard and send it to the keepers of the Gold Copy directory.
- Move the current development file to the User directory and reset to the next version number for a major change. "**LOAN_FIN_108_00.xls**" is replaced with "**LOAN_FIN_109_00.xls.**"
- Move the working development file to the base development file. The version number of this file will reflect the current major/minor version number of the user file.
- If the promotion was only from the working development file to the base development file, you would only change the directory location.

Using Third-Party Software to Manage Access and Promotion

Using vendor software is a convenient, although potentially expensive, way of solving the version control problem. Some are less intrusive than others. The worst require you to essentially place your entire development and user environment within a meta-shell of the program.

All file handling and changes are managed and recorded by the software.

Although this has some advantages of learning yet another set of commands and procedures, the programs are quite up to the type of models described in this book. They would also save a lot of time if you ever have to roll back a version to an earlier one.

EVOLUTION OF THE FORM OF THE MODEL

Beyond the VBA/Excel Construct

As mentioned before, models have life cycles. This is certainly the case for models written in Excel/VBA. A common evolutionary pattern as the model evolves in capacity and sophistication is:

1. An Excel spreadsheet
2. An Excel spreadsheet with recorded macros for simple reports
3. An Excel spreadsheet with VBA subroutines that are purpose designed not recorded. All output is contained within the model
4. An Excel/VBA model that uses menus and external files to input data and template files to output the results
5. Model 4 above with Access to handle very large data input files and some of the reporting

6. Model 4 above with a compiled code such as C or Java to perform the numerically intensive calculations
7. Model 4 above using both Models 5 and 6 features
8. A model with a VBA shell containing a preponderance of compiled code
9. A model in compiled code only

EVOLUTION OF THE STRUCTURE OF THE MODEL

Bifurcation of Collateral Selection Process

The first and obvious bifurcation that could occur is to split the Collateral Selection software completely out of the model and make it a separate program. This makes a lot of sense, especially if the selection process grows in complexity or the collateral files grow in length.

It is just easier to work with smaller single function pieces of software. This is especially true as one moves toward incorporating Microsoft Access into the program. Even without using Access it could make the process more manageable especially with big files.

Let us say we develop an auto loan model using the framework of the model. It is not at all unusual to have upwards of 200,000 loans in a collateral file. If we needed to do a series of collateral cuts, we could have others doing that task while we concentrate on other things. This portion of the model when stripped out of the whole is quite small.

Bifurcation of the Cash Flow Calculation and Structuring Process

If we separate out the Collateral Selection portion of the model, it will be very easy to come up with a specialized cash flow generator. The Collateral Selection model has the capability of producing a file of eligible collateral in the same format as the original data file of the combined model.

The Cash Flow Generator and Structuring model would then use this file as its starting point. There would be no requirements to add any VBA code to the remaining portion of the model.

DELIVERABLES CHECKLIST

The VBA Knowledge Checklist items for this chapter are:

- How to automate a model promotion sequence that moves development code to the users
- How to design and automate a back testing procedure

The Model Knowledge Checklist items for this chapter are:

- What a model Gold Copy is and why you need to have one, even from the beginning
- How to establish the steps of a model promotion sequence

- What model version numbers are, when to change them, and how to manage the change
- Online and offline model version documentation
- How to establish a basic set of back testing scenarios

NEXT STEPS

Take the knowledge and apply it to your first real-world model.

ON THE WEB SITE

On the Web site for this chapter you will find a copy of the **"Auto_Validate.xls"** program.

Risk Assessment and Valuation

Building Portfolio Monitoring Model

OVERVIEW

How time flies!

It is now three months from the date of issuance of the deal. Your boss comes in and says he needs some help. Risk Control has asked him to develop a series of benchmarks for monitoring all the positions in the conduit. They want to understand how the deal is performing relative to its issuance conditions and if there are any signs of credit deterioration in the collateral that might lower the probability of timely payment of coupon and full repayment of principal.

To answer his question you will have to build a risk assessment and valuation model. This model will have to be able to integrate the actual performance of the collateral up to the current time with the "at issuance" projections for the remaining life of the deal. In addition to producing the cash flows, you will have to value these cash flows according to the current market conditions. This valuation will include relative pricing analysis of similar deals that are either being issued at the time of the valuation, or traded actively in the secondary market, or both.

We can see immediately that there are significant portions of the existing structuring model that we can use to build this new application. We can also see that there are going to be major changes in how we do some of this analysis. Fortunately, we have faith in the validity of the structuring model and the integrity of its code so that we are not at all hesitant to use it as a starting point in our development efforts. Some of the functionality it currently contains can be discarded in its entirety, some can be modified to fit the new requirements, and some can be retained in its current form.

The tone of the boss was concerned. We need to establish clear and concise criteria that we can stick to and we need to do it now. Our second major opportunity is upon us.

DELIVERABLES

The VBA Language Knowledge Deliverable for this chapter is:

■ How to construct a model using reusable code that we have written for another or several other applications

The Modeling Knowledge Deliverable for this chapter is:

■ How to build a deal monitoring, risk assessment model that will perform relative value calculations

UNDER CONSTRUCTION

In this chapter we will build a Risk Assessment and Valuation model using the original Structuring model that we completed in Chapter 19, "Building Additional Capabilities," as our starting point. We will need to preserve certain key features of the Structuring model while at the same time completely discarding others that have no relevance to the new application.

We will not be adding any new collateral to the deal as it matures. We therefore do not need the collateral selection process code or any of the reporting related to ineligible loans. We will be able to eliminate the menus and menu checking code that support the collateral selection process as well. We should be careful to purge the "A_Globals" and "A_Constants" modules of unneeded global variables and constants related to this function. Finally, we should also be able to eliminate the Eligibility Report and its supporting code.

However, we will need to produce stratification reports on the current collateral in the deal. As prepayments and defaults occur, we will need to keep track of these loans and understand the composition of those two populations. For this reason it would be wise to retain the collateral stratification report feature of the model.

We will probably want to retain most if not all of the current cash flow calculation code. We will have to modify a number of its calculation subroutines to reflect the mix of information this model will use. The Structuring model projected 100% of its cash flows. The Risk Assessment model will, perforce, use a mix of historical cash flows from the performance of the collateral pool to date and a set of projected cash flows for the future periods of the deal. This model will be an initial attempt to get our arms around the problem and as such we may be able to make some simplifying assumptions about the behavior of the collateral. The impact of the empirical data will also be felt in the fact that our estimates of appraisal values, market value decline percentages, and recovery times will now be empirically determined rather than estimates or assumptions. We will receive "best estimates" from the servicing people in the field and our own appraisers as to what these values will most probably be. We will therefore need to reflect this information on a loan-by-loan basis in the case of defaults rather than at a portfolio basis as we did in the Structuring model.

Our report packages will probably also remain entirely intact, for two reasons. First, all of our constituencies, both internal and external, are used to the current formats and contents of the reports. Many have systems that use these reports directly in their current form. Second it will be much easier to compare the differences of the revised estimates of deal performance with that of the "at issuance" projections if the formats are identical.

With these general guidelines in place, we can proceed to making up a to-do list of program modifications.

An Empirical Performance Monitoring System

To implement the above changes we will need to add, delete, or modify the VBA code in a number of modules throughout the model. The modules affected will be:

- **"A_Constants"**: Delete constants that will no longer be relevant to the new application. This will especially pertain to constants supporting the collateral selection and ineligibility reporting and menu and menu error checking subroutines. We will, however, need to create new constants for the reformatted reports and to support the monitoring function itself.
- **"A_Globals"**: Delete all global variables used by the model in those areas that we will be discarding. As with the comments for the **"A_Constants"** module immediately above, we will concentrate on the collateral selection code and its supporting menu, error checking, and reporting subroutines.
- **"A_Main_Program"**: There will be a number of changes to the Main Program that will recast the subroutine calling sequence to eliminate the collateral selection function while preserving the collateral stratification reports. We will retain, modify, and expand almost all of the other report packages. Those such as the Waterfall Reports, Matrix Summary Reports, and the Single Scenario Reports will look similar to what they were in the structuring model. We will add reports to monitor the speed and magnitude of the collateral prepayment and default activities and a report package to compare the "At Issuance" projected performance of the deal with its current performance at various times in its history.
- **"CollateralCFGenerator"**: Modify the various cash flow calculation subroutines that generate prepayment and default events. We now need to be able to use a mix of empirical information to the current month of the deal and projected information for all periods thereafter. In addition, we will need to be able to integrate empirical estimates of recovery period lags, appraisal values, and market value declines on a loan-by-loan basis.
- **"CollateralPreDefCalcs"**: These subroutines, surprisingly, will probably remain unchanged as they are solely used for producing cash flow projections that we will still use to estimate the cash flows for the future periods of the deal.
- **"CollateralReadDataFile"**: We will need to reflect empirical prepayment and default information. We will also need to store recovery calculation inputs on a loan-by-loan basis.
- **"CollateralSelectionSubs"**: Most but not all of this functionality will be eliminated. We will retain the collateral stratification reporting function and expand it to differentiate between current pay, defaulted, and prepaid collateral.
- **"LoadRunCaptureResults"**: These subroutines will be left intact. We are still going to capture the same results as we did before although later we may need to modify them slightly if additional information is requested by any of out interested parties.
- **"MenusErrorChecking"**: We will need to eliminate the error checking for menus no longer in use and create additional error checking for any new menus we are creating.
- **"MenusReadInputs"**: Some of the input reading subroutines supporting the menus will be eliminated such as the Selection Criteria Menu, the Program

Costs Menu (which are now fixed), and the Geographic selection. Others will be modified like the Main Menu support subroutine.

- **"WriteAssumptionsReport"**: Our original assumption set included collateral selection criteria. We need to eliminate that and add code to reflect the current state of prepayments and defaults of the portfolio life-to-date.
- **"WriteCFTraceReport"**: We retain this functionality to assist in the validation process of the new model.
- **"WriteCollateralReports"**: We will modify this functionality to produce three sets of stratification reports: Current Pay, Prepaid, and Defaulted collateral.
- **"WriteEligibleCollatFile"**: We will eliminate this module in its entirety. We no longer select collateral and therefore do not need to produce a post-selection report.
- **"WriteIneligibilityReports"**: Without the need to perform the collateral selection process, we will eliminate this module also.
- **"WriteScenarioReports"**: These reports will be retained intact as will the code that produces them.
- **"WiteMatrixReports"**: These reports will be retained intact as will the code that produces them.
- **"WriteWaterfallReports"**: These reports are critical to the new application and will be retained unchanged.
- **"Z_ButtonSubs"**: We can eliminate some of the file opening buttons "Peek-A-Boo" function and all of the Geographic Support buttons. We can also eliminate the Coupon Trace code from this module and delete the report feature from the Excel portion of the model.
- **"WritePrepayDefReport"**: This is a new module into which we will put the code for a pair of reports, one for prepayment projections and the other for default projections. The reports will compare the "Expected Case" prepayment and default estimates with the updated empirical/projection estimates.
- **"ReadAtIssueFiles"**: This is a new module into which we will place the code to open and read the contents of the "At Issuance" Cashflow Waterfall Reports and the Matrix Summary Report. The numbers from these reports will serve as the baseline numbers for the monitoring comparison.
- We will also have to change the configuration of the Collateral Data File to allow us to record the changes on a monthly basis and introduce the estimates of the servicing personnel into our cash flow projects of how the portfolio is expected to perform.

HOW MUCH OF THE STRUCTURING MODEL CAN WE USE?

When starting any new modeling exercise it is always a good idea to rummage through the toolkit to determine if you have any previously developed code or menus that you can use in a new application. Many times you do and can immediately reuse, salvage, or copy portions of other models you have written. This is a wonderful thing! No one wants to write the same code more than once. In addition, using code from other applications generally means that you are both familiar with it and you can be assured that it will work correctly the first time.

We are *extremely* lucky in this case that there is a very high degree of commonality of function between the current structuring model and the anticipated monitoring and valuation model. We should be able to use large amounts of the code for the monitoring model.

Before we start we should ask ourselves one other question. Why do we need a second model in the first place?

WHY TWO MODELS?

We clearly have a choice. We can build a new application using much of the code from the structuring model and building a new, separate, and distinct model. The alternative is that we can add a lot of code to the existing structuring model, extensively modifying the old application.

In the real world we would have to give this some thought. Some of the questions that we would have to ask ourselves would be:

- How different is the functionality of the two models?
- Do the functional differences constitute such a divergence that it is unlikely anyone would be running the model and using both functionalities at the same time?
- What is the level of experience and sophistication of the personnel who will be running the model? If we choose to stay with a single model would the result be an overly complicated application? This can directly lead to user dissatisfaction, confusion, mistakes, and frustration. The application is then discarded by the user community in spite of the fact that it effectively meets the needs of the business and is accurate. It is just so darn hard to use everyone gives up!

We also have to be sensitive to the fact that if the model is preserved as a single entity we may have two different sets of users who do not want the results, or even their inputs, viewed by the other. The issuance people may or may not want the monitoring group viewing the structuring process or vice versa. This is especially true when we get to the next process of valuation. In many cases the secondary market participants who are buying and selling the issued security may not wish to share information with the primary issuers.

Based on our survey of what needs to be done, it would appear that the most sensible thing to do is to create a second model. We will begin by working directly off of the existing framework of the structuring model.

There are numerous advantages in this approach. Most of the menus are reusable and superficially very similar to the ones that will be in the new model. In that the menus are similar, we should be able to retain much of the error checking code, modifying it for new menu features we will introduce. In addition we can mimic the structures of the error checking subroutines themselves if we create any new menus or split existing ones! We are sure that the cash flow projection engine is correct. We will still need to load these cash flows into the waterfall spreadsheet, a portion of the code that will not change. Our original data file can be modified to reflect empirical events in the portfolio. We can use the same code to read the file and store the collateral information.

   While we will delete some modules almost in their entirety, such as the collateral selection code, by and large we should be add to modify many of the other modules of the model, leaving them mostly intact. If we work systemically and make small changes each time, we should be able to carve away what we don't need and modify or add to the remaining current model in a fairly straightforward manner. We want to achieve maximum leverage by reusing as much of the original model's code as we can.

   The last and *crushingly convincing argument* in favor of the two model approach is that you will get to both see how its done, and for the serious reader, do it yourself. You may well be faced with the need (or opportunity), to have to do a major development effort against severe time pressure. The ability to inventory the code you have written, determine what you can pull out from your bag of tricks and use immediately, and the experience of having either seen this done once or have done it yourself, will be *critical*. Every second that you can save in development, every minute you can save in the debugging process (because you know that the reused sections of the code will run the first time), will speed you along your way and make the goal that much more attainable!

   As when we started to develop the structuring model, we need to start with the last things first—the report package.

DESIGNING THE NEW REPORT PACKAGE

The fundamental difference between the information that we had been reporting in the structuring model and the information we will report in the monitoring system is simply grasped. The primary focus of the monitoring model is the collection of the empirical performance, or actual performance, from the emerging behavior of the collateral of the portfolio. The prepayment and defaults that occur and the rate of survivorship of those loans currently paying as scheduled will now form a portion of the cash flow streams. The cash flows of the structuring were based entirely on estimates and projections.

   At the beginning of the deal, very little of the cash flows of the monitoring system will be empirical in nature. In the first month of the deal's life, only the cash flows of the first period will be actual. The remaining hundreds of periods of cash flows will continue to be projected using the "At Issuance" assumptions that were used to initially structure and size the deal. In the case of this deal, those assumptions were 200 PSA prepayment speed with a 400 PSA default speed. The actual cash flows of these early periods will have a noticeable impact on the projection stream, however.

   If the early actual prepayments and default rates of the portfolio are lower, or even better yet, substantially lower than those projected in the initial structuring model, the deal will benefit. This is because the departure point for all subsequent periods of the model's cash flow projects will be based on a higher amount of outstanding principal balance. If conversely there are events that serve to increase the prepayment and default activity the deal will show considerably lower principal retention. With lower than expected principal balances in each period, the effect on the aggregate amount of foregone coupon income could become substantial.

   It is to the measurement of the differences we will see emerging between our initial projections and the actual performance of the deal over its life that the monitoring system will be focused on. Each month of successive data from the master servicer of the portfolio will give us more and more insight into the anticipated lifetime performance of the collateral. We will constantly examine all of our original assumptions in regards to the collateral behavior. We will need to produce snapshots on a monthly basis of the divergence, either positively or negatively, away from our initial projections.

As more and more empirical behavior becomes apparent, we may also make adjustments to the portions of the cash flows that are still being projected, those of the remaining term of the deal. If our initial cash flow projections were based on a 200 PSA prepayment and 400 PSA default rate, they may well need to be modified as the portfolio matures. For example, the portfolio may remain robust over a sustained period, say one year, where the prepayment and default activity remains below our initial projections. We may then adjust the lifetime prepayment and default speed downward to 150 PSA and 300 PSA, respectively. If, however, we find ourselves in a challenging economic environment, with a prepayment and default activity level well above what was anticipated, the adjustments could increase the speeds to 250 PSA and 500 PSA, respectively.

The monitoring system will also provide us with empirical economic inputs of another nature. In the event of default by one of the Obligors, we hope to recover a portion of the defaulted principal balance by the ultimate liquidation of our claim through a sale of the asset. If the economy is healthy and financing cheap and available, we may find that the recovery times we estimated are too long and the market value declines too severe. We may also note that the appraisal values of the properties may need to be adjusted upward over time. This creates a stronger LTV ratio for the borrower and more correctly reflects the real risk of loss in a liquidation scenario. Conversely, if the economic situation is weakening or in crisis, the exact opposite would occur. Recovery periods would significantly lengthen. If credit sources became restricted, or for certain kinds of loans and risk profiles, dried up altogether, the net losses would be exacerbated. Long recovery times present more chance of physical damage or deterioration of the asset. Unpaid capitalized interest increases. Selling, servicing, and management costs of bank-owned property increase. The presence of other distressed properties will tend over time to depress values. Their presence on the market will be an unwanted competition to the sale of your own holdings. Appraisal values will be lowered, sometimes precipitously by "fire sales" or sales triggered by special situations. These sales will then serve as lower mark-to-market levels that the lender will be forced to apply to any similar loans in the portfolio.

Local economic conditions would also effect these valuations. Traditionally strong regional and local economies may well evidence below normal default activities with shorter recovery times and less severe market value decline ratios. Traditionally fragile regions, such as the "Rust Belt," or single industry dominated localities may well reflect opposite trends. If the textile mill closes its doors, the local businesses in many surrounding towns may be catastrophically affected.

As the deal matures we may see some or all of these effects manifest themselves over different portions of its life.

In the discussion to this point we have confined ourselves addressing the collateral behavior per se. The monitoring system will also be updating on a monthly basis the effects of changes in the benchmark interest rates that come into play. All of the loans in the deal float off of the Prime Rate. All have fixed spreads to this index. Thus any change in the Prime Rate that carries over a coupon rate reset period or a payment level reset period will have an immediate effect on the collateral cash flows. In addition, the financing costs of the Conduit position are pegged to the LIBOR Rate. Most of the time, these rates move in a highly correlated manner. At times, however, they do not. If the deal were to experience a sustained period of time in which the Prime remained steady or declined while the LIBOR Rate levels increased, the projected performance of the deal would suffer.

I have said all that to now say this. The overriding impetuous for the change in the focus of the reports will be to provide a direct comparison of the *actual* to the *projected*. Repeatedly you will see the current mix of actual/projected behavior compared in varying degrees of detail. We will retain the services of almost all of our old report format friends from the structuring model (with the exception of the Collateral Selection Reports). But like a strong lasting friendship we will expect them to grow with us. Some will remain almost unchanged, most will add an additional section or two, and a few will be wholly new to the process.

Reusing the Reports We Have

Single Scenario Report We will retain the Single Scenario Report. This report will be unchanged. It is the single best report we have for both internal and external presentations. It is a concise summary of the deal on a single page and as such can be used in a wide variety of activities to many different audiences.

We will change the code slightly but only annotate this report as to reflect which portions of the cash flows are based on empirical performance of the collateral as opposed to the surviving original structuring model projections.

Modifying Existing Reports A greater number of the reports that we designed earlier in the process of building the structuring model will be modified and set to similar if not quite identical uses.

Eligible Collateral Reports With the selection process out of the model, the collateral stratification reports are now occupying the top position in the report preparation sequence. Once the deal has begun, we will assume, for simplification purposes, that a loan can be in only one of three states. It can be up-to-date making regular monthly payments, it can be prepaid, or it can be defaulted.

In reality there could easily be another three or four conditions. The loan might be delinquent, less than three full payments in arrears. The loan may be more than three payments in arrears, which in many deals would be the same as a full default. The term for these loans is "deemed default." The loan could be more than three months in arrears but subject to a negotiated or protected "work out." In this case the Obligor and the lender are attempting to arrive at a long-term solution. This may involve recasting the monthly payment amount, spreading the repayment of the current delinquency over a number of future payments, extension of the loan-term to lower payment levels, or any other terms acceptable to both parties. In this case the loan is in a sort of a payment limbo.

For the moment we will drop back to our original three. Based on these categories, current pay, prepaid, or defaulted, the model will produce a full Stratification

Report Package. We will therefore have all the information we had on the initial eligible collateral pool bifurcated by these three categories.

All the stratification reports are retained from our initial package. The "Loan Final Status" report will now differentiate not as it did earlier on "Eligible" and "Ineligible" status but across "Current Pay," "Prepaid," and "Defaulted." We will employ these reports to track clustering behavior especially in regard to geographic concentrations. An example of the report E-11, "Distribution of Current Balances by ZIP Codes," for prepaid loans is shown in Exhibit 22.1.

Cash Flow Waterfall Report   The report that is the champion of excruciating detail is our old stalwart the Cash Flow Waterfall Report. This report is about to move to new heights of exhaustive detail. The Cash Flow Waterfall Report is now composed of five major subsections.

The first three are box score displays that list the performance of the deal at issuance, its current anticipated performance based on the combination of empirical and current projection assumptions, and the difference between the two. There are three sections aligned along the left side of the report in a top to bottom order in the first eight columns of the report spreadsheet. There are, from top to bottom, the current updated projection combining the deal-to-date empirical performance and the original (or revised) prepayment and default assumptions cash flows. The second section is the difference between the Current Summary Section and the "At Issuance" Summary Section. The third section is the At Issuance section.

These three sections allow the reader of the report the ability to rapidly compare the current over or under performance of the deal by looking at less than 25 key numbers and their deal-to-date differences.

There are two remaining subsections. The first is a complete waterfall for the currently projected empirical/projection scenario. The second is another complete waterfall that contains a cell-by-cell difference between the current projected scenario and the at issuance scenario.

In addition to the above report, which is on a single spreadsheet, there is an Assumptions Report spreadsheet and another complete waterfall of the at issuance case on its separate worksheet. Due to the large size of this report a schematic can be found in Exhibit 22.2.

Matrix Summary Report   The Matrix Summary Report Package will also continue on with us from the Structuring model to the monitoring model. This report package will consist of the same five reports that comprised the original. These are the Assumptions Page, the Tenor, Cashflows, Conduit Performance, and Seller Interest reports.

The left-hand portion of the format of the four matrix reports is unchanged. The 100 scenario, 10-by-10 grid has been retained. It will hold the scenarios generated by the monitoring model across a maximum of ten prepayment and ten default assumptions as before.

Each report now has an extended header section at the top left-hand corner. This section contains the key aligned with one grid square of the outputs of the projected performance of the deal based on its issuance assumptions. The information in the Matrix Summary is the result of applying a prepayment rate and default rate assumption of 200 PSA and 400 PSA, respectively. This matrix cell is used as the

Eligible Collateral Report #11
Current Balances in Top 50 ZIP Codes

			1	2	3	4	5	6	7	8	9	10	11	12	13
Rank	ZIP Code	Stat	Number of Loans	Current Loan Balance	Current Loan LTV	% Current Balances	Cum % Current Balances	Average Loan Balance	WtAvg Current Yield	WtAvg Original Term	WtAvg Remain Term	WtAvg Current Seasoning	Equity Balance	Equity % Appraisal	Total Appraisal
			10	882,670									667,330		1,550,000
1	33612	FL	1	320,030	57.148%	36.257%	36.257%	320,030	7.750%	120.00	113.00	7.00	239,970	42.852%	560,000
2	97701	OR	1	201,825	72.080%	22.865%	59.122%	201,825	9.000%	120.00	114.00	6.00	78,175	27.920%	280,000
3	8876	NJ	1	60,494	60.494%	6.854%	65.976%	60,494	9.000%	84.00	76.00	8.00	39,506	39.506%	100,000
4	85032	AZ	1	55,317	55.317%	6.267%	72.243%	55,317	9.000%	84.00	58.00	26.00	44,683	44.683%	100,000
5	29072	SC	1	53,980	53.980%	6.115%	78.358%	53,980	9.000%	84.00	76.00	8.00	46,020	46.020%	100,000
6	30339	GA	1	53,817	67.338%	6.103%	84.642%	53,871	9.000%	83.00	77.00	6.00	26,129	32.662%	80,000
7	6484	CT	1	50,137	41.781%	5.680%	90.142%	50,137	9.000%	84.00	61.00	23.00	69,863	58.219%	120,000
8	20602	MD	1	32,223	40.279%	3.651%	93.792%	32,223	9.000%	83.00	51.00	32.00	47,777	59.721%	80,000
9	6106	CT	1	29,569	42.242%	3.350%	97.142%	29,569	9.000%	84.00	59.00	25.00	40,431	57.758%	70,000
10	90731	CA	1	25,224	42.040%	2.858%	100.00%	25,224	10.000%	84.00	58.00	26.00	34,776	57.960%	60,000

EXHIBIT 22.1   The distribution of current balances at the time of the launch of the deal by state; prepaid loans only

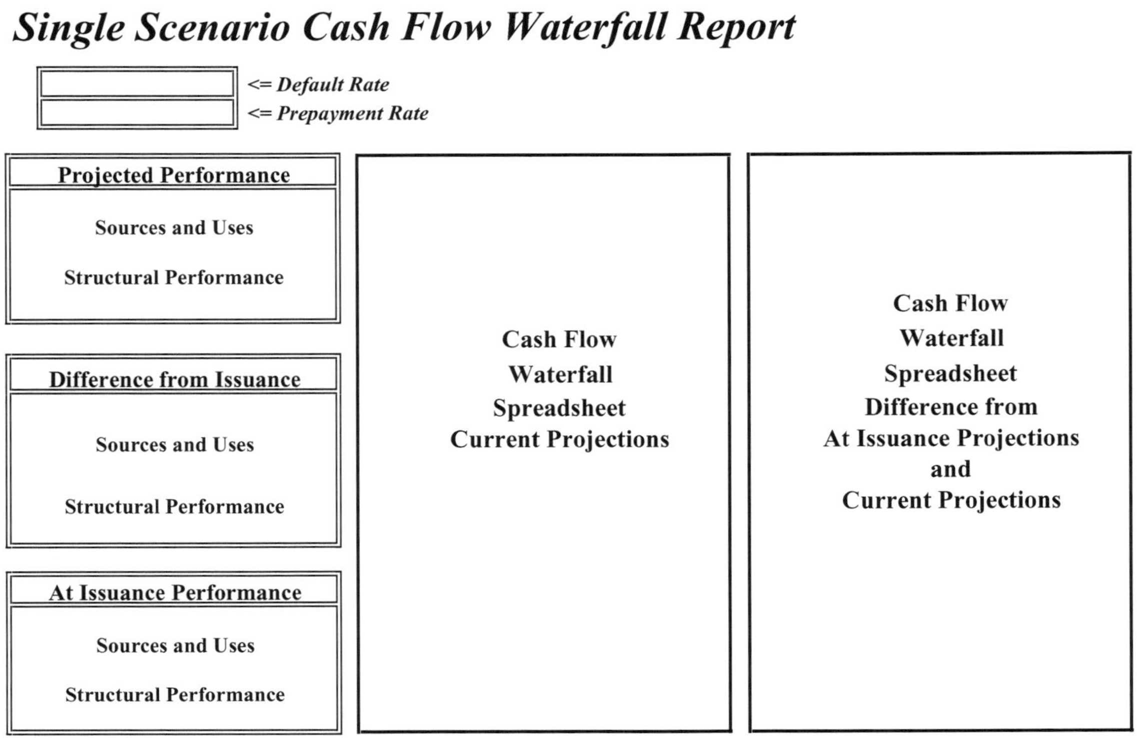

Single Scenario Cash Flow Waterfall Report

	<= *Default Rate*
	<= *Prepayment Rate*

Projected Performance

Sources and Uses

Structural Performance

Difference from Issuance

Sources and Uses

Structural Performance

At Issuance Performance

Sources and Uses

Structural Performance

**Cash Flow
Waterfall
Spreadsheet
Current Projections**

**Cash Flow
Waterfall
Spreadsheet
Difference from
At Issuance Projections
and
Current Projections**

EXHIBIT 22.2 Schematic of the monitoring model single scenario Cash Flow Waterfall Report page (the subsections are *NOT* to scale)

base performance used for the comparison of the currently projected results on each of the four reports with the single matrix cell of the headers.

Another difference grid of a 100-cell matrix in an identical 10-by-10 configuration is now positioned to the right of the current projection grid. The numbers of the current projection are compared to the numbers of the single matrix cell in the issuance case in the header unit. The difference of each cell in the second matrix is the item-by-item comparison with the single cell at the top of the report.

As with the original report, any unused Matrix cell locations are deleted from both the right and left 100 cell starting matrix after the report is populated. Due to the large size of this report, a schematic is shown in Exhibit 22.3.

New Reports

You might think that after running off in high spirits and modifying a number of our existing reports in such a remarkable manner, we would be finished, or at least resting.

Not so! In that the requirements of the monitoring function are significantly different from those of the structuring function, we need to create a few additional reports. These new reports will allow us to examine in more detail the impact that the ongoing prepayment and default activity is having on the deal. Remember that each of the prepayment and default methodologies used in the structuring model are both distributed and fractional in nature. To refresh ourselves, the prepayment and default attrition, regardless of the computational method employed, PSA, CPR, or USER, assess prepayments or defaults from a *portion of each loan* in the portfolio. Once the empirical performance of the portfolio is available to us, this methodology can be used only for the future periods of the deal. The actual collateral pool will default or prepay their entire outstanding balances in one fell swoop.

We will therefore need to keep track of the aggregate of this collective individual attrition and compare it to our earlier projected fractional methods estimates.

On an entirely different note, we will need to be sensitive to developing trends in the performance of the collateral or of the debt structure. A most useful report package would be one that would allow us to take a series of ongoing snapshots in time. We would then compare these snapshots to spot emerging trends or to compare the current periods of activities with others in the past. These snapshots could be taken at a conventional pattern interval such as 1, 3, 6, 12, 18, and 24 months in the past and then successively compared to the at issuance performance estimate.

Alternatively, we might be seeing the beginning of a trend and elect to produce a report that compared the current month, 1, 2, 3, 4, 5, 6, 7, 8, 9, 10, 11, and 12 months ago to the at issuance projection. This monthly time slicing would catch a degree of granularity lost in the more conventional report spacing of the previous paragraph. Yet another pattern we might wish to look at is two intervals, separated in time, but showing what we suspect are similar behaviors. Here the time slicing might be the current month, and 1, 2, 3, 4, and 5 months ago versus at issuance and 23, 24, 25, 26, 27, 28 29, and 30 months ago versus at issuance.

Summary Matrix Report #3
Conduit Note Paydown

Key & Expected Case Performance

| Total P&I Payments |
| Principal Repayments |
| Price |
| Severity of Principal Loss |
| Coverage Ratio |
| Internal Rate of Return |

Default Levels	Prepayment Methodology			
	1	2	3 to 9	10
	0.00%	0.00%	0.00%	0.00%
1				
Up to 10 Scenarios				
10				

DIFFERENCE (CURRENT EXPECTED CASE - BASE CASE)

Default Levels	Prepayment Methodology			
	1	2	3 to 9	10
	0.00%	0.00%	0.00%	0.00%
1				
Up to 10 Scenarios				
10				

EXHIBIT 22.3 Summary Matrix report from the monitoring model

Prepayment and Defaults Projection Report Package These reports are in two separate template files. Their names are **"m_prepay_proj_template.xls"** and **"m_default_proj_template.xls."** The formats of the reports are identical except for the labeling as it relates to contents.

Each report file consists of two worksheets. The first is the Assumptions Report. The second is a worksheet that is replicated once for each projection scenario run by the user. It consists of a table on the left-hand side of the worksheet and a pair of graphs to their immediate right. In both report packages the table measures the period-by-period prepayment or default activity and its cumulative period-to-date totals. The last two columns of the report are the differences between the period-by-period estimates of the issuance versus the current projected and then the differences in the cumulative differences between the two scenarios.

The upper graph plots the period-by-period levels and differences while the lower graph plots the cumulative period-by-period levels and the cumulative differences. Due to the large size of this report, a schematic is shown in Exhibit 22.4.

Historical Period Performance Report Package This report package will allow us to examine selected period performance results for the deal and compare them to the at issuance performance projections. Up to 20 different time intervals can be specified from an entry grid on the new "Files" menu we will discuss shortly.

This report package consists of two worksheets. The first is the Assumptions page and the second is the Historical Cash Flows Report Package. This sheet can be reproduced and filled for up to 20 selected months.

Due to the large size of this report, a schematic is shown in Exhibit 22.5.

YOU CAN'T MAKE AN OMELET WITHOUT BREAKING SOME EGGS

Earlier in this chapter we made the decision to create a separate model to provide at first a portfolio monitoring capability and later a valuation and mark-to-market capability.

As we previously discussed, there is a significant difference between the sum of the actions needed to structure a deal and those needed to monitor a deal. The key to this difference lies primarily in two areas. The first is that once a deal has been created, priced, and launched there are a number of assumptions and sensitivities we no longer need to concern ourselves with. A simple example of this is the program costs and servicing fees associated with running the deal. These fee levels are established at the closing as well as the advance rate of the deal, the Seller Interest, the reserve fund levels, and other things besides. These are no longer subject to estimate and debate. They are now fixed, known quantities, and will remain so for the remaining life of the deal. This is especially true of the composition of the collateral pool. At the beginning of the book we made the assertion that once the deal was finalized the collateral pool was fixed. Loans originally in the deal may prepay or default but no additional collateral could be sold into the structure. The structure must sink or swim based on the collateral that backed it at inception.

Default Activity To Date Plus Projections Collateral Cash Flow Report

Monthly Time Periods	Expected Case Prepayments of Defaults	Projected Prepayments of Defaults	Difference Between At Issuance and Projected

Graph of Month-by-Month Default History

Graph of Cumulative Monthly Default History

EXHIBIT 22.4 Prepayment/Default Report Package schedule page. Table and graphs will plot up to 360 months of data

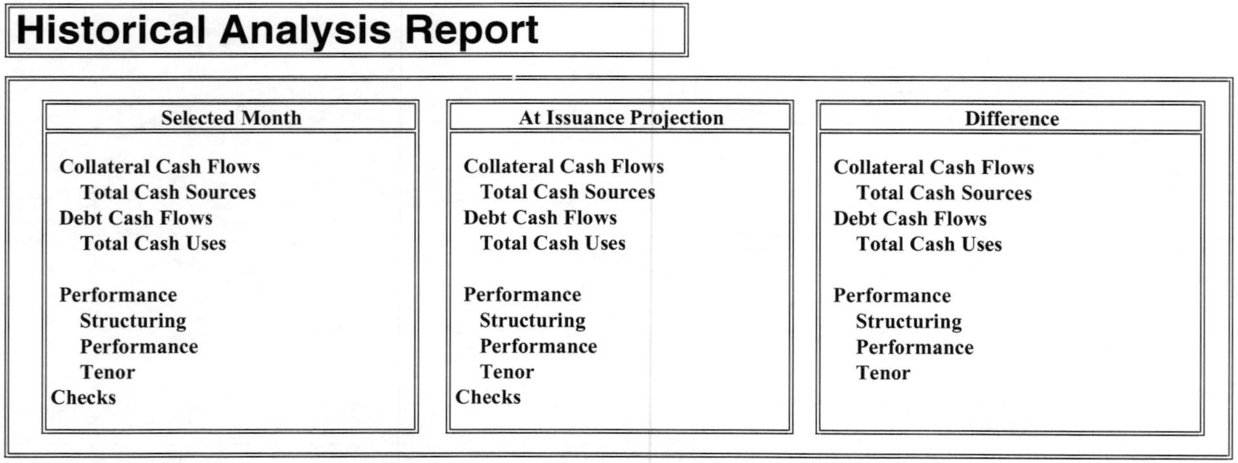

Historical Analysis Report

Selected Month	At Issuance Projection	Difference
Collateral Cash Flows Total Cash Sources Debt Cash Flows Total Cash Uses Performance Structuring Performance Tenor Checks	Collateral Cash Flows Total Cash Sources Debt Cash Flows Total Cash Uses Performance Structuring Performance Tenor Checks	Collateral Cash Flows Total Cash Sources Debt Cash Flows Total Cash Uses Performance Structuring Performance Tenor

EXHIBIT 22.5 Historical Period Performance Report Package

This fact obviates the need for anything resembling a collateral selection process. The collateral is no longer subject to replacement, substitution, or enhancement. "We are all going to heaven or we ain't," in the words of the Western song.

The first step in building the monitoring model will be to strip down the structuring model to the bare essentials whose functionality we can salvage. This will not be as hard as it may sound given that it is almost always easier to remove code than it is to create it. If we address the problem in a systemic manner, starting with the beginning of the model and working our way to the end, we will probably be okay!

Just keep in mind that this is an exercise that could be a lifesaver some day. I also predict that when you will need to do it, you will probably have to do it under some form of duress, time pressure, political pressure, economic pressure, and the like.

If you can pull the rabbit out of the hat in a situation like that, it is worth its weight in gold. It will certainly enforce the concept and value of compartmentalizing your code; writing specific, clear, and focused subroutines; and thinking about what you do before you leap into coding.

Removing the Unneeded Model Functionality

Congruent with all the above remarks, let's start the process from the beginning of the model and work toward its end. As we come upon various issues we will sort them out one at a time. Approaching this exercise in a deliberate manner is of paramount importance! Do not rush. Save your work often and sequentially number the saved copies you have made. If you do that you will not have to go very far to reverse yourself if something goes wrong.

We will start with a copy of the ADD_CAP model that we finished in Chapter 19, "Building Additional Capabilities." We will make a copy of it and rename it, (affectionately), **"ChopShop01.xls."** This will be our base line edit. We will immediately make another copy called **"ChopShop02.xls."** This will be the first version that we make our changes to.

If we start at the Main Program and proceed down the line of subroutine calls, we will delete or modify each portion of the model we need to change as we come to it. After each of these episodes, we will save the program, incrementing the version number by one until we find ourselves at the End Sub statement of the "Loan_Financing_Model." Along the way we will delete (or modify) menus, constants, global variables, subroutines, and many other items whose paths we will cross.

Unnecessary Menus and Their Attendant Support Code   Before we enter the "Loan_Financing_Model" code, we have some very obvious work to do at the Excel level of the model. There are a number of menus and reports that can be immediately eliminated.

The Main Menu   On the Main Menu we will first address the Program Execution Options section at the top. See Exhibit 22.6.

We can eliminate the choice to run the Collateral Selection process by elimination of the choices

```
Perform the Collateral Eligibility Test ? and
Write out Ineligible Collateral Reports ?
```

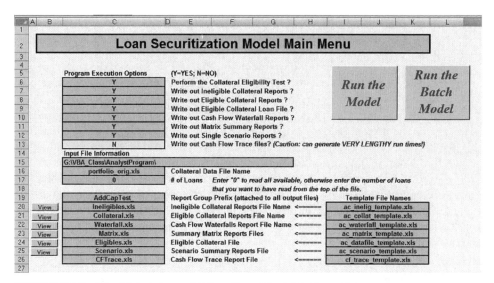

EXHIBIT 22.6 The Main Menu of "ChopShop_02.xls" before editing

Next we can eliminate the option:

```
Write out Eligible Collateral Loan File ?
```

All three of these choices relate to the collateral selection process or its results and are therefore no longer needed. The rest of the reports are both generally and specifically very useful for understanding the cash flows and the structural performance and they will be retained. We can modify them at a later point in time if necessary.

The next section we will visit is the Input Files Section of the menu. The first three fields of this section, the root directory pathway, the name of the collateral file, and the number of loans in the record, will be retained. We will clearly need all of them. Our entire file management code is dependent on the root directory information being in place. The name of the collateral file and the number of loans field will also be used in reading our monthly collateral files sent to us by the loan servicing group.

Below this line we once again have work to do. If we have eliminated the collateral selection process, we can also eliminate the fields of the menu that deal with the template files and reports files that support that activity. Next to go is the Ineligibles Report line and the Eligible Collateral Data File:

```
Ineligible Collateral Reports File Name
Eligible Collateral File
```

We will eliminate these two lines and the "View" report button associated with them. The Main Menu should now look like Exhibit 22.7.

The next thing we need to do is to disconnect any VBA code that was associated with these deleted fields. The first and easy thing to do is to delete the Range names associated with these fields. Using the Insert=>Name=>Define command we will trigger a pop-up menu named "Define Name" with all of the Range names for our model on it in alphabetical order.

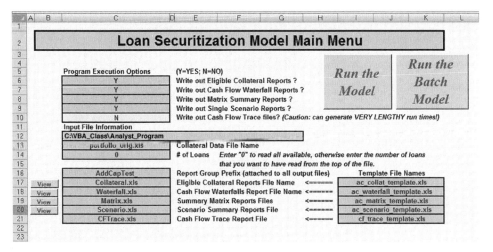

EXHIBIT 22.7   The edited Main Menu

From this menu, we will select each of the Range names for the six fields we deleted from the menu and delete them here. Instead of hunting around for the names in this list and trusting our increasingly fallible memory, we can go to the subroutine "**Read_Main_Menu**" and easily pick them from there. While we are at it we can delete the code from the subroutine as well. See Exhibit 22.8.

Our next stop is the "**A_Globals**" module, where we will delete the declarations of the variables. See Exhibit 22.9.

This is a good start. We have purged the Main Menu and have gotten rid of the unnecessary support variables and Ranges. We will progress to the next menu where we can eliminate the Program Costs Menu.

Program Costs Menu   Once the deal has been launched, nearly all the items in this menu are no longer necessary. In that all the costs and advance rates are now frozen for the remainder of the deal, we can transfer their values to constants declared in the "**A_Constants**" module. We can move the election of the LIBOR and Prime pathways from this menu to the Rates and Dates Menu. We can also designate the Conduit Spread level that we agreed upon at closing to this menu. We will simply put these choices in the header section of the menu at the top of the appropriate columns "C," "D," and "E." See Exhibit 22.10.

The next thing that we will do is eliminate the entire menu by deleting it using the Edit=>Delete Sheet command. We can now eliminate all the Range names of the menu. This is easily done in that they are all prefixed by the character combination "m2." We can now move to "**A_Globals**" and eliminate the variable declarations there. See Exhibit 22.11.

That finishes off the Program Costs menu for the moment.

Eligibility Report Screen   This menu is not an input menu, it is a report screen. It presents the results of the selection process. This function is no longer needed and we can delete the screen in its entirety. We will use the Edit=>Delete Sheet command.

```
Sub Read_Main_Menu()
  Sheets("Main Menu").Select
  Range("A1").Select
  ' Read the program runtime options selections
  g_run_exceptions = UCase(Range("m1CollatElig")) = "Y" 'run exceptions
                                                screening process ?
  g_write_exceptions = UCase(Range("m1WriteCollatInelig")) = "Y" 'write out exceptions
                                                reports ?
  g_write_reports = UCase(Range("m1WritePortReps")) = "Y" 'write out portfolio
                                                reports ?
  g_out_matrix = UCase(Range("m1WriteCFSummary")) = "Y"  'write out matrix cashflow
                                                reports ?
  g_out_cfdetail = UCase(Range("m1WriteCFDetail")) = "Y" 'write out detailed
                                                scenario cashflow reports
  g_out_cftrace = UCase(Range("m1WriteCFTrace")) = "Y"   'write out the loan-by-loan
                                                CF trace
  g_out_collat_file = UCase(Range("m1WriteEligCollatFile")) = "Y" 'write out a file
                                                of the eligibale
                                                collateral
  g_out_scen_file = UCase(Range("m1WriteScenSummary")) = "Y" 'write out a single
                                                scenario file
  ' Read deal name and number of loans in the collateral file
  g_pathway = Range("m1DirectoryPath")           'name of root directory for the code
  g_pathway_template = g_pathway & "template\"   'complete for the template directory
  g_pathway_output = g_pathway & "output\"       'complete for the output file
                                                directory
  g_total_loans = Range("m1CollatNumLoans")      'total loans in the portfolio
  'names of the output report files
  gfn_output_prefix = Range("m1FilePrefix")      'output files prefix
  gfn_collateral_file = Range("m1CollatRepName") 'data file of collateral information
  gfn_accepted_loans_file = Range("m1CollatFileName") 'output file for collateral
                                                reports
  gfn_waterfall_cfs_file = Range("m1CFFileName") 'output file for cashflow reports
  gfn_exceptions_file = Range("m1ExceptRepName") 'output file for ineligible
                                                collateral
  gfn_matrix_file = Range("m1MatrixRepName")     'output file for matrix report
                                                package
  gfn_elig_collat_file = Range("m1EligCollatName") 'output file for eligible
                                                collateral
  gfn_scenario_file = Range("m1ScenarioName")    'output file for single scenario
                                                report package
  gfn_cf_trace_file = Range("m1CFTraceName")     'output file Cash Flow Trace
                                                reports
  'names of the template files
  g_template_collateral = Range("templateCollat") 'template file collateral
                                                selected
  g_template_waterfall = Range("templateWaterfall") 'template file cash flow
                                                waterfall
  g_template_ineligible = Range("templateIneligible") 'template file ineligible
                                                collateral
  g_template_matrix = Range("templateMatrix")    'template file summary matrix
                                                reports
  g_template_elig_file = Range("templateEligCollat") 'template for the eligible
                                                collateral file
  g_template_scenario = Range("templateScenario") 'template for the single
                                                scenario file
  g_template_cf_trace = Range("templateCFTrace") 'template for the cash
                                                flow trace file
End Sub
```

EXHIBIT 22.8 Deleteing references to the eliminated fields of the Main Menu (deleted code in boldface)

```
'MAIN MENU VARIABLES
Public gfn_collateral_file     As String   'Name of the INPUT collateral data file
Public g_run_exceptions        As Boolean  'Run the selection criteria exceptions
                                            report
Public g_write_exceptions      As Boolean  'Write the selection criteria exceptions
                                            report
Public g_write_reports         As Boolean  'Write portfolio collateral reports
Public g_pathway               As String   'Directory level pathway
Public g_pathway_template      As String   'Report templates directory pathway
Public g_pathway_output        As String   'Outputs directory pathway
Public gfn_output_prefix       As String   'Prefix label concatenated to all
                                            output files
Public gfn_accepted_loans_file As String   'Name of OUTPUT collateral reports file
Public gfn_waterfall_cfs_file  As String   'Name of OUTPUT collateral cashflows file
Public gfn_exceptions_file     As String   'Name of OUTPUT exceptions reports file
Public gfn_matrix_file         As String   'Name of OUTPUT matrix summary file
Public gfn_elig_collat_file    As String   'Name of OUTPUT eligible collateral
                                            data file
Public gfn_scenario_file       As String   'Name of OUTPUT single scenario report
                                            file
Public gfn_cf_trace_file       As String   'Name of OUTPUT single scenario report
                                            file
Public g_out_matrix            As Boolean  'Switch to output the cashflow matrix
                                            reports
Public g_out_cfdetail          As Boolean  'Switch to output the period by period
                                            cf reports
Public g_out_cftrace           As Boolean  'Switch to produce file of monthly
                                            loan cash flows
Public g_out_collat_file       As Boolean  'Switch to output the eligible collateral
                                            file
Public g_out_scen_file         As Boolean  'Switch to output the eligible collateral
                                            file
Public g_total_loans           As Long     'Number of loans in the portfolio
Public g_template_collateral   As String   'template for the collateral reports
Public g_template_waterfall    As String   'template for the waterfall reports
Public g_template_ineligible   As String   'template file ineligible collateral
Public g_template_matrix       As String   'template file summary matrix reports
Public g_template_elig_file    As String   'template file name for eligibile
                                            collateral file
Public g_template_scenario     As String   'template file name for single scenarios
                                            file
Public g_template_cf_trace     As String   'template for the Cash Flow Trace report
```

EXHIBIT 22.9 Deletion of global variable declarations supporting the eliminated fields of the Main Menu (deleted code in boldface)

```
Public Const DEAL_SERVICE_FEE = 0.0075
Public Const DEAL_PROGRAM_FEE = 0.002
Public Const DEAL_CLEAN_UP_PCT = 0.1
Public Const DEAL_3_MTH_DEFAULT = 0.05
Public Const DEAL_ADVANCE_RATE = 0.95
Public Const DEAL_LIBOR_PATH = 1
Public Const DEAL_CONDUIT_SPREAD = 1
Public Const DEAL_PRIME_PATH = 1
```

EXHIBIT 22.10 Declarations of the Program Costs Menu contents into constant variables in the "A_Constants" module

```
' PROGRAM COST MENU VARIABLES
Public g_exp_service      As Double    'Percentage rate for servicing
Public g_exp_program      As Double    'Percentage for program expense fees
Public g_trig_cleanup     As Double    'Percentage for clean up call of notes
Public g_trig_3M_delinq   As Double    'Percentage of rolling 3 month delinquencies
Public g_advance_rate     As Double    'Conduit advance rate
Public g_conduit_spread   As Double    'Conduit financing spread
```

EXHIBIT 22.11   Declarations of the Program Cost global variables in the **"A_Globals"** module (all code shown deleted)

All the Range names associated with this screen begin with the character combination of "m3." Using the Inser=>Name=>Define command we can now eliminate them as well. Next we can go to the **"A_Globals"** module and delete the declarations of the variables there. See Exhibit 22.12.

Selection Criteria Menu   The Collateral Criteria Menu is now to be deleted. We note that all the Range names associated with this menu begin with the character code "m5." We delete those Range names first and then the menu itself. We now proceed to the **"A_Globals"** module and delete the following section of it. See Exhibit 22.13.

We can now also delete a number of support constants for the Program Costs Menu and the Collateral Criteria Menu. See Exhibit 22.14.

We have now eliminated three menus entirely, all their Range names, and many if not all of their supporting variables. It is time to save another version of "ChopShop." Let's use the SaveAs command to create **"ChopShop_04.xls."**

Geographic Menu   With ChopShop_04.xls in hand, we now have only two more menus to address. The first is the Geographic Selection Menu. While we will need to use geographic data in the monitoring model, we will not need to do collateral selections using it. To this end, we will delete the menu and the Range names but not the support variables in so much as they do not support the collateral selection process. The Range names for this screen all begin with the character combination "m6."

```
Public g_sum_wac                    As Double    'running total wac
Public g_sum_rem                    As Double    'running total rem term
Public g_sum_sea                    As Double    'running total seasoning
Public g_sum_wac_1                  As Double    'final eligible wac
Public g_sum_rem_1                  As Double    'final eligible wgh rem term
Public g_sum_sea_1                  As Double    'final eligible wgh seasoning
Public g_acc_cur_bal                As Double    'eligible balances
Public g_rej_cur_bal                As Double    'ineligible balances
Public g_grand_total                As Double    'total portfolio balances
Public g_pct_accepted               As Double    '% balances eligible
Public g_pct_rejected               As Double    '% balances ineligible
Public g_number_accepted            As Double    'loan count eligible
Public g_number_rejected            As Double    'loan count ineligible

Public g_inelig_loan(1 To INELIG_SINGLE_REPS) As Long    'by type ineligible loans
Public g_inelig_bals(1 To INELIG_SINGLE_REPS) As Double 'by type ineligible balances
```

EXHIBIT 22.12   Declarations of global variables for the Eligibility Report screen

```
' SELECTION CRITERIA MENU VARIABLES
Public g_crit_min_orig_term         As Double   'Min original term in months
Public g_crit_max_orig_term         As Double   'Max original term in months
Public g_crit_min_rem_term          As Double   'Min remaining term in months
Public g_crit_max_rem_term          As Double   'Max remaining term in months
Public g_crit_min_orig_bal          As Double   'Min original balance
Public g_crit_max_orig_bal          As Double   'Max original balance
Public g_crit_min_rem_bal           As Double   'Min remaining balance
Public g_crit_max_rem_bal           As Double   'Max remaining balance
Public g_crit_max_del               As Double   'Max times delinquent ever
Public g_crit_max_loan              As Double   'Max loan LTV
Public g_crit_min_spread(1 To 6)    As Double   'Min spread to floating rate index
Public g_crit_acc_index(1 To 6)     As String   'Min spread to floating rate index
Public g_crit_max_spread            As Double   'Min spread to floating rate index
Public g_crit_min_coupon            As Double   'Min current yield
Public g_crit_max_coupon            As Double   'Max current yield
Public g_crit_pay_diff              As Double   'Max diff between stated/calculated pmt
```

EXHIBIT 22.13 The global variables, which support the Collateral Criteria Menu (all code deleted)

We can now also delete all the support code behind the buttons that include/exclude portions of the menu listings. See Exhibit 22.15.

Coupon Trace Report The Coupon Trace Report was added during the validation phase of the original model. We have validated that the floating rate reset VBA code is working as designed and we no longer need this feature in the model.

We will delete the report screen and its supporting subroutine. This subroutine is triggered directly from the report and is not part of the Main Program hierarchy. All the VBA support code is found in the "Z_Buttons" module. See Exhibit 22.16.

The trace function takes the information that it is displaying from the subroutine "Calculate_Loan_Floater_Coupon_Levels," so we need to remove the lines from that subroutine as well. See Exhibit 22.17

Although they are not related to the Coupon Trace function, since we are in the neighborhood of the "Z_Button" module we can take this opportunity to delete the button support subroutines for the main menu files we deleted earlier. See Exhibit 22.18.

Once again we have hit a critical mass in deletions. We will take this opportunity to save the file in its current state as the next iteration of ChopShop, "ChopShop05.xls."

Error Checking Subroutines We are now ready to go into the VBA Editor and follow the calls of the main program. As we step through the processes of the model

```
'Selection Criteria Menu
Public Const SEL_CRIT_FIELDS = 11              '# selection criteria parameter fields
Public Const SEL_CRIT_INDEX_SPREADS = 6        '# spread/index fields to check
'Program Costs Menu
Public Const PROG_COSTS_FIELDS = 8             '# fields on Program Costs menu
```

EXHIBIT 22.14 Delete the support constants for the Program Costs Menu and the Collateral Criteria Menu (all code deleted)

```
'=======================================
'    GEOGRAPHIC MENU BUTTON SUBROUTINES
'=======================================
Sub Include_National_Portfolio()
    For i_state = 1 To STATES_PER_COL
        Range("m6States1").Cells(i_state) = "X"
        Range("m6States2").Cells(i_state) = "X"
        Range("m6States3").Cells(i_state) = "X"
    Next i_state
End Sub
Sub Exclude_National_Portfolio()
    For i_state = 1 To STATES_PER_COL
        Range("m6States1").Cells(i_state) = ""
        Range("m6States2").Cells(i_state) = ""
        Range("m6States3").Cells(i_state) = ""
    Next i_state
End Sub
'=======================================
'    Include/Exclude New England
'=======================================
Sub Include_New_England()
    Cells(10, 2).Value = "X"       'Connecticut
    Cells(4, 6).Value = "X"        'Massachusetts
    Cells(6, 6).Value = "X"        'Maine
    Cells(15, 6).Value = "X"       'New Hampshire
    Cells(6, 10).Value = "X"       'Rhode Island
    Cells(13, 10).Value = "X"      'Vermont
End Sub
Sub Exclude_New_England()
    Cells(10, 2).Value = ""        'Connecticut
    Cells(4, 6).Value = ""         'Massachusetts
    Cells(6, 6).Value = ""         'Maine
    Cells(15, 6).Value = ""        'New Hampshire
    Cells(6, 10).Value = ""        'Rhode Island
    Cells(13, 10).Value = ""       'Vermont
End Sub
```

EXHIBIT 22.15   Four of the button support subroutines from the now deleted Geographic Menu (all code deleted)

we will find VBA code related to the functions we have just deleted. We will remove these from the model as well.

The first major step on the main subroutine is the call to subroutine "ErrCheck_All_Menus." We will trace the calls of this subroutine and continue to prepare the model for its transition to a monitoring system.

"ErrCheck_All_Menu" Subroutine   This subroutine is the top subroutine for all the error checking that is done against the menus prior to reading any of the data into the model. It contains the highest level calls to a series of other subroutines that each performs a specialized series of error checking. With many of the original menu deleted, we will need to carefully go through this module and pare out anything no longer needed by the model.

In this subroutine itself we can immediately see that some of the high-level calls and subroutines under them can be eliminated. See Exhibit 22.19.

In addition to deleting the Program Cost, Geographic, and Selection Criteria menu error checking subroutines, we will have to edit both the "errAllMenus_for_IsNumerics" and the "errMainMenu" subroutines.

```
'=========================================================
'   Populate the Loan Coupon Trace Graph
'=========================================================
Sub Populate_Coupon_Trace_Graph()

Dim t_loan              As Long    '# of the loan selected for trace
Dim error_type(1 To 2)  As Boolean 'one of two types of errors

    'Error check the input number before we do anything else so the
    ' program doesn't blow up on the trace
    Call Error_Check_Coupon_Trace_Graph
    'if you get to here the input has passed and we can proceed
    t_loan = Trim(Range("CouponTraceLoan"))
    'clear the current contents of the range if any
    Range("CouponTraceSch").ClearContents
    Calculate
    'load the new contents in based on the loan #
    For i = 1 To PAY_DATES
        If g_val_coup_trace(t_loan, i, 4) > 0# Then
            Range("CouponTraceSch").Cells(i, 1) = g_val_coup_trace(t_loan, i, 1)
                'coupon rate
            Range("CouponTraceSch").Cells(i, 2) = g_val_coup_trace(t_loan, i, 2)
                'index
            Range("CouponTraceSch").Cells(i, 3) = g_val_coup_trace(t_loan, i, 3)
                'period floor
            Range("CouponTraceSch").Cells(i, 4) = g_val_coup_trace(t_loan, i, 4)
                'period cap
            Range("CouponTraceSch").Cells(i, 5) = g_loan_life_floor(t_loan)
                'life floor
            Range("CouponTraceSch").Cells(i, 6) = g_loan_life_cap(t_loan)
                'life cap
        Else
            Calculate
            Exit For
        End If
    Next i

End Sub
```

EXHIBIT 22.16   The subroutine that populated the Coupon Trace Report

The subroutine "Error_Check_Coupon_Trace_Report" will also be deleted from this module.

With these subroutines removed, we can now start to step through the largest of the error checking subroutine trees, the one that checks for numeric entries throughout the menus of the model. The highest level subroutine in this chain is the

```
'if we are doing a coupon rate trace catch that information now
    ' 1 = computed coupon level, 2 = current index level, 3 = period floor
    ' 4 = periodic cap, the life time floor and caps are constant
    If g_val_coup_trace_switch Then
        g_val_coup_trace(iloan, itrace, 1) = beg_rate
        g_val_coup_trace(iloan, itrace, 2) = g_index_levels(itrace, ifloat)
        g_val_coup_trace(iloan, itrace, 3) = beg_rate - g_loan_reset_cap(iloan)
        g_val_coup_trace(iloan, itrace, 4) = beg_rate + g_loan_reset_cap(iloan)
    End If
```

EXHIBIT 22.17   The code that captures the information displayed in the Coupon Trace screen (all code deleted)

```
Option Explicit

Dim irow                As Integer        'generic row counter
Dim icol                As Integer        'generic column counter
Dim i                   As Integer        'generic loop counter
Dim i1                  As Integer        'generic loop counter
Dim i_state             As Integer        'generic state counter


'================================================================
'   Open Output reports
'================================================================
Sub Button_View_Collateral_Reports_File()
Workbooks.Open Filename:=g_pathway_output & gfn_output_prefix & _
                          gfn_accepted_loans_file

End Sub
Sub Button_View_Ineligible_Loans_File()
Workbooks.Open Filename:=g_pathway_output & gfn_output_prefix & _
                          gfn_exceptions_file

End Sub
Sub Button_View_Cash_Flow_Waterfall_File()
    Workbooks.Open Filename:=g_pathway_output & gfn_output_prefix & gfn_waterfall_
                                                                   cfs_file

End Sub
Sub Button_View_Matrix_File()
    Workbooks.Open Filename:=g_pathway_output & gfn_output_prefix & gfn_matrix_file
End Sub
Sub Button_View_Collateral_File()
    Workbooks.Open Filename:=g_pathway_output & gfn_output_prefix & gfn_elig_collat_
                                                                   file

End Sub
Sub Button_View_Single_Scenario_File()
    Workbooks.Open Filename:=g_pathway_output & gfn_output_prefix & gfn_scenario_file
End Sub
```

EXHIBIT 22.18   Deleting the button support code for the Main Menu output files we removed earlier (all code in boldface deleted)

"errAllMenus_for_IsNumerics" subroutine. This subroutine in turn calls four others. Fortunately for us, these calls are organized around the menus they support. Two of these menus we have already eliminated. We can therefore eliminate the calls to these subroutines and the subroutines themselves. See Exhibit 22.20.

To complete the process we need only go to each of the two remaining subroutines, those that support the Rates and Dates menu and the Defaults/Prepayments

```
Sub ErrCheck_All_Menus()

    'Set up of message title
    msgTitle = "MODEL MENUs Input Error"
    Call errAllMenus_for_IsNumerics
    Call errMainMenu
    Call errProgramCostsMenu
    Call errReportsMenu
    Call errGeographicMenu
    Call errSelectionCriteriaMenu
    Call errDefaultsMenu

End Sub
```

EXHIBIT 22.19   The "ErrCheck_All_Menus" subroutine showing deleted lines to high-level error checking subroutines (code in boldface deleted)

```
Sub errAllMenus_for_IsNumerics()

    Call IsNumeric_ProgramCostsInfo      'populates msgInfo(1) & errcase(1)
    Call IsNumeric_CriteriaInfo          'populates msgInfo(2) & errcase(2)
    Call IsNumeric_DefaultPrepayInfo     'populates msgInfo(3) & errcase(3)
    Call IsNumeric_RatesDatesInfo        'populates msgInfo(4) & errcase(4)

    'If there are errors to print -- print them!
    err_total = errcase(1) + errcase(2) + errcase(3) + errcase(4)
    If err_total > 0 Then
        'Error box title -- displayed above any errors
        msgTotal = "Non-numeric Inputs for the following Tables" & Chr(13) & Chr(13)
        'Print the combination of errors based on the error code value
        For iloop = 1 To MENU_CHECK_NUMERIC
            If errcase(iloop) > 0 Then msgTotal = msgTotal & msgInfo(iloop)
        Next iloop
        msgPrompt = msgTotal
        msgResult = MsgBox(msgPrompt, cMsgButtonCode1, msgTitle)
        End
    End If

End Sub
```

EXHIBIT 22.20   We no longer need error checking for the program Costs and the Selection Criteria menus. We reduce the number of locations in the errcase variable from 4 to 2 to reflect this. We will also change the index notation on the **"msgInfo"** array from 3 to 1 and 4 to 2 respectively for the two remaining error checking subroutines

menu and change the references for errcase from 3 and 4, respectively, to 1 and 2, respectively. See Exhibit 22.21.

"errMainMenu" Subrotuine   This subroutine error checks the Main Menu. We had eliminated a number of features and fields from it and will need to adjust this subroutine accordingly. See Exhibit 22.22.

Each of these subroutines follows the same general form. First a list of error messages are declared. Second a set of test criteria, generally embedded in a Select...Case statement, is consulted to verify the existence or nonexistence of the file being referenced. If the test fails, a trigger is set. At the end of the subroutine, the triggers are used to build a compound message made up of the original list of simple messages as to which files are in violation. The subroutines are simple but

```
'combine any or all of the above messages into a compound message
'the compound message will be sent to the calling sub for display
    errcase(3) = False          'no non numerics detected
    For itest = 1 To ISNUMERIC_TESTS_PRE_DEF
        If err_result(itest) = True Then          'got one!
            errcase(3) = errcase(3) + 1           'tell calling sub to print out
            msgInfo(3) = msgInfo(3) & msgComp(itest) 'add detail msg to general
                                                     header msg
        End If
    Next itest
```

EXHIBIT 22.21   This is a portion of the code from the Defaults and Prepayment menu error checking subroutine. We only need to change the reference from errcase(3) to errcase(1) and MsgInfo(3) to MsgInfo(1) and we are finished!

```
Sub errMainMenu()

    Call errMainMenu_FilesCheckTemplate
    Call errMainMenu_FilesCheckOutput
    Call errMainMenu_FieldsFilledIn

End Sub
```

EXHIBIT 22.22 The "errMainMenu" subroutine calls three others, each of which checks either a series of files to protect them from being overwritten when the model is run or that the entries for the Program Execution block have the proper files to complete the actions requested

lengthy. Fortunately, the corrective action merely consists of eliminating the appropriate messages from the initial list and eliminating the unnecessary tests. All that then remains is to renumber the indices of the messages, tests, and triggers to be correctly correlated. We will not cover these in detail here.

That concludes our work with the error checking subroutines. This is a clear stopping place. We now SaveAs **"ChopShop_06.xls"** and we are ready to proceed.

Reading Data from the Menus The next stop, if we continue to follow the flow of the Main Program, will be the set of subroutines that reads the menu and files and transfers the now error checked data into the arrays of the model. It is in a form very similar to the error checking code, as we would expect. There is a call from the Main Program to the subroutine "Read_All_Menu_Input." This subroutine then reads each of the menus in turn collecting the now, we hope, error-free information. See Exhibit 22.23.

We will remove the subroutines highlighted in boldface in Exhibit 22.24 Of the remainder we will have no changes to the Report Selection, the Prepays and Defaults, or the Rates and Dates read menu subroutines. We have, however, modified the Main Menu and need to remove the deleted items from the subroutine "Read_Main_Menu." See Exhibit 22.24.

Our next stop is the collateral selection process. Now would be a good time to save the ChopShop to version 7, **"ChopShop_07.xls."**

Collateral Selection Functionality The last major task in preparing the code for the new model will be to remove any remaining features of the collateral selection

```
Sub Read_All_Menu_Input()

    Call Read_Main_Menu                  'Read Main Menu -- set program run options
    Call Read_Program_Costs_Menu         'Reads the program costs inputs
    Call Read_Selection_Criteria_Menu    'Read tenor, coupon & balance selection
                                          criteria
    Call Read_Report_Selection_Menu      'Read menu for report selections
    Call Read_Geographic_Menu            'Read state code geographic selection criteria
    Call Read_Prepay_Defaults_Menu       'Read prepayment and default schedule to apply
    Call Read_Rates_and_Dates_Menu       'Read the rates and dates menu
    Call Read_Coupon_Trace_Screen        'Read the Coupon Trace report switch

End Sub
```

EXHIBIT 22.23 The "Read_All_Menu_Inputs" subroutine (deleted code is in boldface)

```
Sub Read_Main_Menu()

    (code omitted)
    gfn_collateral_file = Range("m1CollatRepName")   'data file of collateral)
                                                         information
    (code omitted)
    g_template_collateral = Range("templateCollat")  'template file collateral)
                                                         selected

End Sub
```

EXHIBIT 22.24   Lines to be removed from the "Read_Main_Menu" subroutine

process. We have already removed the menu and its Range names and supporting variables. We now must find and remove the selection code itself and separate it from the code that produces the eligible collateral items.

If we return to the "Loan_Financing_Model," we can see that the next step down the main program is a call to "Read_Portfolio_Data_File." There is nothing in this code that we would wish to change; we can use it in an almost unmodified state in the monitoring model. The next subroutine call is very different. Here we have the call to "Select_Deal_Collateral." See Exhibit 22.25. This subroutine does more than select the collateral. It also publishes two report sets, one on the ineligible collateral; and the other on the eligible. We need to remove only the code that performs the selection process and then reports the ineligible loans. To the extent that some of this code supported the Eligibility Report screen, we will also remove it.

The "Clear_Eligibility_Accumulators" subroutine can be removed in that it serves to feed information to the Eligibility Report screen.

The "Run_Selection_Criteria" can also be removed as can all subroutines that are exclusively called by it. The subroutine named "Write_Ineligibility_Reports" can be eliminated in its entirety. Lastly, the subroutine named "Write_Eligible_Collateral_File" will be removed from the model.

The VBA that writes the Ineligible Collateral Reports Package is entirely contained within the module **"WriteIneligibilityReports"** and all we need to do is delete the module.

```
Sub Select_Deal_Collateral()

  Call Clear_Eligibility_Accumulators
  If g_run_exceptions Then Call Run_Selection_Criteria
                                     'run the loans through the criteria
  If g_write_exceptions Then Call Write_Ineligibility_Reports
                                     'write exceptions if any
  Call Setup_Report_Workbook          'set up collateral reports file
  Call Final_Loan_Status_Report(True)  'final loan report for all loans
  g_total_loans = Compress_the_Portfolio 'rewrite portfolio info, selected lons only
  'Write the portfolio demographic reports -- only selected reports will be produced
  If g_write_reports Then Call Write_Portfolio_Demographic_Reports
  If g_out_collat_file Then Call Write_Eligible_Collateral_File

End Sub
```

EXHIBIT 22.25   The "Select_Deal_Collateral" subroutine (deleted code is in boldface)

Writing the Collateral Data File Functionality   The same is true of the VBA code that writes the collateral file of eligible loans only. Removing the module "**Write-CollateralFile**" will eliminate this functionality from the model.

These changes will bring us to another stopping point and another version of ChopShop, "**ChopStop _08.xls.**"

Changing the Format of the Assumptions File   Consistent with the fact that we no longer need to perform the collateral selection, we do not need to inform the user of the selection criteria in the various Assumptions Report pages of the reports. We can eliminate the portion of the report that displays those items, potentially freeing it up for information that will help us in the monitoring model.

The changes to the subroutines in the "**WriteAssumptionsReport**" module follow. See Exhibit 22.26.

Creating and Editing the New Report Template Files   Until we just made those changes to the "Write_Assumptions_Page" subroutine, we have done nothing that will directly impact any of the reports that we will retain from the structuring model and use in the monitoring model. With that change, however, we now need to bring the reformatted Assumptions page into alignment with the VBA code of the model. To do this we will create a series of new template files that are the "monitoring twins" of the report packages that we use for the structuring model.

We will make copies of the templates for Eligible Collateral Reports file, the Cash Flow Waterfall file, the Matrix Summary file, and the Single Scenario Report file. We will preface each of these with the designator "m_" to distinguish them from their predecessors of the structuring model.

On the Assumptions worksheet of each of these template files we will remove the following sections:

- **The Collateral Selection Criteria.** This is the Range of cells from B13 to G21 inclusive.
- **The Indices and Minimum Spread Criteria.** This is the Range of cells from B22 to G29 inclusive.
- **The Collateral Characteristics report.** This is the Range of cells from B32 to J46.
- **The Geographic Selection Table.** This is the Range of cells from P3 to R57.

The "Assumptions" worksheets of the template files are now ready to use with the monitoring model. We will now save the edited program to be "**ChopShop_ 09.xls.**"

A Bit of Final Clean-Up before Moving On   We have now finished with the removal of code from our copy of the old structuring model. At this point we might want to take a moment and compile the code that remains and see if we have left anything hanging loose so to speak. Let's compile "**ChopShop_09.xls**" and see if anything pops out of the woodwork.

We get a clean compile from "**ChopShop_09.xls.**" This is good; it means that the model has hopefully retained all of its old functionality. There is one way to test and that is simply to run the model and observe its activity. If we run the model against the initial collateral file with the selection criteria in place, all the loans will

```
Option Explicit

Dim irow                    As Integer      'generaic row counter
Dim icol                    As Integer      'generic column counter
Dim i_count                 As Integer      'counter
'===============================================================================
' Write_Assumptions_Page
' writes all model assumptions into a single template page which is included in
  all output files
'===============================================================================
Sub Write_Assumptions_Page()

    Sheets("Assumptions").Select

    'SECTION I - Program Costs, Selection Critera, Spread Information
    'load the program costs section
    Cells(4, 2).Value = g_exp_service * 12#    'servicing fee
    Cells(5, 2).Value = g_exp_program * 12#    'program expenses
    Cells(6, 2).Value = g_conduit_spread       'condit financing spread
    Cells(8, 2).Value = 1 - g_advance_rate     'Seller Interest percentage
    Cells(10, 2).Value = g_trig_3M_delinq      'principal reallocation trigger
    Cells(12, 2).Value = g_trig_cleanup        'principal reallocation trigger
    'load the collateral selelction criteria
    Cells(15, 2).Value = g_crit_min_orig_term 'min original term in months
    Cells(15, 4).Value = g_crit_max_orig_term 'max original term in months
    Cells(16, 2).Value = g_crit_min_rem_term  'min remaining term in months
    Cells(16, 4).Value = g_crit_max_rem_term  'max remaining term in months
    Cells(17, 2).Value = g_crit_min_orig_bal  'min original balance
    Cells(17, 4).Value = g_crit_max_orig_bal  'max original balance
    Cells(18, 2).Value = g_crit_min_rem_bal   'min remaining balance
    Cells(18, 4).Value = g_crit_max_rem_bal   'max remaining balance
    Cells(19, 2).Value = g_crit_min_coupon    'min gross coupon
    Cells(19, 4).Value = g_crit_max_coupon    'max gross coupon
    Cells(20, 4).Value = g_crit_max_loan      'max LTV ratio
    Cells(21, 4).Value = g_crit_pay_diff      'allowable difference stated/calc pmt
    'write the spread information
    i_count = 1
    For irow = 24 To 29
        Cells(irow, 2).Value = g_crit_acc_index(i_count)
        Cells(irow, 4).Value = g_crit_min_spread(i_count)
        i_count = i_count + 1
    Next irow

    'SECTION II - Prepayment and default assumptions
    (26 lines of code not displayed from display - all retained)

    'SECTION III - Geographic Selection Parameters
    'load the state and territory selections
    For irow = 1 To 54
        Cells(4 + irow - 1, 16) = g_state_select(irow)
    Next irow

    'SECTION IV - Collateral Selection Results
    'summary statistics
    Cells(34, 2).Value = g_total_loans
    Cells(35, 2).Value = g_grand_total
    Cells(37, 2).Value = g_number_rejected
    Cells(38, 2).Value = g_rej_cur_bal
    Cells(39, 2).Value = g_pct_rejected
    Cells(41, 2).Value = g_number_accepted
```

EXHIBIT 22.26 Removing the collateral selection criteria sections from the "Write_Assumptions_Report" subroutine (*some code not displayed as noted*, deleted code is in bold)

```
    Cells(42, 2).Value = g_acc_cur_bal
    Cells(43, 2).Value = g_pct_accepted
    Cells(44, 2).Value = g_sum_wac_1
    Cells(45, 2).Value = g_sum_rem_1
    Cells(46, 2).Value = g_sum_sea_1
    'ineligibles by rejection condition
    For irow = 1 To INELIG_SINGLE_REPS
        Cells(irow + 35, 6) = ""
        Cells(irow + 35, 7) = ""
        If g_inelig_bals(irow) > 0# Then
                Cells(irow + 35, 7) = g_inelig_bals(irow)
        End If
        If g_inelig_loan(irow) > 0# Then
                Cells(irow + 35, 6) = g_inelig_loan(irow)
        End If
    Next irow

    'SECTION V - Rates and Dates Schedule
    (10 lines of code not displayed from display - all retained)

End Sub
```

EXHIBIT 22.26   (*Continued*)

be eligible. The model will then precisely produce the reports that we generated in the first model run of the sizing exercise!

We can also run cashflows using the structuring model with the selection criteria turned off. This should produce (with identical inputs of course), the same results we get from the now reduced **"ChopShop_09.xls"** model.

MODIFYING SOME OF THE CODE

We have now finished the phase of the project where we are simply removing code from the model. In this next phase we will work within the remaining portions of the structuring model in the direction of developing a fully functional monitoring model. We will need to make changes to several parts of the model to accomplish this.

We will create a total of three new reports and modify all of the surviving structuring model reports in some manner. Each of the new reports will have to have its own template file, a program execution field to allow the user to select it, an output filename field, and all the supporting VBA to move this information from the menus to the model. We will need to add error checking for all of these new fields. We may have to write new calculation or collection subroutines if the specific data for the new reports is not in hand. Lastly, especially with reports, we will have to build new subroutines to find the correct template files, open, populate, and save them.

This is a lot of work but we are confident that with our earlier experience constructing the structuring model, we have the tools to do the job. Not only that, but we have the examples and framework of the earlier model to build from. We will be adding new features, calculation methods, and reports, but it is nothing that we have not done before.

Remember this as you work. The time is ticking away. In a couple of weeks the boss is going to need a monitoring model up and running in time for the first of the new servicing reports that will be arriving. We need to understand what is happening with the deal, and soon.

Modifications to the Main Menu   As discussed earlier in the chapter we are going to add five new reports to the model. These new reports will be in addition to the old four that we are retaining from the structuring model, the Cash Flow Waterfall, the Matrix Summary, the Single Scenario, and the CF Trace report. That means we will have an increased number of Program Execution fields at the top of the Main Menu. Further down, we will have at least five new lines added to the Report File Names section of the menu. This is becoming a very crowded menu! With these additions we may not be able to display the entire menu at once, and even if we can, we need to allow for future growth.

It is time to split the Main Menu into two parts. The first part, which is now the upper one-half of the menu will remain and continue to be called the Main Menu. It will contain the Program Execution fields and the Input File Information blocks as they currently exist. To it we will add any new Program Execution options fields, any additional File Information fields, and a new section called the Update File Information section. It is in this section that we will add a new field that will indicate the number of months of issuance since the inception of the deal. This is a critical field for the model in that it identifies the separation boundary between the empirical (actual) experience of the pool and the still undetermined future that we must continue to estimate.

We will move the remaining fields of the Main Menu into a new menu entitled the File Menu. This menu will contain the names of the template files of the model and their corresponding output file names. It will also contain two new files. These are the designated Base Case files. There are two of them, a Cash Flow Waterfall file and a Summary Matrix, which were run with all the starting assumptions of the deal that we issued six months ago. The prepayment and default assumptions used the PSA methodology and the speeds were 200 PSA and 400 PSA, respectively.

When complete, the two menus will look like those in Exhibits 22.27 and 22.28.

You will note that there are Program Execution Option fields for all the new reports on the Main menu. On the File menu we have fields for each of the new template files, fields for the names of each of the files, a "View" button to look at each of the reports directly from the menu. We also have fields for the two Base Case files that will be the "At Issuance" cases that we will read into the model and use for all our comparisons.

At the bottom of the menu we have a small matrix. This matrix will allow us to specify up to 20 time periods. Each of these time periods is an offset interval. This is to say that if you put a "1" in one of the matrix locations the model will compare the performance of the deal from one month ago, to the at issuance performance and report on the divergence, if any, between the two projections. Let's look at the VBA support code that we need to develop to accommodate this menu splitting. We will take the Main Menu first.

Changes to the Main Menu Support Code   The first thing that we notice is that most of the bottom of the Main Menu is not there anymore. That means that it is no longer

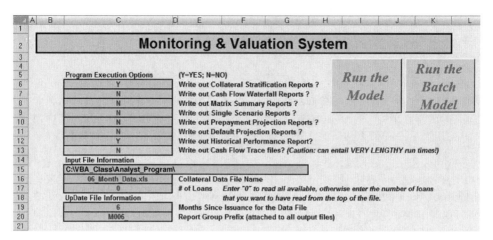

EXHIBIT 22.27   The revised format of the Main Menu

the responsibility of the Main Menu subroutines. Specifically these subroutines are the "errMainMenu" and "Read_Main_Menu."

After the division of the menus, the first subroutine, "errMainMenu," will call two "child" subroutines. The first of these checks the contents of the Program Execution fields and the second checks that there are appropriate entries in the Input File Information fields and the Update File Information fields. The revised error checking subroutine for the Program Execution fields is shown in Exhibit 22.29.

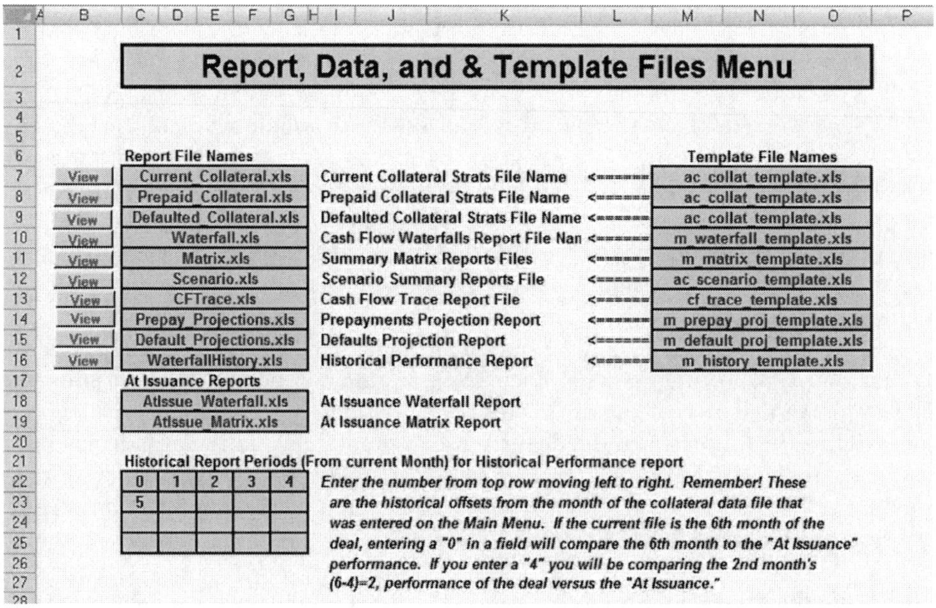

EXHIBIT 22.28   The format of the File Menu

```
Sub errMainMenu_RunOptions_YesOrNo()

(5 variable declaration lines not displayed)

    msgTotal = "MAIN MENU INPUT ERROR MESSAGES " & Chr(13) & Chr(13)
    msgTop = "MUST RESPOND EITHER Y OR N ONLY FOR RUN OPTION FIELDS" _
            & Chr(13)
    msgInfo(1) = " RUN OPTION for Current Collateral Reports" & Chr(13)
    msgInfo(2) = " RUN OPTION for Prepaid Collateral Reports" & Chr(13)
    msgInfo(3) = " RUN OPTION for Default Collateral Reports" & Chr(13)
    (4 lines of msgInfo(4) to msgInfo(7) declarations not displayed)
    msgInfo(8) = " RUN OPTION for Prepayments Performance Report" & Chr(13)
    msgInfo(9) = " RUN OPTION for Defaults Performance Report" & Chr(13)
    msgInfo(10) = " RUN OPTION for Historical Performance Report" & Chr(13)
    (5 lines of comments not displayed)
    For iblock = 1 To OUTPUT_FILE_TESTS
        'load the appropriate messages and conditions for error checking by report
        Select Case iblock
            Case Is = 1: option_test = UCase(Trim(Range("m1WriteStratReports")))
            Case Is = 2: option_test = UCase(Trim(Range("m1WriteStratReports")))
            Case Is = 3: option_test = UCase(Trim(Range("m1WriteStratReports")))
            (4 lines of case Is = N statements not displayed)
            Case Is = 8: option_test = UCase(Trim(Range("m1WritePrepays")))
            Case Is = 9: option_test = UCase(Trim(Range("m1WriteDefaults")))
            Case Is = 10: option_test = UCase(Trim(Range("m1WriteHistory")))
        End Select
        (4 lines of code not displayed)
    Next iblock

    (7 lines of code not displayed)

End Sub
```

EXHIBIT 22.29   The revised error checking code for the Program Execution section of the Main Menu (new code is in boldface)

The second error testing subroutine merely checks that each of the fields in the lower half of the menu have an entry in them.

New Files Menu Error Checking Code   The error checking burden that had been shifted from the structure models Main Menu error checking code had to go some-where (the inputs fields were still being used), and so it ended up in the Files Menu support code.

The main subroutine that checks this code will perform the same functions as those of the Main Menu. See Exhibit 22.30.

As you will note when you look at the first three subroutines called by the "errFileMenu" subroutine, you will see that the only changes have been to accom-modate the five new reports we are adding for the monitoring effort. The fourth call is entirely new and checks for certain consistencies in the 20-cell matrix used to get the historical monthly offsets for use by the Historical Report Package. This grid allows the user to compare up to 20 prior periods of performance to the At Issuance projected performance to determine if there are any trends. If you enter a "0," "1," "2," and "3" into the matrix, you will receive four comparative reports of the most recent information zero months ago, to one, two, and three months ago, to the At Issuance projections.

```
Sub errFilesMenu()

    'checks if the template files are there if the report has been requested
    Call errFilesMenu_FilesCheckTemplate
    'checks if the output file names are there if the report has been requested
    Call errFilesMenu_FilesCheckOutput
    'cross checks if the user has selected a run option there is a corrresponding
     output file
    '  name designated on the File Menu
    Call errFilesMenu_RunOptionCrossCheck
    'check for inconsistencies in the table of Historical Peformance offset months
    Call errFilesMenu_HistoryOffsetMonths)

End Sub
```

EXHIBIT 22.30   The new "errFilesMenu subroutine." The first three error checking subroutines were inherited from the Main Menu, the last check the input matrix for the Historical Report Package

This being the case, we should test for the following:

- No entry is nonnumeric.
- No entry is negative.
- No entry can be greater than the entry in the field on the Main Menu that is named "Months Since Issuance."

To meet these requirements, we have written the following subroutine. See Exhibit 22.31.

The rest of the menu support code for these two menus is fairly straightforward in nature. The subroutines that read the data from the menus are simply bifurcated subroutines of the old "Read_Main_Menu" subroutine with the statements to support the additional five new monitoring reports.

Creating the Portfolio Profile Report   The Portfolio Profile Report is intended to serve as the equivalent of the Eligibility Results Report of the structuring code. In that model, it was of vital importance to understand what the outcome of the collateral selection process looked like. You needed to know how much collateral you had (and what it looked like), and how much collateral you had lost through the selection process.

The key focus of the monitoring model now is how to hold on to the only collateral I will have access to for the rest of the deal. Here it is vital to get an up-to-date picture of the delinquency and prepayment rates the portfolio is experiencing. We want to know how much of the principal balances of the loans of the deal are defaulted as opposed to prepaid, and what percentage both types of these loans are of the total principal of the original portfolio at the time of deal issuance. We especially want to be informed of how these numbers compare to the expected levels of these activities in the "At Issuance" Base Case.

The report will reside in a separate worksheet inside of the model and will not use a template file. It is automatically produced each time the model is run from the historical data file for that period of the deal.

The configuration of the report is seen in Exhibit 22.32.

```
Sub errFilesMenu_HistoryOffsetMonths()

(3 lines of variable declarations not displayed)
  msgTotal = "FILES MENU HISTORICAL OFFSET TABLE " & Chr(13) & Chr(13)
  msgInfo(1) = "    Value must be a Numeric" & Chr(13)
  msgInfo(2) = "    Value must be Greater Than or Equal To Zero" & Chr(13)
  msgInfo(3) = "    Value must be LT/EQ to the Months From Issuance" & Chr(13)

  'age of the information of the data file
  update_history = Range("m1MonthsSinceIssuance")
  'set all the error conditions to false
  For itest = 1 To PERIOD_TESTS
      errcase(itest) = 0
  Next itest
  'read each number of the grid and subject it to the 3 tests
  For irow = 1 To HIST_MENU_ROWS
      For icol = 1 To HIST_MENU_COLS
          sval = Trim(Range("m1HistFromPresent").Cells(irow, icol))
          If sval <> "" Then       ' not blank field
              'if value isNumeric = FALSE then (FALSE=FALSE) = TRUE
              If (IsNumeric(sval) = False) Then errcase(1) = 1
              If IsNumeric(sval) Then
                  If sval < 0 Then errcase(2) = 1
                  If sval >= update_history Then errcase(3) = 1
              End If
          End If
      Next icol
  Next irow
  (20 lines of code and comment not displayed)

End Sub
```

EXHIBIT 22.31 The error checking code for the matrix of offset months from the Files Menu for use by the Waterfall History Report

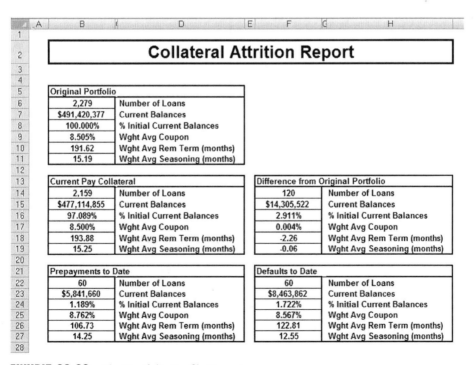

EXHIBIT 22.32 The Portfolio Profile Report

The subroutine "Write_Collateral_Attrition_Report" is contained in the **"Write-CollateralReports"** module. See Exhibit 22.33

Creating the States Information Screen   Although we are not performing Geographic selection on the collateral once the deal has been launched, we still need a table to store this information for use in the Collateral Stratification Reports.

We have reconfigured the menu into a schedule. It contains the ID numbers, postal codes, and common name of each of the 50 states and 4 territories of the United States. This information is read into the model by a replacement subroutine for the "Read_Geographic_Menu" subroutine.

It is called from the "Read_All_Menu_Input" subroutine in the module **"Read-MenuInputs."** See Exhibit 22.34.

Replacing the Program Costs Menu Subroutine   Once the deal is finalized and closed, all the elements of the Program Costs menus cease to be estimates or inputs and become fixed and unchanging. We no longer need a menu to pass the values of these inputs to the model. Since they are now fixed, we can assign their respective values to constant variables and delete the menu. See Exhibits 22.35 and 22.36.

Calculating Empirical Prepayments, Defaults, and Recoveries   One of the most significant differences between the structuring model and our new monitoring model is the presence of actual performance information about the loans in the portfolio. In the context of the structuring model, all of our cash flow estimates have to be based on estimates of future performance of the collateral.

With the advent of the closing of the deal all of this changed. Each month since the anniversary of the deal we have been receiving a report from the serving and surveillance unit hired to manage the deal. We requested, and have been fortunate to receive on a timely basis, a data file that gives us the status of the loans.

As discussed earlier, we will assume that there are only three conditions that each of the loans of the portfolio can assume. These conditions are those of current payment in full, prepayment of the full outstanding principal balance, and default. In the case of default we have asked our servicing unit to provide an estimate of both the estimated recovery time and the market value decline we can expect for the defaulted property.

When we now project the cash flows of the portfolio, we will follow the following rules:

- If the loan is a current payment loan we will amortize the loan until we reach the current month. From the current month onward we will apply the Base Case prepayment and default assumptions for the rest of the life of the loan. The Base Case assumptions are 200 PSA prepayments with 400 PSA defaults.
- If the loan prepays in the current month, we will amortize the cash flows up until the time of prepayment. There will be no fractional prepayments or defaults taken out of the loan balance. At the event of prepayment the entire outstanding balance is shown to be principal received that month. No further principal or interest is due from that point forward.
- If the loan defaults in the current month, it will be considered as current payment until the time of the default. At the month of the default no more principal and

```
Sub Write_Collateral_Attrition_Report()

Dim t               As Integer   'loan type current, prepaid, default
Dim i               As Integer   'loop counter
Dim iloan           As Integer   'loop counter
Dim icase           As Integer   'loop counter
Dim write_output    As Boolean   'must read data file?

    write_output = False
    If g_out_strats Or g_out_waterfall Or g_out_matrix Then write_output = True
    If g_out_scen_file Or g_out_cftrace Or g_out_prepays Then write_output = True
    If g_out_defaults Then write_output = True

    If write_output Then

        'Display the results to the selection screen
        Sheets("Portfolio Profile").Select
        Range("A1").Select
        Erase g_attrit_rep

        For iloan = 1 To g_total_loans
            'original portfolio
            g_attrit_rep(1, 1) = g_attrit_rep(1, 1) + 1
            g_attrit_rep(1, 2) = g_attrit_rep(1, 2) + g_loan_cur_bal(iloan)
            g_attrit_rep(1, 4) = g_attrit_rep(1, 4) + (g_loan_coup(iloan) _
                                                     * g_loan_cur_bal(iloan))
            g_attrit_rep(1, 5) = g_attrit_rep(1, 5) + (g_loan_rem_term(iloan) _
                                                     * g_loan _cur_bal(iloan))
            g_attrit_rep(1, 6) = g_attrit_rep(1, 6) + (g_loan_season(iloan) _
                                                     * g_loan_cur_bal(iloan))
            'increment by current, prepaid, or defaulted
            'these will fill up schedules 2, 3 and 4
            t = g_loan_status_num(iloan) + 1
            g_attrit_rep(t, 1) = g_attrit_rep(t, 1) + 1
            g_attrit_rep(t, 2) = g_attrit_rep(t, 2) + g_loan_cur_bal(iloan)
            g_attrit_rep(t, 4) = g_attrit_rep(t, 4) + (g_loan_coup(iloan) _
                                                     * g_loan_cur_bal(iloan))
            g_attrit_rep(t, 5) = g_attrit_rep(t, 5) + (g_loan_rem_term(iloan) _
                                                     * g_loan_cur_bal(iloan))
            g_attrit_rep(t, 6) = g_attrit_rep(t, 6) + (g_loan_season(iloan) _
                                                     * g_loan_cur_bal(iloan))
        Next iloan

        'calculate the percentages of initial current balance
        For i = 1 To 4
            g_attrit_rep(i, 3) = g_attrit_rep(i, 2) / g_attrit_rep(1, 2)
            (4 lines of code not displayed)
        Next i
        'calculate the difference between original and current pay
        For i = 1 To 6
            g_attrit_rep(5, i) = g_attrit_rep(1, i) - g_attrit_rep(2, i)
        Next i
        'populate the report
        For icase = 1 To 6
            Range("m3OriginalPortfolio").Cells(icase) = g_attrit_rep(1, icase)
            (5 lines of code not displayed)
        Next icase

    End If

End Sub
```

EXHIBIT 22.33   Subroutine that calculates and populates the Portfolio Profile Report screen

```
Sub Read_States_Menu()

Dim istate          As Integer

    Sheets("State Menu").Select
    Range("A1").Select
    For istate = 1 To STATES
        g_state_id_number(istate) = Range("m6StateInfo").Cells(istate, 1)
        g_state_postal(istate) = Range("m6StateInfo").Cells(istate, 2)
        g_state_name(istate) = Range("m6StateInfo").Cells(istate, 3)
    Next istate

End Sub
```

EXHIBIT 22.34 The subroutine that gets the three pieces of information about each state that we need for the various reports of the model

interest will be collected from the loan from that point forward. The estimates of recovery period, appraisal value of the property, equity position, and estimated market value decline will be applied to determine the recovery amount. If, however, in subsequent periods adjustments are made to the factors affecting the recovery amounts and times, these changes will be calculated as if they were in force at the time of the default. For example, if it is decided after the default has occurred but before the recovery period, that the appraisal value of the property is now 20% too high and is adjusted downward and that the recovery period is six months too short, these adjustments will be made to the servicing record we receive.

In the data file we receive each month from the servicing firm, each loan will be designated Current Pay, Prepaid, or Defaulted. If it is Prepaid or Defaulted the month of the action will be noted. In the case of a Defaulted loan, the recovery period lag and the market value decline will be included so that we can use them in our recovery estimates. In addition, the file will contain a appraisal adjustment factor. This factor will be used to adjust the project LTV and equity to value ratios.

To apply these calculation changes in the model, we will implement the following changes.

Additional Fields in the Collateral Servicing Data File   We will read the additional information regarding payment status, month of default or prepayment, recovery lag, estimated market value decline percentage, and the appraisal value adjustment factor

```
Public Const DEAL_SERVICE_FEE = 0.0075
Public Const DEAL_PROGRAM_FEE = 0.002
Public Const DEAL_CLEAN_UP_PCT = 0.1
Public Const DEAL_3_MTH_DEFAULT = 0.05
Public Const DEAL_ADVANCE_RATE = 0.95
Public Const DEAL_LIBOR_PATH = 1
Public Const DEAL_CONDUIT_SPREAD = 1
Public Const DEAL_PRIME_PATH = 1
```

EXHIBIT 22.35   Constant variables now hold the values of the Program Costs

```
Sub Read_Program_Costs()

    ' Read program costs into the model
    g_exp_service = DEAL_SERVICE_FEE / 12#        'servicing fee
    g_exp_program = DEAL_PROGRAM_FEE / 12#        'program expenses
    g_trig_cleanup = DEAL_CLEAN_UP_PCT            'principal reallocation trigger
    g_trig_3M_delinq = DEAL_3_MTH_DEFAULT         'principal reallocation trigger
    g_advance_rate = DEAL_ADVANCE_RATE            'conduit advance rate
    g_spread_path = DEAL_CONDUIT_SPREAD           'spread pathway elected
    g_libor_path = DEAL_LIBOR_PATH                'libor pathway elected
    g_prime_path = DEAL_PRIME_PATH                'prime rate pathway elected

End Sub
```

EXHIBIT 22.36 The "Read_Program_Const" now takes its values from constants instead of a menu

from the data file. The changes needed to the subroutine "Read_Portfolio_Data" to read these additional fields are shown in Exhibit 22.37.

Now that we have this information in the model, we can make use of it in the cash flow calculations code. We will proceed to look at the changes in the cash flow calculations in the order that they appear in the waterfall.

```
Function Read_Portfolio_Data(row_start, row_stop, j)

   g_beg_collateral = 0#
   For i2 = row_start To row_stop
       g_loan_ok(j) = True
       g_loan_num(j) = Trim(Cells(i2, 1).Value)
       (26 lines of code not displayed)
       If (IsNumeric(Cells(i2, 19).Value)) Then g_loan_appraisal(j) _
                                                       = Cells(i2, 19).Value

       'prepayment and default history indicators
       g_loan_status(j) = (UCase(Trim(Cells(i2, 24).Value)))
       Select Case g_loan_status(j)
         Case Is = "": g_loan_status_num(j) = CURRENT_LOANS
         Case Is = "P": g_loan_status_num(j) = PREPAID_LOANS
         Case Is = "D": g_loan_status_num(j) = DEFAULT_LOANS
       End Select
       If (IsNumeric(Cells(i2, 25).Value)) Then g_loan_status_month(j) _
                                                       = Cells(i2, 25).Value
       If (IsNumeric(Cells(i2, 26).Value)) Then g_loan_MVD_est(j) _
                                                       = Cells(i2, 26).Value
       If (IsNumeric(Cells(i2, 27).Value)) Then g_loan_RPL_est(j) _
                                                       = Cells(i2, 27).Value
       If (IsNumeric(Cells(i2, 28).Value)) Then g_loan_stated_pmt(j) _
                                                       = Cells(i2, 28).Value
       If (IsNumeric(Cells(i2, 29).Value)) Then g_loan_app_adjust(j) _
                                                       = Cells(i2, 29).Value
       g_beg_collateral = g_beg_collateral + g_loan_cur_bal(j)
       g_loan_appraisal(j) = g_loan_appraisal(j) * g_loan_app_adjust(j)
       Cells(1, 1).Value = j
       j = j + 1
   Next  i2
   Read_Portfolio_Data = j - 1

End Function
```

EXHIBIT 22.37 Code changes to read the prepayment, default, recovery period, market value decline estimate, and appraisal adjust fields is shown

Modifying the Calculation of Defaulted Principal   The first calculation is that of defaulted principal for the period. Over these next several sections, always keep in mind that there will be two calculation methods for defaulted principal. The first method will amortize the loan until the indicated period of its default. The second method of calculating defaults is used if the loan is in current payment state. For all periods from the origination of the deal until the amortization period, the loan will make principal and coupon payments only. For the period of the monitoring period and thereafter until the end of the term of the loan, the loan will generate fraction defaults of its principal based on the default methodology and the default speed. Let's look at the default calculation code modifications we will make to effect this change for the monitoring model application. See Exhibit 22.38.

Modifying the Calculation of Coupon Income   The next cash flow calculation to follow defaults is that of the coupon calculation. We do not need to modify this

```
Sub Calculate_Default_Effects(iloan As Long)

   'recalculate the beginning period loan-to-value ratio
   If cur_project > 0.01 Then
      cur_ltv = m_loan_cur_bal / cur_project
      Else
      cur_ltv = 0
   End If

   m_loan_defaults = 0#     'initialize the defaulted principal for the period to 0
   If g_loan_status_num(iloan) = CURRENT_LOANS Then
      If iperiod < g_monitor_age Then
         'loan is current pay, prior to the monitoring period, defaults are 0
         m_loan_defaults = 0#
      Else
         'calculate the loan defaults
         If m_loan_cur_bal > 1# Then
         (10 lines of code not displayed calculate the fractional default amount for
            the period)
         End If
         ' Compute what portion of the appraised value these defaults represent
           and subtract it from the beginning appraisal value of the entire project
           (3 lines of code adjust the appraisal amount of the project, not displayed)
      End If
   End If

   'if the loan has prepaid this period there is no defaulted principal
   If g_loan_status_num(iloan) = PREPAID_LOANS Then m_loan_defaults = 0#
   'if the loan has defaulted this period take the entire remaining balance as the
    default
   If g_loan_status_num(iloan) = DEFAULT_LOANS Then
      If g_loan_status_month(iloan) <> iperiod Then
         m_loan_defaults = 0#
         Else
         m_loan_defaults = m_loan_cur_bal
         m_loan_cur_bal = 0#
      End If
   End If

End Sub
```

EXHIBIT 22.38   Defaulted principal period calculation code (modified code shown in bold-face)

subroutine at all. The "Calculate_Coupon_Payment" applies the loan's current coupon level against the current balance of the note. If the note has defaulted in this period or has defaulted or prepaid in a previous period, the coupon amount will be zero.

Modifying the Calculation of Scheduled Principal   As with the calculation of the coupon income for the period, the calculation of the scheduled principal is unaffected by the changes we made to the data file. The scheduled principal retirement amount is predicated on the principal retirement factors we calculate outside of the loop of the cash flow generator.

Modifying the Calculation of Prepayments of Principal   We will next address the question of prepayments. See Exhibit 22.39.

Having not dispensed with the defaults, coupon, scheduled principal, and prepaid principal, we can now move on to revising the recoveries of defaulted principal.

Modifying the Calculation of Recoveries of Defaulted Principal   If the loan is in current pay, continue to calculate the recoveries based on the amounts of fractional defaulted principal assessed all current payment status loans.

If we are in a period prior to the monitoring period we continue to amortize the loan. If at the default period we calculate the recovery amount. Remember, all this subroutine does is calculate the recovery amount. The subroutine that aggregates the cash flows at the portfolio level lags the receipts of recoveries. See Exhibit 22.40.

We have now finished with the modifications to the cash flow calculations. We will next look at changes in the report writing subroutines that will display the results of our portfolio's performance.

```
Sub Calculate_Prepayments_of_Principal()

  ' Compute prepayments on the loan and adjust balance
  m_loan_prepays = 0#
  If g_loan_status_num(iloan) = CURRENT_LOANS Then
    If iperiod < g_monitor_age Then
      m_loan_defaults = 0#
    Else
      (7 lines of code calculate the fractional prepayment, not displayed)
    End If
  End If


  ' If this is NOT the prepayment period set prepays to 0, if it IS the current
  ' set the prepays equal to the current balance of the loan.
  If g_loan_status_num(iloan) = PREPAID_LOANS Then
    If g_loan_status_month(iloan) <> iperiod Then
      m_loan_prepays = 0#
    Else
      m_loan_prepays = m_loan_cur_bal
      m_loan_cur_bal = 0#
    End If
  End If
  'If it prepaid it cannot default, set defaults to 0
  If g_loan_status_num(iloan) = DEFAULT_LOANS Then m_loan_prepays = 0

End Sub
```

EXHIBIT 22.39   Prepayments of principal period calculation code (modified code shown in boldface)

```
Sub Calculate_Recoveries()

Dim loss_factor      As Double

   (16 lines of masthead comments not displayed)
   If g_loan_status_num(iloan) = CURRENT_LOANS Then
      If (1 - g_loss_sever_pct) >= m_loan_ratio Then
         recoveries = m_loan_defaults
      Else
         loss_factor = m_loan_ratio - (1# - g_loss_sever_pct)
         recoveries = m_loan_defaults * ((m_loan_ratio - loss_factor) / m_loan_ratio)
      End If
   End If

   'Prepayments of loans do not generate recovery values
   If g_loan_status_num(iloan) = PREPAID_LOANS Then recoveries = 0
   'Calculate the recovery amounts if appropriate
   If g_loan_status_num(iloan) = DEFAULT_LOANS Then
      If g_loan_status_month(iloan) > iperiod Then
         'this is not the period of the default specified in the file
         recoveries = 0#
      Else
         'this is the period of the default, calculate the recover, if any
         If (1 - g_loan_MVD_est(iloan)) >= m_loan_ratio Then
            recoveries = m_loan_defaults
         Else
            loss_factor = m_loan_ratio - (1# - g_loan_MVD_est(iloan))
            recoveries = m_loan_defaults * ((m_loan_ratio - loss_factor) _
                                                        / m_loan_ratio)
         End If
      End If
   End If

End Sub
```

EXHIBIT 22.40   Recoveries of defaulted principal period calculation code (modified code shown in boldface)

WHAT A BRAVE NEW MODEL THAT HAS SUCH FEATURES IN IT!

We now come to the last phase of the conversion of the structuring model to the monitoring model. As we have repeated, probably ad nauseaum by now, the structuring model was entirely prospective in nature. The monitoring model is a mix of retrospective *and* prospective. We will always be looking back to the inception of the deal as a touchstone for the current performance of the structure. With such a viewpoint we will need to compare the current anticipated performance, which is the combination of however much empirical results we have, with the initial projections, modified by value judgments based on the current economic conditions affecting the portfolio. To that end, we will incorporate the "At Issuance," base case for the deal in many, if not all, of these reports. We will constantly seek to compare and measure the current performance of the deal against our expectations at its inception.

The New History Directory and the "At Issuance" Files   Before we begin to look at the work changes that we have made to the report package, we need to make some changes to the model environment. For the first time since Chapter 6, "Laying the Model Groundwork," we are going to create a new directory. We are going to call this directory the "history" directory.

Into this directory we will eventually place a large number of very important things. This directory will be the repository for the monthly reports of the portfolio servicing unit. It will also be the home to the monthly update reports that we will generate with this monitoring model. All this, however, is in the future. Right now we need to establish a subdirectory named "at_issuance" under the history directory.

Into this new directory we will place a pair of files. The first is a Cash Flow Waterfall Report and the second is a single case, and somewhat modified, Matrix Summary Report. These reports display the final base case run of the deal reflecting 200 PSA prepayments in combination with 400 PSA defaults. Together these will be referenced as the "At Issuance" case by the reports we are now about to create.

The New Collateral Stratification Reports   In that one of the most critical aspects of the performance of the deal is the performance of the collateral, we need to bifurcate the Collateral Stratification Report Package into three parts: current pay loans, prepaid loans, and defaulted loans.

With this division we will be able to compare and contrast each of the subpopulations and with the original stratification loans that we retain from the issuance of the deal. By being able to look at each of these subpopulations as a separate pseudo-portfolio, we should be well-equipped to spot any trends in creditworthiness movement in the portfolio.

One example of this is geographic concentration shifts away from the initial portfolio. If the prepayment and default activity is uniformly distributed across the states, we should see the portfolio retain its initial geographic dispersion. That would be a very positive development. However, if the prepayments of defaults tend to skew the portfolio away from its at issuance distributions, we may see unwanted concentrations emerge. Consider this situation. The initial concentration in a particular state was 5%. The portfolio as a whole prepays or defaults 15% of its collateral in the first two years of the deal. If little or no attrition is experienced in this geographic area, its concentration will increase relative to its concentration level at issuance. In the above example, the initial concentration will increase from 5% to $5\%/85\% = 5.81\%$, a violation of the initial structuring constraints. Even though these loans may all be current pay, the performance risk of the portfolio collateral has increased. What if this concentration of loans was located in California in an area of seismic activity?

Fortunately it will be a straightforward task to modify the collateral stratification reporting code to produce the three portfolios. All we need to do is to create, or cause the program to think that we have created, three separate portfolios and then run the loans through the reporting code we developed for the structuring model. We can retain all of the formats of the original reports and so our changes will be limited. We will need to set up and name three separate reports, but we will only need one template report and the one we have will be just fine. In fact we want to retain the format so that it will be easier to data line the deal later in its life. If the same format is used throughout the stratification package across the three groups, we can build an extraction program similar to the one that we constructed earlier to mine sets of Matrix Summary Reports in Chapter 18, "Running the Model."

We will need to make one other change. We have discarded all the collateral selection code in the model. Previously the stratification code was called from the

```
Sub Write_Collateral_Strat_Reports()

  'Write the portfolio demographic reports -- only selected reports will be produced
  If g_out_strats Then
     Call Setup_Collateral_Workbooks(CURRENT_LOANS)
     Call Final_Loan_Status_Report(True)
     Call Write_Portfolio_Demographic_Reports(CURRENT_LOANS)
     Call Setup_Collateral_Workbooks(PREPAID_LOANS)
     Call Write_Portfolio_Demographic_Reports(PREPAID_LOANS)
     Call Setup_Collateral_Workbooks(DEFAULT_LOANS)
     Call Write_Portfolio_Demographic_Reports(DEFAULT_LOANS)
  End If

End Sub
```

EXHIBIT 22.41   The master subroutine that writes the three sets of collateral stratification reports. Each function is clearly identified by the subroutine name and the constant telling us the category of loans in each report file

module that performed the collateral selection function, **"CollateralSeletionSubs."** We will move it into its report writer module and call it directly from the Main Program.

The subroutine "Write_Collateral_Strat_Reports" has seven calls to other lower-level subroutines. These subroutines produce the three sets of collateral reports. To make the code clearly, we are using a set of constant variables as labels for each of the sub-portfolios. See Exhibit 22.41.

In the structuring model we needed to create only a single collateral report file; here we need three. Thus we will make some changes to the subroutine "Setup_Collateral_Workbooks." See Exhibit 22.42.

The only thing left to do is to print the stratification reports into the appropriate workbook using all the report specific subroutines from the structuring model. See Exhibit 22.43.

The Stratification Report Package is now complete.

```
Sub Setup_Collateral_Workbooks(file_type As Integer)

Dim t_template        As String    'name of the template file
Dim t_outfile         As String    'name of the report file

  Select Case file_type
     Case Is = CURRENT_LOANS:
       t_template = g_template_collat_current
       t_outfile = gfn_current_loans_file
     Case Is = PREPAID_LOANS:
       t_template = g_template_collat_prepaid
       t_outfile = gfn_prepaid_loans_file
     Case Is = DEFAULT_LOANS:
       t_template = g_template_collat_default
       t_outfile = gfn_default_loans_file
  End Select
  Workbooks.Open Filename:=g_pathway_template & t_template
  ActiveWorkbook.SaveAs Filename:=g_pathway_output & gfn_output_prefix & t_outfile
  ActiveWorkbook.Close

End Sub
```

EXHIBIT 22.42   The subroutine that sets up the three stratification templates

```
Sub Write_Portfolio_Demographic_Reports(loan_set As Integer)

  Select Case loan_set
    Case Is = CURRENT_LOANS
      Workbooks.Open Filename:=g_pathway_output & gfn_output_prefix & _
                                            gfn_current_loans_file
    Case Is = PREPAID_LOANS
      Workbooks.Open Filename:=g_pathway_output & gfn_output_prefix & _
                                            gfn_prepaid_loans_file
    Case Is = DEFAULT_LOANS
      Workbooks.Open Filename:=g_pathway_output & gfn_output_prefix & _
                                            gfn_default_loans_file
  End Select

  Call Write_Assumptions_Page
  For irep = 1 To PORTFOLIO_REPORTS
    If g_report(irep) Then
      Select Case irep
        Case Is = 1:  Call Dist_Current_Bal_by_Orig_Term(loan_set)
        (9 lines of code each calling a separate startification report, code not
          displayed)
        Case Is = 11: Call Dist_Current_Bal_by_Zip_Code(loan_set)
      End Select
    End If
  Next
  ActiveWorkbook.Save
  ActiveWorkbook.Close

End Sub
```

EXHIBIT 22.43   The code that writes the Collateral Stratification Report Package

The New Cash Flow Waterfall Comparison Reports   The next report that we will address is the Cash Flow Waterfall Report. As we all recall, the Cash Flow Waterfall Report gives us the period-by-period cash flows of the deal over its life. As our deal develops an empirical history, the early periods of the waterfall will be overwritten with the actual performance of the collateral and the structure. This in turn will change our estimates for the future period's performance as they will, of course, be using the last actual periods as their departure points of extrapolation. The report package consists of three sections.

1. **The Assumptions Report.** This lists the current assumption of the monitoring model.
2. **The "At Issuance" Cash Flow Waterfall report.** This is the at issuance waterfall report that was used to structure the deal. It is predicated on 200 PSA prepayments and 400 PSA defaults.
3. **The "CF-1" worksheet.** This worksheet contains a complete Cash Flow Waterfall Report, three Box Score Summary sections, and a differencing Cash Flow Waterfall worksheet. This worksheet contains in each of its cells the difference between the scenario presented to the left of the page and the At Issuance Cash Flow Waterfall. This allows an immediate comparison of the two schedules and highlights the changes in the cash flows and debt amortization schedules.

The steps in the preparation of this report are:

1. Open and read the contents of the "At Issuance" Cash Flow Waterfall workbook in the "**history****at_issuance**" directory.
2. Open the "**m_waterfall_template.xls**" Cash Flow Waterfall template file and save it to the name entered in the Files Menu. Create one copy of worksheet "CF-1" for each scenario we are to run and rename the new worksheets by their prepayment and defaults projection speed combinations as we did in the structuring model. Save and close the workbook.
3. Successively write each of the newly generated scenarios into the worksheets created to receive them. Push a progress message to the message bar to inform the user of the progress of the model. Calculate the workbook at the end of the loop, save, and close it.

With these steps clearly in mind, let's look at the code. The subroutine that kicks things off is the "Write_Waterfall_Report_Package." The basic difference between the subroutine in the monitoring model and that in the structuring model is the acquisition of the At Issuance waterfall information and the placement of it in a separate worksheet. That worksheet then becomes the base case for the difference section in each of the subsequent scenario worksheets. See Exhibit 22.44.

The monitoring model accesses the Cash Flow Waterfall Report in the "**history****at_issuance**" directory and reads its contents. This consists of the header prepayment and default types and speeds, the contents of the waterfall itself, and the at issuance Box Score summary statistics. See Exhibit 22.45.

The file is now prepared to receive the scenarios of the current monitoring model run. These are loaded into the successive spreadsheets in the same manner as they were in the structuring model. We have seen that process before and do not need to revisit it now.

The New Matrix Summary Comparison Reports   The Matrix Summary Comparison Report is similar in concept to the Cash Flow Waterfall Report Package we just

```
Sub Write_Waterfall_Report_Package()

  'produce the detailed cash flow waterfall reports
  If g_out_waterfall Then
     'get the at issuance porton of the record
     Call Read_At_Issuance_Waterfall_File
     Call Setup_Cashflow_Waterfall_Workbook
     For i_scenario = AT_ISSUE To (g_prepay_levels * g_default_levels)
         Call Write_Single_Case_Waterfall(i_scenario)
         Call Display_Waterfall_ProgressMsg(i_scenario, 1)
     Next i_scenario
     ActiveWorkbook.Save
     ActiveWorkbook.Close
  End If

End Sub
```

EXHIBIT 22.44   The master subroutine that writes the monitoring model Cash Flow Waterfall Report Package

```
Sub Read_At_Issuance_Waterfall_File()

  Workbooks.Open Filename:= _
      g_pathway & "history\at_issuance\" & gfn_at_issue_waterfall

  'read the waterfall contents
  For idate = 1 To PAY_DATES
    For icol = 1 To PAY_COLS
      g_waterfall_info(AT_ISSUE, idate, icol) = Cells(idate + 13, icol + 10).Value
    Next icol
  Next idate
  'prepayment and default headers
  g_waterfall_misc(AT_ISSUE, 1) = Cells(2, 3)      'prepayment rate
  g_waterfall_misc(AT_ISSUE, 2) = Cells(3, 3)      'default rate
  g_waterfall_method(AT_ISSUE, 1) = Cells(2, 4)    'prepayment method
  g_waterfall_method(AT_ISSUE, 2) = Cells(3, 4)    'default method
  'get the components of the Box Score
  Call Get_Waterfall_Box_Score(AT_ISSUE)

  ActiveWorkbook.Close

End Sub
```

EXHIBIT 22.45   The subroutine that reads the at issuance waterfall file

examined. The file consists of an Assumptions Report and four Matrix Summary template worksheets. Each of these individual worksheets has a pair of Matrix grids. The first contains the results of up to 100 current scenarios being run by the monitoring model, the second is a difference grid that compares the results of these scenarios with the At Issuance results. These results are of the 200 PSA prepayment and 400 PSA defaults speed structuring run.

The preparation sequence of this report is identical to that of the preceding report package. See Exhibit 22.46.

The At Issuance performance statistics are contained in a single worksheet of the Matrix Summary Report in the "**history****at_issuance**\" subdirectory. After the contents are read from the file, they are transferred to the header section of each of the appropriate Tenor, Cash Flows, Conduit Note Performance, and Seller Interest

```
Sub Write_Waterfall_Report_Package()

  'produce the detailed cash flow waterfall reports
  If g_out_waterfall Then
    'get the at issuance porton of the record
    Call Read_At_Issuance_Waterfall_File
    Call Setup_Cashflow_Waterfall_Workbook
    For i_scenario = AT_ISSUE To (g_prepay_levels * g_default_levels)
        Call Write_Single_Case_Waterfall(i_scenario)
        Call Display_Waterfall_ProgressMsg(i_scenario, 1)
    Next i_scenario
    ActiveWorkbook.Save
    ActiveWorkbook.Close
  End If

End Sub
```

EXHIBIT 22.46   The master subroutine that writes the Matrix Summary Monitoring Report (new code is in bold)

```
Sub Read_At_Issuance_MatrixFile()

   Workbooks.Open Filename:=g_pathway & "history\at_issuance\" & gfn_at_issue_matriix
   'Read the contents of the file
   icol = 3
   islot = 1
   For irow = 7 To 27
       g_at_issue_matrix01(islot) = Cells(irow, icol).Value
       islot = islot + 1
   Next irow
   'trigger information is boolean
   islot = 1
   For irow = 28 To 30
       g_at_issue_matrix02(islot) = Cells(irow, icol).Value
       islot = islot + 1
   Next irow
   ActiveWorkbook.Close

End Sub
```

EXHIBIT 22.47   The subroutine that reads the content of the at issuance Matrix Summary Report file

Performance worksheets. The difference section then refers to these statistics and compares them to the scenario statistics just generated by the model to populate the differences grid. See Exhibit 22.47.

All the difference calculations of the four spreadsheets of the report package are Excel cell calculations and do not use VBA code. After the scenario grid is populated in each of the worksheets, the workbook is manually calculated displaying the contents of the differences and the content portion of the report is complete.

The only other task we face in finishing the Matrix Summary Report lies in the "Trim_Matrix_Report" function. This function must now eliminate the unused matrix cells from two matrix displays instead of one. Once this has been done, the report is finished.

The New History Report   This report, like the others, is a comparison of the At Issuance scenario performance projections and the combination of the empirical performance of the deal to date and our current expectations of future collateral and structure performance.

This report package consists of the ever present Assumption Report page and a worksheet containing the Box Score of the At Issuance performance and that of the scenario to which it is being compared. It is intended to be a high-level snap shot of the performance of the "At Issuance" deal and various historical update estimates.

The report reads the monthly offsets from a grid on the File Menu. If the content of the grid is 0, 1, 3, 6, 9, 12, and 18, the report package will consist of seven reports. Each of these reports will compare the At Issuance performance with the successive historical performances of, respectively, the 0 or current month offset, and the projections of 1, 3, 6, 9, 12, and 18 months ago if the files have been produced for those time periods.

Each file is opened in turn and the information is stored in a series of Box Score arrays we used in the original structuring model.

```
Sub Write_Attrition_Report_Package(choice As Integer)

  Select Case choice
    Case Is = PREPAY_CHOICE
      If g_out_prepays Then
        'get the at issuance porton of the record
        Call Read_At_Issuance_Waterfall_File
        Call Setup_Report_Workbook(PREPAY_CHOICE)
        For i_scenario = 1 To (g_prepay_levels * g_default_levels)
            Call Write_Prepayment_Projections(i_scenario)
        Next i_scenario
        ActiveWorkbook.Save
        ActiveWorkbook.Close
      End If
    Case Is = DEFAULT_CHOICE
      If g_out_defaults Then
        'get the at issuance porton of the record
        Call Read_At_Issuance_Waterfall_File
        Call Setup_Report_Workbook(DEFAULT_CHOICE)
        For i_scenario = 1 To (g_prepay_levels * g_default_levels)
            Call Write_Defaults_Projections(i_scenario)
        Next i_scenario
        ActiveWorkbook.Save
        ActiveWorkbook.Close
      End If
  End Select

End Sub
```

EXHIBIT 22.48   The master subroutine for both the Prepayments and the Defaults Comparison reports

The New Default and Prepayment Comparison Reports   We are finally at the last of the new reports. This one is completely new and does not build off of any of the structuring model reports in the least. Each page of the report consists of a table displaying the empirical prepayments or defaults to date, the projected prepayments or defaults as estimated at issuance of the deal, and the difference.

The VBA code reads the At Issuance default and prepayment cash flow columns from the At Issuance Cash Flow Waterfall Report. It then reads the same data columns from the scenarios being run through the monitoring model. Both the At Issuance and the Current projections are then pasted into the table and the differences are calculated. The graphs display a period-by-period or a cumulative difference between the two projections. See Exhibit 22.48.

The rest of the code consists of reading in the contents of the **"g_waterfall_info"** array that we have populated by reading the at issuance file Cash Flow Waterfall file in the **"\history\at_issuance\"** directory and the contents of the **"g_waterfall_info"** array positions holding the results of the scenarios generated by the monitoring program.

With the development of this last report, we are done.

VALIDATING THE MODEL

The validation of this model is very straightforward. The key elements of change between the structuring and the monitoring models are the cash flow calculations.

Simply follow the pattern that we used in validation of the cash flows of the structuring model. Create a collateral file with a single prepaid loan and a single defaulted loan. Set these events in separate, but early, months of the deal. Set the "Months Since Deal Issuance" field in the Main Menu to a period slightly past the event.

Both loans should trigger. Principal and coupon will be recorded with the prepaid loan. Defaulted principal and a delayed recovery will be recorded when looking at the defaulted loan.

DELIVERABLES CHECKLIST

The VBA Knowledge Checklist items for this chapter are:

- How to think about mixing empirical and projected data
- How to design a report package to compare "to date" performance with original projections

The Model Knowledge Checklist for this chapter is:

- How to transform a structuring model into a monitoring model

NEXT STEPS

In Chapter 23, we will build a Valuation module to perform a mark-to-market on the cash flows we have generated here.

In Chapter 24 we will put the deal through it first 24 years of life, recording the changes to the collateral and valuing the conduit financing against other secondary market deals.

ON THE WEB SITE

This was a busy chapter for items on the Web site. You will find the following:

- Several way-point ChopShop in-progress versions of the structuring model as we removed code and transitioned to the monitoring model
- The completed monitoring model, **"MONITOR_Ver01.xls"**
- The report templates for all the report packages developed or modified in this chapter
- A test file of collateral information for one month out into the deal
- The stratification reports for the "at one month past issuance" portfolio file
- The At Issuance Cash Flow Waterfall and Matrix Summary reports
- Examples of all reports for one month into the life of the deal

## CHAPTER 23

Valuation Techniques: How Do We Determine Price?

OVERVIEW

By the time you have gotten to this point in the book, you have achieved two considerable accomplishments. The first is the building of a structuring model to generate a fixed income security out of a collateral pool. The second is to build a monitoring model to track the performance of the collateral and the debt structure after the deal was created.

Guess what? **All of this work was designed only to get you ready to understand the contents of the next two chapters! This is where the value of what you have learned to date can be applied to the real-world situation we find ourselves in today.** You can view the entire preceding 22 chapters as a very long training and practice period before you get to understand several key aspects of the current credit crisis. What we will do in this chapter is apply the structuring and surveillance software and knowledge we have acquired over the last several hundred pages to embark on the exercise of valuing the security we have created.

There are many ways of performing a security valuation that are characterized by the type of security you wish to value; the amount, type, accuracy, appropriateness, and completeness of the data you have available; and the degree of sophistication you wish to employ in the pricing calculation. Pricing calculations can cover a complexity Range from the very straightforward for many debt instruments to extremely complicated, mathematically advanced, and computationally burdensome. In that this is not a book on pricing or valuation methods, and given the attendant space constraints of a general work, we will take a middle-of-the-road approach.

The pricing method we will apply will be more straightforward rather than complex in nature. We will make certain simplifying assumptions for the sake of familiarizing the reader with many of the assumptions and work that goes into getting a valid price. We will discuss in general a number of more sophisticated approaches, including Option Adjusted Spread (OAS) models and Monte Carlo simulation. While we will not implement them into the model, you should be aware that they exist and what steps you would need to take to convert the model to produce this analysis.

In the course of this discussion, we will make use of the monitoring reports to gauge the sensitivity of the deal structure to various perturbations of the cash flows away from out original assumptions.

By the end of the chapter we will be able to apply what we have learned here to the events we will see unfold in Chapter 24. In that chapter, our management will call on us to value and price, on a monthly basis, the security we have created in Chapters 3 through 19. The time span for this analysis will cover the first two years of the life of the deal and be conducted at three-month intervals (although in the real world we would mark the deal to market on a daily basis, if possible).

DELIVERABLES

In this chapter we will cover the answers to the following financial knowledge questions:

- What are the basic input elements of a pricing calculation for a fixed-income security?
- How can these elements change over time based on collateral performance, investor preferences, rating agency guidelines, and market conditions?
- What are the most common pricing methods, and how do they vary in sophistication for a security similar to the one we have?
- How can I use the structuring and monitoring models to identify which factors of collateral risk will have the biggest impact on the pricing exercise?

We will also cover the following modeling questions:

- How to use the outputs of the structuring and monitoring models to help us in the pricing exercise
- Changes we need to make to the monitoring model to derive a price given a straightforward pricing method
- Changes we need to make to the monitoring model to produce a report of pricing sensitivities

UNDER CONSTRUCTION

In this chapter we will add the ability to price our deal and to display this information across a number of the monitoring reports. To accomplish this we will have to make the following changes to the model and various template files we created in the last chapter.

In the "A_Constants" module, we will declare some new constant variables and modify the values of others. We are going to increase the number of columns in the "CFWaterfall" worksheet. This worksheet is read into the "g_waterfall_info" array on a one-to-one correspondence of cells-to-array positions. As a result, we need to redimension the array to accommodate these incremental columns. In addition, we will replace the loop counters that read in the contents of the three sections of the Box Score portion of the CFWaterfall spreadsheet. We will globally replace the loop terminus for these three sections with the constants BXSCR1_ROWS, BXSCR2_ROWS, and BXSCR3_ROWS.

In the "A_Globals" module, we will declare three new variables for the calculated price for a single scenario, a vector of prices for all scenarios run, and the pricing risk premium spread. We will also use the constants we declared for the Box Score information to change the variable declarations for the arrays that hold that information.

In the "ErrCheckAllMenus" module, we will need to add the conduit pricing spread field to the "IsNumerics_RatesDatesMenu" subroutine.

In the "ReadMenusInputs" module, we will need to add the price vector to the subroutine "Redim_All_SummaryMatrixReport_Vectors." This subroutine performs the redimensioning of the array sizes for all the matrix report variables.

In the "WriteMatrixReports" module, we need to change two subroutines, one that captures the price information from the Cash Flow Waterfall spreadsheet and the second that writes the price information of the VBA matrix variables to the report.

In the "WriteWaterfallReports" module, we will redimension the three Box Score module variables using the BXSCR#_ROWS constants. We will also need to make changes to the "Write_Waterfall_Box_Score" subroutine to reflect the addition of the "Price" field.

In the "WriteHistoricalReports" module, we will rewrite the looping controls using the BXSCR#_ROWS constants. We will also have to modify the code to include the addition of the "Price" field in the second session of the Box Score.

In the report template files we will create a new format for those report files that have Box Score sections within them. We will need to reformat the Box Score sections in the "m2_waterfall_template.xls," "m2_matrix_template.xls," "m2_scenario_template.xls" and "m2_historical_template.xls." In the "m2_matrix_template.xls" file, we will edit the ConduitNotePerformance worksheet and replace the field "Debt Service Paid" and replace it with a field named "Price." We will then need to reformat the worksheet to reflect the "Price" entry in both the initial display and the differences sections of the report.

INTRODUCTION TO PRICING A SECURITY

All pricing models employ a small number of key elements. How people arrive at the value of the elements in a pricing calculation can be fairly simple, in the case of some types of Treasury bonds, or mind numbingly complicated in the case of credit derivatives.

Nevertheless, all of these methods rely on the basic inputs that we are about to examine. One of the most important issues to keep in mind as we go through this process is that no pricing exercise is performed in isolation from the market. This act of pricing is referred to as the "mark-to-market" valuation process. Some securities reference hundreds, if not thousands, of prices for identical or broadly similar instruments. We will need to be cognizant of relative performance. Is our collateral performing above or below expectations? How does the magnitude and timing of the cashflows of our deal compare at the present time to those we generated in our "At Issuance" estimate? Is our structure better or worse at protecting the investor (even if the sole investor is us!)? What is the sensitivity to change in these factors where we stand now in the history of the life of the deal versus at the point of its inception?

Regardless of the sophistication of the methodology, there are four irreducible steps in the pricing of a security:

1. Generating the periodic cash flows under the performance assumptions for the pricing exercise to be conducted.
2. Determining the discount rate to be used at present valuing the cash flows stream.
3. Applying the discount rate to the cash flows to determine their present values and summing the now discounted cash flows.
4. Dividing the sum of the discounted cash flows by the original principal balance of the instrument and multiplying the result by 100 to attain a dollar price.

Let's look at these components one by one.

Expected Cash Flows of the Instrument

The first step in the pricing process is to arrive at the stream of periodic cash flows that will ultimately determine the value of the security. These cash flows will be present valued to determine the sum of their time-weighted value.

Our starting position for the cash flow analysis is the At Issuance assumptions. These cash flows will be affected by the behavior of the Obligors of our collateral pool. If the businesses are successful, the risks of defaults will be lower. If there are issues stressing the businesses holding these loans, the cash flows may be impaired by adverse Obligor credit behavior. This will result in a greater number of defaults than we initially estimated.

Changes to the initially anticipated rate of loan prepayments will also affect the timing and magnitude of the cash flows. Every loan that prepays earlier than expected will diminish the total amount of coupon income received by the deal. If there are significant changes in the lending terms available to these borrowers, they may refinance. If these terms are sufficiently attractive to the pool as a whole prepayments may far exceed our original estimates.

The evolution of general economic conditions will also affect the cash flows. If the economy is robust and the value of property and equipment increase, the project appraisals for the collateral will improve. For example, if there is an appreciation of 15% in the appraisal value of a $100,000 property, the current value becomes $115,000. The property, at the original valuation of $100,000 had an original loan balance of $60,000, giving it an initial loan-to-value (LTV) of 60%. With the increase in project value, with no other repayment of principal, the owner's equity of the loan will increase from its original level of:

$$\text{Equity} = (\$100,000 - \$60,000)/\$100,000 = 40\%$$

to

$$\text{Equity} = (\$115,000 - \$60,000)/\$115,000 = 48\%!$$

If, however, the economy moves into a recession and the project appraisal value of the same $100,000 property drops by 15%, from $100,000 to $85,000 the effect is quite the opposite! Now we have the same initial $60,000 indebtedness but the

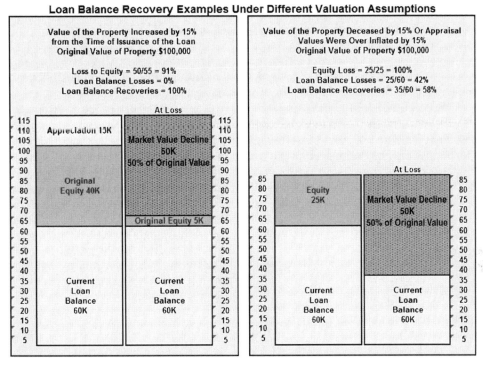

Loan Balance Recovery Examples Under Different Valuation Assumptions

Value of the Property Increased by 15% from the Time of Issuance of the Loan Original Value of Property $100,000	Value of the Property Deceased by 15% Or Appraisal Values Were Over Inflated by 15% Original Value of Property $100,000
Loss to Equity = 50/55 = 91% Loan Balance Losses = 0% Loan Balance Recoveries = 100%	Equity Loss = 25/25 = 100% Loan Balance Losses = 25/60 = 42% Loan Balance Recoveries = 35/60 = 58%

EXHIBIT 23.1 An example of two loans, one with appreciation, the other with depreciation or phantom equity created by an inflated appraisal estimate

equity position has shrunk from 40% to 29%!

$$\text{Equity} = (\$85{,}000 - \$60{,}000)/\$85{,}000 = 29\%$$

Now assume that both Obligors default. We apply a market value decline assumption of 50% of the $100,000 original value of the project. In the first case this event would result in a full recapture of the defaulted principal with 0% losses. In the second case the loan would have a loss severity of 42%, failing to recover a substantial portion of its balance. See Exhibit 23.1.

Furthermore, in a robust economy our assumptions about recovery lag period may be unchanged or even shortened. Foreclosed or abandoned properties of business may be quickly sold at or near their asking price. In that they will not have sat vacant or unattended for long, repair and refurbishment costs will be minimal. Conversely, in a depressed economy, with the property inventories rising, purchasers may anticipate lower prices in the immediate future. They may defer purchasing a property thereby lowering demand and increasing recovery lag periods.

When we construct our pricing assumptions for the deal we need to keep all of these things in mind.

Using One Prepayment/Default Assumption or Many? The model runs that we will conduct use the most basic form of prepayment and default assumption, a single constant rate for the remaining life of the deal. This is a state of affairs in the real world that is very unrealistic. Individual prepayment and default actions are triggered by a myriad of conditions.

If we wanted to make later improvements to the model we might allow the user to use a vector of varying prepayment or default assumptions that could be described and entered into the model on a month-to-month basis.

For prepayments, the next refinement of this approach is the Option Adjusted Spread (OAS) model. This model uses the current interest rate environment as the departure point and simulates a series of interest rate pathways using a selected rate. The model consults the current level of the interest rate as a starting point. Using this starting point, it consults a transition table indicating the probability that the rate will stay the same, increase, or decrease. A random number is generated and the new rate level is determined for the future period. This pathway is constructed through the end of the deal. Once complete, the pathway is revisited on a month-by-month basis. At each month the prepayment rate is reset for the loan based on the difference between the current index level and the loan itself. The index level is much greater than the loan coupon level the probability of a prepayment is decreased reflecting a lower probability that the loan will prepay. If the index level is significantly less than the current coupon of the loan, there is a much higher probability of a prepayment event.

Similar multivariate models exist for estimating the probability of defaults. These models look at both macro and micro economic factors including family income and property value trends to estimate ongoing default rates.

Alternatively, prepayments and defaults may be directly generated by the use of a Monte Carlo simulation. In this approach the simulation consults a table or series of tables as the probability of the prepayment or default of each specific loans or group of loans on a period by period basis. A random number is generated and if the result falls within the band of outcomes the loan is either prepaid or not.

Choosing a Discount Rate

The next item on the list that we need to specify is the discount rate used to present value the stream of payments that we generated above. Again, in the model we will take a simple approach and assume a single discount rate. In this approach the discount rate is a combination of a benchmark rate, LIBOR in this case, and a pricing spread. The pricing spread is driven by two components. The first is the performance of the deal to date against its At Issuance expected performance and other deals of its type. The second is the general market pricing of all deals in that class, such as credit cards, home equity lines of credit, or autos and the rest of the ABS market.

The alternatives are to employ a forward curve of values and tailor the discount rates to be the respective value of the index at the point on the curve corresponding to the time period when the cash flow is received. The index will be adjusted for a risk premium. This risk premium is an incremental spread premium that is added to the interpolated forward curve rate to arrive at the discount rate for the period. Deals that are performing better than expected may be priced at lower spreads while other deals performing poorly may attract high pricing spreads.

Keep in mind that the size of the spread is directly linked to the relative risk of the deal to a hypothetical "risk free" rate of a benchmark government security or an index such as LIBOR. For example, let's assume that the 2-year forward LIBOR rate is 2.5% as the base rate for a cash flow received 24 months from now. If the deal was low risk, the capital markets liquid and functioning, and the demand for the security robust, the risk premium spread of the deal might be 0.5%, or 50 basis points. However, the security may have experienced significant credit deterioration from higher than expected default rates, longer recovery times, and much higher market value decline numbers. In this case the risk premium spread may be 4.0% or 400 basis points. If these conditions are systemic to the markets, liquidity is nonexistent, and demand levels for yield are at rapacious levels, the risk premium spread might be 10% or 1,000 basis points!

Present Value of the Cash Flows at the Discount Rate

Once we have the cash flows and our agreed on discount rate in hand, the rest is easy! All we need to do is generate a sequence of monthly Present Value factors using our discount rate. We can then multiply those discount factors by the values of the corresponding cash flows for the period to arrive at the net present value of the cash flow for that period.

We then sum the net present valued cash flows to arrive at the now risk adjusted expectation of repayment. It is this that we use in the next step of the process. In Exhibit 23.2, we have a schedule of a hypothetical $100,000,000 portfolio. All amounts are expressed in thousands of dollars. To facilitate the display of the calculations, the portfolio consists of newly originated loans. Recoveries are at 50%

Joint Effects of Prepayments & Defaults on Price
Prepayment Rate = 200 PSA
Default Rate = 400 PSD
Recovery Period = 3 months; Recovery Rate = 50%　　　　　　　　　　Price = 99.657

Month	Beginning Balance	Defaulted Principal	9.000% Coupon Payment	Scheduled Principal	Prepaid Principal	Recovery of Defaulted Principal	Total Cash Flows Received	PV Factor 9.000%	NPV Total CF's 9.000%
Totals =>		$ 730	$ 9,442	$ 95,968	$ 3,301	$ 365	$ 109,077		$ 99,657
1	100,000.00	6.67	749.95	3,818.22	32.12		$ 4,600	0.992556	$ 4,566
2	96,142.99	12.83	720.98	3,845.06	61.75		$ 4,628	0.985167	$ 4,559
3	92,223.36	18.46	691.54	3,870.53	88.82	3.33	$ 4,654	0.977833	$ 4,551
4	88,245.54	23.57	661.66	3,894.60	113.27	6.41	$ 4,676	0.970554	$ 4,538
5	84,214.11	28.12	631.39	3,917.23	135.02	9.23	$ 4,693	0.963329	$ 4,521
6	80,133.73	32.12	600.76	3,938.39	154.03	11.78	$ 4,705	0.956158	$ 4,499
7	76,009.19	35.56	569.80	3,958.05	170.23	14.06	$ 4,712	0.949040	$ 4,472
8	71,845.35	38.43	538.55	3,976.18	183.59	16.06	$ 4,714	0.941975	$ 4,441
9	67,647.15	40.72	507.05	3,992.75	194.06	17.78	$ 4,712	0.934963	$ 4,405
10	63,419.61	42.44	475.33	4,007.74	201.62	19.22	$ 4,704	0.928003	$ 4,365
11	59,167.81	43.57	443.43	4,021.13	206.24	20.36	$ 4,691	0.921095	$ 4,321
12	54,896.88	44.11	411.40	4,032.88	207.89	21.22	$ 4,673	0.914238	$ 4,273
13	50,611.99	44.07	379.26	4,042.98	206.58	21.78	$ 4,651	0.907432	$ 4,220
14	46,318.36	43.45	347.06	4,051.41	202.29	22.06	$ 4,623	0.900677	$ 4,164
15	42,021.21	42.25	314.84	4,058.16	195.03	22.04	$ 4,590	0.893973	$ 4,103
16	37,725.77	40.48	282.64	4,063.20	184.80	21.73	$ 4,552	0.887318	$ 4,039
17	33,437.28	38.13	250.49	4,066.53	171.64	21.13	$ 4,510	0.880712	$ 3,972
18	29,160.98	35.23	218.44	4,068.14	155.55	20.24	$ 4,462	0.874156	$ 3,901
19	24,902.07	31.76	186.53	4,068.01	136.57	19.07	$ 4,410	0.867649	$ 3,826
20	20,665.73	27.76	154.78	4,066.14	114.75	17.61	$ 4,353	0.861190	$ 3,749
21	16,457.08	23.22	123.25	4,062.53	90.12	15.88	$ 4,292	0.854779	$ 3,669
22	12,281.20	18.16	91.97	4,057.18	62.75	13.88	$ 4,226	0.848416	$ 3,585
23	8,143.12	12.59	60.98	4,050.07	32.69	11.61	$ 4,155	0.842100	$ 3,499
24	4,047.76	6.53	30.31	4,041.23	-	18.64	$ 4,090	0.835831	$ 3,419

EXHIBIT 23.2 Price of a portfolio experiencing 200 PSA prepayments, 400 PSD defaults over its life. All loans have a two-year term, none are seasoned

of defaulted amounts and lagged three months. The last period cash flow is allowed to capture the recoveries from periods 22, 23, and 24. The total cash flows for each period consist of the coupon payments, the scheduled amortization of principal, prepayments of principal, and recoveries (if any). The coupon rate of the note is 9% and the discount rate applied to the cash flows is also 9%. Review Appendix B, "Bond Math," for other pricing examples if this is not clear. See Exhibit 23.2.

Calculating the Price

With the risk adjusted sum of the Net Present Values (NPVs) of the cash flow streams, we need only do one more thing.

We divide the sum of these risk adjusted cash flows by the current outstanding balance of the indebtedness. The result, essentially a ratio of the NPV of the cash flows and balance of the note is then multiplied by 100 to arrive at a dollar price.

This is our price, taking into consideration our estimates of the deal performance and the conditions of the marketplace.

ASSESSING RISK

Well, when we look at it like that it seems simple.

If only that were true! It seems all too easy and you have a right to be suspicious, after all we are not at the end of the chapter so the author must have additional things to say.

You are right, I do. In this section we will look at some of the issues, information, judgments, and guesswork that constitute the pricing activity. Don't worry; I will be merciful in this regard. There are probably entire chapters in other books written on just these issues. In fact, I would not be at all surprised to find that there are entire books written on some of them! I will, however, confine my remarks to a few sentences at most.

The Expectations at Issuance

There are three broad categories of expectations that we hold at the time of issuance. The first is the expectations concerning the performance of the collateral over the life of the deal. The second is the performance of the structure of the deal and how it will perform given variations of the collateral cash flows in retiring the debt. A third set of expectations, in regard to price, are the market conditions that will influence the deal in a manner only partially related to its own performance.

Collateral Performance   Collateral performance is about maximizing the cash flows from a pool of loans that support the debt structure of the deal. Anything that results in the receipt of less cash flow than originally anticipated at the time of the issuance of the deal is *bad*! Anything that results in more cash flow is *good*! It's about that simple.

Also, it should be painfully obvious, if we have to choose between two scenarios where we receive the identical total amount of cash flow from the collateral pool, we would prefer to receive it earlier in the deal rather than later. First, each dollar of cash flow in excess of the coupon costs and expenses of the deal will be applied to the task of principal retirement. In general the faster you retire the debt outstanding, the safer the deal becomes. This is not always true, but it's a safe way to bet. An exception is if you were to receive an extraordinary amount of prepayments in an early month of the deal. The excess collections after payment of the coupon expenses and other deal expenses would be applied to the outstanding principal balance of the note indebtedness reducing it substantially. We prefer this situation to many others for two reasons. The first is that it is impossible to default on any dollar of principal that you have already retired. The second is that the deal is relieved of the attendant debt service on the principal retired from the point of its retirement to the end of the deal. This then allows the future cash flows to be applied to the remaining principal as overall debt service cost decline.

If, however, the coupon rate of the prepaid loans were higher than the coupon rate on the debt, and if the prepayments were a very large amount, the model may have expected much more coupon income from the collateral. In the case that the deal size was predicated on the receipt of this incremental coupon income arriving in some form, the deal may come up short.

All in all we must be constantly aware that the performance of the deal is dynamic and not static. In some months the deal will improve in favorable economic conditions, in some months it will decline because of poor economic conditions.

Characteristics of the Collateral Portfolio   The first thing to do is to establish a clear view of the salient characteristics of the collateral at the time of the deal issuance. This is our base line against which we will measure any subsequent variation.

We need to be aware of any clustering or concentrations. Concentrations are almost always unfavorable. They tend to make a collection of loans vulnerable to a single phenomenon that could trigger a default or loss event. These characteristics can be related to coupon distributions, term distributions, geographic distributions, or balance distributions. Fortunately for us, we have both the initial conditions of the deal and the month-by-month updates of the collateral portfolio provided by the servicing unit. We can compare the original Collateral Stratification Reports to those we will run against the collateral pool data file of the monthly update. If necessary, we may even design a series of specialty comparative reports on the stratification changes to date. These reports would compare the existing current payment loans against the original stratification reports and look at the change in demographics.

Coupon Dispersion   The lack of coupon dispersion can negatively influence pricing assumptions if the coupons are concentrated in an area that makes them vulnerable to prepayment events. In the case of floating rate mortgages, we need to be sensitive to rate and payment reset shock.

One thing to also remember is that it is not necessarily how much prepayment activity you experience. What is more important is where in the coupon level distribution of the portfolio you **do** experience it. If you lose a disproportionate balance of your high coupon, high spread loans, your absolute prepayment rate may be low but the effect on your cash flows may be severe.

Seasoning and Cohort Distribution   If the collateral is concentrated in regard to seasoning you may be vulnerable to exposure to underwriting or credit standards risk. Here you may find standards may have relaxed especially in an economic period similar to the one we have just experienced. Available credit, raising property values, and a strong economy tend to loosen credit standards. If a large number of loans have seasoning concentration this risk is a distinct possibility. This is a very young and unseasoned portfolio! Over 50% of the At Issuance current balances are contained in loans less that a year old. If we look to loans two years old or less, the percentage climbs to 80% of the At Issuance current balances. If we extend this count out to three years or less we find that 95% of the current loan balances fall into this limit.

What this means is that we have very little empirical experience with the credit performance of this segment of the portfolio. We know that these are loans on the property and chattel of small businesses. High failure rates of small businesses are clustered in the greater than 12 months and less than 48 months period of their lives. We should therefore be wary of extrapolating the current portfolio behavior over the life of the deal. In addition, we should track defaults closely and be ready to change our projection assumptions if we see trends developing in this regard.

Balance Concentration Issues   If a small number of loans comprise a large portion of the portfolio, the loss of some or all of those loans may have a negative effect on the creditworthiness of the deal. This is especially true if they share a secondary concentration characteristic such as coupon or spread rate, or a geographic concentration. Although early in the collateral selection process we deemed ineligible for inclusion in the deal all loans with current balances over $1,100,000, we still have somewhat of a concentration issue here. The largest 146 loans (6% by count), comprise 23% of the current balances at the time of issuance. We may need to keep an eye on the attrition of loans that had initial current balances of over $500,000.

Appraisal Valuations   Appraisal valuations are especially critical. Earlier in this chapter we looked at the effect that a 10% increase and 25% decrease in the value of the project had on loss severity. If there is a systemic overestimation of the property values, the degree of owner's equity in each of the projects of the portfolio would be immediately suspect. If, in addition to an initial overvaluation, the portfolio were to experience a sharp decline in the project, values of the expected loss severities could increase sharply. If there were evidence of this, would we need to consider a subcomponent of the pricing spread to be added into the risk premium spread?

The Effects of Interest Rate Movement   Aside from the fact that interest rate movements can trigger payment shock at a reset period as mentioned above, they can affect the portfolio in other ways as well. A steadily increasing coupon rate can lead to defaults if the businesses are not outperforming relative to their peers for any reason. Here the business is just hanging on, or has been affected by a nonfinancial issue such as a regulatory action or a technological change, and simply may be unable to make a higher payment.

The Effects of Changes in Assumed Prepayment Rates   If the portfolio's empirical prepayment rate is lower than the At Issuance modeled rate, all other things being equal, there will be more cash flow available to the deal. It will come in more slowly and over a longer period of time, but it will be available.

If, however, prepayments are more robust than predicted, the cash flows will arrive earlier in the deal, but be lower in volume. Selected prepayments may have the adverse effect of reducing the excess spread between the coupon rates of the notes and that of the loans if the high spread loans disproportionately pay off.

Monitoring prepayments is critical to making pricing estimates since much of the cash flow volatility is related to this factor and defaults.

The Effects of Changes in Assumed Default Rates Deals can be very sensitive to changes in default rate. A defaulted loan immediately deprives the deal of any immediate payments of interest or principal. After a recovery period lag, some, or all, of the defaulted principal may be realized in the sale of the assets of the project. If there is a combination of higher defaults and lower recovery rates, the deal can suffer accordingly.

Tracking, reporting, and analysis of the default rates are critical to arriving at a well-reasoned set of pricing criteria.

Default Principal Recovery Assumptions The percentage market value decline estimate combined with the recovery lag period assumptions determine when, or even if, the deal will realize any recoveries from a liquidation of a project.

If market value declines increase and at the same time the recovery period lengthens, you will need to integrate this change into your pricing assumptions. If conversely recovery rates rise and the recovery period shortens over time, the deal is becoming stronger. These developments would serve to improve the cash flow assumptions and lower at least a portion of the risk premium spread adjustment.

Structure Performance In this section we have only looked at the pricing considerations related to the performance of the collateral. We will now take a brief overview of structural considerations that affect pricing.

Advance Rates Advance rates translate immediately to investor protection. The higher the advance rate the lower the protection. The lower the advance rate the higher the protection. This deal has a high advance rate, 95% of the At Issuance current balances. If we have sustained credit deterioration in the portfolio, we could eat through the Seller Interest, our passive credit protection. At our expected economic performance criteria of 200 PSA prepayments and 400 PSA defaults, we have a 24.83% overcollateralization of cash flows. This is a pretty healthy coverage ratio as long as none of our basic assumptions are incorrect.

Reserve Accounts The presence of large, adequately funded reserve accounts is a definite pricing plus that will lower the risk premium spread. Reserve funds can acquire their cash in several ways but all of the methods fall into one of three camps. They can be either funded at the onset of the deal, or funded over time as the deal begins to operate, or some combination of these two methods.

In order of preference you should look for, from best to worst:

1. Fully funded at issuance, no release of funds to the Seller Interest until late in the deal
2. Fully funded at issuance, release to the Seller Interest contingent upon superior collateral performance or accelerated retirement of the senior notes
3. Fully funded at issuance, then subject to a nonperformance scheduled release

4. Partially funded at issuance, dependant on ongoing deal cash flows to provide additional top off funding, triggers tightly defined
5. Partially funded at issuance, dependant on ongoing deal performance to fund, triggers not tightly defined
6. Reserve funds not funded at issuance, tight triggers
7. Not funded at issuance, loose or poorly designed triggers
8. No reserve funds at all

This was by no means an exhaustive list, but the pattern is evident at a glance. Cash is king in reserve funds. The more you have sooner, the better you are. The more delayed or conditional the funding of the reserves, the more likely you are to find yourself not having the reserves established when you need them the most. The larger they are in regard to the anticipated risks to the deal, the more value they should bring to the pricing. Remember that the advance rate is in itself establishing an immediate reserve by placing the repayment of the Seller Interest in a subordinate position to the Investor Interest.

Our deal has a modest reserve feature and should it encounter collateral performance away from the expected case, it will probably suffer in regards to an increase in the risk premium.

Performance Triggers   Performance triggers serve to shut off cash payments to the Seller Interest and divert the full cash flow of the deal into the senior Investor Interest. To the extent that the performance triggers of the deal activate early and it is hard to perform this function, the deal should benefit from a reduced risk premium. If, however, such triggers are missing, weak, ill, or poorly designed, the deal should be rated as having more risk and pricing adjusted accordingly.

The Effects of the Market   The market's perception of the deal on an individual basis, or the asset class the deal belongs to, or the entire structured products market, also has a direct impact on the determination of the risk premium spread used in the pricing exercise. If the deal is robust, the issuer has a solid reputation for underwriting, the asset class as a whole is in demand by investors, there is a secondary market for the security (or the commercial paper it backed by the asset pool), and the capital markets are functioning smoothly, the risk premiums will tend to be low. This was the condition of the markets from 2003 to the beginning of 2007. If the reverse of all these things is representative of the current market conditions, the risk premiums will rise until conditions change. If liquidity dries up, investors harbor justifiable and demonstrated concerns about the creditworthiness of the collateral backing the investments, or the structural features of the investments themselves, the spreads will increase. If in addition to these pressures, secondary trading in distressed deals puts severe downward pressure on the mark-to-market comparables, risk premiums can skyrocket to unprecedented levels. These are the conditions of the market from early 2007 to the present.

Some asset classes have seen their pricing spreads from AA-rated deals move from a spread of 60 basis points (.60%) over LIBOR in early 2007 to 900 basis points (9.00%) over LIBOR in a little more than a year. If an incremental move in the risk premium is applied to the pricing exercise, an instrument might lose as much as 25% of its value from this effect alone.

ADDING THE PRICING FUNCTIONALITY
TO THE MONITORING MODEL

Having discussed how to calculate a price and the elements we need to consider in our approach to pricing, it is time to implement the VBA code that will produce a price!

As is our standard approach we will start with considering how we will output the pricing results first and only then work our way backwards through the input and calculation stages to see how we will produce the numbers that we need.

Changes to the Excel "CFWaterfall" Spreadsheet

As we mentioned earlier, before we can produce a price we need to be able to do the following:

- **Produce the stream of periodic cash flows that will be paid to the holder of the investment.** We already have these in the model in the form of a column in the Cash Flow Waterfall spreadsheet. This is column BS of the Waterfall spreadsheet entitled "Total Conduit CF's."
- **Produce a matching series of present value discount factors for each of the cash flow periods.** These present value factors are generated by applying a discount rate that is a combination of the pricing benchmark, in this case the current three-month LIBOR rate, and a risk premium spread. We have similar columns to these in which we calculate discount rates for the purpose of arriving at the Internal Rate of Return of the investment. We will replicate these existing columns in the spreadsheet BQ, BR, and BT and place them at the end of the spreadsheet.
- **Be able to enter the risk premium spread, or "pricing spread," into the model, and use it and the benchmark rate to produce the pricing discount rate.** We will create a field on the Rates and Dates Menu into which we can enter our pricing risk premium spread. This spread will then be displayed at the top of the column in the Waterfall spreadsheet in which we will calculate the discount factors. This will be column BQ.
- **Calculate the Net Present Value of the stream of cash flows and sum the stream.** We will create a column that will contain the discounted cash flows. The present value factor for the period is based on the benchmark rate assumption (LIBOR) plus the risk premium spread reflecting the deal risk and market conditions at the time. We will place this calculation in column BT. A sum function at the top of the column will tell us the aggregate balance of these cash flows.
- **Calculate the price based on the principal outstanding and the sum of the discounted cash flows.** We will create a "Price" field in the cell F32, the region of the waterfall we have labeled the "Box Score" section.

These are the changes we need to make to the Cash Flow Waterfall spreadsheet.

The very first step is to create and place the field where we will display the "Price" information. The Box Score section of the worksheet is the obvious best choice. We will insert a line in the "Performance" section of the Box Score sub-report in the

Summary Report

Collateral Cash Flows

Scheduled Amortization	95,805,059	19.50%
Prepayments to Principal	329,756,846	67.10%
Total Principal Retired	425,561,905	
Defaulted Principal	65,858,473	13.40%
Recoveries of Principal (& rate)	56,801,007	86.25%
Coupon Income	126,234,543	
Total Cash Sources	**608,597,454**	

Debt Cash Flows

Program Fees	10,354,589	
Servicing Fee	2,988,772	
Conduit Debt Service	51,772,943	
Conduit Principal Payments	466,849,358	
Released to Seller	76,631,792	
Total Cash Uses	**608,597,454**	

Performance	Conduit	Seller Interest
Structuring		
Beginning Balance	466,849,358	24,571,019
Ownership Interest	95.00%	5.00%
Performance		
Principal Outstanding	$0	0.00%
Severity of Loss	0.000%	0.00%
IRR	3.750%	36.695%
Price	92.278	
Tenor		
Average Life (yrs)	2.957	
Final Maturity (yrs)	9.333	

EXHIBIT 23.3   Adding the "Price" field to the Waterfall spreadsheet Box Score section

CFWaterfall spreadsheet. We will give this field the Range name "CFConduitPrice."
See Exhibit 23.3.

The next step is to build some columns into the Cash Flow Waterfall to provide us with a series of pricing rate discount factors. We would also like to apply these factors against the stream of conduit financing payment cash flows. We will therefore create three columns at the far right of the spreadsheet in the 64th, 65th, and 66th rows of the waterfall. These will allow us to calculate the periodic discount factors and discount the payments received by the conduit position. See Exhibit 23.4.

The Conduit Pricing Section contains three columns. They perform the following functions:

- **Pricing Conduit Period PV Factor.** Column BU. This is the single period discount factor based on the Conduit Pricing Spread (displayed at the top of the column) added to the value of the LIBOR rate vector for the period. In the displayed case, the Conduit Pricing Spread is 400 basis points or 4.000%. This spread is added to the underlying LIBOR benchmark rate for the period of 2.75% to produce a period discount factor of 6.75%. The discount factor is calculated from this rate. The formula for the cell is: "= 1/ (1+(($BU$12+'RatesDatesMenu'!D8)/12))."

	BS	BT	BU	BV	BW	BX
1						
2						
3						
4						
5	62	63	64	65	66	67
6			Conduit Pricing Section			
7						
8	Total	NPV	Pricing		Pricing	
9	Conduit	Conduit	Conduit	Pricing	NPV	
10	CFs	CFs	Period PV	Cum PV	Conduit	
11			Factor	Factor	CFs	
12	518,622,301	466,849,358	4.000%		430,797,051	
13	(466,849,358)					
14	6,291,196	6,271,597	0.994406	0.994406	6,256,005	1
15	5,378,499	5,345,040	0.994406	0.988844	5,318,498	2
16	5,582,119	5,530,112	0.994406	0.983313	5,488,970	3
17	5,995,624	5,921,261	0.994406	0.977813	5,862,598	4
18	6,397,960	6,298,923	0.994406	0.972343	6,221,015	5
19	6,787,649	6,661,761	0.994406	0.966905	6,563,009	6
20	7,163,644	7,008,880	0.994406	0.961496	6,887,817	7
21	7,524,191	7,338,704	0.994406	0.956118	7,194,014	8
22	7,868,786	7,650,895	0.994406	0.950770	7,481,405	9
23	8,196,111	7,944,330	0.994406	0.945452	7,749,028	10
24	8,505,204	8,218,246	0.994406	0.940163	7,996,282	11
25	8,794,757	8,471,556	0.994406	0.934905	8,222,258	12

EXHIBIT 23.4   The three pricing columns: the periodic discount, the cumulative discount factor, and the net present value of the discounted cash flows

- **Pricing Cumulative PV Factor.** Column BV. This column consists of the schedule of cumulative present value discount factors at the rate of the pricing coupon. It takes the first period discount rate and multiples the current period cumulative discount rate to find the current period cumulative discount rate. The formula for this column is: "= Product($BU$14:BU14)."
- **Pricing NPV Conduit Cash Flows.** Column BW. This column discounts the per period cash flows by multiplying them with the Pricing Cumulative PV Factor. We will sum these cash flows at the top of the column for use in the pricing calculation. The relevant cash flows are the total payments to the conduit interest contained in column BS. The formula for this column is: "= BV14 * BS14."

While we are here we will give the Conduit Pricing Spread cell the Range name of "CFConduitPricingSpread." We now have almost all the components we need to complete the pricing calculation.

Changes to the Rates and Dates Menu

With the changes to the Cash Flow Waterfall spreadsheet complete, we can now turn our attention on how to get the Conduit Risk Pricing Spread into the model and over to the Waterfall spreadsheet to do its work.

		Rates Used in Model Run					Alternative Libor Pathways						Alternative Conduit Financing Spreads	
		Prime	**Libor**	**Spread**	**Conduit**									
		1	**1**	**1**	**Fund Rate**		**1**	**2**	**3**	**4**	**5**		**Spreads**	
8	1	5.250%	2.750%	1.000%	3.750%	1	2.750%	2.900%	3.000%	3.250%	3.500%	1	1.000%	1
9	2	5.250%	2.750%	1.000%	3.750%	2	2.750%	2.900%	3.000%	3.250%	3.500%	2	2.000%	2
10	3	5.250%	2.750%	1.000%	3.750%	3	2.750%	2.900%	3.000%	3.250%	3.500%	3	3.000%	3
11	4	5.250%	2.750%	1.000%	3.750%	4	2.750%	2.900%	3.000%	3.250%	3.500%	4	4.000%	4
12	5	5.250%	2.750%	1.000%	3.750%	5	2.750%	2.900%	3.000%	3.250%	3.500%	5	5.000%	5
13	6	5.250%	2.750%	1.000%	3.750%	6	2.750%	2.900%	3.000%	3.250%	3.500%			6
14	7	5.250%	2.750%	1.000%	3.750%	7	2.750%	2.900%	3.000%	3.250%	3.500%			7
15	8	5.250%	2.750%	1.000%	3.750%	8	2.750%	2.900%	3.000%	3.250%	3.500%		Conduit	8
16	9	5.250%	2.750%	1.000%	3.750%	9	2.750%	2.900%	3.000%	3.250%	3.500%		Pricing	9
17	10	5.250%	2.750%	1.000%	3.750%	10	2.750%	2.900%	3.000%	3.250%	3.500%		Spread	10
18	11	5.250%	2.750%	1.000%	3.750%	11	2.750%	2.900%	3.000%	3.250%	3.500%	1	4.000%	11
19	12	5.250%	2.750%	1.000%	3.750%	12	2.750%	2.900%	3.000%	3.250%	3.500%			12

Day Count Factors and Rates

EXHIBIT 23.5 The Conduit Pricing Spread field on the Rates Dates Menu

This spread is a rate that is critical to the analysis of the deal. It will be especially so in the activities we will undertake in the following chapter. Thus we will put it with all the other rates of the model on the Rates Dates Menu.

We will position just under the Conduit Financing Spread box. See Exhibit 23.5. We will give this field the Range name "m11ConduitPricingSpread."

Changes to the VBA Code

There are also a number of numerous but thankfully small changes we will need to make to various parts of the VBA code as we outlined in the "Under Construction" section of the chapter earlier.

Constant Variable Declarations The first and most important thing we need to do is to increase the value of the constant variable PAY_COLS, which is one of the dimensions of the Cash Flow Waterfall calculation grid. We have added three new columns, so this variable needs to be incremented from 63 to 66. See Exhibit 23.6.

The next thing we need to do is to correct something that we should have fixed some time ago. We need to establish a set of three constant variables to govern the printing size of each of the three sections of the Box Score report. Once we began to incorporate the Box Score section into a number of reports where it had not been used in the structuring model, we should have taken this step immediately. Rapping ourselves on the knuckles with a ruler (although lightly), we will do this now. See Exhibit 23.7.

Global Variable Declarations We have two distinct tasks we need to perform in the "A_Globals" module. The first is that we need to declare three new global variables used in the pricing process. They are the names for the pricing spread we will read

```
Public Const PAY_COLS = 66      'maximum Excel model columns in Cash Flow Waterfall
```

EXHIBIT 23.6 Increasing the value of the PAY_COLS constant to keep it in line with the dimensions of the Cash Flow Waterfall calculation area

```
Public Const BXSCR1_ROWS = 14    'rows in the cash flows section
Public Const BXSCR2_ROWS = 12    'rows in the deal performance section
Public Const BXSCR3_ROWS = 3     'rows in the triggers section
```

EXHIBIT 23.7 Creating three new constant variables for use in printing the sub-sections of the Box Score Report

in from the Rates Dates Menu, the variable for the conduit price we will generate, and the array of calculated prices we will display in the Matrix Summary Report.

The second task is to edit the declarations of the Box Score arrays to include the use of the three constant variables we created above. See Exhibits 23.8 and 23.9.

While we are mucking about with Box Score arrays and the three newly created constant variables, we need to adjust the data arrays that hold the comparative information between the At Issuance case and the Current case in the Waterfall Report. These are module variables and reside at the top of the **"WriteWaterfall-Reports"** module, not in the **"A_Globals"** module. See Exhibit 23.10.

Changes to the Error Checking Subroutines Now that we have the conduit pricing spread available to the model we must make sure that it is okay to use. We will run it through the usual drill of error checking to make sure that we are introducing something into the program that will blow up! One of the subroutines called by the "IsNumerics_AllData" is "IsNumerics_RatesDatesMenu." The **"ErrCheckMenus"** module holds both of these subroutines.

The changes to the "IsNUmerics_RatesDatesMenu" are shown below in Exhibit 23.11.

Changes to the Read Rates and Dates Menu Subroutine Having error checked the conduit pricing spread, we can now read it into the model and put it to work. See Exhibit 23.12.

Capturing the Price Information The next step is to load the conduit pricing spread onto the cash flow spreadsheet and perform the calculation. See Exhibit 23.13.

The model now has everything it needs to perform the price calculation. The conduit pricing spread can be error checked, read off the menus, and then loaded onto the Cash Flow Waterfall to trigger the net present value discount factors calculation. With the factors calculated, the price can be calculated in one easy formula. The price is now out on the Waterfall spreadsheet. We need to capture it, store it, and display it on the appropriate reports.

Changes to the Box Score Read and Write Subroutines Once the price result has been generated, we need to get it off the waterfall spreadsheet and into VBA arrays so

```
Public g_conduit_price_spread    As Double    'conduit financing spread
Public g_cond_price              As Double    'calculated conduit price
Public g_out_cond_price()        As Double    'matrix report array to hold price
```

EXHIBIT 23.8 Creating two new global variables to store the pricing spread and to record the results of the price calculation

```
Public g_waterfall_bxscr1(0 To MAX_SCEN, 1 To BXSCR1_ROWS, 1 To 2)
                                         As Double  'box score field group 1
Public g_waterfall_bxscr2(0 To MAX_SCEN, 1 To BXSCR2_ROWS, 1 To 2)
                                         As Double  'box score field group 2
Public g_waterfall_bxscr3(0 To MAX_SCEN, 1 To BXSCR3_ROWS)
                                         As String  'box score field group 3

Public g_scen_bxscr1(1 To MAX_SCEN, 1 To BXSCR1_ROWS, 1 To 2)
                                         As Double  'box score field group 1
Public g_scen_bxscr2(1 To MAX_SCEN, 1 To BXSCR2_ROWS, 1 To 2)
                                         As Double  'box score field group 2
Public g_scen_bxscr3(1 To MAX_SCEN, 1 To BXSCR3_ROWS)
                                         As Double  'box score field group 3
```

EXHIBIT 23.9 Using the new created constant variables BXSCR1_ROWS, BXSCR2_ROWS, and BXSCR3_ROWS, to dimension the arrays holding the Box Score Information

that we can present the results in our report packages. Most of the activity that must be changed lies in reading the fields in the second section of the Box Score report. We are going through a loop of 12 lines, the value of BXSCR2_ROWS. Lines 3 and now 8 are headers and contain no information. By inserting the line that contains the "Price" field we have moved the position of the "Performance" header line down one. This also means that we will need to change the offset from 37 to **38** (as in boldface) below for the Triggers sections. By adding the price line we moved the entire Trigger section down one line. See Exhibit 23.14.

We now have the contents of the Box Score in "**g_waterfall_bxscr#**" arrays. This means that all we have to do is make the similar corrections to the subroutines that write the Box Score. We can populate any template file that has had the "Price" field added to its Box Score section. See Exhibit 23.15.

Changes to the Report Template Files   In the Waterfall Report we will need to add the "Price" field to not one but three separate Box Scores on the report worksheet. We will also need to insert the field into the At Issuance waterfall spreadsheet. We will also need to add the three new columns of the pricing calculations at the end of the At Issuance and Current Month worksheets as well as to the Difference waterfall spreadsheet to the right of the Current scenario.

In the Matrix Summary Report we are replacing the "Debt Service Paid" field in the "ConduitNotePerformance" worksheet with the "Price" information. The original field is a dollar field with no decimal places that is right justified. We will be expressing the price in a three-decimal, centered format. We must therefore change the presentation of the price output fields of the report and of the Differences report to its right. See Exhibit 23.16.

```
Dim bxscr1_diff(1 To BXSCR1_ROWS, 1 To 2)   As Double   'box score field group 1
Dim bxscr2_diff(1 To BXSCR2_ROWS, 1 To 2)   As Double   'box score field group 2
Dim bxscr3_diff(1 To BXSCR3_ROWS)           As Double   'box score field group
```

EXHIBIT 23.10 Using the new created constant variables BXSCR1_ROWS, BXSCR2_ROWS, and BXSCR3_ROWS, to dimension the arrays holding the Box Score Information for the Waterfall Reports Package

```
Sub IsNumeric_RatesDatesInfo()


Const NUM_TABLES = 3              'number of rates tables
(7 lines of code not displayed, these are other constant and variable declarations)

   msgInfo(3) = "Rates  & Dates Menu   => non-numeric entry in table" & Chr(13)
   (3 lines of code not displayed, other error message content)
   msgComp(4) = " Conduit Pricing Spread "
   msgComp(5) = Chr(13)
   errcase(2) = 0     'tells the calling subroutine we have error if = 1

   'set all error counts for the columns and tables to zero
   (6 lines of code not displayed)
   'The Libor and Prime Tables
   (23 lines of code not displayed)
   'Conduit Spread Table
   (12 lines of code not displayed)

   'Conduit Pricing Coupon Table
   condt_value = Range("m11ConduitPricingSpread")
   err_result(4) = False        'specific error tag for this table
   If condt_value <> "" Then err_result(4) = (IsNumeric(condt_value) = False)
   'if we find an error, increment the counter and table of the error
   If err_result(4) Then
      column_err(1, 4) = column_err(1, 4) + 1
      table_total(4) = table_total(4) + 1
      errcase(2) = 1            'error detected
   End If

   'assemble the error message
   For itest = 1 To NUM_TABLES + 1  '1=Libor,2=Prime,3=Conduit Spread,4=PricingSpread
     If table_total(itest) > 0 Then          'got one!
        msgInfo(2) = msgInfo(2) & msgComp(itest) 'add detail msg to general header msg
        For icase = 1 To 5
          If column_err(icase, itest) > 0 Then    'add the pathway(s) numbers
             msgInfo(2) = msgInfo(2) & " " & icase & ","
          End If
        Next icase
        msgInfo(2) = msgInfo(2) & msgComp(5)         'close with a line return
     End If
   Next itest

End Sub
```

EXHIBIT 23.11 Modifying the "IsNumerics_RatesDatesMenu" subroutine to error check the conduit pricing spread input field

```
Sub Read_Rates_and_Dates_Menu()

  Sheets("Rates Dates Menu").Select
  Range("A1").Select
  Sheets("Rates Dates Menu").Calculate
  'read the day count factors for 30/360, Act/360, Act/Act
  (7 lines of code not displayed,For...Next loop that reads these schedules)
  'index interest level;  Prime, LIBOR, spread
  (5 lines of code not displayed,For...Next loop that reads these schedules)
  g_conduit_spread = Range("m11IndexLevels").Cells(1,3)
  g_conduit_price_spread = Range("m11ConduitPricingSpread")
  'funding rates for the conduit
  (3 lines of code not displayed)

End Sub
```

EXHIBIT 23.12 Reading the conduit pricing spread from the Rates Dates Menu

```
Sub Load_Funding_Rate_Levels()

  Application.Calculation = xlCalculationManual
  Sheets("CFWaterfall").Select
  Range("cfFundConduit").ClearContents
  For irow = 1 To PAY_DATES
    Range("cfFundConduit").Cells(irow) = g_fund_conduit(irow)
  Next irow
  Range("CFConduitPricingSpread") = g_conduit_price_spread

End Sub
```

EXHIBIT 23.13 Loading the conduit pricing spread into the cash flow waterfall spreadsheet

In the Single Scenario reports and the Historical reports we will insert the "Price" field into the Box Scores.

In the At Issuance Waterfall Reports we will need to insert the three new pricing calculations columns in the right side of the Waterfall spreadsheet and the "Price" field in the Box Score section.

In the At Issuance Matrix Summary Report we will need to replace the third entry in the third block of the "At Issuance" spreadsheet with "Price" and reformat the field as noted above.

Changes to the Report Generating Subroutines The CF Waterfall report generating subroutine will have very little change. Only the reformatted Box Score is affected by the inclusion of the "Price" line. The report generator is already adjusted

```
Sub Read_Waterfall_Box_Score(scen As Integer, row_offset As Integer, col_offset As
Integer)

  'Box Score Section 1 -- Cash Flow Summary
  (8 lines of code not displayed, this section is unaffected by the
       addition of the "Price" field lower in the report)
  'Box Score Section 2 -- Performance of the Notes and Seller Interest
  For irow = 1 To BXSCR2_ROWS
    For icol = 1 To 2
      'these are the title lines for Performance and Tenor
      If irow = 3 Or irow = 8   Then Exit For
      g_waterfall_bxscr2(scen, irow, icol) = _
           Cells(irow + 25 + row_offset, icol + 5 + col_offset)
      'For the 8th row and onwards there is no Seller Interest
      ' information so we do not have to print a second column
      If irow >= 8 Then Exit For
    Next icol
  Next irow
  'Box Score Section 3 -- Triggers
  For irow = 1 To BXSCR3_ROWS
      If Cells(irow + 38 + row_offset, icol + 5 + col_offset) = 0 Then
          g_waterfall_bxscr3(scen, irow) = "False"
      End If
  Next irow

End Sub
```

EXHIBIT 23.14 Modifications to the subroutine that reads the contents of the Waterfall Box Score, which now includes our price

```
Sub Write_Waterfall_Box_Score(scen As Integer, row_offset As Integer, col_offset As
Integer)

  'Box Score Section 1 -- Cash Flow Summary
  (8 lines of code not displayed, this section is unaffected by the
         addition of the "Price" field lower in the report)
  'Box Score Section 2 -- Performance of the Notes and Seller Interest
  For irow = 1 To BXSCR2_ROWS
      For icol = 1 To 2
          'rows 3 and 8 are header rows
          If irow = 3 Or irow = 8 Then Exit For
          Cells(irow + 25 + row_offset, icol + 5 + col_offset) = _
                                          g_waterfall_bxscr2(scen, irow, icol)
          'conduit information only on these lines so immediately leave the loop
          If irow = 8 Then Exit For
      Next icol
  Next irow
  'Box Score Section 3 -- Triggers
  For irow = 1 To BXSCR3_ROWS
      Cells(irow  + 38 + row_offset, icol + 5 + col_offset) = _
                                          g_waterfall_bxscr3(scen, irow)
  Next irow

End Sub
```

EXHIBIT 23.15 Modifications to the subroutine that writes the contents of the Waterfall Box Score to the various template files of the report package

by our earlier change in the declaration of the constant variable PAY_COLS. This modified all of the code that read the results from the spreadsheet automatically as it did the subroutines that we use to write the results to the template files. As long as we change the Waterfall template file to include the additional three columns of price calculations, we are fine.

The situation with the Matrix Summary Report requires a bit more work. We first need to change the Base Case statistics block at the upper right-hand of the

Summary Matrix Report #3
Conduit Note Paydown

Key & Expected Case Performance	
Total P&I Payments	622,923,116
Principal Repayments	466,849,358
Price	100.000
Severity of Principal Loss	0.000%
Coverage Ratio	30.16%
Internal Rate of Return	6.375%

Default Levels	PSA Prepayment Methodology 1	2	3
	200.00%		
1 400.00% PSA	621,386,315 466,849,358 92.337 0.000% 28.50% 6.376%		

Comparison of At Issuance to Current Month			
Default Levels	PSA Prepayment Methodology 1	2	3
	200.00%		
1 400.00% PSA	(1,536,801) (0) -7.663 0.000% -1.665% 0.001%		

EXHIBIT 23.16 Reformatted Matrix Summary Report. This report has been run and trimmed down from the template configuration of 100 possible cases

```
Sub Redim_All_SummaryMatrixReport_Vectors()

    'If we are going to produce the summary matrix cashflows
    If g_out_matrix Then
        ReDim g_out_avg_life(1 To g_prepay_levels, 1 To g_default_levels) As Double
        (12 lines omitted)
        ReDim g_out_cond_debt_service(1 To g_prepay_levels, 1 To g_default_levels) As
        Double
        ReDim g_out_cond_price(1 To g_prepay_levels, 1 To g_default_levels) As Double
        (8 lines omitted)
        ReDim g_out_coupon_short(1 To g_prepay_levels, 1 To g_default_levels) As Double
    End If

End Sub
```

EXHIBIT 23.17 This subroutine redimensions all the Matrix Summary Report variables. We will add the variable g_out_condt_price to it

"ConduitNotePerformance" spreadsheet. Before we can populate the report with the price information we must make sure the program has the capacity to capture this information for our use. The following subroutine redimensions all of the "g_out_" variables used by the Matrix Summary Report. See Exhibit 23.17.

Now that we have a place to store the information we can get it from the model runs. See Exhibit 23.18.

Now we have everything and can write it to the Matrix Summary Report! See Exhibit 23.19.

With the Matrix Summary Report taken care of, we are finished. The new and improved mark-to-market monitoring model can now be deployed to track our deal in the months ahead!

DELIVERABLES CHECKLIST

The VBA Knowledge Checklist item for this chapter is:

- How to modify the monitoring model to price a deal or to provide a mark-to-market estimate

```
Sub Capture_Matrix_Report_Results()

    g_out_avg_life(i_prepay, i_default) = Range("AvgLifeConduit")
    (10 lines omitted)
    g_out_cond_debt_service(i_prepay, i_default) = Range("sumConduitDebtService")
    g_out_cond_price(i_prepay, i_default) = Range("CFConduitPrice")
    g_out_cond_sol(i_prepay, i_default) = Range("SolConduit")
    (22 lines omitted)

End Sub
```

EXHIBIT 23.18 This reads the price information from the Range "CFConduitPrice" on the waterfall spreadsheet into arrays used by the Matrix Summary Reports

```
Sub Write_Conduit_Financing_Performance()

   Sheets("ConduitNotePerformance").Select
   (omitted 3 lines of code that writes the Base Case performance)
   icol = 3
   For i_p = 1 To g_prepay_levels
      irow = 14
      For i_d = 1 To g_default_levels
         Cells(irow + 1, icol).Value = g_out_cond_repay(i_p, i_d)
         Cells(irow + 2, icol).Value = g_out_cond_price(i_p, i_d)
         Cells(irow + 3, icol).Value = g_out_cond_sol(i_p, i_d)
         (12 lines of code omitted that finish the report and format it)
      Next i_d
   Next i_p
   Calculate
End Sub
```

EXHIBIT 23.19 This writes the price information to "ConduitNotePerformance" report of the Matrix Summary Reports

The Financial Knowledge Checklist items for this chapter are:

- What are the basic components needed to produce a price on an ABS security
- That the pricing of the deal is based on anticipated performance against other deals of its type, the "At Issuance" projections and the conditions in the market

NEXT STEPS

In Chapter 22 we built the monitoring model based on our original structuring model. In this chapter we added a pricing feature to it.

We are now ready to use the monitoring model to perform surveillance on our deal and to additionally perform the mark-to-market function on an as-needed basis.

In Chapter 24 we will monitor the deal over its first 24 months and see how it does. We will perform surveillance of the assets and the structure. In addition, using the deal performance and the market conditions, we will perform a monthly mark-to-market pricing exercise.

ON THE WEB SITE

On the Web site you will find **"MONITOR_Ver02.xls"** and the four new report template files for the Cash Flow Waterfall, the Matrix Summary, the Single Scenario, and the History reports. These are respectively **"m2_waterfall_2template .xls," "m2_matrix_template.xls," "m2_scenario_template.xls,"** and **"m2_history_template.xls."**

## CHAPTER 24

Challenging Times for the Deal

OVERVIEW

We now have a working monitoring model that we can apply to tracking and valuing our deal. We will look at the first two years of the life of our deal and see how it performs. This performance will be measured against our initial expectations at issuance; how other similar deals are performing; how the structure appears to be functioning; and how the market conditions affect the pricing and valuation of the deal.

DELIVERABLES

VBA Modeling Knowledge:

■ Using the monitoring model to track our deal over the first 24 months of its life

Finance Knowledge:

■ What types of comparison, judgments, and measurements are appropriate when monitoring a structured finance deal in a difficult market?

UNDER CONSTRUCTION

We have the day off. We will be running the monitoring program to update both others and ourselves as to the progress of the deal. We will not, hopefully, need to write any more code!

USING THE MONITORING MODEL TO ASSESS THE PERFORMANCE AND VALUE OF THE DEAL

We have a monitoring model. It is now three months since the issuance of our deal in October 2006. For the purposes of this exercise, the deal that we will be tracking over the next two years will be somewhat different than the deal that we structured earlier in the book.

All the loans of our portfolio are indexed off of the Prime Rate. The cost of debt to the Seller is the conduit financing rate, which consists of the three-month LIBOR Rate and a spread. In order to illustrate the performance of the deal over the previous two years, we will need to structure the deal using the rates that were applicable in October 2006, not now. At that time the three-month LIBOR Rate was 5.371% and the Prime Rate was 8.25%. Using a 95% advance rate, the same beginning collateral portfolio which had a current At Issuance balance of $491 million and identical program costs and deal expenses, we will issue the identical amount of funding to the client, $466 million. This issuance has a 1.00% pricing spread making the initial coupon rate equal to LIBOR + 1% = 6.371%. The coupons of the loans have spreads to Prime ranging from 2.25 to 4.75%. This would mean that the initial gross coupons for the portfolio would Range from a low of 10.5 to 13.00%.

The two deals are very similar with one noticeable exception. The deal that we initially structured with a 200 PSA Prepayment speed and a 400 PSD default speed versus the deal that we will use in this chapter have one very different cash flow component: The aggregate coupon income. The total cash flows for the original deal are $701 million while the cash flows for the deal we will follow in this chapter are $788 million! The preponderance of this difference is the coupon income difference caused by the much higher index levels for Prime and LIBOR that pertained at the time. As can be clearly seen, the extra income that comes to the deal from the Prime Rate driven loans is then almost immediately paid back out in conduit debt service! The effect on the retirement of the principal is minimal. If we look at the average life and final maturity of the two deals, we will see that they are virtually identical. The detailed results can be seen in Exhibit 24.1.

The Next 24 Months

Over the rest of the chapter we will look at the life of the deal for its first 24 months. This span will include some highly contrasted conditions. In the fourth quarter of 2006 the capital markets were in high gear and the investor community was eagerly purchasing a wide Range of structured financial products. At the end of the two-year period, the capital markets are essentially shut down. We have experienced several large banks failing or surviving only on government sponsored or supported bailouts. The sellers' markets of late 2006 are now characterized by asset holding liquidations triggered by mark-to-market and capital constraints on the part of the banks and other investors. The valuation of assets has become unsure and is at times driven by the only prices available, that of distressed or liquidity driven sales. These sales then benchmark a new and higher risk premium for all subsequent valuations of deals in the same asset class. These devaluations then lead to further markdowns in value triggering a vicious cycle. Into this picture now step liquid investors, including hedge funds, who "bottom fish" driving the spreads even higher.

Factors That Influence Performance and Valuation

In the course of the rest of the chapter, we will use the monitoring program to examine the performance of our deal. As part of this exercise we will use the monitoring model

400%	PSD	<= Default Rate
200%	PSA	<= Prepayment Rate

Originally Structured Deal Chapter 18		
Summary Report		

Collateral Cash Flows		
Scheduled Amortization	197,427,612	42.29%
Prepayments to Principal	252,247,689	54.03%
Total Principal Retired	449,675,300	
Defaulted Principal	41,745,077	8.94%
Recoveries of Principal (& rate)	35,765,295	85.68%
Coupon Income	216,235,379	
Total Cash Sources	**701,675,975**	
Debt Cash Flows		
Program Fees	4,739,182	
Servicing Fee	19,216,364	
Conduit Debt Service	88,859,663	
Conduit Principal Payments	466,849,358	
Released to Seller	122,011,408	26.14%
Total Cash Uses	**701,675,975**	

		Seller
Performance	Conduit	Interest
Structuring		
Beginning Conduit Balance	466,849,358	24,571,019
Ownership Interest	95.00%	5.00%
Performance		
Principal Outstanding	$ -	0.00%
Severity of Loss	0.000%	0.00%
IRR	3.750%	49.880%
Price	100.00	
Tenor		
Average Life (yrs)	5.076	
Final Maturity (yrs)	17.000	
Modified Duration	4.418	
Macauley Duration	4.259	

Monitor Model Deal Chapter 24		
Summary Report		

Collateral Cash Flows		
Scheduled Amortization	185,410,203	39.72%
Prepayments to Principal	263,299,530	56.40%
Total Principal Retired	448,709,733	
Defaulted Principal	42,710,644	9.15%
Recoveries of Principal (& rate)	36,582,308	85.65%
Coupon Income	303,236,913	
Total Cash Sources	**788,528,954**	
Debt Cash Flows		
Program Fees	4,896,432	
Servicing Fee	19,889,241	
Conduit Debt Service	156,073,758	
Conduit Principal Payments	466,849,358	
Released to Seller	140,820,166	30.16%
Total Cash Uses	**788,528,954**	

		Seller
Performance	Conduit	Interest
Structuring		
Beginning Balance	466,849,358	24,571,019
Ownership Interest	95.00%	5.00%
Performance		
Principal Outstanding	$0	0.00%
Severity of Loss	0.000%	0.00%
IRR	6.375%	54.176%
Price	100.000	
Tenor		
Average Life (yrs)	5.244	
Final Maturity (yrs)	16.917	
Modified Duration	4.154	
Macauley Duration	3.905	

EXHIBIT 24.1 Comparison of the Summary Box Scores for the deal we originally structured in Chapter 18 and the deal we will use for this chapter

to generate prices based on three things:

1. The intrinsic performance of the deal itself, the performance of the collateral in the context of prepayments and defaults, and the prospects for recoveries of defaults. We will want to keep an eye out for any changes in the risk profile of the collateral due to changes in geographic, balance, or spread concentrations. We will also compare the speed at which the collateral is being retired. We will take reports from the financial and field servicers who will work with the Obligors if necessary to help liquidate collateral in the case of defaults. Finally, we compare how the deal is amortizing relative to our At Issuance assumptions and look at changes in average life and final maturity as the deal ages.
2. Performance of the deal relative to other deals of the same type in regards to collateral and structure. Our benchmarks here are public deals issued into the market and other deals of this asset class we hold in the conduits.
3. The last factor will be the general economic and market conditions. Is the economy robust or weak? The majority of the Obligors in our portfolio are running small businesses that are in the first three to five years of their existence. This is the most stressful time for these firms. How is the value of the deal reflected in the conditions of the marketplace? Is there a healthy balance of buyers and Sellers? How is this deal perceived as having relative value to other similar deals and other deals of other asset classes, or any other potential investments? Finally what is the market appetite for risk/return relative to the characteristics of the deal?

Looking at the Deal in a Quarterly Framework

The job of monitoring and valuation is an ongoing one. Most types of securities that are traded in a liquid secondary market are priced throughout the deal, several or many times a day, as needed, in response to changing market conditions. Monitoring is usually performed in conjunction with the payment cycle of the deal. If it is a deal backed by the major asset types such as credit cards, auto loans, mortgages or home equity loans, manufactured housing, or leases, the monitoring cycle has a monthly frequency.

In this chapter we will use a time period of three months. This will give us a total of eight snapshots of the deal over the first two years of its life. We will have three sections for each of these quarterly updates. The first will consist of how well the deal is performing relative to its At Issuance expectations. The second will be a brief section of how other deals of its type are performing, especially collateral performance. The third will be the impact of market conditions on valuation.

We will take the viewpoint that we are reporting to our internal risk personnel and, in addition, a rating agency surveillance group that is periodically reviewing the conduit holdings.

Due to space constraints, this analysis will not be as detailed as it would be in its actual practice. I will, however, try to cover the core essentials of the process and show you how to employ the information we have to support our positions.

Inputs to the Monitoring Process

To help us with the monitoring and valuation process we have a number of parties that we can draw on for their particular expertise. These are:

- The field servicing team. These are the people who visit the Obligors if there are problems and serve as our closest to the source font of information on how the portfolio is doing. They will also provide us with market information and local color as it relates to liquidation sales, workouts, and the like.
- The financial servicing team who handles the payments and see that the cash gets to the right parties, at the right time, with the right accounting. They will also provide us with all the portfolio information including the current balances of the loans, default and prepayment rates, market value decline percentages, and recovery lag periods and amounts.
- The trading desk for public deals of this or similar asset classes in the secondary market.
- The syndicate desk that can inform us as to what the state of the market is, what current levels of issuance spreads are, and which investments are in and out of favor. They are also a good source of information on client likes and dislikes for future demand because of their frequent interaction with the sales force.
- The risk control and accounting personnel who will tell us what the current corporate view is to valuation guidelines.

All of these sources will be polled and utilized as necessary in the months ahead.

THREE MONTHS FROM ISSUANCE

Time Period: October through December 2006.

　　General Economic Conditions: Very good. The capital markets are wide open. There is strong investor demand driven by the approaching year-end to put the last of the targeted money to work.

　　Pricing Inputs: Spreads are low and stable. The pricing spread applied by the conduit for our deal at 100 bps over LIBOR, is in line with other "A" rated deals both in the conduit and in the secondary market. Outlooks are optimistic. Rates for both LIBOR and Prime are stable. Prime is at 8.25% for all three months of the quarter, while LIBOR is 5.371%, 5.370%, and 5.360%. This means that the spread between the two Ranges is from 2.80% and 2.89%.

　　Inputs from the Servicing Groups: The market's demand for real estate is strong due to the fact that financing is cheap and readily available. At issuance we had estimated that our Market Value Decline (MVD) numbers would be about 50%, but evidence suggests that 25% is closer to the actual case. This is due to the fact that many properties are being sold near or at asking price with minimal repair and refurbishment needed. Most properties are being completely turned around in well under a year, some as soon as six months from the event of default. It is reasonable to assume that we could use nine months as our recovery lag assumptions with a 25% MVD Factor. We also note that it is believed that the project values of the portfolio might be as much as 4 to 6% too low based on appreciation since we began the deal process. We will therefore adjust the project values upward to reflect this fact.

　　Collateral Performance: Collateral performance for the first three months remains strong. Our At Issuance model suggested that we would experience $0.98 million in prepayments and $1.57 million in defaults. We have in fact experienced $1.47 million of prepayments and $1.33 million of defaults over the first quarter. A snapshot of the portfolio performance in this regard can be seen in Exhibit 24.2.

　　Structure Performance: The structure appears to be outperforming our at issuance expectations. If we look at the Box Score Summary comparison of the three months from issuance versus the At Issuance report, we note several things. The first is that our Current rate for recoveries is 100%. This is due to the current economic environment, which allows the foreclosed and repossessed properties to be disposed of quickly. We have also increased the project values of the properties by 4% to reflect the rise in values over the last three months when this information was last evaluated. The combination of the lower-than-predicted MVD, faster recovery periods, and increased valuation means that *none* of the losses will be greater than any of the equity positions on the loans. We will have an incremental $5.3 million in the deal from these additional recovered sums. See Exhibit 24.3.

　　Market Conditions: Excellent. The financial markets are finishing another strong year. Although there is some concern over the large number of adjustable rate mortgages that will be resetting their coupons in the next 6 to 12 months, the economic outlook remains strong. Spreads remain historically low. The 1.00% pricing spread on our deal appears congruent with the market and pricing of comparable deals. With full repayment of principal and timely receipt of interest expected, our deal remains priced at par.

　　Running the Model: We will run the model for each of these three months using a 25% MVD number and a nine-month Recovery Lag Period (RLP). We will use

Collateral Attrition Report
3 Months Since Issuance

Original Portfolio	
2,279	Number of Loans
$491,420,377	Current Balances
100.000%	% Initial Current Balances
11.505%	Wght Avg Coupon
191.62	Wght Avg Rem Term (months)
15.19	Wght Avg Seasoning (months)

Current Pay Collateral			Difference from Original Portfolio	
2,272	Number of Loans		10	Number of Loans
$481,507,985	Current Balances		$9,912,392	Current Balances
97.983%	% Initial Current Balances		2.017%	% Initial Current Balances
11.504%	Wght Avg Coupon		0.000%	Wght Avg Coupon
192.45	Wght Avg Rem Term (months)		(0.83)	Wght Avg Rem Term (months)
15.20	Wght Avg Seasoning (months)		(0.01)	Wght Avg Seasoning (months)

Prepayments to Date			Defaults to Date	
5	Number of Loans		5	Number of Loans
$1,466,244	Current Balances		$1,332,017	Current Balances
0.298%	% Initial Current Balances		0.271%	% Initial Current Balances
11.285%	Wght Avg Coupon		11.017%	Wght Avg Coupon
223.68	Wght Avg Rem Term (months)		190.84	Wght Avg Rem Term (months)
7.58	Wght Avg Seasoning (months)		12.44	Wght Avg Seasoning (months)

EXHIBIT 24.2 The prepayment and default Portfolio Attrition Report for the first three months of the deal

1.00% as the pricing spread for each of the three months. We will also increase the project values by 4% to reflect higher-than-average price appreciation in the real estate market since the Obligors bought the properties.

SIX MONTHS FROM ISSUANCE

Time Period: January through March 2007.

General Economic Conditions: Good. The capital markets are open. There is strong investor demand driven by the beginning of the year.

Pricing Inputs: Spreads continue to be both low and stable. Prime remained at 8.25% across this period, LIBOR moved generally lower at 5.36%, 5.48%, and finally 5.35% over the three-month period.

Inputs from the Servicing Groups: The market's demand for real estate is strong. There are a few instances in which unusual or specialty property such as we have in some sectors of the portfolio are not moving as quickly or as well (pricewise as others). These are specifically hotels, motels, and storage facilities. It is suggested that we leave the recovery lag assumption at nine months but increase the MVD number slightly from 25% to 30%.

Collateral Performance: Collateral performance for the first six months remains strong. Our At Issuance model suggested that we would experience $2.41 million in prepayments and $1.87 million in defaults. We have in fact experienced

Current Month - 3 Months Since Issuance

Collateral Cash Flows		
Scheduled Amortization	185,047,522	
Prepayments to Principal	263,470,551	53.61%
Total Principal Retired	448,518,073	
Defaulted Principal	42,902,304	8.73%
Recoveries of Principal (& rate)	42,901,918	100.00%
Coupon Income	302,417,821	
Total Cash Sources	**793,837,811**	
Debt Cash Flows		
Program Fees	4,882,165	
Servicing Fee	19,831,754	
Conduit Debt Service	155,609,754	
Conduit Principal Payments	466,849,358	
Released to Seller	146,664,780	31.42%
Total Cash Uses	**793,837,811**	

Performance	Conduit	Seller Interest
Structuring		
Beginning Conduit Balance	466,849,358	24,571,019
Ownership Interest	95.00%	5.00%
Performance		
Principal Outstanding	$ -	0.00% 0.00%
Severity of Loss	0.000%	0.00%
IRR	6.375%	58.284%
Price	100.000	0.000%
Tenor		
Average Life (yrs)	5.229	
Final Maturity (yrs)	16.917	
Modified Duration	4.142	
Macauley Duration	3.894	

At Issuance Projection

Collateral Cash Flows		
Scheduled Amortization	185,410,203	
Prepayments to Principal	263,299,530	53.58%
Total Principal Retired	448,709,733	
Defaulted Principal	42,710,644	8.69%
Recoveries of Principal (& rate)	36,582,308	85.65%
Coupon Income	303,236,913	
Total Cash Sources	**788,528,954**	
Debt Cash Flows		
Program Fees	4,896,432	
Servicing Fee	19,889,241	
Conduit Debt Service	156,073,758	
Conduit Principal Payments	466,849,358	
Released to Seller	140,820,166	30.16%
Total Cash Uses	**788,528,954**	

Performance	Conduit	Seller Interest
Structuring		
Beginning Conduit Balance	466,849,358	24,571,019
Ownership Interest	95.00%	5.00%
Performance		
Principal Outstanding	$ -	0.00% 0.00%
Severity of Loss	0.000%	0.00%
IRR	6.375%	54.176%
Price	100.000	0.000%
Tenor		
Average Life (yrs)	5.244	
Final Maturity (yrs)	16.917	
Modified Duration	4.154	
Macauley Duration	3.905	

Difference: At Issuance and Current Month

Collateral Cash Flows		
Scheduled Amortization	-362,682	
Prepayments to Principal	171,021	0.06%
Total Principal Retired	-191,661	
Defaulted Principal	191,661	0.45%
Recoveries of Principal (& rate)	6,319,610	17.28%
Coupon Income	-819,092	
Total Cash Sources	**5,308,857**	
Debt Cash Flows		
Program Fees	-14,266	
Servicing Fee	-57,487	
Conduit Debt Service	-464,004	
Conduit Principal Payments	0	
Released to Seller	5,844,614	1.25%
Total Cash Uses	**5,308,857**	

Performance	Conduit	Seller Interest
Structuring		
Beginning Conduit Balance	0	0
Ownership Interest	0	0
Performance		
Principal Outstanding	0	0.000%
Severity of Loss	0.000%	0.000%
IRR	0.000%	-4.108%
Price	0.000	
Tenor		
Average Life (yrs)	0.015	0.000
Final Maturity (yrs)	0.000	0.000
Modified Duration	0.012	0.000
Macauley Duration	0.011	0.000

EXHIBIT 24.3 Comparison of the Summary Box Scores for the At Issuance performance versus the Current Month, three months from issuance

Collateral Attrition Report
6 Months From Issuance

Original Portfolio	
2,279	Number of Loans
$491,420,377	Current Balances
100.000%	% Initial Current Balances
11.505%	Wght Avg Coupon
191.62	Wght Avg Rem Term (months)
15.19	Wght Avg Seasoning (months)

Current Pay Collateral			Difference from Original Portfolio	
2,255	Number of Loans		24	Number of Loans
$469,930,055	Current Balances		$21,490,323	Current Balances
95.627%	% Initial Current Balances		4.373%	% Initial Current Balances
11.504%	Wght Avg Coupon		0.001%	Wght Avg Coupon
193.15	Wght Avg Rem Term (months)		(1.53)	Wght Avg Rem Term (months)
15.23	Wght Avg Seasoning (months)		(0.04)	Wght Avg Seasoning (months)

Prepayments to Date			Defaults to Date	
16	Number of Loans		8	Number of Loans
$3,881,282	Current Balances		$3,208,358	Current Balances
0.790%	% Initial Current Balances		0.653%	% Initial Current Balances
11.176%	Wght Avg Coupon		11.310%	Wght Avg Coupon
229.70	Wght Avg Rem Term (months)		202.38	Wght Avg Rem Term (months)
9.36	Wght Avg Seasoning (months)		11.00	Wght Avg Seasoning (months)

EXHIBIT 24.4   The prepayment and default Portfolio Attrition Report for the first six months of the deal

$2.40 million in prepayments and $1.98 million in defaults over the last quarter. A snapshot of the portfolio performance in this regard can be seen in Exhibit 24.4.

Structure Performance: The structural performance of the deal remains strong. According to the projections based on the March 2007 data, the deal will have an incremental $4.70 million to work with over its life. At 30% MVD and keeping the RLP assumption at nine months, our recovery rate is very, very high. It is, in fact, 99.92%.

The average life of the deal has come in from 5.24 years to 5.22 years as a result of the slightly better than prepayment rate and the incremental recovery money. See Exhibit 24.5.

Running the Model: We will run the model for each of these three months using a 30% MVD number and leave the RLP assumptions at nine months. The pricing spreads remain at 1.00% for each of the months. We will make no further adjustments to the project appraisals as our field personnel, real estate department, and others have seen little or no price appreciation of the properties of the portfolio. We have a price of par, **100.00.**

NINE MONTHS FROM ISSUANCE

Time Period: April through June 2007.

General Economic Conditions: Weakening. The capital markets are open. Many investors have now taken a step back a bit. Deals are still getting done across all of the asset classes, even exotics.

Current Month - 6 Months Since Issuance

Collateral Cash Flows		
Scheduled Amortization	185,107,531	
Prepayments to Principal	263,313,408	53.58%
Total Principal Retired	448,420,939	
Defaulted Principal	42,999,438	8.75%
Recoveries of Principal (& rate)	42,964,698	99.92%
Coupon Income	301,849,786	
Total Cash Sources	**793,235,423**	
Debt Cash Flows		
Program Fees	4,872,439	
Servicing Fee	19,790,547	
Conduit Debt Service	155,274,252	
Conduit Principal Payments	466,849,358	
Released to Seller	146,448,827	31.37%
Total Cash Uses	**793,235,423**	

Performance	Conduit	Seller Interest
Structuring		
Beginning Conduit Balance	466,849,358	24,571,019
Ownership Interest	95.00%	5.00%
Performance		
Principal Outstanding	$ -	0.00%
Severity of Loss	0.000%	0.00%
IRR	6.373%	58.194%
Price	100.000	0.000%
Tenor		
Average Life (yrs)	5.218	
Final Maturity (yrs)	16.917	
Modified Duration	4.135	
Macauley Duration	3.887	

At Issuance Projection

Collateral Cash Flows		
Scheduled Amortization	185,410,203	
Prepayments to Principal	263,299,530	53.58%
Total Principal Retired	448,709,733	
Defaulted Principal	42,710,644	8.69%
Recoveries of Principal (& rate)	36,582,308	85.65%
Coupon Income	303,236,913	
Total Cash Sources	**788,528,954**	
Debt Cash Flows		
Program Fees	4,896,432	
Servicing Fee	19,889,241	
Conduit Debt Service	156,073,758	
Conduit Principal Payments	466,849,358	
Released to Seller	140,820,166	30.16%
Total Cash Uses	**788,528,954**	

Performance	Conduit	Seller Interest
Structuring		
Beginning Conduit Balance	466,849,358	24,571,019
Ownership Interest	95.00%	5.00%
Performance		
Principal Outstanding	$ -	0.00%
Severity of Loss	0.000%	0.00%
IRR	6.375%	54.176%
Price	100.00	0.000%
Tenor		
Average Life (yrs)	5.244	
Final Maturity (yrs)	16.917	
Modified Duration	4.154	
Macauley Duration	3.905	

Difference: At Issuance and Current Month

Collateral Cash Flows		
Scheduled Amortization	-302,672	
Prepayments to Principal	13,878	0.01%
Total Principal Retired	-288,794	
Defaulted Principal	288,794	0.68%
Recoveries of Principal (& rate)	6,382,390	17.45%
Coupon Income	-1,387,127	
Total Cash Sources	**4,706,469**	
Debt Cash Flows		
Program Fees	-23,993	
Servicing Fee	-98,693	
Conduit Debt Service	-799,506	
Conduit Principal Payments	0	
Released to Seller	5,628,662	1.21%
Total Cash Uses	**4,706,469**	

Performance	Conduit	Seller Interest
Structuring		
Beginning Conduit Balance	0	0
Ownership Interest	0	0
Performance		
Principal Outstanding	0	0.000%
Severity of Loss	0.000%	
IRR	0.002%	-4.017%
Price	0.000	
Tenor		
Average Life (yrs)	0.026	0.000
Final Maturity (yrs)	0.000	0.000
Modified Duration	0.019	0.000
Macauley Duration	0.018	0.000

EXHIBIT 24.5 Comparison of the Summary Box Scores for the At Issuance performance versus the Current Month, six months from issuance

Pricing Inputs: Spreads have started to come up in response to the first serious rumblings of the sub-prime debacle. The Prime Rate has remained stable at 8.25%, while LIBOR has been 5.35%, 5.60%, and 5.60% for the three months of the quarter, respectively.

Inputs from the Servicing Groups: The market's demand for real estate is now stable, with prices moving neither upward nor downward. The group is noticing that there is a pronounced slowdown of lending activity. There are fewer buyers and they are beginning to assert themselves. The recommendation is therefore, to raise the MVD to 50% from 30%, just to be conservative, and to increase the RLP from its current value of 9 months to 12 months. Appraisal values will also be lowered by 4% in a small number of loans due to lower current appraisal values caused by the sales of other distressed properties by other desperate owners.

Collateral Performance: Collateral performance for the first nine months remains strong. Our at issuance model suggested that we would experience $3.78 million in prepayments and $1.98 million in defaults. We have in fact experienced $2.82 million of prepayments and $3.44 million of defaults over the first quarter. In this quarter the state of Florida was hit by a Category 5 storm. The storm destroyed ten properties of the portfolio over an area of five ZIP codes in the southeastern part of the state. The defaults from this event alone will be $2.60 million. See Exhibits 24.6 and 24.7. These losses move Florida to the top of the defaulted loans listing.

A snapshot of the default and prepayment activity of the entire portfolio can be seen in Exhibit 24.8.

Structure Performance: The structure has, for the first time in its history dipped below the At Issuance expectations. Aggregate cash flows are now estimated to be $3.0 million worse than the at issuance case. The recovery rate has fallen from 100% in quarter 1 to 96.6% in quarter 2 to 83.27%, below the at issuance value of 85.65%.

The average life of the deal has come in from 5.24 years to 5.21 years as a result of Florida activity. See Exhibit 24.9.

Running the Model: We will run the model for each of these three months using a 50% MVD number along with a 12-month recovery lag. The pricing spread will be raised to 1.50%.

With these changes the value of the deal falls below par, with a dollar price of 97.98.

TWELVE MONTHS FROM ISSUANCE

Time Period: July through September 2007.

General Economic Conditions: Fair. The capital markets are beginning to experience the first wave of sub-prime defaults as cohorts of one-, two-, and three-year ARMs, and Alt-A mortgages reset. The vintage analysis of the 2006 and early 2007 residential mortgages are showing the highest first-year delinquency and default rates yet seen. Prime remains at 8.25% for this quarter and LIBOR is 5.359%, 5.621%, and 5.229% for the three months, respectively.

Pricing Inputs: There is the beginning of an upward pressure on spreads. "AAA" rated and "AA" CDOs are experiencing greater than expected credit deterioration from the mortgages contained in their collateral pools. There is a beginning understanding that the investors are not completely sure what the composition of some of

Defaulted Collateral Report #11 Current Balances in Top 50 Zip Codes							
			1	2	3	4	5
			Number of Loans	Current Loan Balance	Current Loan LTV	% Current Balances	Cum % Current Balances
Rank	Zip Code	State	21	6,652,387			
1	32256	FL	3	1,394,133	53.009%	20.957%	20.957%
2	10010	NY	1	712,269	63.595%	10.707%	31.664%
3	35967	AL	1	672,017	67.202%	10.102%	41.766%
4	72703	AR	1	619,748	63.760%	9.316%	51.082%
5	67114	KS	1	592,459	65.829%	8.906%	59.988%
6	32257	FL	2	553,226	62.867%	8.316%	68.304%
7	32504	FL	2	397,840	56.034%	5.980%	74.285%
8	27513	NC	1	376,658	58.126%	5.662%	79.947%
9	30075	GA	1	351,034	46.433%	5.277%	85.223%
10	28277	NC	1	281,749	61.250%	4.235%	89.459%
11	19003	PA	1	234,835	55.913%	3.530%	92.989%
12	32501	FL	1	177,508	46.713%	2.668%	95.657%
13	35243	AL	1	121,274	55.124%	1.823%	97.480%
14	32514	FL	2	73,795	56.765%	1.109%	98.589%
15	95035	CA	1	54,235	54.235%	0.815%	99.405%
16	41056	KY	1	39,605	49.506%	0.595%	100.00%

EXHIBIT 24.6 The distribution of defaulted loans by Postal ZIP code. Note that there are no less than four Florida ZIP codes in this listing

the asset pools backing their investments are comprised of. This fuels uncertainty, putting further pressure on spreads. There is a general widening of spreads across all structured products. Our deal will see the spread widen by another 150 basis points to 3.00% in this quarter.

Inputs from the Servicing Groups: The market's demand for real estate is down significantly. Housing starts for the quarter are lower. We are at the beginning of the first signs of tighter credit, it is suggested that the recovery lag period be moved from 12 to 18 months. Project values (appraisals) of the properties are now seen to have been somewhat aggressive over the last two to three years and are adjusted downward by 5%. Defaults have increased over the quarter and 60- and 90-day delinquencies are up sharply.

Collateral Performance: Collateral performance for this quarter shows signs of weakening. Our at issuance model suggested that we would experience $5.1 million in prepayments and $2.1 million in defaults. Actual results are disappointing. We experience $5.3 million of prepayments which is right in line with expectations. However, we experience $3.9 million of defaults in this quarter. This default rate is

Defaulted Collateral Report #10
Current Balances Distribution by State or Territory

			4	5	6	7	8
			Number of Loans	Current Loan Balance	Current Loan LTV	% Current Balances	Cum % Current Balances
#	Name	Postal	21	6,652,387			
1	Florida	FL	10	2,596,503	54.894%	39.031%	39.031%
2	Alabama	AL	2	793,291	65.024%	11.925%	50.956%
3	New York	NY	1	712,269	63.595%	10.707%	61.663%
4	North Carolina	NC	2	658,407	59.423%	9.897%	71.560%
5	Arkansas	AR	1	619,748	63.760%	9.316%	80.877%
6	Kansas	KS	1	592,459	65.829%	8.906%	89.782%
7	Georgia	GA	1	351,034	46.433%	5.277%	95.059%
8	Pennsylvania	PA	1	234,835	55.913%	3.530%	98.589%
9	California	CA	1	54,235	54.235%	0.815%	99.405%
10	Kentucky	KY	1	39,605	49.506%	0.595%	100.000%

EXHIBIT 24.7 The state-by-state ranking of defaults. The state of Florida has assumed the leadership in the total damage figures

Collateral Attrition Report
9 Months Since Issuance

Original Portfolio	
2,279	Number of Loans
$491,420,377	Current Balances
100.000%	% Initial Current Balances
11.505%	Wght Avg Coupon
191.62	Wght Avg Rem Term (months)
15.19	Wght Avg Seasoning (months)

Current Pay Collateral			Difference from Original Portfolio	
2,224	Number of Loans		55	Number of Loans
$456,240,729	Current Balances		$35,179,648	Current Balances
92.841%	% Initial Current Balances		7.159%	% Initial Current Balances
11.503%	Wght Avg Coupon		0.002%	Wght Avg Coupon
194.49	Wght Avg Rem Term (months)		(2.87)	Wght Avg Rem Term (months)
15.21	Wght Avg Seasoning (months)		(0.02)	Wght Avg Seasoning (months)

Prepayments to Date			Defaults to Date	
34	Number of Loans		21	Number of Loans
$6,699,206	Current Balances		$6,652,387	Current Balances
1.363%	% Initial Current Balances		1.354%	% Initial Current Balances
11.395%	Wght Avg Coupon		11.225%	Wght Avg Coupon
189.69	Wght Avg Rem Term (months)		201.91	Wght Avg Rem Term (months)
11.91	Wght Avg Seasoning (months)		12.95	Wght Avg Seasoning (months)

EXHIBIT 24.8 The prepayment and default Portfolio Attrition Report for the first nine months of the deal

Current Month - 9 Months Since Issuance

Collateral Cash Flows

Scheduled Amortization	184,414,543	
Prepayments to Principal	262,504,323	53.42%
Total Principal Retired	446,918,866	
Defaulted Principal	44,501,512	9.06%
Recoveries of Principal (& rate)	37,058,031	83.27%
Coupon Income	301,518,081	
Total Cash Sources	**785,494,978**	

Debt Cash Flows

Program Fees	4,866,506	
Servicing Fee	19,766,942	
Conduit Debt Service	155,115,224	
Conduit Principal Payments	466,849,358	
Released to Seller	138,896,946	29.75%
Total Cash Uses	**785,494,978**	

Performance	Conduit	Seller Interest
Structuring		
Beginning Conduit Balance	466,849,358	24,571,019
Ownership Interest	95.00%	5.00%
Performance		
Principal Outstanding	$ -	0.00%
Severity of Loss	0.000%	0.00%
IRR	6.375%	52.272%
Price	97.981	0.000%
Tenor		
Average Life (yrs)	5.212	
Final Maturity (yrs)	16.917	
Modified Duration	4.130	
Macauley Duration	3.882	

At Issuance Projection

Collateral Cash Flows

Scheduled Amortization	185,410,203	
Prepayments to Principal	263,299,530	53.58%
Total Principal Retired	448,709,733	
Defaulted Principal	42,710,644	8.69%
Recoveries of Principal (& rate)	36,582,308	85.65%
Coupon Income	303,236,913	
Total Cash Sources	**788,528,954**	

Debt Cash Flows

Program Fees	4,896,432	
Servicing Fee	19,889,241	
Conduit Debt Service	156,073,758	
Conduit Principal Payments	466,849,358	
Released to Seller	140,820,166	30.16%
Total Cash Uses	**788,528,954**	

Performance	Conduit	Seller Interest
Structuring		
Beginning Conduit Balance	466,849,358	24,571,019
Ownership Interest	95.00%	5.00%
Performance		
Principal Outstanding	$ -	0.00%
Severity of Loss	0.000%	0.00%
IRR	6.375%	54.176%
Price	100.00	0.000%
Tenor		
Average Life (yrs)	5.244	
Final Maturity (yrs)	16.917	
Modified Duration	4.154	
Macauley Duration	3.905	

Difference: At Issuance and Current Month

Collateral Cash Flows

Scheduled Amortization	-995,661	
Prepayments to Principal	-795,207	-0.30%
Total Principal Retired	-1,790,868	
Defaulted Principal	1,790,868	4.19%
Recoveries of Principal (& rate)	475,723	1.30%
Coupon Income	-1,718,832	
Total Cash Sources	**-3,033,977**	

Debt Cash Flows

Program Fees	-29,925	
Servicing Fee	-122,298	
Conduit Debt Service	-958,533	
Conduit Principal Payments	0	
Released to Seller	-1,923,219	-0.41%
Total Cash Uses	**-3,033,977**	

Performance	Conduit	Seller Interest
Structuring		
Beginning Conduit Balance	0	0
Ownership Interest	0	0
Performance		
Principal Outstanding	0	0
Severity of Loss	0.000%	0.000%
IRR	0.000%	1.905%
Price	2.019	
Tenor		
Average Life (yrs)	0.032	0.000
Final Maturity (yrs)	0.000	0.000
Modified Duration	0.025	0.000
Macauley Duration	0.023	0.000

EXHIBIT 24.9 Comparison of the Summary Box Scores for the At Issuance performance versus the Current Month, nine months from issuance

Collateral Attrition Report
12 Months Since Issuance

Original Portfolio	
2,279	Number of Loans
$491,420,377	Current Balances
100.000%	% Initial Current Balances
11.505%	Wght Avg Coupon
191.62	Wght Avg Rem Term (months)
15.19	Wght Avg Seasoning (months)

Current Pay Collateral			Difference from Original Portfolio	
2,187	Number of Loans		92	Number of Loans
$440,530,245	Current Balances		$50,890,132	Current Balances
89.644%	% Initial Current Balances		10.356%	% Initial Current Balances
11.502%	Wght Avg Coupon		0.003%	Wght Avg Coupon
195.40	Wght Avg Rem Term (months)		(3.77)	Wght Avg Rem Term (months)
15.10	Wght Avg Seasoning (months)		(0.10)	Wght Avg Seasoning (months)

Prepayments to Date			Defaults to Date	
52	Number of Loans		40	Number of Loans
$11,082,749	Current Balances		$10,449,037	Current Balances
2.255%	% Initial Current Balances		2.126%	% Initial Current Balances
11.355%	Wght Avg Coupon		11.346%	Wght Avg Coupon
199.19	Wght Avg Rem Term (months)		200.42	Wght Avg Rem Term (months)
15.45	Wght Avg Seasoning (months)		15.19	Wght Avg Seasoning (months)

EXHIBIT 24.10   The prepayment and default Portfolio Attrition Report for the first 12 months of the deal

85% greater than expected. Other collateral pools are experiencing similar levels of defaults. In fact our deal is in the middle of the Range for the experience of this group and consistent with the delinquency rates seen in Small Business Administration (SBA) loans that are broadly similar. A snapshot of the portfolio performance in this regard can be seen in Exhibit 24.10.

Structure Performance: The structure performance of this quarter is under performing in regard to the At Issuance expectations. Deal to date, we have now experienced $3.5 million more defaults than modeled. The coverage ratio of the deal, the Cash Released to Seller/ Beginning Conduit Balance, has fallen from 30.16% to 28.50%. On a remaining balance basis, the coverage ratio predicted for month 12 using the At Issuance projection was 32.3% and it is currently 30.8%. This is not an alarming drop, but it is one that is not encouraging given all the other things that are happening at this time. See Exhibit 24.11.

Running the Model: We will run the model for each of these three months using a 55% MVD number, and an RLP of 18 months. The pricing spread will now be 3.00%, which is consistent with the rest of the deals of this type in the secondary markets, and in fact, better than some of the poorer performing ones with higher default rates. Using these inputs we arrive at the price of **92.34**. This represents a decline of 5.46 from the previous ending quarter price. It should be noted that so far all of the price volatility is a result of changes in the pricing risk premium. The cash flows of the collateral provide 30.8% over collateralization to the conduit indebtedness.

Current Month – 12 Months Since Issuance

Collateral Cash Flows

Scheduled Amortization	184,038,994	
Prepayments to Principal	261,189,096	53.15%
Total Principal Retired	445,228,090	
Defaulted Principal	46,192,287	9.40%
Recoveries of Principal (& rate)	33,209,043	71.89%
Coupon Income	300,543,613	
Total Cash Sources	**778,980,746**	

Debt Cash Flows

Program Fees	4,847,387	
Servicing Fee	19,701,141	
Conduit Debt Service	154,536,957	
Conduit Principal Payments	466,849,358	
Released to Seller	133,045,903	28.50%
Total Cash Uses	**778,780,746**	

Performance	Conduit	Seller Interest
Structuring		
Beginning Conduit Balance	466,849,358	24,571,019
Ownership Interest	95.00%	5.00%
Performance		
Principal Outstanding	$ -	0.00%	0.00%
Severity of Loss	0.000%	0.00%
IRR	6.376%	46.102%
Price	92.337	0.000%
Tenor		
Average Life (yrs)	5.192	
Final Maturity (yrs)	16.833	
Modified Duration	4.116	
Macauley Duration	3.869	

At Issuance Projection

Collateral Cash Flows

Scheduled Amortization	185,410,203	
Prepayments to Principal	263,299,530	53.58%
Total Principal Retired	448,709,733	
Defaulted Principal	42,710,644	8.69%
Recoveries of Principal (& rate)	36,582,308	85.65%
Coupon Income	303,236,913	
Total Cash Sources	**788,528,954**	

Debt Cash Flows

Program Fees	4,896,432	
Servicing Fee	19,889,241	
Conduit Debt Service	156,073,758	
Conduit Principal Payments	466,849,358	
Released to Seller	140,820,166	30.16%
Total Cash Uses	**788,528,954**	

Performance	Conduit	Seller Interest
Structuring		
Beginning Conduit Balance	466,849,358	24,571,019
Ownership Interest	95.00%	5.00%
Performance		
Principal Outstanding	$ -	0.00%	0.00%
Severity of Loss	0.000%	0.00%
IRR	6.375%	54.176%
Price	100.00	0.000%
Tenor		
Average Life (yrs)	5.244	
Final Maturity (yrs)	16.917	
Modified Duration	4.154	
Macauley Duration	3.905	

Difference: At Issuance and Current Month

Collateral Cash Flows

Scheduled Amortization	-1,371,209	
Prepayments to Principal	-2,110,434	-0.80%
Total Principal Retired	-3,481,643	
Defaulted Principal	3,481,643	8.15%
Recoveries of Principal (& rate)	-3,373,265	-9.22%
Coupon Income	-2,693,300	
Total Cash Sources	**-9,548,208**	

Debt Cash Flows

Program Fees	-49,045	
Servicing Fee	-188,099	
Conduit Debt Service	-1,536,801	
Conduit Principal Payments	0	
Released to Seller	-7,774,263	-1.67%
Total Cash Uses	**-9,548,208**	

Performance	Conduit	Seller Interest
Structuring		
Beginning Conduit Balance	0	0
Ownership Interest	0	0
Performance		
Principal Outstanding	0	0.000%	0
Severity of Loss	0.000%	8.074%
IRR	-0.001%	
Price	7.663	
Tenor		
Average Life (yrs)	0.053	
Final Maturity (yrs)	0.083	
Modified Duration	0.038	
Macauley Duration	0.036	

EXHIBIT 24.11 Comparison of the Summary Box Scores for the At Issuance performance versus the Current Month, 12 months from issuance

FIFTEEN MONTHS FROM ISSUANCE

Time Period: October through December 2007.

General Economic Conditions: Poor. Sub-prime mortgage contagion has now established itself across all areas of the structured products spectrum. Major banks are taking large write downs in inventory and product holding based on ever increasing delinquency and default rates across products backed by mortgage securities. This market uncertainty is now cascading into any mortgage-related products. Spreads have significantly widened due to investor concerns over the composition and creditworthiness of the collateral backing the paper they have purchased over the last three to four years. The Prime Rate for these three months falls as policy makers attempt to improve the liquidity of the capital markets. Prime Rates for the three months are 7.75%, 7.50%, and 7.50%. The monthly rates for LIBOR also decline to 4.89%, 5.13%, and 4.70%.

Pricing Inputs: Spreads continue to widen as markets weaken and seize up. Issuance of new structured products has declined precipitously in this quarter. The pricing spread on our product has risen from 300 basis points at the end of the last quarter to 375 bps, 450 bps, and finally 500 bps at the end of the quarter.

Inputs from the Servicing Groups: The sales in the real estate market have slowed tremendously. In addition, there are now massive influxes of new inventory from projects that have failed in the construction phase through owner-occupied properties that have been owned for three years. As more and more people hit their reset triggers and default, a sustained deflationary price spiral has set in. Individuals who purchased properties speculating on selling into a raising market are also strongly contributing to this trend. As liquidity dries up, banks raise underwriting criteria, further reducing the pool of buyers and aggravating the existing conditions. For this quarter we will adjust the project values downward by another 5%. An examination of the current appraisals would appear that even after the adjustment they are at least 10% too high. We are also moving the RLP from 18 to 24 months. MVDs on foreclosed property will be set at 60%.

Collateral Performance: Our At Issuance model suggested that we would experience $6.3 million in prepayments and $2.2 million in defaults. We have in fact experienced $5.3 million of prepayments, an amount lower than expected but consistent with the developments of the quarter, and $3.2 million of defaults, 145% the number forecast in the At Issuance model. See in Exhibit 24.12.

Structure Performance: The current projection for the cash flows is now a total of $15.6 million less than the base case estimate. This represents a loss of only 2% of the expected cash flows from the initial structured deal. The deal is now projecting $47.2 million in lifetime defaults as opposed to $42.7 million At Issuance, an increase of $4.5 million. The estimate for prepayments has dropped from $263.3 million to $260.3 million, slightly over 1% less than the At Issuance projections. The deal is outperforming others in its class most likely due to very high LTVs. In addition, it appears that the defaults are not clustered, but are distributed about the portfolio without any systemic pattern. This means that the geographic and business sector diversity of the pool is serving as a loss deterrent. See Exhibit 24.13.

Running the Model: We will run the model for each of these three months using a 60% MVD, an RLP of 24 months, and a pricing spread as indicated above. The

Collateral Attrition Report
15 Months Since Issuance

Original Portfolio	
2,279	Number of Loans
$491,420,377	Current Balances
100.000%	% Initial Current Balances
11.505%	Wght Avg Coupon
191.62	Wght Avg Rem Term (months)
16.10	Wght Avg Seasoning (months)

Current Pay Collateral		Difference from Original Portfolio	
2,139	Number of Loans	140	Number of Loans
$424,650,510	Current Balances	$66,769,868	Current Balances
86.413%	% Initial Current Balances	13.587%	% Initial Current Balances
11.503%	Wght Avg Coupon	0.002%	Wght Avg Coupon
196.39	Wght Avg Rem Term (months)	(4.77)	Wght Avg Rem Term (months)
15.10	Wght Avg Seasoning (months)	0.09	Wght Avg Seasoning (months)

Prepayments to Date		Defaults to Date	
81	Number of Loans	59	Number of Loans
$16,396,074	Current Balances	$13,621,157	Current Balances
3.336%	% Initial Current Balances	2.772%	% Initial Current Balances
11.345%	Wght Avg Coupon	11.338%	Wght Avg Coupon
204.91	Wght Avg Rem Term (months)	195.92	Wght Avg Rem Term (months)
14.77	Wght Avg Seasoning (months)	14.84	Wght Avg Seasoning (months)

EXHIBIT 24.12 The prepayment and default Portfolio Attrition Report for the first 15 months of the deal

price for the security at the end of the quarter is **85.607**. This is a decline of **6.74** from the fourth quarter ending in September 2007.

EIGHTEEN MONTHS FROM ISSUANCE

Time Period: January through March 2008.

General Economic Conditions: Poor. The capital markets are, for all intents and purposes, shut down. Any trading activity that is taking place is motivated by the necessity to offload assets from the balance sheets of large financial institutions thus relieving pressure on capital caused by large losses on mortgage-related investments. The Prime Rate for these three months was 7.25%, 6.00%, and 6.00%, and the LIBOR rate was 3.11%, 3.06%, and 2.69%.

Pricing Inputs: Spreads are being driven by distressed sales. Mark-to-market activity is producing a downward spiral of prices and valuations as investors who are liquid command wider and wider returns.

Inputs from the Servicing Groups: The continued tightening of the credit markets is forcing more and more buyers from the market. We are going to leave the appraisal values of the properties unchanged for this quarter. We will also leave unchanged the 60% market value decline factor and the 24-month recovery lag time. Clustered defaults of sub-prime and Alt-A mortgages are affecting local economies. This is especially true in areas already under previous economic stress. Delinquency rates have risen significantly in our portfolio and we are being increasingly pressed for

Current Month - 15 Months Since Issuance

Collateral Cash Flows		Seller Interest
Scheduled Amortization	183,872,123	
Prepayments to Principal	260,327,965	52.97%
Total Principal Retired	444,200,088	
Defaulted Principal	47,220,289	9.61%
Recoveries of Principal (& rate)	28,896,753	61.20%
Coupon Income	299,789,293	
Total Cash Sources	**772,886,134**	
Debt Cash Flows		
Program Fees	4,843,100	
Servicing Fee	19,682,675	
Conduit Debt Service	153,908,640	
Conduit Principal Payments	466,849,358	
Released to Seller	127,602,360	27.33%
Total Cash Uses	**772,886,134**	

Performance	Conduit	Seller Interest
Structuring		
Beginning Conduit Balance	466,849,358	24,571,019
Ownership Interest	95.00%	5.00%
Performance		
Principal Outstanding	$ -	0.00%
Severity of Loss	0.000%	0.00%
IRR	6.352%	42.230%
Price	85.607	0.000%
Tenor		
Average Life (yrs)	5.187	
Final Maturity (yrs)	16.833	
Modified Duration	4.117	
Macauley Duration	3.870	

At Issuance Projection

Collateral Cash Flows		Seller Interest
Scheduled Amortization	185,410,203	
Prepayments to Principal	263,299,530	53.58%
Total Principal Retired	448,709,733	
Defaulted Principal	42,710,644	8.69%
Recoveries of Principal (& rate)	36,582,308	85.65%
Coupon Income	303,236,913	
Total Cash Sources	**788,528,954**	
Debt Cash Flows		
Program Fees	4,896,432	
Servicing Fee	19,889,241	
Conduit Debt Service	156,073,758	
Conduit Principal Payments	466,849,358	
Released to Seller	140,820,166	30.16%
Total Cash Uses	**788,528,954**	

Performance	Conduit	Seller Interest
Structuring		
Beginning Conduit Balance	466,849,358	24,571,019
Ownership Interest	95.00%	5.00%
Performance		
Principal Outstanding	$ -	0.00%
Severity of Loss	0.000%	0.00%
IRR	6.375%	54.176%
Price	100.00	0.000%
Tenor		
Average Life (yrs)	5.244	
Final Maturity (yrs)	16.917	
Modified Duration	4.154	
Macauley Duration	3.905	

Difference: At Issuance and Current Month

Collateral Cash Flows		Seller Interest
Scheduled Amortization	-1,538,080	
Prepayments to Principal	-2,971,565	-1.13%
Total Principal Retired	-4,509,645	
Defaulted Principal	4,509,645	10.56%
Recoveries of Principal (& rate)	-7,685,555	-21.01%
Coupon Income	-3,447,620	
Total Cash Sources	**-15,642,820**	
Debt Cash Flows		
Program Fees	-53,331	
Servicing Fee	-206,566	
Conduit Debt Service	-2,165,118	
Conduit Principal Payments	0	
Released to Seller	-13,217,805	-2.83%
Total Cash Uses	**-15,642,820**	

Performance	Conduit	Seller Interest
Structuring		
Beginning Conduit Balance	0	0
Ownership Interest	0	0
Performance		
Principal Outstanding	0	0.000%
Severity of Loss	0.000%	0.00%
IRR	0.023%	11.947%
Price	14.393	
Tenor		
Average Life (yrs)	0.057	
Final Maturity (yrs)	0.083	
Modified Duration	0.038	
Macauley Duration	0.035	

EXHIBIT 24.13 Comparison of the Summary Box Scores for the At Issuance performance versus the Current Month, 15 months from issuance

Collateral Attrition Report
18 Months Since Issuance

Original Portfolio

2,279	Number of Loans
$491,420,377	Current Balances
100.000%	% Initial Current Balances
11.505%	Wght Avg Coupon
191.62	Wght Avg Rem Term (months)
15.19	Wght Avg Seasoning (months)

Current Pay Collateral

2,041	Number of Loans
$399,629,135	Current Balances
81.321%	% Initial Current Balances
11.495%	Wght Avg Coupon
198.33	Wght Avg Rem Term (months)
15.02	Wght Avg Seasoning (months)

Difference from Original Portfolio

238	Number of Loans
$91,791,242	Current Balances
18.679%	% Initial Current Balances
0.010%	Wght Avg Coupon
(6.70)	Wght Avg Rem Term (months)
0.17	Wght Avg Seasoning (months)

Prepayments to Date

104	Number of Loans
$22,217,273	Current Balances
4.521%	% Initial Current Balances
11.424%	Wght Avg Coupon
201.33	Wght Avg Rem Term (months)
16.46	Wght Avg Seasoning (months)

Defaults to Date

134	Number of Loans
$25,786,081	Current Balances
5.247%	% Initial Current Balances
11.463%	Wght Avg Coupon
185.75	Wght Avg Rem Term (months)
14.42	Wght Avg Seasoning (months)

EXHIBIT 24.14 The prepayment and default Portfolio Attrition Report for the first 18 months of the deal

workouts or accommodations. The economic stress to our collateral portfolio is not caused by the payment reset shock. The portfolio is being stressed by secondary economic effects triggered by reduced consumer spending.

Collateral Performance: Collateral performance has started to deteriorate. Our At Issuance model suggested that we would experience $7.5 million in prepayments and $2.3 million in defaults. We have in fact experienced $5.8 million of prepayments and $12.2 million of defaults over the quarter. A snapshot of the portfolio performance in this regard can be seen in Exhibit 24.14.

Structure Performance: The deal is now expected to have $29.7 million less in cash flows than our estimate at issuance. Our recovery rate has slipped from 85.6% to 53.4%, which will cost us $6.2 million in forgone recoveries. The model cash flow projections indicate that a total of $118.4 million of excess servicing will be released to the Seller. We are now, however, in the 18th month of the deal. Of the $118 million, a total of $7 million has already been released and is gone from the deal. Relative to our remaining $400 million in conduit indebtedness outstanding, there is only $111 million of coverage left giving us a 111/400 = 27.7% coverage ratio. Our original coverage ratio at issuance was 30.2%. We have, therefore, lost about 1/10th of the total original credit enhancement of the deal in the first 18 months. See Exhibit 24.15.

Running the Model: We will run the model for each of these three months using a 60% MVD number, and a 24-month RLP. In that we have seen an enormous spike in defaults, we will consider increasing the base default assumptions over the next quarter but for now we will leave it at 400% PSD.

Current Month - 18 Months Since Issuance

Collateral Cash Flows

Scheduled Amortization	179,475,726	
Prepayments to Principal	254,938,674	51.88%
Total Principal Retired	434,414,400	
Defaulted Principal	57,005,977	11.60%
Recoveries of Principal (& rate)	30,432,367	53.38%
Coupon Income	294,011,983	
Total Cash Sources	**758,858,750**	

Debt Cash Flows

		Seller Interest
Program Fees	4,778,619	
Servicing Fee	19,417,889	
Conduit Debt Service	149,386,989	
Conduit Principal Payments	466,849,358	
Released to Seller	118,425,895	25.37%
Total Cash Uses	**758,858,750**	

Performance	Conduit	Seller Interest
Structuring		
Beginning Conduit Balance	466,849,358	24,571,019
Ownership Interest	95.00%	5.00%
Performance		
Principal Outstanding	$ -	0.00%
Severity of Loss	0.000%	0.00%
IRR	6.233%	36.679%
Price	82.675	0.000%
Tenor		
Average Life (yrs)	5.118	
Final Maturity (yrs)	16.833	
Modified Duration	4.083	
Macauley Duration	3.839	

At Issuance Projection

Collateral Cash Flows

Scheduled Amortization	185,410,203	
Prepayments to Principal	263,299,530	53.58%
Total Principal Retired	448,709,733	
Defaulted Principal	42,710,644	8.69%
Recoveries of Principal (& rate)	36,582,308	85.65%
Coupon Income	303,236,913	
Total Cash Sources	**788,528,954**	

Debt Cash Flows

		Seller Interest
Program Fees	4,896,432	
Servicing Fee	19,889,241	
Conduit Debt Service	156,073,758	
Conduit Principal Payments	466,849,358	
Released to Seller	140,820,166	30.16%
Total Cash Uses	**788,528,954**	

Performance	Conduit	Seller Interest
Structuring		
Beginning Conduit Balance	466,849,358	24,571,019
Ownership Interest	95.00%	5.00%
Performance		
Principal Outstanding	$ -	0.00%
Severity of Loss	0.000%	0.00%
IRR	6.375%	54.176%
Price	100.000	0.000%
Tenor		
Average Life (yrs)	5.244	
Final Maturity (yrs)	16.917	
Modified Duration	4.154	
Macauley Duration	3.905	

Difference: At Issuance and Current Month

Collateral Cash Flows

Scheduled Amortization	-5,934,477	
Prepayments to Principal	-8,360,856	-3.18%
Total Principal Retired	-14,295,333	
Defaulted Principal	14,295,333	33.47%
Recoveries of Principal (& rate)	-6,149,941	-16.81%
Coupon Income	-9,224,930	
Total Cash Sources	**-29,670,204**	

Debt Cash Flows

		Seller Interest
Program Fees	-117,813	
Servicing Fee	-471,352	
Conduit Debt Service	-6,686,768	
Conduit Principal Payments	0	
Released to Seller	-22,394,271	-4.80%
Total Cash Uses	**-29,670,204**	

Performance	Conduit	Seller Interest
Structuring		
Beginning Conduit Balance	0	0
Ownership Interest	0	0
Performance		
Principal Outstanding	0	0.000%
Severity of Loss	0.000%	0.000%
IRR	0.142%	17.498%
Price	17.325	
Tenor		
Average Life (yrs)	0.126	
Final Maturity (yrs)	0.083	
Modified Duration	0.071	
Macauley Duration	0.066	

EXHIBIT 24.15 Comparison of the Summary Box Scores for the At Issuance performance versus the Current Month, 18 months from issuance

The price for the security at the end of the quarter is **82.68**. This is a decline of 2.93 from the sixth quarter of the deal ending in December 2007.

TWENTY-ONE MONTHS FROM ISSUANCE

Time Period: April through June 2008.

General Economic Conditions. This quarter was characterized by dismal financial news. All the major equity indices fell. Several of the largest banks announced massive losses. A major investment bank failed. A second major investment bank was purchased before it failed. The government completed the bailout of FHLMC and FNMA while backstopping a global insurance company that had taken catastrophic losses in credit default swaps. The Prime Rate for these three months was 5.25%, 5.00%, and 5.00%, and the LIBOR rate was 2.85%, 2.68%, and 2.783%.

Pricing Inputs: With the continued deterioration of the portfolio, spreads are now set at 6.50%, 7.25%, and 8.00% for the three months of the quarter. The only buyers are a limited number of firms with liquidity, many of them hedge funds. Most sales are of distressed assets by distressed Sellers. This tends to continue to fuel the downward trend.

Inputs from the Servicing Groups: The market's demand for real estate is very poor. There is a five- to seven-year inventory of small homes and multiple use structures.

Collateral Performance: Collateral performance for the first three months continues to weaken. Our at issuance model suggested that we would experience $8.5 million in prepayments and $2.3 million in defaults. We have in fact experienced $5.6 million of prepayments, less than expected, and another large rise in defaults to $15.6 million. That number is almost 700% of the expected default levels. A snapshot of the portfolio performance in this regard can be seen in Exhibit 24.16.

Structure Performance: The deal is now expected to have $61.1 million less in cash flows than our estimate at issuance. Our recovery rate has slipped from 85.6% to 44.6%. This is particularly important as we have increased the default rate assumptions on the remaining current pay collateral over each of the last three months. The model cash flow projections now indicate that a total of $95.5 million of excess servicing will be released to the Seller. We are now, however, in the 21st month of the deal. Of the $95.5 million, a total of $7.1 million has already been released and is gone from the deal. Relative to our remaining $383 million in conduit indebtedness outstanding, there is only $88.4 million of coverage left giving us a 88/383 = 23.0% coverage ratio. Our original coverage ratio at issuance was 30.2%. We have therefore lost about one-quarter of the total credit enhancement of the deal in the first 21 months. We are also very close to hitting one of the deal triggers. With the surge in defaults in month 21, the projected rolling three-month default rate is over 4.00%; our default trigger is set at 5.00%! See Exhibit 24.17.

Running the Model: We will run the model for each of these three months using a 70% MVD number, and a 24-month RLP. In that we have seen a second enormous spike in defaults, we revised our projection assumptions. For the three months of this quarter, we will raise the default rates used on the current payment collateral to 450% PSD, 500% PSD, and 650% PSD. We will also adjust the project values of the portfolio downward 5%.

Collateral Attrition Report
21 Months Since Issuance

Original Portfolio	
2,279	Number of Loans
$491,420,377	Current Balances
100.000%	% Initial Current Balances
11.505%	Wght Avg Coupon
191.62	Wght Avg Rem Term (months)
15.19	Wght Avg Seasoning (months)

Current Pay Collateral			Difference from Original Portfolio	
1,943	Number of Loans		336	Number of Loans
$371,854,321	Current Balances		$119,566,056	Current Balances
75.669%	% Initial Current Balances		24.331%	% Initial Current Balances
11.487%	Wght Avg Coupon		0.018%	Wght Avg Coupon
199.52	Wght Avg Rem Term (months)		(7.89)	Wght Avg Rem Term (months)
15.06	Wght Avg Seasoning (months)		0.13	Wght Avg Seasoning (months)

Prepayments to Date			Defaults to Date	
134	Number of Loans		202	Number of Loans
$27,807,028	Current Balances		$41,367,444	Current Balances
5.659%	% Initial Current Balances		8.418%	% Initial Current Balances
11.456%	Wght Avg Coupon		11.505%	Wght Avg Coupon
199.66	Wght Avg Rem Term (months)		191.54	Wght Avg Rem Term (months)
15.97	Wght Avg Seasoning (months)		14.18	Wght Avg Seasoning (months)

EXHIBIT 24.16 The prepayment and default Portfolio Attrition Report for the first 21 months of the deal

The price for the security at the end of the quarter is 77.53. This is a decline of 5.15 from the seventh quarter of the deal ending in March 2008.

TWENTY-FOUR MONTHS FROM ISSUANCE

Time Period: July through September 2008.

General Economic Conditions: Catastrophic. The capital markets are nearly shut down completely. Then late in the quarter the Congress passes a bailout plan! The worst may be over. This does not mean immediate recovery but it does mean that there is a chance to reverse the negative pricing momentum. We will just have to await developments. The Prime Rate for these three months was steady at 5.00%. The LIBOR rates were 2.791%, 2.811%, and 4.053%.

Pricing Inputs: Spreads are exorbitantly high, getting higher, and highly volatile. There is however hope in sight, we think!

Inputs from the Servicing Groups: The conditions are little changed from the last quarter, which is to say they are terrible. We are going to stick with the 70% market value decline due to the high inventories of properties in the market. Our recovery lag period will remain at 24 months. We will decrease the appraisal values of the portfolio another 5%. This will be our third 5% adjustment downwards this year.

Collateral Performance: Collateral performance for the first three months remains strong. Our At Issuance model suggested that we would experience $9.4 million in prepayments and $2.3 million in defaults. We have in fact experienced

Current Month – 21 Months Since Issuance

Collateral Cash Flows

Scheduled Amortization	170,912,217	
Prepayments to Principal	240,690,083	48.98%
Total Principal Retired	411,602,300	
Defaulted Principal	79,818,077	16.24%
Recoveries of Principal (& rate)	35,251,360	44.16%
Coupon Income	280,561,283	
Total Cash Sources	**727,414,943**	

Debt Cash Flows

Program Fees	4,618,482	
Servicing Fee	18,708,284	
Conduit Debt Service	141,748,577	
Conduit Principal Payments	466,849,358	
Released to Seller	95,490,242	20.45%
Total Cash Uses	**727,414,943**	

Performance	Conduit	Seller Interest
Structuring		
Beginning Conduit Balance	466,849,358	24,571,019
Ownership Interest	95.00%	5.00%
Performance		
Principal Outstanding	$ - 0.00%	0.00%
Severity of Loss	0.000%	0.00%
IRR	6.106%	25.709%
Price	77.523	0.000%
Tenor		
Average Life (yrs)	4.946	
Final Maturity (yrs)	16.500	
Modified Duration	3.989	
Macauley Duration	3.751	

At Issuance Projection

Collateral Cash Flows

Scheduled Amortization	185,410,203	
Prepayments to Principal	263,299,530	53.58%
Total Principal Retired	448,709,733	
Defaulted Principal	42,710,644	8.69%
Recoveries of Principal (& rate)	36,582,308	85.65%
Coupon Income	303,236,913	
Total Cash Sources	**788,528,954**	

Debt Cash Flows

Program Fees	4,896,432	
Servicing Fee	19,889,241	
Conduit Debt Service	156,073,758	
Conduit Principal Payments	466,849,358	
Released to Seller	140,820,166	30.16%
Total Cash Uses	**788,528,954**	

Performance	Conduit	Seller Interest
Structuring		
Beginning Conduit Balance	466,849,358	24,571,019
Ownership Interest	95.00%	5.00%
Performance		
Principal Outstanding	$ - 0.00%	0.00%
Severity of Loss	0.000%	0.00%
IRR	6.375%	54.176%
Price	100.000	0.000%
Tenor		
Average Life (yrs)	5.244	
Final Maturity (yrs)	16.917	
Modified Duration	4.154	
Macauley Duration	3.905	

Difference: At Issuance and Current Month

Collateral Cash Flows

Scheduled Amortization	-14,497,986	
Prepayments to Principal	-22,609,447	-8.59%
Total Principal Retired	-37,107,434	
Defaulted Principal	37,107,434	86.88%
Recoveries of Principal (& rate)	-1,330,948	-3.64%
Coupon Income	-22,675,630	
Total Cash Sources	**-61,114,011**	

Debt Cash Flows

Program Fees	-277,950	
Servicing Fee	-1,180,956	
Conduit Debt Service	-14,325,181	
Conduit Principal Payments	0	
Released to Seller	-45,329,924	-9.71%
Total Cash Uses	**-61,114,011**	

Performance	Conduit	Seller Interest
Structuring		
Beginning Conduit Balance	0	0
Ownership Interest	0	0
Performance		
Principal Outstanding	0	0.000%
Severity of Loss	0.000%	28.468%
IRR	0.269%	
Price	22.477	
Tenor		
Average Life (yrs)	0.298	
Final Maturity (yrs)	0.417	
Modified Duration	0.165	
Macauley Duration	0.154	

EXHIBIT 24.17 Comparison of the Summary Box Scores for the At Issuance performance versus the Current Month, 21 months from issuance

Collateral Attrition Report
24 Months Since Issuance

Original Portfolio	
2,279	Number of Loans
$491,420,377	Current Balances
100.000%	% Initial Current Balances
11.505%	Wght Avg Coupon
191.62	Wght Avg Rem Term (months)
15.19	Wght Avg Seasoning (months)

Current Pay Collateral			Difference from Original Portfolio	
1,841	Number of Loans		438	Number of Loans
$346,138,921	Current Balances		$145,281,456	Current Balances
70.436%	% Initial Current Balances		29.564%	% Initial Current Balances
11.490%	Wght Avg Coupon		0.015%	Wght Avg Coupon
200.59	Wght Avg Rem Term (months)		(8.96)	Wght Avg Rem Term (months)
15.03	Wght Avg Seasoning (months)		0.17	Wght Avg Seasoning (months)

Prepayments to Date			Defaults to Date	
169	Number of Loans		269	Number of Loans
$32,707,482	Current Balances		$56,121,941	Current Balances
6.656%	% Initial Current Balances		11.420%	% Initial Current Balances
11.465%	Wght Avg Coupon		11.460%	Wght Avg Coupon
194.84	Wght Avg Rem Term (months)		197.45	Wght Avg Rem Term (months)
15.85	Wght Avg Seasoning (months)		14.43	Wght Avg Seasoning (months)

EXHIBIT 24.18 The prepayment and default Portfolio Attrition Report for the first 24 months of the deal

$4.9 million in prepayments and $14.7 million in defaults. A snapshot of the portfolio performance in this regard can be seen in Exhibit 24.18.

Structure Performance: The deal is now expected to have $92.3 million less in cash flows than our estimate At Issuance. Our recovery rate has slipped from 85.6% to 41.8%; given that we have $62.7 million more defaults than anticipated, this will cost us about $27.5 million. The model cash flow projections indicate that from an At Issuance estimate of $140 million of excess servicing, we can now only expect $71.5 million. Relative to our remaining $368 million in conduit indebtedness and less the $7 MM of excess servicing paid out prior to this time, our current coverage ratio is now 64/368 = 17.4%. We have also breached our three-month rolling default trigger of 5%. The level reached in the last month of the quarter was 6.811%. See Exhibit 24.19.

Running the Model: We will run the model for each of these three months using a 70% MVD number, a 24-month RLP, and with default rates of 600% PSD, 700% PSD, and 800% PSD for the three months. Our pricing spreads will be 9%, 10%, and 11%. The quarter ending price was **70.65**, a decline of **6.88**, our largest quarterly decline yet! We should note that after the last valuation exercise, the news of the bailout was announced and pricing spreads have pulled back considerably!

END OF THE EXERCISE

We have now reached the end of the 24-month valuation period. What a ride! From this point we all hope that the monitoring model will be used to track the

Current Month - 24 Months Since Issuance

Collateral Cash Flows		
Scheduled Amortization	161,415,390	
Prepayments to Principal	224,532,540	45.69%
Total Principal Retired	385,947,930	
Defaulted Principal	105,472,448	21.46%
Recoveries of Principal (& rate)	44,036,083	41.75%
Coupon Income	266,246,077	
Total Cash Sources	**696,230,089**	
Debt Cash Flows		
Program Fees	4,484,647	
Servicing Fee	17,966,901	
Conduit Debt Service	135,467,599	
Conduit Principal Payments	466,849,358	
Released to Seller	71,461,583	15.31%
Total Cash Uses	**696,230,089**	

Performance	Conduit	Seller Interest
Structuring		
Beginning Conduit Balance	466,849,358	24,571,019
Ownership Interest	95.00%	5.00%
Performance		
Principal Outstanding	$ -	0.00%
Severity of Loss	0.000%	0.00%
IRR	6.002%	16.052%
Price	70.645	0.000%
Tenor		
Average Life (yrs)	4.803	
Final Maturity (yrs)	16.167	
Modified Duration	3.918	
Macauley Duration	3.686	

At Issuance Projection

Collateral Cash Flows		
Scheduled Amortization	185,410,203	
Prepayments to Principal	263,299,530	53.58%
Total Principal Retired	448,709,733	
Defaulted Principal	42,710,644	8.69%
Recoveries of Principal (& rate)	36,582,308	85.65%
Coupon Income	303,236,913	
Total Cash Sources	**788,528,954**	
Debt Cash Flows		
Program Fees	4,896,432	
Servicing Fee	19,889,241	
Conduit Debt Service	156,073,758	
Conduit Principal Payments	466,849,358	
Released to Seller	140,820,166	30.16%
Total Cash Uses	**788,528,954**	

Performance	Conduit	Seller Interest
Structuring		
Beginning Conduit Balance	466,849,358	24,571,019
Ownership Interest	95.00%	5.00%
Performance		
Principal Outstanding	$ -	0.00%
Severity of Loss	0.000%	0.00%
IRR	6.375%	54.176%
Price	100.000	0.000%
Tenor		
Average Life (yrs)	5.244	
Final Maturity (yrs)	16.917	
Modified Duration	4.154	
Macauley Duration	3.905	

Difference: At Issuance and Current Month

Collateral Cash Flows		
Scheduled Amortization	-23,994,814	
Prepayments to Principal	-38,766,990	-14.72%
Total Principal Retired	-62,761,804	
Defaulted Principal	62,761,804	146.95%
Recoveries of Principal (& rate)	7,453,775	20.38%
Coupon Income	-36,990,836	
Total Cash Sources	**-92,298,865**	
Debt Cash Flows		
Program Fees	-411,785	
Servicing Fee	-1,922,340	
Conduit Debt Service	-20,606,159	
Conduit Principal Payments	0	
Released to Seller	-69,358,583	-14.86%
Total Cash Uses	**-92,298,865**	

Performance	Conduit	Seller Interest
Structuring		
Beginning Conduit Balance	0	0
Ownership Interest	0	0
Performance		
Principal Outstanding	0	0.000%
Severity of Loss	0.000%	0.00%
IRR	0.373%	38.124%
Price	29.355	
Tenor		
Average Life (yrs)	0.441	
Final Maturity (yrs)	0.750	
Modified Duration	0.236	
Macauley Duration	0.220	

EXHIBIT 24.19 Comparison of the Summary Box Scores for the At Issuance performance versus the Current Month, 24 months from issuance

improvement in our deal! What I would like you to take away from this exercise is how we transformed the structuring model into a model that performed an equally complex and equally necessary task.

This transformation was achieved because of the hard work we put into the structuring model. We had clearly segregated and identified all of its components and were therefore able to get to work quickly. We were able to sort out the code that would be helpful to us, and to put aside the code we did not need for the new task. We were then able to apply a large amount of tested, modular code as a basic framework for the new model. We could also use the existing subroutines as guides and logical templates for the new code that we now needed to write. This was especially true in that annoying but necessary subject of menu management and error checking.

Well, we are finally done!

I, for one, hope that you don't feel that way! I hope you feel this is just the beginning of applying what you have learned here to help you in your careers. The next steps are for you to take what you have learned in this book and apply it to the challenges of the real world. If you have learned the fundamental principles of using VBA, and how to organize and build models, you will have added a powerful tool to your problem solving kit.

I wish you the best of luck, interesting problems to work on, and success as you apply what you have learned here to the challenges you will encounter.

ON THE WEB SITE

On the Web site you will find the following:

- The monthly collateral files used to run the model
- The results of each of these quarterly analyses

# PART Nine

Farewell

## CHAPTER 25

Parting Admonitions

WHAT WE HAVE LEARNED

It is now over 600 pages from when you read the first paragraph of the Preface. What have you learned?

You should have grasped the following:

1. Understand the advantages and disadvantages of learning VBA
2. Understand the basic concepts of securitization as a financing strategy
3. Understand the functionality and structure of the Excel Waterfall Spreadsheet
4. Learned how to write a basic model outline in pseudo code
5. How to build the model framework by creating and naming VBA modules
6. How to read and, by editing, make recorded VBA macros more efficient
7. How to design menus and what the components of well-designed menu are
8. How to move information from menus into the VBA model using Range names
9. How to error check the menu inputs and produce error messages as necessary
10. How to use VBA to manipulate Excel objects such as cells, Ranges, and workbooks
11. The various data types of the VBA language and when it is appropriate to use them
12. The flow control statements of the VBA language
13. How to build and use messaging capabilities of VBA
14. How to design and build report packages for collateral and waterfall results
15. What a Main Program is; what an effective Main Program looks like
16. How to write collateral selection code using VBA arrays to hold ineligibility conditions
17. How to calculate the cash flows of the collateral under many different conditions
18. The "onion strategy" for building complex looping calculation sequences from the inside out
19. How to make looping code more efficient by moving operations out of the inner loops wherever possible
20. What the cash flow components of a typical loan portfolio are
21. What the basic prepayment and default calculation methodologies are
22. What the standard measures of deal performance are: average life, final maturity, duration, yield, internal rate of return, coverage ratios, severity of loss, and so on

23. How to load information, in this case collateral cash flows, into an Excel spreadsheet, trigger its calculation, and capture the results, from within a VBA looping structure
24. What are template files, what are the advantages of their use
25. How to use VBA to build pathways to the template file, open it, rename it, save it, write to it, and save it again
26. How to open data files external to the model, such as the collateral pool data file, and read their contents into VBA arrays for use by the model
27. How to interactively redesign report packages as you are creating them by deleting unused report worksheets or by modifying their appearance after they have been written by changing cell font and background colors
28. How to compile your VBA code
29. What are the standard, and most frequently used commands in the VBA Debugger
30. How to control the operation of a VBA program by the use of Breakpoints
31. How to read the contents of VBA variables, vectors, and arrays using the VBA Debugger
32. What are the most common VBA compiler error messages and what are the conditions that most frequently generate them, and how to fix the conditions causing the error
33. The general steps in the validation of a model of this type
34. How to write a function to allow you to track the period by period cash flows of the collateral portfolio and write them into a separate file by cash flow component details
35. How to use a series of tests, simple at first, and then of increasing complexity, to validate the collateral selection process VBA code
36. How to run the model and produce collateral demographic reports for an unselected pool of collateral
37. How to apply the initial collateral selection criteria and produce the eligible collateral demographic reports
38. How to produce the ineligible collateral report package
39. How to use the collateral selection function to avoid a geographic concentration issue for the deal
40. How to produce a fully eligible collateral pool that can be used as the starting point for structuring the deal
41. How to run the base Expected Case cash flows of the portfolio
42. How to run the initial key parameter sensitivity studies, using Market Value Decline, Recovery Lag Period, and the Conduit Financing Spread
43. Find the "breaking point" of the deal
44. Run the internal credit stress reports, which modify the timing of the default patterns
45. Run the rating agency stress studies, which modify all significant parameters to produce stress case conditions
46. Determine the advance rate for the final deal structure we want to receive a rating on
47. What is a post-processing program, how to build it, and how to use it to summarize data from large numbers of files of related runs
48. What is a model control environment and how to use it

49. The importance of back testing the model after changes, and the use of the compare program to analyze the results
50. The expected steps in the maturation and growth of the model

Well, I think that covers MOST of the highlights of what we have just learned!

I am absolutely sure that I could add at least one additional point in between every item on this list (and I would hope that you could too!)! If you can, you have done a GREAT job with the material. If you have only learned everything on this list you have done a GREAT job too!

If you understand and follow the basic principles of model design and implementation contained in this book, you will have the skills to tackle a wide variety of modeling challenges. You should be able to take a stab at any of the models I described in the Preface.

Just remember a few things:

1. Make use of the available expertise to understand the problem that you are going to model as much as possible before you start. This can be human, experiential, scholastic, or academic in nature.
2. Get sign off with everyone about what the model is and is not expected to do; its scope and design; the use of resources, money, and time needed to develop the model; and the expected delivery date.
3. Identify the critical components of the system.
4. Outline the steps the model will take to explore and solve the problem.
5. Write the Excel/VBA code you need.
6. Debug the initial model (stay calm, no code ever works as designed the first time).
7. Validate the model.
8. Run the model, get the initial results.
9. Share the results with the audience of the model. Make sure that they agree that the results are in a form and scope that is congruent with their needs as decision makers. If not, redesign the model to THEIR wishes but be sure to preserve model integrity.
10. Use the model to do the deal.
11. Over time improve the model, keeping it in touch with the changing environmental conditions and the needs of its users.
12. Protect and document the model, if for no one else, yourself.

If you follow these guidelines you cannot go very far wide of the mark.

NEXT STEPS

The "Next Steps" are all up to you.

You now have all the basic skills you need to model at an introductory level. Take this knowledge and confidently apply it to your first real world model.

Just remember:

FORTUNE FAVORS THE BRAVE!

You have my best regards and fondest hopes for success!

Mortgage Math

OVERVIEW

I have included this section as a quick introduction to (or, for those of you who are already familiar with the material, a quick review of) the cash flow characteristics of loans and how to calculate them. In this book we are dealing with a collection of loans to small business. Even though these are loans to commercial entities or business establishments, they are no different in their cash flow characteristics than ordinary residential mortgages.

Each loan at its inception has a starting balance. This balance is to be retired through the application of a monthly payment. The monthly payment will be the minimum amount to pay both the current month's interest charges on the balance of the mortgage and a portion of the principal. There are a fixed number of payments (e.g., 30 years × 12 payments per month = 360), and a beginning payment amount that is set at the time of the issuance of the loan.

If the coupon rate of the mortgage is fixed—that is, if the interest rate is not subject to change over the life of the loan, this combined monthly interest/portion of principal payment is fixed for the life of the loan.

If the coupon rate is floating, the coupon may change periodically. The periodicity of these changes and the amount by which the payment is allowed to change are specified in the terms of the loan agreement. A typical floating rate loan is described as a "spread to an index;" an example might be "200 basis points over Prime." In that case, the initial rate of the loan, unless otherwise specified, will be the rate of the Prime Rate on the day the loan was issued, and the contractual spread, in this case set at 2.00%. Thus, if on the day of issuance of the loan, the Prime Rate was 6.00% the interest rate of the loan (or its coupon rate) would be 6% + 2% = 8%. The payment of the loan can be reset at specific intervals based on the issuance date of the loan. At these times, the spread is applied to the index and a new coupon rate for the loan is determined. It is not, however, the only calculation that needs to be accomplished. The new coupon rate is compared to a series of limits that may govern the manner in which this adjustment is made. There are, with all the loans in this portfolio, a set of caps and floors. These are minimum and maximum limits that the coupon rate is subject to at the time of adjustment. These levels take two broad forms: limits on what can happen at the reset date, and limits that apply to the lifetime of the loan. Once the new coupon rate is applied, the payment is recalculated to ensure that the loan's balance can be repaid in the number of payments remaining until maturity.

After we have determined what the new regular monthly payments are, we should also be aware of other loan payment behaviors. These are loan prepayment and loan default. In the case of prepayment, the Obligor makes a payment larger than the minimum monthly amount required by the current conditions of the contract. This extra money is always applied to the outstanding balance of the loan's principal. Often, this extra payment is the entire outstanding balance of the loan. Once the loan is paid in full via prepayment, the contract of indebtedness between the lender and the Obligor is no longer in force— the principal has been fully retired and the scheduled future interest payments are obviated.

The second type of payment behavior with which to concern ourselves is non-payment. In this case, the Obligor defaults on the loan and stops making monthly payments altogether. The lender then moves to seize the property and sell it, with the goal of receiving enough money through the sale to repay the loan. It may take an appreciable period of time for this process to occur, especially if the Obligor contests the proceedings. If there is a subsequent realization of cash from a sale, it is called a "recovery of principal." The lender is usually allowed to recover an amount equal to the cost of repayment of the loan, all interest due from the time of the default to the time of the recovery, and any costs involved in the repossession, repairs, and selling. Anything in excess of those amounts are returned to the Obligor.

In this section, we start with how to calculate the monthly payment on a loan, both fixed and floating, and then look at how coupon income is calculated and principal is retired. We then will learn how to calculate prepayments and anticipate their effects on the cash flows. Lastly, we will look at the issue of defaults and recoveries.

LOAN AMORTIZATION TERMS

Before we start learning how to crunch mortgage numbers, we should review the language of mortgage math.

Original Term. The number of months from the date mortgage issuance to the final payment date. For the purposes of these discussions, we will assume that all the mortgages we are dealing with are monthly payment mortgages. That is, the borrower will make one payment per month until all principal is retired, the loan prepays, or the loan defaults. For example, the original term of a 20-year mortgage is 240 months.

Remaining Term. The number of months remaining until the end of the loan. For example, the original term of the mortgage is 300 months. A total of 120 monthly payments have been made to date. The remaining term of the loan is therefore $300 - 120 = 180$ months.

Seasoning or Age. The age of a mortgage is the difference between the original term and the remaining term. To continue our example, the age or seasoning of the mortgage above is the original term less the remaining term, or 300 months minus the remaining term of $180 = 120$.

Original Balance. The initial amount lent by the lender to the Obligor, the amount to be repaid over the life of the loan through the monthly payments.

Remaining Balance. The current, also referred to as "outstanding," balance of the loan principal.

Appraisal Amount. The value of the property and chattel that secures the mortgage. This lender makes an estimation of the value of the property and its contents, then uses this as a "backstop," a final source of liquidity (through sale of the asset) in case the Obligor defaults on the mortgage.

Loan-to-Value (LTV) Ratio. This is the ratio between the remaining balance of the mortgage and the appraisal value of the property and chattel securing the loan. Thus, if the appraisal value of the Obligor's property and chattel is $1,000,000 and the remaining balance of the loan is $700,000, the LTV ratio is $700,000/$1,000,000 = 70%. The LTV ratio will change as both the appraisal value changes and the mortgage balance of the mortgage decreases through payment activity.

Equity. This is the difference between the remaining balance of the mortgage and the current appraisal value. In the previous example, the equity is $1,000,000 − $700,000 = $300,000. Equity can be expressed either as a dollar amount or a percentage. When expressed as a percentage it is the ratio between the equity amount and the appraisal amount, $300,000/$1,000,000 = 30%.

Payment Amount. The level of the current monthly payment.

Scheduled Amortization. The amount of the payment that is applied to retire the remaining balance of the loan.

Coupon Income. The interest expense component of the monthly payment.

Prepaid Principal. The payment of remaining balance that exceeds the minimum monthly amount required by the loan terms. It is any extra money received, usually with the monthly payment, once all previously scheduled principal payment and current month's coupon income payment are met.

Defaulted Principal. Defaulted principal is the amount of remaining balance when the Obligor stops making the monthly payment.

Principal Recovery. A principal recovery is the amount of money realized through the disposition of the property and chattel, less any expenses incurred by the lender during the recovery period, but not greater than the remaining balance plus any capitalized interest added to the balance during the default period of the mortgage at the time of the default.

Coupon Reset Frequency. Applicable to floating rate notes, this is the interval, in months, between the recalculation of the mortgage's coupon level based on the spread of the mortgage and the current level of the index.

Payment Reset Frequency. Again for floating rate notes, the interval, in months between the times that the monthly payment is recalculated to reflect the current coupon level of the mortgage. "Applicable to floating rate notes, this is the number of times each year that the loan's payment amount may be adjusted."

Periodic Floor and Periodic Cap. Respectively, the lowest point and the highest point to which the mortgage coupon rate can be reset.

Lifetime Floor and Lifetime Cap. Respectively, the lowest and highest coupon rate levels allowable at any time in the life of the mortgage.

COMPONENTS OF THE CASH FLOWS OF A LOAN

Having tied down the basic language we are about to use, let's get to the task of understanding how to calculate mortgage cash flows!

Calculating the Monthly Payment

One of the first things we have to do is calculate the monthly payment of the mortgage. In that the payments of fixed-rate mortgages are much easier to explain and calculate, we will start with them.

Fixed Rate Mortgage Payment Calculation   To calculate the level monthly payment for a fixed-rate mortgage one merely sums the following series where:

> N = number of payments
>
> r = periodic interest rate (9.00% annual = (9%/12)monthly rate)
>
> n = current period, from 1 to N

$$\text{Sum} = (1/(1+r)^{1st}) + (1/(1+r)^{2nd}) + (1/(1+r)^{3rd}) + \ldots (1/(1+r)^{Nth})$$

> Payment = original balance/sum

Thus, the payment calculation for a fixed-rate 9% mortgage with a 24-month original term and a $100,000 balance is $4,568.47. See Exhibit A.1 for the calculation of the payment.

If we look at cell "C9" we can see that $1/(1+r) = 0.992556$.

The sum of this series for the 24 months of the loan is shown in cell "C10" = 21.889146.

The payment is therefore $100,000/21.889146 = \$4,568.47$.

If we apply this payment monthly to the outstanding loan balance, we see that the mortgage amortizes to zero in month 24, as scheduled. We also see that the total coupon payments are $9,643.38, the principal payments are $100,000.00, and the total cash flows are $109,643.38, the combination of the two.

Floating-rate Mortgage Calculation   To calculate the payment of a floating-rate mortgage, we will need to know more information than we did for a fixed-rate mortgage. With a floating-rate mortgage, we will need to know the following:

1. The current index level
2. The spread to the index
3. The remaining term of the mortgage
4. The coupon reset schedule
5. The payment reset schedule (if it is different than the coupon reset schedule)
6. The periodic reset floor and cap
7. The lifetime reset floor and cap

	A	B	C	D	E	F	G	H	I	J	K

2	9.000%	Coupon Rate		0.00%	Prepayment Rate
3	$100,000.00	Beginning Balalnce		0	Prepayment Method (1=CPR,2=PSA)
4	24	Total # Payments		0.00%	Default Rate
5	12	Payments per Year		0	Default Method (1=CPR,2=PSA)
6	$4,568.47	Monthly Payment

	1/(1+r)	Totals => $ -				$ 9,643.38	$100,000.00	$ -		$ 109,643.38
	0.992556	Beginning	Defaulted	Period Prin	Coupon	Scheduled	Prepaid	Ending	Total
	21.889146	Balance	Principal	Post Defaults	Payment	Principal	Principal	Balance	Cash Flows
0	1.000000								
1	0.992556	$ 100,000.00	$ -	$ 100,000.00	$ 750.00	$ 3,818.47	$ -	$ 96,181.53	$ 4,568.47
2	0.985167	$ 96,181.53	$ -	$ 96,181.53	$ 721.36	$ 3,847.11	$ -	$ 92,334.41	$ 4,568.47
3	0.977833	$ 92,334.41	$ -	$ 92,334.41	$ 692.51	$ 3,875.97	$ -	$ 88,458.45	$ 4,568.47
4	0.970554	$ 88,458.45	$ -	$ 88,458.45	$ 663.44	$ 3,905.04	$ -	$ 84,553.41	$ 4,568.47
5	0.963329	$ 84,553.41	$ -	$ 84,553.41	$ 634.15	$ 3,934.32	$ -	$ 80,619.09	$ 4,568.47
6	0.956158	$ 80,619.09	$ -	$ 80,619.09	$ 604.64	$ 3,963.83	$ -	$ 76,655.26	$ 4,568.47
7	0.949040	$ 76,655.26	$ -	$ 76,655.26	$ 574.91	$ 3,993.56	$ -	$ 72,661.70	$ 4,568.47
8	0.941975	$ 72,661.70	$ -	$ 72,661.70	$ 544.96	$ 4,023.51	$ -	$ 68,638.18	$ 4,568.47
9	0.934963	$ 68,638.18	$ -	$ 68,638.18	$ 514.79	$ 4,053.69	$ -	$ 64,584.50	$ 4,568.47
10	0.928003	$ 64,584.50	$ -	$ 64,584.50	$ 484.38	$ 4,084.09	$ -	$ 60,500.41	$ 4,568.47
11	0.921095	$ 60,500.41	$ -	$ 60,500.41	$ 453.75	$ 4,114.72	$ -	$ 56,385.69	$ 4,568.47
12	0.914238	$ 56,385.69	$ -	$ 56,385.69	$ 422.89	$ 4,145.58	$ -	$ 52,240.10	$ 4,568.47
13	0.907432	$ 52,240.10	$ -	$ 52,240.10	$ 391.80	$ 4,176.67	$ -	$ 48,063.43	$ 4,568.47
14	0.900677	$ 48,063.43	$ -	$ 48,063.43	$ 360.48	$ 4,208.00	$ -	$ 43,855.43	$ 4,568.47
15	0.893973	$ 43,855.43	$ -	$ 43,855.43	$ 328.92	$ 4,239.56	$ -	$ 39,615.87	$ 4,568.47
16	0.887318	$ 39,615.87	$ -	$ 39,615.87	$ 297.12	$ 4,271.36	$ -	$ 35,344.52	$ 4,568.47
17	0.880712	$ 35,344.52	$ -	$ 35,344.52	$ 265.08	$ 4,303.39	$ -	$ 31,041.13	$ 4,568.47
18	0.874156	$ 31,041.13	$ -	$ 31,041.13	$ 232.81	$ 4,335.67	$ -	$ 26,705.46	$ 4,568.47
19	0.867649	$ 26,705.46	$ -	$ 26,705.46	$ 200.29	$ 4,368.18	$ -	$ 22,337.28	$ 4,568.47
20	0.861190	$ 22,337.28	$ -	$ 22,337.28	$ 167.53	$ 4,400.94	$ -	$ 17,936.33	$ 4,568.47
21	0.854779	$ 17,936.33	$ -	$ 17,936.33	$ 134.52	$ 4,433.95	$ -	$ 13,502.38	$ 4,568.47
22	0.848416	$ 13,502.38	$ -	$ 13,502.38	$ 101.27	$ 4,467.21	$ -	$ 9,035.18	$ 4,568.47
23	0.842100	$ 9,035.18	$ -	$ 9,035.18	$ 67.76	$ 4,500.71	$ -	$ 4,534.47	$ 4,568.47
24	0.835831	$ 4,534.47	$ -	$ 4,534.47	$ 34.01	$ 4,534.47	$ -	$ -	$ 4,568.47

EXHIBIT A.1 Amortization table of a fixed-rate mortgage with a 9% coupon and 24-month original term

There is an excellent example of a series of calculations that show the step-by-step payment reset process in Chapter 14, so no need to replicate that work here. It is important to point out that the process is broadly similar to that of a fixed-rate loan.

There are two obvious differences. The first is that with a fixed-rate loan the coupon is fixed and never changes, while with a floating rate note we must calculate what the new coupon is at each reset period. To do this:

1. Take the current index level and add the mortgage spread to it. This is our provisional new coupon. We don't know if this is the coupon level we will use yet, because it is subject to two tests.
2. Compare the provisional coupon to the reset floor or cap limits. If the change in the coupon limit is greater than the cap it is limited in its increase by the cap amount. If the decrease is greater than the floor, it is limited in its decline by the floor amount. For example, assume the cap increase is 2.00% and the previous coupon level is 7.00%. The index is at 9.00% and the spread is 3.00%, so the provisional coupon would then be 9% + 3% = 12%. The most that the coupon can increase, however, is the previous level plus the reset cap of 7% + 3% = 10%, which is lower than 12%. The new provisional coupon level is therefore limited to 10%.

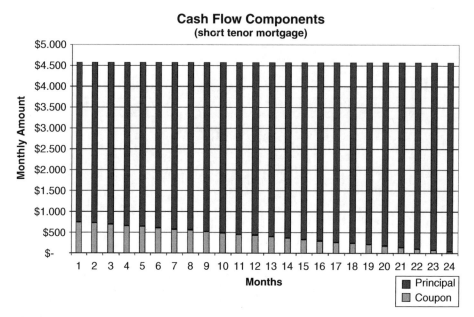

EXHIBIT A.2   Principal and coupon components of the payment over 24 months of the loan

3. Compare the provisional coupon level to the lifetime floor and cap constraints. The lifetime floor and cap on this mortgage are 5.5% and 22.0% respectively. Since the provisional coupon level is now at 10% and fits well within the 5.5% to 22.0% Range, we are fine to leave it the way it is.
4. Now, using exactly the same formulas we used for the fixed rate mortgage, we calculate the new payment level, based on 10% as the new coupon rate to be applied for the remaining term of the mortgage.

Exhibit A.3 illustrates the above example in table form. The initial coupon level at the issuance of the mortgage was 7.00%. Instead of being a fixed-rate mortgage, as we saw in the earlier example, where the coupon did not change over the life of the loan, the current mortgage is a floating-rate note. The first reset period is at month 13, at which point the loan resets to a 10% coupon for months 13 to 24. Looking at Exhibit A.3, we then see the new cash flows.

If we apply the earlier formulas for calculating the payment, we will use the following values to determine our new reset payment level:

$$N = 12 \text{ remaining term}$$

$$R = 10\%/12 \text{ periodic interest rate}$$

$$\text{Periodic Factor} = 1/(1 + r) = 0.991736$$

$$\text{Sum of the Periodic Factors} = 11.374508$$

$$\text{Remaining Balance} = \$51,744.21$$

$$\text{Monthly Payment} = \$51,744.21/11.374508 = \$4,549.14$$

	10.000%	Coupon Rate		0.00%	Prepayment Rate				
	$100,000.00	Beginning Balalnce		0	Prepayment Method (1=CPR,2=PSA)				
	24	Total # Payments		0.00%	Default Rate				
	12	Payments per Year		0	Default Method (1=CPR,2=PSA)				
	$4,549.14	Monthly Payment							

	1/(1+r)	Totals =>	$ -		$ 8,316.75	$100,000.00	$ -		$ 108,316.75
	0.991736	Beginning Balance	Defaulted Principal	Period Prin Post Defaults	Coupon Payment	Scheduled Principal	Prepaid Principal	Ending Balance	Total Cash Flows
	11.374508								
0									
1		$ 100,000.00	$ -	$ 100,000.00	$ 583.33	$ 3,893.92	$ -	$ 96,106.08	$ 4,477.26
2		$ 96,106.08	$ -	$ 96,106.08	$ 560.62	$ 3,916.64	$ -	$ 92,189.44	$ 4,477.26
3		$ 92,189.44	$ -	$ 92,189.44	$ 537.77	$ 3,939.49	$ -	$ 88,249.95	$ 4,477.26
4		$ 88,249.95	$ -	$ 88,249.95	$ 514.79	$ 3,962.47	$ -	$ 84,287.48	$ 4,477.26
5		$ 84,287.48	$ -	$ 84,287.48	$ 491.68	$ 3,985.58	$ -	$ 80,301.90	$ 4,477.26
6		$ 80,301.90	$ -	$ 80,301.90	$ 468.43	$ 4,008.83	$ -	$ 76,293.07	$ 4,477.26
7		$ 76,293.07	$ -	$ 76,293.07	$ 445.04	$ 4,032.21	$ -	$ 72,260.86	$ 4,477.26
8		$ 72,260.86	$ -	$ 72,260.86	$ 421.52	$ 4,055.74	$ -	$ 68,205.12	$ 4,477.26
9		$ 68,205.12	$ -	$ 68,205.12	$ 397.86	$ 4,079.39	$ -	$ 64,125.73	$ 4,477.26
10		$ 64,125.73	$ -	$ 64,125.73	$ 374.07	$ 4,103.19	$ -	$ 60,022.54	$ 4,477.26
11		$ 60,022.54	$ -	$ 60,022.54	$ 350.13	$ 4,127.13	$ -	$ 55,895.41	$ 4,477.26
12	1.000000	$ 55,895.41	$ -	$ 55,895.41	$ 326.06	$ 4,151.20	$ -	$ 51,744.21	$ 4,477.26
13	0.991736	$ 51,744.21	$ -	$ 51,744.21	$ 431.20	$ 4,117.94	$ -	$ 47,626.27	$ 4,549.14
14	0.983539	$ 47,626.27	$ -	$ 47,626.27	$ 396.89	$ 4,152.25	$ -	$ 43,474.02	$ 4,549.14
15	0.975411	$ 43,474.02	$ -	$ 43,474.02	$ 362.28	$ 4,186.85	$ -	$ 39,287.16	$ 4,549.14
16	0.967350	$ 39,287.16	$ -	$ 39,287.16	$ 327.39	$ 4,221.74	$ -	$ 35,065.42	$ 4,549.14
17	0.959355	$ 35,065.42	$ -	$ 35,065.42	$ 292.21	$ 4,256.93	$ -	$ 30,808.49	$ 4,549.14
18	0.951427	$ 30,808.49	$ -	$ 30,808.49	$ 256.74	$ 4,292.40	$ -	$ 26,516.09	$ 4,549.14
19	0.943563	$ 26,516.09	$ -	$ 26,516.09	$ 220.97	$ 4,328.17	$ -	$ 22,187.92	$ 4,549.14
20	0.935765	$ 22,187.92	$ -	$ 22,187.92	$ 184.90	$ 4,364.24	$ -	$ 17,823.68	$ 4,549.14
21	0.928032	$ 17,823.68	$ -	$ 17,823.68	$ 148.53	$ 4,400.61	$ -	$ 13,423.08	$ 4,549.14
22	0.920362	$ 13,423.08	$ -	$ 13,423.08	$ 111.86	$ 4,437.28	$ -	$ 8,985.80	$ 4,549.14
23	0.912756	$ 8,985.80	$ -	$ 8,985.80	$ 74.88	$ 4,474.26	$ -	$ 4,511.54	$ 4,549.14
24	0.905212	$ 4,511.54	$ -	$ 4,511.54	$ 37.60	$ 4,511.54	$ -	$ -	$ 4,549.14

EXHIBIT A.3 Floating rate mortgage with an initial coupon of 7% that reset to a coupon of 10% in the second year

We can see that this monthly payment, extended out, retires the last of the outstanding principal balance just when it should, in the 24th month of the mortgage.

Just remember that when you are calculating the new payment levels for each of the payment reset dates, you simply follow the steps above until you determine a new coupon level and then treat the loan as if it were a fixed-payment loan.

In the case of multiple payment reset dates prior to the remaining term, you just need to treat each as though it is independent of the others. If you have a 120-month loan with annual reset dates, you simply assume the current coupon is to be the coupon in effect for the rest of the life of the mortgage. As each subsequent reset date occurs, just follow the same procedures to readjust the monthly payment.

Cash Flow Components of a Long-Tenor Loan The graph of the components of scheduled principal amortization and coupon income for the monthly payments of the example 24-month term loan in Exhibit A.2 is typical of those of a short-tenor loan. The preponderance of the monthly payment will be used to retire the outstanding principal.

The story is quite different for long-term mortgages. If instead of an original term of 24 months we have a mortgage with an original term of 360 months, you will see that coupon income is the predominate component of the monthly payment until well into the 25th year of the mortgage. See Exhibit A.4.

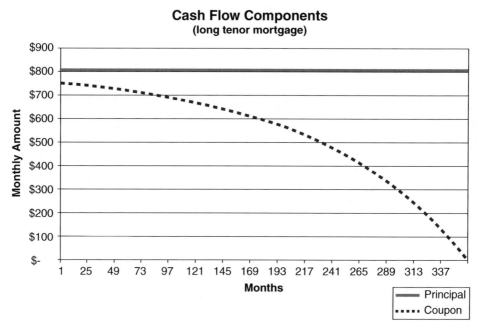

EXHIBIT A.4   Relative components of coupon income and scheduled amortization for a long-term mortgage, in this case 360 months, fixed-rate, level payment, and 9% coupon. The amount of the coupon income is the area below the curve, the amount of the principal paid is above it to the $800 line

Coupon Income

Coupon income is one of the easiest of the cash flow components to compute. In any given period simply multiply the prorated coupon rate by the current remaining principal balance of the period.

For the purposes of simplification, the above examples simply prorated the coupon to the monthly level by dividing it by 12. Depending on the convention of the mortgage, there may be several ways of determining the prorated coupon based on the number of days in the period.

The model allows the use of three different types of day count. The types are 30/360, which is to say 30 days per month in a 360-day year, or 12 payments. The second is Actual/Actual which is the number of days in each month, (corrected for Leap Years) divided by the actual days of that year, also Leap Year-corrected. The final method is Actual/360. In this method the actual number of days in the month are divided by 360 days for the year.

On individual months the differences can be small, but can add up quickly if you are not aware of this possibility. See Exhibit A.5.

Scheduled Amortization

A discussion of the calculation of the scheduled amortization portion of a mortgage loan payment is also given in Chapter 14.

EXHIBIT A.5 Calculation of 9% coupon on $1,000,000,000 for the month of February 2008, (a Leap Year)

February 2008 Interest		
Balance Outstanding		$ 1,000,000,000
Coupon Rate		9.00%
Methodology	**Factor**	**Interest**
30/360	0.0833333	$ 7,499,997.00
Actual/360	0.0805600	$ 7,250,400.00
Actual/Actual	0.0794500	$ 7,150,500.00

The formula for the percentage of outstanding principal retired by scheduled payment activity in any given period is:

N = total number of remaining term period

n = period of the principal retirement

$n - 1$ = period immediately prior to the retirement period

r = periodic coupon rate

Principal amortization of period n:

$$\text{Amort Factor} = \frac{\{[(1 + r)^{Nth} - (1 + r)^{nth}]}{[(1 + r)^{Nth} - (1 + r)^{nth} - 1]\}}$$

This is a particularly useful formula because it makes the calculation of the period principal a function of the remaining principal balance outstanding. Thus, all you ever need to know is the remaining balance of the mortgage at the beginning of the period, the coupon rate, the current period, and the original period of the sequence.

A tabular display of this calculation can be seen in Exhibit A.6. This is the table of principal retirement factors for the original 9%, 24-month, $100,000 mortgage we looked at in the payment calculation section.

In columns "M," "N," and "O" we can see the calculation of the factors for the principal retirement for each period. Column M contains the monthly factors of the hopefully now familiar series of

$$(1/(1 + r)^{1st}), \ (1/(1 + r)^{2nd}), \ (1/(1 + r)^{3rd}), \ \dots (1/(1 + r)^{Nth})$$

	A	B	C	D	G	H	J	K	M	N	O
1											
2			9.000%	Coupon Rate							
3			$100,000.00	Beginning Balance							
4			24	Total # Payments							
5			12	Payments per Year							
6			$4,568.47	Monthly Payment					Principal Payment Section		
7											
8			1/(1+r)	Totals =>	$ 9,643.38	$100,000.00		$ 109,643.38	1.007500	1.196414	
9			0.992556	Beginning	Coupon	Scheduled	Ending	Total	Monthly	Principal	Principal
10			21.889146	Balance	Payment	Principal	Balance	Cash Flows	Factors	Retired	Retired
11		0	1.000000						1.000000		
12		1	0.992556	$ 100,000.00	$ 750.00	$ 3,818.47	$ 96,181.53	$ 4,568.47	1.007500	0.038185	$ 3,818.47
13		2	0.985167	$ 96,181.53	$ 721.36	$ 3,847.11	$ 92,334.41	$ 4,568.47	1.015056	0.039998	$ 3,847.11
14		3	0.977833	$ 92,334.41	$ 692.51	$ 3,875.97	$ 88,458.45	$ 4,568.47	1.022669	0.041977	$ 3,875.97
15		4	0.970554	$ 88,458.45	$ 663.44	$ 3,905.04	$ 84,553.41	$ 4,568.47	1.030339	0.044145	$ 3,905.04
16		5	0.963329	$ 84,553.41	$ 634.15	$ 3,934.32	$ 80,619.09	$ 4,568.47	1.038067	0.046531	$ 3,934.32
17		6	0.956158	$ 80,619.09	$ 604.64	$ 3,963.83	$ 76,655.26	$ 4,568.47	1.045852	0.049167	$ 3,963.83
18		7	0.949040	$ 76,655.26	$ 574.91	$ 3,993.56	$ 72,661.70	$ 4,568.47	1.053696	0.052098	$ 3,993.56
19		8	0.941975	$ 72,661.70	$ 544.96	$ 4,023.51	$ 68,638.18	$ 4,568.47	1.061599	0.055373	$ 4,023.51
20		9	0.934963	$ 68,638.18	$ 514.79	$ 4,053.69	$ 64,584.50	$ 4,568.47	1.069561	0.059059	$ 4,053.69
21		10	0.928003	$ 64,584.50	$ 484.38	$ 4,084.09	$ 60,500.41	$ 4,568.47	1.077583	0.063236	$ 4,084.09
22		11	0.921095	$ 60,500.41	$ 453.75	$ 4,114.72	$ 56,385.69	$ 4,568.47	1.085664	0.068011	$ 4,114.72
23		12	0.914238	$ 56,385.69	$ 422.89	$ 4,145.58	$ 52,240.10	$ 4,568.47	1.093807	0.073522	$ 4,145.58
24		13	0.907432	$ 52,240.10	$ 391.80	$ 4,176.67	$ 48,063.43	$ 4,568.47	1.102010	0.079951	$ 4,176.67
25		14	0.900677	$ 48,063.43	$ 360.48	$ 4,208.00	$ 43,855.43	$ 4,568.47	1.110276	0.087551	$ 4,208.00
26		15	0.893973	$ 43,855.43	$ 328.92	$ 4,239.56	$ 39,615.87	$ 4,568.47	1.118603	0.096671	$ 4,239.56
27		16	0.887318	$ 39,615.87	$ 297.12	$ 4,271.36	$ 35,344.52	$ 4,568.47	1.126992	0.107819	$ 4,271.36
28		17	0.880712	$ 35,344.52	$ 265.08	$ 4,303.39	$ 31,041.13	$ 4,568.47	1.135445	0.121756	$ 4,303.39
29		18	0.874156	$ 31,041.13	$ 232.81	$ 4,335.67	$ 26,705.46	$ 4,568.47	1.143960	0.139675	$ 4,335.67
30		19	0.867649	$ 26,705.46	$ 200.29	$ 4,368.18	$ 22,337.28	$ 4,568.47	1.152540	0.163569	$ 4,368.18
31		20	0.861190	$ 22,337.28	$ 167.53	$ 4,400.94	$ 17,936.33	$ 4,568.47	1.161184	0.197022	$ 4,400.94
32		21	0.854779	$ 17,936.33	$ 134.52	$ 4,433.95	$ 13,502.38	$ 4,568.47	1.169893	0.247205	$ 4,433.95
33		22	0.848416	$ 13,502.38	$ 101.27	$ 4,467.21	$ 9,035.18	$ 4,568.47	1.178667	0.330846	$ 4,467.21
34		23	0.842100	$ 9,035.18	$ 67.76	$ 4,500.71	$ 4,534.47	$ 4,568.47	1.187507	0.498132	$ 4,500.71
35		24	0.835831	$ 4,534.47	$ 34.01	$ 4,534.47	$ -	$ 4,568.47	1.196414	1.000000	$ 4,534.47
36											

EXHIBIT A.6 Calculation of the scheduled principal amortization factors, (some columns hidden for clarity)

for each of the periods. In cell "N9" we take the maximum value of the sequence that will be the term:

$$(1/(1+r)^{\text{Nth}})$$

We now have everything we need to populate the "Principal Retired" column "N." Once these monthly factors are in hand, we need only multiple them by the previous period remaining balance of the mortgage to arrive at the scheduled principal amortization for the month. We can then take these numbers from column "O" and place them into the mortgage amortization table column "H."

Prepayments of Principal

If the world were a simple place, we could stop right here! If everyone sent in each payment month after month, we could drop the subject of mortgage math at this point and go home. Fortunately for us, the world is much more complicated. I say fortunately, because if it were simple, we would not be needed as bankers, risk analysts, etc. (and therefore not get paid the *big bucks*).

Prepayments can occur for both financial and non-financial reasons. A business may prepay an existing mortgage because it has sold its current location and is expanding. It may prepay because it wants to take advantage of a relatively better financing rate. Regardless of the reason, prepayments in a mortgage portfolio occur and can at times significantly change the expected cash flows.

There are two basic prepayment methodologies discussed in this book and our model. The first is called the Constant Percentage Rate, or CPR method. The second uses CPR factors as its base and constructs a ramped table over time. This is the Public Securities Administration (PSA) method and the method that is used in most of the structuring activity outlined in Chapter 18.

Let's look at each in turn

Constant Prepayment Rate (CPR) Method   The CPR is an annual rate. We are producing monthly cash flows for the model. What we need to do is to first restate the annual rate of the CPR prepayment speed into a one-month prepayment speed that we can use here in our spreadsheet, and later in our VBA calculations. To reduce the annual rate to a monthly one-month rate we can use the following formula:

$$\text{One Month Rate} = 1 - (1 - \text{CPR})^{1/12}$$

Thus, an 8% annual CPR represents a one-month percentage prepayment attrition of:

$$\text{One Month Rate} = 1 - (1 - .08)^{.083333}$$

$$\text{One Month Rate} = 1 - (.92)^{.083333}$$

$$\text{One Month Rate} = .006924 \text{ or } 0.6924\%$$

This means that 0.6924% of the outstanding principal balance of the mortgage will prepay in a given month. Keep in mind that prepayments occur only after the retirement of the scheduled amortization of the mortgage, and are assessed against the post-scheduled amortization balance, not the beginning balance of the period. Once we have determined the one-month factor, we are practically done! All that is left to do is to multiple this factor against the post-scheduled amortization outstanding balance—then we will have our prepayments for the period.

Public Securities Administration (PSA) Method   As the loan securitization industry grew, it became clear that the CPR methodology could be improved upon. What was needed was a way to account for the fact that the probability of a loan prepaying grows as the loan ages. The more time passes, the greater chance there was that some set of circumstances would emerge that would favor a prepayment event.

As a result, the PSA method was invented. The PSA method uses a series of CPR factors to construct a graduated increase of prepayment activity in the first 30 months of the life of the mortgage, and then levels out to a plateau rate that stays constant for the remaining life of the loan (no matter *how* long that is).

The pattern starts with a base rate of 0.2% CPR for the first month. It then increases by 0.2% CPR each month thereafter, until it reaches the 30th month, when it reaches the plateau rate of 6% CPR for the remaining life of the mortgage. This pattern is called 100% PSA. If the analyst wishes to apply a more robust prepayment assumption, a multiple of the curve can be used; if a less robust speed assumption is made, a fraction of the curve can be used. An example of using multiples or fractions

EXHIBIT A.7   Table of PSA curve multiples expressed in
monthly CPR speeds

Month	PSA Rate (Monthly Speeds in CPR%)				
	50%	100%	150%	200%	300%
1	0.10%	0.20%	0.30%	0.40%	0.60%
6	0.60%	1.20%	1.80%	2.40%	3.60%
12	1.20%	2.40%	3.60%	4.80%	7.20%
18	1.80%	3.60%	5.40%	7.20%	10.80%
24	2.40%	4.80%	7.20%	9.60%	14.40%
30	3.00%	6.00%	9.00%	12.00%	18.00%
36	3.00%	6.00%	9.00%	12.00%	18.00%
48	3.00%	6.00%	9.00%	12.00%	18.00%
60	3.00%	6.00%	9.00%	12.00%	18.00%
72	3.00%	6.00%	9.00%	12.00%	18.00%
84	3.00%	6.00%	9.00%	12.00%	18.00%
96	3.00%	6.00%	9.00%	12.00%	18.00%
108	3.00%	6.00%	9.00%	12.00%	18.00%
120	3.00%	6.00%	9.00%	12.00%	18.00%
132	3.00%	6.00%	9.00%	12.00%	18.00%
144	3.00%	6.00%	9.00%	12.00%	18.00%
156	3.00%	6.00%	9.00%	12.00%	18.00%
168	3.00%	6.00%	9.00%	12.00%	18.00%
180	3.00%	6.00%	9.00%	12.00%	18.00%
192	3.00%	6.00%	9.00%	12.00%	18.00%
204	3.00%	6.00%	9.00%	12.00%	18.00%
216	3.00%	6.00%	9.00%	12.00%	18.00%
228	3.00%	6.00%	9.00%	12.00%	18.00%
240	3.00%	6.00%	9.00%	12.00%	18.00%

of the PSA base curve is shown in Exhibit A.7. The CPR speeds for selected months of
a 20-year mortgage at various multiples of the base PSA curve are shown in Exhibits
A.7 and A.8.

Exhibit A.8 shows the monthly speeds, expressed in CPR, of the various multiples
of the base PSA curve. PSA speeds are often quoted in multiple units of the basic
curve. To use a PSA-based prepayment speed, we first need to convert the PSA speeds
to CPR speeds and then convert the CPR speeds to the one-month prepayment
percentages.

The Effects of Prepayments on a Pool of Mortgages   When a prepayment occurs,
the entire remaining principal balance of the loan is immediately retired. Unfortunately, that means that there will be no more coupon income from that loan. This

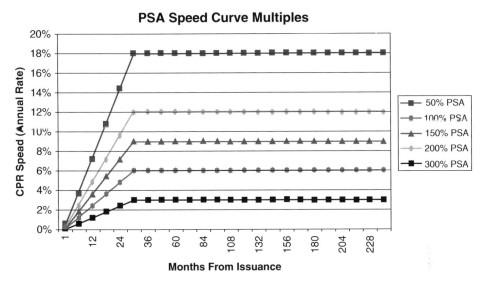

EXHIBIT A.8 Graph of PSA curve multiples expressed in monthly CPR speeds

can be an especially nasty little problem if the mortgages that start to prepay rapidly are those that have the highest margin to the funding costs of your deal.

What this means is the following: If you are borrowing funds at a rate of 5% and the average coupon on the mortgages is say, 8%, you have a 3% margin. If, however, the top coupon mortgages all prepay in a group because of a change in interest rates and the yield drops to 6.5%, then your margin has collapsed to 1.5% and the aggregate amount of cash flows will be greatly reduced. They may be so reduced that you may have trouble making up the cash flows missing from the defaulted mortgages in the pool and the deal might collapse.

Quantifing Prepayment Effects   We will now expand our sample mortgage from 24 periods to 180 periods. The effect of prepayments is to accelerate the receipt of principal payments and dilute or lessen the receipt of coupon payments. Exhibit A.9 shows the effects of various CPR prepayment speeds on the receipt of scheduled amortization, coupon income, and total cash flows.

Here we can clearly see the reduction in coupon income from a pool of mortgages subject to higher and higher prepayment rates. Exhibit A.10 displays this material in a graphic format.

Principal Defaults

The discussion of prepayment activity is a natural lead in to the next subject on the list of mortgage cash flow analysis, defaults of principal. The effects of defaults on total cash flows are much more severe than that of prepayments. See Exhibit A.11.

In Exhibit A.12 we can see the devastating effects that defaults can inflict on the cash flows of a mortgage portfolio. With a 25% CPR prepayment rate, we retained

EXHIBIT A.9   The decrease in total cash flows from an increase in prepayments

	Effects of Prepayment Activity on Cash Flow Components				
CPR Rate	**Coupon Payments**	**Scheduled Principal**	**Prepaid Principal**	**Total Cash Flows**	**% of 0% Cash Flows**
0%	$ 82,567.99	$ 100,000.00	$ -	$ 182,567.99	100.00%
1%	$ 78,195.70	$ 91,347.99	$ 8,652.01	$ 178,195.70	97.61%
2%	$ 74,115.15	$ 83,517.52	$ 16,482.48	$ 174,115.15	95.37%
5%	$ 63,419.35	$ 64,206.70	$ 35,793.30	$ 163,419.35	89.51%
10%	$ 49,727.73	$ 42,410.67	$ 57,589.33	$ 149,727.73	82.01%
25%	$ 26,925.77	$ 15,319.02	$ 84,680.98	$ 126,925.77	69.52%

69.52% of the total 0% prepayment rate. Here, with a 25% CPR default rate, we retained 22.59% of the original cash flows.

The difference is even more striking when we put Exhibits A.12 and A.13 together.

In Exhibit A.13, we see the difference most clearly between the effect of a prepayment and a default. If the default rate and prepayment rate are both 10%, we will lose an incremental 31.99% of our original cash flows. Almost 1/3 of the original cash flow-generating power of the collateral is gone. The total amount of foregone payments is $58.4 thousand dollars on an original amount of $182.6 thousand.

The fortunate thing about defaults is that it is rare that, as we are assuming in the tables above, there are no recoveries whatsoever. If we have a recovery rate of even 25%, we can realize a definite improvement in these results.

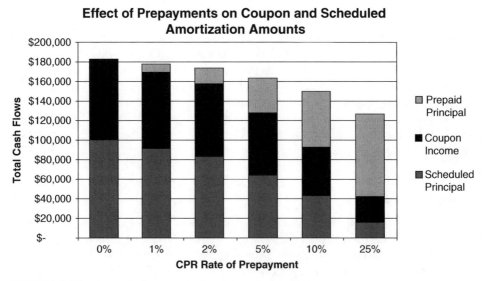

EXHIBIT A.10   A graph showing the loss of total cash flows as prepayment rates increase

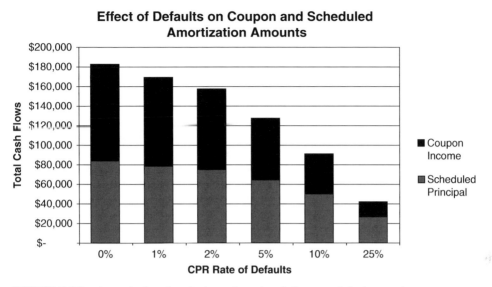

EXHIBIT A.11   A graph showing the loss of total cash flows as default rates increase

EXHIBIT A.12   A table showing the loss of total cash flows as default rates increase

Effects of Default Activity on Cash Flow Components					
Default CPR Rate	Defaulted Principal	Coupon Payments	Scheduled Principal	Total Cash Flows	% of 0% Cash Flows
0%	$ -	$ 82,567.99	$ 100,000.00	$ 182,567.99	100.00%
1%	$ 6,301.51	$ 78,130.24	$ 91,271.51	$ 169,401.75	92.79%
2%	$ 12,224.59	$ 73,990.48	$ 83,377.03	$ 157,367.51	86.20%
5%	$ 27,920.53	$ 63,148.85	$ 63,932.83	$ 127,081.68	69.61%
10%	$ 48,224.02	$ 49,293.03	$ 42,039.94	$ 91,332.97	50.03%
25%	$ 80,509.05	$ 26,287.94	$ 14,956.14	$ 41,244.08	22.59%

EXHIBIT A.13   A table showing the comparative loss of total cash flows between identical default and prepayment rates

Difference in Effects of Default vs Prepayment Activity on Cash Flow Components						
CPR Rate	Prepayment Scenarios	Default Scenarios	Loss of Cash Flows	Prepayment % Original	Default % Original	Difference % Original
0%	$ 182,567.99	$ 182,567.99	$ -	100.00%	100.00%	0.00%
1%	$ 178,195.70	$ 169,401.75	$ 8,793.95	97.61%	92.79%	4.82%
2%	$ 174,115.15	$ 157,367.51	$ 16,747.64	95.37%	86.20%	9.17%
5%	$ 163,419.35	$ 127,081.68	$ 36,337.67	89.51%	69.61%	19.90%
10%	$ 149,727.73	$ 91,332.97	$ 58,394.76	82.01%	50.03%	31.99%
25%	$ 126,925.77	$ 41,244.08	$ 85,681.69	69.52%	22.59%	46.93%

Recoveries of Principal

The last elements of mortgage portfolio cash flows that we will address are recoveries. When a mortgage default occurs, the lender has the right to move to secure the pledged interest of the borrower. Most commonly this interest is in the form of real property, a home, a building, equipment, materials, and other chattel.

Unless the Obligor voluntarily relinquishes use and holding of the asset, the lender must resort to some type of legal proceedings to recover principal. The first move is to establish the lender's right to gain legal control over the pledged property. In the case of residential and commercial mortgages, this usually means a foreclosure. Once the property is under the lender's control, it can attempt to liquidate the property. Upon liquidation the lender can apply the realized proceeds to the outstanding loan balance, plus any allowable expenses. Depending upon the laws of the state in which the legal action takes place, these expenses can vary. They generally, but may not necessarily, include:

1. *Legal expenses.* Foreclosure and legal notice service, title policy expenses, eviction expenses.
2. *Capitalized interest.* This is interest that is charged to the loan between the time of the default and the time of the liquidation of the assets. The interest is added to the loan balance outstanding at the time of the loan default.
3. *Servicing expenses.* Any expenses involved in monitoring and servicing the loan or the property, e.g., hiring a premises protection service for a commercial property.
4. *Rehabilitation expenses.* The expenses are typically repairs and renovations required to make the property conform with building codes, and to prepare the property for sale.
5. *Selling expenses.* These expenses are typically realty fees of various sorts, and sales commissions paid to real estate brokers.

In aggregate these expenses can be significant. Recoveries are dependent upon the amount of net proceeds that can be realized relative to the outstanding balance of the mortgage at the time of the default, plus any or all of these expenses. If the lender is in a position in which there is sufficient Obligor equity in the property and these expenses are reasonable, recoveries can be substantial.

At this point I would direct the reader to the illustrations in Exhibits 3.4 and 3.5 in Chapter 3, "Securitizing a Loan Portfolio," for a graphic depiction of the relationship between loan-to-value ratios, severity of loss upon liquidation, and the recovery amount.

A set of example cases in Exhibits A.14 and A.15 will illustrate these points. Exhibit A.14 is representative of normal economic times, while Exhibit A.15 is representative of a recessionary period.

Recoveries of whatever level are an additional source of cash flows for a deal. The one other aspect that needs to be considered when dealing with the subject of recoveries of defaulted principal is the timing of their receipt. How quickly the property or chattel can be disposed of is of critical importance. The longer the delay between seizure of the property and the liquidation activity, the

EXHIBIT A.14 Various recovery scenarios based on differing loan-to-value ratios during normal economic times

\multicolumn{6}{c}{**Calculation of Recovery Amounts & Percents**}
#	Item	Calc	Case 1	Case 2	Case 3
1	Original Appraisal Value		125,000	125,000	125,000
2	Outstanding Mortgage Balance		00,000	60,000	40,000
3	Current Owners Equity	1–2	45,000	65,000	85,000
4	Loan-to-Value Ratio	2/1	64.00%	48.00%	32.00%
5	Market Value Decline 20%	1*20%	25,000	25,000	25,000
6	Net Owners Equity	3–5	20,000	40,000	60,000
7	Liquidation Expenses		15,000	15,000	15,000
8	Net Proceeds Upon Liquidation	6–7	5,000	25,000	45,000
9	Recovery Amount	Min(2,8)	5,000	25,000	40,000
10	Recovery Percentage	9/2	6.25%	41.67%	100.00%

greater the possibility of damage to the property or other events that might trigger a value decline. In addition, the longer the period the more capitalized interest accrues.

The model allows the user to input assumptions about the Recovery Lag Period. A reasonable recovery lag time assumption for residential and commercial real estate is a minimum of 12 months, and more likely 18 months. In recessionary environments, 24 to 30 months is not an unreasonable assumption.

EXHIBIT A.15 Various recovery scenarios based on differing loan-to-value ratios during moderately stressed economic times

\multicolumn{6}{c}{**Calculation of Recovery Amounts & Percents**}
#	Item	Calc	Case 4	Case 5	Case 6
1	Original Appraisal Value		125,000	125,000	125,000
2	Outstanding Mortgage Balance		80,000	60,000	40,000
3	Current Owners Equity	1–2	45,000	65,000	85,000
4	Loan-to-Value Ratio	2/1	64.00%	48.00%	32.00%
5	Market Value Decline 30%	1*30%	37,500	37,500	37,500
6	Net Owners Equity	3–5	7,500	27,000	47,500
7	Liquidation Expenses		25,000	25,000	25,000
8	Net Proceeds Upon Liquidation	6–7	–17,500	2,500	22,500
9	Recovery Amount	Min(2,8)	0	2,500	22,500
10	Recovery Percentage	9/2	0.00%	4.17%	56.25%

NEXT STEPS

This concludes our discussion of mortgage math. All of these exercises concerned the behavior of the loan collateral. Appendix B will address the measurement of the performance of the debt side of the deal.

In Appendix B we will learn the specifics of calculating a series of measurements, such as average life, final maturity, duration, internal rate of return, and several other statistics. We will do this to be able to compare the performance of the debt under various scenarios. These terms, in addition to what we have learned here, will allow us to better describe the performance of the deal in more succinct and precise ways.

Bond Math

OVERVIEW

Hopefully you have survived reading Appendix A or have now found yourself directed here from one of the chapters of the book. This appendix will cover the basic elements of the calculations that we will use to describe the performance of the Conduit Financing notes and the Sellers Interest. Appendix A focused on the calculations used to determine the performance of the collateral; Appendix B will focus on the calculations related to the performance of the financing or liability side of the deal. To think of it in a simpler way, the collateral is "Source of Funds" and the financing is the "Use of Funds."

The statistics in this section broadly relate to three measurement issues. The first is tenor, or in other words, how long does it take for the investor to receive repayment for his indebtedness. The second is return, how can we compare this investment against others using a common yardstick. The third is sufficiency, which is another way to say how well the cash flows retire the outstanding balances of the Conduit Financing notes and the Seller Interest. Here we will want to measure if the cash flows are sufficient for the full repayment of the notes and what our relative payoff is in the form of a percentage return. If the cash flows are insufficient to retire the notes we will want to measure what losses will result and how severe those losses will be.

The tenor measurements are:

- Final Maturity
- Average Life

The yield and return calculations will be:

- Macaulay Duration
- Modified Duration
- Internal Rate of Return
- Total Rate of Return

The loss and coverage statistics will be the following:

- Coverage Ratio and Net Present Value (NPV) of the Coverage Ratio
- Severity of Loss and NPV Severity of Loss
- Frequency of Loss

Before we start to construct these various statistics we will need to take a quick look at two broad financial concepts that underpin much of the theory of modern finance: Future Value and Present Value.

FUTURE VALUE

Since ancient times it has been known that one of the most important components of money and wealth is time. Since the invention of the concept of interest several thousand years ago, the time that a sum of invested or borrowed money is at risk has been of critical importance. The reward for taking the risk of lending money is your return. How do we calculate it?

Calculation of Annual Interest Over Time

In a simple example let us assume that a savings account in the amount of $100,000 is established that will pay an interest rate of 8% per year for a five-year period. The account holder will not remove any funds from the account until the end of the five-year period. The interest is paid once a year on the anniversary of the establishment of the account. After the first year the 8% will be paid not only on the initial deposit but on all retained interest in the account.

In Exhibit B.1 we see the Future Value of the investment over its five-year life equals $146,932.81.

It is abundantly clear that each year we will have 8% more money than when we began the year! Another way we can say this is that there will be 1.08 times as much money in the end of the year as there was at the beginning. Therefore if the investment were of a two-year term, the amount of money we would have at the end of the second year would be:

$$\$100,000 * 1.08 * 1.08 = \$116,640$$

For the entire period it would be:

$$\$100,000 * 1.08 * 1.08 * 1.08 * 1.08 * 1.08 = \$146,932.81$$

EXHIBIT B.1 The Future Value of a $100,000, five-year investment paying 8% per year

Year	Beginning Year Balance	Annual Interest Rate	Interest Paid	Ending Year Balance
1	$ 100,000.00	8.000%	$ 8,000.00	$ 108,000.00
2	$ 108,000.00	8.000%	$ 8,640.00	$ 116,640.00
3	$ 116,640.00	8.000%	$ 9,331.20	$ 125,971.20
4	$ 125,971.20	8.000%	$ 10,077.70	$ 136,048.90
5	$ 136,048.90	8.000%	$ 10,883.91	$ 146,932.81
Total			$ 46,932.81	

A more concise way of mathematically stating the above is:

$$\$100,000 * (1.08)^5$$

Which can then be generalized to the following equation:

$$FV = Amt * (1 + r)^n$$

Where:

Future Value $= FV$

Invested Amount $= Amt$

Annual Interest Rate $= r$

Number of years $= n$

Thus we can rewrite our exercise above as:

$$FV = \$100,000 * (1.08)^5$$
$$FV = \$100,000 * (1.46932807)$$
$$FV = \$146,932.81$$

Future Value for Interest Payment Dates Less Than One Year

What happens if the interest period is less than one year? If we take the previous example and modify the terms of the agreement to reflect interest payments on a semi-annual basis we would arrive at the following, as seen in Exhibit B.2.

EXHIBIT B.2   The Future Value of a $100,000, five-year investment paying 8% semi-annually

Year	Beginning Year Balance	Period Interest Rate	Compound Factor	Interest Paid	Ending Year Balance
0.5	$ 100,000.00	4.000%	1.00	$ 4,000.00	$ 104,000.00
1.0	$ 104,000.00	4.000%	2.00	$ 4,160.00	$ 108,160.00
1.5	$ 108,160.00	4.000%	3.00	$ 4,326.40	$ 112,486.40
2.0	$ 112,486.40	4.000%	4.00	$ 4,499.46	$ 116,985.86
2.5	$ 116,985.86	4.000%	5.00	$ 4,679.43	$ 121,665.29
3.0	$ 121,665.29	4.000%	6.00	$ 4,866.61	$ 126,531.90
3.5	$ 126,531.90	4.000%	7.00	$ 5,061.28	$ 131,593.18
4.0	$ 131,593.18	4.000%	8.00	$ 5,263.73	$ 136,856.91
4.5	$ 136,856.91	4.000%	9.00	$ 5,474.28	$ 142,331.18
5.0	$ 142,331.18	4.000%	10.00	$ 5,693.25	$ 148,024.43
Total				$ 48,024.43	

A more concise way of mathematically stating the above is:

$$\$100,000*(1.04)^{10}$$

Thus we can rewrite our exercise above as:

$$FV = \$100,000*(1.04)^{10}$$

$$FV = \$100,000*(1.48024428)$$

$$FV = \$148,024.43$$

Here we have simply adjusted for the change in periodicity of the interest rate payment by increasing the compounding periods from 5 to 10 and the effective interest rate per period from 8% to 4%.

If we wished to change the interest payment frequency to monthly we would restate the equation in the following manner:

$$FV = \$100,000*(1.02)^{20}$$

$$FV = \$100,000*(1.48594740)$$

$$FV = \$148,594.70$$

Fractional Interest Payment Periods

We can further generalize this equation to take into effect the problem opposed by partial or irregular ending of beginning interest calculation periods. If, for example, we are offered an annual interest rate payment for a four-year-three-month period, we can calculate the future value using the generalized formula above with the modification shown in Exhibit B.3.

Using the formula we arrive at the same result:

$$FV = \$100,000*(1.08)^{4.25}$$
$$FV = \$100,000*(1.38691856)$$

$$FV = \$138,691.86$$

EXHIBIT B.3   The Future Value of a $100,000, 4.25-year investment paying 8% semi-annually

Year	Beginning Year Balance	Period Interest Rate	Compound Factor	Interest Paid	Ending Year Balance
1.00	$ 100,000.00	8.000%	1.00	$ 8,000.00	$ 108,000.00
2.00	$ 108,000.00	8.000%	2.00	$ 8,640.00	$ 116,640.00
3.00	$ 116,640.00	8.000%	3.00	$ 9,331.20	$ 125,971.20
4.00	$ 125,971.20	8.000%	4.00	$ 10,077.70	$ 136,048.90
4.25	$ 136,048.90	8.000%	4.25	$ 2,642.96	$ 138,691.86
Total				$ 38,691.86	

PRESENT VALUE

Present Value is the exact opposite of Future Value! It is, in its simplest terms, the amount of money that must be invested in the present to recognize a targeted Future Value.

The formula for computing Present Value (PV) is as follows:

$$PV = FV^*(1/(1 + r)^{Nth})$$

Where:

PV = Present Value

FV = Future Value

r = Annual Interest Rate

N = Number of Annual Time Periods

Present Value of a Series of Future Values

A school district has an escrow account that has been funded over a number of years to meet a series of construction and expansion projects over the next four years. The costs of these projects in the years they will be undertaken are estimated as the following:

Year 1	$1,000,000
Year 2	$3,500,000
Year 3	$2,500,000
Year 4	$5,000,000
Total	$12,000,000

The escrow fund manager can invest funds at 7% interest. The escrow fund has a balance of $10.25 million at the present date. Is this amount sufficient to fund the expansion program? (See Exhibit B.4.)

EXHIBIT B.4 The Present Value of the projects is $9.8 million, the school district does not have to raise the taxes, the escrow fund is sufficient to cover the expenses if invested at 7% interest!

Years in the Future	Present Value Factor at 7%	Project Cost	Net PV of Project Cost
1	0.934579439	$ 1,000,000	$ 934,579
2	0.873438728	$ 2,500,000	$ 2,183,597
3	0.816297877	$ 3,500,000	$ 2,857,043
4	0.762895212	$ 5,000,000	$ 3,814,476
Totals		$ 12,000,000	$ 9,789,695

Present Value Calculations When the Period Is Less Than One Year

To adjust the calculation of Present Value to those situations in which the Future Value payments are received, we need to make two adjustments to the calculation.

1. We must multiply the number of annual periods by the frequency of the new payment stream. Thus if we are receiving monthly payments for 10 years, the value of N, the number of payments changes from 10 to 120.
2. We need to prorate the interest rate to reflect the more frequent periodicity of the compounding effects. Thus if the original discount rate was 9% and we are moving from a yearly schedule to a monthly schedule our new value for "r" the interest rate would be 9% / 12 = 0.75%.

Thus if we are going to find the present value of a set of monthly cash flows from two-year, monthly pay mortgage, discounted at 7.5% we would have the set of calculations shown in Exhibit B.5.

EXHIBIT B.5 In these calculations "N" has been adjusted from 2 to 24, and the value for "r" has been adjusted from 7.5% to 0.625%

	Totals => $ 9,643.38	$ 100,000.00	$ 109,643.38		$ 101,522.57
	Beginning Balance	Coupon Payment	Scheduled Principal	Total Cash Flows	PV Factor at 7.5%	Net PV of Cash Flows
1	$ 100,000.00	$ 750.00	$ 3,818.47	$ 4,568.47	0.9937888	$ 4,540.10
2	$ 96,181.53	$ 721.36	$ 3,847.11	$ 4,568.47	0.9876162	$ 4,511.90
3	$ 92,334.41	$ 692.51	$ 3,875.97	$ 4,568.47	0.9814820	$ 4,483.88
4	$ 88,458.45	$ 663.44	$ 3,905.04	$ 4,568.47	0.9753858	$ 4,456.02
5	$ 84,553.41	$ 634.15	$ 3,934.32	$ 4,568.47	0.9693275	$ 4,428.35
6	$ 80,619.09	$ 604.64	$ 3,963.83	$ 4,568.47	0.9633068	$ 4,400.84
7	$ 76,655.26	$ 574.91	$ 3,993.56	$ 4,568.47	0.9573236	$ 4,373.51
8	$ 72,661.70	$ 544.96	$ 4,023.51	$ 4,568.47	0.9513774	$ 4,346.34
9	$ 68,638.18	$ 514.79	$ 4,053.69	$ 4,568.47	0.9454683	$ 4,319.35
10	$ 64,584.50	$ 484.38	$ 4,084.09	$ 4,568.47	0.9395958	$ 4,292.52
11	$ 60,500.41	$ 453.75	$ 4,114.72	$ 4,568.47	0.9337598	$ 4,265.86
12	$ 56,385.69	$ 422.89	$ 4,145.58	$ 4,568.47	0.9279600	$ 4,239.36
13	$ 52,240.10	$ 391.80	$ 4,176.67	$ 4,568.47	0.9221963	$ 4,213.03
14	$ 48,063.43	$ 360.48	$ 4,208.00	$ 4,568.47	0.9164684	$ 4,186.86
15	$ 43,855.43	$ 328.92	$ 4,239.56	$ 4,568.47	0.9107760	$ 4,160.86
16	$ 39,615.87	$ 297.12	$ 4,271.36	$ 4,568.47	0.9051191	$ 4,135.01
17	$ 35,344.52	$ 265.08	$ 4,303.39	$ 4,568.47	0.8994972	$ 4,109.33
18	$ 31,041.13	$ 232.81	$ 4,335.67	$ 4,568.47	0.8939103	$ 4,083.81
19	$ 26,705.46	$ 200.29	$ 4,368.18	$ 4,568.47	0.8883580	$ 4,058.44
20	$ 22,337.28	$ 167.53	$ 4,400.94	$ 4,568.47	0.8828403	$ 4,033.23
21	$ 17,936.33	$ 134.52	$ 4,433.95	$ 4,568.47	0.8773568	$ 4,008.18
22	$ 13,502.38	$ 101.27	$ 4,467.21	$ 4,568.47	0.8719074	$ 3,983.29
23	$ 9,035.18	$ 67.76	$ 4,500.71	$ 4,568.47	0.8664918	$ 3,958.55
24	$ 4,534.47	$ 34.01	$ 4,534.47	$ 4,568.47	0.8611099	$ 3,933.96

TENOR MEASUREMENTS

Having laid the groundwork with the sections on Future and Present Value, we can now move on to other measures of financial performance of cash flows.

A Set of Bond Cash Flows

We will use the principal and coupon payments in Exhibit B.5 as the basis for our examples of the calculations of the four tenor measurements in this section. While these cash flows are from the amortization of a mortgage, they could just as well have been the payment pattern on any type of pass-through asset backed security. (See Exhibit B.6.)

Final Maturity

Final Maturity for a bond or mortgage is the last date that any principal payments are received. It is generally expressed in years to two decimal places. In the above example the last cash flows have been received in month 24. The Final Maturity is therefore $24/12 = 2.00$ or 2.00 years. If these cash flows had been altered by prepayment or default activity, the Final Maturity would have been either before or after two years. If the final principal payment were received in month 21, the Final Maturity would have been $21/12 = 1.75$; if in month 28, $28/12 = 2.33$.

Average Life

Average Life is the measure of the time-weighted receipt of principal. This measurement is expressed in two digits, in the form of years. If we look at the sixth column of Exhibit B.6, Time Weighted Period Principal, we can see that it is the product of the first column, the Time Period, and the fourth column, the Scheduled Principal column. The sixth column is summed to get the number $1,370,542. This is the sum of the time weighted principal cash flows. We divide this number by the principal payments received and adjust it from a monthly statistic to an annual statistic by dividing by 12.

Thus the Average Life for this set of cash flows is equal to:

$$\$1,285,784/100,000 = 12.858 \text{ months}$$

$$12.858/12 = 1.071 \text{ years}$$

Macaulay Duration

Macaulay Duration was initially developed by Frederick Macaulay in 1938 as a tenor measurement but is now more frequently used as an input to calculating the next statistic we will talk about, Modified Duration. Be that as it may, Macaulay Duration is the sum of the Present Value adjusted cash flows, times their period weighting, divided by the price of the bond. In this case we will assume that the price of the bond is par. Therefore, the sum of the time weighted present valued cash flows is given at the top of the eighth column in Exhibit B.6, entitled "Time Weighted PV Factor at 10%," divided by the NPV of the principal.

EXHIBIT B.6 Principal and coupon payments from a two-year, 9% coupon, mortgage pass through security. We will use these cash flows as the basis for our discussion of tenor measurements

Month	Beginning Balance	9.00% Coupon Payment	Scheduled Principal	Total Cash Flows	Time Wght Period Principal	PV Factor 10%	NPV Total Cash Flows 10%	Cash Flow Time Wght PV Factor 10%
Totals =>		$ 9,643	$ 100,000	$ 109,643	$ 1,285,784		$ 99,003	$ 1,198,192
1	$ 100,000	$ 750	$ 3,818	$ 4,568	$ 3,818	0.991736	$ 4,531	$ 4,531
2	$ 96,182	$ 721	$ 3,847	$ 4,568	$ 7,694	0.983539	$ 4,493	$ 8,987
3	$ 92,334	$ 693	$ 3,876	$ 4,568	$ 11,628	0.975411	$ 4,456	$ 13,368
4	$ 88,458	$ 663	$ 3,905	$ 4,568	$ 15,620	0.967350	$ 4,419	$ 17,677
5	$ 84,553	$ 634	$ 3,934	$ 4,568	$ 19,672	0.959355	$ 4,383	$ 21,914
6	$ 80,619	$ 605	$ 3,964	$ 4,568	$ 23,783	0.951427	$ 4,347	$ 26,079
7	$ 76,655	$ 575	$ 3,994	$ 4,568	$ 27,955	0.943563	$ 4,311	$ 30,175
8	$ 72,662	$ 545	$ 4,024	$ 4,568	$ 32,188	0.935765	$ 4,275	$ 34,200
9	$ 68,638	$ 515	$ 4,054	$ 4,568	$ 36,483	0.928032	$ 4,240	$ 38,157
10	$ 64,584	$ 484	$ 4,084	$ 4,568	$ 40,841	0.920362	$ 4,205	$ 42,047
11	$ 60,500	$ 454	$ 4,115	$ 4,568	$ 45,262	0.912756	$ 4,170	$ 45,869
12	$ 56,386	$ 423	$ 4,146	$ 4,568	$ 49,747	0.905212	$ 4,135	$ 49,625
13	$ 52,240	$ 392	$ 4,177	$ 4,568	$ 54,297	0.897731	$ 4,101	$ 53,316
14	$ 48,063	$ 360	$ 4,208	$ 4,568	$ 58,912	0.890312	$ 4,067	$ 56,943
15	$ 43,855	$ 329	$ 4,240	$ 4,568	$ 63,593	0.882954	$ 4,034	$ 60,506
16	$ 39,616	$ 297	$ 4,271	$ 4,568	$ 68,342	0.875657	$ 4,000	$ 64,007
17	$ 35,345	$ 265	$ 4,303	$ 4,568	$ 73,158	0.868420	$ 3,967	$ 67,445
18	$ 31,041	$ 233	$ 4,336	$ 4,568	$ 78,042	0.861243	$ 3,935	$ 70,822
19	$ 26,705	$ 200	$ 4,368	$ 4,568	$ 82,995	0.854125	$ 3,902	$ 74,139
20	$ 22,337	$ 168	$ 4,401	$ 4,568	$ 88,019	0.847067	$ 3,870	$ 77,396
21	$ 17,936	$ 135	$ 4,434	$ 4,568	$ 93,113	0.840066	$ 3,838	$ 80,594
22	$ 13,502	$ 101	$ 4,467	$ 4,568	$ 98,279	0.833123	$ 3,806	$ 83,734
23	$ 9,035	$ 68	$ 4,501	$ 4,568	$ 103,516	0.826238	$ 3,775	$ 86,817
24	$ 4,534	$ 34	$ 4,534	$ 4,568	$ 108,827	0.819410	$ 3,743	$ 89,843

Thus the calculation for Macaulay Duration is as follows:

> PV rate (Yield to Maturity) = 10%
>
> Sum of PV of the Cash Flows = $99,003
>
> Sum of Period Wght PV of Cash Flows = $1,198,192
>
> Macaulay Duration = 1,198,192/99,003
>
> Macaulay Duration = 12.11 months
>
> Macaulay Duration = 1.01 years

Modified Duration

We have computed the Macaulay Duration as the first step in computing the Modified Duration. Modified Duration is used as a good first term approximation of the change in price expected from a percentage change in yield. To compute Modified Duration we take Macaulay Duration and divide it by the prorated discount factor +1.

> Time Periodicity of the Cash Flows = 12
>
> PV rate (Yield to Maturity) = 10%
>
> Time Periodicity adjusted discount factor = 10%/12 = 0.008333
>
> Denominator = 1 + 0.008333 = 1.008333
>
> Macaulay Duration = 12.11 months
>
> Modified Duration = 12.11/1.00833
>
> Modified Duration = 12.002591 months
>
> Modified Duration = 1.00 years

If we now want to find out what the expected price impact of a 0.20% change in yield would be, we have the following:

$$-1.00 * (+0.0020) = -0.002 = -0.2\% \text{ change in price}$$

YIELD AND RETURN MEASUREMENTS

Internal Rate of Return

The Internal Rate of Return for an instrument is the discount rate that when used to present the value of the cash flows of the investment over its life, results in the sum of the Present Valued cash flows being equal to a target price.

In Exhibit B.6, if we assume the price of the notes to be at par, 100.00, then the Present Valued target of the cash flows are the initial amount of the issuance of

EXHIBIT B.7 Two scenarios in which the IRR = 9.00%, full return of coupon and principal

Month	Beginning Balance	9.00% Coupon Payment	Principal Retired	Total Cash Flows
Totals =>		$ 7,918	$ 100,000	$ 107,918
1	$ 100,000	$ 750	$ 5,500	$ 6,250
2	$ 94,500	$ 709	$ 5,400	$ 6,109
3	$ 89,100	$ 668	$ 5,300	$ 5,968
4	$ 83,800	$ 629	$ 5,000	$ 5,629
5	$ 78,800	$ 591	$ 4,900	$ 5,491
6	$ 73,900	$ 554	$ 4,000	$ 4,554
7	$ 69,900	$ 524	$ 3,994	$ 4,518
8	$ 65,906	$ 494	$ 4,024	$ 4,518
9	$ 61,883	$ 464	$ 4,054	$ 4,518
10	$ 57,829	$ 434	$ 4,084	$ 4,518
11	$ 53,745	$ 403	$ 6,000	$ 6,403
12	$ 47,745	$ 358	$ 7,500	$ 7,858
13	$ 40,245	$ 302	$ 8,000	$ 8,302
14	$ 32,245	$ 242	$ 4,208	$ 4,450
15	$ 28,037	$ 210	$ 4,240	$ 4,450
16	$ 23,798	$ 178	$ 4,271	$ 4,450
17	$ 19,526	$ 146	$ 4,303	$ 4,450
18	$ 15,223	$ 114	$ 4,336	$ 4,450
19	$ 10,887	$ 82	$ 4,368	$ 4,450
20	$ 6,519	$ 49	$ 4,401	$ 4,450
21	$ 2,118	$ 16	$ 2,118	$ 2,134
22				
23				
24				

Month	Beginning Balance	9.00% Coupon Payment	Principal Retired	Total Cash Flows
Totals =>		$ 9,643	$ 100,000	$ 109,643
1	$ 100,000	$ 750	$ 3,818	$ 4,568
2	$ 96,182	$ 721	$ 3,847	$ 4,568
3	$ 92,334	$ 693	$ 3,876	$ 4,568
4	$ 88,458	$ 663	$ 3,905	$ 4,568
5	$ 84,553	$ 634	$ 3,934	$ 4,568
6	$ 80,619	$ 605	$ 3,964	$ 4,568
7	$ 76,655	$ 575	$ 3,994	$ 4,568
8	$ 72,662	$ 545	$ 4,024	$ 4,568
9	$ 68,638	$ 515	$ 4,054	$ 4,568
10	$ 64,584	$ 484	$ 4,084	$ 4,568
11	$ 60,500	$ 454	$ 4,115	$ 4,568
12	$ 56,386	$ 423	$ 4,146	$ 4,568
13	$ 52,240	$ 392	$ 4,177	$ 4,568
14	$ 48,063	$ 360	$ 4,208	$ 4,568
15	$ 43,855	$ 329	$ 4,240	$ 4,568
16	$ 39,616	$ 297	$ 4,271	$ 4,568
17	$ 35,345	$ 265	$ 4,303	$ 4,568
18	$ 31,041	$ 233	$ 4,336	$ 4,568
19	$ 26,705	$ 200	$ 4,368	$ 4,568
20	$ 22,337	$ 168	$ 4,401	$ 4,568
21	$ 17,936	$ 135	$ 4,434	$ 4,568
22	$ 13,502	$ 101	$ 4,467	$ 4,568
23	$ 9,035	$ 68	$ 4,501	$ 4,568
24	$ 4,534	$ 34	$ 4,534	$ 4,568

the note, $100,000. The following two schedules in Exhibit B.7 outline two cases in which the full coupon of the Note is retired on or before the final maturity (24 months) of the note. In the case in the left of the Exhibit, the Note pays coupon and principal right on schedule and the last principal is retired in month 24. In the schedule on the right of Exhibit B.7 the Note receives accelerated payments from the collateral that allow it to pay the coupon expense due at each month and retire the principal of Note at an accelerated rate.

In both cases above the Internal Rate of Return is equal to 9.00%. Why? Even though the cash flows have dramatically different patterns, the case on the right is clearly benefiting from an accelerated payment of cash flows in the form of prepayments or other collateral behaviors. Both cases pay full coupon and all principal. Discounting their cash flows at 9.00%, the coupon rate of the Note will quickly confirm this. As we can see from Exhibit B.8 the sum of the Present Valued cash flows at 9% is equal to the initial price of $100,000 at par.

Not all stories have a happy ending. In the next two scenarios we will see in Exhibit B.9, the cash flows are insufficient to retire the notes over their life. In both

EXHIBIT B.8   Discounting the cash flows for both these cases gives us the target amount $100,000 at par

		$ 100,000	$ 100,000
Month	PV Factor 9%	Case B.7-1 Sum of PV CF's	Case B.7-2 Sum of PV CF's
1	0.992556	$ 4,534	$ 6,203
2	0.985167	$ 4,501	$ 6,018
3	0.977833	$ 4,467	$ 5,836
4	0.970554	$ 4,434	$ 5,463
5	0.963329	$ 4,401	$ 5,290
6	0.956158	$ 4,368	$ 4,355
7	0.949040	$ 4,336	$ 4,288
8	0.941975	$ 4,303	$ 4,256
9	0.934963	$ 4,271	$ 4,224
10	0.928003	$ 4,240	$ 4,193
11	0.921095	$ 4,208	$ 5,898
12	0.914238	$ 4,177	$ 7,184
13	0.907432	$ 4,146	$ 7,533
14	0.900677	$ 4,115	$ 4,008
15	0.893973	$ 4,084	$ 3,978
16	0.887318	$ 4,054	$ 3,948
17	0.880712	$ 4,024	$ 3,919
18	0.874156	$ 3,994	$ 3,890
19	0.867649	$ 3,964	$ 3,861
20	0.861190	$ 3,934	$ 3,832
21	0.854779	$ 3,905	$ 1,824
22	0.848416	$ 3,876	$ -
23	0.842100	$ 3,847	$ -
24	0.835831	$ 3,818	$ -

EXHIBIT B.9 Cash flows of failed scenarios; there is significant principal unpaid at the end of the deal

	Totals =>	$ 9,363	$ 94,855	$ 104,218
Month	Beginning Balance	9.00% Coupon Payment	Principal Retired	Total Cash Flows
1	$ 100,000	$ 750	$ 2,300	$ 3,050
2	$ 97,700	$ 733	$ 2,200	$ 2,933
3	$ 95,500	$ 716	$ 3,000	$ 3,716
4	$ 92,500	$ 694	$ 5,000	$ 5,694
5	$ 87,500	$ 656	$ 4,900	$ 5,556
6	$ 82,600	$ 620	$ 4,000	$ 4,620
7	$ 78,600	$ 590	$ 3,994	$ 4,583
8	$ 74,606	$ 560	$ 4,024	$ 4,583
9	$ 70,583	$ 529	$ 4,054	$ 4,583
10	$ 66,529	$ 499	$ 4,084	$ 4,583
11	$ 62,445	$ 468	$ 6,000	$ 6,468
12	$ 56,445	$ 423	$ 7,500	$ 7,923
13	$ 48,945	$ 367	$ 8,000	$ 8,367
14	$ 40,945	$ 307	$ 4,200	$ 4,507
15	$ 36,745	$ 276	$ 4,200	$ 4,476
16	$ 32,545	$ 244	$ 4,200	$ 4,444
17	$ 28,345	$ 213	$ 4,200	$ 4,413
18	$ 24,145	$ 181	$ 4,100	$ 4,281
19	$ 20,045	$ 150	$ 4,000	$ 4,150
20	$ 16,045	$ 120	$ 3,500	$ 3,620
21	$ 12,545	$ 94	$ 3,000	$ 3,094
22	$ 9,545	$ 72	$ 2,000	$ 2,072
23	$ 7,545	$ 57	$ 1,500	$ 1,557
24	$ 6,045	$ 45	$ 900	$ 945

	Totals =>	$ 12,818	$ 56,873	$ 69,691
Month	Beginning Balance	9.00% Coupon Payment	Principal Retired	Total Cash Flows
1	$ 100,000	$ 750	$ 1,380	$ 2,130
2	$ 98,620	$ 740	$ 1,320	$ 2,060
3	$ 97,300	$ 730	$ 1,800	$ 2,530
4	$ 95,500	$ 716	$ 3,000	$ 3,716
5	$ 92,500	$ 694	$ 2,940	$ 3,634
6	$ 89,560	$ 672	$ 2,400	$ 3,072
7	$ 87,160	$ 654	$ 2,396	$ 3,050
8	$ 84,764	$ 636	$ 2,414	$ 3,050
9	$ 82,350	$ 618	$ 2,432	$ 3,050
10	$ 79,918	$ 599	$ 2,450	$ 3,050
11	$ 77,467	$ 581	$ 3,600	$ 4,181
12	$ 73,867	$ 554	$ 4,500	$ 5,054
13	$ 69,367	$ 520	$ 4,800	$ 5,320
14	$ 64,567	$ 484	$ 2,520	$ 3,004
15	$ 62,047	$ 465	$ 2,520	$ 2,985
16	$ 59,527	$ 446	$ 2,520	$ 2,966
17	$ 57,007	$ 428	$ 2,520	$ 2,948
18	$ 54,487	$ 409	$ 2,460	$ 2,869
19	$ 52,027	$ 390	$ 2,400	$ 2,790
20	$ 49,627	$ 372	$ 2,100	$ 2,472
21	$ 47,527	$ 356	$ 1,800	$ 2,156
22	$ 45,727	$ 343	$ 1,200	$ 1,543
23	$ 44,527	$ 334	$ 900	$ 1,234
24	$ 43,627	$ 327	$ 500	$ 827

EXHIBIT B.10   Disappointing IRRs from two
battered collateral portfolios

Month	PV Factor 9%	−4.638% Case B.8-1 Sum of PV CF's	−43.753% Case B.8-2 Sum of PV CF's
1	0.992556	$ 3,027	$ 2,114
2	0.985167	$ 2,889	$ 2,029
3	0.977833	$ 3,634	$ 2,474
4	0.970554	$ 5,526	$ 3,607
5	0.963329	$ 5,352	$ 3,500
6	0.956158	$ 4,417	$ 2,937
7	0.949040	$ 4,350	$ 2,894
8	0.941975	$ 4,317	$ 2,873
9	0.934963	$ 4,285	$ 2,851
10	0.928003	$ 4,253	$ 2,830
11	0.921095	$ 5,958	$ 3,851
12	0.914238	$ 7,244	$ 4,621
13	0.907432	$ 7,593	$ 4,828
14	0.900677	$ 4,059	$ 2,706
15	0.893973	$ 4,001	$ 2,669
16	0.887318	$ 3,943	$ 2,632
17	0.880712	$ 3,886	$ 2,596
18	0.874156	$ 3,742	$ 2,508
19	0.867649	$ 3,601	$ 2,421
20	0.861190	$ 3,118	$ 2,129
21	0.854779	$ 2,645	$ 1,843
22	0.848416	$ 1,758	$ 1,309
23	0.842100	$ 1,311	$ 1,039
24	0.835831	$ 790	$ 691

cases there is an unretired principal balance of the notes at the end of the stated final maturity of the deal, 24 months. As we apply the discount rates, we find that in order to calculate a Present Value that will make the stream of received payments equal to the price of the Notes, $100,000, we find that the rate will go through zero and then into negative returns. This is what we should expect. These scenarios are symptomatic of high default rate situations where the reserves of the deal are insufficient to replace the cash flows lost through default attrition of the collateral portfolio.

Both cases in Exhibit B.9 are indicative of a failed deal.

If we now apply the discount rates for these two scenarios, we arrive at the following IRR's: −4.638% and −43.753%. See Exhibit B.10.

LOSS AND COVERAGE MEASUREMENTS

The next set of performance measurements look at two sides of the same question: Has the principal outstanding been repaid in full? If it has, there are usually cash flows in excess of that amount needed to retire the principal. These excess cash flows are the coverage level of the principal. In the case where the cash flows were insufficient to provide for the full retirement of the Notes, we need to be able to measure the degree of the shortfall. Was the shortfall severe, moderate, or diminimus? The following performance statistics will answer these questions.

Gross Coverage Ratio and NPV Coverage Ratio

In many cases of securitized finance, the liabilities of the deal are retired while the assets of the deal continue to generate additional cash flows. The most common name for these excess cash flows is *residual*. Residual can be thought of as the excess cash flow generating ability of the collateral in relationship to the amount of Notes or other liabilities securitized in the deal.

Sometimes these residual cash flows are significant relative to the liabilities, sometimes they are moderate, and sometimes they are trivial. It all depends on the conditions affecting the performance of the collateral. If the collateral portfolio experiences large amounts of prepayments and defaults, the aggregate cash flows may be lower or even much lower than expected at the inception of the deal.

There was a need to specifically describe the degree of this protection, or surplus of cash flows in relationship to the originally issued Notes. Thus was the statistic Coverage Ratio invented and its companion in crime the Net Present Value Coverage Ratio. Let us see how we calculate these ratios. In Exhibit B.11 we can see that the cash flows from the collateral are coming in very quickly and in large amounts. The stated final maturity of the deal is fixed at 24 months, but the collateral has managed to retire the Notes in 17 months! The remaining collateral cash flows are not needed to pay either coupon expense or retire the principal balance outstanding of the Notes and are therefore Excess Collections or Residual Collections.

The sum of the Future Value of the Residual Collections divided by the original principal balance of the liabilities is the Gross Coverage Ratio. If we sum the discounted Residual cash flows, using the Note Coupon as the discount rate, and divide by the original principal of the Notes, we arrive at the NPV Coverage Ratio.

Gross Residual Cash Flows = $24,171

NPV 9% Residual Cash Flows = $20,857

Note Original Principal Balance = $100,000

Gross Coverage Ratio = 24,171/100,000 = 24.17%

NPV Coverage Ration = 20,857/100,000 = 20.86%

Severity of Loss and NPV Severity of Loss

In the cases where the deal does not produce a coverage condition you have a loss. The Severity of Loss statistic can be computed on a Future Value basis without discounting or on a Present Value basis with discounting. If computed on the Present Value basis, the discount rate used is the coupon rate of the liabilities.

In Exhibit B.12, the collateral pool has generated only 70% of the cash flows in Exhibit B.11.

EXHIBIT B.11 Excess Collections, or Residual, provides this deal with a set of Coverage Ratios

Month	Collateral Pool Cash Flows	Beginning Balance	9.00% Coupon Payment	Principal Retired	Total Cash Flows	Residual Cash Flows	PV Factor 9%	NPV Residual Cash Flows
Totals =>			$ 6,429	$ 100,000	$ 106,429	$ 24,171		$ 20,857
1	$ 8,050	$ 100,000	$ 750	$ 7,300	$ 8,050	$ -	0.992556	$ -
2	$ 7,800	$ 92,700	$ 695	$ 7,105	$ 7,800	$ -	0.985167	$ -
3	$ 7,500	$ 85,595	$ 642	$ 6,858	$ 7,500	$ -	0.977833	$ -
4	$ 6,800	$ 78,737	$ 591	$ 6,209	$ 6,800	$ -	0.970554	$ -
5	$ 6,500	$ 72,528	$ 544	$ 5,956	$ 6,500	$ -	0.963329	$ -
6	$ 6,400	$ 66,572	$ 499	$ 5,901	$ 6,400	$ -	0.956158	$ -
7	$ 6,200	$ 60,671	$ 455	$ 5,745	$ 6,200	$ -	0.949040	$ -
8	$ 6,000	$ 54,926	$ 412	$ 5,588	$ 6,000	$ -	0.941975	$ -
9	$ 5,600	$ 49,338	$ 370	$ 5,230	$ 5,600	$ -	0.934963	$ -
10	$ 6,500	$ 44,108	$ 331	$ 6,169	$ 6,500	$ -	0.928003	$ -
11	$ 6,400	$ 37,939	$ 285	$ 6,115	$ 6,400	$ -	0.921095	$ -
12	$ 6,300	$ 31,823	$ 239	$ 6,061	$ 6,300	$ -	0.914238	$ -
13	$ 5,400	$ 25,762	$ 193	$ 5,207	$ 5,400	$ -	0.907432	$ -
14	$ 4,600	$ 20,555	$ 154	$ 4,446	$ 4,600	$ -	0.900677	$ -
15	$ 3,600	$ 16,109	$ 121	$ 3,479	$ 3,600	$ -	0.893973	$ -
16	$ 5,500	$ 12,630	$ 95	$ 5,405	$ 5,500	$ -	0.887318	$ -
17	$ 7,900	$ 7,225	$ 54	$ 7,225	$ 7,279	621	0.880712	$ 547
18	$ 6,200					6,200	0.874156	5,420
19	$ 5,300					5,300	0.867649	$ 4,599
20	$ 4,800					4,800	0.861190	$ 4,134
21	$ 3,400					3,400	0.854779	$ 2,906
22	$ 2,200					2,200	0.848416	$ 1,867
23	$ 1,050					1,050	0.842100	$ 884
24	$ 600					600	0.835831	$ 501

EXHIBIT B.12 The deal fails to repay $18,410 of original principal

Month	Collateral Pool Cash Flows	Beginning Balance	9.00% Coupon Payment	Principal Retired	Ending Balance	Total Cash Flows	PV Factor 9%	NPV of Unpaid Principal
Totals =>			$ 9,845	$ 81,590		$ 91,435		$ 15,387
1	$ 5,635	$ 100,000	$ 750	$ 4,885	$ 95,115	$ 5,635	0.992556	
2	$ 5,460	$ 95,115	$ 713	$ 4,747	$ 90,368	$ 5,460	0.985167	
3	$ 5,250	$ 90,368	$ 678	$ 4,572	$ 85,796	$ 5,250	0.977833	
4	$ 4,760	$ 85,796	$ 643	$ 4,117	$ 81,680	$ 4,760	0.970554	
5	$ 4,550	$ 81,680	$ 613	$ 3,937	$ 77,742	$ 4,550	0.963329	
6	$ 4,480	$ 77,742	$ 583	$ 3,897	$ 73,845	$ 4,480	0.956158	
7	$ 4,340	$ 73,845	$ 554	$ 3,786	$ 70,059	$ 4,340	0.949040	
8	$ 4,200	$ 70,059	$ 525	$ 3,675	$ 66,385	$ 4,200	0.941975	
9	$ 3,920	$ 66,385	$ 498	$ 3,422	$ 62,962	$ 3,920	0.934963	
10	$ 4,550	$ 62,962	$ 472	$ 4,078	$ 58,885	$ 4,550	0.928003	
11	$ 4,480	$ 58,885	$ 442	$ 4,038	$ 54,846	$ 4,480	0.921095	
12	$ 4,410	$ 54,846	$ 411	$ 3,999	$ 50,848	$ 4,410	0.914238	
13	$ 3,780	$ 50,848	$ 381	$ 3,399	$ 47,449	$ 3,780	0.907432	
14	$ 3,220	$ 47,449	$ 356	$ 2,864	$ 44,585	$ 3,220	0.900677	
15	$ 2,520	$ 44,585	$ 334	$ 2,186	$ 42,399	$ 2,520	0.893973	
16	$ 3,850	$ 42,399	$ 318	$ 3,532	$ 38,867	$ 3,850	0.887318	
17	$ 5,530	$ 38,867	$ 292	$ 5,238	$ 33,629	$ 5,530	0.880712	
18	$ 4,340	$ 33,629	$ 252	$ 4,088	$ 29,541	$ 4,340	0.874156	
19	$ 3,710	$ 29,541	$ 222	$ 3,488	$ 26,053	$ 3,710	0.867649	
20	$ 3,360	$ 26,053	$ 195	$ 3,165	$ 22,888	$ 3,360	0.861190	
21	$ 2,380	$ 22,888	$ 172	$ 2,208	$ 20,680	$ 2,380	0.854779	
22	$ 1,540	$ 20,680	$ 155	$ 1,385	$ 19,295	$ 1,540	0.848416	
23	$ 750	$ 19,295	$ 145	$ 605	$ 18,689	$ 750	0.842100	
24	$ 420	$ 18,689	$ 140	$ 280	$ 18,410	$ 420	0.835831	$ 15,387

As a result the collateral cash flows, for whatever reason, are not sufficient to retire the full amount of the issued Notes. These are $18,410 of principal still outstanding at the end of the deal at 24 month. Applying the PV factor for month 24 to this figure we come out with a discounted amount of $15,387.

$$\text{Gross Severity of Loss} = \$18,410/\$100,000 = 18.41\%$$
$$\text{NPV Severity of Loss} = \$15,387/\$100,000 = 15.39\%$$

Frequency of Loss   The final loss statistic is the Frequency of Loss. This loss measurement refers to the number of scenarios that fail to repay all principal amounts or fail to pay timely interest. If, for example, you are running a set of 100 scenarios and 32 produce losses the Frequency of Loss for the group as a whole is 32%. In other words:

$$\text{Loss Frequency} = \text{Loss Cases/Total Cases}$$
$$\text{Loss Frequency} = 32/100 = 32\%$$

This statistic is more appropriate for Monte Carlo analysis where large numbers of cases, call trials, are produced. If the model has run 5,000, 10,000, or 100,000 trials, the Frequency of Loss may be one of the most important statistics calculated (in spite of its simplicity).

We will use the Frequency of Loss to look at the number of cases that fail in a designated set of runs when we are engaged in the structuring exercise in Chapter 18, "Running the Model."

NEXT STEPS

This concludes our discussion of bond math. I strongly encourage you to make an effort to become familiar with these terms and their attendant formulas. You will find that they are widely used and critical to your understanding of the performance of this model and structured finance in general.

Exhibits Index

Note: All references to exhibits are to the exhibit number. In addition, the following capitalization conventions have been used in this index:

VBA keywords:	Dim, Public
VBA Commands:	Exit, Clear Contents, SaveAs
VBA Editor Features:	Properties Window
VBA Debugger Features:	Data Tips, Add Watch
Subroutine names:	Calculate Loan Floater Coupon Level
Report names:	Summary Matrix report
Menu names of the models:	Program Costs menu
Financial Acronyms:	CPR, PSA, USER, SOL, MVD

All other terms are displayed in lower case.

Printed and bound by CPI Group (UK) Ltd, Croydon, CR0 4YY

24/04/2025